Integrating Doctrine and Diversity

Integrating Doctrine and Diversity

Beyond the First Year

Edited by

Nicole P. Dyszlewski

DIRECTOR OF SPECIAL PROJECTS, ACADEMIC AFFAIRS
ROGER WILLIAMS UNIVERSITY SCHOOL OF LAW

Raquel J. Gabriel

PROFESSOR OF LAW AND DIRECTOR OF THE LAW LIBRARY
CUNY SCHOOL OF LAW

Suzanne Harrington-Steppen

CLINICAL PROFESSOR OF LAW AND
ASSOCIATE DIRECTOR OF PRO BONO PROGRAMS
ROGER WILLIAMS UNIVERSITY SCHOOL OF LAW

Anna Russell

LIBRARIAN
NINTH CIRCUIT COURT OF APPEALS LIBRARY

Genevieve B. Tung

ASSOCIATE DIRECTOR FOR EDUCATIONAL PROGRAMS
BIDDLE LAW LIBRARY, UNIVERSITY OF PENNSYLVANIA CAREY LAW SCHOOL

CAROLINA ACADEMIC PRESS

Durham, North Carolina

LIBRARY OF CONGRESS CATALOGING-IN-PUBLICATION DATA

Names: Dyszlewski, Nicole, editor.
Title: Integrating doctrine and diversity : beyond the first year / edited by Nicole P. Dyszlewski, Raquel J. Gabriel, Suzanne Harrington-Steppen, Anna Russell, and Genevieve B. Tung.
Description: Durham, North Carolina : Carolina Academic Press, 2024. | Includes bibliographical references and index.
Identifiers: LCCN 2023042630 | ISBN 9781531024505 (paperback) | ISBN 9781531024512 (ebook)
Subjects: LCSH: Law--Study and teaching--United States. | Law schools--United States. | Bar examinations--United States.
Classification: LCC KF272 .I58 2024 | DDC 340.071/173--dc23/eng/20231002
LC record available at https://lccn.loc.gov/2023042630

CAROLINA ACADEMIC PRESS
700 Kent Street
Durham, North Carolina 27701
(919) 489-7486
www.cap-press.com

Printed in the United States of America

Contents

Acknowledgments ix

Foreword · *Erwin Chemerinsky* xi

Introduction · *Nicole P. Dyszlewski* xiii

Part I
Looking Across the Curriculum

Using Feminist Judgments in Upper-Level Law Courses: Teaching Justice and Equality Across the Curriculum · *Kathryn M. Stanchi & Bridget J. Crawford (with Olympia Duhart, Elena Marty-Nelson, Ann C. McGinley & Eloisa C. Rodriguez-Dod)* 3

Teaching Indian Law in the Twenty-First Century · *Matthew L.M. Fletcher* 17

A Lesson Plan for Teaching Gender-Inclusive Language · *Amanda Elyse* 27

Using Prose to Create Legal Pros · *Brandon Stump* 37

Mitigating Stereotype Threat in Upper Division Academic Support and Bar Preparation Courses · *Kiyana Kiel* 47

White Letter Law · *Varro J. Clarke* 59

Cultural Competence, Humility, Empathy, and Active Learning as Critical Features of Teaching Diversity, Equity, Belonging, and Inclusion in the Classroom · *Jocelyn Kennedy* 73

Part II
Dedicated Courses on Race, Injustice, and Professional Identity

Race and the Foundations of American Law: Creating a New Three-Credit Class at Roger Williams University School of Law · *Nicole P. Dyszlewski, Diana Hassel & Nadiyah J. Humber* 83

Incorporating Critical Perspectives in Law and Professional Identity into the 1L Curriculum at Boston College Law School · *Reena Parikh & Cheryl Bratt* 95

Race and the Equal Protection of the Laws Program (REPL) · *Dermot Groome* 109

The Power of the Narrative: Building Empathy, Allyship, and Belonging Within (or Despite) an Exclusionary Profession · *Tanya Johnson* 121

Part III
Professional Responsibility

Rethinking Professional Responsibility (PR) Materials: Insights from a New-to-PR Teacher · *Nicole P. Dyszlewski* 133

Exploring Two Sides of the DEI Coin in Professional Responsibility: Access to Justice and Access to the Profession · *Brooks Holland* 141

Beyond Fear: Bringing Mental Health into the Professional Responsibility Classroom While Empowering Students · *Sarah J. Schendel* 151

Diversity, Equity, and Inclusion Resources to Foster a More Inclusive Professional Identity: A Select Annotated Bibliography · *Jessica Almeida & Alisha Hennen* 161

Part IV
Integrating Doctrine and Diversity in the Second and Third Year Curriculum

SECTION 1 · ADMINISTRATIVE LAW

Teaching the Americans with Disabilities Act's Constitutionality without Othering People with Disabilities · *Katherine A. Macfarlane* 171

Administrative Law Through a Social Justice Lens · *Natalie M. Chin* 181

Dismantling Discriminatory Zoning: *City of Edmonds v. Oxford House, Inc.*— A Case Study on Defeating City-Imposed Family Composition Mandates · *D.O. Malagrinò* 193

SECTION 2 · BUSINESS, COMMERCIAL, AND LABOR

De-Neutralizing Business, or Teaching Business Organizations for Inclusive Engagement · *Lua Kamál Yuille* 205

Business Law and Racism · *Robert R. Statchen* 217

Doctrine and Diversity in the Labor Law Syllabus and Classroom · *Kerri Lynn Stone* 231

Equity and Inclusion at the Intersection of Law, Money and Technology · *Rohan Grey & Julia Ricciardi* 241

Identifying Bias, Inequity, and Discrimination in Insurance Law (with Some Thoughts on Doing the Same in a Business Associations Course) · *Deborah L. Johnson* 253

Doctrine and Diversity in the Employment Law Syllabus and Classroom · *Kerri Lynn Stone* 265

SECTION 3 · REMEDIES

Widening the Lens of Consciousness: Strategies to Broaden Students' Agency in Considering Remedies as a Vehicle for Systemic Change · *Patricia Winograd* 277

SECTION 4 · CRIMINAL PROCEDURE

Using Images and Videos in Criminal Procedure · *Tung Yin* 289

SECTION 5 · EVIDENCE

Teaching Antiracism in Evidence Law · *Jasmine B. Gonzales Rose* 301

Trial by Fire: Lessons Learned from Teaching Race and Evidence in a Hostile Environment · *Montré D. Carodine* 309

Making Evidence Meaningful: Diversity and Realism in Action · *Deborah Ahrens* 321

Creating a Space of Possibility in the Evidence Law Classroom · *Pavel Wonsowicz* 329

Evidentiary Support · *Malikah Hall Retteen* 339

SECTION 6 · FAMILY LAW

Teaching Family Law Through the Lens of Minoritized Identities · *Jeffrey A. Dodge* 359

Teaching Reproductive Justice Lawyering in Family Law: Moving Toward a Race-Conscious Curriculum · *Brittany L. Raposa* 371

Family Law Bibliography · *Margaret (Meg) Butler* 381

SECTION 7 · INDIGENOUS AND INTERNATIONAL LAW

Decolonizing the Legal Academy (Is the Future) · *Nazune Menka* 397

Native American and Indigenous Law: A Selected, Annotated Bibliography of Sources for Promoting and Maintaining Native American Law as Part of the Core Curriculum in Law School · *Rebecca Chapman* 409

Engaging with Equity in International Law—Personal Reflections · *J. Nilmini Silva-Send* 421

SECTION 8 · WRITING, RESEARCH, AND SIMULATIONS

Reconstructing Advanced Legal Research · *Kristin C. McCarthy* 437

The Unstandardized Client: Collaborating with an Actor on Lessons About Diversity, Equity, and Inclusion · *Carol M. Suzuki* 453

Incorporating Federal Indian and Tribal Law into Litigation-Drafting Curricula · *Gail Stephenson & Michael D.O. Rusco* 463

Grappling with DEI Issues Through an Environmental Negotiation Case Study · *Robin L. Juni* 473

Index 483

Acknowledgments

Nicole Dyszlewski would like to thank her co-editors for all their amazing work on this book. You inspire me to dream bigger and also ground me when needed. Thanks for being a great team.

She would also like to thank all of the authors of the different essays for giving their time and talents to this project, especially her co-authors, Diana and Nadiyah. Your wisdom, courage, and vulnerability is remarkable.

Nicole would like to thank her mom and dad, her Paccione family, her Manlove family, her Bos/Crofter family, her RWU Law family, her law librarian family, Lauren, Jonas, Alisha, and Mike for the tireless and continued support. Always and without question.

Finally, Nicole would like to thank RWU Law, CUNY Law, Berkeley Law, GW Law, and Jurist for their support for the ID&D Speaker Series. There are so many moving parts to this series that are hard to see as an attendee (unless things go horribly wrong) so thank you to the many people who assist with tech support, speaker management, planning, marketing, and just plain helping out when needed.

Raquel J. Gabriel thanks her co-editors, who took on the lion's share of this volume as she took on added responsibilities at work and home. Their support, understanding, and commitment to this volume was a true inspiration. Many thanks to the fantastic team in Academic Affairs at CUNY Law, who have been patient as I navigated a new role, and to my colleagues in the Library patiently awaiting my return. As always, I am grateful to my family for their love, especially my mom.

Genevieve Tung thanks our contributing authors for their generosity, insight, and creativity. Thanks also to our authors, the editorial team, and everyone at Carolina Academic Press, for their patience and good humor as we put this book together.

Suzanne Harrington-Steppen thanks her co-editors, the contributing authors, and law students all over the country who push us to be better teachers. Many thanks to RWU Law's administration, faculty, and staff who have supported the IDD series.

Anna Russell wants to extend her deep gratitude to her editorial team colleagues for their unflagging dedication. This has been a true labor of love with many thanks to the thoughtful and trailblazing contributions from all our authors as well as the excitement at Carolina Academic Press for this project.

Foreword

*Erwin Chemerinsky**

Law schools were tragically late in recognizing the importance of diversity. Now, thankfully, there is an increasing realization that diversity is central to our mission. In part, this is about ensuring that we have diverse student bodies and faculties. And we must be constantly vigilant that our instruction is inclusive, making all students feel they belong, and preparing all to practice law in a diverse society and world.

At the same time, it is important that in all of our courses we recognize the ways in which racism, sexism, homophobia, antisemitism, and other pernicious biases have infected the law. No longer can we pretend that the law is neutral. Quite the contrary, it always has reflected a myriad of choices that favor the privileged and the powerful. We must systematically explore this in our classes in order for our students to understand the law.

Important insights come from bodies of scholarship that did not exist when I went to law school or became a law professor. There is much to learn and much for us to teach from the insights of critical race theory, feminist jurisprudence, and other critical perspectives on the law.

But how to go about doing this? *Integrating Doctrine and Diversity: Beyond the First Year* is a wonderful place to start. It is a sequel to an earlier book that focused on first year subjects. Both books have a practical focus, exploring how teachers can effectively teach a diverse student body and teach about the countless ways in which matters of identity affect the law and the practice of law.

The book is a collection of essays, almost all from experienced teachers discussing how to approach matters of diversity in upper-level law school subjects. The book is organized so that it can be read from front-to-back or one can focus on teaching a par-

* Dean and Jesse H. Choper Distinguished Professor of Law, University of California, Berkeley School of Law.

ticular topic. Although the essays are by different authors, they fit beautifully together. Bibliographies for additional readings are particularly useful.

Part I is a series of essays about topics that cut across particular fields of academic study. They focus on issues common throughout the curriculum, such as teaching the use of gender-neutral language and teaching cultural competency. It also includes how to incorporate insights from feminist jurisprudence and Indian law, as well chapters on more specific subjects such as legal writing and academic skills.

The remainder of the book focuses on specific subjects within the curriculum. There are several chapters about teaching race and the law courses, and several chapters on teaching professional responsibility. Part IV of the book focuses on many specific subjects: administrative law, business and labor law, remedies, criminal procedure, evidence, family law, indigenous law and international law, and research, writing, and simulations. Virtually every major upper-level subject is considered, some with multiple chapters offering differing perspectives on particular areas of the law.

But all the chapters share much in common. All are written by individuals, almost all professors, who are deeply committed to improving our students' legal education. All are sharing their personal experiences. All offer concrete, practical suggestions on how we can do a better job. Both experienced teachers and those early in their academic careers have much to learn from this excellent collection of essays.

Introduction

*Nicole P. Dyszlewski**

> *The classroom remains the most radical space of possibility in the academy.*[1]

> *The first law of Library Science, like the first law of any other science, embodies an elemental truth. In fact, it is so self-evident that one may be inclined to say that it is trivial. But, that is an invariable characteristic of all first laws.... The first law of Library Science is: BOOKS ARE FOR USE.*[2]

This book, like the one that came before it, is *for use.* It is not intended to be theoretical.

This book is intended to be used by law teachers, wherever they may fall within the legal education hierarchy, to move American legal education in a direction where diverse perspectives are fully integrated into every law school classroom. The essays in the book are intended to be read, considered, annotated, discussed, bookmarked, and re-read. The teaching innovations included here, large and small, are intended to be adopted, changed, engaged with, tossed aside, reconsidered, and reworked. We hope this book gets dog-eared pages, cracked bindings, and stained with coffee. This book is *for use.*

When we created *Integrating Doctrine and Diversity: Inclusion and Equity in the Law School Classroom*, we had no idea if anyone would use it. We were, and continue to be thrilled, that someone (many someones, in fact) did use it. Beyond just reading the book, teachers and law schools are using the book to teach in a way that more accurately reflects American history and jurisprudence and the diverse interests, backgrounds, and needs of law students. Truthfully, this has been exciting and astonishing. But more

---

* Nicole P. Dyszlewski is the Director of Special Programs, Academic Affairs at Roger Williams University School of Law. Nicole would like to thank her colleagues at RWU Law, her friends, her family, her co-editors, her students, her partner, and Stephany Nuggs.

1. BELL HOOKS, TEACHING TO TRANSGRESS: EDUCATION AS THE PRACTICE OF FREEDOM 12 (1994).

2. S.R. RANGANATHAN, THE FIVE LAWS OF LIBRARY SCIENCE 1 (1931).

than the spirit of fellowship, it has been affirming that the need for practical teaching advice on these topics and information for law professors, by law professors, is real. And so it is with this deeper awareness we began work on the second book.

This volume brings the editorial team back together with some of the same amazing contributors, as well as some fantastic new faculty, around the same general theme: diversity skills and social justice content should be integrated within all law school classes. Which classes, and how that is accomplished, is the major difference between the first volume and this one. The first volume focused on law school classes typically found in the 1L curriculum. This volume focuses on classes taught beyond the first year.[3]

Like volume one, this book takes an expansive view of what "diversity" means in legal education and the facets of identity to which it can refer. As editors, we choose "diversity" as an umbrella term to include a variety of issues that may touch diversity but are also distinct, such as equity, equality, inclusion, belonging, racial injustice, gender discrimination, and other forms of social inequality. We also intend diversity to be defined broadly to include race, ethnicity, religion, spirituality, national origin, citizenship, age, domicile, gender identity, ability, gender expression, sexual orientation, status, culture, difference, and the many places where those descriptors intersect.

The organization of this book is key to its use. As in volume one, this book contains a must-read first chapter about cross-curricular issues. This part of the book includes essays that are widely applicable to law school faculty and not tied to a specific topical area. Part II of the book contains essays from law teachers at schools that have implemented classes on race, injustice, professional identity, and the law. Part III of the book includes essays on professional responsibility classes. Part IV contains essays organized by topics commonly taught in the second and third year of law school (i.e., all of the evidence essays are found together in one chapter). This book also contains annotated bibliographies for those hoping to go beyond the scope of each contributor's essay. While we would love readers to enjoy the book in its entirety, it is organized to allow readers to skip ahead to the subjects they find most relevant to their teaching.

We wish to give our profound thanks to the contributing authors who share their wisdom in these pages. The authors come from a variety of institutions across the country and have diverse backgrounds, diverse perspectives, and diverse approaches. We solicited and selected authors to maximize diversity of identity, style, institutional affiliation, and experience. Like in volume one, we have sought to create something that is approachable, accessible, and not pedantic. Our focus is, and has always been, on presenting tools and relevant examples to law professors willing to do, or at least consider, this work. This book is not about convincing the unwilling or indoctrinating those who do not value diversity and social justice in the doctrinal law school curriculum. It *is* about celebrating the creativity and possibility in those who do or want to try.

---

3. If you are someone who reads footnotes and you have gotten this far you may be excited to hear that we hope there is a future volume in the series about clinical education.

Since the first volume was published, we have been very gratified by the interest from law faculties nationwide, recognizing the urgency of this work. Gratitude goes to the co-sponsors of the speaker series that accompanies this work: RWU Law, CUNY Law, Jurist, GW Law, and Berkeley Law.[4] This work is messy, and at times it is far more dynamic than a static written essay can convey. Authors, editors, and friends of our book series have gotten together to present a series of webinars on topics related to the work of integrating doctrine and diversity. Those sessions are free, recorded, and available on YouTube. Again, the engaged conversations on these topics could not happen without speakers being willing to share of themselves and institutions being willing to support our work. Thank you to all who have sponsored, spoken, attended, or shared our sessions. This work comes alive in these webinars in an engaging and authentic way that complements the essays in these volumes.

Finally, I personally want to express my gratitude to my co-editors. We started this work together in 2018 and we have continued it into 2023. We have seen job changes, status changes, institution changes, home moves, sicknesses, losses, and a pandemic. But throughout it all we have continued to laugh and edit and support each other. While I do tire of the reminders to update the spreadsheets, I couldn't imagine a more supportive group of women to work alongside (virtually speaking). May our readers enjoy volume two, and may the future bless us with more ways to advance the conversation.

---

4. *See* Roger Williams School of Law, *Integrating Doctrine & Diversity*, https://law.rwu.edu/student-experience/diversity-and-outreach/integrating-doctrine-diversity.

Part I

Looking Across the Curriculum

Using Feminist Judgments in Upper-Level Law Courses: Teaching Justice and Equality Across the Curriculum

*Kathryn M. Stanchi** *& Bridget J. Crawford***
*(with Olympia Duhart,**** *Elena Marty-Nelson,*† *Ann C. McGinley*†† *& Eloisa C. Rodriguez-Dod)*†††

Introduction

Across the United States, law faculties are seriously considering how to incorporate issues of diversity and social justice in the law school curriculum. This move comes at a time when more people than ever before are acknowledging the persistent problem of police violence against people of color,[1] as well as decisions of the United States Supreme Court that undermine voting rights, substantive due process, and the right to

* E.L. Cord Professor of Law, University of Las Vegas-Nevada, William S. Boyd School of Law.

** University Distinguished Professor, Elisabeth Haub School of Law at Pace University.

*** Associate Dean for Faculty Development, Professor of Law, and Director of the Legal Research and Writing Program, Shepard Broad College of Law at Nova Southeastern University.

† Associate Dean for Academic Affairs and Professor of Law, Shepard Broad College of Law at Nova Southeastern University.

†† William S. Boyd Professor of Law, University of Las Vegas-Nevada, William S. Boyd School of Law.

††† Associate Dean for Academic Affairs and Professor of Law, Florida International University College of Law.

1. *See, e.g.*, Larry Buchanan, Quoctrung Bui & Jugal K. Patel, *Black Lives Matter May Be the Largest Movement in U.S. History*, N.Y. Times (July 3, 2020), https://www.nytimes.com/interactive/2020/07/03/us/george-floyd-protests-crowd-size.html (estimating that between 15 million and 26 million people in the U.S. participated in Black Lives Matter demonstrations in 2022, making the protests in the wake of the death of George Floyd "the largest movement in the country's history").

bodily autonomy. Historically speaking, social justice concerns—meaning interest in the rights, well-being, and flourishing of those who have been traditionally excluded and marginalized by law—have not been front and center of most law school classrooms in the United States. For years, the law school curriculum has focused on legal doctrine. Even in courses designed to cultivate critical perspectives on law, whether alongside traditional rules or as stand-alone "perspective" courses, course material often centers law review articles, books, or sources from other disciplines. Students know that this material is not "law"; it is not written in the language or form of legal documents that are integral to the practice of law. In this way, the materials through which critique is taught encourage a sort of false separation between the study of legal "doctrine" and considerations of "justice," or improving the law through a perspective that takes into account issues of race, sexual orientation, and gender identity, to name just a few identity axes. Erecting an artificial wall between *doctrine* and *justice* sets students on a pathway of assuming that the work of lawyers, lawmakers, and judges is about rules only. Unless we can disrupt the notion that racism, homophobia, misogyny, and even politics generally are somehow "separate" from the law, these same students will carry the belief over into their future careers. For these reasons, it is our view that the very structure of the law school curriculum and the materials we use to teach contribute to the failure of many members of the legal profession to understand that law can be a means for achieving a more just society.

Law professors should teach students clearly, explicitly, and unequivocally that many of the rules students are learning are not neutral.[2] Very often, those rules may be unfair or unjust. Furthermore, there is nothing inevitable about the law, the way it is now. Very often, legal rules that might appear neutral upon first (or even repeated) consideration are not mandated by legal authority. They are the product of decisions made by lawmakers and judges who, for centuries in the United States, have come from a small segment of society that is unrepresentative of the multitude of races, ethnicities, genders, abilities, and socioeconomic classes that make up this country.[3] The most effective way to challenge the notion of law's neutrality and to show students how a more just and equitable society can be achieved under existing legal precedent, is to teach with rewritten judicial opinions—"shadow opinions"—that are bound by all the same conventions as the opinions in their casebooks, but are informed by a deep commitment to racial and gender justice. The goal of teaching with rewritten judicial opinions is to show that perspective matters. While in law school, students can develop their own vision for how to create a more just society.

---

2. *See, e.g.*, Carlos A. Singer, *The Stultification of the Fourteenth Amendment*, 13 TEMP. POL. & CIV. RTS. L. REV. 875, 875 (2004) ("The gospels of 'neutrality' and 'color-blindness' have substituted clever statutory construction and crafty language for blatant reference to prejudice in laws that continue to reinforce long-standing group inequalities.").

3. *See, e.g.*, Kathryn M. Stanchi, Bridget J. Crawford & Linda L. Berger, *Why Women? Judging Transnational Courts and Tribunals*, 34 CONN. J. INT'L L. 317, 332 (2019) ("The more than 1300 sitting federal judges overwhelmingly attended Harvard (140 judges) and other elite law schools. These elite law schools—including Yale, Columbia, Stanford, Berkeley, NYU—tend to skew white and wealthy.").

Feminist Judgments

Under the broad title of the Feminist Judgments Project, several hundred law professors, lawyers, and even judges all over the world have banded together to rewrite hundreds of key judicial decisions. These projects are now moving beyond the realm of judicial writing to reimagine legislation, constitutions, investigative reports, and policy white papers, too. Feminist judgments use the factual record and legal precedents in effect at the time of the original decision, but incorporate reasoning informed by a commitment to social justice. Practically speaking, depending on the particular author and project, that reasoning draws on multiple theoretical traditions, including (but not limited to, despite the name "feminist judgments"): feminist legal theory, critical race theory, anti-poverty analysis, queer legal theory, and disability rights frameworks.

In this country, contributors to the United States Feminist Judgments Project have rewritten approximately two hundred judicial opinions in a wide array of fields, including: torts, property, criminal law, health law, trusts and estates, taxation, employment discrimination, immigration, corporations, family law, and reproductive justice. These feminist judgments provide a rich array of teaching material for professors who wish to show (not tell) students that many legal outcomes are far from inevitable. Because these decisions cover some of the most widely taught cases, are written in judicial language and read like "real" judicial opinions, they fit seamlessly into most traditional doctrinal classes. The instructor can choose to reveal the assigned material as a "shadow" opinion, either before or after the students have read and discussed it. By using the same vehicle (cases) that are traditionally used to teach "doctrine," law professors creatively stimulate students to think more deeply about law's present non-neutrality, and how to transform the law to do justice. By placing an original opinion directly in dialogue with a feminist judgment and asking students to compare them, a professor enables students to understand how greater social justice can be achieved through legal channels. The law does not need to turn a blind eye to the diversity of human identities and experiences.

This chapter takes a deep dive into how to use rewritten judicial opinions in upper-level law school classes. We invited four national colleagues teaching three different types of courses to offer their perspectives on the power of rewritten judicial opinions to teach students that achieving social justice and combating racism, misogyny, homophobia, and poverty are concerns that should be shared broadly in the legal profession.

Using Feminist Judgments in Upper-Level Real Estate Transactional Courses

Law professors, lawyers, and judges might look at the title of this section and think "what does feminism have to do with real estate law?" Even those committed to social justice might think that courses like employment discrimination or constitutional law are the more appropriate places in the law curriculum to discuss racism and misogyny. Courses like real estate, tax, securities, and trusts and estates, so the argument goes, are neutral and don't have anything to do with social justice issues. But this belief is misguided and dangerous. *All* law courses implicate gender, race, ableism, and other social justice issues. In the discussion that follows, Professors Elena Marty-Nelson and Eloisa Rodriguez-Dod show how the rewritten opinions and commentaries in *Feminist Judgments: Rewritten Property Opinions* can be used in upper-level property-based courses such as land use, real estate transactions, and others, to expose patriarchal biases in, and the impact of racial and class-based inequities on, the development of property law.[4]

Discussion (Professors Elena Marty-Nelson and Eloisa C. Rodriguez-Dod)

We suggest, as one example, using the rewritten opinion by Professor Guadalupe Luna in *Botiller v. Dominguez*, 130 U.S. 238 (1889). We use *Botiller* in our advanced real estate transactions course because *Botiller* is a powerful and effective vehicle for introducing students to the reality that United States property law is anything but neutral. Unlike the first year property course, which generally only briefly addresses issues regarding title, the real estate transactions course allows for in-depth exploration of the concepts of title and many of its nuances, including determining the validity of deeds and evaluating competing claims based on the derivation of title. The rewritten opinion of *Botiller* and its commentary serve to illustrate how the claims of title by women, Indigenous peoples, and other marginalized persons were treated much more harshly than weaker claims to title made by white men.

Examining *Botiller* in the upper-level real estate transactions course dovetails nicely with, and expands on, the concepts of inclusion and equity hopefully introduced to law students in the first year property course through other feminist rewritten property opinions. *Botiller* can be used on its own in the advanced class, but it works best if the feminist judgment in *Johnson v.*

4 Feminist Judgments: Rewritten Property Opinions (Eloisa C. Rodriguez-Dod & Elena Maria Marty-Nelson eds., 2021).

M'Intosh, 21 U.S. 543 (1823) was included in the first year Property course as a foundation.[5] Nevertheless, here we will focus on *Botiller.*

In *Botiller*, a landowner, Dominga Dominguez, brought an ejectment action against trespassers who were attempting to obtain settler status on land referred to as Rancho Las Virgenes, which had long been held by Dominga Dominguez and her ancestors. There was no dispute that Dominga Dominguez had perfect title to the land pursuant to Mexican law. Moreover, the Treaty of Guadalupe Hidalgo, which ended the Mexican-American War of 1846 to 1848, provided that existing private property rights in the territories that the United States had newly acquired from Mexico would be inviolably respected.

After the Treaty of Guadalupe Hidalgo, however, an act of Congress, the Land Claim Act of March 3, 1851 (the "Land Act"), created the Land Claims Commission and required landowners whose title derived from Mexican law, but whose land was within California, to present claims to their property to the Commission. Dominga Dominguez did not present a claim before the Commission during the required period. Despite the guarantee in the Treaty of Guadalupe Hidalgo to respect existing land titles, the U.S. Supreme Court in *Botiller* rejected the argument that the Land Claim Act applied only to imperfect title and held that it had no power to enforce the provisions of the Treaty if Congress chose to disregard these rights enunciated in the Treaty of Guadalupe Hidalgo when it enacted the Land Act. Thus, the case, in effect, validated the rights of squatters over the titleholder notwithstanding the Treaty. The treatment of Dominga Dominguez is in sharp contrast to how the Court analyzed claims to title to tracts of lands asserted by John Charles Fremont, a white male. In Marc-Tizoc González's insightful commentary on the rewritten opinion of *Botiller v. Dominguez*, he notes that the U.S. Supreme Court in *Fremont v. U.S.*, 58 U.S. (17 How.) 542 (1854), "lent the law's protection to racially white male John Charles Fremont, a U.S. colonel whose inability to prove perfect title derived in part from his participation in the 'Bear Flag Revolt' and the consequent destruction of deeds possessed by the

5. Almost all first-year property law casebooks include the U.S. Supreme Court case of *M'Intosh* and, in many first-year Property courses, *M'Intosh* is the first case the students are assigned. Thus, the feminist rewritten opinion of *M'Intosh* can be seamlessly interwoven in the first-year readings and serve as a solid introduction to exploring inclusion and equity topics regarding property rights. In *M'Intosh*, the Supreme Court devalued tribal property rights to land. In effect, the *M'Intosh* Court found that the property rights claimed by Indigenous nations were inferior to those of Christian European nations and held that the tribes could only alienate their lands to the U.S. government and lacked the power to alienate to private persons. In her brilliant commentary to the rewritten opinion of *M'Intosh*, Stacey L. Leeds explains that, unlike the U.S. Supreme Court's opinion, the "feminist rewritten opinion rejects Chief Justice Marshall's paternalistic and Euro-centric view of the Indigenous peoples and, using a feminist lens, focuses on, and equalizes, the Indigenous perspective." Stacey L. Leeds, *Commentary on* Johnson v. M'Intosh, *in* FEMINIST JUDGMENTS: REWRITTEN PROPERTY OPINIONS, *supra* note 4, at 35, 42.

Mexican *alcalde* (mayor) at Sonoma, which interfered with some grantees' ability to prove the validity of their claims."[6]

Including the feminist rewritten opinion of *Botiller* and its commentary facilitates discussion of the lack of equity and inclusion in numerous rulings where white male squatters were favored over women who had documents evidencing their superior property rights and where jurists rewarded non-Mexican, non-Spanish, and non-Indigenous claimants. *Botiller* had wide-ranging consequences for land ownership in California and other territories acquired from Mexico. *Botiller* and similar rulings led to impoverishment of the women claimants and their descendants. The rewritten opinion of *Botiller* and the commentary work extremely well for raising issues regarding competing claims to land title. Both illustrate how power dynamics played a role in the development of property law and the denial of land titles held by Mexican-American women.

Including a discussion of *Botiller* in upper-level property courses such as real estate transactions signifies a rejection of the curriculum choices of the past, which have done generations of law students a disservice. As Professor Joseph Singer has noted, "We participate in racial injustice if we act in ignorance of the ways land titles originated in the United States. Our ignorance of the past will lead us to repeat it."[7] *Botiller* allows for an equitable and inclusive analysis of title and the development of property law. It also allows for a comparison of how women in Mexico had more rights to land ownership and title than women in the United States at the time. Finally, it allows for teaching the effect of the Mexican-American War, a topic that bears more attention in the development of our laws, including property law.

Using Rewritten Employment Discrimination Opinions in a Judicial Writing Course to Enhance Understanding of Inequality and Judicial Bias

In this portion of the chapter, Professor Ann McGinley describes her seminar titled Employment Discrimination Law and Judicial Writing: Feminist, Masculinities, and Critical Race Theories, which uses *Feminist Judgments: Rewritten Employment Discrimination Opinions*[8] as the primary text. In this course, her students not only read the rewritten judgments, but draft a rewritten judgment. In this way, the students not

6. Marc-Tizoc González, *Commentary on* Botiller v. Dominguez *in* FEMINIST JUDGMENTS: REWRITTEN PROPERTY OPINIONS, *supra* note 4, at 61, 70.

7. Joseph William Singer, *Indian Title: Unraveling the Racial Context of Property Rights, or How to Stop Engaging in Conquest*, 10 ALB. GOV'T L. REV. 1, 48 (2017).

8. FEMINIST JUDGMENTS: REWRITTEN EMPLOYMENT DISCRIMINATION OPINIONS (Ann C. McGinley & Nicole Buonocore Porter eds., 2020).

only read how another author attempted to achieve a more just opinion, but they also do the hard work of creating a just opinion. The students learn through multiple processes: reading, writing, doing. Professor McGinley's course strives to teach students to understand that stereotypes and implicit biases influence judicial decision making and to learn that they can write a judicial opinion that furthers equality while respecting precedent and using appropriate organization, syntax, and voice.

Discussion (Professor Ann C. McGinley)

Students begin by analyzing the original opinions in several fundamental employment discrimination cases—*Meritor v. Vinson*, *Oncale v. Sundowner Offshore Services*, *Desert Palace v. Costa*, *Jespersen v. Harrah's*, *E.E.O.C. v. Catastrophe Management*, and *City of Philadelphia v. Webb*[9]—and the corresponding rewritten opinions and commentaries from *Rewritten Employment Discrimination Opinions*. They also examine articles on judicial writing and on feminist, masculinities, and critical race theories. This lays the foundation for the second half of the course in which students rewrite opinions and write commentaries on their own rewritten opinions.

The opinions assigned from *Rewritten Employment Discrimination Opinions* are meant to teach students about gender stereotypes, implicit biases, and intersectional discrimination in law. For example, in *Meritor*, *Oncale*, and *Desert Palace*, although plaintiffs won, the original decisions by the Supreme Court omitted or distorted important facts, thereby obscuring the link between the plaintiffs' protected characteristics and the discriminatory behavior. The rewritten judgments, read side-by-side with the originals, starkly demonstrate the Supreme Court's omissions and obfuscations. Reading the opinions together teaches students how important the narrative rhetorical choices of judges are in the development of the law and how just one omission, or one deceptive word choice, can change the whole narrative: it can make a victim a villain, or discrimination seem trivial or silly.

For example, in the original *Meritor*, the Supreme Court never mentions that the plaintiff and her harassing supervisor were both African-American. The rewritten *Meritor* reveals this fact and argues its legal significance, reasoning that the young African-American female plaintiff was more vulnerable to workplace harassment because her harasser was a respected businessman from the African-American community. *Meritor* and its rewrite can stimulate an excellent class discussion about why it might be important—and legally relevant—for the race of the parties of a case to be disclosed. Students

9. Meritor Savings Bank, FSB v. Vinson, 477 U.S. 57 (1986); Oncale v. Sundowner Offshore Services, Inc., 523 U.S. 75 (1998); Desert Palace, Inc. v. Costa, 539 U.S. 90 (2003); Jespersen v. Harrah's Operating Co, 444 F.3d 1104 (9th Cir. 2006) (en banc); Webb v. City of Philadelphia, 562 F.3d 256 (3d Cir. 2009); E.E.O.C. v. Catastrophe Mgt. Solutions, 852 F.3d 1018 (11th Cir. 2016).

can be asked about the Court's omission of the races of the parties and whether they made assumptions about the race of the parties based on that omission (students can be asked directly whether they assumed the parties were white). This in turn can lead to an excellent discussion about who benefits from the Supreme Court's "colorblind" approach to racial inequality.

Reading the original *Meritor, Jespersen, Catastrophe Management*, and *Webb* decisions alongside the feminist judgments also shows students how courts' consideration of intersectional identities when determining violations of Title VII could have real and practical impact. For example, in the original *Catastrophe Management* decision, the court held that refusing to hire the plaintiff because she wore her hair in "dreadlocks"[10] was not illegal race discrimination. Ignoring the long historical connection between the law's treatment of Black hair and racism, the original decision was able to dismiss the plaintiff's locs as merely a hairstyle: an easily changeable cultural trait. For students, the opinion's reasoning can be seductively persuasive—after all, who hasn't had to change something for a job? But the rewritten opinion by Professor Wendy Greene provides an eye-opener for students. Professor Greene details the history of enslaved peoples and how this history connects to the particularly racial burden that Black women bear when their employment depends on appearance standards of a predominately white society. Students see, in real terms, how locs aren't just a hairstyle and how banning them is substantially different from an employer's asking employees to wear a collared shirt.

In the next phase of the course, students play the role of judge and rewrite a different decision, choosing from a list that includes *Bostock v. Clay County, Georgia*,[11] and *Hosanna-Tabor Evangelical Lutheran Church and School v. E.E.O.C.*[12] While *Bostock* laudably held that Title VII forbids employment discrimination based on the "homosexuality" and transgender identity of the plaintiffs, it lionizes biological sex, ignores stereotyping, and never uses the term "sexual orientation." Moreover, *Bostock* leaves a gaping hole in the protection of employees of religious employers, emphasizing that the Religious Freedom Restoration Act[13] may trump Title VII and signaling approval for future application of the broad ministerial exception to federal anti-discrimination law.

Rewriting these cases and explaining their reasoning in commentaries requires students to understand the structural forces that lead to discrimination

10. The rewritten opinion and commentary use the term "locs" because of the racist history of the term "dreadlocks."

11. 140 S. Ct. 1731 (2020).

12. 565 U.S. 171 (2012) (holding that the ministerial exception precluded plaintiff's discrimination claim under the Americans with Disabilities Act).

13. 42 U.S.C. 2000bb *et seq.*

based on intersectional identities and to grapple with how to protect employees from discrimination, given the legitimate constraints of judicial power.

Reading and discussing the original and rewritten opinions in the first half of the seminar, along with articles on theory and judicial writing, provide the tools to analyze opinions, a grounding in how those opinions can differ if using feminist methods and perspectives, and practical information about judicial precedent, organization, and tone of judicial opinions. In the second half of the seminar, students must go further: when rewriting an opinion, they engage with the doctrine and perspectives represented by the original opinion and decipher how to rewrite the opinion in a more egalitarian way. This process leads to deeper analysis and understanding.

Moreover, if students are assigned to write a draft of the commentary even before the first draft of the rewritten opinion is due, they will be forced to think deeply about the goals they wish to achieve and how to organize the rewritten opinion to reach those goals. Faculty feedback on the draft commentary, as well as on the draft rewritten opinion, provides students the ability to grapple with how to improve their analysis, organization, and written work product as they progress.

Using Feminist Judgments to Teach Public Policy and the Value of Diverse Voices and Views

In this section, Professor Olympia Duhart demonstrates how feminist judgments can be used across the curriculum in almost any course in which judicial opinions are the primary teaching vehicles (i.e., most law school courses with casebooks). In Professor Duhart's view, students too often rush through reading an opinion without thinking critically about the speaker or author. Students tend to overlook the reality that every author, including the judicial author, brings a unique perspective to the writing process. To be sure, students tend to fixate on doctrine and rules, because that focus is encouraged in most law courses. Yet underlying rationales, especially public policy concerns, are an important part of any judicial opinion. The most robust legal analysis must take these concerns into account.

As a pedagogical matter, a focus on a judicial opinion's underlying rationales is an effective way to bring diverse voices and viewpoints into the conversation. A professor can assign rewritten opinions of judgments that they have already encountered in that course or a previous course. The instructor can then encourage students to identify the multiple ways that the two opinions differ, having due regard for how the perspective of the author shapes the judgment. This is a critical lesson for lawyers: perspective tends to influence the context, theme, and values underlying a legal opinion. By focusing on the author's "voice," it is possible to illuminate both implicit and explicit public policies undergirding the judgment.

None of this is to say that the identity of the speaker is the sole determinant of the content of an opinion. That is overly simplistic and inaccurate. Yet it is true that traditional legal analysis is made more nuanced and complex by understanding who is speaking and what the speaker's priorities are. Rewritten judgments suggest that viewpoint matters in judging. Rules matter. Doctrine matters. But how one interprets those rules and that doctrine may depend on the perspective that one brings to the process of judging. Feminist judgments amplify voices and views historically excluded from the bench.

Discussion (Professor Olympia Duhart)

A professor may assign both the original majority opinion and the feminist judgment in a particular case to highlight differences between the authors and the underlying public policies advanced in the two opinions. If a professor decides to use excerpts from cases, instead of full-length opinions, the instructor may need to provide students with a summary of the case. The professor should explicitly convey to students that the purpose of the exercise is to study the public policy arguments in both opinions—not necessarily to extract the "law." Prior to the class in which the students will compare the two opinions, the professor should assign a short reading on the major types of public policy arguments that judges tend to make;[14] even a simple primer will make it easier for students to identify the policy arguments in the two opinions.

In class, the professor should begin by reviewing major types of public policy arguments, such as economic arguments, institutional competence arguments, and moral arguments. Working in pairs, students should then identify and track at least two policy arguments advanced in the original opinion and two in the feminist judgment. Students could do this simply by highlighting or circling policy arguments or using a chart to track the arguments across the two opinions.

Below is a chart with a sample entry to illustrate how students might begin taking notes on the rewritten feminist judgment in *Loving v. Virginia*[15] by Professor Teri McMurtry-Chubb:

14. *See, e.g.*, Ellie Margolis, *Teaching Students to Make Effective Policy Arguments in an Appellate Brief*, 9 PERSPECTIVES: TEACHING LEGAL RSCH.& WRITING 73, 74 (2001); Ellie Margolis, *Closing the Floodgates: Making Persuasive Policy Arguments in Appellate Briefs*, 62 MONT. L. REV. 59 (2001).

15. 388 U.S. 1 (1967).

Original opinion or feminist judgment	Type of public policy argument	Sample text from opinion illustrating that argument (one or two sentences)	What does this suggest about the speaker's core values?	Will this policy positively or negatively impact a marginalized group? How?
Feminist judgment	Economic Argument	"Civil, contractual marriage was a legal impossibility in slavery, because slave owners required full control over the bodies of slaves to make a plantation profitable."[16]	For the author of the opinion, plantation profits are more valuable than autonomy for Black bodies	Black people are severely, negatively impacted by this policy analysis. Under this policy, Black people are stripped of their independence and bodily integrity.

Students would take similar notes on the original opinion. Students could use Padlet, an internet-based digital bulletin board, to quickly post their findings and share them with the class. Then, after about 20 minutes working together, the class can reconvene to discuss the work.

In prompting a discussion of the feminist judgment in *Loving v. Virginia*, the professor might ask questions such as these:

1. Why does the author of the rewritten judgment include an economic argument in a discussion of marriage rights?
2. What does that emphasis placed on plantation profits suggest about the author's view of autonomy for Black people?
3. How is the importance of bodily integrity for Black women consistent with feminist theory?
4. How are plantation profits addressed in the original opinion?
5. If plantation profits are not included, why would the author of the original opinion choose to ignore this point?
6. What, if anything, can you infer about the authors of the original opinion and their view of bodily autonomy for Black people?
7. How does the author of a particular opinion impact the public policy advanced or ignored in the opinion?
8. What impact does this have on the development of the law, especially its protection for marginalized communities?

16. *See* Teri McMurtry Chubb, *Rewritten Opinion in* Loving v. Virginia *in* FEMINIST JUDGMENTS: REWRITTEN OPINIONS OF THE UNITED STATES SUPREME COURT 125 (Kathryn M. Stanchi, Linda L. Berger & Bridget J. Crawford eds., 2016).

The instructor might add follow-up questions for consideration. Alternatively, an instructor may prefer to use PowerPoint or a whiteboard to write down group responses as students offer them.

Because public policy instruction is essential to all kinds of law courses, including casebook courses, writing courses, and clinics, this exercise can be incorporated into virtually any course.[17] The exercise also provides a seamless way to raise and explore the impact of public policy on diverse populations; it highlights the value of diverse voices and views. Importantly, it reveals the value of bringing diverse backgrounds and considerations to the bench and bar. For example, the author's perspective in the feminist judgment in *Loving v. Virginia* was especially instructive. Through the economic policy argument cited above, students are reminded of the corrupt societal values that once elevated plantation profits over the integrity of Black bodies—a hard but painful truth. In other words, the commitment to feminism, broadly understood as a justice project that includes Black people, gives the opinion a distinct authorial "voice." This distinction serves as a powerful reminder of the value of diverse perspectives and the need to ensure that the bench more closely resembles the population it serves.

The incorporation of feminist judgments into upper-level courses provides a platform for considering the relationship among the author's perspective, public policies, and reasoning—all especially important concerns when examining the impact of judicial decisions on minoritized communities. Further, using rewritten opinions is a dynamic way of teaching public policy arguments to students; it is more engaging than assigning academic readings about norm-building. The best policy analysis instruction "doesn't assume that there is an objectively correct policy that requires a particular outcome" in a given case.[18] By grounding students in the specifics of a particular case, students are challenged to assert policies that advance a client's interest.[19] They may also choose to advance policies that promote a society goal or value.[20]

One of the hallmarks of feminist practical reasoning, which one can see throughout the Feminist Judgments Project, is "the use of narrative to illuminate the effects of law on individual plaintiffs."[21] This use constitutes anoth-

---

17. It would work as effectively in bioethics, constitutional law, or tax, for example.

18. Margolis, *Teaching Students to Make Effective Policy Arguments*, *supra* note 14, at 74.

19. *Id.*

20. Camille Campbell & Olympia Duhart, Persuasive Legal Writing: A Storytelling Approach 38 (2017) (explaining that core societal values are "things, ideas, or concepts that a society believes are so important that they justify legal protections.").

21. Kathryn M. Stanchi, Linda L. Berger & Bridget J. Crawford, *Introduction*, *in* Feminist Judgments: Rewritten Opinions of the United States Supreme Court, *supra* note 16, at 15. *See also* Inga N. Laurent, *Commentary on* Loving v. Virginia, *in* Feminist Judgments: Rewritten Opinions of the United States Supreme Court, *supra* note 16, at 115.

er pedagogical benefit of placing more emphasis on the underlying perspective or values of the judicial author. Such emphasis invites critical examination of how a decision impacts the real people in a case, as well as the broader legal implications for the public. When parties to a legal action are members of historically minoritized or disenfranchised communities, an emphasis on personal stories and perspectives reveals the humanity that is too often suppressed or even denied. Under their robes, judges are human beings with their own values, strengths, biases, experiences, and biases. And behind the names of cases, so are the plaintiffs and defendants, too.

Conclusion

There are seemingly unlimited ways to teach with rewritten judicial opinions. Because feminist judgments take the recognizable form of judicial opinions, students can readily absorb a key message: the perspective of the decisionmaker matters. Too often the language of neutrality—in judging, in lawmaking, in policy discussions, and even in legal scholarship—makes it difficult to see bias where it exists. The multiple books comprising the U.S. Feminist Judgments Series seek to make that bias plain. As books are available as part of the Cambridge Core, to which many universities have subscriptions, instructors can easily assign selected opinions without additional cost to students.

In this discussion of perspective, it is fair to ask whether "feminist" judgments themselves are not riddled with bias, albeit of a different kind than they seek to unmask. Feminist judgments *are* biased, unapologetically so. Their bias is in favor of "justice for all people, particularly those historically oppressed or marginalized by or through law."[22] As analytic tools go, we believe that feminism is a mode of inquiry that encourages human flourishing—not of one group at the expense of another, but of all people in the world.

---

22. Kathryn M. Stanchi, Linda L. Berger & Bridget J. Crawford, *Introduction*, *in* FEMINIST JUDGMENTS: REWRITTEN OPINIONS OF THE UNITED STATES SUPREME COURT, *supra* note 16, at 3.

Teaching Indian Law in the Twenty-First Century

*Matthew L.M. Fletcher**

Introduction

Since the first Indian[1] law classes were offered in the late 1960s and early 1970s, law teachers mostly have considered the field a niche specialty, even a backwater, unnecessary to anyone not likely to go into law practice in Indian country. In those days, law teachers focused on treaty rights fights. Treaty rights are a critical but small part of Indian country practice. Lawyers in modern-day Indian country handle virtually every kind of matter taught in law schools in addition to the Indian law-specific subject matters. Beginning in the 1990s, American Indian tribal nations started to become critical factors in governmental and economic activity throughout much of the United States.

In the twenty-first century, many law schools offer Indian law—and occasionally offer additional, specialized courses—but generally are still far behind the curve. Worse, when it is offered, the Indian law canon tends to be taught in ways that ignore contemporary tribal agency by emphasizing historical events over modern issues. Modern tribal nations make their own laws. Here, I give examples of tribal court cases

---

* Matthew L.M. Fletcher is the Harry Burns Hutchins Collegiate Professor of Law at Michigan Law. He teaches and writes in the areas of federal Indian law, American Indian tribal law, Anishinaabe legal and political philosophy, constitutional law, federal courts, and legal ethics, and he sits as the Chief Justice of the Pokagon Band of Potawatomi Indians and the Poarch Band of Creek Indians. Professor Fletcher also sits as an appellate judge for the Cabazon Band of Mission Indians, the Colorado River Indian Tribes, the Grand Traverse Band of Ottawa and Chippewa Indians, the Hoopa Valley Tribe, the Lower Elwha Klallam Tribe, the Mashpee Wampanoag Tribe, the Match-E-Be-Nash-She-Wish Band of Pottawatomi Indians, the Nottawaseppi Huron Band of Potawatomi Indians, the Rincon Band of Luiseño Indians, the Santee Sioux Tribe of Nebraska, and the Tulalip Tribes. He is a member of the Grand Traverse Band.

1. I use the word "Indian" with full awareness of the impropriety of the term, but I use it because my own tribal nation has appropriated it (the Grand Traverse Band of Ottawa and Chippewa Indians) and for clarity, given that federal law from the United States Constitution on down uses the term.

and tribal statutes law teachers can use to incorporate Indian law into virtually any common law course.

Indian Law Instruction

The dominant metaphor used to describe Indian affairs is the miner's canary. Felix S. Cohen introduced the metaphor in the 1940s when he wrote, "Like the miner's canary, the Indian marks the shifts from fresh air to poison gas in our political atmosphere; and our treatment of Indians, even more than our treatment of other minorities, reflects the rise and fall in our democratic faith."[2] That metaphor certainly served a purpose then and for many decades after, but the role of weakness and passivity it assigns to Indian people is now a serious problem. To describe Indian people in the twenty-first century as sacrificial canaries whose whole purpose is to serve as a warning to non-Indians is really quite offensive.

Indian law instruction often replicates the treatment of Indian people as passive underdogs with no agency. Indian law classes usually start with an extensive review of Indian affairs history, which is essential to understanding how Indian law fits into greater American law. The foundational principles of Indian law derive from critically important historical events. Moreover, the United States Constitution, as we will see below, is structured the way it is, in part, because of the geopolitical role played by Indian tribes at the Founding. One cannot learn Indian law without this history.

But this focus on Indian affairs history sets a trap with two sides. The first part of the trap is that the myth of the vanishing Indian—the "romantic" notion that Indian people were substantially inferior to white Americans, that Indian people would inevitably fade away, die out, vanish, and that the passive withering away of Indian people actually occurred—really did prevail.[3] Most Americans just don't know anything about Indians and tribes. They certainly don't learn about Indian affairs history in school and when they do, it is often wildly inaccurate.

The second part of the trap is that scholars and instructors focus on the history of dispossession of Indian people of their lands, resources, children, and powers, not the modern-day lived reality of Indian people. Since dispossession is relatively well documented, scholars have a wealth of information to draw from in researching colonization and loss. It also feeds into the expectation that Indian people have disappeared. Moreover, most Indian law scholars and instructors have little experience navigating the lived reality of Indian country. Other than a very few of us, Indian law instructors have not worked inside Indian country. They know what they know from reading, not experiencing. In law school, the primary sources are almost exclusively United States

---

2. Felix S. Cohen, *The Erosion of Indian Rights, 1950–1953: A Case Study in Bureaucracy*, 62 Yale L.J. 348, 390 (1953).

3. *See generally* Kathryn E. Fort, *The Vanishing Indian Returns: Tribes, Popular Originalism, and the Supreme Court*, 57 St. Louis U. L.J. 297, 299 (2013).

Supreme Court decisions.[4] Outside of the former Solicitors General who argued an Indian law case or two in the Supreme Court, only a very small number of Supreme Court Justices in the entire history of the Court have had much actual experience in Indian law.[5] As a judge the Tenth Circuit, Justice Gorsuch heard numerous Indian law cases.[6] What they know of Indian country they learn from reading as well, and only the things brought to them by adversarial parties in litigation with vested interests in persuading the Court to adopt a particular narrative.

It is all too easy to offer an Indian law class that skips over the lived realities of Native people living in Indian country. The classic Indian law class covers the horrific history of American Indian affairs as told through the prism of Supreme Court decisions. The Court notoriously emphasizes the otherness of Indian people, labeling Indian people as weak and incompetent and Indian tribes dangerous and anti-democratic.[7] The world that Indians and tribes inhabit, as described by the Supreme Court and other federal and state courts, would be comical if the real-world implications were not so dire.

I much prefer the metaphor of the muskrat instead of the miner's canary.[8] In Anishinaabe creation stories, the muskrat is the hero. The muskrat is not the strongest or the smartest, but is the most devoted and giving. The muskrat has agency and foresight. The muskrat *sacrifices for* others, and is not *sacrificed by* others. Indian people and tribal nations are much more like a muskrat, an underdog with enormous capacity to make great positive change.

What modern tribal nations are doing right is not the easiest thing to discover. General law reviews rarely touch upon the subject.[9] It is absolutely difficult for any Indian law instructor to blast through the history to get to the lived realities of Indian people, but it is absolutely necessary. In my view, the best approach is to skip the Supreme

---

4. The casebook I teach from and serve as lead editor, DAVID H. GETCHES ET AL., CASES AND MATERIALS ON FEDERAL INDIAN LAW (7th ed. 2017), is a good example of how Supreme Court decisions serve as the focus of the class.

5. *E.g.*, Matthew L.M. Fletcher, *What Does a Justice Kagan Mean for Indian Country?* TURTLE TALK BLOG (May 10, 2010), https://turtletalk.blog/2010/05/10/what-does-a-justice-kagan-mean-for-indian-country/ ("Solicitor General Kagan has almost no paper record of scholarship on Indian law, no judicial opinions, and little else in the way of a paper trail.").

6. Matthew L.M. Fletcher, *Neil Gorsuch Indian Law Record as Tenth Circuit Judge*, TURTLE TALK BLOG (Feb. 1, 2017), https://turtletalk.blog/2017/02/01/neil-gorsuch-indian-law-record-as-tenth-circuit-judge/.

7. One of the most harmful examples of this phenomenon was Justice Souter's separate writing in a tribal court jurisdiction case where he characterized tribal law as "unwritten," derivative of "customs, traditions, and practices ... handed down orally or by example from one generation to another," and acontextually citing to a non-lawyer's description of tribal peacemaking processes. Nevada v. Hicks, 533 U.S. 353, 384–85 (2001) (Souter, J., concurring) (quoting Ada Pecos Melton, *Indigenous Justice Systems and Tribal Society*, 79 JUDICATURE 126, 130–131 (1995)).

8. Matthew L.M. Fletcher, *Muskrat Textualism*, 116 NW. U. L. REV. 963, 968 (2022).

9. Sonia K. Katyal, *Encouraging Engaged Scholarship: Perspectives from an Associate Dean for Research*, 31 TOURO L. REV. 53, 64–65 (2014). Professor Liz Reese's recent work is a rare exception. *See* Elizabeth A. Reese, *The Other American Law*, 73 STAN. L. REV. 555 (2021).

Court decisions and go directly to the source, tribal law. Tribal nations are leading the way in the development of the law. They are real laboratories of democracy.

Choice of Law/Commercial Law

Indian tribes contribute many billions of dollars to the national economy. Indian tribes are large federal government contractors, through congressional appropriations for tribal governmental services under the Indian Self-Determination and Education Assistance Act (also known as Public Law 648),[10] and through Section 8(a) contracting preferences as well.[11] Indian tribes also control untold billions of dollars of natural resources, such as coal, natural gas, petroleum, mining products, forestry products, and other materials. Finally, Indian gaming, which benefits less than half of Indian tribes, is nearly a $40 billion a year industry.[12] Many Indian tribes own corporate entities chartered under tribal, federal, or state law to operate their businesses.

Indian tribes and their corporate entities engage in highly complicated commercial transactions, borrowing common law principles from state law. Consider *Lake of the Torches Economic Development Corp. v. Saybrook Tax Exempt Investors, LLC*, a case decided by the Lac du Flambeau Band of Lake Superior Chippewa Indians trial-level court in 2013.[13] The case was brought by the tribe's Section 17 corporation, a corporate entity chartered by the Secretary of the Interior for the benefit of the tribe under § 17 of the Indian Reorganization Act of 1934.[14] The underlying dispute involved an off-reservation gaming development deal between the parties that had gone bad (off-reservation tribal gaming deals are extremely speculative). The parties had reached agreement on a series of transaction documents in which the tribe and its corporate entity waived sovereign immunity in Wisconsin federal and state courts to enforce the deal, agreeing to a forum selection clause allowing for suit in those courts as well. When the deal went south, the tribe's former business partners brought a whole series of suits in federal and state court.[15] The tribe and its corporate entity attempted to short-circuit these suits by suing in tribal court. The tribe's argument was that nothing in the transaction

---

10. 25 U.S.C. § 5301 et seq.

11. *See generally* Robert Jay Dilger & R. Corinne Blackford, Cong. Rsch. Serv., R44844, SBA's "8(a) Program": Overview, History, and Current Issues (2022), https://sgp.fas.org/crs/misc/R44844.pdf (describing the origins and scope of the 8(a) program).

12. Nat'l Indian Gaming Comm'n, *2021 Indian Gaming Revenue Jumps to Record High $39 billion, Increases 40%* (Aug. 10, 2022), https://www.nigc.gov/news/detail/2021-indian-gaming-revenue-jumps-to-record-high-39-billion-increases-40.

13. No. 13 CV 115 (Lac du Flambeau Band of Lake Superior Chippewa Indians Tribal Ct. 2013). The decision is unpublished, but it is available here: https://turtletalk.files.wordpress.com/2013/05/lake-of-the-torches-v-saybrook-tax-exempt-investors.pdf. Disclosure: the author served as the trial judge in the matter.

14. 25 U.S.C. § 5124.

15. *E.g.*, Wells Fargo Bank v. Lake of the Torches Econ. Dev. Corp., 658 F.3d 684, 686 (7th Cir. 2011); Stifel, Nicolaus, & Co., Inc. v. Lac du Flambeau Band of Lake Superior Chippewa Indians, 980 F. Supp. 2d 1078 (W.D. Wis. 2013).

documents prevented it from suing in tribal court because the forum selection clause was a permissive clause, rather than a mandatory clause. Some states apply a contrary rule that requires courts to construe forum selection clauses against the bringer of the suit. The transaction documents required the court to apply Wisconsin law. The court applied a Wisconsin Court of Appeals decision that adopted the rule advanced by the tribe.[16] In this century, this type of complex commercial transaction between Indian tribes, their corporate entities, and non-Indian businesses is the norm.

If one focuses on the Supreme Court decisions on the application of tribal law in a commercial context like this one, one would come away with the impression that tribal courts apply a kind of "unwritten law" that is "unusually difficult for an outsider to sort out."[17] This oversimplification and misunderstanding is common unless one learns about commercial law on the ground. I worked in-house for several Indian tribes in addition to my current work as a tribal judge. I've never seen a tribal business deal where the law was unusual or rooted in unknowable tribal custom and tradition. Tribes want to do business with outsiders, not scare them away.

Tribal court decisions dealing with commercial and business activities inside Indian country are legion. Examples of prominent cases include *Neptune Leasing, Inc. v. Mountain States Petroleum Corp.*,[18] a repossession action against a helium plant purchaser; *Wolf Point Organization v. Investment Centers of America, Inc.*,[19] a business fraud action; and *Cabazon Band of Mission Indians v. Lexington Insurance Co.*,[20] a claim for business losses arising from the COVID-19 pandemic.

Family Law

Family law, on the other hand, often *is* rooted in tribal custom and tradition. For centuries, tribal nations suffered the loss of generation after generation of Native children.[21] There were those orphaned and made homeless by the dispossession of tribal lands and resources. Then there were federal boarding schools that removed Native children from their homes and cultures. Then there was state removal of Native children from their homes and their adoption into non-Indian homes. But now, because of

16. The non-tribal parties brought suit in federal court shortly thereafter, seeking relief from tribal court jurisdiction. They prevailed, with the Seventh Circuit following its own precedents. *Stifel, Nicholas, and Company, Inc.*, 807 F.3d at 192–93 (citing Altheimer & Gray v. Sioux Manufacturing Corp., 983 F.2d 803 (7th Cir. 1993)). It is my understanding that, ultimately, the tribe reached a confidential settlement with its former business partners.

17. Nevada v. Hicks, 533 U.S. 353, 384–85 (2001) (Souter, J., concurring).

18. 11 Am. Indian Tribal L. 162, 2013 WL 2393054 (Navajo Nation S. Ct. 2013).

19. 3 Am. Indian Tribal L. 290, 2001 WL 36152106 (Fort Peck Ct. App. 2001).

20. No. CBMI 2020-0103 (Cabazon Band of Mission Indians Ct. App. 2022). The decision is unpublished but can be accessed here: https://turtletalk.files.wordpress.com/2021/11/final-opinion-cbmi-2020-0103-1.pdf. Disclosure: the author wrote the opinion in this matter.

21. *See generally* Margaret D. Jacobs, White Mother to a Dark Race: Settler Colonialism, Maternalism, and the Removal of Indigenous Children in the American West and Australia, 1880–1940 (2009).

the Indian Child Welfare Act of 1978,[22] tribal nations have led the way toward reform of child welfare systems, not just in Indian country, but throughout the United States. After losing generations of children, tribal nations were motivated to correct these injustices.

One key feature of tribal laws in child welfare is an emphasis on family and culture, too often missing in state child welfare systems that emphasize making children available for adoption.[23] The child welfare laws of the Nottawaseppi Huron Band of the Potawatomi elevate culture to the status of public policy. First, the code acknowledges that child welfare matters are not to be compartmentalized, impliedly referencing *Mno-Bmadzen*, the Anishinaabe philosophy of interconnectedness and inter-generational respect:

> *Bode'wadmi* traditions and values recognize the interconnectedness of every person and everything in this world and that the actions of one individual, or of a group of individuals, will have an impact on the whole of our community. In all things we do as a government, it is our obligation to promote *Bode'wadmi* traditions and values by seeking consensus so that decisions that are made will benefit the whole of our community for this and the next seven generations.[24]

The code also instructs the tribal government and tribal judiciary to interpret the child welfare code in light of *Noeg Meshomsenanek Kenomagewenen* (the Seven Grandfather Teachings):

> In carrying out the powers of self-government in a manner that promotes and preserves our *Bode'wadmi* values and traditions, the Tribe strives to be guided by the Seven Grandfather Teachings in its deliberations and decisions. The rights and limitations contained in this chapter are intended to reflect the values in the Seven Grandfather Teachings to ensure that tribal youth and community and other persons participating in youth development within the jurisdiction of the Tribe will be guided by the Seven Grandfather Teachings:
>
> *Bwakawen*—Wisdom
>
> *Debanawen*—Love
>
> *Kejitwawenindowen*—Respect
>
> *Wedasewen*—Bravery
>
> *Gwekwadzewen*—Honesty
>
> *Edbesendowen*—Humility
>
> *Debwewin*—Truth

---

22. 25 U.S.C. § 191 et seq.

23. The work of Dorothy Roberts is helpful in understanding this point. *E.g.*, Dorothy E. Roberts, *Is There Justice in Children's Rights: The Critique of Federal Family Preservation Policy*, 2 U. PA. J. CONST. L. 112 (1999).

24. Nottawaseppi Huron Band Tribal Code § 7.3-4.

In a recent opinion of the Nottawaseppi Huron Band Supreme Court, *Wright v. Nottawaseppi Huron Band of the Potawatomi*,[25] we applied *Noeg Meshomsenanek Kenomagewenen* in holding the tribe to a higher obligation to guarantee due process. The government must do more than merely provide the bare minimum; the government must "do justice."[26]

Many tribal nations, including the *Bode'wadmi* nations, treat children as supernatural creatures. They attempt to do justice to children, parents, extended family, and the entire community. The word in the language for child, *Penojé*, means "young spirit coming forth."[27] *Mno Bmadzen* assumes that all people are connected to all things: land, water, air, living creatures, inanimate objects, powerful forces like thunder, and spirits. Tribal child welfare cases take seriously the interconnectedness of a community.

Other interesting family law decisions include *In re the Guardianship of a Tulalip Minor*,[28] where a split appellate court decided a dispute over whether custody with the paternal or maternal grandparents was in the child's best interest, and *Matter of K.M.C.*,[29] another child custody dispute.

Criminal Law

Tribal criminal law is dominated by Acts of Congress and United States Supreme Court decisions, but what has become very clear is that tribal governments often provide greater procedural and substantive protections to criminal defendants, even where they don't have to. Congressional intervention takes the form of the Indian Civil Rights Act of 1968 (ICRA).[30] ICRA is designed to ensure that Indian tribes comply with federal constitutional rights norms.

However, ICRA is a creature of its time and is limited by that era. In the congressional hearings leading up to the enactment of ICRA, the United States Departments of Justice and the Interior opposed the inclusion of a guaranteed right to counsel for indigent criminal defendants, claiming to be worried about the cost (perhaps believing President Nixon's appointees to the Supreme Court would overrule or severely limit federal precedents guaranteeing the right to counsel and not wanting to see the right to

25. No. 21-154-APP (Nottawaseppi Huron Band of the Potawatomi S. Ct. 2022). The tribe has published the opinion here: https://nhbp-nsn.gov/wp-content/uploads/2022/06/2022-6-3-Filed-NHBP-Supreme-Court-Opinion-Order-in-Wright-et-al-v-NHBP-et-al-21-154-APP.pdf. Disclosure: the author wrote the opinion in the matter.

26. *Id.* at 11.

27. *Putting Our Minds Together for Our Children*, THE PUNDIT (Dec. 20, 2017) (quoting Michael D. Petoskey, Chief Judge of the Pokagon Band of Potawatomi Indians and the Match-E-Be-Bash-She-Wish Band of Pottawatomi Indians), https://michildsupportpundit.blogspot.com/2017/12/putting-our-minds-together-for-our.html.

28. 13 NICS App. 12 (Northwest Intertribal Ct. App.—Tulalip Tribes 2015), https://www.codepublishing.com/WA/NICS/.

29. 15 Am. Tribal Law 278, 2017 WL 10832146 (Fort Peck Ct. App. 2017).

30. 25 U.S.C. §§ 1302, 1304.

counsel codified by Congress in any form). It remains easy for observers to complain that because ICRA doesn't protect the full right to counsel present in state and federal prosecutions, tribal prosecutions are suspect. But in fact, tribal judges tend to come from underprivileged backgrounds, meaning they or those close to them have first-hand experience with the criminal justice system, and take seriously the enforcement of individual rights.[31]

In *Navajo Nation v. Rodriguez*,[32] the Navajo Nation Supreme Court was confronted with the question of whether to adopt the *Miranda* warnings in their tribal context. The court parsed through the *Miranda* decision, which catalogued the long history of police use of coercion and abuse to obtain confessions from criminal suspects. That long history served as partial justification for the suppression of confessions obtained through coercion. But the Navajo court knew of no similar tradition in the Navajo context and worried that to adopt Anglo-American policies would undercut their own legal traditions. That said, the court acknowledged that the tribal government (likely influenced to do so by American colonizers) had introduced coercive police tactics into Navajoland. The court ultimately adopted a more stringent test for determining whether confessions and other evidence obtained by police could be admissible on the ground.

In *People of the Little River Band of Ottawa Indians v. Champagne*,[33] the criminal defendant claimed that the tribe's assimilation of the state criminal code violated tribal public policy. The court invoked an *aadizookaan*, a traditional story of the Anishinaabe called *Nanaboozhoo and the Duck Dinner* where the trickster god Nanaboozhoo suffers a comeuppance resulting from his own poor choices, to show that the assimilation of state law comported with tribal custom and tradition.

Other representative and fascinating tribal court decisions in criminal law and procedure include *Lonjose v. Pueblo of Zuni*,[34] a decision about a defendant's competency to stand trial; *Southern Ute Tribe v. Peña*;[35] *Muscogee (Creek) Nation v. Johnson*,[36] a case involving a criminal suspect who confessed his "Indian" status to tribal police and whether that confession was admissible; and *People v. Rangel*,[37] where the court invoked

---

31. *E.g.*, Ann E. Tweedy, *Hon. Ronald J. Whitener: Chief Judge, Tulalip Tribal Court*, FED. LAW., Apr. 2017, at 23 (describing Judge Whitener's background as part of a family subject to criminal prosecution for treaty fishing in the 1970s).

32. 5 Am. Tribal Law 473, 8 Nav. R. 604 (Navajo Nation S. Ct. 2004).

33. 35 Indian L. Rep. 6004, 2007 WL 6900484 (Little River Band of Ottawa Indians Ct. App. 2004). Disclosure: the author wrote the opinion in the matter.

34. 28 SWITCA 1 (Southwest Intertribal Ct. App.—Zuni Tribe 2015), available at https://www.ailc-inc.org/our-work/switca/switca-reporter/.

35. 16 NICS App. 10 (Northwest Intertribal Ct. App.—Southern Ute Tribe 2018), available at https://www.codepublishing.com/WA/NICS/.

36. No. SC 11-13 (Muscogee (Creek) Nation S. Ct. 2013). The tribe has published the opinion here: http://www.creeksupremecourt.com/wp-content/uploads/SC_11-13.pdf.

37. No. 13-002-AP (Pokagon Band of Potawatomi Indians Ct. App. 2014). The tribe has published the opinion here: https://www.pokagonband-nsn.gov/sites/default/files/assets/group/tribal-court/2014/13-002-ap-decision-1653.pdf. Disclosure: the author wrote the opinion in this matter.

the Bode'wadmi principle of *Mno-Bmadzewen* in analyzing an issue involving the right to counsel.

Procedure

Tribal court judges often speak seriously about access to justice. Indian people rarely have resources to retain lawyers and, until a few decades ago, Indian tribes could not retain counsel without the approval of the Secretary of the Interior.[38] Keeping open the courthouse doors to people without resources is a critical public policy for modern tribal nations. Conversely, despite the platitudes of the judiciary, state and federal procedural rules often limit access to the courts for those with limited or no resources.[39]

In *Wright v. Nottawaseppi Huron Band of the Potawatomi*,[40] a tribal membership case mentioned above, the parties sparred over the specificity of the arguments made by the membership petitioners. The tribe also claimed that the plaintiffs, who were petitioning for tribal membership, had not provided any legal authority for their claims. These were defenses rooted in procedural default, a feature of state and federal litigation. The court sided with the plaintiffs, invoking *Edbesendowen*, the *Bode'wadmi* principle of humility, and *Bwakawen*, wisdom. The court concluded that to punish the petitioners for the actions of their counsel was unfair, absent a showing of prejudice by the opposing party.

For many years, I have served on the appellate court of the Pokagon Band of Potawatomi Indians. We have had few appeals over the years, but we have had the opportunity to draft and approve court rules after public comment. We have attempted to draft streamlined rules that are accessible to the general tribal public, but also are effective in ensuring fairness. For example, our evidence rules are only a few pages long, with the presumption favoring the introduction of just about any relevant information.[41]

Tribal Law and the Future

In many respects, Indian tribes have only just begun to experiment with their cultures and the law. Most tribes continue to assimilate state and federal common law in the first instance. But there are tribes that are truly on the cutting edge of law reform. For example, citizens of the White Earth Nation of Ojibwe brought a claim in tribal court against the Minnesota Department of Natural Resources, citing a tribal law rec-

---

38. Matthew L.M. Fletcher & Wenona T. Singel, *Lawyering the Indian Child Welfare Act*, 120 Mich. L. Rev. 1755, 1758 (2022) (discussing a now-repealed statute codified at 25 U.S.C. § 476(e) that subjected tribal retention of counsel to the approval of the Secretary of the Interior).

39. *See generally* Deborah L. Rhode, Access to Justice (2004) (surveying how federal and state laws limit access to justice for underprivileged litigants).

40. No. 21-154-APP (Nottawaseppi Huron Band of the Potawatomi S. Ct. 2022).

41. Pokagon Band of Potawatomi Indians, Rules of Evidence (2009), https://www.pokagonband-nsn.gov/government/tribal-courts/court-rules.

ognizing the legal personhood of *manoomin*, or wild rice. The tribal appellate court dismissed the claim,[42] but the claim could serve as a harbinger of similar claims in the future. This is just one example.

I sometimes (only a little bit facetiously) tell my students that American Indian tribal courts are a little bit like an alternate universe where political, sexual, and racial minorities actually get their day in court, where fairness and justice are paramount, and wealth and privilege don't mean much. Law teachers would do well to learn what they could about tribal laws.

42. Minnesota Dept. of Natural Resources v. Manoomin, No. AP21-0516 (White Earth Band of Ojibwe Ct. App. 2022), https://turtletalk.files.wordpress.com/2022/03/manoomin-opinion-ap21-0516.pdf.

A Lesson Plan for Teaching Gender-Inclusive Language

*Amanda Elyse**

Introduction

Below I've shared my step-by-step lesson plan for teaching gender-inclusive language to law students in both 1L and upper-level legal writing courses; it would also fit well in courses on client interviewing and counseling, pretrial and trial advocacy, and social movement lawyering, as well as in clinics and externships. Additionally, I've used this lesson plan when invited to conduct workshops for judge groups, public defender offices, and private law firms, as the recognition of the importance of gender-inclusive language is percolating through the legal profession. Here, this lesson plan is intended to serve as whatever you want it to be for teaching your own students, whether as a blueprint to follow, as a menu from which you select some items, as a supplement to materials you've already put together, or as a foundation for developing your own lesson plan. The lesson plan that I've shared can be taught in twenty to thirty minutes (depending on the amount of time for student discussion), but can be extended into other areas of a course (such as practicing use of gender-inclusive language with a non-binary character in a problem, developing a client-intake form, considering how to revise legislation to be gender-inclusive, or practicing how to advocate for a client or talk to a jury in court). I hope this lesson plan is merely a starting point.

* Former Visiting Assistant Professor of Lawyering Skills at Seattle University School of Law. The author thanks Emma Daniels and Lauren Butrim for their assistance with research, as well as everyone in SU's Legal Writing Program for their support over the years. She also thanks her partner for their support and encouragement of her work, and the two dogs and cat who are her constant writing companions.

Lesson

I start the lesson about gender-inclusive language by holding up the children's book *A More Graceful Shaboom*. I tell my students that we're taking a little break from law school and having story time (an announcement that is met with smiles and some relief), and then I explain that this children's book has a main character, Harmon, with they/them pronouns, and read from what the book has titled "A note about the use of they as a singular pronoun in this book":

> Some people are girls. Some people are boys. Some people are somewhere in between, everything all at once, or neither. "They" can be used to refer to a person whose gender is non-binary, gender-expansive, intersex, or gender-fluid, like the main character of this book. For instance, Harmon loves going downtown; they go there often.[1]

This passage thereby becomes our introduction to discussing singular they pronouns and other gender-inclusive language.

From there, I pose the following questions to my students to discuss either in small groups or with the class as a whole:

> *Why is it important for law students and lawyers to understand progress in the evolution of gender-inclusive language?*[2]
>
> *How might such knowledge relate to client-centered lawyering and cultural humility?*[3]
>
> *How might such knowledge be considered a power skill in the legal profession? How might it be part of a professional identity?*[4]

---

1. Jacinta Bunnell & Crystal Vielula, A More Graceful Shaboom (2020). This book was one of the first children's books to feature a main character with they/them pronouns, so I started using it in my classes soon after its publication and then kept using it given the positive reception from students and the effective explanation of singular they.

2. Having students read or discuss content such as shared in "Legal Language" by Professor Sheila Hyatt (available on the University of Denver Strum College of Law website at https://www.law.du.edu/index.php/law-school-learning-aids/legal-language) about the importance of precision in the meaning of words in legal language can be a helpful primer to considering this question. *See also* Kadija Kabba, *Gender Neutral Language: An Essential Language Tool to Serve Precision, Clarity and Unambiguity*, 37 Commw. L. Bull. 427 (2011) (studying how gender-neutral language serves precision, clarity, and unambiguity, and it is an essential tool in drafting legislation).

3. Prior to this class day, my students would have read sections of "Addressing Cultural Bias in the Legal Profession" by Debra Chopp. The article discusses cultural humility and explains, "Cultural humility emphasizes self-reflection and treats each person as an expert on [their] own cultural experience. It … can help lawyers respect the cultural backgrounds of their clients, communicate with them more successfully, and tell their stories to decision-makers and negotiation partners with greater fidelity to the client's lived experience." Debra Chopp, *Addressing Cultural Bias in the Legal Profession*, 41 NYU Rev. of L. & Soc. Change 367, 370 (2017).

4. "Power skills" is a rebranding of "soft skills" and refers to "human-centered skills, such as communication, social and emotional intelligence, critical thinking, problem-solving, teamwork, leadership, professional attitude, work ethic, career management, and intercultural fluency." Natalie Runyon,

How might such knowledge relate to persuasive writing and advocacy on behalf of a client?

The discussion of these questions lays a foundation for the information that I then share about singular they pronouns and other gender-inclusive language.

In sharing information, I first establish the baseline that using the correct gendered language for someone—whether a future client or colleague, current classmate,[5] or anyone else—is not merely a preference but a requirement. For example, while the term "preferred pronouns" has often been used in order to indicate a respect for using the correct pronouns for someone, the "preferred" part of the term has quickly become outdated, which has been highlighted everywhere from stickers and buttons[6] to articles in global media outlets.[7] Someone's pronouns—and other gendered language—are not a mere preference, as we may think of preferring chocolate or vanilla ice cream, but just what they are.

What are your pronouns?

My pronouns are ______.

I also model this phrasing, both during this particular discussion, as well as at other times. For example, prior to the start of a course, I send out a student information sheet and one of the questions I include is "What are your pronouns?" We repeat this process again on the first day of class when I have everyone share their name and pronouns. I also include my pronouns in my email signature and on my Zoom name, and I encourage my students to do so as well.

After establishing that someone's pronouns are what they are and not a preference, I then teach the grammar basics of how singular "they" pronouns work—when referring to an individual by name, use singular verb conjugation with the name ("Charlie Kim is our client."), and when referring to an individual by a they/them/theirs pronoun, use plural verb conjugation with the pronoun ("They are stopping by the office."). Here I also highlight that someone whose pronouns are them/them/theirs likely will not want to be referred to with a gendered honorific such as Ms. or Mr., and so the gender-neu-

---

Why "Power Skills" Is the New Term for Soft Skills in the Hybrid Work World, THOMSON REUTERS (Feb. 8, 2022), https://www.thomsonreuters.com/en-us/posts/legal/power-skills-rebranding/.

5. As of 2016, 56% of people in Gen Z in the U.S. (people who were then thirteen to twenty years old—which means people who are of an age that are currently or soon to be law students, or who are new lawyers) said that they knew someone who went by gender-neutral pronouns such as they/them/theirs. Zing Tsjeng, *Teens These Days Are Queer AF, New Study Says*, VICE (Mar. 10, 2016), https://www.vice.com/en/article/kb4dvz/teens-these-days-are-queer-af-new-study-says.

6. *See, e.g.*, ETSY.COM, cpikoart, *My Pronouns Are Not Preferred Button // Transgender Nonbinary Pride*, https://www.etsy.com/ie/listing/1109072752/my-pronouns-are-not-preferred-button?external=1&ref=lp_collection_recs-listing-3 (last visited Dec.8, 2022).

7. *See, e.g.*, A.C. Fowlkes, *Why You Should Not Say 'Preferred Gender Pronouns,'* FORBES (Feb. 27, 2020), https://www.forbes.com/sites/ashleefowlkes/2020/02/27/why-you-should-not-say-preferred-gender-pronouns/?sh=3d0176c1bd60.

tral "Mx." (pronounced "mix," like "mix the cake batter") is available.[8] So, Charlie Kim could be referred to as Mx. Charlie Kim or Mx. Kim.

From there, I delve into illustrating ways in which the legal profession and world around my students require them—as current law students and future lawyers—to understand use of singular "they" pronouns. First, to consider the general evolution of language, I share that Merriam-Webster selected singular "they" as its Word of the Year in 2019 due to how often it was looked up on Merriam-Webster.com,[9] the AP Stylebook began to include singular "they" in its 2017 edition,[10] and singular "they" was the word of the year from the American Dialect Society in 2015.[11] Additionally, the online version of the Oxford Dictionary includes singular "they" as well as a blog post providing a history of its use.[12] Furthermore, a variety of mainstream media outlets—from *The Washington Post* to NPR to *New York Times* to *The Atlantic*—have featured pieces about the use of gender-neutral pronouns.[13]

Not only has singular "they" received these broad forms of acknowledgement in relation to the progress in language, but it has received attention that is specific to the legal profession as well. As one sign of the times: inclusion in a legal drama. The CBS show *All Rise*, which follows the stories of characters who are lawyers and judges, aired an episode in which one of the lawyers represents a client whose pronouns are they/them/theirs—and in one court scene, the lawyer has to advocate for her client's correct pronouns to be used in court.[14] The scene clip is only thirty-eight seconds long, so I'm able to show it to my students without taking up very much time. I'm also able to use the clip to address the concern that using they/them/theirs pronouns to refer to an individual will create confusion. In the scene, the judge says that the character's pronouns will be respected, but she also says that doing so is "gonna wreak havoc on the record." So, I point out to my students that we deal with language and clarity all the time in legal writing and oral advocacy. In a case that involves two people who both have the pronouns "she/her/hers," we sometimes have to use each person's name to clarify who we're referring to. The same thing is true with they/them/theirs—we can use the person's name when needed in order to make clear that we're referring to that

---

8. The first use of "Mx." as a gender-neutral honorific dates to 1977, so it has a history that is much longer than more recent (and overdue) formal recognition. Heidi K. Brown, *Get with the Pronoun*, 17 Legal Comm. & Rhetoric: JAWLD 61, 67 (2020).

9. *They Is Merriam-Webster's Word of the Year 2019*, Merriam-Webster.com (https://www.merriam-webster.com/words-at-play/woty2019-top-looked-up-words-they.

10. Laura Easton, *Making a case for a singular "they,"* AP (Mar. 24, 2017), https://blog.ap.org/products-and-services/making-a-case-for-a-singular-they.

11. *2015 Word of the Year is singular "they,"* Am. Dialect Soc'y (Jan. 8, 2016), https://www.americandialect.org/2015-word-of-the-year-is-singular-they.

12. Dennis Baron, *A brief history of singular "they,"* Oxford Eng. Dictionary (Sept. 4, 2018), https://public.oed.com/blog/a-brief-history-of-singular-they/.

13. *See, e.g.*, Miriam Berger, *A guide to how gender-neutral language is developing around the world*, Wash. Post (Dec. 15, 2019), https://www.washingtonpost.com/world/2019/12/15/guide-how-gender-neutral-language-is-developing-around-world/.

14. The scene is available to watch at https://www.facebook.com/AllRiseCBS/videos/we-see-you-jax-everyone-should-have-the-freedom-to-live-herhistheir-truth-pronou/961709404319055/.

individual rather than a group of people. I also remind my students that they can make use of brief parentheticals or footnotes if needed to explain someone's pronouns.

I then move the lesson from the fictional realm of a legal drama to the real world of the legal profession. I start by showing my students that the American Bar Association itself has shown concern about recent state bills across the U.S. that target transgender youth. Articles in the *ABA Journal* include coverage of the ABA House voting to oppose laws that ban transgender student athletes and "the association adopt[ing] a resolution that opposes all legislation, regulations and policies that discriminate against individuals who are transgender or nonbinary on the basis of gender identity or that impose barriers to obtaining or providing medical care to affirm individuals' gender identity."[15]

From there, I cover some examples of how laws have changed to account for non-binary gender identification. So far, twenty-two states plus Washington, D.C., allow an X gender marker (in addition to F and M) on a driver's license, and sixteen states plus Washington, D.C., allow an X gender marker on a birth certificate.[16] Additionally, some cities have addressed gender identity and expression; for example, the New York City Commission on Human Rights prohibits discrimination on the basis of gender by "most employers, housing providers, and public accommodations" and provides that "gender 'shall include actual or perceived sex, gender identity, and gender expression including a person's actual or perceived gender-related self-image, appearance, behavior, expression, or other gender-related characteristic, regardless of the sex assigned to that person at birth.'"[17]

I then turn to the judicial realm to illustrate to my students how teachings and practices for judges are advancing to reflect respect for people's pronouns and gender identities. According to attorney Francesco G. Salpietro, the first time a court directly ruled on a transgender pronoun issue was in Chelsea Manning's[18] case in 2015 when the U.S. Army Court of Appeals stated that all orders and decisions in the case should use gender-neutral terms (such as Private First Class Manning or Appellant) or pronouns she/her/hers.[19] Furthermore, Salpietro asserts that if a judge refuses to respect a transgender individual's pronouns, the judge may be in violation of canons in the ABA's Model Code of Judicial Conduct: "Integrity, Impartiality, and the Manifestation

---

15. Amanda Robert, *ABA House votes to oppose laws that ban transgender student athletes*, ABA J. (Aug. 9, 2021), https://www.abajournal.com/news/article/resolution-609-aba-opposes-laws-that-ban-transgender-student-athletes.

16. *Identity Document Laws and Policies*, Movement Advancement Project, https://www.lgbtmap.org/equality-maps/identity_document_laws (last visited Dec. 8, 2022).

17. *Gender Identity/Gender Expression: Legal Enforcement Guidance*, NYC Comm'n on Human Rts., https://www1.nyc.gov/site/cchr/law/legal-guidances-gender-identity-expression.page (last visited Dec. 8, 2022).

18. Chelsea Manning describes herself as "Security Consultant. Fmr. Intel Analyst. Player of Vijyagames. Trans femme (she/they)" on her Twitter profile at https://twitter.com/xychelsea (last visited Dec. 8, 2022).

19. Francesco G. Salpietro, *R-E-S-P-E-C-T: Transgender Pronoun Preference and the Model Code of Judicial Conduct*, 53 Ct. Rev.: J. Am. Judges Ass'n. 590 (2017), https://digitalcommons.unl.edu/cgi/viewcontent.cgi?article=1629&context=ajacourtreview.

of Bias."[20] I point out that this assertion can be extended to a non-binary individual as well (along with the pronouns they/them/theirs). Then I remind my students that, as soon-to-be lawyers, they will operate under Rules of Professional Conduct and the ABA Model Rule 8.4 provides, "It is professional misconduct for a lawyer to ... engage in conduct that the lawyer knows or reasonably should know is harassment or discrimination on the basis of ... sex ... sexual orientation, [or] gender identity...."[21]

Additionally, judges receive specific guidance about pronouns, including singular "they" pronouns and gender-inclusive language. For example, the QLaw Association (The LGBTQ+ Bar Association of Washington) provides a Judges' Bench Guide on the LGBTQ Community and the Law as a resource for judges, as well as lawyers and the broader community. The guide states:

> The words used in court—whether by a judge or anyone else—matter, as does a respectful and inclusive tone. The use of pejorative terms, incorrect gender-signifying pronouns, or the use of a transgender person's former name can indicate disrespect, ignorance, or bias. It is not enough for a judicial officer to use inclusive language. The judge and all court personnel must ensure that all participants in the legal process show respect to one another.[22]

It also instructs, "If unsure of which pronoun to use to refer to a person, ask the person, use the gender-neutral 'they/them,' or simply use their last name."[23] In line with this advice, some judges have become proactive in asking about pronouns. For example, Magistrate Judge S. Kate Vaughan's Courtroom Rules include: "The parties and counsel are encouraged to advise the Court of their pronouns and may do so by including their pronouns in signature lines or advising the in-court deputy clerk of pronouns and honorifics before a hearing begins, either via email or in person."[24] This rule prompted me to have my students practice including their pronouns in their signature blocks on assignments such as a Motion Brief.

I also select an example of gender-inclusive language that is something other than singular "they" pronouns to share with my students. A common example that I use is language around pregnancy and who can become pregnant. Just referring to "women," as is often done, is not gender-inclusive language. I start by showing them that mainstream publications, such as *Parents*, recognize the importance of language in being

---

20. *Id.*

21. Model R. Pro. Conduct R. 8.4 (Am. Bar Ass'n 2020). *See also* Chan Tov McNamarah, *Misgendering as Misconduct*, 68 UCLA L. Rev. Discourse 40 (2020) (arguing that bar associations should address discriminatory behavior relating to misgendering people through the RPCs).

22. QLaw Foundation of Washington & QLaw Association: The LGBTQ Bar Association of Washington, Judges' Bench Guide on the LGBTQ Community and the Law § 2 (3d. ed. 2017), https://www.courts.wa.gov/committee/pdf/LGBTQ%20Bench%20Guide.pdf.

23. *Id.* at § 4.

24. Jude Vaughan's Courtroom Rules are available online at https://www.wawd.uscourts.gov/judges/vaughan-chambers.

inclusive of trans and non-binary people in discussing who can become pregnant.[25] Then, to move into the legal profession, I highlight how law review authors have dealt with the importance of gender-inclusive language in relation to making sure that laws about pregnancy and reproductive health care actually include everyone who may become pregnant.[26] This past school year, I also showed them an example in the media of the relationship between gender-inclusive language and the law in how Representative Alexandria Ocasio-Cortez referenced "any person with a menstrual cycle" in discussing who a Texas abortion ban would impact.[27] We then discussed other possible gender-inclusive language that could be used, such a "people who may become pregnant" or "pregnant person."

We also look at some examples of frequently used terms in the legal profession that falsely assume a gender binary—and how to easily change the terms. For example, instead of referring to "Ladies and gentlemen of the jury," one can refer to "members of the jury." We can also update saying "he or she" to saying "he, she, or they" or just "they," and we can avoid calling people "Sir" or "Ma'am" unless we know that they want to be referred to by one of those gendered terms.

As the lesson nears the end, I go over some "Tips for Representing Clients" with my students. We talk about how client-centered lawyering guides us to communicate with a client, follow their direction, and back them up—to normalize asking and sharing about pronouns and other gender-inclusive language in a space of support and learning. We can use footnotes or parentheticals to clarify names, pronouns, and other language as needed. We can explain names, pronouns, and other language as needed to colleagues, judges, juries, opposing counsel, etc. and advocate that the appropriate language is used for clients. We need to respect names, pronouns, and other language for all parties, regardless of who we represent, and if we accidentally use the wrong language take that as a learning opportunity in which we apologize, say thank you for being corrected, and move on—and work on practicing, remembering, and continued learning for using the correct language in the future. These tips can also help to guide the tone we set in the classroom so that it is an inclusive space for students of all genders.[28]

---

25. "Transgender men (men who were assigned female at birth based on their biological sex) and nonbinary folks like me (those who don't identify as either male or female) can and do get pregnant. When talking about reproduction, reproductive rights, and gynecological health, transgender folks deserve the same inclusive and affirming care as cisgender folks. That starts with language." Amber Leventry, *Trans and Nonbinary People Can Be Pregnant Too*, PARENTS (Oct. 21, 2021), https://www.parents.com/pregnancy/my-body/pregnancy-health/trans-and-nonbinary-people-can-be-pregnant-too/.

26. *See, e.g.*, Jessica Clarke, *Pregnant People?* 119 COLUM. L. REV. FORUM 6 (2019).

27. Paul LeBlanc, *Alexandria Ocasio-Cortez slams Texas GOP governor's "deep ignorance" on abortion*, CNN (Sept. 8, 2021), https://www.cnn.com/2021/09/07/politics/aoc-texas-abortion-law-greg-abbott-cnntv/index.html.

28. See the article *Creating a Gender-Inclusive Classroom* by Sarah McKibben (available at https://www.ascd.org/el/articles/creating-a-gender-inclusive-classroom) for additional ideas about thinking about how gendered language arises in classrooms and impacts students' experiences, and how to re-shape the classroom to be more gender-inclusive.

I then finish the lesson by bringing it back into the law school classroom. I emphasize that this time we're spending on gender-inclusive language helps to put them in a similar space on this topic as students at many other law schools (as well as practicing lawyers!)—so they are not behind in being able to use singular "they" pronouns and other gender-inclusive language as legal professionals. I share with them that I've presented about gender-inclusive language at legal writing conferences, as well as to judges, law firms, and public defender offices, and that the overwhelming response is that this content is important in the legal profession. Furthermore, in addition to the importance stretching across the U.S. legal profession, it stretches internationally. For example, the British Columbia Law Institute, a non-profit law reform agency in Vancouver, B.C., Canada, is creating a guide to "Gender Diversity in Legal Writing: Pronouns, Honorifics, and Gender-Inclusive Techniques." The overview of the reasons behind the guide explains,

> Like the law, language and styles of writing evolve over time to meet the needs of new generations. One such shift is towards language that reflects a modern understanding of gender and gender identity. Inclusivity can no longer be limited to masculine and feminine but must be extended to include people who identify as non-binary, agender, two spirited, or genderqueer.[29]

And then the lesson concludes with, "Questions? Thoughts to share?"

Conclusion

After the lesson, I then get to see the impact. The immediate impact has largely been defined by students expressing a lot of appreciation and feeling more comfortable, including: (1) students saying thank you for going over gender-inclusive language because they were aware of it and wanted to use it but weren't sure how, (2) students expressing that they were glad that gender-inclusive language was part of class because they came to law school wanting an educational experience that reflected social progress, and (3) a student deciding that the lesson set up a space that felt good for them to share with their classmates that their pronouns had changed to they/them. I have not heard any negative comments from students, and I credit that to the material in the lesson that makes clear that the broader legal profession values understanding and properly using gender-inclusive language, regardless of what any one person may feel individually. Beyond the immediate impact, I see students actively practice using singular they pronouns and other gender-inclusive language in their discussions and writing, ask follow-up questions to me and have further conversations with each other, and think beyond the assignments in a course. They show themselves to be ready and eager to apply gender-inclusive language in the classroom and beyond, and they are primed to think critically about other areas of language as well (such as referring to

---

29. *Gender Diversity in Legal Writing: Pronouns, Honorifics, and Gender-Inclusive Techniques*, British Columbia L. Inst. (2022), https://papers.ssrn.com/sol3/papers.cfm?abstract_id=4161161.

someone by name rather than objectifying them through a term like defendant or inmate) that impact how people are viewed, treated, and made to feel in the legal system and our society as a whole. I hope this lesson plan can serve as a starting point for not only what you do in class, but also for so much more.

Using Prose to Create Legal Pros

*Brandon Stump**

Introduction

Every law professor and law student contain, as Walt Whitman eloquently wrote, "multitudes."[1] We are each the sum of our identities and experiences. And those identities and experiences gain meaning through story. Sometimes, though, we allow our own multitudes, the intersections of our identities, to dictate the content we deliver to students. One way that we as law professors can add diverse voices to our course content and foster other challenging discussions is to incorporate fiction, particularly novels, into our courses. In this essay I will explore the benefits of using novels to create Problem Based Learning (PBL) in upper-level law school courses, including family law, remedies, and intellectual property, and how relying on fiction can: (1) incorporate diverse voices and perspectives into the class and (2) prepare students for a wide array of clients.[2] In particular, I will focus on my own experiences using fiction to teach legal writing.

In 2021, 32 percent of law students were students of color.[3] Additionally, women comprised 55.3 percent of all enrolled students.[4] While the American Bar Association

---

* Brandon Stump, Professor of Legal Writing, Cleveland State University College of Law.

1. Walt Whitman, Song of Myself 104 (Stephen Mitchell, ed. 1998) ("Do I contradict myself?/ Very well then I contradict myself,/ (I am large, I contain multitudes.)").

2. Raymond A. Mar, Keith Oatley & Jordan B. Peterson, *Exploring the Link Between Reading Fiction and Empathy: Ruling out Individual Differences and Examining Outcomes*, 34 Commc'ns 407, 409 (2009) ("There is growing evidence that reading narratives, even those explicitly labeled as fiction, is far from a meaningless leisure activity that ends when one closes the cover of a book. Several researchers have demonstrated that exposure to narrative fiction can influence our attitudes toward various issues.... [E]vidence is accumulating that the reading of narrative fiction can have important consequences[.]"). *See also* Stacey A. Tovino, *Incorporating Literature Into a Health Law Curriculum*, 9 Mich. St. U. J. Med. & L. 213, 255 (2005) (explaining that the use of literature in a law and health course can "help [law students] understand and identify with different types of people.").

3. Am. Bar Ass'n, ABA Legal Profile: Legal Education, https://www.abalegalprofile.com/legal-education.php (last visited Dec. 20, 2022).

4. *Id.*

does not collect data on the number of disabled or LGBTQ law students enrolled, employment data shows 1.2% percent of practicing lawyers are disabled and 3.7 percent are openly LGBTQ.[5] Obviously, at some point, these queer and disabled attorneys matriculated through an American legal classroom. But how many of these students ever saw themselves reflected in the materials? Furthermore, how many students, in general, were ever prepared to work with and for diverse clients? One way to make diverse students feel seen and incorporated into the fabric of the historically white and patriarchal law school classroom (and legal profession), while also preparing every student to competently and empathetically[6] represent diverse clients, is to design courses around works of fiction that include three-dimensional characterizations of marginalized people. Reading a novel or two during a semester of law school, outside of the benefits of reading in general, allows students to immerse themselves in the facts of a story the same way they would a case file.

A Novel Idea: Literary-Based PBL

When I walk into my legal writing classroom for the first time each fall semester, I know that I stand at the center of an intersection most of my students have never witnessed before. I am an Autistic, queer, male-bodied professor who grew up in overwhelmingly white Appalachia and practiced law in predominantly Black Detroit. However, I am still only one person. My experiences, as unique and diverse as they might be from the experiences of a majority of my students and colleagues, do not encompass all the various diversity intersections of my classroom or the world of clients they will someday represent.

Law professors traditionally teach students "the law" through a "case-based method, [where] students acquire legal knowledge and skills by dissecting the arguments and reasoning in appellate case opinions and responding to questions and comments from the professor that challenge student viewpoints, highlight important points in case opinions, and identify errors made by students."[7] Conversely, "Project Based Learning is a teaching method in which students gain knowledge and skills by working for an extended period of time to investigate and respond to an authentic, engaging, and complex question, problem, or challenge."[8] In law school, this means that the student

---

5. Am. Bar Ass'n, ABA Legal Profile: Demographics, https://www.abalegalprofile.com/demographics.php (last visited Dec. 20, 2022).

6. Jennifer L. Cornell, *Reading Cases for Empathy*, 17 U. St. Thomas L.J. 772, 782 (2022) (explaining that empathy, like legal analysis, is a "core lawyering skill"). Specifically, some "courses use literary fiction itself as a means of stimulating empathy[.]").

7. Shirley Lung, *The Problem Method: No Simple Solution*, 45 Willamette L. Rev. 723, 724 (2009).

8. PBL Works, *What Is PBL?* https://www.pblworks.org/what-is-pbl (last visited Dec. 20, 2012).

"must determine which part of their legal knowledge base is relevant and use that knowledge appropriately to solve the problem."[9]

Some law professors, including myself, use fiction (or literary non-fiction) as a form of PBL to "more realistically portray the practice of law[.]"[10] In fact, Capital University Law School's Professor Scott A. Anderson uses Tim O'Brien's *In the Lake of the Woods* to teach his criminal litigation drafting. "The novel is not a typical legal writing fact pattern. In its 300 pages, there is not one passage designed to elicit a response from students about which legal issues are relevant."[11] In part, Anderson uses *In the Lake of the Woods* to teach students how "to identify with their client over the semester-long case. They begin to see dry legal rules as tools for protecting [the main character's] interests.... The students begin to learn lessons about persuasion."[12] Students in my class apply case law to the facts and scenarios in the novel, albeit with my guidance.

Critics of using novels might contend that the use of stories/narrative loses effectiveness after the first year of law school as students become more familiar with the structure of law school courses, thus eliminating their need for familiar pre-law school narrative.[13] Scant empirical evidence regarding the effectiveness of using novels to teach law school courses exists. However, in a study conducted at Florida Coastal School of Law, a group of students enrolled in a first-year contracts class were compared to upper-level students, both second and third year, enrolled in a sales class (Article 2 of the Uniform Commercial Code).[14] The students in both courses received supplemental materials in two forms: (1) story form and (2) expository form.[15] Students had one week to review the materials, and at the end of the semester students took a multiple-choice

9. Lung, *supra* note 7, at 724.

10. Scott A. Anderson, *A Novel Teaching Practice: Using Nonlegal Fiction to Instill Legal Values*, 21 PERSPECTIVES: TEACHING LEGAL RSCH. & WRITING 28, 31 (2012). This "case method approach" to learning is common in medical and business schools, referred to as "problem based learning (PBL)." While outside of the context of the legal classroom, researchers studying high school Advanced Placement (AP) courses found that "nearly half of students in project-based classrooms passed their AP tests, outperforming students in traditional classrooms by 8 percentage points." *Id. See also* Youki Terada, *New Research Makes a Powerful Case for PBL*, EDUTOPIA (Feb. 21, 2021), https://www.edutopia.org/article/new-research-makes-powerful-case-pbl (describing "a new generation of classes that transform traditional teacher-led instruction into a more student-centered, project-based approach—requiring students to work together as they tackle complex, real-world problems that emphasize uncertainty, iterative thinking, and innovation.").

11. Anderson, *supra* note 10, at 29.

12. *Id.* at 31. As an added bonus, Anderson finds that because students rely on a literary work for their fact patterns, they are less likely to use legalese in their drafting because such language did not form the basis of their understanding of the case. *Id.*

13. Scott DeVito, *The Power of Stories and Images in Law School Teaching*, 53 WASHBURN L.J. 51, 67 (2013).

14. *Id.* at 61–62.

15. DeVito, *supra* note 13, at 64. Story form supplements included: Doctrinal information written into a script, the script forming the basis for a cartoon, and the script forming the basis of a movie. *Id.* at 62 n.80. Expository form supplements included: outlines of doctrinal information, flowcharts of doctrinal information, and hornbook sections. *Id.*

exam.[16] The study revealed that both groups of students benefited from "visual formats" whether they were story form or expository form. "Ultimately, visual supplementation was thirty-percent better at improving learning than text supplementation for first-year students."[17] For upper-level students, "visual supplementation was fifty-percent better at improving learning than text supplementation[.]"[18]

The study also revealed that for first-year students, "story supplementation improved learning by twelve percent while expository supplementation improved learning by eleven percent (as compared to no supplementation)."[19] Upper-level students benefited from story supplementation, 12 percent, but not as much as they benefited from expository supplements, 13 percent.[20] First-year law students seem to benefit the most from a law professor's use of story because they are "naïve learners—they are unfamiliar with both the material and how to learn it."[21] Conversely, "[u]pper-level students are sophisticated learners in the sense that they already know how to learn the law."[22] Importantly, the study involved "story," taking doctrinal information and creating a script; whereas I propose using novels to supplement and create three-dimensional background facts to which students can apply doctrinal concepts, the same way attorneys apply the law to the facts of client cases. I posit that using a novel, a form of art, might produce similar learning improvements as the use of illustrations.

While student understanding, achievement,[23] and success in a course are paramount, they should not be the sole motivator for a professor designing a course, especially if that professor wants to achieve the two goals stated at the outset of this essay: (1) incorporate disparate and marginalized experiences into the classroom and (2) prepare students to empathetically[24] work with diverse clients.

---

16. *Id.* at 62.
17. *Id.* at 63.
18. *Id.*
19. *Id.* at 64.
20. *Id.*
21. *Id.* at 67.
22. *Id.*
23. *See* Zahr K. Said, *Incorporating Literary Methods and Texts in The Teaching of Tort Law*, 3 Cal. L. Rev. Circuit 60, 70 (2012) (finding value in "[g]rounding larger humanistic concerns in substantive law shows students how relevant these approaches are to what they are learning, and what they may be doing in practice for the rest of their lives").
24. In adopting a "humanist" approach to Tort law, Prof. Said "aim[ed] to learn from complex representations of those who commit torts, those who suffer injury therefrom, and those who seek to represent the various parties." *Id.* at 68.

Personal Experiences Using Fiction to Teach Legal Writing

Each spring semester my students immerse themselves in author Dennis Lehane's mystery thriller, *Mystic River*.[25] All of the novel's main characters are white and mostly working-class.[26] Most of the main characters live at the margins of society because of forces beyond their control.[27] The novel begins with three working-class boys playing in a Boston neighborhood. Two men approach the boys and kidnap one of them, 11-year-old Dave Boyle.[28] His friends Jimmy Marcus and Sean Devine are spared.[29] A manhunt ensues, and during this time, Dave is raped over a period of days in a shack in the woods.[30] Dave physically escapes, but he never mentally escapes what his kidnappers did to him.[31] The three boys are reunited in 2000 when their stories all intersect, and Boyle becomes a prime suspect in the murder of Marcus's daughter.[32] The novel weaves in and out of perspectives, but most readers are taken with Boyle's internal life, his childhood trauma informing who he is in the present.[33] Boyle's inner, and at times audible, dialogue involves his emotional and mental reckoning with his rape and kidnappers.[34] In fact, Boyle, to survive the trauma, creates a life narrative that he is the Boy who survived an attack by the evil Wolves.[35] We see how Boyle's trauma shapes his marriage, his relationship with his son, his ability to work, etc.[36] After reading the 400-plus page novel, I provide students with a supplemental record informing them to accept the events of the book as real (outside of Boyle's ultimate fate). I then provide a fictional complaint that Boyle filed against one of his kidnappers for sexual abuse of a minor in Massachusetts. In providing the supplemental record, students see how three-dimensional characters with complicated lives—the contents of the novel—get reduced to a legal filing.

Emotionally, students deeply care for Boyle who, by the novel's end, is the heart and soul of *Mystic River*. They want some form of justice for Boyle. But the assignment is significantly more morally complex than representing Boyle.[37] Students are challenged

25. Dennis Lehane, Mystic River (2021).
26. *Id.*
27. *Id.*
28. *Id.*
29. *Id.*
30. *Id.*
31. *Id.*
32. *Id.*
33. *Id.*
34. *Id.*
35. *Id.*
36. *Id.*
37. Admittedly, this assignment involves complex and difficult issues. In my own teaching, I find the following guidance useful:

> [T]he best learning and unlearning often comes with great discomfort, and this discomfort is not equivalent to trauma. With this, students should also be given guidelines and taught how to engage with difficult and, at times, potentially triggering material, and how to know

with representing the alleged child rapist.[38] I remind students that real and true justice requires zealous representation on both sides. In representing the defendant in the case, students must balance their emotional empathy for the opposing party with favorable application of the law for the defendant. The assignment is practical, the answer hinging on the application of a statute of limitations. Students are allowed to use the contents of the book to build their case—that Boyle knew or should have known the various injuries alleged in his complaint are not recent injuries; instead, the injuries are linked to the 1975 sexual abuse. Thus, Boyle's claims are untimely filed. While students are hesitant to zealously represent the defendant, within a week of beginning the assignment, students begin to see how the narrative, dialogue, plot, etc.—like a record in any civil or criminal case—helps them make their own case.

> within their own bodymind the difference between discomfort/injury and trauma/triggering. This work may be done by including general statements in the class syllabus, opening a conversation, brainstorming potential responses or self-care skills one might utilize in the event of an overwhelming affective experience, or perhaps engaging activities that model how to speak with one another when the connections between systemic injustices and deeply personal experiences are felt and known in the bodymind. For example, the instructor might initiate a discussion on the necessity of discomfort in learning about difficult material and guide students through thinking about the differences between personal discomfort and institutionally sanctioned, epistemic violence. Statements on the syllabus, or in other handouts, might include instructions on how to talk about difficult topics, and disagree without demeaning or disrespecting one another. While this may seem unnecessarily, or overly laborious for instructors such measures are actually methodological in nature—instructing students on how to learn with one another not just what to learn. Similarly, various kinds of acknowledgements could be given before in-class readings, videos, discussions, or activities. These could take the form of a trigger warning, a content note, or brief descriptions. Instructors might make note of the most common kinds of triggering material (rape/sexual assault, extreme violence, suicide/murder, and self-harm). Or, at the beginning of the term, instructors may ask that students anonymously submit any potentially triggering topics they may have. As educators, there is no way to predict what may trigger one student or another, but we can provide the space needed for the bodyminds in the room to share their truths. Rather than place the responsibility of student's affective responses on the instructor, these measures would serve to remind students of their own power, and agency over their bodyminds. Instructors would make note of potentially triggering material, not to "protect" their students, but to allow their students to prepare in whatever way is necessary for participation.

Angela M. Carter, *Teaching with Trauma: Trigger Warnings, Feminism, and Disability Pedagogy*, 35 Disability Stud. Q. 1, 13 (2015) (internal endnotes removed), https://uwethicsofcare.gws.wisc.edu/wp-content/uploads/2019/10/Carter_Teaching-with-Trauma-Disability-Pedagogy-Feminism-and-the-Trigger-Warnings-Debate.pdf.

38. As a survivor, myself, I am aware of the unique challenges posed by teaching potentially triggering materials. Before students read the novel, I explain that the book contains sexual abuse of a child and murder. I allow any student hesitant to begin the assignment to meet with me. Ultimately, I explain to students that during my legal career, I was assigned numerous child sex abuse, rape, kidnapping, and murder cases. Nothing in law school prepared me to take on such painful topics. I explain to students that the assignment is designed to allow students to work on an emotionally difficult case for a professor who intentionally creates a safe space for measured and mindful conversations on the involved topics.

Incorporating Marginalized Voices Through Literature

Over the course of the semester, students digest Lehane's novel, revisiting many chapters for evidence they will need to answer the problem. Given the intimacy of fiction, students who have never spent much time with working-class people or survivors of sexual abuse become thoroughly acquainted with characters so poignantly drawn that they seem real. For students in my class who grew up poor or working-class, as well as students who are survivors of sexual abuse, I make sure to address the moral complexities of the case, and urge students turned off by the likely outcome of the civil suit (the case will be dismissed because it was filed outside the statute of limitations) to focus on changing the law to protect people like Boyle, like themselves.

But it is not lost on me that no matter how narratively and intellectually stimulating this assignment might be, the novel involves all white, heterosexual men.[39] If one of my goals is to help create an environment where marginalized students feel seen,[40] I am succeeding on some fronts (economic class and survivors of sex crimes), but failing on others. Professor Brooke Baker's mission in teaching is similar to my own: "If we want our diverse student body to learn better, to succeed in law school, and to pluralize and reform the legal community, then we will have to do a better job addressing their intra-psychic needs and the concerns of their constituent communities."[41] One way to achieve this goal: PBL.

I do not want to be reductive and imply that marginalized students, particularly students of color, LGBTQ students, and disabled students cannot relate to or feel seen by immersing themselves in *Mystic River*, but a downside of choosing PBL is that any person, let alone a busy law student, can only read so much in a given course before the load becomes unbearable. While the length and depth of novel-based PBL is a benefit that enriches the educational experience, it also limits the professor to the diversity

39. During the first semester of my legal writing course (objective/predictive writing), I do not rely on novels. Instead, I rely on my skills as a creative writer to divide the semester into two, interwoven stories—a record larger than 40 pages. I intentionally create a diverse universe that includes disabled, LGBTQ, and BIPOC characters.

40. While research of the impact on multicultural literature on adult readers is scant, "[T]he idea that multicultural literature is most appropriate or only useful for children of historically marginalized groups is now outdated. Weaving multicultural literature throughout the curriculum has the potential to promote cultural pluralism and challenge assimilation to dominant belief systems and canons of knowledge." Ernest Morrell & Jodene Morrell, *Multicultural Readings of Multicultural Literature and the Promotion of Social Awareness in ELA Classrooms*, 47 New England Reading Ass'n J. 10, 10–11 (2012).

41. Brook K. Baker, *Incorporating Diversity and Social Justice Issues in Legal Writing Programs*, 9 Perspectives: Teaching Legal Rsch. & Writing 51, 52 (2001). Baker proposes several methods for how to "incorporate issues of diversity and social justice": (1) creating virtual realities and compelling contexts; (2) creating and interacting with clients with realistic identities; (3) putting issues of equality and social justice center stage, etc. *Id.* All of these goals can be accomplished with novel-based PBL.

contained in the novel itself. In choosing one novel, I preclude myself from teaching another novel that features other/different diversity.

Preparing Students for Diverse Clients and Complicated Issues

"Unlike judicial opinions and government advisory opinions, in which the judge or administrative agency succinctly summarizes only the most relevant facts of the case into a paragraph or two ..., longer works of literature generally tell complex and multi-staged stories."[42] In turn, this complexity helps "law students to provide better legal advice[.]"[43] In fact, "literature is valuable precisely for its tendency, like real life, to include complicated fact patterns and unpredictable human emotions and behavior."[44] The realistic nature of this form of PBL helps students to better understand their clients, and opposing parties, by fleshing out what we in law school and practice tend to call the *human element*. Intentionally choosing literature that features diverse characters, then, better prepares all students to understand the real, complicated, diverse parties they will work with in practice. Furthermore, by better understanding the power of narrative storytelling, students are better prepared to construct compelling persuasive writing for their clients.[45] Novels like *Mystic River*, which unsparingly deal with issues like child rape and trauma, also help students prepare for difficult conversations in practice.[46]

Employing Novel-Based PBL in Upper-Level Law Courses

Reading a 250–400 page novel is an investment in general, but reading a novel as a first-year law student is an even greater investment. While first-year professors will likely feel limited to assigning only one novel per semester given the amount of reading that novice students must complete on a daily and weekly basis, upper-level professors who choose to employ the use of novels in their teaching could assign more than one novel in a given course. Presumably, upper-level students are more familiar with law school, its demands, and how to read caselaw; thus, reading a second novel would not

---

42. Tovino, *supra* note 2, at 245.

43. *Id.*

44. *Id.* at 247.

45. Judith D. Moran, *Families, Law, and Literature: The Story of a Course on Storytelling*, 49 U.S.F. L. Rev. 1, 9–10 (2015).

46. Jeena Cho, *10 Lessons Law School Didn't Teach You*, Montana Lawyer, Jun.–Jul. 2015, at 20 ("I could not have imagined the incredibly difficult conversations I would have with my clients over the years.... We constantly deal with incredibly delicate issues and are charged with delivering life altering news yet we don't receive any training on how to do this. We also don't receive any training on ways to manage our own internal challenges of being in these difficult situations.").

cause the same hardship as for first-year law students, but would have the net benefit of allowing the professor to choose two novels of varying subject matter to create a more enriched, diverse PBL.[47]

Furthermore, the use of novels is particularly ripe for upper-level courses, allowing professors who want to facilitate a safe environment to discuss issues particular to marginalized people to outsource the storytelling creation to writers, particularly marginalized authors. This is especially true for white professors traditionally hesitant to wade into examples and discussions of race, gender, sexuality, etc.[48] Professors can rely on the author's work and characterization while focusing on the legal aspect of the PBL. For those upper-level professors enticed by such an idea, the opportunities are seemingly endless: A remedies professor could require students to read, among other novels, a murder mystery, requiring students to rely on what was revealed about the victim and the assailant to develop a potential wrongful death claim and an assessment of damages.[49] An intellectual property professor could design a course that relies on both non-fiction and fiction. For example, why not explore the myriad and tragic legal woes of Superman's creators, Jerry Siegel and Joel Shuster, in trying to earn any substantial money off their creation?[50] This intellectual property professor could also use comics to illustrate the various copyrighted materials at issue. Further, what if a family law professor used *Detransition Baby* by Torrey Peters[51] and *A Home at the End of the World* by Michael Cunningham?[52] Both are stories about non-traditional queer family structures where children are involved—such a scenario would provide endless hypothetical opportunities.

Conclusion

Moving forward, professors with the resources should begin to study the empirical benefits of using novels to teach law school classes. However, even if these results show that novels negligibly impact student improvement, professors should consider the other benefits to using novels in the legal classroom, including creating empathy. Furthermore, professors can intentionally diversify their pedagogy by relying on marginalized authors whose art can fill a void in the legal classroom. The depth of characterization and the complexities of plot unique to novels help students see potential parties as human beings.

---

47. *See, e.g.,* Tovino, *supra* note 2 (advocating for the use of literature in teaching health law).

48. *See e.g.,* Margalynne J. Armstrong & Stephanie M. Wildman, *Teaching Race/Teaching Whiteness: Transforming Colorblindness to Color Insight*, 86 N.C. L. Rev. 635 (2008).

49. Professors can add diversity by intentionally choosing novels written by and that feature BIPOC characters. *See, e.g.,* Bluebird, Bluebird, Attica Locke (2017).

50. Brad Ricca, Super Boys (2013).

51. Torrey Peters, Detransition Baby (2021).

52. Michael Cunningham, A Home at The End of The World (1990).

Mitigating Stereotype Threat in Upper Division Academic Support and Bar Preparation Courses

Kiyana Kiel *

Acknowledgment, Validation, and Empowerment

Academic support and bar preparation educators (ASEs) play a unique role in the education of law students. We serve as teachers, advisors, and administrators. We work with students in small and large groups, one-on-one, and in the classroom. As a result, it is imperative that ASEs acknowledge and address issues of diversity, equity, and inclusion (DEI) in and outside of law school classrooms. Frequently associated with stigma and sometimes viewed as remedial, academic support/bridge-to-the-bar (ASP) and bar exam preparation (BP) courses are uniquely situated in law school curricula, which optimally places ASEs to use teaching strategies that ameliorate stereotype threat in upper division ASP and BP courses as a way of supporting DEI in law school classrooms. Though discussed in the context of upper-division academic support and bar preparation curriculum, the pedagogic techniques employed are relevant to all legal educators who want to "[be] skilled at ensuring that students from all backgrounds feel safe and can succeed academically in their classrooms."[1]

---

* Assistant Dean for Academic Achievement, California Western School of Law. Thank you to my colleague, William J. Aceves, for reading and providing invaluable feedback on this piece. Thanks also to my colleagues, Paula J. Manning and Kris Franklin, for encouraging me to write. Heartfelt thanks to my mother, Felicia Jackson, for her review and feedback on each version of this piece.

1. Sean Darling-Hammond & Kristen Holmquist, *Creating Wise Classrooms to Empower Diverse Law Students: Lessons in Pedagogy from Transformative Law Professors*, 17 Berkeley J. Afr.-Am. L. & Pol'y 47, 57 (2016) [hereinafter *Creating Wise Classrooms*] (describing the authors' aim to "catalogue and explain the techniques [transformative law] professors employ to ... reduce stereotype threat, create a sense of safety and belonging, and provide the kind of legal education that allows students from all backgrounds to have successful legal careers.").

The impact of stereotype threat on law students remains a hot topic and is defined as the suppression of an individual's performance ability when they belong to a group associated with a negative stereotype and the individual fears confirming the stereotype.[2] Studied in varied contexts, underperformance induced by stereotype threat persists regardless of "gender, race, age, social class, athletic ability," so long as a negative stereotype exists about a group to which the individual belongs.[3] For example:

1. When confronted with the stereotype that women possess "poor math skills," women performed worse than men despite having "comparable math SAT scores, good grades in calculus, and for whom math was an important personal and professional goal."[4]
2. Stereotype threat also affects members of majority groups. When told they were being tested on "natural athletic ability" on a miniature golf course, white men performed poorly, but when they were told it was a test of "sports strategic intelligence," they performed well.[5] The inverse was true for Black men, when told "natural athletic ability" was tested, they performed well, but when they were told it was a test of "sports strategic intelligence," they performed poorly.[6]
3. Numerous studies show that African-Americans perform worse when confronted with a task that primes the negative stereotype that Blacks are less intelligent than whites; "the effect is still real and measurable: subjects confronted with the threat do worse. On the other hand, when the primer is eliminated, performance improves."[7]
4. When primed with the "stereotype that persons from lower socioeconomic backgrounds are not as intelligent as those from higher socioeconomic classes, persons from lower socioeconomic classes performed worse on tests. When the primer was removed, performance improved."[8]
5. "When primed with the stereotype that aging people have worse memories, older people performed worse than those who were not primed with the stereotype."[9]

---

2. *See* Catherine Martin Christopher, *Eye of the Beholder: How Perception Management Can Counter Stereotype Threat Among Struggling Law Students*, 53 Duq. L. Rev. 163 (2015).

3. *Id.* at 163.

4. *Id.* at 166 (referencing experiments conducted by Claude M. Steele: Claude M. Steele, Whistling Vivaldi: How Stereotypes Affect Us and What We Can Do (2010)).

5. Christopher, *supra* note 2, at 168.

6. *Id.*

7. Russell A. McClain, *Helping Our Students Reach Their Full Potential: The Insidious Consequences of Ignoring Stereotype Threat*, 17 Rutgers Race & L. Rev. 1, 13–14 (2016).

8. *Id.* at 18–19; *see also* Jean-Claude Croizet & Theresa Claire, *Extending the Concept of Stereotype Threat to Social Class: The Intellectual Underperformance of Students from Low Socioeconomic Backgrounds*, 24 Personality & Soc. Psych. Bull. 588 (1998).

9. McClain, *supra* note 7, at 19.

6. When primed with the "stereotype ... that whites are worse than Asians at math, white men performed worse on a math test when told the purpose of the test was to evaluate why Asians outperform [w]hites in math."[10]
7. When primed with the stereotype that "college students from underrepresented high schools are not as capable as others academically, students performed worse when told that students from their high schools were not as highly represented at the university level as students from other schools."[11]

Research demonstrates that, as a general psychological process, stereotype threat "can impact anyone who belongs to a group for which there exist negative stereotypes."[12] Fortunately, research in this area also shows that positive stereotypes can lead to positive results, coined "performance boost."[13]

> One researcher demonstrated that when a group of Asian-American women were given a math test, those who were subtly reminded beforehand that they were female (thereby triggering the stereotype that women are bad at math) underperformed as compared to a control group. But those who were reminded of their Asian heritage (and thus the corresponding stereotype that Asians are good at math) actually *over-performed* when compared to the control group.[14]

Stereotype threat poses a threat to law students "who suffer the solo status that accompanies being a member of an underrepresented group, the stereotype threat that accompanies being a member of a stereotyped group, and the challenges that attend lacking a background in the law before beginning law school."[15] This is particularly true for law students who also find themselves struggling academically[16] and, as such, directly relates to ASP and BP curricula because, though ASEs provide programming for all students, they interact most often with struggling, low-performing students. These students know their grades suggest they will not pass the bar exam and the pressure to overcome this negative stereotype prevents them from performing up to their capacity and believing in their ability to improve.[17] As such, it is imperative that ASEs incorporate transformative teaching methods to combat this and other negative stereotypes in and outside of the classroom.[18] "When it comes to combating stereotype threat ... interventions [adjust] the students' self-concept and their experience of the

---

10. *Id.*

11. *Id.* at 19–20.

12. Christopher, *supra* note 2, at 168 (quoting Jeff Stone, *A Hidden Toxicity in the Term "Student-Athlete": Stereotype Threat for Athletes in the College Classroom*, 2 WAKE FOREST J.L. & POL'Y 179, 182 (2012) (internal footnotes omitted)).

13. *Id.* at 169 (referencing Jerry Kang, *Trojan Horses of Race*, 118 HARV. L. REV. 1489, 1520 (2005)).

14. *Id.* (internal citations omitted).

15. *Creating Wise Classrooms*, *supra* note 1, at 47.

16. Christopher, *supra* note 2, at 165–67.

17. *Id.*

18. *See* McClain, *supra* note 7, at 45–46.

threat."[19] The following list, developed by Professors Sean Darling-Hammond and Kristen Holmquist, outlines 10 habits employed by transformative law teachers:[20]

1. Use E&E. Approach teaching with a sense of **Empathy and Enthusiasm**. Aim to understand the student experience and inspire passion.
2. Communicate **high expectations** while creating **safe classroom environments**.
3. **Provide context** for comprehension. Assume intelligence of every student, but never assume prior experience or legal skills.
4. **Give it structure** to make it stick. Structure the semester around a narrative arc or web of related themes or techniques and be transparent about how concepts fit together.
5. **Get feedback**. Use tools like clickers, breakouts, office hours, and mid-semester evaluations to understand and adapt to your students' progress and needs.
6. **Give feedback**. Provide assessment opportunities throughout the semester to help students learn and self-correct.
7. **Get practical**. Provide opportunities for students to learn practical and academic skills by assigning and reviewing briefs and motions and by reviewing practice exams in class and outlines during office hours.
8. Use the Socratic method to **teach, not intimidate**. Create an environment where **compassionate cold calling** is the norm.
9. **Modernize**. Transcend classical cases and embrace discussions about the modern political and social phenomena that attracted many students to law school.
10. **Learn from your fellow professors** as much as possible.[21]

The remainder of this essay will explore classroom assignments designed to minimize the impact of negative stereotypes on students in upper-division ASP/BP courses.

---

19. *Id.* at 46.

20. *See Creating Wise Classrooms, supra* note 1, at 66–67 ("The eleven [transformative] teachers interviewed include a diverse range of personalities and teaching styles. They teach a variety of core doctrinal and bar courses with different pedagogical demands, including Criminal Law, Evidence, Contracts, Constitutional Law, Legislation, Civil Procedure, Trusts and Estates, Family Law, and others. They represent different racial groups, religions, genders, socio-economic backgrounds, and, political beliefs. And all of them were regarded [by their students] as being able to create environments that helped students from all backgrounds thrive.").

21. *Id.* at 67 (emphasis in the original).

Setting the Tone

Since participation is predicated on low academic performance, students in upper division ASP and BP courses are threatened by at least one negative stereotype: they will not succeed in law school or on the bar exam due to their grades. Stereotype threat is compounded for ASP/BP students encumbered by overlapping negative stereotypes: e.g., race, gender, socioeconomic background, citizenship, sexual orientation, first-generation status, etc. ASEs can counter these threats by: (1) holding all ASP/BP students to rigorous academic standards to increase their students' trust in them;[22] (2) explicitly stating classroom goals;[23] (3) sharing relevant personal experiences;[24] (4) understanding triggers and seeking to undermine their impact; (5) expressing their belief in each student's individual ability to meet their expectations;[25] and (6) infusing growth mindset and grit in all classroom activities and assignments.[26]

Normalizing academic struggles through the frameworks of growth mindset and grit reduces stereotype threat by guiding students to believe their natural abilities can be improved and developed through hard work, perseverance, and the passion to reach one's long-term goals.[27] The more students continue to do the work and persevere through academic struggles, the more they will improve and move closer to achieving the higher levels of learning needed to "think like a lawyer."

---

22. McClain, *supra* note 7, at 48 ("Pedestrian, skills-only courses or courses containing only as much substance as is necessary to teach a skill, standing alone, run the risk of leading the student participants to think that we believe they are capable only of pedestrian tasks. *On the other hand, focusing students on skill mastery has been shown to ameliorate stereotype threat.* These kinds of skills courses should be coupled with challenging course material to be the most effective. ASPs should not "dumb down" course material.") (emphasis added).

23. *See* Nicole P. Dyszlewski, *Wisdom for Teachers on the Journey to Integrating Diversity in the Law Classroom*, in Integrating Doctrine and Diversity: Inclusion and Equity in the Law School Classroom 5–6 (Nicole P. Dyszlewski, et al. eds. 2021); *see also* Vernellia R. Randall, *Teaching Diversity Skills in Law School*, 54 St. Louis U. L.J. 795, 798 (2010).

24. *See* Dyszlewski, *supra* note 23, at 9–10.

25. McClain, *supra* note 7, at 47–48.

26. *See* Dyszlewski, *supra* note 23, at 10–11.

27. Alli Gerkman & Milana L. Hogan, *Accelerating Talent: Grit and Growth Mindset Fuels Lawyers' Success Throughout Their Careers*, N.Y. St. B.J., Nov.–Dec. 2018, at 49 (quoting Angela Duckworth et al., *Grit: Perseverance and Passion for Long-Term Goals*, 92 J. Personality & Soc. Psych. 1087, 1087 (2007).

Framing the Discussion with Personal Experience

During law school, I believed grades dictated my intellectual ability. My mindset became fixed and was further compounded by negative stereotypes associated with my identity: low-income, first-generation, Black, female, attending a top 10 law school (UC Berkeley School of Law) six years after California voters passed 1997's Proposition 209.[28] Also in 1997, only one Black law student joined the first-year entering class.[29] I was bombarded by destructive thoughts: "you don't belong here," "without guidance you will not succeed," "men are better law students and lawyers than women," "Blacks have inferior intellectual capacity than other races," "law school and lawyering is set up by wealthy people for wealthy people," "I did not attend boarding school or an Ivy League college, so I will be unable to compete with my law school peers."

Fortunately, recent research suggests that "directly acknowledging the existence of stereotype threat has the effect of neutralizing [primers]."[30] In one study, when presented with a difficult math test, one set of women was told the test's purpose was to study gender performance differences in math.[31] The other set of women was "told to consider that any anxiety they experienced on the test might be the result of stereotype threat."[32] The women in this set performed much better than the women in the first set, "nearly eliminating the gender performance gap."[33] This led researchers to conclude that "informing members of stereotyped groups about the effects of stereotype threat can buffer their performance on stereotype-relevant tasks."[34]

To counter stereotype threat, at the beginning of my upper division ASP course, I provide the following summary of my personal background:

> Welcome! I look forward to working with each of you this semester. I realize many of you were not happy to receive a letter requiring enrollment in this course. I truly understand because I too received a letter my 1L year stating that I needed to improve. Unfortunately for me, my alma mater did not have ASP educators or courses at the time, so I had to figure it out on my own which is why I dedicated my career to demystifying law school. The good news: I promise if you meaningfully engage in this course, you will improve your academic performance. The news you may not want to hear: it is going

28 *See* Thomas Peele & Daniel J. Willis, *Dropping affirmative action had huge impact on California's public universities*, EdSource (Oct. 29, 2020), https://edsource.org/2020/dropping-affirmative-action-had-huge-impact-on-californias-public-universities/642437?amp=1.

29. *See generally* Andrew Cohen, *Two Decades Later: Assessing Prop 209's Impact on Legal Education in California*, Berkeley Law, https://www.law.berkeley.edu/article/two-decades-later-assessing-prop-209s-impact-on-legal-education-in-california/.

30. McClain, *supra* note 7, at 24.

31. *Id.* at 24–27.

32. *Id.* at 24.

33. *Id.*

34. *Id.*

to be uncomfortable at times, but I implore you to "grit your teeth" and push through these times.

ASEs should demystify the meaning of "thinking like a lawyer" through simulation. I begin this process by framing future assignments through the lens of Bloom's 2001 Revised Taxonomy (Bloom's)[35] and Webb's Depth of Knowledge (DOK).[36] I use these frameworks because they are relatively well known by legal educators and make themselves accessible to students by establishing and defining a common language for educators to discuss learning and assessment.

I explain that to excel in law school, one must "remember, understand, and apply," and more significantly "analyze, evaluate, and create"[37] to achieve higher-level strategic and extended thinking.[38]

Using Self-Assessment to Attack Stereotype Threats

Self-assessment is a "systematic process of data-driven self-reflection" that "occurs when students judge their own work to improve performance as they identify discrepancies between current and desired performance."[39] To be successful, ASEs must provide students straightforward criteria "to gauge their performance," what they are doing well and areas that require improvement.[40] Effective self-assessment exercises empower students to take ownership of their learning because "[w]hen students establish goals, identify criteria that will propel them toward those goals, reflect on their learning, and then generate strategies for additional learning, they show improved [academic] performance."[41]

Essay Assessment

I offer numerous practice opportunities in my upper division ASP course. During class, students complete ungraded, mini-practice essays after which I explain the relevant rules, how those rules should be applied to the facts, and where ambiguity exists. After my lecture, students grade their responses using a rubric prepared by me that

35. *See* BloomsTaxonomy.net, https://bloomstaxonomy.net (last visited Dec. 19, 2022) [hereinafter Bloom's Taxonomy]. (In 2000, a group of cognitive psychologists, curriculum theorists and instructional researchers, and testing and assessment specialists published a revision of Bloom's Taxonomy; *see* Lorin Anderson et al., A Taxonomy for Teaching, Learning, and Assessment (2000).)

36. *See* https://www.synergiseducation.com/blooms-taxonomy-and-webbs-depth-of-knowledge/ [hereinafter Webb's Depth of Knowledge].

37. *See* Bloom's Taxonomy, *supra* note 35.

38. *See* Webb's Depth of Knowledge, *supra* note 36.

39. Katherine A. Gustafson, *From Self-Assessment to Professional Effectiveness: Five Steps to Teaching Students to Effectively Self-Assess*, 88 Miss. L.J. Supra 49, 59 (2019) (internal citations omitted).

40. *Id.*

41. *Id.* at 60 (internal citations omitted).

includes a sample answer to each question presented and the associated numerical points. After grading themselves, they complete a self-assessment questionnaire[42] that asks them to assess the following for each question presented:

<u>Issues</u>

1. Did you include all the issues in the sample answer?
   i. If you did not include an issue in your essay, which issue(s) were missing?
   ii. Do you understand why you did not identify the issue (explain)?
2. Did you include an issue absent from the sample answer in your essay?
   i. If so, what issue did you include?
   ii. What was your reasoning for including it? Do you understand why it was not included in the sample answer (explain)?
3. Consider your identification of issues as a whole:
   i. What did you do well?
   ii. In what areas do you need to improve?
   iii. Identify ways you can improve in these areas.

<u>Rules</u>

1. Did you identify all the relevant rules?
   i. If your essay was missing any rules, which rules were missing?
   ii. Do you understand why you did not identify the rules (explain)?
2. Were the rules as written in your essay thorough and accurate?
   i. Were they under- or over-inclusive?
   ii. If your essay included rules that were under- or over-inclusive, explain why they were.
3. Consider your rule statements as a whole:
   i. What did you do well?
   ii. In what areas do you need to improve?
   iii. Identify ways you can improve in these areas.

<u>Application</u>

1. Compare your response to the sample answer. Did your response include all relevant facts from the hypothetical?

42. The self-assessment questionnaire is a living document compiled from content I created while teaching, as well as other sources, including but not limited to multiple presentations by ASEs at the Association of Academic Support Educators annual conference since 2013, SUZANNE DARROW-KLEINHAUS, MASTERING THE LAW SCHOOL EXAM (2006), and MARY BASICK, ESSAY EXAM WRITING FOR THE CALIFORNIA BAR EXAM (2012).

   i. If you did not include each relevant fact in the hypothetical, which facts were missing?
   ii. If you did not include each relevant fact in the hypothetical, why did you not include the fact(s)?
2. If the sample answer included counterarguments, did you include them in your response?
   i. If you did not, explain why you did not include them.
3. Is your analysis conclusory?
   i. Do you explain how/why the rule should be applied to the hypothetical facts?
   ii. Do you use signals (e.g., because, since, so, etc.) to explain the connection between the rules and facts?
4. Consider your application of the law to the facts as a whole:
   i. What did you do well?
   ii. In what areas do you need to improve?
   iii. Identify ways you can improve in these areas.

<u>Conclusion</u>

1. Did you include a conclusion for each issue?
2. Did you include an overall conclusion for each question presented?

<u>Studying and Study Aid Reflection</u>

1. Explain what you were missing from your essay and identify at least two (2) ways you can adjust your studying techniques or study aids to avoid doing this in the future.
2. What areas in your response could be improved? Identify at least two (2) ways you can adjust your studying techniques or study aids to improve these areas in the future.

Multiple-Choice Assessment

Self-assessment does not end with essay practice; it is essential to improve performance on multiple-choice exams. Unfortunately, many students do not know how to improve and if they seek guidance the guide may be unable to articulate a strategy to improve. Enter my multiple-choice distillation self-assessment, which requires students to extract the essential meaning or most important aspects of each multiple-choice question answered. Specifically, I require students to review every multiple-choice question answered, regardless of accuracy. I require this to ensure students differentiate the questions they answered:

1. Correctly for the correct reasons.

2. Correctly, but for the *incorrect* reasons.
3. Incorrectly.

After review of an individual question's answer explanation, students must explain, in two sentences or less, why their answer selection is correct, correct for the incorrect reason(s), or incorrect. This requires students to focus on their performance by distilling the typically 1–2 paragraphs answer explanation. It also allows their personal performance and knowledge to guide any alterations to their studying or study aids to improve their performance on future multiple-choice practice exams.

The final step of this process requires ASEs to provide students feedback on their self-assessments: "The key ... is not grading the exercise; rather [it] is evaluating the students' assessment of their work on the exercise ... determining how accurately the students identified the strengths and weaknesses of their work on the exercise."[43] This can be done in several ways: (1) individualized feedback provided by the ASE, (2) individualized feedback provided by the ASE's teaching assistant, (3) ASE-guided peer assessment completed in class so the ASE can respond to questions of students being assessed and those assessing them.

These self-assessment exercises effectively combat stereotype threat and improve student learning because they guide students through the process in a low-stakes environment and require them to self-identify their own strengths and areas that need additional learning.[44] They model growth mindset and grit by framing mistakes as opportunities to learn how to avoid making them again.

You Become the Professor: Students as Question Drafters

Improving performance in stereotype-threatened students can be as simple as shifting the focus from performance/grades to skills and subject matter mastery.[45] The same way self-assessment allows the student to become the "grader," this exercise allows them to become the professor. In class, using small groups of 4–6, participants must draft mini-exams. Each group is assigned a distinct issue for which they must draft a practice exam and sample answer that they will present to the class and have proofed by me (their ASE). For essays, students are instructed to include the explanatory citations they believe support their sample answer. For multiple-choice exams, students are instructed to provide explanatory citations for each answer choice indicating why the answer choice is or is not the best of the answer choices available.

This exercise requires students to think deeply about the law because question drafting requires a depth of knowledge that must pass group, non-group peer, and ASE muster. The construction of this exercise is productive because, during group presen-

43. Gustafson, *supra* note 39, at 66–67.
44. *Id.* at 59–60 (internal citations omitted).
45. McClain, *supra* note 7, at 24–27.

tations, what students within the group do not catch, members of another group or the ASE will. To ensure this exercise undermines stereotype threats, it is presented as the process law professors use to draft and proof exams.

Conclusion

This is not an exhaustive list or explanation of exercises that could be used to effectively combat stereotype threat in the law school classroom. Instead, the intention of this essay is to continue the nationwide discussion and prompt more quantitative and qualitative study of transformative pedagogical techniques that possess the potential to ameliorate stereotype threat.[46] As exercises are implemented in different ways, law teachers should publish their findings, thereby "[enabling] schools to learn from each other and, over time, generate data that will help determine the best practices for mitigating [stereotype threats]."[47] The authors of *Creating Wise Classrooms* furthered this work by contacting campus law student groups to ask:

> which professors they considered to be the most effective at conveying complicated concepts and creating classrooms where all students (regardless of gender, race, or other group status) can learn.... Using the list of professors recommended by students as a baseline, a smaller list of teachers was developed by utilizing quantitative end of semester student evaluation scores.... Professors were chosen for the study [of transformative law teaching] if they were both recommended by multiple students in the initial [student feedback request], and garnered average scores between 4.5 and 5 on most of the student assessment criteria in courses with over 50 students.[48]

As law teachers, we should be mindful of how students learn and the barriers to student learning, and integrate pedagogical techniques that foster, not undermine, learning. As the integrations occur in our individual classrooms, I encourage you to gather and analyze both qualitative and quantitative data in order to add to the growing body of literature that demonstrates that transformative law teaching does, in fact, lead to enhanced student learning regardless of an individual student's identity group(s).

---

46. *Id.* at 54.

47. *Id.*

48. *Creating Wise Classrooms, supra* note 1, at 65–66 ("Of the thirteen professors who fit both criteria, eleven professors participated in in-depth interviews regarding their teaching practices. The perspectives of these eleven individuals inform this article. While there are clearly many ways to determine what constitutes excellent teaching, the eleven interviewed individuals are referred to as "transformative professors" throughout the article. This is meant to facilitate economy, convey the way many of their students perceive these professors, and suggest that embracing their pedagogical approaches may help transform legal instruction to ensure students from all backgrounds can learn and thrive.").

White Letter Law

Varro J. Clarke *

Introduction

Who are the authors of your textbooks?

In the spring of my 1L year, I heard a professor, Dr. Heather Moore Roberson, explain that she always asks this question of her students at the start of every semester.[1] I gave no thought to the names listed on the covers of my textbook prior to her question. It was enough for me to know that I trusted my professors and my professors trusted these authors (at least enough to assign their book). Like most students, I considered these texts to be credible simply because they were printed,[2] without consideration of the authors' qualifications or perspectives. Dr. Moore Roberson surprised me when she explained that her students "get a very monolithic homogeneous introduction to the world through the vantage point of only white authors."[3]

Wondering if the same was true for law students, I quickly Googled the 23 authors listed on the seven books I had been assigned in my first year and was surprised to see only one person of color. Hoping this was a statistical anomaly, I reached out to students in other sections, asked for their syllabi, and Googled the authors of their textbooks. All said, my law school assigned 13 different books to 1Ls, written by 37 authors—36 of whom were white. Those two hours of Googling were the start of an ongoing research project. This essay shares what I have learned so far in trying to answer that seemingly simple question: *who are the authors of your textbooks?*

---

* Varro Clarke will graduate Samford University Cumberland School of Law in April 2023. He serves as an editor of the *Cumberland Law Review*. Special thanks to Professors Ramona Albin and Lynn Hogewood who assisted in this process.

1. Allegheny College, *Dr. Andre Perry '93 and Dr. Heather Moore Roberson—President's Lecture Series on Social Justice*, YouTube (Feb. 16, 2021), https://www.youtube.com/watch?v=IxcKppeTmCo [https://perma.cc/VFC9-7LDL] (beginning at minute 44, although the entirety of the discussion is well worth the time spent) [hereinafter Allegheny College, *President's Lecture Series on Social Justice*].

2. *See* Yuan Chen et al., *Exploring Perceptions of E-Books Among CEGEP Students and Faculty*, 45 Can. J. Learning & Tech. 1, 16 (2019).

3. Allegheny College, *President's Lecture Series on Social Justice*, *supra* note 1, at 46:37.

My answer is neither perfect, nor complete. Still, I hope that it inspires more rigorous investigation and, more importantly, thoughtful change in legal pedagogy. The lack of diversity within the ranks of legal textbook authors should be concerning to students, educators, and the legal community writ large.[4] When this problem is ignored, the consequences are simultaneously vast and clandestine, reinforcing racial, gender, and sex stereotypes in nearly every corner of the law. This essay first aims to identify possible diversity issues in the legal casebook publishing industry by attempting to quantitatively measure the ethnic and gender demographics of legal textbook authors. Next, I turn my focus to the consequences that a lack of diversity causes in the classroom and beyond. Finally, I suggest strategies to address these disparities.

Measuring Race, Ethnicity, Sex, and Gender

Accurately measuring the gender and racial demographics of a population requires voluntary completion of a carefully designed survey.[5] Unfortunately, to my knowledge, that survey has not been done. Instead of embarking on such a survey, I have chosen a more casual approach. Although not perfect, my approach is intended to give the reader two new tools to confront this iteration of bias at law schools. First, it offers something resembling qualitative data that describes an abstract problem. Second, it offers a student's perspective on the status quo and the effectiveness (or lack thereof) of strategies to confront bias.

To start, identifying and defining the terms being measured poses several challenges. For example: what is the difference between race and ethnicity?[6] Is one more relevant in this application? Should it be?

---

4. While the problems caused by a lack of diversity are substantial, many practitioners and educators are rising to meet that challenge. *The Feminist Judgments Series* published by UNLV law school, and Lolo Serrano's *Frugging KCP* are great examples.

5. *See generally* Jonathan Burton et al., *Measuring Ethnicity: Challenges and Opportunities for Survey Research*, 33 Ethnic & Racial Stud. 1332 (2010) [hereinafter *Measuring Ethnicity*].

6. It is important to recognize the concept of "race" as "the result of a process of social construction rather than a naturally occurring phenomenon within human populations." Kenneth Smith, *Some Critical Observations on the Use of the Concept of 'Ethnicity' in Modood et al.*, Ethnic Minorities in Britain, 36 Socio. 399, 401 (2002). The result of this social construct is the use of the term to communicate the perception of visible differences thought to be caused by geographic origins of a person's ancestors. *See generally* Tariq Modood et al., *'Race', Racism and Ethnicity: A Response to Ken Smith*, 36 Socio. 419–427 (2002). While measuring race can be an exercise in futility by "treating a multi-dimensional, fluid and contextually and relationally specific concept as if it were unidimensional fixed and stable," it offers insights nonetheless. Measurements of race matter, not because the distinctions supposedly delineating groups are justified by any biological or genetic distinction. *Measuring Ethnicity*, *supra* note 6, at 1334; *see also* Interview with Pilar Ossorio, *RACE—the Power of an Illusion, Background Readings* (2003), https://www.pbs.org/race/000_About/002_04-background-01-03.htm [https://perma.cc/T8DN-HQCR] [hereinafter Ossorio Interview] ("We can't find any genetic markers that are in everybody of a particular race, and in nobody of some other race."). Rather, as Justice Sotomayor has explained, race "matters because of persistent racial inequality in society—inequality that cannot be

Black's Law Dictionary opted against weighing in on this topic and does not provide definitions of race or ethnicity.[7] Offering a frustratingly circular definition, *The Essential Dictionary of Law* defines "race" as "an ethnic group," but provides no definition of "ethnicity."[8] The absence or flaws of these terms' definitions highlights a fundamental challenge faced by demographic researchers.[9] As professor of law and bioethics Dr. Pilar Ossorio explained, "[i]n our popular conceptions, we have a notion of race as being sort of simple divisions of people—divisions among people that are deep, that are essential, that are somehow biological or even genetic, and that are unchanging, that these are clear-cut, distinct categories of people. And that is not the case."[10]

Similar challenges emerge when considering gender. While "[s]ex refers to a label assigned at birth—usually female or male ... sex can also encompass nonbinary characterizations including intersex."[11] On the other hand, "gender is self-defined and associated with the emotional, social, and psychological traits that identify someone."[12] Observation has been proven to be an ineffective method of measuring gender within a population.[13] This makes sense because, as previously mentioned, gender is *self*-defined.[14]

I point all of this out to be candid and forthright with the flaws of my approach. First, I attempted to measure race and sex, which are imperfect indicators of popula-

---

ignored." Schuette v. Coal. to Def. Affirmative Action, Integration & Immigrant Rts. & Fight for Equal. By Any Means Necessary (BAMN), 572 U.S. 291, 380 (2014) (Sotomayor, J., dissenting). At bottom, two facts about group racial measurements bear highlighting. In a vacuum, racial distinctions are devoid of scientific justification. Nonetheless, the existence of these cultural fabrications continues to cause demonstrable harm on members of certain racial groups. The reality of the latter, despite the truth of the former, compels attention and correction. Even so, a more meaningful statistic, especially for this research, may be a population member's "ethnicity and ethnic group identification [which] are contingently located in one or more characteristic or expression of shared belonging." *Measuring Ethnicity, supra* note 6, at 1335. Ethnic identity encompasses a wider swath of variables including, "race (or colour or visibility), national identity, parentage or ancestry, nationality, citizenship, religion, language, and country of birth (or being an immigrant)," and culture. *Id.* Because ethnicity necessarily encompasses more self-identified identity markers than race, it may offer a more complete picture of the perspectives represented in a population.

7. *See, e.g.*, Black's Law Dictionary (11th ed. 2019).

8. Essential Dictionary of Law 104, 251 (Amy Hackney Blackwell ed., 2004).

9. *See generally* Kenneth Prewitt, What Is Your race? The Census and Our Flawed Efforts to Classify Americans (2013).

10. Ossorio Interview, *supra* note 6.

11. Jeremy W. Jacobs et al., *The Importance of Accurately Defining Gender and Sex in Pathology*, 158 Am. J. Clinical Pathology 153, 153 (2022).

12. *Id.*

13. Trixie Cartwright & Clive Nancarrow, *A Question of Gender: Gender Classification in International Research*, 64 Int'l J. Mkt. Rsch. 575, 583 (2022).

14. Peter M. Smith & Mieke Koehoom, *Measuring Gender When You Don't Have a Gender Measure: Constructing a Gender Index Using Survey Data*, 15 Int'l J. for Equity in Health, May 28, 2016, at 6, https://doi.org/10.1186/s12939-016-0370-4 ("[D]ata analyses where direct measures of gender, such as [questionnaires], have not been collected is challenging.").

tion diversity.[15] Second, I relied on subjective observational assessments rather than eliciting voluntary survey responses from authors. While this requires taking the metrics offered in section two with a grain (or more) of salt, allow me to briefly make the case that these findings are not entirely devoid of merit.

It bears pointing out that there is no publicly available data on the authors of legal textbooks. This is not limited to race and gender data. Currently there is no centralized repository in which a person, researcher or otherwise, could learn about the backgrounds of legal textbook authors. While some publishers offer brief biographies, these consist largely of resume information without any indication of an author's unique perspective.[16] To that end, a law professor, inspired by this book to be more thoughtful about diversity when assigning textbooks, would find the same dearth of information that I did. Without question, this issue deserves rigorous investigation on the part of an experienced social science researcher. Until then, interested students, professors, and administrators will be confronted with the same choices I did while writing this essay. They could: (A) rely on their own flawed subjective assessment of authors ethnic and gender identity, (B) accept the status quo and hope that a textbook is devoid of racial or gender bias, or (C) attempt to reach out to each author in the hopes they are willing and able to candidly answer personal questions from a stranger about their ethnic and gender identity. None of these options is particularly desirable. This information vacuum should be seen by publishers as an opportunity to be transparent about diversity while empowering students and faculty to make more informed purchasing decisions.

Further, there is reason to believe the methods outlined below accurately identify macro patterns (if not precise population rates). Although individuals generally struggle to identify the race of strangers, observational assessments are "most accurate in identifying the race of white" individuals.[17] Similarly, observational assessments of race were most accurate when the observer is of "the same race" as the person they are observing.[18] To that end, I made several choices in conducting this research in an effort to improve its reliability.[19]

First, I did not attempt to identify any authors' ethnic or gender identity. Rather, this research attempts to identify patterns in the race and sex of authors. Second, I did not attempt to measure the frequency with which specific non-white racial groups authored textbooks. Rather, I attempted to answer a simpler question: how many legal

---

15. In addition to the reasoning laid out above, reliance on these statistics also ignores other meaningful data like educational background, geographic diversity, disability, etc.

16. *See, e.g.*, Constitutional Law: Cases in Context, Fourth Edition, https://www.aspenpublishing.com/Barnett-ConLaw4 (last visited Jan. 28, 2023) (offering a headshot and brief biography of the two authors of the textbook, Randy E. Barnett and Josh Blackman).

17. Anna Brown, *Many Poll Respondents Guess Wong on Their Interviewer's Race or Ethnicity*, Pew Research (Sept. 27, 2017), https://www.pewresearch.org/social-trends/2016/06/27/methodology-6/ [https://perma.cc/QU3L-5877].

18. *Id.*

19. Some judgments may be incorrect. Skeptical readers should, for argument's sake, double the number of racial minorities counted. Doing so would increase the number of non-white authors identified to 18%. Whether the number is 9% or 18%, it remains shockingly low.

textbook authors are white? Finally, although I researched websites, recorded lectures, and publicly available CVs to find descriptive pronouns and self-reported racial identity for each author, this frequently failed to produce any new information. As such, when I was unable to find an author's gender or racial identity, I made a subjective observational assessment of race and/or sex.[20] With the large sample size of 455 authors and limitation of focus to race and sex, I am confident in the large-scale patterns that emerged from my research.

Selecting a Sample

Developing a population of authors to study proved to be an easier challenge than the one described above. I considered it important that the population included the authors of the textbooks most commonly assigned to law students. Three publishers, Thomson Reuters (with subsidiaries including Foundation Press and West Academic), Wolters Kluwer (with subsidiaries including Aspen Publishing), and Carolina Academic Press, publish most legal textbooks assigned in American law schools. However, none offers public information on the sales of their books, which would be a good indicator of the frequency with which they are assigned by professors. It would have been possible to search each publisher's entire catalog and identify the author of each book listed. However, that would have meant including the authors of infrequently assigned books. Because authors incorporate their implicit bias into their writing,[21] and because readers are prone to accept bias as true when it is disguised as fact,[22] the consequence and impact of an author's implicit bias is correlated to the classroom use of their textbook. For that reason, I aimed to limit the population of authors to those who write the most commonly assigned textbooks.

Luckily, the list of the mostly commonly assigned legal textbooks already existed. *Quimbee* is a frequently used website that offers a variety of study aids to law students.[23] The site maintains a library of case briefs designed to supplement casebook readings.[24] Users have the option to search for a specific case or they can search for their assigned casebook and find briefs for all the cases in that book.[25] When a student is unable to find their textbook on the site, they are encouraged to alert *Quimbee*'s staff researchers

---

20. If you are an author of a textbook included in this study and I have obviously misidentified you, I sincerely apologize.

21. *See* Keith Payne et al., *How to Think About 'Implicit Bias'*, Sci. Am. (Mar. 27, 2018), https://www.scientificamerican.com/article/how-to-think-about-implicit-bias/ [https://perma.cc/5SBE-SG6V]; Kris Goffin & Stacia Friend, *Learning Implicit Biases from Fiction*, 80 J. Aesthetic & Art Criticism 129, 133 (2022).

22. *See generally* Gayle L. Nelson & John M. Murphy, *Peer Response Groups: Do L2 Writers Use Peer Comments in Revising Their Drafts?* 27 TESOL Q. 135 (1993).

23. Quimbee, *Casebook Coverage*, https://www.quimbee.com/casebooks (last visited Nov. 30, 2022).

24. *Id.*

25. *Id.*

who then assemble the case briefs needed for that textbook.[26] This feedback system has allowed *Quimbee* to create a thorough list of textbooks reported by the students that use them.[27] For this study, I gathered each textbook that *Quimbee* listed for seven classes commonly taken by first-year law students: torts, criminal law, property, constitutional law, evidence, civil procedure, and contracts.[28]

After researching 455 authors of 174 textbooks, the observation of Dr. Roberson Moore proved correct. The number of white authors dwarfed the number of non-white authors. While the difference was less dramatic for male and female authors, it was still large.

Author Observation

This observational study included 174 different legal textbooks.[29] Of that, 27 covered criminal law, 33 contracts, 22 property, 23 torts, 19 evidence, 26 constitutional law, and 24 civil procedure.[30] The 174 books most frequently assigned to first-year law students were written by a total of 455 authors.[31] Of those 455 authors, only 42, or 9%, were not white and 78, or 17% were not men.

---

26. *Request that Quimbee cover your casebook*, QUIMBEE, https://www.quimbee.com/casebooks /request (last visited Nov. 30, 2022) ("Is Quimbee missing your casebook? Please submit a request below, and our staff authors will do their best to cover it.").

27. Because *Quimbee* claims to have served 504,000 law students since its founding in 2007, I expect the list maintained by the cite to be fairly reflective of the national patterns. *Who is Quimbee*, QUIMBEE, https://www.quimbee.com/about#:~:text=16%2B%20years%2C%20616%2C000%2B%20 law,of%20quality%20online%20study%20aid (last visited Jan. 23, 2023). However, it does not publicize current user numbers or which schools users attend. However, with monthly subscriptions ranging from $19 to $29, it is may not be accessible to all students. *Pricing and Free Trial*, QUIMBEE, https ://www.quimbee.com/pricing/study-aids (last visited Jan. 28, 2023).

28. When a book did not have a doctrinal focus, like Conley's *Scientific and Expert Evidence*, or was not nationally focused, like Grey's *An Anatomy of Louisiana Evidence Law*, they were not included. Additionally, if Quimbee reported an older edition of a textbook, the newest edition of the same book was included in this study.

29. *Id.*

30. *Id.*

31. Authors were counted every time they authored a book. For example, David Crump, who authored five different textbooks covering different subjects—civil procedure, constitutional law, criminal law, property, and evidence—was counted five times for his five authorship credits.

In order from most diverse to least[32] are civil procedure (54%),[33] criminal law and torts (48%), evidence (42%), property (36%), contracts (33%), and constitutional law (23%) when considering racial and gender diversity together.[34] The average was 41%. Put another way, only 41% of textbooks were written by a team of authors that were not *exclusively* white men.

Looking exclusively at the percentage of books that have at least one non-male author produced similar results: 26% of criminal law textbooks were written by at least one non-male author, civil procedure 23%, contracts 21%, torts 17%, property 14%, evidence 10%, and constitutional law 7%.[35] The average for all the books was 17%. This means that 83% of the legal textbooks studied were written exclusively by men. The pattern continued when looking at racial presentations in isolation. Nineteen percent of criminal law books had at least one non-white author, while torts had 13%, evidence 10%, contracts 9%, property 8%, and civil procedure and constitutional law both 3%. The average was only 9%, meaning 91% of legal textbooks had an all-white authorship team.

	Total Books	Books with ANY Diversity	Total Authors	Non-White Authors		Non-Male Authors	
Criminal Law	27	48%	62	12	19%	16	26%
Contracts	33	33%	78	7	9%	16	21%
Property	22	36%	64	5	8%	9	14%
Torts	23	48%	70	9	13%	12	17%
Evidence	19	42%	51	5	10%	5	10%
Con Law	26	23%	60	2	3%	4	7%
Civil Procedure	24	54%	70	2	3%	16	23%
Totals	174	41%	455	42	9%	78	17%

Because much of this work serves to highlight the deficiencies in scholarship and publishing, it is worthwhile at the outset to highlight stand-out texts. Lee and Harris's *Criminal Law, Cases and Materials, Fourth* was written by two non-white female au-

32. To start, each book was assigned a score of one or zero. If any of the authors appeared to be either non-white or non-male, the book scored a one. For purposes of consistency, books scoring a one, were termed "diverse," although it does not necessarily mean that all authors of a given text presented as neither white nor male. Only when a textbook was written exclusively by authors presenting as white men would the book receive a score of zero. Next, books received a score that was determined by the sex of the authors. A textbook scored a zero if it was written by an all-male team of authors. If any authors did not present as male, the book scored a one. Finally, books were scored for the diversity of the racial presentation of its authors. If any author did not present as white, the book scored a one while an all-white presenting team of authors earned the book a zero.

33. A complete appendix of results is available here: https://perma.cc/6RR9-SW7A.

34. *Id.*

35. *Id.*

thors: Cynthia Lee and Angela Harris.[36] For contracts professors looking for a book that features the scholarship of diverse authors, consider *Contracting Law, Fifth Edition*[37] by Amy Kastely, Deborah Waire Post, Nancy Ota, and Deborah Zalesne. The torts casebook by Meredith J. Duncan, Ronald Turner, and Rory D. Bahadur, *Torts, A Contemporary Approach, Third Edition*,[38] is also remarkable and represents diverse scholarship.

The Impact of Authorship Diversity

Results of studies investigating the impact of gender and racial diversity in educational settings are "almost uniformly consistent" in identifying a wide range of benefits.[39] Underrepresented students in diverse classrooms report completing higher levels of education than those in homogenously white classrooms[40] while students of all backgrounds demonstrate higher retention rates overall.[41] This pattern applies across gender and race lines and is not unique to specific fields of study.[42] Studies also find a statistically significant positive correlation between more classroom diversity and greater critical thinking,[43] improved cognitive development,[44] and higher rates of academic self-confidence among white and non-white students alike.[45] Again, this pattern is not limited to higher education[46] and is found where racial and gender diversity are

---

36. Cynthia Lee & Angela P. Harris, Criminal Law Cases and Materials (4th ed. 2019).

37. Amy Kastely, Deborah Waire Post, Nancy Ota & Deborah Zalesne, Contracting Law (5th ed. 2015).

38. Meredith J. Duncan, Ronald Turner & Rory D. Bahadur, Torts, A Contemporary Approach (3d ed. 2018).

39. Patrick T. Terenzini et al., *Racial and Ethnic Diversity in the Classroom*, 72 J. Higher Educ. 509, 511 (2001).

40. *Id.*

41. Mitchell J. Chang et al., *Considering the Impact of Racial Stigmas and Science Identity: Persistence Among Biomedical and Behavioral Science Aspirants*, 82 J. Higher Educ. 564, 585 (2011) (discussing the impact of diversity on participants in graduate science programs).

42. Juan C. Garibay & Shirley Vincent, *Racially Inclusive Climate within Degree Programs and Increasing Student of Color Enrollment: An Examination of Environmental/Sustainability Programs*, 11 J. Diversity in Higher Educ. 201, 211 (2018) (discussing the impact of diversity within environmental science programs).

43. Maurianne Adams & Yu-Hui Zhou-McGovern, *The Sociomoral Development of Undergraduates in a "Social Diversity" Course: Developmental Theory, Research and Instructional Applications*, at 27 (Apr. 1994), http://files.eric.ed.gov/fulltext/ED380345.pdf (paper presented at the Annual Meeting of the American Educational Research Association).

44. Sylvia Hurtado, *Linking Diversity and Educational Purpose: How Diversity Affects the Classroom Environment and Student Development*, *in* Diversity Challenged 187, 199–200 (Gary Orfield ed., 2001) [hereinafter *Linking Diversity*].

45. Terenzini et al., *supra* note 39, at 511.

46. David MacPhee et al., *Infusing a Diversity Perspective into Human Development Courses*, 65 Child Dev. 699, 713 (1994).

developed.[47] Further, students educated in a diverse classroom report more "openness to diversity and challenge."[48]

However, on-campus diversity—what most consider the primary goal of diversity programs—is not enough. To fully access the potential benefits that diversity offers, it must be reflected and "embodied in the curriculum."[49] Textbooks are a fundamental part of the curriculum. The curriculum plays an outsized role in the students' perception of the institutional diversity[50] and, consequently, the educational outcome for both minority and non-minority students.[51]

In addition, when a textbook's authors hold diverse perspectives, the quality of the book can improve. This is because the bias, or "systematic errors" in decision making,[52] authors carry with them as they write impacts their final product.[53] Increased representation can decrease how frequently an author's narrow scholarly focus is mistaken for the breadth of the legal landscape; how conventional application of a doctrine is confused as its strict limit; how bias is presented as fact. Homogeneity of authors can create an environment in which the author's perspective "masquerades as colorless, raceless, and systematically devoid of bias," when it may be anything but.[54] The real harm of this defect occurs when law students accept the author's bias as the black letter law it's presented to be—an all-too-common occurrence given the demands of legal education and ignorance to the mere existence of other viewpoints.[55]

For example, when a property textbook covers the civic republicanism defense of property rights,[56] the authors' perspectives can influence how much, if any, attention is given to what kinds of "property" the idea's proponents were seeking to protect. Representation of more perspectives may highlight the pro-slavery motivation that popularized civic republicanism in the late 1700s.[57] Similarly, when a contracts textbook covers

47. Ernest T. Pascarella et al., *Influences on Student' Openness to Diversity and Challenge in the First Year of College*, 67 J. Higher Educ. 174, 183–92 (1996).

48. *Id.*; *see also generally* Terenzini et al., *supra* note 39.

49. *On the Importance of Diversity in University Admissions*, N.Y. Times, Apr. 24, 1997, at A27 (reprinting a statement adopted by the Association of American Universities at its annual spring meeting held on April 14, 1997).

50. Matthew J. Mayhew et al., *Curriculum Matters: Creating a Positive Climate for Diversity from the Student Perspective*, 46 Rsch. in Higher Educ. 389, 408 (2005) (discussing the role curriculum plays in how undergraduate students experience campus diversity).

51. *Id.*; *see also Linking Diversity*, *supra* note 44, at 200.

52. *See* Daniel Kahneman, Thinking Fast and Slow 3–4 (2011).

53. Kathleen D. Fletcher, *Casebooks, Bias, and Information Literacy—Do Law Librarians Have a Duty?*, 40 Legal Reference Servs. Q. 184, 185 (2021).

54. Jasmine B. Gonzales Rose, *Toward a Critical Race Theory of Evidence*, 101 Minn. L. Rev. 2243, 2252 (2017) (internal quotation marks omitted).

55. *See* Kahneman, *supra* note 52, at 3–4 (2011).

56. John G. Sprankling & Raymond R. Coletta, Property A Contemporary Approach 2 (4th ed. 2018).

57. Civic Republicanism, the idea that property owners are better citizens, was advanced by Thomas Jefferson, who owned hundreds of slaves. *See* Donald Last, *Private Property Rights with Responsibilities: What Would Thomas Jefferson Say about the "Wise Use" Movement?*, *in* Who Owns

unconscionability, unchecked implicit bias may frame the litigants who relied on the doctrine as low-income people of color,[58] "lacking the capacity to contract fully."[59] The scope of this problem compounds over the course of a law student's 3 years—roughly 30 courses and 90 credit hours—in law school.

Fixing the Textbook Problem

Everyone in the legal community plays a role in improving legal education. Many new pedagogical approaches to law school have been considered, especially since COVID-19. In searching for a solution, it's easy to assign blame. Barriers to authoring and editing textbooks are extensive. Authors frequently require years to complete a textbook.[60] Because compensation is usually paid in royalties, authors may not be paid for their work for years.[61] More fundamentally, authoring and editing a textbook is a challenging endeavor that demands rigorous scholarship as well as knowledge of a publishing industry that may be inaccessible to all but experienced authors.[62] Additional barriers exist for non-white, non-male prospective authors, including the lack of diversity within the legal academy[63] and shouldering the additional responsibilities of mentoring marginalized students.[64] In light of these barriers, the publishers of legal textbooks can, and should, do a better job of supporting more diverse authors. This could include developing new compensation plans that pay authors more up-front, recruiting authors from underrepresented communities by monitoring periodicals, and assembling new authorship teams when updating editions rather than allowing the previous edition's authors exclusive editorial rights. There are many steps available to publishers while this long-term goal is underway.

At their online bookstore, Aspen Publishing includes pictures and biographies of most authors. Carolina Academic Press provides shoppers with a very brief biography

---

America 45, 48 (Harvey M. Jacobs ed., 1998); *see also* The White House Historical Association, The Enslaved Household of President Thomas Jefferson, https://www.whitehousehistory.org/slavery-in-the-thomas-jefferson-white-house#:~:text=Despite%20working%20tirelessly%20to%20establish,most%20of%20any%20U.S.%20president [https://perma.cc/2RRV-4HA2].

58. *E.g.*, Williams v. Walker-Thomas Furniture Co., 350 F.2d 445 (D.C. Cir. 1965).

59. E. Allan Farnsworth et al., Contracts—Cases and Materials 531 (8th ed. 2013).

60. *See* Oxford Univ. Press, *How a textbook is made*, https://www.oup.com.au/higher-education/publish-with-us/how-a-textbook-is-made#:~:text=A%20lot%20of%20work%20goes,from%20idea%20to%20published%20book [https://perma.cc/W4DA-3BNC] (last visited Dec. 8, 2022).

61. Learn.org, *What Will I Earn as a Textbook Author?*, https://learn.org/articles/What_Will_I_Earn_as_a_Textbook_Author.html#:~:text=In%20general%2C%20authors%20are%20paid,contractor%20with%20a%20flat%20fee [https://perma.cc/S6NX-4X8U] (last visited Dec. 8, 2022).

62. Nicole Mansfield Wright, *Overcoming the 4 Pain Points of Publishing*, Inside Higher Ed (Jun. 29, 2021) https://www.insidehighered.com/advice/2021/06/29/how-navigate-key-obstacles-getting-your-academic-book-published-opinion [https://perma.cc/L2NZ-EECZ].

63. *See generally* Meera D. Deo, Unequal Profession: Race and Gender in Legal Academia (2019).

64. *See* Kimberly Mutcherson, *Taking Our Space: Women of Color and Antiracism in Legal Academia*, 73 Rutgers U. L. Rev. 869, 869, 880 (2021).

of the authors of their textbooks. West Publishing offers no authorship information beyond names. Publishers should be transparent about who is writing and editing the books they publish. For their part, professors should be mindful of the authors' identities when assigning a textbook. While it would be best if more professors assigned books written by authors that bring diverse perspectives, professors and students can start by being fully aware of the bias that may come from a book written by a team of all white men. Law school administrators and accrediting institutions should also be aware of the pervasive lack of diversity within their schools.[65] As long as "the low numbers of Black tenured professors and other professors of color contribute to ongoing biases in legal academia," it remains difficult for new ideas and diverse perspectives to enter law school classrooms.[66]

For professors interested in diversifying their curriculum, "there are a multitude of important and helpful materials" that can augment or replace traditional casebooks.[67] While abandoning printed textbooks wholesale may seem daunting, it offers several significant benefits. Open Educational Resources (OER) have proven to be a great alternative to traditional textbooks.[68] This method may lead to more engaged students. Because textbooks come at a significant cost for students, less expensive options may lead to more reading.[69] Less expensive options remove financial barriers to law students who are graduating with an average of $150,000 in debt.[70] Students can reasonably expect to pay between $4,000 and $6,000 on textbooks in addition to what they pay for tuition.[71] In addition to the cost savings, adoption of OER leads to "better or similar student educational outcomes than commercial textbooks. For example, there were higher final examination scores and a lower withdrawal rate in the semester an open-source textbook was adopted compared to the previous semester for the same course with a commercial textbook."[72]

My conviction regarding the efficacy of OER stems from personal experience. I can confidently say that I have learned more from OER than any printed textbook. Adoption of OER in the classroom should be met with solidarity by law school ad-

65. *See generally* Stephanie Francis Ward, *How Many Tenured Law Professors are Black? Public Data Does Not Say*, ABA J. (Oct. 28, 2020), https://www.abajournal.com/web/article/how-many-tenured-law-professors-are-black-public-data-doews-not-say [https://perma.cc/T66E-325D] (last visited Dec. 8, 2022).

66. *Id.*

67. Stephen E. Henderson & Joseph Thai, *Crowdsourced Coursebooks*, 51 Alberta L. Rev. 907, 908 (2014).

68. Thanuja Chandani Sandanayake, *Promoting Open Educational Resources-Based Blended learning*, 16 Int'l J. Educ. Tech. in Higher Educ. 1 (2019).

69. *Id.* at 3.

70. Am. Bar Ass'n Young Laws. Div. & AccessLex Inst., *Student Debt: The Holistic Impact on Today's Young Lawyer* 2 (2021) https://www.americanbar.org/content/dam/aba/administrative/young_lawyers/2021-student-loan-survey.pdf [https://perma.cc/J2UC-849L].

71. Kyle McEntee, *Law Books for the Price of Printing?* Above the Law (Jun. 30, 2016) (https://abovethelaw.com/2016/06/law-books-for-the-price-of-printing/) [https://perma.cc/TM9Z-QJ9G].

72. Virginia Clinton, *Savings Without Sacrifice: A Case Report on Open-Source Textbook Adoption*, 33 J. Open, Distance & E-Learning 177, 178 (2018).

ministrators; tenure decisions should not weigh publication of a traditional textbook more heavily than OER and other similar educational resources. Some professors I've spoken with suggest a compromise short of dismissing all textbooks: "What if I just send out more supplemental materials—law review articles, recorded lectures, and podcasts—that were produced by people from marginalized backgrounds?"

While this may expose some students to new perspectives, I cannot endorse the "textbook + supplement" strategy. In my experience, the vast majority of students, regardless of year or academic standing, do not read supplements whether "required" or "suggested."[73] Requiring students to purchase a textbook written by one (or more) author(s), but then later delivering other scholarship for free, communicates a message that the textbook is more valuable than the supplement. Further, it entrenches the race and sex disparity outlined above by paying textbook authors for their work while allowing the author from a marginalized background to go uncompensated. Discussing frequent requests to offer free lessons about racism, one Black author reflecting on the experiences of women of color wrote, "[w]e've already given you enough of our free labor. Don't ask us for anymore."[74] I think the sentiment applies here as well.

Avoiding these "textbook plus supplements" pitfalls, faculty unready to abandon textbooks should try to find a textbook written by authors that are not exclusively white men. Short of that, professors could adopt a "supplements plus textbook" approach, deliberately and conspicuously elevating the scholarship of authors from marginalized backgrounds. Make it clear that students should focus on non-textbook readings by identifying them as the primary reading assignment. Assign the textbook a less conspicuous place on your syllabus. Require older editions of the textbook, thereby directing students' funds in such a way that lessens the "free labor" problem outlined above. Most importantly, explain why you are doing this. A positive and accessible approach includes evaluating the perspectives of the authors when assigning textbooks, judicial opinions, or law review articles and encouraging your students to do the same. When introducing new concepts in the classroom, consider discussing the role that bias, gender, and ethnicity may play in a reading and the concept more generally. Conversations of race and sex need not, and should not, be limited to legal concepts explicitly focused on race and sex. When textbooks are assigned, professors should endeavor to highlight the perspectives not represented within their pages.

Finally, students should seek out the perspectives not represented in their reading. Just because your professor does not assign OER does not mean you cannot use them. Reach out to your school's law librarian if you don't know where to start. If your professor does not foster a classroom environment that allows for candid conversations about bias, consider starting these conversations yourself. Most importantly, consider

73. Obviously, I refer exclusively to other students. I would never do this.

74. *White People, Stop Asking Us to Educate You About Racism*, MEDIUM (May 27, 2017), (https://medium.com/@realtalkwocandallies/white-people-stop-asking-us-to-educate-you-about-racism-69273d39d828) [https://perma.cc/T5ZV-UVK9].

Dr. Moore Roberson's question at the start of every semester and look up the authors of your textbooks.

Conclusion

The purpose of this essay is not to condemn the character of textbook authors. Nor is it to cast aspersions on the publishers of these books. Instead, this essay advocates for improving legal education by incorporating more perspectives and improved pedagogical methods into the curriculum. Fundamentally, this essay was designed to invite you to:

> [i]magine what your educational experience would look like if we centered voices of color—if most of the people on your syllabus were people of color, women, LGBTQ+ folks, low income identified folks—what would your educational experience look like if we decentered white people for a moment, including them in the conversation but decentered them a bit, and privileged, so to speak, voices of color.[75]

When law students depend exclusively on a textbook written exclusive by white men, they are given an incomplete picture of doctrinal subjects. They carry that incomplete picture with them into subsequent classes and ultimately into practice. They also lose out on the benefits of diverse classroom experiences—critical thinking, cognitive development, and self-confidence. With neither these perspectives or the benefits they carry, these students are hindered from becoming truly excellent lawyers. Thinking about textbook authors is a small step toward making the legal community a more equitable place.

75. Allegheny College, *President's Lecture Series on Social Justice*, *supra* note 1, at 47:10 (remarks of Dr. Heather Moore Roberson).

Cultural Competence, Humility, Empathy, and Active Learning as Critical Features of Teaching Diversity, Equity, Belonging, and Inclusion in the Classroom

Jocelyn Kennedy *

Introduction

In law school, most experiential learning involves direct client interaction through clinical and externship programming. Other forms of experiential learning within the law school curriculum include courses on trial advocacy, contract drafting, negotiation and mediation, and courses exploring policy and legislative drafting. As experiential, rather than lecture-based "doctrinal" courses, the instructor can utilize methods of teaching that help students develop and internalize the skills necessary to embody equity, inclusion, and belonging into their future work. These less "traditional" law teaching methods and structures make experiential classrooms ideal spaces to develop expertise in cultural awareness as a first step toward internalizing diversity, equity, and inclusion in the practice of law.

This bibliography summarizes a selection of materials from multiple disciplines and in particular highlights material focused on the importance of cultural awareness or cultural competence within the classroom to create a more inclusive learning environment; methods for developing empathy and self-reflection; and the use of active learning methods to create inclusive classrooms. It does not include material relating to teaching in the clinical setting.

* Executive Director, Harvard Law School Library, and Lecturer in Law.

Setting the Stage

CULTURAL COMPETENCE IN HIGHER EDUCATION: VOL. 28, INNOVATIONS IN HIGHER EDUCATION TEACHING AND LEARNING (Tiffany Puckett and Nancy S. Lind, eds., 2020).

In this book, the authors offer a deeper exploration of the importance of cultural awareness in higher education. The editors and contributors write from a U.S. educational lens as members of higher education institutions solely within the United States. The first part of the book articulates how institutions of higher education are working to develop cultural competence in their students and faculty. They emphasize the experiences of international students as well as cultural humility and cross-cultural mindfulness and understanding. Part two presents four chapters exploring research, including the impact of multiculturalism, intercultural frameworks, and the experiences of graduate students. Parts three and four provide both best practices and challenges by exploring lessons learned in teaching cultural competence as well as ideas for future development of teaching practice. Of particular interest to the law teacher will be Chapter 13, in which Mikah K. Thompson advocates for introducing self-awareness and positionality in the first year, as well as ideas for implementation, as part of a framework for introducing cultural competence in the 1L curriculum.

Articles on Culture Competence

Verlyn F. Francis, *Infusing Dispute Resolution Teaching and Training with Culture and Diversity*, 33 OHIO STATE JOURNAL ON DISPUTE RESOLUTION 171 (2018).

In this article, Francis provides a brief history of alternative dispute resolution, explores the difficulty of defining culture, and offers a rationale for approaching teaching from a place of cultural awareness into the alternative dispute resolution (ADR) curriculum. Without settling on a specific definition, Francis highlights the essence of culture as "the lens through which we see ourselves and view the world" (191) and posits that the successful ADR instructor who "fails to acknowledge their own worldview and ignores or diminishes the culture or worldview of the learner is inviting disputes and misunderstanding into the classroom" (*Id.*). Because dispute resolution is inherently grounded in conflict and conflict resolution, the author offers models for understanding the ways culture can create conflict and methods for evaluating and developing cultural competence as an instructor. The article offers ideas to develop culturally responsive teaching methods that enable both the teacher and learner to develop "rapport and empathy with learners" and a learning environment in which both the teacher and learner "participate in and are vulnerable to each other" (229). While directed at teachers of ADR, this article offers a grounding in the rationale for, and methods to develop, cultural competence for all teachers and is valuable to anyone teaching in an experiential framework.

Anastasia M. Boles, *Seeking Inclusion from the Inside Out: Towards a Paradigm of Culturally Proficient Legal Education*, 11 CHARLESTON LAW REVIEW 209 (2017).

Referencing Interpretation 302-1 of the ABA Standard 302(d), which includes cultural competency as one of the "other professional skills needed for competent and ethical participation as a member of the legal profession," the author argues law faculty are ill-prepared to teach cultural competence because they have not been trained to be culturally competent. In Part III of the article, the author discusses a cultural proficiency paradigm as an "inside-out approach" in which the administration and faculty engage in cultural proficiency work under a five-part framework to "(1) assess culture, (2) value diversity, (3) manage the dynamics of difference, (4) adapt to diversity, and (5) institutionalize cultural knowledge"[1] (246). The author also explores barriers to developing and sustaining cultural proficiency and concludes by arguing that while individual instruction in the classroom is beneficial, true modelling of cultural proficiency in all facets of legal education are necessary to transform the legal profession.

L. Danielle Tully, *The Cultural (Re)Turn: The Case for Teaching Culturally Responsive Lawyering*, 16 STANFORD JOURNAL OF CIVIL RIGHTS & CIVIL LIBERTIES 201 (2020).

In this article, the author calls for the implementation of culturally responsive lawyering across the profession. The author offers a discussion of culture and explores how cultural and social cognition are interrelated. What follows in Parts III and IV is a lengthy exploration of the tenets of culturally responsive lawyering and a detailed framework to incorporate these tenets into the classroom, the curriculum, and the law school environment.

1. Citing Carolyn Copps Hartley & Carrie J. Petrucci, *Practicing Culturally Competent Therapeutic Jurisprudence: A Collaboration Between Social Work and Law*, 14 WASH. U. J. L. & POL'Y 133, 172 (2004).

Using Active Learning via Simulation, Community Engagement, Games, and Other Methodologies to Build Emotional Intelligence Skills, Including Empathy, Compassion, and Cultural Competency

Olga Chernikova et al., *Simulation-Based Learning in Higher Education: A Meta-Analysis*, 90 REVIEW OF EDUCATIONAL RESEARCH 499 (2020).

In an analysis of 145 empirical studies reviewing the use of simulation-based learning in various professional domains, this study looks at a variety of simulation methodologies and structures to posit that the use of simulation in higher education, particularly in areas where complex decision making is critical, is beneficial to learners. The study evaluates the need for instructional support and intervention throughout the simulation process and points to both successful and unsuccessful simulation models. This meta-analysis suggests that simulation is effective where complex skills are necessary for graduate success. While studies of simulation in legal education were not included in this meta-analysis, the inclusion of studies in "high-touch" fields such as medicine, nursing, and social work can be extrapolated to the legal profession. While complex skills in the STEM field are more scientific in nature, the complex skills learned through simulation within this meta-analysis include decision-making, negotiation, and client counsel. This meta-analysis will familiarize educators with core educational concepts of simulation.

Catherine Bramble and Rory Bahadur, *Actively Achieving Greater Racial Equity in Law School Classrooms*, 70 CLEVELAND STATE LAW REVIEW 709 (2021).

This article argues that the Socratic Method, the prevalent teaching method in law school education, is insufficient and perhaps harmful to learners. The authors argue that this method is a form of passive learning for all but the students interacting in the moment with a faculty member. They further argue that the current form of lecture-based teaching creates and perpetuates a hierarchical and systemically harmful learning environment. The article offers an analysis of active learning and its history, as well as practical methods for incorporating active learning in the classroom. In addition, the article reviews the literature that suggests students from diverse backgrounds benefit greatly from the incorporation of active learning techniques in the classroom, which foster inclusive learning environments and the opportunity for all students to participate in the learning endeavor. The authors offer several forms of active learning, with examples of how to incorporate them into both doctrinal and experiential courses.

Simulations

Margaret Bearman et al., *Learning Empathy Through Simulation: A Systematic Literature Review*, 10 SIMULATION IN HEALTH CARE 308 (2015).

In this systematic literature review, the authors evaluated over 800 articles that explore the use of simulations in health care education to teach empathy in healthcare students. The findings indicate that simulation courses can increase empathy in learners and are most successful in simulations where the learner is placed in the patient's shoes. The review also reveals that measuring empathy as an overall outcome is difficult. The review in the healthcare field suggests that simulations to develop empathy in law school courses may or may not have efficacy.

Laure West Steck et al., *Doing Poverty: Learning Outcomes Among Students Participating in the Community Action Poverty Simulation Program*, 39 TEACHING SOCIOLOGY 259 (2011).

This article analyzes the learning outcomes of students who participated in the Missouri Community Action Poverty Simulation. It includes a discussion on the value of simulation to facilitate knowledge transfer, skill development, and application of both. The article provides a detailed description of the simulation, created to "educate everyone, from policy makers to community leaders, about the day-to-day realities of life with a shortage of money and an abundance of stress" (262). Following the simulation, which places students in the role of an impoverished person with a defined identity (child, parent, disabled person, elderly person, extended family member), students engage in a written critical reflection, as well as large and small group discussion. The researchers found that students "reported an enhanced and sometimes changed understanding of people who are living in poverty and deeper recognition of the many factors that affect impoverished families" (270). This article demonstrates that placing students in the shoes of a particular person, coupled with course readings and materials on the subject, enhances and deepens the student's understanding of underlying issues.

Oral Histories and Storytelling

Tina Maschi et al., *Moving Stories: Evaluation of an MSW Experiential Learning Project on Aging and Diversity*, 49 JOURNAL OF SOCIAL WORK EDUCATION 461 (2013).

This article discusses a study of an oral history research project, "Moving Stories: Older Adults Share Their Experiences Before, During, and After Immigration" in a Masters of Social Work (MSW) program at Fordham University. This project paired MSW students with older adults from diverse ethnic backgrounds. The curriculum for the project included reading material on issues of aging and diversity. Students were instructed in how to conduct culturally competent oral histories. "Students ... learned to understand what it means to listen across culture or race" (471) and to contextualize lived experiences.

Maria Saltzez Wyant Cuzzo et al., *How Do You Effectively Teach Empathy to Students?* 151 New Directions for Teaching and Learning 61 (2017).

In this article, the authors explore both the more structured modernist approach and the student-centered postmodernist approach to teaching. They acknowledge the difficulty of incorporating empathy education into the classroom, while offering a variety of best practices to do so. They use examples such as incorporating storytelling, multimedia, student written role-plays, and community of practice feedback sessions, to demonstrate the benefit of these practices in the classroom.

Study Away Programs

Melinda L. Lewis et al., *Creative Teaching and Reflection in Nontraditional Settings: Regional, National and International Experiences*, 39 Social Development Issues 29 (2017).

This article examines a three-pronged study-away program. Particularly interesting is the discussion of regional study-away as community immersion. The authors, professors in the social work discipline, describe the value of study away and study abroad courses that engage "students within diverse communities, identifying social justice issues, exploring solutions, and developing skills to advocate for social change" (30). They discuss four immersive courses that include both on-campus and off-campus components, while exploring social justice history, policy making, and cultural adaptability. The courses described in the article offer opportunities for law faculty to reconsider how to bring real-world issues and experience into their non-clinical classrooms. One course included traveling portions of the Underground Railroad. Post-course assessment of learning outcomes "appear to have increased student willingness to engage with vulnerable populations (as change agents who ... advocate for the dignity and worth of all human beings" (36). The immersive learning techniques described in this article offer a frame for adapting courses to incorporate community engagement and immersion into instruction.

Fiction, Literature, and Writing

Ilene L. Ingram & Toni S. Walters, *A Critical reflection model to teach diversity and social justice*, 2 Journal of Praxis in Multicultural Education 23 (2007).

The authors developed a Social Justice Critical Reflection Model (SJCRM) as a model for engaging in classroom-based critical thinking. In particular, the authors use this model in literature courses to explore diversity and social justice issues. The article discusses the long-supported value of literature as a teaching tool and a lens through which students can examine different worldviews and experiences. The SJCRM may offer teachers a framework to interrogate texts in the classroom and guide learners toward deeper reflection and transformation.

Johanna Shapiro et al., *Teaching Empathy to First Year Medical Students: Evaluation of an Elective Literature and Medicine Course*, 17 EDUCATION FOR HEALTH 73 (2004).

The authors found a significant improvement of empathy in students who participated in an elective course on Literature and Medicine. Studies have shown that in the field of medicine, empathy declines over time. Empathy is in the curriculum "in a cognitive behavior format as part of a communications skills course." By turning to the humanities, and in particular literature, the authors speculated "reading and discussing literature about patient experiences of illness and the doctor-patient relationship could significantly improve medical student empathy. . . ." (74). The study, while inconclusive on the long-term effect of teaching empathy in medical school, it suggests that incorporating literature into the law school curriculum may increase students' capacity for empathy.

Teri A. McMurtry-Chubb, *The Practical Implication of Unexamined Assumptions: Disrupting Flawed Legal Arguments to Advance the Cause of Justice*, 58 WASHBURN LAW JOURNAL 531 (2019).

In this article, Professor McMurty-Chubb describes "teaching legal writing as a practice of liberation", and an opportunity to examine the systemic inequities of law and legal education. She provides examples of integrating complex issues of power and privilege through an "anti-racist and feminist pedagogies that aim to reflect the unexamined assumptions students make and employ in structuring legal arguments"(536). She explains her methodology, course design, and learning outcomes for a required course in legal writing. This article interrogates the systemic inequities of legal education and the legal system while providing a vehicle to incorporate that inquiry into legal writing instruction.

Part II

Dedicated Courses on Race, Injustice, and Professional Identity

Race and the Foundations of American Law: Creating a New Three-Credit Class at Roger Williams University School of Law

Nicole P. Dyszlewski, Diana Hassel† & Nadiyah J. Humber‡*

> *Judging from the delightful array of recent writings on curriculum reform in the* Journal of Legal Education, *it is much more fashionable to talk about the nature and scope of potential reforms than to address the more pragmatic concerns that will determine whether they are adopted. Indeed, it is not uncommon for a proposal to be put forth without comment on its costs or its effects on existing resources, especially existing faculty resources. But the "process" of curriculum reform will have a significant impact on the configuration of any reforms ultimately accepted. Thus, while the current reform agenda is quite full, many of the proposals lose their luster when they confront the constraints that define the present potential of legal education.*[1]

---

* Nicole P. Dyszlewski is the Director of Special Programs, Academic Affairs at Roger Williams University School of Law. Nicole would like to thank her brilliant co-authors, Diana and Nadiyah, for their creativity, kindness, innovative spirit, and patience.

† Diana Hassel is a Professor of Law at Roger Williams University. Thank you to the best team—Nadiyah Humber and Nicole Dyszlewski and for the support of the RWU Law faculty.

‡ Nadiyah J. Humber is an Associate Professor of Law at University of Connecticut School of Law. Thank you, Diana and Nicole, for inviting me to co-create this course with you, the opportunity to contribute to this chapter, and for sharing with me your continual wisdom.

1. John C. Weistart, *The Law School Curriculum: The Process of Reform*, 1987 Duke L.J. 317, 329 (1987).

Introduction

This essay will not be fashionable in the ways described above. Instead, its aim is to plainly discuss the nuts and bolts of how one school, Roger Williams University School of Law (RWU Law), underwent a significant curricular reform by creating, testing, and rolling out a mandatory three-credit class for all JD students on the topic of systemic racism in U.S. law. This essay is not intended to be a call for curricular upheaval, nor is it intended to provide step-by-step instructions for other schools. It is intended to discuss, briefly, the way in which one school recognized a need for change and made that change. The three authors of this piece were all involved in this change by working to develop the original draft syllabus for this new class, as well as co-teaching the first iteration of the class, offered as a three-credit elective for upper-level students. We all have a different specialty, identity, and place within the academic hierarchy that inform our perspective and role within the project. Our diversity of perspective has been crucial to the success of the endeavor. Because we are not a professorial monolith, we have been able to take the lead in different aspects of the course design based on our areas of expertise, share our differing perspectives on chosen readings, and navigate classroom discussion hurdles using our different styles and approaches. This essay will discuss the history of the creation of the class, give an overview of the class structure, and provide some advice for those who are considering adopting a similar class.

In the wake of the murders of George Floyd, Breonna Taylor, Ahmaud Arbery, and countless others, the RWU Law faculty, staff, and administration met to respond to demands from the law school's students, particularly from students of color. One of the major issues raised by the students was a perceived lack of coverage in the curriculum on issues of racial inequality. One specific request was a dedicated course on critical race theory. As the faculty grappled with these requests,[2] the idea of a dedicated course on the role of race in the development of the law emerged and was adopted. One reason for the faculty's approval of the course was the sense of urgency based on student demands and the rise of the Black Lives Matter movement. We understood that we needed to take concrete action and not just express concern. At this meeting, the faculty, staff, and administration voted to create a required class on race and the law. While the usual process of approving a class, even an elective class, requires a syllabus, this class was approved based on concept alone. The class was also approved within the context of the school's amended mission statement[3] and the school's diversity strategic plan.[4]

---

2. One issue deliberated by faculty concerned the term "white supremacy" in the course title. While the course focuses on white supremacist institutions, labeling the course in this way gave the faculty pause because of the potential for divisiveness. "Race and the Foundations of American Law" was adopted because notionally it was less antagonistic.

3. "Provide an excellent legal education that is focused on the development of students' analytical, ethical, and other practice skills through the exploration of legal doctrine, policy, history, and theory, *including the relationship between law and social inequality.*" Roger Williams School of Law, *Our Mission*, https://law.rwu.edu/why-rwu-law/our-mission (last visited Jan. 4, 2023) (emphasis added).

4. "Continue to develop and offer courses that focus specifically on issues of inequality and social justice AND Address inequality and social justice issues in courses across the curriculum, identify

One of the questions we faced was whether a dedicated course was appropriate or if integrating diversity issues into the broader curriculum would be a better approach. We concluded that the dedicated course would be a foundation and not a substitute for bringing issues of diversity to all aspects of the curriculum. Another concern was whether the breadth of student views about issues of racial inequality would be respected. Would the course be seen as "indoctrination" of a particular political view? This concern was addressed by carefully including materials from a variety of perspectives in the course readings. We made it clear that students would not be graded on their political viewpoint, but rather on the quality of their engagement with and analysis of the issues raised by the course. An additional concern was whether RWU Law had the resources to support an ambitious required course and whether the school's limited resources could better be used in other areas. The administration made clear that resources would be made available to hire additional faculty and to provide administrative support for the course. This reassurance and support from the law school and the university gave confidence to the faculty that we could successfully roll out the course without taking needed resources away from other aspects of the curriculum.

While there was not unanimity in support for the course on race and the law, a large majority of the faculty backed the initiative. The discussions on the subject alone were useful and allowed the faculty to learn about each other's hopes and concerns as we embarked on the exciting new project. The deliberations and the decision to adopt the course led to a renewed sense of unity and purpose at the law school.

Once the class was voted into existence, the work of creating and executing the class began and decisions needed to be made. Given that this class would be developed as a required class for all JD students, the process of class creation took about two years to complete. That two-year period consisted of discussions, negotiations, research, two pilot offerings of the class as an elective, and a semester-long training session for the faculty involved. As a result of this period of innovation and preparation, it was decided that that class would be team taught by three faculty members and would be situated in the first semester of the second year.[5] It was decided that the class would be three credits and be graded on the same mandatory curve as other second-year required classes. It is

---

teaching materials that facilitate consideration of those issues, and provide students the opportunity, where appropriate to evaluate faculty members on the effectiveness of their efforts." Roger Williams School of Law, *Strategic Plan for Diversity & Inclusion*, https://law.rwu.edu/student-experience/diversity-and-outreach/strategic-planning-diversity-inclusion (last visited Jan. 4, 2023).

5. Where the course should be placed in the curriculum was a major topic of discussion. Should we add another required course without cutting back on current requirements? The goal of adequately preparing students for bar success was seen as critical, so any changes should not interfere with that effort. After many alternative proposals were examined, a decision was made to place the course in the third semester of law school. This placement took the course out of the already challenging first year list of required courses and allowed students to have some legal grounding before taking on a legally and socially complex subject.

important to note that these decisions were made based on a variety of considerations; a pragmatic appraisal of available resources, though, stands out as necessary factor.[6]

Defining the Class

It is helpful to understand what the class is and is not. Again, available resources and constraints have been foundational to the definition of the class. The class at RWU, in its earliest iterations and current version, is not a survey class on race and the law in a traditional sense where we engage students on the way in which different racial or ethnic groups have been impacted by U.S. laws. Instead, it is envisioned to be more limited in scope, as we look specifically at ways in which systemic racism against BIPOC people has and continues to be fundamentally baked into the American legal system. The narrative thread is systemic racism, not individual moments of racist behavior or animus. This focus is responsive to the student demands and narrow enough to be manageable. It is also strategic in that it allows students to focus less on their own individual bias or the bias of individual classmates, but on the systemic bias of the legal system.[7]

Another foundational guiding principle to what the class is, and is not, is the context of student and faculty expectations of what a law class is and should be. Another way of stating this principle is that we were continually mindful of how similar or dissimilar the class would be to other more traditional courses at the law school and student and faculty expectations. For example, we had many conversations about the class materials. We extensively debated the use of cases,[8] the use of a textbook,[9] and the use of multimedia assignments.[10] Understanding that the class is limited in scope and created to fit within the expectations of what a law school class is, we designed it with

---

6. For example, team teaching was a fundamental part of the plan because this would allow interested faculty to teach on subjects that they were comfortable teaching. It would also allow for flexibility with regard to the way in which the Associate Dean managed the faculty credit load and the hiring of adjuncts, diversity in professorship identity with regard to who was available for student support and connectivity because the instructors would have a support network within the classroom. Another example is where it was placed in the curriculum in that it was impossible to shoehorn three credits into the first year without cutting other important credits so even though it was seen as desirable to engage with students on this topic at the beginning of their law school experience, we were unable to fit three additional credits into the curriculum.

7. It is not as if the class ignores identity and implicit bias. The hope is that taking the focus from the individual student, teacher, judge, legislator, etc., allows the students the ability to engage with the material in a way that creates distance and allows for critical thinking beyond the self.

8. How many cases should the class include? Will the use of cases make some students feel more comfortable with the subject matter? Will using more cases give the appearance that this is more legal and less social science?

9. Does having an open education resource create the illusion that this class is less important than other classes? Does not using an expensive casebook make the class materials more accessible to others?

10. Does the use of magazine articles from *The Atlantic* and podcasts allow for increased diversity of authorship of key texts? Does the use of podcasts and documentary films increase the feeling that this class is less important or less legal to students who may be already resistant to this subject matter?

traditional legal pedagogy in mind but also considered how to teach beyond those parameters. The next section will give more specifics of the class design.

The Class Structure

The course, *Race and the Foundations of American Law*, is divided into three sections: Historical Origins of White Supremacy; Systems of Racism; and Going Forward. This approach—addressing the past, the present, and the future—seemed like the best structure to expose students to important legal history, the relevance of that history to present legal doctrine, and the possibility of reform and repair. This sequence allows students to move from the rage and despair that sometimes develop in response to a confrontation with our history of racial hierarchy to contemplating steps that can be taken, particularly by lawyers, to address this legacy.

Along with introducing students to specific cases and doctrine, another major goal of the course is to provide students with analytic tools that can be used in other areas of their legal education. To do that we look at cases that students may be familiar with—such as *Plessy v. Ferguson*—and examine the background of the litigants, the legal context in which the decision was issued, and the concrete impact of the case on the lives of the enslaved. This approach, looking beyond the abstract legal ruling set forth in a court decision and asking what lies behind the holding, is a critical tool that students can bring to all areas of legal study and praxis. This tool is especially important when students are confronted with legal doctrine that is seemingly unrelated to race. Asking more questions, and finding out whose lives are impacted, reveals the racial implications of seemingly neutral legal rules.

The assignments have been constructed to allow students to engage with the materials in a variety of ways. Students submit weekly short reflections, contribute to forum discussions, write three short papers, and participate in class-wide and small group discussions. The frequency and variety of methods of engagement and assessment are designed to keep the level of student interest and participation high. We also believe these frequent methods of contact help support students through the sometimes frustrating and painful examination of racial hierarchy in the law.

Three questions: (1) what the law did; (2) what the law is doing; and (3) what the law should do, are helpful to frame why the three modules make sense for a race and the law course. Starting a race and the law course with historical origins is a worthwhile strategy because it centers knowledge accumulation. Students are eager to understand the past, and by focusing on what the law did, you can more easily ground students in facts, which is beneficially linked to building trust in the classroom. There is little room for debate when discussing facts. What the law is doing and what it should do are questions reserved for later classes.[11] The contextualization of history creates a natural scope

11. We understand that what the law should do is relative. In these later discussions, we introduce ideas for reform as a starting point and welcome a variety of viewpoints. The goal is to ignite discussion

for the direction of class discussion. From our perspective, the role of the instructor is not to convince students about the existence of structural racism. Rather, by reading historical records and primary sources that explicitly detail how the law controlled the social and political will of BIPOC people in America, discussions of systems of racism are more informed and less contentious.

Having taught this course as an elective, we are frequently surprised by the lack of knowledge law students have of American history and specifically racial history. The first section of the course aims to address some of these deficits. We start with the history of North American colonialism and the Supreme Court's adoption of the Doctrine of Discovery providing the legal justifications for loss of control of land by Native Americans.[12] We look at how the early establishments of colonies by European empires were based on the assertion of white supremacy and how that assumption continued into the formation of the United States. The establishment of slavery in colonial America accelerates the central role racial injustice has played in the history of our country. The Supreme Court cases and provisions of the U.S. Constitution that provide the legal framework to support the enslavement of African peoples, including *Dred Scott v. Sanford* and the Fugitive Slave Clause, are closely analyzed and the concrete details of the lives of the enslaved are confronted. We conclude the history section with the Amendments to the Constitution adopted after the Civil War that created some hope for equality and the brief history of Reconstruction, which brought some reform and the possibility of a more racially just political and legal system in the decade after the war.[13] Finally, we examine the failure of the goals of Reconstruction and the reimposition of terror, disenfranchisement, and criminalization of the formerly enslaved.

As the first third of the course unfolds, students begin to speak more freely in class, in reflective journal writing, or both, and do so with respect for their classmates and professors.[14] During the second phase of the course where the current state of the law is front and center, while students may, and frequently do, experience emotional distress,[15] they do so as a collective and they begin to let their guard down when discuss-

but not place value judgements on ideas. We do, however, encourage thoughtful articulation of these ideas.

12. The Doctrine of Discovery, originated by European colonialists, deprived native peoples of the Americas ownership of the land they occupied. This doctrine was adopted by the United States Supreme Court in *Johnson v. M'Intosh*, 21 U.S. 543 (1823).

13. We do not cover the Civil War itself in any detail. Rather, we focus on the pressures leading up to the war and the possibility of an expanded American democracy following the defeat of the Confederacy.

14. As a point of context, we have chosen in our class materials to skip over the Civil War. This allows us to focus on the beginnings (and swift ending) of the multi-racial democracy during Reconstruction. In our experience, most students have context about the Civil War but lack fundamental historical information about Reconstruction.

15. Class material may invoke emotional reactions in a variety of ways. The primary avenue for digesting the material is reflective journals. Another way to help ground students is to assign material at the beginning of the semester that explains common psychological and emotional responses to discussions of race in the classroom. For example, Beverly Daniel Tatum's article *Talking About Race, Learning About Racism: The Application of Racial Identity Development Theory in the Classroom* is

ing ideas or asking questions. The new focus becomes the students' digestion of the material in the now and they begin to question the purpose of law—if the law is a tool for progress or oppression and how their professional identity fits within the legal profession. Their thinking shifts from how individuals are situated within legal, political, social, and economic hierarchies to thinking about systems and the effects of those systems on people of color.

The goal of the section on current systems of racism is to pick up the historical thread and examine how our current legal policies have been influenced by our previous history of explicit white supremacy. How do our current, seemingly more neutral, legal regimes continue to reinforce racial hierarchy? We chose to address mass incarceration, voter suppression, housing, education, and the legal profession, but other topics, such as immigration, policing, or health law, would also be appropriate. This portion of the course allows instructors to take advantage of their expertise by delving into an area of law that is of most interest to them. In analyzing different legal systems, we address the question of systemic racism rather than individual intent. While deliberate racial discrimination has largely been outlawed due to the reforms in the Civil Rights Era, racial inequality remains. What are the forces that keep it in place if consciously racist policy decisions are rare? We encourage the practice of looking behind the seemingly neutral and evenhanded language of legal decisions and policy to unearth the origins of the doctrine and find the real-world implications on the lives of people based on their race.

Module three gives students an opportunity to learn how others have used the law to dismantle or challenge systems. This is a natural final step because students often feel compelled to act by the end of the semester. We survey and critique current efforts to address systemic racial inequality. We look at topics such as reparations, reparative justice, and truth telling closely through the concrete efforts of different communities and organizations. In analyzing the strengths and flaws of the various reform efforts, we pay particular attention to the role lawyers and the legal profession have in creating a more just legal system. Students are encouraged to think critically and independently about their role as lawyers. This section strives to give agency to students in their own learning and professional development. Paying attention to the students' development of professional identities and future roles in the community provides a central theme of the last few weeks of the semester.

Moving through the themes of history, current legal doctrine, and possible routes to reform provides a pathway for students to confront the realities of our history, develop tools to critically engage with other areas of law, and begin to develop strategies and goals as they create their own places in the legal profession.

---

helpful for grounding students in race law discussions. 62 HARV. EDUC. REV. 1 (1992). Students have also taken comfort in having small group discussions and learning from their personal experiences. We also have an open-door policy if students want to discuss material in a deeper way in a more private setting, though this is more feasible with limited class sizes. As a required course, referral sources for professional counseling can be shared.

When structuring classes, employing backward design methods was a helpful approach. First, we drafted learning goals and objectives, then related instructional procedures to learning goals, and finally, we determined the most applicable formative and summative assessments. We asked: (1) what is the goal for this class? (2) what instruction should be provided to accomplish the goal? and (3) how should we assess if the goal is achieved? In the *Historical Origins of White Supremacy* section, the *Constitution/ Views of the Framers* class is instructive. For this class, the goal is for students to read the Constitution and understand the historical underpinnings of selected sections. To accomplish this goal, students are instructed to read an article that summarizes and directly quotes discussion from the Constitutional Convention. Students also engage in a textualist exercise to examine literal meaning. To assess if the goal is achieved, we engage in group discussion and journal writing. Large and small group discussions help us decipher if students draw their own conclusions about the constitutional text and the institution of slavery.

The format for the class is a brief lecture, a reading review, and small group discussion. Groups are pre-assigned depending on the number of students with one instructor assigned to each group The assignment for the class includes one law review article, Juan F. Perea, *Race and Constitutional Law Casebooks: Recognizing the Proslavery Constitution,*[16] and a shorter read by Robert Cohen, *Was the Constitution Pro-slavery? The Changing View of Frederick Douglass.*[17] *Prigg v. Pennsylvania*[18] and sections of the U.S. Constitution are also assigned. The lecture is about events leading up to the Constitutional Convention, and overviews of relevant legal text, such as the Fugitive Slave Act, are provided and are often surprising to the students. The three-fifths compromise is another attention-grabbing lesson. Students gather for themselves that their conventional wisdom about federalism is a more superficial understanding of the dynamic between slave-holding states and northern states in the framing of the Constitution.

For small group discussions, students are provided two questions for small group discussion:

1. How can you reconcile Frederick Douglass's point of view that We the People, meant ALL the people, and the Constitution was drafted for all, with Perea's point of view about race-neutral language having harmful outcomes in Black communities?
2. Do you think the Constitution was a political, not a moral, union? That is, was it more like an economic treaty or compact than a rule of law?

As with any examples provided in this chapter, there is always room for improvement, but we provide the example because these questions resulted in rich discussion. But of course, adjust accordingly.

---

16. Juan F. Perea, *Race and Constitutional Law Casebooks: Recognizing the Proslavery Constitution*, 110 MICH. L. REV. 1123 (2012).

17. Robert Cohen, *Was the Constitution Pro-slavery? The Changing View of Frederick Douglass*, 72 SOC. EDUC. 246 (2008).

18. 41 U.S. 539 (1842).

After class, we provided students with question prompts for their reflection journals. Some questions for this class were:

1. What do you think about Juan Perea's conclusions about the Constitution and its influence on structural racism at the end of his article?
2. Law students are generally surprised to learn about the Fugitive Slave Act of 1793/1850 and the impact these statutes had on events leading up to the Civil War. Do you think law schools should address constitutional law from a critical race perspective in first-year courses, or do you think these discussions are better served in a seminar with self-selected audiences? Why or why not?
3. How did the framers reconcile two diametrically opposed visions of America? Were they successful?

Students have a myriad of reactions to this class. In response to question two, one student wrote:

> At the end of his article, Perea concludes that one of the consequences of not utilizing a critical race perspective in the discussion of law and the Constitution is "widespread ignorance" about the role of slavery and racism in the Constitution and a generation of "Colorblind warriors" (Perea 16). While I definitely agree with his conclusions, I do not believe just teaching Constitutional Law from a critical race perspective is enough to prevent this consequence. Because of the existing incentives in law school and student focus on ultimately passing the rules-based Bar exam, a critical race perspective needs to be applied across the doctrinal courses, and there should be required engagement with these topics at a deeper level in a seminar-style class.

When students reflect on the class material, we always comment on their reflection papers. We comment to acknowledge we are listening and learning the student's perspectives. We also engage in this practice to build trust in the private space of writing so students know we are not judging their opinions; rather, we are engaging them in dialogue where they feel more comfortable to speak freely as illustrated by the following excerpt:

> Two points were made in class that I wanted to disagree with here. First, one note was made that the framers did not necessarily want slavery and that the northerners at the least thought it was bad. For the reasons stated above, [she described why she thought the Constitution was a pro-slavery document] as to why my group believes the document to be antislavery, I disagree.... Second, one group talked about how they thought the framers were intentionally vague in order to allow slavery to be rid of. I disagree. I think that they were vague because they realized that they did not have all the answers. And regardless of whether they left the world 'slavery' out intentionally, it was still at the forefront of each framer's mind.... Most importantly, though, these comments were interesting to me because of what they reminded me of (which is why I want to note them). Please note that I do not mean any of this towards

> the students directly, it is just some thoughts I had after class. Basically, these views and comments are ones I believed in as well prior to our readings.

We make clear that students are not graded on content or comments, but their writing and quality of reflection. Rubrics are provided for students, so they understand grades are uniform, neutral, and serve the purpose of enriching classroom discussion in another medium.

Practical Advice

Teaching and learning about the legacy and presence of white supremacy in our legal system is hard work. "Learning how to communicate about such topics as white privilege, police violence, economic inequality and mass incarceration requires practice, and facilitating difficult conversations demands courage and skill—regardless of who we are, our intentions or how long we've been teaching."[19] This hard work, courage, and skill building requires support. Based on our experiences creating and teaching the class described, it is important to build in extracurricular support for faculty and students. Currently, RWU Law has an optional weekly "talk back" session where we facilitate conversations with students outside of the classroom. This is an opportunity for students to vent, learn more, form community, and obtain additional support. These additional opportunities to engage with the class content have been underutilized but it is a message to students that the instructors (and institution) are committed to providing a space for additional support outside of class time.

Beyond additional support for the students, this class may, and frequently does, require additional support for the teachers. This is not a class you just show up to teach. It can be demanding and emotional work, dissimilar to other doctrinal subjects in intensity. As we have grown from three faculty teaching an elective to a cadre of faculty[20] teaching this class as a required course, the nature of this support has grown and changed. The teachers meet once or twice a week as a "pod" and at least once a month as a full Race and the Foundations of American Law faculty. This class is particularly demanding of resources from both the teachers and the institution.[21]

---

19. *Let's Talk! Discussing Race, Racism and Other Difficult Topics with Students*, LEARNING FOR JUSTICE, https://www.learningforjustice.org/sites/default/files/general/TT%20Difficult%20Conversations%20web.pdf.

20. In fall 2022, the mandatory class was rolled out with five sections of students, each taught by a team of three instructors, which were each a combination of full-time faculty, staff, and adjunct professors.

21. Beyond the scope of this essay, but very fitting in the practical advice section, is the "what went wrong" of things. There were some expected bumps in the road as this class grew from the elective version to the mandatory version. Changing the nature of the students taking the class from voluntary to mandatory changed some of the class dynamics. Growing the faculty from the three authors of this essay to a dozen or so faculty and five TAs changed some of the class dynamics. As we continue to refine the class and teach it every year we will likely write another piece that discusses and dissects some of these changes.

Conclusion

As promised, this essay has focused on the pedagogical choices and programmatic nuts and bolts of one school's efforts to change their curriculum in a meaningful way to include a required three-credit class, *Race and the Foundations of American Law*. Decisions were made with intentionality but not perfection. It is our continued hope that this class, and its design, are iterative, that it will change and grow with this area of law and the societal context in which it blossomed. We also celebrate all of the other institutions who are engaging in these efforts and look forward to seeing how other schools embrace antiracism in the law school curriculum.

Incorporating Critical Perspectives in Law and Professional Identity into the 1L Curriculum at Boston College Law School

Reena Parikh & Cheryl Bratt†‡*

Introduction

Law schools are uniquely situated to educate students on how the law and the legal system can perpetuate racism and inequality, and yet these institutions have largely failed to provide new lawyers with the necessary tools to critique the law and transform it in order to advance racial and social justice. The ABA's revised Standard 303, instituted in the 2022–2023 edition of the Standards and Rules of Procedure for Approval of Law Schools, has started to address this gap, now requiring all law schools to "provide education to law students on bias, cross-cultural competency, and racism."[1] However, Boston College Law School (BC Law) took steps to address this hole in the traditional law school curriculum before the latest ABA reform. Indeed, our Jesuit tradition demands proactive efforts to combat inequality, as "it is not enough to refrain from injustice," but rather, "one must go further and refuse to play its game."[2] BC Law's ongoing efforts to live up to this ideal are reflected in a new, required 1L course titled "Critical Perspectives: Law, Context, and Professional Identity," which launched in the

* Assistant Clinical Professor, Boston College Law School.

† Associate Professor of the Practice, Boston College Law School.

‡ Co-authors Cheryl Bratt and Reena Parikh contributed equally to this essay, reject the hierarchy imputed by any particular ordering of co-author names, and request that both names be included in any full or short citation to this essay.

1. Am. Bar Ass'n, Standards and Rules of Procedure for Approval of Law Schools 2022–2023, Standard 303(b).

2. Pedro Arrupe, S.J., Superior General of the Society of Jesus, *Men and Women For Others*, Ignatian Solidarity Network (1973), https://ignatiansolidarity.net/men-and-women-for-others-fr-pedro-arrupe-s-j/. (last visited Dec. 8, 2022).

fall of 2021 following a powerful student organizing effort to institute a required course on race and the law.

The Critical Perspectives course, which occurs during the first semester of the 1L year, introduces students to critical legal theories,[3] helps students explore how a critical lens can offer a deeper understanding of the cases they read in their 1L doctrinal courses, and acknowledges ways in which the law can be both a tool of oppression and liberation. The course also invites students to reflect upon their own professional identities and goals as both law students and future lawyers, in light of the topics and issues that the course covers.

Designing and instituting this course has been an iterative and evolving endeavor that is exhilarating, risky, and extremely fulfilling. It has taken countless hours, teamwork, and collaboration across all facets of the law school, and presented myriad substantive, administrative, financial, and logistical challenges along the way. But it has also grown to be a pivotal addition to our curriculum, shedding light on narratives typically left in the shadows, contextualizing doctrine that otherwise leaves new law students feeling alienated, and strengthening our community bonds. We are eager to share what we did with the course and what we learned through our iterations with the hope that our story might encourage, and also ease the transition of, other institutions introducing similar programs. Although each school has its own needs and particularities, we hope that the blueprint below and the lessons we learned will help other schools embrace the risks of evolving their own curriculum, and likewise begin to transform their campuses.

Part I: History Behind the Course

Like many law schools and other higher education institutions around the country, BC Law has grappled with adequately reflecting, both on its campus and in its curriculum, its commitment to promoting diversity, equity, inclusion, and belonging (DEIB).[4] Indeed, a campus-wide survey conducted in 2019 reflected that although BC Law overall had a strong sense of community, DEIB efforts were lacking within the 1L curriculum, as elective offerings, and with respect to faculty and student fluency both inside and outside the classroom.[5] The curricular holes left some students, particularly 1L students of color, feeling alienated at the law school and ambivalent about their ambitions to become lawyers.

4. *See, e.g.*, Danielle M. Conway, *Antiracist Lawyering in Practice Begins with the Practice of Teaching and Learning Antiracism in Law School*, 2022 Utah L. Rev. 723 (2022); Eduardo R. C. Capulong, Andrew King-Ries & Monte Mills, *Antiracism, Reflection, and Professional Identity*, 18 Hastings Race & Poverty L.J. 3 (2021).

5. BC Law hired Diversity @ Work to gather data through surveys and meetings with various constituencies, which reported its findings and recommendations to the administration, which in turn reported that information to the faculty and staff.

After digesting the 2019 survey findings, BC Law recommitted to better translating its DEIB values into concrete efforts. It undertook numerous initiatives, including: a series of town hall and community meetings, an all-day retreat for the faculty and staff, multiple trainings facilitated by outside diversity consultants, and the hiring of a Director of Diversity, Equity, and Inclusion Programs. But, while all of this important institutional work was occurring to improve the *campus* experience, the *classroom* experience remained mostly unaltered, creating a dissonance between BC Law's articulated commitment to DEIB and its actual core curriculum.

The successive murders of Elijah McClain, Breonna Taylor, and George Floyd, among others, however, sparked a national reckoning that reached the walls of campus and inspired a widespread, student-initiated, grassroots campaign that demanded action.[6] Student leaders and activists formed the Student Action Group for an Inclusive Curriculum[7] to urge BC Law to adopt a mandatory course that would speak to the realities of our world and interrogate the ways in which the law has been used to construct and uphold hierarchies that subjugate marginalized communities. During an April 2021 faculty meeting, members of the student group then presented their well-researched and reasoned request for a required course on race and the law.[8] They argued that such a course would not only help the entire student body better confront and critique issues of race and power that underlie the doctrine they learn, but it would also help them make sense of the present-day injustices that the law enables and perpetuates, and give them an opportunity to examine their own roles as law students and future lawyers who will inevitably shape our future laws and legal systems.

The presentation was a compelling call to action. And the faculty overwhelmingly affirmed the students' work. But deciding next steps and actualizing the students' vision proved more complicated. At a faculty meeting the following month, colleagues raised a myriad of issues, including: whether a race and law course should be optional or required, in what year it should be situated, how many credit hours it should reflect, whether it should be graded pass-fail or with a traditional letter grade, what role students and faculty should have in creating and teaching the course, and whether our faculty had the necessary training and expertise to facilitate crucial conversations about racism and bias within our legal systems and institutions.[9] Several faculty mem-

6. Students in the past, and especially leaders of the Black Law Student Association, had also voiced a desire for race and law courses, mandatory trainings, and more, and the administration adopted some of those suggestions over the years. But the student effort in spring 2021 was the most comprehensive collaboration demanding specific action.

7. The organizers included, among others, Jessica Barbaria, Daniel Basuk, Isabella Forcino, Indigo Harris, Rosa Kim, Vannessa Lawrence, Louise Lyall, Erin McLaughlin, and Osman Yasin.

8. Presentation on file with the authors and student organizers.

9. Questions about our faculty's expertise in race and the law, in critical legal theories, and in facilitation pedagogy, coupled with the fear of making missteps or unwittingly saying something hurtful, weighed on us. Ultimately, however, we realized that any harm flowing from these abstractions were far outweighed by the more certain harm of doing nothing, which students had repeatedly expressed perpetuated feelings of alienation and disillusionment.

bers also questioned whether a separate course was problematic in itself, asserting that these issues should be taught organically through our existing curriculum.

After extensive discussions about these many important complications, the faculty passed several measures, which included long-term and short-term goals. In the long-term, the faculty would consider reforms to the first-year curriculum to ensure a systematic and thorough engagement with critical approaches to the law. But in the short-term, the faculty also approved creating an interim task force to design a fall-semester, required, 1L, pass-fail, one-credit course on critical perspectives and the law, facilitated by faculty members but with opportunities to involve upper-class students. That gave BC Law exactly three months to meet the moment and realize the student demand.

The course-design task force came together quickly and organically, without oversight or appointment.[10] And, through a summer of hard work and deep thinking, we created *Critical Perspectives in Law and Professional Identity.*

Part II: Jumping In—Pilot 1.0 in Fall 2021—Critical Perspectives in Law and Professional Identity

The objectives of the fall 2021 pilot course were twofold. First, we endeavored to provide students with an introduction to a few foundational critical perspectives related to race, gender, sexuality, class, and power and privilege, in order to give them the tools to better encounter, understand, and critique the legal concepts that they were learning in law school and would soon be practicing. The second and related goal was to have students notice and reflect on how their social identities and law school experiences were forming their professional identities and shaping their interactions with colleagues and others in the legal system. These dual goals were represented in the title of the pilot course: Critical Perspectives in Law and Professional Identity.

With only three months to design this new course, create a curriculum, recruit faculty instructors, and handle the myriad logistics that spring from a course designed for 353 students, we made a series of strategic decisions in terms of both structure and curriculum. We decided to have the course operate on two independent tracks, one consisting of two-hour plenary lectures delivered live every few weeks to the entire first-year student body, and the other consisting of three 90-minute small group meetings that were spread out over the semester.[11] The course met sporadically—sometimes

10. After the faculty meeting, Cheryl Bratt and Daniel Farbman approached DEIB Task Force co-Chair Evangeline Sarda to work on the course, and then solicited Claire Donohue Prono, Laurel Davis, and Reena Parikh, who eagerly joined. Each person has played a crucial role in the course's existence and success.

11. Our oversized incoming 1L class during the fall of 2021, which many schools also experienced, additionally created a host of unique logistical and administrative challenges. For example, after designing the course to include plenary lectures, we learned that our campus had no classroom large enough to accommodate all of our students in person, which led us to use an overflow room

every week, and sometimes with weeks off between sessions—mostly based on student and faculty availability and bandwidth.

The purpose of the plenaries was to provide context and teach content. We had an introductory plenary session where each member of the task force and some of the student organizers spoke about how and why the course emerged, what it entailed, and why it mattered to each of us personally. We also organized an inaugural plenary featuring a student-moderated discussion with two preeminent critical race theorists, Professors Khiara Bridges[12] and Patricia Williams,[13] who shared with students their insights on CRT and the law school experience.[14] Then, for the remainder of the term, we held four lectures delivered by individual professors that explored a range of critical theories in the contexts of intersectionality, family law, criminal law, and constitutional law.

Separately, the small groups were meant to be a space for deeper engagement, personal reflection, and professional identity formation. Students met in groups of no greater than 20, along with a faculty facilitator and, for some, an upper-class student.[15] The first small group session focused on exploring identity, intersectionality, and privilege. The second small group session focused on deepening an understanding of critical race, feminist, poverty, and queer theory, and applying the theories to hypothetical client situations. The third and final small group session explored the features of structural racism and invited students to analyze various social challenges using structural racism as an analytical tool. The course-design task force provided draft lesson plans for each of the small group sessions, but we encouraged facilitators to modify and innovate as they saw fit.

Although the small groups were complementary to the plenaries, they were untethered to them, given certain practicalities. First, our truncated planning time made it difficult to align the curriculum of these two course features, since much of our lesson planning was still occurring during the semester. Second, because our small-group facilitators were being provided only a modest stipend without other teaching relief,

---

and then eventually shift to a hybrid model. In addition, finding available classrooms and scheduling the small groups to fit each 1L section's schedule and that of the faculty facilitator was inordinately time-consuming and challenging, given our limited physical space.

12. Professor of Law, UC Berkeley School of Law.

13. University Distinguished Professor of Law and Humanities, Northeastern University School of Law.

14. Before the presentation, we posted on our course website a suggested reading list in order to introduce Profs. Bridges and Williams to our students. That list included, among others: KIARA BRIDGES, CRITICAL RACE THEORY: A PRIMER (2019), *Code Switch: The Folk Devil Made Me Do It*, NPR (Sept. 1, 2021) (featuring Prof. Bridges), https://www.npr.org/2021/08/20/1029775224/the-folk-devil-made-me-do-it; PATRICIA WILLIAMS, THE ALCHEMY OF RACE AND RIGHTS (1991); and Patricia Williams, *Stop Getting Married on Plantations*, THE NATION (Sept. 26, 2019), https://www.thenation.com/article/archive/plantation-wedding-slavery. After the presentation, we then posted an annotated bibliography of works which the speakers mentioned during their discussion.

15. The upper-class students volunteered to support the small groups in various ways, as agreed upon by the student and facilitator, with responsibilities ranging from co-facilitating to silently observing and providing constructive feedback.

and had little lead-time to plan for and facilitate the small groups, we opted to cap the number of these sessions to only three throughout the term, such that they occurred sometimes multiple weeks after a plenary session.

In terms of course policies, the class was one credit and exclusively pass-fail. We assigned short readings before plenary lectures and a few pre-work assignments before small group meetings, but because the course was only one credit, we endeavored to keep the student workload light. Students were required to attend all sessions, participate in any written component, complete any assigned readings and pre-work, and actively participate in their small group meetings. However, as a practical matter, so long as a student attended and participated in the majority of sessions and assignments, they passed the course. The decisions regarding how to credit and grade the course were driven by a few factors, including our desire to avoid adding stress to overburdened 1Ls, and to ease the workload on course lecturers and facilitators who lacked the time and administrative infrastructure to assist with more detailed grading. This choice also helped us build support and buy-in for the course from students, participating faculty, and staff, especially in this pilot stage.

Part III: Feedback and Lessons Learned

As the pilot semester came to an end, we recognized the need to obtain widespread, targeted, and meaningful feedback from the students, lecturers, and facilitators about their experiences with the course. To gather student feedback, we designed a custom survey (opting out of the University's course evaluations), and provided in-class time during the last small group meeting for students to complete it, without the facilitator present. With respect to the strengths of the course, students reported that they appreciated the exposure to important topics and critical lenses that they would not otherwise be learning. Additionally, students valued the small group environment, sharing that it helped them reflect on their own identity and the identity of others. Lastly, a majority of students surveyed believed that the course should remain in the first-year curriculum as opposed to the second or third years.

Students also identified several weaknesses of the course and made suggestions for improvement. With respect to course administration, they reported that the last-minute rollout of the course,[16] along with the irregular class schedule, caused confusion and anxiety, and they suggested a more consistent schedule for the future. Students also shared the difficulties of focusing for two hours during the large plenary sessions and noted their preference for more frequent small group meetings. With respect to content, students shared that they craved a more obvious connection between this course and their other 1L doctrinal courses, and between the plenaries and the small group sessions within the Critical Perspectives course itself. Lastly, some students shared that

16. Because of the fast turnaround to create the course, we experienced several logistical and administrative hiccups, one being that students did not receive notice about the course until Orientation.

they needed more community-building within the small groups to feel comfortable discussing personal topics related to their own social identities.

To gather lecturer and facilitator feedback, we held a series of listening sessions. From those, we learned that the facilitators, us included, deeply valued the community we forged together as we jointly executed this new course. Indeed, facilitators took up the practice of regularly emailing the cohort with ideas to innovate the lessons and personal reflections after their sessions. We were humble, supportive, and generous in these communications, which helped break down hierarchical barriers among us (as junior and senior colleagues, and as long-term contract and doctrinal faculty), and created a much-needed sense of unity and belonging. Additionally, the facilitators expressed gratitude for the opportunity to learn something new: by accompanying our students and learning alongside them, we both lived and modeled that personal and professional growth is a lifelong journey. Lastly, the facilitators affirmed our "in-house" model. They reflected that had the small groups been facilitated by adjunct professors with expertise in critical theories, rather than full-time faculty who had varying degrees of experience with the content, we might have missed a critical opportunity to build knowledge internally and deepen bonds between students and faculty.

With respect to suggestions for improvement, facilitators expressed that three small group sessions of 90 minutes each presented too little time to adequately build community and explore critical theories, structural inequality, and professional identity formation. Rather, facilitators craved more class sessions, coupled with commensurate compensation for a higher workload. Similar to the student feedback, facilitators also shared the need for a more coherent connection between the fall 1L classes and the course itself, and between the plenary lectures and small group sessions. Many also noted that they would benefit from additional training on how to facilitate productive conversations about race and identity. Lastly, some facilitators acknowledged that those teaching in the course were disproportionately junior, long-term contract faculty, and that it would be valuable to have more tenured faculty, particularly those teaching in the first year, participate.

Finally, the course-design task force held a full-day retreat to reflect upon the feedback we received from students and faculty, share our own experiences from teaching the course, and outline a pilot 2.0 course for fall 2022 that would build upon the strengths of the previous year and incorporate the collective suggestions. In doing that work, we were struck by how crucial it was for all levels of the school—administrators, faculty, and staff members—to actively embrace this course into the curriculum. For the course to survive, it would need to be seamlessly messaged to incoming students alongside their other 1L fall courses; receive comprehensive administrative, financial, and logistical support; and involve more senior faculty members (particularly 1L faculty) who would share their expertise, legitimize the course, and deepen the connection between the critical perspectives curriculum and the doctrinal coursework. Through a second summer of hard work and deep thinking, much of this came together in Critical Perspectives 2.0, which launched in fall 2022.

Part IV: Learning to Swim—Pilot 2.0 in Fall 2022—Critical Perspectives: Law, Context, and Professional Identity

For fall 2022, the course was newly retitled "Critical Perspectives: Law, Context, and Professional Identity."[17] It had three objectives, building off of the initial pilot and what we learned from that experience. First, it aimed to create a community for constructive and respectful conversations around social identities and positionality. Second, it sought to introduce critical legal theories as additional lenses to view doctrine alongside more privileged legal theories, such as law and economics, that already surface in the 1L curriculum. Third, it attempted to connect theory to professional identity formation by giving students space to reflect on how themes raised in the course related to their visions for themselves as law students and lawyers.[18]

The course structure was also refashioned, based on student and facilitator feedback.[19] It met more consistently throughout the semester for shorter periods, with extra opportunities to come together in small groups, and with low-maintenance measures to ensure student accountability. Specifically, under the redesign, the course met weekly for one hour, at the same time each week, from the start of the semester until the week before Thanksgiving break.[20] Students met both as a larger 1L section of approximately eighty students (no longer in plenaries for the full 1L class), and in smaller groups of about 15 students, alternating each week, but with small groups bookending the semester. Each small group was led by co-facilitators—a faculty member and an upper-class student Teaching Assistant (TA). This new structure satisfied the students' and facilitators' preference for predictability, shorter class sessions, and more opportunities for small-group meetings. Additionally, we used mandatory exit tickets after each session, lectures and small groups alike, to mark attendance and provide instant feedback as to how the material was landing.

The substance of the course was also revamped based on the feedback to align more intentionally with the 1L fall doctrinal subjects, and to create more coherence between the lectures and small groups that comprised the course. Students attended four section-wide lectures. The first introduced students to critical legal theories generally and the history of critical legal thought. The three lectures that then followed were specific

17. The name change was both cosmetic, to simplify the previously wordy title, and intentional, to better articulate the aims of the course: contextualizing legal doctrine and connecting it to our roles and duties as lawyers.

18. In view of these objectives, the course satisfies the newly revised ABA Standards 303(b) and 303(c), which require that a law school "provide substantial opportunities to students for ... the development of a professional identity," and "provide education to law students on bias, cross-cultural competency, and racism: (1) at the start of the program of legal education, and (2) at least once again before graduation." *See supra* note 1.

19. *See* Appendix A for a weekly sketch of the course.

20. The course intentionally finished early to allow students to focus exclusively on their graded coursework at the end of the term, while still complying with ABA Standard 310.

to the three doctrinal courses the students were enrolled in at that time—Contracts, Civil Procedure, and Torts or Property[21]—and applied a critical lens to one or more cases classically taught in those subjects. Several senior doctrinal faculty members who teach 1L courses delivered those lectures, which helped further affirm the connection between critical theories and traditional doctrine. Additionally, the small group sessions that followed the previous week's lectures were tethered to them, allowing students to dig more deeply into the issues raised within the lecture, this time in a smaller and less formal setting, and to apply those concepts to other cases, contexts, and their own lived experiences.

By way of example, during the Contracts lecture, Professor Frank Garcia discussed three excerpted cases traditionally covered in a Contracts course: *Hawkins v. McGee*, where a plaintiff won for breach of contract after his doctor botched a skin-grafting surgery;[22] *Batsakis v. Demotsis*, involving a question of sufficient consideration when the plaintiff agreed to pay the defendant $25 in exchange for the defendant later paying him back $2,000 plus interest;[23] and *Williams v. Walker-Thomas Furniture Co.*, involving a cross-collateralization clause in a contract between a customer and a rent-to-own furniture store.[24] Each case is often taught to illustrate a particular doctrine in contracts law: damage calculations (*Hawkins*), sufficiency of consideration (*Batsakis*), and unconscionability (*Williams*). In applying a critical lens to the cases and widening the frame, however, Garcia excavated the backstories of the parties and judges, and situated the disputes within their historical contexts. In doing so, he demonstrated the tension in contract law between a desire to honor people's autonomy to contract, while also protecting against exploitation. He also explored the question of how to protect against exploitation while not reinforcing stereotypes about marginalized communities. Law is a tool of both emancipation and oppression, he offered, but determining which principle a case is furthering can be fraught with uncertainty. The following week's small group meetings then dug deeper into these themes, giving students an opportunity to reflect, raise questions, and draw connections among other cases they had read.[25]

---

21. At BC Law, the fall semester for every 1L consists of Law Practice (the introductory lawyering skills course), Civil Procedure, and Contracts. Additionally, two of the three 1L sections receive instruction in Torts, while one section receives instruction in Property. The 2022 Critical Perspectives course tracked the students' actual schedules: each section received a lecture on critical perspectives in Contracts and Civil Procedure, with two sections additionally receiving a Torts lecture and one additionally receiving a Property lecture.

22. 146 A. 641 (N.H. 1929).

23. 226 S.W.2d 673 (Tex. Civ. App. 1949).

24. 350 F.2d 445 (D.D.C. 1965).

25. To assist small-group facilitators, we created a lesson plan template for each small group session, which included specific discussion questions facilitators might introduce in their groups, teachers' notes as to what responses those questions might elicit, and different media examples (e.g., short videos, news articles, or podcast excerpts) that highlighted a particular theme or concept that the lecture covered. Additionally, we provided facilitators with an explanation of various small-group discussion techniques that they might employ to engage their students.

We also scheduled three small group meetings untethered to a lecture to enhance community-building, knowledge application, and professional identity formation. In the first small group session, which introduced the course, students wrote a letter to themselves, articulating personal goals related to their law school experience and their roles as future lawyers. That letter was then returned to the students during the last small group session, which concluded the course, so that students could reflect on their journey through the term. Additionally, the second-to-last small-group session consisted of students presenting a capstone project that required students to work collaboratively in teams to apply a critical legal analysis to a case they had already read that semester outside of the Critical Perspectives course. The students researched the social identities of the parties and judges involved, the national and international climate and events at the time of the decision, and the impact the decision had on the parties to the dispute and others more broadly. They then presented what they learned; surmised how this context may have informed the holding, reasoning, and outcome of the case; and led a brief class-wide discussion.[26]

Finally, all students attended an end-of-semester plenary presentation, where a panel of BC Law alumni from different sectors discussed how critical approaches to the law impacted their day-to-day work.

As we write this chapter, we are still gathering and digesting feedback from students, lecturers, and facilitators about this second version of the course, but already we know that this year's iteration was a substantial improvement and overall success. Students completed a comprehensive, custom course evaluation that we designed to capture meaningful feedback about each aspect of the course and inform how we continue to move forward. Those evaluations overwhelmingly demonstrated that students found the course deepened their understanding of critical perspectives on the law; exposed them to new ways of thinking about the possibilities and limits of the law and legal institutions; contextualized their 1L doctrinal coursework; created an engaged, respectful, and comfortable learning community, particularly in the small groups; helped students reflect on their own professional identities; and was overall a positive part of their experience adjusting to law school. We are also organizing separate debriefing sessions with faculty facilitators, student facilitators, and lecturers to gather their insights. Finally, we will again be holding a day-long retreat for the course-design task force to synthesize all that we learn and make a plan for fall 2023.

---

26. See Appendix B for our capstone project description that we distributed to students.

Conclusion: Our Continued Collective Evolution

Our course is still evolving, and we suspect it will continue to do so as we learn how best to integrate critical theories into our curriculum, make incoming students feel less alienated or excluded by the 1L doctrinal courses, and train all of our students to be culturally competent and reflective attorneys. Nonetheless, our pilot years taught us the importance of taking that first step, even when we knew it would be imperfect. Indeed, we firmly believe that by doing something, we did less harm than by doing nothing at all. Although it would have been easier to allow our curriculum to persist unchanged, a lack of action would continue to chip away at our students' education and overall experience, and ultimately leave them unprepared for their future careers. We look forward to continuing this work as we think about the years ahead and what they mean for the long-term future of our 1L curriculum.

We hope that our narrative gives other schools both courage and ideas as to how to innovate their own curriculum. Indeed, even if our model is not suitable for your institution, we hope that our story inspires your own innovations and sparks new ideas that we can learn from, too.

Appendix A: Semester Sketch of Critical Perspectives: Law, Context, and Professional Identity (Pilot 2.0)

Week	Format
1	*Small Group:* Icebreakers & Getting to Know You, Course Walk-Through, Capstone Project Explanation
2	*Section-Wide Lecture:* Intro to Critical Perspectives: What They Are and Why They Matter
3	*Small Group:* Introductory Lecture Debrief
4	*Section-Wide Lecture:* Critical Perspectives in Civil Procedure
5	*Small Group:* Civil Procedure Lecture Debrief
6	*Section-Wide Lecture:* Critical Perspectives in Contracts
7	*Small Group:* Contracts Lecture Debrief
8	*Section-Wide Lecture:* Critical Perspectives in Torts or Property
9	*Small Group:* Torts or Property Lecture Debrief
10	*Small Group:* Capstone Project Presentations
11	*Closing Plenary Event:* Alumni Panel—Critical Perspectives in Action
12	*Small Group:* Close Out and Reflection

Appendix B: Capstone Project Description

Critical Perspectives: Group Presentation Details

Description

Students will work in teams of 3 or 4 to prepare a 10–15 minute presentation that will occur during the small group meetings held during the week of October 31, 2022. Small group facilitators will decide each team's composition.

Each team will identify *one case* that has been assigned to them in any of their 1L classes that has not yet been covered in the larger Critical Perspectives lectures. They will then conduct research into the case to present a critical analysis of it to their small group.

To critically analyze the case, teams might, for example, research:

- Who the parties were, including their social identities, histories, and lived experiences;
- Who the judge(s) were, including their social identities, histories, and lived experiences;
- What was happening in our country and/or the world while the case was being decided;
- What happened to the parties after the decision was issued, and what impact the decision had on others/the country more generally;
- How the answers to the above questions affect how one might think about the holding, reasoning, or outcome of the case; and
- Anything else that students find relevant.

The teams will then use what they learn from their research to offer a critical perspective on the decision. Students are not expected to tether their critiques to a particular critical theory framework (e.g., feminist theory, critical race theory, etc.), but rather use their presentations to provide context for the decision and question what dynamics, motivations, or other aspects contributed to the court's opinion.

The teams will assign to their small group colleagues: (1) the case itself, and (2) a short additional piece that somehow relates to the team's critique. That piece might be a news or magazine article, a book chapter excerpt, an audio or video clip, or anything else that would be helpful for the class to read or experience before the presentation.

[Students were provided with a link to additional resources if they wanted to dig a little deeper into various critical theories.]

Deadlines:

Oct 14 (week 7)—Proposals

Each team will email their facilitators with a proposal for their presentation. That proposal should include:

- a copy of the case they intend to critically analyze,
- A paragraph explaining why they chose that case, and
- A copy of (or link to) the supplemental material they choose to assign.

The facilitators will review the proposals and provide any necessary feedback. They will then distribute the supplied cases and supplemental materials to the small group.

Week of October 31, 2022 (week 10)—Presentations

Each team will have between 10–15 minutes to present their analysis and offer space for a group discussion. All members of the team are expected to speak.

Completion of the group project is a requirement for passing the course.

Race and the Equal Protection of the Laws Program (REPL)

*Dermot Groome**

The History of Penn State Dickinson Law's REPL Program

In June 2020, in response to the murder of George Floyd, the faculty of Penn State Dickinson Law adopted two resolutions related to race.[1] The second of these, titled Race and Our Educational Mission ("REM"), operationalized the first by recognizing that the faculty had "a unique opportunity and important responsibility to combat racism and inequality through its educational mission."

In REM, the faculty resolved to develop an annual plan of antiracist education and to develop focused programing addressing structural racism. This resolution requires an annual internal review of the effectiveness of its antiracist efforts and an external review every five years. To facilitate the internal annual review, the Dean created an ad hoc committee that reports to the faculty twice each year. Dickinson Law will engage an outside scholar with relevant experience to conduct the five-year review. With the 2020 resolutions, Dickinson Law has incorporated antiracist education into its core educational mission, a commitment that "shall remain in effect until such time that the faculty deems, by resolution, that it is no longer necessary."[2]

Concurrent with these two resolutions, the Race and the Equal Protection of the Laws course ("REPL") came into existence. Starting in the fall of the 2020–21 academic year, REPL became a required course for all first-year students. This one-credit,

---

* Professor Dermot Groome is the Harvey A. Feldman Distinguished Faculty Scholar at Penn State Dickinson Law. https://dickinsonlaw.psu.edu/dermot-groome.

1. *See* Penn State Dickinson Law Faculty, Faculty Resolution (2020), https://dickinsonlaw.psu.edu/sites/default/files/2020-06/faculty-resolution.pdf. *See also* Penn State Dickinson Law Faculty, Race and Our Educational Mission (REM) (2020), https://dickinsonlaw.psu.edu/sites/default/files/2020-07/Race-and-Our-Educational-Mission.pdf.

2. *Id.*

eight-session course examines the relationship between race and our legal system and how mostly race-neutral laws have been used to shape and perpetuate structural racism in areas like criminal justice, education, health care, and housing. The course is graded credit/no credit and students are required to complete a reflection paper at the end of the course. Although Dickinson Law has incorporated REPL into its first-year curriculum, it would work equally well for upper-level students.

Developing the Substantive Content of REPL

Many in the first-year class of 2020 were questioning themselves and their decision to become lawyers in light of the renewed consciousness about systemic inequality precipitated by George Floyd's murder. There was a consensus among the faculty that there was an urgent need to develop a program for our incoming students.

A diverse group of over fifty individuals, including faculty, staff, upper-level students, and alumni, volunteered to work together to pool their knowledge, personal experiences, and skills to create the content for REPL, give presentations to students, and guide them in the sometimes difficult conversations we have asked them to have with each other.[3] Recognizing the importance of role models, REPL has also invited lawyers who can speak authoritatively and authentically about the issues we examine in the program.

The course objectives are twofold:

1. To help students begin the process of discerning how they will respond as a lawyer to this moment in our country's history; and
2. To cultivate within them an enduring commitment to equality in all they do as lawyers.

Critical Pedagogy

Central to the REPL program is its teaching methodology. REPL considers that how we teach is as important as what we teach. REPL's goal is not only to impart substantive knowledge regarding the relationship between race and our legal system, but also to help students consider what kind of lawyer they will be when they become part of that legal system. In order to "cultivate within students, a principled, enduring commitment

3. The two faculty resolutions proved to be an important prerequisite to the REPL course. The drafting, discussion, and adoption of the two resolutions created a consensus among the faculty with respect to our opportunities and obligations as educators. Dickinson Law faculty see the incorporation of discussions about the relationship between race and the law as a joint responsibility and not something assigned to a segment of the faculty. The Dean has reinforced this important dynamic by incorporating a review of each faculty member's contribution as part of their annual review meeting with the Dean.

to work for true equality in our society over the course of their careers,"[4] we must engage students in considering how the text and spirit of the Fourteenth Amendment calls them to practice law. To do this, REPL has developed a unique teaching method and structure that incorporates principles of Critical Pedagogy.

Critical Pedagogy, developed by Paulo Freire, is an educational theory that arose out of the social justice movements in South America in the 1960s. These movements, which paralleled our own Civil Rights Movement, sought to ameliorate the systemic injustices suffered by indigenous and historically oppressed peoples. Critical Pedagogy's essential insight is the idea that a goal of education should be to create an "opportunity for students to be able to reflectively frame their own relationship to the ongoing project of an unfinished democracy."[5]

Critical Pedagogy calls us as legal educators to include in all our courses the opportunity for students to reflect on our nation's shared experience of the area of the law under consideration. Coursework should not be insulated from what is happening in our country but fully immersed in it so that students not only learn settled principles of law and theory but understand their unique opportunities and responsibilities to address societal problems as lawyers. As educators, we must nurture their nascent inclinations towards justice, so that they are vigilant to inequalities in whatever corner of our legal system they ultimately work and prepare them to be guardians of true equality in all they do as lawyers.

Paulo Freire was born in Brazil in 1921 and grew up in poverty. He attended law school, and although he was admitted to the bar, he chose instead to teach secondary school in poor communities. While teaching literacy, Freire discovered that he could achieve better results when he taught students to become critically aware of social issues that impacted their lives.[6] This realization of the relationship between social consciousness and pedagogy led him to a lifelong study of the synergy between the two.

As an educator and philosopher, Freire thought deeply about systemic inequality and how education might address it. His most famous work, *Pedagogy of the Oppressed*, sets out his understanding of the relationship between education and social change and how that understanding should inform the work of educators. Core to his theory is the notion that educators must help students "develop their power to perceive critically the way they exist in the world with which and in which they find themselves; they come to see the world not as a static reality, but as a reality in progress, in transformation."[7] A student aware of their place in a reality capable of change by them, will, over time, discern their own role in that change. To Freire, the most effective way to nurture this process was not through a traditional pedagogy that "banked" information in the mind of students as if they were passive receptacles, but through a Socratic-like dialogue

4. Penn State Dickinson Law School Faculty, REM, *supra* note 1.

5. Henry A. Giroux, On Critical Pedagogy 181 (2020).

6. Peter McLaren, *Pablo Freire's Legacy of Hope and Struggle*, 14 Theory, Culture & Soc'y, 147, 147–53 (1997), https://www.chapman.edu/education/_files/freire-legacy.pdf.

7. Paulo Friere, Pedagogy of the Oppressed 83–84 (4th ed. 2018).

with students. Freire emphasized the importance of a give-and-take about an epochal generative theme, an important contemporary social issue that cried out for redress. Further, Freire proposed a dialogue in which participants, instructors and students alike, engage each other as co-investigators and critical thinkers in a reflective process, unmasking the reality and causes of oppression, and imagining how to be agents of social change.[8]

If Freire were alive at this moment, he undoubtedly would see systemic racism as a social injustice to be addressed with Critical Pedagogy. He would propose to address injustice through a critically reflective dialogue between teacher and students about the relationship between race and our legal system,[9] reasoning that the more active the conversation and collaboration, the deeper students' understanding will be. Freire calls this deeper shared understanding *conscientização*. Roughly translated, *conscientização* is a critical consciousness that is disposed and determined to act for necessary change.[10] Through this process of investigation and reflection, "[h]umankind *emerge* from their *submersion* and acquire the ability to *intervene* in reality as it is unveiled."[11]

Overview of the REPL Teaching Method

Informed by Critical Pedagogy, each of the eight sessions of REPL is designed with a four-part structure. Each of the four elements works with the others to guide students to a deeper understanding of an important issue and helps them develop their own response as lawyers.

Selecting a Generative Theme for Individual Classes

The first task in designing the REPL course was to identify the themes we would focus on in each of the eight sessions. For assistance, we looked to Freire's concept of the generative theme. Generative themes as defined by Freire, are, by their very nature, important life issues that are likely to engage participants' interest. According to Freire, a generative theme arises from the situation bounded by the time and place in which students find themselves.

For this first iteration of REPL, we selected seven generative themes related to race and our legal system. The last session did not focus on a generative theme but shifted the focus to a reflection by students about their capacity to be agents of change as lawyers. Students were required to submit a paper articulating their personal reflections

---

8. *Id.* at 92 *et seq.*

9. *Id.* at 96.

10. *Id.* at 109. "Conscientização is the deepening of the attitude of awareness characteristic of all emergence." *Id.*

11. *Id.* (emphasis in original).

on the issue of the relationship between the law and race and how they, in their work as lawyers, might contribute to greater equality in the United States.[12]

Generative themes can exist in concentric circles moving from the general to the particular.[13] The generative themes of our program include both broad issues related to our entire legal system and more focused examinations of particular areas of the law. In our first session, *Historic and Modern Privilegia* ("*Privilegia*"),[14] we started with the broadest possible focus—the outermost circle of possible themes—by examining the foundational documents of our country and the various laws that have created structural advantages for some, and structural disadvantages for others.[15]

The next six sessions were built around more granular generative themes. In these sessions, we addressed important areas of the law that have daily, significant impacts on us all. These generative themes included: capitalism, criminal justice, housing, health care, education, and democracy.

Element One: Turning Our Attention to the Issue

Every REPL session begins with a Focusing Activity. The Focusing Activity establishes the curriculum for the session around a generative theme. Here, the intent is twofold: (a) to engage students as active participants in an interactive teaching/learning dynamic, and (b) to focus students on the generative theme of the class. "The focusing activity turns people to their own 'being' in place and time, to their present praxis, and establishes a focus for the curriculum."[16] The Focusing Activity must establish the session's theme as vital, urgent, and deserving of attention.[17]

In REPL, we use a two-part Focusing Activity. The first is the Playlist. One week before the session, students receive a playlist of multimedia links. These links direct students to podcasts, music videos, speeches, poetry readings, short readings, and works of art. The items are chosen because they will engage students with the theme, present them with perspectives that may be different from their own, and begin the process

---

12. Students also had the opportunity to provide public reflections on the courses. Some of these were incorporated in a webinar. *See* Penn State Dickinson Law, *The First Look, Race and the Equal Protection of the Laws*, YouTube (Apr. 9, 2021), https://youtu.be/s6pnVPfz8gg.

13. Freire, *supra* note 7, at 103.

14. The term *Privilegia*, from Roman Law, is "[a] special constitution by which the Roman emperor conferred on some single person some anomalous or irregular right, or imposed upon some single person some anomalous or irregular obligation, or inflicted on some single person some anomalous or irregular punishment." Black's Law Dictionary (2d ed. 1910).

15. For example, we examined such laws as: The Fugitive Slave Acts of 1793 and 1850 (requiring northern states to return people who escaped from slavery); Black Codes and Jim Crow laws; cash bail laws and targeted fines; The Housing Act of 1937 (authorized segregation in public housing); and the FHA's use of racially restrictive covenants (some property deeds still contain these restrictions although the Supreme Court deemed them unenforceable in *Shelley v. Kraemer* (1948).

16. Thomas H. Groome, Sharing Faith: A Comprehensive Approach to Religious Education and Pastoral Ministry 146 (1991).

17. *Id.*

of thinking about their lived experience with respect to that theme. For *Privilegia*, the playlist included an address by Chief Justice Cheri Beasley of the North Carolina Supreme Court addressing the killing of George Floyd.[18] For the Criminal Justice session, we included a slam poem about a Black man talking to his nephew as the police approach the car they are in. Students who listen to the Playlist arrive at the session better prepared to thoughtfully immerse themselves in the issue.

The second component of the Focusing Activity happens at the start of each class session itself and is called "Turning our Attention to the Issue." We introduce the issue with a compelling video or story that shifts students from their busy day to a sharp focus on the generative theme of the class. For *Privilegia*, we showed a six-minute film depicting young descendants of Frederick Douglass reading excerpts of "What to the Slave Is the Fourth of July," a speech Douglass gave on July 5, 1852.[19] In *Race and Criminal Justice*, a second-year student described an encounter he and his brother had with police officers when he was eight years old.

Element Two: The Lesson

After the Turning our Attention to the Issue segment, we move to the Lesson. In developing this course, we considered—how can we engage students in a critical reflection on race and our legal system when they, like us, probably do not know our own history in sufficient detail to have a reasonably informed discussion about it? In this segment, members of the faculty and upper-level students give a series of presentations designed to provide essential information about the generative theme. A session typically includes five or six ten-minute sessions. Each is a concise exposition of the generative theme. It is not intended as a comprehensive treatment of the subject.[20] Whenever possible, we endeavor to trace modern phenomena to the Antebellum period. For example, in the *Capitalism* session, we traced a timeline that began with a discussion of the slave market on Wall Street and continued with: slave mortgages and the collateralization of human life; "40 Acres and a Mule"; the New Deal; redlining; and finally the impediments Black-owned businesses faced in accessing Payroll Protection Payments (PPP) during the COVID-19 pandemic.

In the Lesson segment, we also try to introduce students to the work of renowned Black thinkers such as Dr. Martin Luther King Jr., W.E.B. Du Bois, and James Baldwin through presentations about their work and short excerpts of their writings.[21]

---

18. C.J. Cheri Beasley, *Special Announcement*, FACEBOOK (June 2, 2020), https://www.facebook.com/NCcourts/videos/chief-justice-beasley-june-2-2020-special-announcement/251903529564824/.

19. *See* NPR, *'What To The Slave Is The Fourth Of July?': Descendants Read Frederick Douglass' Speech*, YOUTUBE (July 3, 2020), https://www.youtube.com/watch?v=NBe5qbnkqoM&ab_channel=NPR.

20. These short presentations are supplemented by a more complete treatment of the subject matter in an essay written by the presenter and included in the handout for that session.

21. While REPL's primary focus has been on the legal system's disparate impacts on Black and Brown people, we have addressed inequality more broadly in response to anti-Semitic and anti-Asian attacks that occurred during this period in our country.

PennState
Dickinson Law

RACE AND THE EQUAL PROTECTION OF THE LAWS

SESSION 1, HISTORIC AND MODERN PRIVILEGIA

Group Number: Group Members:

Instructions: The group will collectively draft a review of our legal system. Use the task to prompt discussions about our legal system.

Great For: the individuals it was originally written for

United States Supreme Court

United States Legal System

Has formed a "more perfect union"
"insure[s] domestic tranquility"
"Promote[s] the general Welfare."
"Secure the Blessings of Liberty to ourselves and our Posterity"

U.S. Constitution

OVERALL RATING

★★★

Verified citizen

Rate our legal system using the following criteria:

2.5/5

Creates a more perfect union

2/5

Preserves domestic tranquility

2/5

Promotes General Welfare

2.5/5

Has secured the "Blessings of Liberty" for the descendants of the Framers

1/5

Laws facilitating structural racism easily corrected.

2/5

Best legal system possible

Liked: Checks and balances, principles of life, liberty, happiness

Disliked: Not living up to the standards we set, inequality, amendments can be repealed

Describe group's assessment of our legal system.	The overall ideals that have been set are admirable, but they have not lived up to their standards. We each have different lived experiences, but we can all recognize that the ideals set out were positive. There just needs to be more work to make sure they are attainable for all Americans.
What are the root causes of any problems you describe?	There has been a "religious-like" view of the constitution for so long. The original document has been so revered that people fear addressing and adapting to new issues we face as a society. It was meant to be a "living, breathing document," but it is not currently behaving as such. We are also losing touch with separation of church and state. Morality differs among individuals and it can create a variety of different issues.
What needs to be done to correct these problems?	The first step to correcting issues is addressing that they are present. So many policies are not concerning on their face, but are once the "veil" is lifted. Addressing the fact that things are in need of repair and improvement will allow us as a country to begin the process of change. We also all agree that the system itself needs to reflect the rule "treat other the way you want to be treated."

For *Historic and Modern Privilegia*, we developed an Airbnb-type review for students to rate our constitution and whether it has lived up to what it "advertises" in its preamble. The above example is a completed form.

Element Three: Small Group Discussions

After completing the Lesson segment, students gather in small groups to engage with a discussion prompt. The groups are made intentionally diverse and are moderated by a member of the faculty and an upper-level student. The moderator's primary role is to help create an environment where complex and difficult discussions about race can take place in a constructive and respectful way.[22] We structure these discussions and provide prompts designed to achieve the aims of Critical Pedagogy. Most prompts are some variation of, "What are our opportunities and responsibilities as lawyers to promote greater equality within this area of law and our legal system?"

In the context of *Privilegia*, students were asked to reflect on whether or not the Constitution has lived up to the promises in its preamble. In *Race and Housing*, students developed a ten-year plan to encourage greater racial integration in the local community. Students engaged in such a cooperative exercise must necessarily draw from some of the material presented in the Lesson, reflect on the group's shared experience of race and housing, and develop strategies designed to respond to the generative theme in their particular time and place.

Critical Race Theory

During the discussion, moderators can pose the questions asked by Critical Race (CRT) theorists about why the promise of the Civil Rights Movement and its legal victories before the Supreme Court have not translated into fundamental changes in the lived experience of Black and Brown Americans. The CRT movement began in the 1970s as scholars recognized that the advances made during the Civil Rights Movement had slowed, stopped, and in some respects "were being rolled back."[23] The potential for improving the lived experience of Black Americans promised by favorable precedents such as *Brown v. Board of Education* were diminished by lower court decisions that narrowed their rulings and by administrative and bureaucratic "slow rolling" of their mandate.[24] Similarly, the Supreme Court's ruling in *Shelby County v. Holder* rendered largely ineffective the legislative accomplishment of the Voting Rights Act of 1965.[25]

The work of Critical Race theorists can inform the task of REPL moderators and help facilitate more constructive discussions. Although REPL does not attempt to ad-

---

22. The moderators were volunteers and received some limited training by members of staff with relevant experience. We continue to think about how best to engage students in these difficult discussions and are considering more intensive training for moderators.

23. Richard Delgado & Jean Stefancic, Critical Race Theory 3–4 (3d ed. 2018). Delgado summarizes Critical Race Theory as:

> The critical race theory (CRT) movement is a collection of activists and scholars engaged in studying and transforming the relationship among race, racism, and power. The movement considers many of the same issues that conventional civil rights and ethnic studies discourses take up but places them in a broader perspective that includes economics, history, setting, group and self- interest, and emotions and the unconscious. Unlike traditional civil rights discourse, which stresses incrementalism and step-by-step progress, critical race theory questions the very foundations of the liberal order, including equality theory, legal reasoning, Enlightenment rationalism, and neutral principles of constitutional law.

Id.

24. *Id.* at 5. *See also* Derrick Bell, Brown v. Board of Education *and the Interest-Convergence Dilemma*, 93 Harv. L. Rev. 518, 523–28 (1980); Mario L. Barnes, *"The More Things Change . . .": New Moves for Legitimizing Racial Discrimination in a "Post-Race" World*, 100 Minn. L. Rev. 2043, 2082–83 (2016).

25. Shelby Cnty., Ala. v. Holder, 570 U.S. 529, 553 (2013).

dress CRT comprehensively, one of its objectives is to introduce students to some of CRT's core concepts and principles to help them recognize and react to systems of inequality they may encounter as lawyers.

Element Four: The Story and Vision

While the small group discussion is a collaborative process, a featured speaker takes center stage in the Story and Vision segment. In this element, the pedagogical task is to tell the story of how the law has addressed, does address, and can address the generative theme as now developed. For this element, we invite a prominent lawyer or activist who can speak both authoritatively and authentically on the subject. For example, Professor Deborah Archer, the president of the ACLU, addressed the students during the session on *Race and Democracy*. Possible speakers are chosen by the faculty and students developing the particular session and for the most part have been lawyers from our region. These speakers have volunteered their time, although we do reimburse expenses they incur.

The task of the featured speaker is to guide students with clarity and accuracy through the ways our laws have and can be brought to bear to address inequality. During this element, students should be "awakened" to the power of the law to address inequality. Their understanding of the relationship between the issue and the relevant law should deepen, seeing the law as a powerful tool to combat inequality.

This element also includes a candid retelling of its failures, where it has fallen short of ensuring equality, or when it has been an accomplice in the oppression of Black people and people of color. Again, the sources of law and justice from which the instructor may draw are varied.

The Story and Vision segment presents students with an explicit invitation to consider the implications of what they have learned for their own lives, their lives now as law students, and their lives ultimately as lawyers. This element invites students to consider how their emerging understanding of the law calls them to act differently, to see themselves differently. What is their response as lawyers to the issue? What will they do to promote greater justice and equality?

REPL does not advocate for students to adopt any particular response and does not require students to voice what their response might be. Each student's response is the product of their own discernment—a process for which the autonomy and privacy of the individual is respected in the REPL program. Having said that, it has become a common occurrence for students to engage with each other, REPL presenters, and featured speakers after the session about the possibilities they see for themselves.

The Handout

Each session is accompanied by a Handout, which includes original essays and reprinted excerpts. The Handout is not the typical handout an instructor might prepare for a class. Rather, the Handouts are more akin to book chapters and serve more ambitious objectives than class handouts. The Handout supplements The Lesson and provides students with relevant case law, excerpted articles, historic speeches, and other materials designed to facilitate a deep, thoughtful exploration of the generative theme.

Student Reaction

Most students, as measured by anonymous feedback solicited at the end of each course, see the value of REPL; the need to engage them in these discussions; and the importance of incorporating a study of the relationship between race, equality, and the law in their legal education.[26] Many offer suggestions for future iterations, suggestions the faculty considers carefully. As might be expected in the deeply polarized times in which we live, there have some strong reactions both for and against the program. Some students think that the law school must expand our efforts with more compulsory courses similar to REPL.[27] Others accuse the faculty of trying to "indoctrinate" them to a particular point of view they do not share.[28]

It is worth noting that our work in REPL, as well as our Antiracist Development Institute,[29] has caught the attention of prospective students and our admissions staff is regularly asked for information about these programs. In response to the growing number of inquiries, for the first time in 2023, we are including an information session about these efforts during our open houses for prospective students. We interpret this interest as an indication that a growing number of aspiring lawyers are seeking legal education that comprehensively incorporates the study of race, inequality, and the law.

---

26. For some student reactions to REPL *see* Penn State Dickinson Law, *The First Look, Race and the Equal Protection of the Laws*, *supra* note 12.

27. We are in the process of developing upper-level electives that will explore the relationship between the law and other areas of inequality including: anti-Semitism, anti-Asian discrimination, and discrimination based on gender, gender identity, and sexual orientation.

28. A small vocal group of students in the first REPL course took this view. We responded by inviting them to join the design team for the following year to ensure that all points of view were reflected. Although they initially accepted the invitation to help design subsequent iterations of the course, ultimately, they declined to participate.

29. The Antiracist Development Institute (ADI) is a long-term initiative of Dickinson Law that seeks to dismantle structures that scaffold systemic racial inequality in all facets of legal education and the legal profession. For more information, *see* Penn State Dickinson Law, Antiracist Development Institute, https://dickinsonlaw.psu.edu/antiracist-development-institute.

Conclusion

Our task as legal educators today is greater than it has been in the past. In this important period of our national history, our country requires of us something that only we can provide: a generation of lawyers who will dismantle the remaining vestiges of systemic racism in our nation. We must educate the next generation of lawyers to finish the job of rooting out systemic racism wherever it continues to live and breed. We must equip our students not simply with the knowledge and skills they will need for this task but with a sense of their place and role in our changing, imperfect, struggling democracy and with the enduring passion they will need to sustain their efforts. Penn State Dickinson Law's Race and the Equal Protection of the Laws program is our humble contribution to this effort.

The Power of the Narrative: Building Empathy, Allyship, and Belonging Within (or Despite) an Exclusionary Profession

*Tanya Johnson**

Introduction

I have been co-teaching a three-credit course called Diversity and Inclusion in the Legal Profession at the University of Connecticut School of Law since 2019. In this essay, I wanted to focus on the importance of narrative as a way to foster empathy and inclusivity. I chose to emulate the style of critical race theorists and present this as a story and dialogue in which readers will join the fictional newly appointed Associate Dean for Academic Innovation, Jack Park, in his observation of our class.[1] I ask you to engage openly with the style and critically examine your assumptions.

---

* Research and Instruction Librarian, UConn School of Law. Innumerable thanks to Karen DeMeola, without whom this class would never have been so successful.

1. On the power of storytelling and narrative, *see* Richard Delgado, *Storytelling for Oppositionists and Others: A Plea for Narrative*, 87 Mich. L. Rev. 2411 (1989). For some of the many narratives that inspired us, *see Chronicles of the Space Traders*, in Derrick Bell, *Racism: A Prophecy for the Year 2000*, 42 Rutgers L. Rev. 93 (1989) and Richard Delgado, *Rodrigo's Final Chronicle: Cultural Power, the Law Reviews, and the Attack on Narrative Jurisprudence*, 68 S. Calif. L. Rev. 545 (1995). For excellent examples of the power of narrative to expose inequities in academic culture, *see* Presumed Incompetent: The Intersections of Race and Class for Women in Academia (Angela P. Harris, Carmen G. González, Gabriella Gutiérrez y Muhs, Yolanda Flores Niemann eds., 2012), and its follow-up, Presumed Incompetent II: Race, Class, Power, and Resistance of Women in Academia (Carmen G. González, Gabriella Gutiérrez y Muhs, Yolanda Flores Niemann eds., 2020).

Story and Dialogue

TJ and CT (co-teacher) meet with Jack in his office.

CT: Thank you for reaching out, Jack.

Jack: It's great to see you both. I'm curious about your class. How do you go about teaching this topic?

CT: First and foremost, we try to open students' minds to different perspectives and emphasize the importance of people and stories. We use storytelling as a vehicle to develop students' potential and help them think differently about their professional trajectory. We invite guest speakers to almost every class; each of them contributes to the narrative of our profession and allows students to see themselves in a variety of roles.

TJ: We designed the class so that students can learn about and discuss the problems within the profession as a whole and to allow students to be authentic within the classroom, to experience what it might be like to exist as themselves within their future legal workplaces, in a space that has far fewer consequences. We try to show students the possibilities that exist for them, the ways that they can help work toward changing the system and dismantling barriers.

Jack: Conversations on these issues must be very difficult. How do you handle that in the classroom?

TJ: You're right, there are *a lot* of difficult conversations that happen in our classroom, but I see them as opportunities for the students—and for us—to practice discussing awkward or sensitive topics, which come up frequently in legal practice and everyday life. I try to think through the possibilities and prepare in advance, but students have generally been very respectful of each other, and of us.

CT: And being respectful of others is one of the ground rules that the whole class agrees upon at the beginning of the semester. We found that taking a student-centered approach helps students develop their own professional identities and allows them to contextualize their experiences. Plus, our class fits the recent ABA Standards requiring law schools to provide training and education to law students on bias, cross-cultural competency, and racism.[2]

Jack: It's hard to believe you can include all of that in one course.

CT: Jack, why don't you observe our class tomorrow and see it for yourself? You are welcome to participate and solicit feedback from the class. This semester, we have 19 students enrolled in our seminar, and because of the con-

2. *See* Am. Bar Ass'n, Revisions to the 2021–2022 ABA Standards and Rules of Procedure for Approval of Law Schools (Feb. 2022), https://www.americanbar.org/content/dam/aba/administrative/legal_education_and_admissions_to_the_bar/standards/2021-2022/21-22-standards-book-revisions-since-printed.pdf [https://perma.cc/KN24-QCNR] (Section 303: Curriculum).

sistently long waiting list, students often request that we teach the class more often.

Jack: Alright, I'll see you tomorrow.

On the following day, the class meets in a seminar room and is seated in a large circle.

TJ: Before we begin, I want to acknowledge that we have a special guest in class tonight, Associate Dean Jack Park. Welcome to our class.

Jack: Thank you both for inviting me. I hope that everyone can treat me like a student today, since I am here to learn.

CT: OK, welcome everyone, and let's get started. Last week we focused on DE and I in law firms and heard from managing partners about the challenges of meeting client demands for diverse teams and the firms' ability to hire and support diverse talent. The business case for diversity[3] is one that many of you questioned, and we appreciate your candor with our guests. Each of the panelists reached out expressing their thanks for your insight, suggestions, and thoughtful contributions to the discussion. Contact information for our guests was posted in the student portal. Tonight, we will look at DE and I from the lens of the judicial branch. I am honored to introduce Judge Mare Bristol.

Judge Bristol: Good evening, I am honored to join you tonight. I want to start by acknowledging that you belong here. We all come from different backgrounds, experiences, and identities. No matter the journey, what you look like, or believe in, our profession needs you.

This class would not and could not have been offered when I was in law school. I grew up in our largest and poorest city. But for the grace of my family, and one opportunity, I would be a statistic, lost to systemic racism, misogyny, homophobia, bias, and hatred. But instead, someone saw something in me. I am a product of public schools and hung out at what was called the Recreation Center. We played basketball, cards, talked, and learned. We were mostly Black and Brown kids, but those of us who weren't were still poor. One day, some folks came through to ask why we came—in retrospect, it was likely an election year, but I didn't think about politics then, I just existed. I am not shy, and always had something to say, still do, and I told them exactly what I thought. Apparently, that worked. One of the big shots there was amused by my boldness and saw my potential. He encouraged me, sponsored me, and gave me the financial and educational support my family

3. For an explanation of the business case, *see* Sheryl L. Axelrod, *Banking on Diversity: Diversity and Inclusion as Profit Drivers—The Business Case for Diversity*, AM. BAR ASS'N (June 12, 2014), https://www.americanbar.org/groups/litigation/committees/diversity-inclusion/articles/2014/diversity-inclusion-profit-drivers/ [https://perma.cc/B7AE-4WJ2]. For critiques of the business case, *see, e.g.*, Robin J. Ely & David A. Thomas, *Getting Serious About Diversity: Enough Already with the Business Case*, HARVARD BUS. REV. (Nov./Dec. 2020), https://hbr.org/2020/11/getting-serious-about-diversity-enough-already-with-the-business-case [https://perma.cc/VT5N-QPR2].

couldn't. He was the first person I called when I was admitted to this law school, and though he missed my nomination to the bench, he always believed I would ascend to this position; a position that, when much younger, I didn't think was open to me. I spent years in the public defender's office, tried a big firm, and then, when I grew tired of seeing young, straight, white males, far less seasoned than me, elevated to the bench, I finally applied. The rest is history.

The judicial branch is not diverse—at least the judges aren't—but things are changing. If we do not have a diverse bench and bar, what will our clients see, experience, or merely perceive? Criminal defendants should see, *must see* themselves represented in the faces of attorneys—no matter the side—and should also see themselves reflected in the judiciary. The first time a young Black man saw me on the bench, his eyes widened, and he proclaimed, 'you're the judge?' When I said yes, his shoulders relaxed. *Relaxed.* He had no idea how I would rule, what his sentence would be, but regardless of the outcome, he knew that I would be fair, that I would see *him* and not merely the color of his skin.

We spend time debating the merits of DE and I; many still do not agree that there is a problem. But in order to effectuate justice, we must have diverse perspectives, identities, and experiences on the bench. To see the totality of someone's circumstances, to hear and see them, to understand that not everyone has equal opportunity or access, is critical to our justice system. Even if it wasn't imagined in that way. What you are learning and considering in this class is critically important to the profession, and to access to justice.

Thank you for listening. I am happy to answer any questions you might have.

Tedde: Thank you, Judge Bristol. I appreciate you sharing your story and framing the issue for us. Recognizing the ways in which Black men in particular are disproportionately charged, arrested, and convicted of crimes, I entered law school wanting to be a public defender. As we moved through this class, my mindset shifted a bit and am now considering the prosecutor's office. Can you please talk about why you chose to work as a public defender and talk a bit about the impact of prosecutorial discretion?

Judge Bristol: Great question, Tedde. The first part is easy. Too many of my friends were arrested. You should know, as a young kid, the cops were in and of my community. Sure, there were issues with some, but they knew us, knew our families, and had no problem dragging us home and letting our parents dole out the punishment. Something changed. Poverty grew, more people moved in, as did gangs and drugs, and the cops moved out of our neighborhoods and "fought crime." I went off to college and every letter from home was an account of the goings-on in the neighborhood. Too many of my friends were arrested. I thought I could make a change—what they needed was someone who looked more like them, someone who understood where they came from, to defend them.

Like you Tedde, I wanted to change the lives of the Black and Brown people who were arrested and who didn't get a fair shot at a defense because of bias within in the defense bar. Have you discussed implicit bias yet? Of course, you have. Okay, so you understand that we all have unconscious bias based on our experiences within this country, our families, faith communities, the profession, schools, media, and the list goes on. My bias saw white men in the defense bar, and I assumed a lack of care for my communities. This was not always the case. Again, we all have bias, both positive and negative, and each must be explored and checked. While working in the system, I realized that prosecutors also had bias.

Prosecutorial discretion is necessary for the criminal justice system to flow and proceed. But that discretion is not immune from the impact of bias. A prosecutor's bias may impact how they see alleged offenders, who they charge, who is believable, who is guilty, who is worthy of a plea, and the length of a recommended sentence. Prosecutors have significant power in the criminal justice system—*this* is where the power lies. So, Tedde, what I realized was there was greater power to effect change in the prosecutor's office. Given the work you are doing in this class, and your desire to impact change, I am not surprised you are reconsidering.

CT: Thank you so much for joining us, Judge Bristol.

The class gives Judge Bristol a round of applause and then takes a short break.

TJ: OK, everyone, now it's time for our student-led discussion.

Parker: I'm the discussion leader tonight. Since tonight's topic is the judiciary, I'd like to focus on the recent nomination of Ketanji Brown Jackson for the Supreme Court.[4] In our readings, we saw how awfully Anita Hill was treated when she testified about Clarence Thomas's sexual harassment of her, and how Christine Blasey Ford was treated differently, though still harshly, for covering the same sorts of behavior by a nominated Supreme Court Justice, during the Kavanaugh confirmation hearings.[5] Given all of this, I think that things have improved in the sense that allegations by women are being taken

4. This was written prior to Justice Jackson's confirmation on April 7, 2022. *See* Katie Rogers, *'We've Made It': Jackson Celebrates Confirmation With Poetry and a Pledge*, N.Y. Times, Apr. 9, 2022, at A14.

5. *See, e.g.*, Sarah E. Heck, *From Anita Hill to Christine Blasey Ford: A Reflection on Lessons Learned*, 39 Equality, Diversity & Inclusion 101 (2019); John Blake, *The unspoken reason Christine Blasey Ford may be viewed differently than Anita Hill*, CNN (Sept. 27, 2018), https://www.cnn.com/2018/09/26/us/kavanaugh-ford-anita-hill-race/index.html [https://perma.cc/BG5U-NLD8]; Julia Jacobs, *Anita Hill's Testimony and Other Key Moments From the Clarence Thomas Hearings*, N.Y. Times (Sept. 20, 2018), https://www.nytimes.com/2018/09/20/us/politics/anita-hill-testimony-clarence-thomas.html [https://perma.cc/M37J-SKSS]; Haley Sweetland Edwards, *How Christine Blasey Ford's Testimony Changed America*, Time (Oct. 4, 2018), https://time.com/5415027/christine-blasey-ford-testimony/ [https://perma.cc/HU73-JMGT].

more seriously, but Kavanaugh was still confirmed, and there is already pushback on Jackson's nomination, even before any confirmation hearings.[6] So overall, it seems to me that Congress needs to do better. What does everyone else think of this?

Alex: I wonder how much of this is because the majority of Congress is still white men, and particularly wealthy white men. I don't think this would be a problem, or at least not as much of a problem, if Congress—especially the judiciary committee—was more diverse.

Blake: You're assuming that it's problematic for there to be pushback, though. There is an argument to be made that Jackson was only chosen because she's a Black woman, and Biden promised to pick a Black woman. Isn't that like reverse discrimination, to pick someone based on their race and not on their qualifications?

TJ: Why are you assuming that Jackson is not qualified?

Blake: I'm not saying that. I'm saying that it's possible she was only picked because she's a Black woman.

TJ: But by saying that, you're implying that Jackson is less qualified than other candidates, that the standards must have been lowered so that she could be nominated since she wouldn't have been qualified if she was white.

Blake: Oh, I didn't think about it that way.

Jack: Even if we assume equal qualifications, though, how is it not discrimination to choose someone because of their race?

Parker: Respectfully, Dean, I think you're only saying it that way because you're assuming that equal qualifications would mean an equal chance of being nominated, but it doesn't. Look at the incredibly low number of Black women who have ever served as federal judges—only 2% of all federal judges ever—and the fact that no Black woman has ever even been nominated for the Supreme Court before.[7] It's pretty clear that there is systemic discrimination going on, but it's not against white people.

Alex: In addition, there's true value to having diverse viewpoints on the Supreme Court. In previous classes, we've talked about how groups with diverse members make more reasoned decisions.[8] I would hope that Biden—in his

6. *See, e.g.*, Carl Hulse, *As Hearing Approaches, Republicans Step Up Objections to Jackson*, N.Y. TIMES, Mar. 20, 2022, at A25.

7. For a summary of relevant statistics, *see* Chandelis Duster & Priya Krishnakumar, *Ketanji Brown Jackson's nomination brings renewed attention to lack of Black judges on the federal bench*, CNN (Apr. 3, 2022), https://www.cnn.com/2022/04/02/politics/ketanji-brown-jackson-diversity-federal-bench-black-judges/index.html [https://perma.cc/J8NY-TVHJ].

8. *See, e.g.*, David Rock & Heidi Grant, *Why Diverse Teams Are Smarter*, HARV. BUS. REV. (Nov. 2016), https://hbr.org/2016/11/why-diverse-teams-are-smarter [https://perma.cc/JBE2-HTSM]; Dev Stahlkopf, *Why Diversity Matters in the Selection and Engagement of Outside Counsel: An In-House Counsel's Perspective*, ABA LITIG. J. (Spring 2020), https://www.americanbar.org/groups/litigation

discretion to choose a nominee—considered that as a factor in choosing Jackson.

Jack: Those are excellent points, and I hadn't considered the analysis in that way before.

Parker: That's why you always tell us to do all of the reading, right, Dean Park?

Jack: Even I need to be reminded of that sometimes!

CT: This is a good example of why it's important to look beyond the traditional narrative. There is always context behind judicial appointments, and you have to look at the systemic factors that create less obvious barriers to progress.

After a bit more discussion, the class moves on to a small group activity.

TJ: For our activity today, you're each going to take on the role of either a judge or an attorney, who primarily works on either civil or criminal cases. From that perspective, I'd like for you to identify three DE and I-related issues that you think exist in the courtroom and come up with one action step that your group, meaning people in your role, could take to address that issue. We're going to take 15 or 20 minutes to work on this in small groups, and then we'll discuss it as a class.

The students and Jack divide up into their groups, and while they work, CT and TJ listen to the discussions, chiming in when necessary and answering questions. When the class comes back together, each group briefly explains one of their ideas, and then TJ begins the larger discussion.

TJ: So now that we've heard at least one idea from each group, let's consider the barriers to taking these actions.

Alex: As one of the civil attorneys, I think the real barrier is money. No one has or is willing to dedicate enough money to these initiatives so that they can be successful.

CT: Well, are there any ideas that wouldn't cost a lot?

Alex: In our group, the criminal judges, we talked about limiting peremptory challenges in order to hopefully increase the diversity of juries, and that would just be a rule change, which shouldn't cost anything other than time.

Jack: In my group, Parker had an interesting idea for all of the judges on the court to commit to raising issues of bias—both procedurally and in the law itself—in written opinions, which would require some commitment to collective and individual action but wouldn't cost any money.

TJ: Why do you all think it's so difficult to get funding for these initiatives?

/publications/litigation_journal/2019-20/spring/why-diversity-matters-the-selection-and-engagement-outside-counsel-inhouse-counsels-perspective/ [https://perma.cc/GP6U-9K2V].

Alex: Funding is just so scarce generally that I think sometimes it's all they can do to keep the courts open and functioning.

Parker: That's just the courts, though, and maybe the legislature, but what about outside organizations? Why doesn't legal services have enough money to provide representation in more cases? Why are the public defenders so underfunded, with such a huge caseload? I think it's a larger, systemic issue that people may want to improve things like the criminal justice system, but they don't want to pay for it.

CT: So what do you think can be done about that?

Blake: I think education is key. We need to make people more aware of why this is important and the consequences for not changing things.

Drew: Take to the streets in protest!

The class laughs for a moment.

Spencer: You all laugh, but actually, I think demonstrations are a great idea. I've interned for a state senator, and if it's done at the right time, publicly showing that kind of widespread support among constituents could have a real impact on legislative votes.

TJ: That's a very creative idea, but unfortunately, it's time to wrap up for today. Next week, we'll be talking about DE and I in law schools and doing an activity where you get to be the admissions committee.

Conclusion

Even with institutional support, excellent student evaluations, and engagement from the bench and bar, sometimes I receive questions about the nature of the class and the efficacy of the pedagogical approach we employ. The class allows us to question systems, including the profession, the legal academy, and law schools. Because of this, I intentionally create an anti-hierarchical and collaborative space that further supports open dialogue and growth.[9] Students understand that I am a professor, and that our guest speakers are deans, judges and justices, managing partners, and other members of the bar. Although the atmosphere remains professional, due to the structure of the class, the power differentials are broken down, and students are more willing to engage in difficult conversations about the topic at hand. They are vocal about the whys and ways that this course has changed their perspective, impacted their view of the profession, and continued to inform their work in law school and beyond. They leave feeling empowered to change the system.

9. For a thorough discussion of critical pedagogical practices in law school, *see, e.g.*, Sheila I. Velez Martinez, *Towards an Outcrit Pedagogy of Anti-Subordination in the Classroom*, 90 Chi.-Kent L. Rev. 585 (2015).

Realistically, as is the nature of the legal academy, this class is one that is widely accepted by those who engage in and support diversity, equity, and inclusion, and generally ignored by others. I have had informative and enriching conversations about our class with a variety of people, and I continue to strive for more inclusion in our class and the wider legal community. As the institution creates its ABA Section 303 plan, this course and others like it will be elevated.

Part III

Professional Responsibility

Rethinking Professional Responsibility (PR) Materials: Insights from a New-to-PR Teacher

*Nicole P. Dyszlewski**

Introduction

Teaching professional responsibility (PR) is hard work, especially for a new-to-the-subject adjunct professor. I felt a lot of pressure to swiftly "get it right" when I volunteered, during the COVID-19 pandemic, to teach a mostly asynchronous, online 9-week summer course.

As I was wrestling with the breadth and depth of the materials I could assign and cover in class, and was awash with rules, cases, news stories, and scholarly articles, I did some basic research to see what other PR professors were doing. During this process, I came across this observation: "Professional responsibility is unique, at least among core courses in law school, in being essentially contested in its definition."[1] This quote, which made me laugh, also made me feel a bit directionless. How should I decide not just what to teach, but how to cram all the "right" content into the class, and when to teach each of the tested and important concepts?

Adding to the difficulty, I grappled with student expectations about what PR should be or should not be. There seems to be a popular sentiment among students that PR should be an MPRE prep class, focusing mostly on the rules and practice questions for

---

* Nicole P. Dyszlewski is the Director of Special Programs, Academic Affairs at Roger Williams University School of Law. To take risks and make changes, professors need to feel safe, stable, and supported by their community. Thank you to those members of the RWU Law community who support this work and provide a safe space each and every Friday morning for creativity, innovation, and growth to occur.

1. W. Bradley Wendel, Strategics and Techniques for Teaching Professional Responsibility 2 (2013).

the exam.[2] However, focusing only on the rules is shortsighted and paints an incomplete picture.

Looking beyond the doctrine, and putting aside the perception that "PR is just an MPRE prep class," PR is also a good place to address professional identity development, specifically with regard to mental health and well-being.[3] This seemed especially true during the COVID-19 pandemic, when students were feeling shut in, disconnected, and fearful.

As a guiding principle for my class preparation, I chose to look within, instead of beyond, myself. As author Leah Wortham stated in her 1993 article, *Teaching Professional Responsibility in Law School*, "For a course to be effective, decisions on what to teach and the perspective from which to teach it must reflect the teacher's background and convictions."[4] Following this sage advice, I decided to structure my PR class in a way that reflected my own convictions; I decided to prioritize equality, equity, and social justice as key narratives within the ethical rules, cases, examples of practical decision-making, and real-world lawyering. This decision felt risky because I was afraid my class would be considered less serious or less important by students because it looked less traditional.

At the same time I was prepping for my class, PR professors in several schools were using diversity, equity, equality, and social justice as a way to further build connections and context for the model rules and fundamental ethical decisions in our field. In a journalistic flourish, which may both overstate and understate this phenomenon, one article provides: "Standard legal ethics courses, long considered dry and theoretical by many students, have experienced a renaissance over the past two years due to the pandemic and an increased focus on social justice."[5] In this essay, I am hoping to celebrate this "renaissance" and detail a few decisions I made about course content and delivery. Perhaps other PR professors will find some wisdom and inspiration to make changes to their course content.

---

2. "If I had a dollar for every time someone asked me, "Will this course help me prepare for the MPRE?" I'd be flying around in my own private jet." *Id.* at 13.

3. *See* Rhonda V. Magee, *"If You Plant Corn, You Get Corn": On Mindfulness and Racial Justice in Florida and Beyond*, FLA. BAR J. (Apr. 2016) at 36, https://www.floridabar.org/the-florida-bar-journal/if-you-plant-corn-you-get-corn-on-mindfulness-and-racial-justice-in-florida-and-beyond/.

4. Leah Wortham, *Teaching Professional Responsibility in Law School*, DEL. LAW. (Winter 1993), at 18, 19

5. Melissa Heelan, *Law School Ethics Becomes "Real," Tackles Covid, Social Justice*, BLOOMBERG LAW (Jan. 25, 2022), https://news.bloomberglaw.com/social-justice/law-school-ethics-becomes-real-tackles-covid-social-justice.

Choosing a Textbook

According to an article from the *Journal of Multicultural Education*, "Some educators have begun to adopt open textbooks and other OER learning materials as a way to increase equity by improving student access, particularly with an eye to those who are struggling with basic need insecurities."[6] I was delighted to find an OER resource for PR and chose Frye and Schiller's *Professional Responsibility: An Open-Source Casebook* for my class.[7] Because the OER book was about 2 years old at the time, I made it clear in the syllabus and class website what rules had changed since the publication of the OER book.[8]

Textbook affordability is an equity and social justice issue. Law students, especially during the COVID-19 pandemic, may struggle with food insecurity, housing insecurity, and inability to pay their bills.[9] These concerns are further compounded by the high cost of tuition. Law students also often struggle with the rising costs of textbooks. LSSSE data bears out that, during the COVID-19 pandemic, these financial concerns "weighed heavily on students' minds. Almost two-thirds (63%) of all student respondents had increased concerns about their ability to pay their bills, with both gender and race-based disparities increasing challenges for already vulnerable populations."[10] Choosing an OER textbook can eliminate some of these costs and help alleviate student anxiety about these costs. As one study definitively concluded:

> In the end, the unjust burden created by course material costs on historically underserved students—combined with the cost-savings potential of OER and the current oligopolistic state of academic publishing—reveal the United States' education system to be far from the meritocratic bastion it proposes to be. Rather, educational institutions and academic publishers in the United States have created a systemic condition in which students' learning potential is limited by their purchasing power. This realization exposes a social mandate for universities to take more concerted efforts toward their increased use of no-cost course materials.... Accordingly, university staff, faculty, and administrators should include textbook affordability as part of their broader efforts to promote student equity. Said differently: Universities must heed this study's empirical results by using OER and/or other no-cost

6. Jennifer Van Allen & Stacy Katz, *Teaching with OER During Pandemics and Beyond*, 14 J. for Multicultural Educ. 209, 211 (2020).

7. *See* Brian L. Frye & Elizabeth Schiller, Professional Responsibility: An Open-Source Casebook (2019), https://open.umn.edu/opentextbooks/textbooks/865.

8. Practically, there were very minimal changes to the rules themselves, so this was a fairly easy lift. I added this just as a reminder. Like print resources, OER books can sometimes lag behind the most recent changes to the rules or case law.

9. Meera E. Deo et al., *LSSSE 2021 Annual Report: The Covid Crisis in Legal Education*, LSSSE, https://lssse.indiana.edu/wp-content/uploads/2015/12/COVID-Crisis-in-Legal-Education-Final-10.28.21.pdf

10. *Id.*

course materials to pursue a more socially just classroom, university, and higher education system writ large.[11]

Supplementing the Textbook

Choosing a textbook was an important first step, but I wanted to include sources and perspectives from beyond just Frye and Schiller. I organized the content into weekly lessons that I presented on my school's learning management system. This allowed me to diversify my lessons in form and perspective, and provide access to all of the class content in one place. I chose to supplement the casebook with a variety of multimedia resources, CALI lessons, library-licensed materials, and sample test questions, some of which I will highlight in this section.[12] When selecting this supplemental content, I tried to focus on issues and perspectives related to diversity, equality, equity, and social justice.

Gender in the Workplace

One example of a topic on which I supplemented the casebook was gender in the practice of law. I assigned all students two episodes from the *Women in the Law* podcast.[13] This podcast describes itself as having "advanced the conversation on the many challenges, both professional and personal, that women continue to face as members of the legal profession. Through first-person narratives, thoughtful conversations, and synthesis of economic and social science research, this show adds to the myriad of work fighting against decades of systemic problems."[14] I assigned the students to listen to one episode of their choosing and the final episode titled "Solutions."[15] This episode specifically discusses ABA Model Rule of Professional Conduct 8.4(g), which states that it is professional misconduct to "engage in conduct that the lawyer knows or reasonably should know is harassment or discrimination on the basis of race, sex, religion, national origin, ethnicity, disability, age, sexual orientation, gender identity, marital status or socioeconomic status in conduct related to the practice of law."[16]

When discussing the podcast in class I also discussed gender stereotypes in the legal profession and the so-called double bind of gender norms. As summarized by authors Jessica M. Salerno and Hannah J. Phalen:

---

11. J. Jacob Jenkins et al., *Textbook Broke: Textbook Affordability as a Social Justice Issue*, 2020 J. Interactive Media Educ. 3 (2020) (internal citations omitted).

12. I also required the students to purchase a rule book.

13. *Women in the Law Podcast mini-series*, Law School Transparency, https://www.lstradio.com/women/#theshow (last visited Feb. 8, 2023).

14. *Id.*

15. *Id.*

16. Model Code of Pro. Conduct r. 8.4 (Am. Bar Ass'n 2022).

> Legal scholars have theorized that women's success in the field might be stunted by the contradictory expectations for how a good attorney should behave and how women should behave. Female attorneys might be penalized both for failing to exhibit masculine traits when acting feminine but also for violating gender stereotypes when exhibiting masculine traits. This "double bind" might put women in the legal profession at a disadvantage while attempting to advance their careers, as there is no way for women to meet both sets of contradictory expectations.[17]

I spoke of my own experiences with gender norms and communication, specifically via written communication. I asked the students, many of whom were working in legal offices for the summer, to notice differences, if any, in how female-identified attorneys communicated in contrast to how male-identified attorneys communicated.[18] The students who chose to speak on this issue in class pointed out that it appeared to them that many male-identified attorneys communicated assignments via email in short, direct language free of (sometimes necessary) context and without greetings or pleasantries. In contrast, the students who volunteered to speak on this issue reported that many female-identified attorneys communicated assignments with more information, more conversational pleasantries, and with expressions of gratitude. The students seemed to enjoy this conversation and several students spoke with me outside of class about the impact this discussion had on their perceptions of their workplace.

Indigenous Identities and Tribal Nations

Another example of supplemental content I shared with the students was on the topic of representing tribal nations. I shared with them a series of slides that were part of a 2016 presentation titled *Ethical Considerations When Representing Tribal Nations.*[19] The slides examine several of the model rules from the perspective of an attorney representing a tribal nation. With these slides I shared an ABA article that explains, "There are only 2,640 Native American attorneys in the United States, comprising 0.2 percent of the more than 1.2 million attorneys in the United States."[20] Before class I asked students to reflect on this question—"Had you considered how the rules might apply to members of a tribe or members with a different legal system or cultural understand-

---

17. Jessica M. Salerno & Hannah J. Phalen, *Traditional Gender Roles and Backlash Against Female Attorneys Expressing Anger in Court*, 16 J. EMPIRICAL LEG. STUD. 909 (2019).

18. In future classes I will include those who identify across the gender spectrum.

19. D. Michael McBride, III, *Ethical Considerations When Representing Tribal Nations*, presentation at the 20th Annual Tribal Law and Government Conference, Mar. 11, 2016, https://perma.cc/6MMF-EDQR.

20. Mary Smith, *Native American Attorneys Systematically Excluded in the Legal Profession*, HUMAN RTS. MAG. (Oct. 1, 2014), https://www.americanbar.org/groups/crsj/publications/human_rights_magazine_home/2014_vol_40/vol--40--no--1--tribal-sovereignty/native-american-attorneys-systematically-excluded-in-the-legal-p/.

ing?" These slides and this discussion may be most appropriate for a class specifically about Model Rule 1.13.[21]

Mass Incarceration

Because of my own research and teaching interests, I tend to consider legal topics through the lens of mass incarceration. PR is no different. Still another way I chose to supplement my coursebook was through the use of an article from *Prison Legal News* (PLN) about the role of prosecutors as related to the mass incarceration phenomenon.[22] PLN has regular contributing writers, most of whom are currently or formerly incarcerated and 65–70% of PLN's subscribers are currently incarcerated.[23] I think it is important to use sources, even nontraditional sources, that are proximate to the issues we are discussing and using an article from PLN not only makes the students aware of the nexus between professional conduct and mass incarceration, but also about the existence of *Prison Legal News* itself. This article can be a way to discuss judgement, discretion, charging decisions, and the ABA's *Criminal Justice Standards for the Prosecution Function.*[24] I used this article as part of an online class discussion between in-person classes.[25] Later in the semester we revisited the nexus of mass incarceration and the model rules when we discussed Model Rule 8.4 and undercover investigations.[26]

Outside Speakers

Beyond just diversifying the assigned readings in my class, I brought in a few outside speakers. As one scholar noted, "Outside speakers can send the message that 'real lawyers' in the 'real world' have heard of this stuff and actually use it. They also can offer texture and richness in the specialized areas about which a teacher lacks experience."[27]

---

21. Model Rules Pro. Conduct r. 1.13 (Am. Bar Ass'n 2022).

22. Jayson Hawkins, *The Role of Prosecutors in Mass Incarceration*, Prison Legal News (Dec. 1, 2020), https://www.prisonlegalnews.org/news/2020/dec/1/role-prosecutors-mass-incarceration/. Prison Legal News (PLN) is "an independent 72-page monthly magazine that provides cutting edge review and analysis of prisoners' rights, court rulings and news concerning criminal justice-related issues." PLN is managed by editor Paul Wright, executive director of the Human Rights Defense Center, PLN's parent organization.

23. *See* Prison Legal News, FAQ, https://www.prisonlegalnews.org/faq/#faq-15.

24. Am. Bar Ass'n, Criminal Justice Standards for the Prosecution Function (4th ed. 2017). Also consider local rules such as R.I. Sup. Ct. R. 3.8 (Special Responsibilities of a Prosecutor).

25. Specifically, I asked students, "Do you think the rules need to be changed in light of the mass incarceration epidemic? Why or why not? If you think they should be changed based on the study described, what changes to you suggest? If you think they should not be changed based on this study, what about this article/study did you find not convincing?"

26. *See Supreme Court referee: Hurley didn't break ethics rules*, Pioneer Press (Feb. 5, 2008), https://www.twincities.com/2008/02/05/supreme-court-referee-hurley-didnt-break-ethics-rules/amp/; Hope C. Todd, *Lies, Damn Lies, and D.C. Rule 8.4(c)*, Wash. Law. (Jan. 2015) at 8, https://dcbar.org/getmedia/d6ca5548-a8f4-468a-941c-60d622b4d4d3/EthicsColumnJanuary2015

27. Wortham, *supra* note 4, at 20.

This was a keen way to inject some real-life context to the rules and to allow students to hear perspectives from someone beyond their cisgender, female, white professor. Inviting one of the co-chairs of the Rhode Island Bar Association's Ethics and Professionalism Committee allowed students to hear about how the bar's committee is structured and learn about its work. The students were excited to hear from a "real lawyer" and this guest speaker broke up some of the hyperfocus on the rules themselves.

Student Evaluations and Final Thoughts

Given that I made choices to provide a diversity of perspectives, lean into social justice as a theme, and to use an OER resource as the main casebook, I wondered if these decisions would impact my teaching evaluations or my students in a negative way. As a newer teacher, these teaching evaluations seem important, and I felt like I was possibly risking criticism for my decisions. Below are three different student perspectives from those evaluations:

> Student 1: The podcasts and articles for the forum posts were helpful to relate the rules to actual situations and helped me internalize the Information.
>
> Student 2: I found it not so effective that all the material was online.... I am more of a hands-on reader.
>
> Student 3: I like that we were given multiple sources of material to read from. I think in other classes it's primarily from what the casebook which limits your perspective.

Another metric of success or failure I considered was if the students who took my class would perform similarly to those who had taken another professor's class on the MPRE. Unfortunately, I do not have any data about the comparative MPRE scores.

PR is truly a welcome home for innovation, social justice, and creativity. As I prepped my class, I was constantly inspired by the work of other PR professors, especially Dean Spade's *Writing Assignment: Ethical Roadmap Zine.*[28] In the development and presentation of my class I made some decisions to prioritize social justice, diversity, and equity, but I could have done more and pushed farther. Depending on who is reading this and where we find ourselves in the academy, I imagine some will read this essay and think these changes were substantial, and some will read this essay and think these changes don't go far enough. The decisions I made felt risky based on my identity and academic status, but I hope as legal education continues to progress and to confront the realities of bias, oppression, inequality, and injustice our profession has long cast out of the doctrinal classroom, the risks we feel comfortable taking become greater. For myself,

28. Dean Spade, *Ethical Roadmap Zine Assignment Instructions*, http://www.deanspade.net/ethical-roadmap-zine-assignment-instructions/ (last visited Feb. 8, 2023).

I know my journey in the PR classroom is not complete; I look forward to the next iteration of my class with more innovation and more risk.

Exploring Two Sides of the DEI Coin in Professional Responsibility: Access to Justice and Access to the Profession

*Brooks Holland**

Introduction

In my fifteen years of teaching professional responsibility (PR), I have routinely experimented with how to incorporate diversity, equity, and inclusion (DEI) values into the course as a learning objective. For example, for a number of years, I gave students an access-to-justice group exercise exploring law firm *pro bono* policies. Students increasingly recognized, however, that an underinclusive legal profession itself will be less capable of delivering inclusive access, revealing a two-sided and dominant DEI coin in our commodified legal profession. This two-sided DEI coin controls not just who can purchase keys to the law's palace gates as a consumer, but also who guards the palace gates of our law's monopolistic kingdom in the first place.[1]

As a result, I have broadened this access-to-justice exercise to prompt students to think critically about intersectional systems of bias—between service provider and consumer—that maintain hierarchies in who gives and receives the law. This essay shares my exercise, and explores and reinforces the values of diversity, equity, and

* Professor of Law and J. Donald and Va Lena Scarpelli Curran Professor of Legal Ethics and Professionalism, Gonzaga University School of Law. Contributing to this essay was Mirela L.A. Timóteo, a law student at Universidade Salgado de Oliveira in Brazil, and a participant in the Justice Initiative at Harvard and Howard University Law Schools.

1. *Cf.* Francisco Valdes, Steven W. Bender & Jennifer J. Hill, Critical Justice: Systemic Advocacy in Law and Society 678 (2021) (hereinafter Critical Justice) (observing that "[t]he legal 'profession' is a for-profit industry, with owners, workers, customer, and regulators in constant socio-economic play. Law, like other industries, increasingly obeys economic rules of capitalism. . . .").

inclusion, as well as professional identity formation, which increasingly are expected and even required in legal education.

DEI and Professional Identity Values in PR

The rigors and career incentives of law school can lead some students to adopt an instrumentalist approach to legal studies: embrace formalist legal analysis to maximize grades, jobs, and bar passage prospects, and relegate mushy values to episodic "policy" or "theory" units that a professor may impose. Yet intuitively, PR should resist this instrumentalism, because PR is about being an "ethical" lawyer. Ethics-centered learning objectives *sound* values-driven.

PR, however, teaches ethical lawyering largely from a legal code, the American Bar Association (ABA) Model Rules of Professional Conduct (Model Rules).[2] This code is subject to a standardized licensure test, the Multi-State Professional Responsibility Exam (MPRE).[3] The Model Rules and the MPRE often express ethical issues of whether a lawyer's conduct would subject the lawyer to *discipline*—not a particularly aspirational paradigm. Counterintuitively, PR can amplify the siren call of instrumentalist legal studies. Many students thus may enroll in PR with the goals of avoiding professional discipline, passing the MPRE, and fulfilling a graduation requirement.[4]

No PR professor would dismiss these necessary learning objectives. But these objectives are far from sufficient for ethical lawyering. Ethical lawyering necessitates constant engagement with values. The important but sometimes overlooked Preamble to the Model Rules emphasizes this necessity, acknowledging that in the real world, despite the black letter doctrine of the Model Rules, "many difficult issues of professional discretion can arise."[5] These discretionary "issues must be resolved through the exercise of sensitive professional and moral judgment,"[6] judgment that is "guided by personal conscience and the approbation of professional peers."[7]

The ABA Standard requiring PR education makes explicit that PR must wrestle with these values in some form.[8] Moreover, recent amendments to the ABA Standards

---

2. *See* Am. Bar Ass'n, Model Rules of Professional Conduct (2020) (hereinafter Model Rules), https://www.americanbar.org/groups/professional_responsibility/publications/model_rules_of_professional_conduct/model_rules_of_professional_conduct_table_of_contents/.

3. *See* Nat'l Conf. of Bar Examiners, Multistate Professional Responsibility Examination, https://www.ncbex.org/exams/mpre/ (last visited Jan. 11, 2023).

4. *See* Am. Bar Ass'n, Standards and Rules of Procedure for Approval of Law Schools 2022–2023 (hereinafter "ABA Standards"), Standard 303(a)(1) (requiring minimum of two credit hours of professional responsibility).

5. Model Rules, Preamble, at ¶ 9.

6. *Id.*

7. *See id.* at ¶ 7.

8. *See* ABA Standards, *supra* note 4, at Standard 303(a)(1) (mandating "substantial instruction in rules of professional conduct, and values and responsibilities of the legal profession and its members").

reinforce the necessity of embedding DEI-related values in PR. For example, ABA Standard 303 now requires law schools "to provide substantial opportunities to students for ... the development of a professional identity."[9] The ABA's interpretation of this Standard explains professional identity:

> Professional identity focuses on what it means to be a lawyer and the special obligation lawyers have to their clients and society. The development of professional identity should involve an intent and exploration of the values, guiding principles, and well-being practices considered foundational to successful legal practice.[10]

PR is a natural place for students to explore these questions of professional identity: what kind of lawyer students want to be, and what systems are necessary to support that identity.

The ABA's conception of professional identity also extends naturally to DEI values—especially professional identity's focus on "the special obligations lawyers have to their clients and society." ABA Standard 303 reinforces this connection by further mandating that law schools "provide education to law students on bias, cross-cultural competency, and racism ... at the start of the program of legal education, and ... at least once again before graduation."[11] This Standard does not "prescribe the form or content" of this education,[12] but "courses incorporating these topics" can satisfy this requirement if they include "substantial activity designed to reinforce the skill of cultural competency and [students'] obligation as future lawyers to work to eliminate racism in the legal profession."[13]

Training in DEI values as a component of professional identity thus is critical for students to practice law ethically in a diverse and complex society.[14] But the Model Rules and ABA Standards do not exactly provide practical insight for students in how to identify and navigate these issues in the real world. I thus constructed this practical exercise that I hope widens the aperture for PR students to the systemic, intersectional nature of bias in obstructing access to the law and what students can do as lawyers to advocate critically for reform. In the process, I hope this exercise sharpens students'

---

9. *Id.* at Standard 303(b)(3).

10. *Id.* at Interpretation 303-5.

11. *Id.* at Standard 303(c).

12. *Id.* at Interpretation 303-8.

13. *Id.* at Interpretation 303-7.

14. *Cf.* Exec. Order No. 14,035, *Diversity, Equity, Inclusion, and Accessibility in the Federal Workforce*, 86 Fed. Reg. 34,593 (June 25, 2021) (directing a "workforce that reflects the diversity of the American people," and noting that "[a] growing body of evidence demonstrates that diverse, equitable, inclusive, and accessible workplaces yield higher-performing organizations"); *cf.* David L. Douglass, Amber C. Thompson & Eliazar Chacha, *Signposts in the Road: The Lawyer's Ethical Obligation to Promote Diversity in the Profession*, IILP Rev. 2019–2020 at 52, https://www.theiilp.com/resources/Documents/IILP_2019_FINAL_web.pdf; *cf.* David Douglass, *The Ethics Argument for Promoting Equality in the Profession*, ABA J. (Nov. 1, 2019), https://www.abajournal.com/magazine/article/the-ethics-argument-for-promoting-equality-in-the-profession (making moral, business, and ethical cases for diversity commitments).

doctrinal understanding of key Model Rules, and enhances students' ability to practice collaboratively with shared responsibility.

The Two-Sided DEI Coin: Access to Services and Access to the Profession

I have students engage in a number of exercises during PR as formative assessments and to provide students with the experience of a practical workflow during the term. Several of these assignments are individual in nature, but certain exercises are group "law firm" exercises. I organize students into these law firms at the start of the term so students undertake the collaboration and shared responsibility that they quickly learn is an essential aspect of most law practices.[15] For these exercises, I give each student law firm a practical problem to address. The firms submit a group memorandum addressing the problem, and the firms discuss the problem in class, either collectively or as a firm group presentation to the class.

As an equity values-centered culmination to the course, I developed an access-to-justice exercise for student firms that focuses on lawyer *pro bono* duties.[16] I give the firms a demographic profile as a private law practice, and ask students to meet as the firm's management committee to deliberate on a firm *pro bono* policy. Although fairly traditional, this exercise has been productive in prompting firms to explore the access-to-justice crisis, *pro bono* duties under the Model Rules,[17] and how to incorporate a more inclusive practice into the firm's business model.

Student firms thus research the familiar and dispiriting data about the access-to-justice crisis in the United States, where in 2017, "86% of the civil legal problems reported by low-income Americans received inadequate or no legal help, [when] 71% of low-income Americans had experienced at least one civil legal problem in the last year."[18]

15. *See, e.g.*, Model Rules 5.1, 5.2, 5.3, and 1.10. Student law firms can vary in size depending on the class size, but I typically assign eight firms with six to eight students in each firm.

16. *See* Model Rules, Preamble ¶ 6 and Rule 6.1 and comments.

17. *Pro bono* work under Model Rule 6.1 also can raise unique issues, for example, of competence and diligence; *see* Rules 1.1 and 1.3; client and lawyer decision-making, Rules 1.2 and 2.1; lawyer and staff supervision, Rules 5.1, 5.2, and 5.3; and conflicts of interest, Rules 1.7, 1.8, 1.9, 1.10, 6.3, 6.4, and 6.5.

18. Legal Aid Interagency Roundtable, *Access to Justice in the Age of COVID-19: A Roundtable Report*, at 13 (Sept. 2021), https://www.justice.gov/ag/page/file/1445356/download; *see also* Inst. for the Advancement of the Am. Legal Sys., *US Justice Needs* (2021), https://iaals.du.edu/projects/us-justice-needs (last visited Jan. 13, 2023). Access to justice is not a uniform issue from state-to-state. *See* Karen Sloan, *New Report Highlights Which States Are Leading on Access to Justice and Which Are Falling Short*, Law.com (May 18, 2021), https://www.law.com/2021/05/18/new-report-highlights-which-states-are-leading-on-access-to-justice-and-which-are-falling-short/. Further, access to justice is a global juridical issue; *see* World Justice Project, *Measuring the Justice Gap* (2019), https://worldjusticeproject.org/our-work/research-and-data/access-justice/measuring-justice-gap, although the nature of local access issues may vary. *See, e.g.*, Felipe Probst Werner, *A Critical View of the Access to Justice in Brazil*,

Firms add their emerging awareness of law firm billing and management practices,[19] and learn about exemplar *pro bono* programs and opportunities they can emulate.[20] Firms as a result have engaged in sometimes spirited debates about these issues—such as whether to make *pro bono* work mandatory or optional, or to have no policy at all; how to distribute the costs of *pro bono* work in the firm; firm control over lawyers' *pro bono* cases and clients; and *pro bono* brand management.

These class discussions about access to justice, however, have turned often to more systemic DEI questions, which localized problem-solving through *pro bono* work alone seems inadequate to address. The access-to-justice problem looks a lot like a societal bias problem—the for-profit legal system is systemically biased against poor and low-income communities,[21] which in turn disproportionately impacts individuals by race, gender, and other factors.[22] At the same time, lawyers' parsimonious monopoly over law practice[23] manifests very similar hierarchies in the people who control this monopoly for delivering legal services. These student discussions thus surface the other side of the DEI coin: whether the access-to-justice crisis merely replicates and reinforces inequitable hierarchies in the legal profession itself.[24]

Recent data demonstrate that "while law firms in the United States have made some progress in increasing diversity and inclusion, it has been relatively modest,"[25] and "people of color remain woefully underrepresented in major U.S. law firms in relation to their presence in the total population in the U.S."[26] Instead of prioritizing diverse hiring practices, "many law firms stick to their comfort zone when it comes to hir-

---

3 INT'L J. L. & SOC'Y 1 (2020) (arguing for reform despite Brazil's more generous civil legal services system due to systemic delays in case resolution and incentives for litigation).

19. *See, e.g.*, MODEL RULES, Rules 1.5, 1.15, and 5.4.

20. *See e.g.*, Am. Bar Ass'n, *Pro Bono Now*, https://www.americanbar.org/groups/probono_public_service/projects_awards/probononow/ (last visited Jan. 13, 2023); Wa. State Bar Ass'n, *Public Service Toolkit*, https://www.wsba.org/connect-serve/volunteer-with-wsba/toolkit-for-public-service-volunteers (last visited Jan. 13, 2023).

21. *See* Deborah L. Rhode, *Access to Justice*, 69 FORDHAM L. REV. 1785, 1785–86 (2001) (observing "[w]e tolerate a system in which money often matters more than merits and equal protection principles are routinely subverted in practice").

22. *Cf., e.g.*, 2015 *Washington State Civil Legal Needs Study Update*, WA. STATE SUP. CT., at 10–12 (Oct. 2015), https://ocla.wa.gov/wp-content/uploads/2015/10/CivilLegalNeedsStudy_October2015_V21_Final10_14_15.pdf (finding poor and low-income persons "suffer higher degrees of discrimination and unfair treatment because of race, ethnicity, and other status-based characteristics").

23. *See* Leslie Levin, *The Legal Profession's Monopoly on the Practice of Law: The Monopoly Myth and Other Tales about the Superiority of Lawyers*, 82 FORDHAM L. REV. 2611, 2613 (2014) ("The [lawyer] monopoly problem is problematic not simply because lawyers are unfairly advantaged in the marketplace for legal services. It contributes to a more fundamental problem: many poor, near-poor, and middle-class individuals cannot afford a lawyer.").

24. *Cf.* Rhode, *supra* note 21, at 1812–1815 (noting intersection between the justice gap, *pro bono* failures, and the lawyer monopoly on law practice); CRITICAL JUSTICE, *supra* note 1, at 678, 694, and 701.

25. Kirtana Kalavapudi, *Being Seen & Heard: How Can We Create More Space for Diversity & Inclusion in the Legal Market?*, 105 WOMEN L.J. 17, 17 (2021) (citing National Association for Law Placement 2020 Report on Diversity in U.S. Law Firms).

26. *Id.*

ing practices and career development."[27] In this "comfort zone," women, the LGBTQ+ community, and persons with disabilities also are all underrepresented.[28] For example, a recent ABA study reports:

- White men still super-dominate the field, with only 17% of attorneys self-identifying as "minority," 35.2% self-identifying as female, 2.8% as LGBTQ+, and .6% as disabled
- Despite a decrease in hiring generally, white attorneys were almost twice as likely to be hired into partnership roles
- Male attorneys were twice as likely to be hired into partnership roles, whereas female attorneys were substantially more likely to be hired as associates
- Most law firms for the most recent year did not report hiring a single attorney who self-identified as Native American, Pacific Islander, or LGBTQ+, or as having a disability.
- Black and Asian American lawyers experienced the highest attrition rates[29]

Significantly, these disparities are most pronounced at the leadership and management levels, where firm policies and practices are set.[30]

I therefore have expanded my access-to-justice exercise more fully to explore exclusionary bias in the legal profession from both sides of the coin—access to services and access to the profession, as an intersectional discussion. The goal is for students in a practical, law firm setting to explore and attempt to address this dilemma of one exclusionary dynamic feeding the other to "reproduce dominant hierarchies, not to produce equal justice,"[31] and where "social identities ... maintain the profession based on social and economic castes."[32]

My PR course culminates with student firms meeting as the management group for their firm to respond to critiques from clients, the state bar, and junior associates that the firm has not been active enough on access-to-justice or diversity. Each student group takes either the access-to-justice prompt or the diversity prompt, and prepares

---

27. *Id.* at 18. The data are more positive with respect to DEI *training* in law firms, particularly in the years since the murder of George Floyd raised awareness in some sectors of racial injustice. *See Findings on Racial Justice and DEI Efforts at U.S. Law School and Legal Employers*, NALP Bulletin (Oct. 2020), https://www.nalp.org/1020research.

28. *See generally* Am. Bar Ass'n, Commission on Racial and Ethnic Diversity in the Profession, *2021 ABA Model Diversity Survey* (2021), https://www.americanbar.org/content/dam/aba/administrative/diversity-inclusion-center/2021-md-survey-2nd-edition.pdf.

29. *See id.* at 16–19, 77–166.

30. *See id.* at 16–17; *see also* Amanda Robert, *Law Firm Leaders Are Still Mostly White and Male, ABA Diversity Survey Says*, ABA J. (May 16, 2022), https://www.abajournal.com/web/article/law-firm-leaders-are-still-mostly-white-and-male-aba-diversity-survey-says (citing 81–93% figure for white equity partners in all firms, and 80% figure for male equity partners).

31. Critical Justice, *supra* note 1, at 731.

32. *Id.* at 701.

a written proposal.[33] The following are selected elements of this exercise as I recently administered it:

> You are members of a successful private law firm in Seattle, Washington. The firm's lawyers practice in a variety of areas, including civil litigation and transactional work. Your firm has 20 partners, 50 associate lawyers, and 35 staff in different roles. Your firm expects associate lawyers to bill a minimum of 1,800 hours annually to be eligible for the firm's annual bonus—an important component of associates' anticipated income, and a critical marker for anyone seeking partnership. To be considered a "high-value" lawyer, an associate should bill 2,000+ hours a year.

Student groups receive detailed information about their firm's current *pro bono* work and diversity based on the firm's annual review process and an internal survey. The problem offers a mixed bag on *pro bono* within the firm, and the internal "survey" reveals a demographic mix that might be common for a Seattle law firm regarding race and ethnicity, sex, gender identity and expression, sexual orientation, disability, and other factors, such as religion and political views. The problem differentiates in the survey between partners, associates, interns, and staff.

Student groups receive this direction:

> Your student group should convene as a firm management subcommittee to discuss, explain, and propose one of these policies to the firm, pro bono or diversity. Your policy should not express simply an abstract statement about pro bono work or diversity values. Rather, identify whether pro bono work or diversity initiatives will be required, discretionary but supported, or not supported, and explain how and with what goals. If you will not support these initiatives, explain why to the firm. Address both the ethical and economic implications of your decision to the firm's practice. Moreover, in drafting your policy, prepare to discuss how your policy may impact not only practices in your firm, but also *access to the legal system as a whole.*

I invite students to research existing policy models on which their firm groups would wish to draw, so long as each firm identifies its sources. Firms also do not need to research the implications of the policy under other areas of law. For example, firms do not need to research the tax implications of a *pro bono* policy, or whether a firm's diversity policy complies with EEOC standards. The point is for the firm to identify and discuss access and diversity values in the legal profession, and the impact that a law firm can and should prioritize within its business model.

Once student groups submit written proposals, I share them with the entire class, and we meet for our final class session to review. This review takes the form of a law firm management meeting, where we consider, debate, and seek to harmonize the different proposals. We conclude with the question, "Will we make a difference?"

---

33. I typically set the proposal length at three or four single-spaced pages.

Outcomes and Takeaways

Student law firm responses have been illuminating, and sometimes highly divergent in the prescriptions that they propose. Student groups, however, largely have appreciated that a profession which is not fully inclusive in who can make the law likely will be no more inclusive in who can access the law. These parallel hierarchies will persist without greater interventions.

The group proposals have offered a broad mix of interventions, from mandatory diversity and *pro bono* policies to discretionary but supported policies. For example, seeking to leverage private law firm culture, many proposals have focused on incentives and collaborations that firms could pursue to reward or compel *pro bono* and diversity work within the firm's for-profit business model. The ability of lawyers to incorporate this work into billable hours often has played a prominent role. The proposals thus linked lawyer productivity and remuneration to *pro bono* and diversity outcomes, and sometimes sought to partner with bar associations, civic organizations, and even clients in these initiatives.

For diversity, student groups naturally have addressed recruitment strategies, such as pipeline and mentorship programs. But many groups also have emphasized retention as a critical issue, particularly by bringing more diverse lawyers to leadership positions. Some groups have varied, however, on how broadly and explicitly to define "diversity," such as whether to identify racial and ethnic diversity as an explicit priority, or to whether to define diversity more generally across numerous identities, experiences, and perspectives without prioritizing or ordering any particular diversity factors.

In the process of this class review, students have learned a lot about their responsibility as lawyers to access-to-justice and diversity issues, and also about the limits of what private-sector firms can accomplish in isolation without more systemic reforms. However we harmonize these proposals into a student firm policy, we further realized we had to answer the question, "Will we make a difference?" with humility. The goal here is not to dispirit students, considering that this work is a drop in the bucket in the face of these systemic issues. Rather, the goal is to open students to the idea that these systemic problems necessitate system reform as well, and they as lawyers have unique skills and knowledge to *do something about it*. Systemic reform opportunities we have discussed include legal education reform, pipeline programs, licensure reform, and opening law practices to non-lawyer models.[34]

Moreover, from this exercise students deepened their understanding of relevant Model Rules. Model Rules 6.1 (*pro bono*) and 8.4(g) (bias) are the most directly related. But students also explored how *pro bono* and diversity policies could support fuller compliance, for example, with Model Rules 1.1 (competence), and 5.1 and 5.3 (lawyer and staff supervision), and the Preamble's "public citizen" role for lawyers.[35] Students

34. The Society of American Law Teachers is an excellent resource for many of these reforms. *See* https://www.saltlaw.org (last visited Jan. 13, 2023).

35. MODEL RULES, Preamble, at ¶ 6.

further learned much more about real-world law firm billing, budgeting, recruitment, and retention practices. And the exercise supported students in developing professional identity by fostering cultural competence and empowering students to eliminate racism and other systemic biases in the legal profession.

Beyond Fear: Bringing Mental Health into the Professional Responsibility Classroom While Empowering Students

*Sarah J. Schendel**

Introduction

Having read no further than the table of contents for an article about lawyer well-being, I felt overwhelmed and somewhat deflated: "Depression"; "Anxiety and other Mental Illness"; "Alcoholism and Drug Abuse"; "Divorce...." This article was hardly an outlier: in 2022, after survey upon survey, seemingly endless startling statistics, and alarm bells of concern going off at the highest decibels, there can be little question that the legal profession is having to reckon with the state of lawyer mental health.[1] Recognizing this, I've worked to incorporate material on mental health—and the related issues of

---

* Associate Professor of Academic Support, Suffolk University School of Law, Boston, MA. My thanks to Elizabeth Stillman, Sarah Fender, Sarish Siddiqui, and Christina Guccione for their comments. And, as always, my gratitude to every student who has trusted me to be a part of their educational experience.

1. *See, e.g.*, NAT'L TASK FORCE ON LAWYER WELL-BEING, THE PATH TO LAWYER WELL-BEING: PRACTICAL RECOMMENDATIONS FOR POSITIVE CHANGE 7 (2017) (hereinafter THE PATH TO LAWYER WELL-BEING). The Survey of Law Student Well-Being found that:

> 17 percent experienced some level of depression, 14 percent experienced severe anxiety, 23 percent had mild or moderate anxiety, and six percent reported serious suicidal thoughts in the past year. As to alcohol use, 43 percent reported binge drinking at least once in the prior two weeks and nearly one-quarter (22 percent) reported binge-drinking two or more times during that period. One-quarter fell into the category of being at risk for alcoholism for which further screening was recommended.

Id. I will also note that this "crisis" is not just about lawyers—paralegals, legal secretaries, and others are also impacted; this essay focuses only on lawyers and law students.

well-being and professional identity formation—into my Professional Responsibility (PR) course.[2]

Professional Responsibility is a natural home for these topics as it's one of the few classes required[3] following a student's 1L year and because the material (ideally) addresses the realities of not only studying, but also practicing law. Among the wealth of suggestions for how the legal profession might address well-being issues, there is a reoccurring focus on the potential role for both PR and the Model Rules of Professional Conduct (Rules). One report, for instance, recommended that the Rules be modified to "endorse well-being as part of a lawyer's duty of competence."[4] The American Bar Association (ABA) has been deep in conversation about changes to Standards 303 and 508,[5] and law schools will undoubtedly continue to investigate where and how to tackle the complex issues of student and attorney well-being. However, even if there is a consensus that these issues should be addressed in the law school curriculum, there remains much to learn about the best ways to expose students to these issues and help them prepare for practice, without adding to their anxiety, shifting responsibility for systemic failures onto their already-burdened shoulders,[6] or increasing their fear of legal practice. While the legal profession can certainly be challenging, it can also be

---

2. Beyond my individual efforts, in 2022 our law school approved a pilot program expanding our Professional Responsibility classes from 2 to 3 credits, with the purpose of addressing these issues generally.

3. AM. BAR ASS'N, STANDARDS AND RULES OF PROCEDURE FOR APPROVAL OF LAW SCHOOLS 2022–2023, Standard 303(a)(1): "A law school shall offer a curriculum that requires each student to satisfactorily complete at least the following: (1) one course of at least two credit hours in professional responsibility that includes substantial instruction in rules of professional conduct, and the values and responsibilities of the legal profession and its members."

4. THE PATH TO LAWYER WELL-BEING, *supra* note 1, at 26 (Recommendation 20.2). It is worth noting that some experts have been understandably wary about creating a basis for disciplining a lawyer who struggles to maintain their mental, emotional, or physical abilities.

> Notably, we do not recommend discipline solely for a lawyer's failure to satisfy the well-being requirement or the essential eligibility requirements. Enforcement should proceed only in the case of actionable misconduct in the client representation or in connection with disability proceedings under Rule 23 of the ABA Model Rules for Disciplinary Enforcement. The goal of the proposed amendment is not to threaten lawyers with discipline for poor health but to underscore the importance of wellbeing in client representations. It is intended to remind lawyers that their mental and physical health impacts clients and the administration of justice, to reduce stigma associated with mental health disorders, and to encourage preventive strategies and self-care.

Id. See also Alex B. Long, *What the Lawyer Well-Being Movement Could Learn From the Americans with Disabilities Act*, 63 WILLIAM & MARY L. REV. Online 63 (2023) for an important discussion about the ways "the lawyer well-being movement has sometimes perpetuated harmful stereotypes concerning disability," suggesting "that in order to more effectively improve lawyer well-being, the organized bar should look more carefully at the text of the Americans with Disabilities Act (ADA) as well as the policies that underly it."

5. Midyear Meeting 2022 House of Delegates Res. 300, Am. Bar Ass'n (Feb. 14, 2022), https://www.americanbar.org/content/dam/aba/directories/policy/midyear-2022/300-midyear-2022.pdf (amending Standard 303: Curriculum and Standard 508: Student Support Services).

6. *See, e.g.*, Christian B. Sundquist, *Beyond the "Resiliency" and "Grit" Narrative in Legal Education: Race, Class, and Gender Considerations*, 50 J. MARSHALL L. REV. 271 (2016):

incredibly fulfilling and dynamic, and law students should enter with a (realistic) sense of responsibility, excitement, and hope.

This essay reflects on the challenges of teaching law students about "the well-being crisis" and offers several concrete, practical ways for professors to incorporate discussions of mental health into the PR curriculum. Beyond simply scaring students with dire statistics and disciplinary decisions, there exist powerful opportunities to carefully weave mental health and wellness issues into the PR classroom as well as create space for dynamic and relevant discussions of professional identity development, bias, addiction, professionalism, and the future of legal education. These discussions are perhaps even more important for BIPOC[7] students who face the additional challenges of seeking education in a "white space."[8] Through the structure of the class, the readings I assign, and how we engage with the materials, I seek to incorporate mental health into the PR curriculum in a way that will engage students, encourage honest discussions about the legal profession, and ideally leave them with reason to feel encouraged and forward-looking.

From the Jump

Professors who teach PR structure the class in a wide variety of ways. In addition to variations in content (no one has time to cover every Rule, for example, and while some professors focus more on guest speakers, others provide more preparation for the MPRE), the order of presenting material varies too. One of the most important decisions I have made is to start the class with a topic and readings that immediately engage students, and which let them know this is a class where we will not only be learning about the complexities of legal practice, but also critiquing them. I do this by beginning with admission to the bar, assigning students the following readings for Week 1: Rules 8.1, 8.3, and 8.4 (as well as the oft-ignored Scope and Preamble), and a *New York Times*

> The narrative on modifying legal education to produce entrepreneurial students with resiliency and 'grit' ... often has a troubling class and race-regarding dimension. The 'grit' reform initiative has the potential to rationalize future disparities, by shifting the focus in education from responding to the continuing impact of poverty and identity bias (race, religion, gender) on student outcomes to bolstering individual character traits and resiliency. Our country has a long and troubling history of adopting such post-racial 'distancing moves' in order to discount the effect that systemic bias has on legal outcomes and social justice by focusing on personal responsibility and individual deficit. The 'grit' and 'resiliency' narrative, by way of example, has been regularly deployed this year to silence the voices of minority students protesting systemic racism at colleges and law schools throughout the nation.

Id. at 272.

7. I want to acknowledge the shortcomings of the term BIPOC, and that the experiences of students of color in law school are varied and not universal. *See, e.g.*, Meera E. Deo, *Why BIPOC Fails*, 107 Va. L. Rev. Online 115 (2021).

8. See generally Bennett Capers' excellent essay, *Law School as White Space*, 106 Minn. L. Rev. 7 (2021).

article by attorney and "ex-convict" Reginald D. Betts, "Could an Ex-Convict Become an Attorney? I Intended to Find Out."[9]

Rule 8.1 is effective for teaching how to read the Rules[10] and prompts discussion of one of the big, broad questions over-arching much of PR: who "deserves" to be a lawyer and who judges worthiness? Immediately beginning with discussions of gatekeeping, access, privilege, and belonging sets the stage for the whole semester, and can be affirming for students who have felt excluded during law school due to disability, race, class, and/or gender identity. Having these barriers and challenges acknowledged in a classroom can confirm for students that they are not alone, that their experiences might not be as simple as "imposter syndrome"[11] but rather the result of some very real and wide-reaching systemic barriers. Betts' piece is fantastic not only for discussing barriers to admission, but also creates the opportunity for the class to discuss juvenile sentencing, terms like "superpredator,"[12] and ideas like exceptionalism.[13]

Starting with bar admission also allows us to discuss the character and fitness[14] portion of the bar admission process. The immediacy of this issue is critical, because I want to let students know as soon as possible where to find more information about what their state will ask with regard to mental health and criminal history, to dispel myths they might have about what would prevent admission, and to reassure them that

---

9. Reginald Dwayne Betts, *Could an Ex-Convict Become an Attorney? I Intended to Find Out*, N.Y. Times Mag., Oct. 16, 2018, https://www.nytimes.com/2018/10/16/magazine/felon-attorney-crime-yale-law.html.

10. For example, instructing students to not only read the text of the Rule but also to refer to Rule 1.0 Terminology for further clarification, cross-reference internal references (for example, pointing out that Rule 8.1(b) refers to Rule 1.6), and the importance of also reading the comments.

11. *See, e.g.*, on the inadequacy of "imposter syndrome" as a diagnosis or explanation for feelings of exclusion, Ruchika Tulshyan & Jodi-Ann Burey, *Stop Telling Women They Have Imposter Syndrome*, Harv. Bus. Rev. (Feb. 11, 2021), https://hbr.org/2021/02/stop-telling-women-they-have-imposter-syndrome ("For many women, feeling like an outsider isn't an illusion—it's the result of systemic bias and exclusion").

12. For example, I ask students: even if it's permitted by the Rules, is it ethical for a prosecutor to use such terms? In addition to sparking conversation, the purpose of asking this is to set an expectation that the Rules are not the "end-all be-all" of determining our own, individual ethics. I sometimes show this video for further context around the term and its impact: *Correcting the Myth of the Superpredator* (PBS 2019), https://www.pbs.org/video/retro-report-on-pbs-season-1-episode-8-correcting-myth-superpredator/.

13. It's easy to get most students to agree that Betts should be admitted but then I push them further—does an applicant have to be exceptional, a YLS grad, a MacArthur "genius," to have his past convictions "forgiven"? What if Betts had been an average student at a non-Ivy law school, who hadn't published books and won awards?

14. For more on the character and fitness requirement, *see, e.g.*, David L. Hudson, Jr. & Andrea Gemignami, *The Other Bar Hurdle: An Examination of the Character and Fitness Requirement for Bar Admission*, 48 Mitchell Hamline L. Rev. 500, 501 (citing Deborah L. Rhode, *Moral Character as a Professional Credential*, 94 Yale L.J. 491, 508–09 (1985)): ("In her seminal work in 1985, Professor Deborah Rhode explained the dual purposes of the character and fitness requirement: (1) protecting the public given their inherent vulnerability created by the disproportionate knowledge of lawyers and the required trust for essential matters, and (2) protecting the courts and administration of justice from those who are dishonest (disposed to perjury or bribery)."

they should still seek out support and treatment as needed.[15] Studies show that 3Ls are less likely than 1Ls to seek help because of fear around how such help might impact their bar admission and career search, so it is crucial that we reassure them early and often.[16] I also tie this discussion of character and fitness into our study of the Rules more broadly by discussing the fact that, in general, disciplinary actions arise from attempts to *hide* conduct or history, rather than the conduct or history itself.

I repeat these themes again in Week 5, which is specifically devoted to mental health and addiction in the legal community. The students read the article, "The Lawyer, The Addict" as well as Prof. Hannon's short essay, "Why the character and fitness requirement shouldn't prevent law students from seeking mental health treatment."[17] In that class I also let them know about ABA Resolution 102, which called for "character and fitness questions to address conduct rather than treatment or diagnoses when inquiring into an applicant's mental health history,"[18] and recommend they reach out to our Dean of Students Office with any specific concerns about required disclosures on their character and fitness applications.

---

15. I know our wonderful Dean of Students office also emphasizes this in orientation (consistent with the recommendation by Jerome Organ et al. that "[f]irst-year orientation is one of the most important times to address law student wellness issues." Jerome M. Organ, David B. Jaffe & Katherine M. Bender, *Suffering in Silence: The Survey of Law Student Well-Being and the Reluctance of Law Students to Seek Help for Substance Use and Mental Health Concerns*, 66 J. Legal Educ. 116, 148 (2016).

16. 3Ls may be less likely than 1Ls to seek help because of fears about imminent applications to jobs and the bar exam, as well as misinformation about the character and fitness requirements. In one survey, 49% of all respondents indicated: "If I had a drug or alcohol problem, my chances of getting admitted to the bar are better if the problem is hidden." *Id.* at 141, 142. Also, regarding the need to address substance use as early as possible, one study concluded that alcohol use among lawyers is at highest rates among attorneys early to practice. *See* Patrick R. Krill, Ryan Johnson & Linda Albert, *The Prevalence of Substance Use and Other Mental Health Concerns Among American Attorneys*, 10 J. Addiction Med. 46, 51 (2016) (noting that "attorneys in the first 10 years of their practice now experiencing the highest rates of problematic use" and "[t]his trend is further reinforced by the fact that of the respondents who stated that they believe their alcohol use has been a problem (23%), the majority (44%) indicated that the problem began within the first 15 years of practice.... Taken together, it is reasonable to surmise from these findings that being in the early stages of one's legal career is strongly correlated with a high risk of developing an alcohol use disorder.") It is also important to note the racial disparities in mental health treatment. Barriers may include: "Different cultural perceptions about mental illness and well-being; [r]acism and discrimination; [b]eing more vulnerable to being uninsured; [c]ultural differences in help-seeking behavior; [l]anguage and other communication barriers; [f]ear and mistrust of treatment." Simmons Univ., *Racial Disparities in Mental Health Treatment*, https://online.simmons.edu/blog/racial-disparities-in-mental-health-treatment/ (last visited Jan. 13, 2023).

17. Eilene Zimmerman, *The Lawyer, the Addict*, N.Y. Times (June 15, 2017), https://www.nytimes.com/2017/07/15/business/lawyers-addiction-mental-health.html; Margaret Hannon, *Why the character and fitness requirement shouldn't prevent law students from seeking mental health treatment*, ABA for Law Students (July 9, 2018), https://abaforlawstudents.com/2018/07/09/character-fitness-requirement-and-seeking-mental-health-treatment/. Please note: I also give a content warning before assigning these materials, for issues of substance abuse, mental illness, and suicide.

18. Midyear Meeting 2015 House of Delegates Res. 102, Am. Bar Ass'n, https://www.americanbar.org/news/reporter_resources/annual-meeting-2015/house-of-delegates-resolutions/102/.

While not required in order to lead discussions about mental health, sometimes I choose to disclose in passing that I have been diagnosed and live with depression and anxiety, hoping I can play a small role in destigmatizing these diagnoses and demonstrate that they did not negatively impact my ability to be admitted to the bar or practice law.[19] While decisions about what and whether to disclose health diagnoses are personal (and political) decisions, they can be powerful for students and new lawyers.[20] Reports by both the National Task Force for Lawyer Well-Being and the Massachusetts Steering Committee on Lawyer Well-Being emphasize the importance of supervising attorneys and leaders modeling well-being by discussing their personal commitments to it, including discussing how they personally nurture their own mental health.[21]

---

19. *See, e.g.*, Devon Price, *Laziness Does Not Exist*, MEDIUM.COM (Mar. 23, 2018), https://humanparts.medium.com/laziness-does-not-exist-3af27e312d01 (discussing how frank discussions about the stereotypes attributed to people with mental illnesses helped students open up about these issues, feel more comfortable to engage in class, and even succeed academically); Heidi S. Alexander, *Creating a Culture of Well-Being: Recommendations for Leaders*, L. PRAC. TODAY (Feb. 15, 2022), https://www.lawpracticetoday.org/article/creating-a-culture-of-well-being-recommendations-for-leaders/ ("Leaders can create and support change through their own demonstrated commitment to core values and well-being in their own lives and by supporting others in doing the same.") (internal quotations omitted); Organ, *et al*, *supra* note 15, at 151 n. 108 ("A number of faculty around the country have set examples by addressing wellness issues, as well as sharing their personal experiences."). Similarly, in the medical education setting, "97.4% [of] residents agreed that faculty sharing their personal struggles destigmatizes mental health issues during training, and the same percentage reported engaging in post conference self-reflection regarding their own mental health and well-being." Brianna E. Vaa Stelling & Colin P. West, *Faculty Disclosure of Personal Mental Health History and Resident Physician Perceptions of Stigma Surrounding Mental Illness*, 96 ACAD. MED. 682, 682 (2021). The experience of disabled law students is beyond the scope of my knowledge and beyond this article; however, when mentioning diagnoses and disclosures of any kind, it is important to acknowledge that "[l]aw schools remain unwelcoming spaces for many people with disabilities—a phenomenon that no doubt is perpetuated by the dearth of openly disabled law faculty." Katie Eyer, *Am I Disabled? Disability Identity and Law Faculty*, J. LEGAL ED. (forthcoming), https://papers.ssrn.com/sol3/papers.cfm?abstract_id=4095004.

20. Alexander, *supra* note 19. *See also* Katie Rose Guest Pryal, *Disclosure Blues: Should You Tell Colleagues About Your Mental Illness?* (2014), https://papers.ssrn.com/sol3/papers.cfm?abstract_id=4158926 ("Should higher education faculty with mental disabilities disclose their disabilities to their colleagues or institutions? In this essay, drawing on interviews, research, and my own experience as a disabled person, I show why disclosure is rarely the right choice. Stigma attached to mental disability in higher education is still too strong. In particular, the risk of repercussions for graduate students, contingent faculty, and pre-tenure faculty is especially high because of their lack of institutional power.").

21. *See* THE PATH TO LAWYER WELL-BEING, *supra* note 1; Massachusetts Supreme Court Steering Committee On Lawyer Well-Being, *Report to the Justices* (July 15, 2019), https://www.mass.gov/doc/supreme-judicial-court-steering-committee-on-lawyer-well-being-report-to-the-justices/download. *See also* Prof. Katie Eyer's fantastic essay, *supra* note 19, discussing the lack of "identifiably disabled law professors" and the "important consequences" of this "dearth":

> In contexts where there are no identifiably disabled law faculty, students with disabilities—themselves a substantial but mostly hidden group within law schools—may feel especially stigmatized or unwelcome. Such stigmatization can further have material costs, as students may not seek needed accommodations because of the actual or perceived stigma of doing so. The type of mentoring and support networks that we know are important to students of all underrepresented backgrounds are also unavailable where faculty of such backgrounds are not present or not identified. The cost of the absence of identifiably dis-

Finally, I emphasize that the question of how and whether to include mental health questions on character and fitness applications is very much a "live" matter,[22] and that it has changed over the years because of advocacy by students and lawyers alike. My hope is that this emphasizes to students—as early as during Week 1 of class—both the changes that need to be made, and the power they possess to make those changes. I bookend the semester with a similar sentiment regarding changes to the bar exam, particularly acknowledging the incredible advocacy of law students and recent graduates during the COVID-19 pandemic.[23]

The Skill of Self-Assessment

In addition to assigned readings and quizzes, I've created two basic self-assessment worksheets that I ask students to complete and submit to me.[24] These assignments arose both from my interest in self-assessment as a valuable skill for law students to develop,[25] and my desire to create an opportunity to learn more about my students and provide them with individualized feedback. The first of the assessments is a Professional Skills Self-Assessment based on the IAALS Foundations for Practice: The Whole Lawyer and the Character Quotient.[26] The second self-assessment focuses explicitly on well-being,

---

> abled law professors does not extend to students with disabilities alone. Law professors teach those who will go on to be the gatekeepers of disability equality: judges, law clerks....

Id. (internal citations omitted).

22. For example, under discussion in Ohio during the writing of this article: Anonymous, *Mental Health Question May Be Axed In Ohio*, LEGAL PROFESSION BLOG, https://lawprofessors.typepad.com/legal_profession/2022/06/mental-health-question-may-be-axed-in-ohio.html.

23. *See, e.g.*, Kelsey J. Griffin, *Harvard Law School Students Advocate for Licensing without Bar Exam*, HARV. CRIMSON (Apr. 3, 2020), https://www.thecrimson.com/article/2020/4/3/Harvard-coronavirus-law-school-petition-bar-exam/; Karen Sloan, *National Momentum Builds for Diploma Privilege as Oregon Makes Bar Exam Optional*, Law.com (June 30, 2020), https://www.law.com/2020/06/30/national-momentum-builds-for-diploma-privilege-as-oregon-makes-bar-exam-optional/?slreturn=20221102151448; Sarah J. Schendel, *Listen!: Amplifying the Experiences of Black Law School Graduates in 2020*, 100 NEB. L. REV. 73 (2021).

24. I'm happy to share these with other professors, please feel free to email me at sschendel@suffolk.edu.

25. *See, e.g.*, Sarah J. Schendel, *What You Don't Know (Can Hurt You): Using Exam Wrappers to Foster Self-Assessment Skills in Law Students*, 40 PACE L. REV. 154 (2020) ("Given a widespread weakness in accurate self-assessment, the desire to produce self-regulated learners, and a consensus about the need for more formative assessment of law students, there is a persuasive argument for combining these needs through student-involved assessment activities."); the lesson of self-awareness and self-assessment is also conveyed through reading Cassandra Burke Robertson, *Online Reputation Management in Attorney Regulation*, 29 GEO. J. LEG. ETHICS 97 (2016) (describing the psychological reasons for inappropriate and/or unprofessional attorney overreacting to online critiques).

26. Alli Gerkman & Logan Cornett, *Foundations for Practice: The Whole Lawyer and the Character Quotient*, INST. FOR THE ADVANCEMENT OF THE AM. LEG. SYS. (July 26, 2016), https://iaals.du.edu/publications/foundations-practice-whole-lawyer-and-character-quotient.

asking students to reflect on their emotional, physical, and social self-care, as well as suggestions for how to create effective goals[27] focused on self-care.[28]

The worksheets are assigned mid-semester (generally during weeks 4–5 in a 12-week semester). By this point, my hope is that I will have gained some of their trust, and they will feel more comfortable being honest with me (and themselves) in their answers. I emphasize that their responses will not be shown to anyone else, and that the worksheets are graded for completion only. These worksheets are a crucial opportunity for me to learn more about my students, and to provide them with individualized feedback. I have anywhere from 25–110 students in Professional Responsibility each semester, so this is often the only one-on-one exchange I have with every one of them. I create a template email, and customize it for each student, thanking them for telling me more about themselves, noting one interesting thing they wrote, and offering them one resource (for ex, a short video on procrastination, a link to an online Pomodoro timer, a free meditation podcast).

My hope is that these self-assessments provide variety (the rest of the class assignments are a mix of readings, CALI and BARBRI lessons, and quizzes using MPRE questions) and that they give students an opportunity to remember that professional identity development and well-being are most powerful when they come from self-reflection and not external motivation. In both the class dedicated to mental health and well-being, and the class dedicated to reflecting on legal education, we explicitly discuss the 1L shift from intrinsic to extrinsic motivation.[29] All opportunities for feedback—whether personalized via comments in response to the self-assessments, quantitative in the form of ungraded quiz scores, or graded like the midterm—are also an attempt to help manage student anxiety.[30]

---

27. This focus on goal-setting is, in my opinion, a part of well-being, due in part to the connection between planning fallacy, and procrastination. *See, e.g.*, Sarah J. Schendel, *Due Dates in the Real World*, 35 Geo. J. Leg. Ethics 203 (2022) (discussing procrastination and time management).

28. Discussing the fact that law school students take pride in allowing law school to consume their entire lives. Studies cited indicate that students sleep little, relax little, and this is even more often the case for students of color. *See* Jonathan Todres, *Work-Life Balance and the Need to Give Law Students a Break*, 83 Univ. Pitt. L. Rev. Online 1, 4 (2022).

29. Additional resources I use to prepare and also share with students surrounding this discussion include: Kennon M. Sheldon & Lawrence S. Krieger, *Does Legal Education Have Undermining Effects on Law Students? Evaluating Changes in Motivation, Values, and Well-Being*, 22 Behav. Sci. & L. 261 (2004); Deborah L. Rhode, The Trouble with Lawyers (2015); Nancy Levit & Douglas O. Linder, The Happy Lawyer: Making a Good Life in the Law (2010); Jeena Cho & Karen Gifford, The Anxious Lawyer (2022); Shailini Jandial George, The Law Student's Guide to Doing Well and Being Well (2021); Tara Brach, Guided Meditations, https://www.tarabrach.com/guided-meditations/ (last visited Jan. 13, 2023); Massachusetts Supreme Court Steering Committee On Lawyer Well-Being, *supra* note 21.

30. A lack of feedback has been cited as a source of anxiety for students. *See, e.g.*, Olympia Duhart, *"It's Not for a Grade": The Rewards and Risks of Low-Risk Assessment in the High-Stakes Law School Classroom*, 7 Elon L. Rev. 491, 494 (2015) ("[F]requent opportunities to practice that do not have any or much impact on grades can also be valuable. They can alleviate student anxiety and help prepare students for a more effective practice performance."). *See also* (in non-law school settings) François Molin et al., *Toward Reducing Anxiety and Increasing Performance in Physics Education: Evidence from*

Imagining Our Collective Future

In our final class together, I ask students to take what they have learned about the Rules, the rewards and demands of the profession, admission to the bar, and professionalism, and to look back at their law school education. Is law school adequately preparing them for the profession? Is that the primary role of law school? Has law school taught them any useful tools for managing stress and preparing for the challenges of practice? What would they change? What has been the most helpful?

We usually end up discussing the curriculum broadly (what classes should be required and when) as well as classroom pedagogy and dynamics in quite specific ways. The specific experiences in the classroom that students are still processing—and that they report have impacted their mental health, well-being, and sense of self—often include cold calling;[31] "gunners" or other students who dominate classroom dynamics (and how professors respond);[32] being a Brown or Black student when issues of race are discussed (or omitted;[33] and how/whether professors discuss current events.[34] In a small way, I hope that moving these discussions from private ones between students to the broader classroom, into a required class, a class about what the profession has been and could be, is part of a broader project of reimagining law school and the profession.[35]

---

a Randomized Experiment, 51 RSCH. IN SCI. EDUC. 233 (2021) ("[F]ormative assessments significantly reduce anxiety in physics and improve academic performance in physics in comparison with traditional teaching.").

31. Kathryne M. Young, *Understanding the Social and Cognitive Process in Law School that Creates Unhealthy Lawyers,* 89 FORDHAM L. REV. 2575, 2590 (2021) ("My interviews suggest that, in addition to being ineffective equalizers of gender dynamics in the classroom, cold calls affect women disproportionately in at least two ways. For one, insofar as they reported their experiences in the first half of their first 1L semester, only 15–20 percent of students described extreme trepidation about cold calls. However, of those students, all but one were women, and all but one of these women were nonwhite."); *see also* Elizabeth Bodamer, *Do I Belong Here? Examining Perceived Experiences of Bias, Stereotype Concerns, and Sense of Belonging in U.S. Law Schools*, 69 J. LEG. EDUC. 455, 457 (2020) ("[M]inoritized students—particularly women of color— must contend with marginalizing perceptions and concerns as they navigate through law school and negotiate their sense of belonging.").

32. *See, e.g.*, Thea Johnson, *Taking up Space in the Criminal Law Classroom*, in INTEGRATING DOCTRINE AND DIVERSITY: INCLUSION AND EQUITY IN THE LAW SCHOOL CLASSROOM 179–80 (Nicole Dyszlewski et al. eds., 2021) ("I start the first day of every criminal law class with a plea that students be mindful about whether they are taking up space in the classroom in an effective way.").

33. *See e.g.*, Capers, *supra* note 8, at 31 ("The problem is not that race is absent from the classroom. It is that the whiteness of the curriculum goes unsaid and unremarked upon.")

34. *See, e.g.*, Young, *supra* note 31 (discussing disconnect between what students expected their professors to talk about and the reality, including student expectations of discussions about current events with regard to the intersection of race and the law).

35. I am in debt to those who are braver and bolder in their reimagining, and who push me forward, including Prof. Bennett Capers, who writes "My hope is that law schools will have the courage and audacity to reimagine themselves as a different kind of white space—a blank page, a tabula rasa—and to untether themselves from so much that weighs them down. That they will reinvent themselves from the bottom up in a way that is cosmopolitan and then some, as a place where intellectual curiosity thrives, where change and challenge are celebrated, where education itself is a practice of freedom, and where there is no need to tout inclusivity, because everyone already belongs." Capers, *supra* note 8, at 57–58.

Conclusion

A course in Professional Responsibility should be an opportunity for students to form a clear vision. A vision of their career aspirations and prospective obligations, the type of person they want to be, and even what it might look like to be "an officer of the legal system and a public citizen having special responsibility for the quality of justice."[36] Rather than leaving the semester discouraged, I hope students feel a renewed dedication to being an active member of the profession, to breaking cycles of stress, overwork, and substance abuse that plague so many lawyers, and to paving the way for those behind them.

36. Am. Bar Ass'n, Model Rules of Professional Conduct, Preamble and Scope; I will also note here that not all students want this from a PR class. I've gotten one or two comments on evaluations from students who don't think it's appropriate to discuss personal issues or structural issues like race in PR, and wish I focused only on the MPRE. They are in the minority, but worth noting.

Diversity, Equity, and Inclusion Resources to Foster a More Inclusive Professional Identity: A Select Annotated Bibliography

Jessica Almeida & Alisha Hennen†*

Introduction

This annotated bibliography covers materials and resources on the topics of diversity and inclusion in professional responsibility. Works were chosen based on their benefit to a teaching method that incorporates diversity issues, or as supplementary materials for use beyond the classroom. For instance, the book chapter "The Legal Profession: Bar Admission, History, and Diversity" discusses the history of discrimination in the legal profession. Women, people of color, and other underrepresented groups have struggled to be accepted in law schools, licensed by states, and employed as attorneys. This chapter could be used to give students a deeper understanding of how discrimination is systemic in the legal profession.

Many of the articles and book chapters examine inclusive thinking and cultural competency, not always in the context of teaching professional responsibility, but in ways that could be adapted into a course to promote discussion or encourage reflection. Two of the book chapters tackle inclusive thinking. Both chapters ask students to be aware of their cultural biases and look at problems from all perspectives. Working

---

* Associate Librarian, University of Massachusetts School of Law. Thank you to my colleagues at UMass Law for their support, thank you to my mentor and friend Nicole Dyszlewski for her guidance, thank you to my co-author Alisha Hennen for being a thoughtful and kind friend, and a huge thanks to Mike, Makayla, and Michael for their love and support.

† Research & Instructional Librarian, Mitchell Hamline School of Law. Thank you to my co-author Jessica Almeida for her patience and diligence, thank you to my colleagues at the Warren E. Burger Library, thank you to Nicole Dyszlewski for being a thoughtful colleague and friend, and thank you to my family for all the love they give.

through the steps for inclusive thinking and discussing real-world examples will transition students into the profession with a better understanding of how to include all voices and perspectives.

Cultural competence in professional responsibility is the core of many works highlighted here. In "Lawyers Beware: You Are What You Post," the author promotes being aware and mindful of diverse audiences before posting to social media. In the book chapter "Five Habits for Cross-Cultural Lawyering," the authors challenge lawyers to "develop awareness, knowledge, and skills that enhance the lawyers' and clients' capacities to form meaningful relationships and to communicate accurately." [1]

Lastly, we examine innovative teaching methods and an open source resource to encourage educators to explore and consider incorporating these ideas into their classrooms. For example, in "Teaching Professional Responsibility through Theater," professors asked students to produce a play that examines ethical issues in real-life cases while organically addressing issues of race and injustice. In "Teaching Diversity Skills in Law School," the author discusses how to incorporate diversity issues throughout a law school class like professional responsibility. "We Are All on the Journey: Transforming Antagonistic Spaces in Law School Classrooms" uses storytelling as a way to include diverse voices in the professional responsibility classroom. The author also suggests the use of interview and reflection to contemplate legal ethical issues. We've also included a free open access resource, the ABA Toolkit, to make your class resources more accessible, and make your class more equitable and inclusive.

Articles

Jan L. Jacobowitz, *Lawyers Beware: You Are What You Post—The Case for Integrating Cultural Competence, Legal Ethics, and Social Media*, 17 SMU Science & Technology Law Review 541 (2014).

> In this article, Jan Jacobwitz examines the inappropriate use of social media by legal professionals, which can lead to disciplinary actions and sanctions, and describes how lawyers should actively work toward cultural competency and awareness when using social media. To begin, Jacobwitz defines cultural awareness and competency, discusses research on the stages of cultural competence, and how progression is measured. The author then looks at the perception of lawyers in pop culture and scholarly research to define the culture of the legal profession. This definition includes "normative values of analytical thinking, confidentiality and respect" (561), which is found to be in opposition to the culture of social media. The article gives a variety of examples of inappropriate use of social media, including public defenders using de-

1. Sue Bryant & Jean Koh Peters, *Five Habits for Cross-Cultural Lawyering, in* Race, Culture, Psychology & Law (Kimberly Holt Barrett & William H. George eds., 2005).

rogatory language when discussing their clients in a blog post and a judge removed from the bench for biased comments about people of color and the LGBTQ+ community on an online message board. The article finishes with a discussion of the International Bar Association's six principles of online cultural competence in the legal profession. The author concludes by encouraging legal professionals to be more aware and mindful of ethical rules and cultural differences before posting on social media.

Lois R. Lupica, *Professional Responsibility Redesigned: Sparking a Dialogue Between Students and the Bar*, 29 JOURNAL OF THE LEGAL PROFESSION 71 (2005).

In this article, Professor Lupica redesigns her professional responsibility class to include diverse voices from the legal profession. Students are challenged to present and discuss a variety of ethical topics over the course of the semester. In conjunction, Lupica invites guest speakers from the local bar to talk about how they work through those same ethical dilemmas in practice.

Natasha Martin, *Role, Identity, and Lawyering: Empowering Professional Responsibility*, 3 CALIFORNIA LAW REVIEW CIRCUIT 44 (2012).

In this article, Professor Martin details how she incorporates identity into the traditionally rule-heavy professional responsibility class. Her goal is to take a holistic approach to the subject, which includes showing students how their personal identity and role as a lawyer combine to inform their professional judgment. She details her use of critical reflective exercises throughout the course and illustrates other materials utilized to make students think critically, including the use of films to introduce students to the tensions lawyers face as fiduciaries, officers of the court, and self-interested professionals in what she calls a "self-integrative" approach to professional responsibility (48).

Michael Millemann, Elliott Rauh & Robert Bowie Jr., *Teaching Professional Responsibility through Theater*, 17 HASTINGS RACE & POVERTY LAW JOURNAL 399 (2020).

This article discusses the University of Maryland Carey School of Law's professional responsibility course in which students collaboratively wrote and performed plays that examined legal ethics in real-life cases. By using cases in which the defendant was tried during a time of prevalent race discrimination, the professors and students organically discussed issues of injustice and racial bias while investigating legal realism and critical race theory. Students developed cross-cultural competence through their portrayal of people in the play, empathizing with Black men who were wrongly sent to jail, the crime victims, and their family and friends. Students learned through role playing how irresponsible actions by a lawyer can send innocent people to jail and affect the lives of people in their community.

Spencer Rand, *Social Justice as a Professional Duty: Effectively Meeting Law Student Demand for Social Justice by Teaching Social Justice as a Professional Competency*, 87 UNIVERSITY OF CINCINNATI LAW REVIEW 77 (2018).

Citing the Preamble to the ABA Model Rules of Professional Conduct and Rule 6.1, the author argues that social justice should be taught throughout the law school curriculum to develop lawyers who give power to the powerless. As part of this curriculum, students create their own social justice credo that cultivates their professional identity. The formation of law students through a curriculum with a social justice lens promotes lawyers who seek to represent marginalized groups and concentrate on delivering basic human needs.

Vernellia R. Randall, *Teaching Diversity Skills in Law School*, 54 St. Louis University Law Journal 795 (2010).

In this article, Professor Vernellia Randall is interviewed about her methods of including diversity skills in her classes. Professor Randall defines diversity skills as "incorporating the outsider's view and perspective into the analysis of the law" (796). She discusses making her students aware of her "diversity conscious pedagogy" (799) and how, through class participation and weekly reflections, she is able to train students to think critically about diversity issues. At the end of the interview, she highlights a variety of diversity assignments for classes in professional responsibility, health law, and more.

Tarra Simmons, *Transcending the Stigma of a Criminal Record: A Proposal to Reform State Bar Character and Fitness Evaluations*, 128 Yale Law Journal 759 (2018–2019).

This article details Tarra Simmons' journey from life as a "formerly justice-involved individual" (760) to becoming an attorney. Simmons overcame many barriers, including addiction and incarceration, to get to law school. Once there, Simmons excelled. However, her bar application was rejected the first time around due to barriers imposed by state character and fitness evaluations. Simmons argues that state bar associations should use a "conditional approval process" (762) to let potential law students know whether their state bar intends to admit them prior to the start of law school.

Palma Joy Strand, *We Are All on the Journey: Transforming Antagonistic Spaces in Law School Classrooms*, 67 Journal of Legal Education 176 (2017).

In this article, Professor Strand discusses her work on equity and inclusion in the law school classroom, including some specific teaching strategies for integrating equity and inclusion into "regular" doctrinal classes. Strand's thesis is that there are tangible ways to "counter antagonistic space in law schools for students from traditionally underrepresented groups and that concurrently stretch students across the board" (177). This includes the power of using stories[2] that can help deepen diversity into inclusivity and belonging by illustrating the value of others' experiences and stories as well as affirming the value of the students' own stories and experiences. Strand incorporated storytelling fundamentals in her professional responsibility class by including an

2. *See* Chimamanda Adichie, *The Danger of a Single Story*, TED.com (Oct. 2009), https://www.ted.com/talks/chimamanda_ngozi_adichie_the_danger_of_a_single_story.

assignment tasking students to interview a practicing attorney and ask about ethical challenges they have encountered in practice. Students were also asked to write a reflection paper about the experience. Strand also discusses how she has formatted their professional responsibility class in a way that introduces students to "inequities and isms and their systemic nature" (191).

Books/Book Chapters

Sue Bryant & Jean Koh Peters, *Five Habits for Cross-Cultural Lawyering, in* Race, Culture, Psychology & Law (Kimberly Holt Barrett & William H. George eds., 2005).

Based on a 2001 law review article[3] written by one of the authors, this book chapter introduces lawyers to five habits that help "engage in effective, accurate cross-cultural communication" (47). The authors discuss how culture plays a part in communication and how through establishing trust, accurate understanding, and conceptualizing facts, lawyers can work through cultural misunderstandings to determine the best legal strategy for the client. The chapter then delves into the five specific habits: awareness of cultural similarities and differences, analyzing the similarities and differences in regard to the legal system, identifying alternative interpretations based on culture, working on culturally communicating with your client, and proactively eliminating bias. Incorporating these habits can help students become more effective communicators, aiding in the development of their professional identity.

Derrick Bell, Ethical Ambition: Living a Life of Meaning and Worth (2002).

This book, written by the late prominent lawyer, law professor, and activist, Derrick Bell, discusses his professional journey and provides insight into how others can achieve success while maintaining their ethical convictions. Bell's goal with this work is to "inspire and encourage people, whatever their color or status, to achieve their full potential while simultaneously affirming for them and with them that the road they travel to success is often filled with barriers" (15). Along the way, Bell highlights the benefits of making honorable choices and demonstrates how it takes diligent effort, with the foundation of good intentions, to succeed in the pursuit of ethical ambition. These themes lend themselves well to a professional responsibility course and this title could be a good supplemental text.

Paul A. Haskins & Arin N. Reeves, *Inclusive Thinking: Essential Professional Value/Powerful Professional Advantage, in* Essential Qualities of the Professional Lawyer (2013).

This book chapter discusses inclusive thinking, the practice of pushing past our cognitive bias, and seeking out diverse perspectives. The chapter begins

3. Susan Bryant, *The Five Habits: Building Cross-Culture Competence in Lawyers*, 8 Clinical L. Rev. 33 (2001).

with a definition of inclusive thinking, gives examples of why it is important, and how it works. Through the use of fables and real-world examples, the author tackles the challenges of thinking inclusively. The chapter concludes with the seven steps to thinking inclusively, including expanding your personal network, identifying all perspectives in problem solving, and creating conflict in your thought process.

Toni Jaeger-Fine, Becoming a Lawyer: Discovering and Defining Your Professional Persona (2019).

This book includes a section on working across boundaries, which discusses "developing cross-cultural competence, understanding generational issues, being aware of the significance of race and gender, appreciating other differences, and recognizing our implicit biases and thinking inclusively" (187). The section contains generational definitions (e.g., boomer vs. millennial), the need for understanding between the generations, and advice for working with individuals from each generation. The author also discusses how being aware of our assumptions and appreciating each other's differences can lead to equivalent opportunities for all. Lastly, the chapter explains implicit bias and gives advice on how to achieve inclusive thinking.

Lisa G. Lerman, Philip G. Schrag & Robert Rubinson, Ethical Problems in the Practice of Law (2020).

Pages 46–64 of this legal ethics textbook include a chapter that details the history of discrimination in the legal profession through a question-and-answer format with examples. For instance, it gives the history of how women were excluded from the profession until the 1970s, when women began to file discrimination lawsuits, and tells the story of Myra Bradwell, who was denied an Illinois license to practice law in 1869. Portions of the chapter also discuss the current climate in the legal profession for women, younger lawyers, people of color, LGBTQ+, and disabled lawyers. It discusses issues of sexual harassment, bullying, discrimination, and gives statistics showing that minoritized groups are underrepresented in the legal profession.

Deborah L. Rhode & David J. Luban, Legal Ethics Stories (2006).

This book contains stories related to ten significant legal ethics rulings. Most of the stories are related to reported cases. However, the introduction of the book states that the authors and editors did not choose them because they are "landmark" cases, but because they illustrate "the pressures lawyers face, the ethical decisions they confront, the institutions they work in, and the choices they make" (2). All in all, these cases typify issues that most lawyers confront in one form or other during their careers. Chapters of particular interest include: "Race, Ethics, and the First Amendment: Should a Black Lawyer Represent the Ku Klux Klan? by David B. Wilkins (17–53); "'What's Sex Got To Do With It?': Diversity in the Legal Profession" by Deborah L.

Rhode (233–253); and "*In re Arons*: The Plight of the Unrich in Obtaining Legal Service" by David C. Vladeck (255–286).

Eliza Vorenberg, Cynthia F. Adcock, Eden E. Harrington, Elizabeth Kane, Lisa Bliss, Robin Boyle, Conrad Johnson, Susan Schechter & David Udell, *Teaching the Newly Essential Knowledge, Skills, and Values in a Changing World, in* BUILDING ON BEST PRACTICES: TRANSFORMING LEGAL EDUCATION IN A CHANGING WORLD (2015).

This comprehensive book chapter covers a wide variety of topics, including professional identity formation, relational skills, and problem solving and conflict resolution. While all of the topics covered could be incorporated in the professional responsibility classroom, the sections most relevant are: "Learning Professional Responsibility" by Clark D. Cunningham (280–296); "Intercultural Effectiveness" by Mary A. Lynch with Robin Boyle, Rhonda Magee & Antoinette Sedillo López (337–359); and "Social Justice Across the Curriculum" by Susan Bryant (360–368).

Websites

Toolkits, Trainings, and Other Resources, AMERICAN BAR ASSOCIATION, https://www.americanbar.org/groups/diversity/resources/toolkits/.

This collection, assembled by the American Bar Association, provides a variety of diversity, equity, and inclusion resources. The website has materials to help educate lawyers on the barriers underrepresented communities face (e.g., the 21-day Habit Building Challenges) and materials to help institutions develop meaningful conversations around obstacles in the workplace for women, people of color, and the LGBTQ+ communities (e.g., the Black Lawyers in America Toolkit, The Guided Conversation Project, and How to Be an Ally). The toolkit also includes the Harvard Implicit Bias Test and implicit bias training videos for use in the classroom.

Videos

Minnesota Journal of Law & Inequality, *Preventing Bias with the Model Rules of Professional Conduct: An Interview with Professor Jon J. Lee*, YOUTUBE (Dec. 6, 2021), https://www.youtube.com/watch?v=fRnVdD-NwXM.

Professor Jon J. Lee discusses his scholarship around state rules regulating the sanctions of attorneys in the area of harassment and discrimination.[4] Professor Lee gives a brief history of Model Rule 8.4, which outlines violations of professional misconduct and the fit to practice provision. He discusses the construction and scope of Model Rule 8.4(g) as well as the risks of not adopt-

4. Jon J. Lee, *Catching Unfitness*, 34 GEO. J. LEGAL ETHICS 355 (2021).

ing the rule. Rule 8.4(g) aims to curb incidents of bias, harassment, and discrimination in the practice of law. Lee also discusses the history of public versus private sanctions and the lack of transparency in the grievance process, including the absence of protections for reporters.

Part IV

Integrating Doctrine and Diversity in the Second and Third Year Curriculum

Section 1

Administrative Law

Teaching the Americans with Disabilities Act's Constitutionality without Othering People with Disabilities

*Katherine A. Macfarlane**

Introduction

The Americans with Disabilities Act (ADA) is taught across the law school curriculum, appearing in Federal Courts, Constitutional Law, Civil Rights Litigation, and Disability Law classes. This essay focuses on how the ADA's constitutionality arises in federal courts and Constitutional Law, where students read *Alabama v. Garrett*[1] and *Tennessee v. Lane*[2] in the context of Eleventh Amendment immunity. *Garrett* and *Lane* discuss disability as though it affects people other than those who are reading the cases. But people with disabilities represent twenty-five percent of the U.S. population.[3] There are disabled lawyers, judges, law professors, and law students. The COVID-19 pandemic has only increased the number of disabled Americans—people with Long COVID are people with disabilities who need accommodations in higher education and at work. Disability and the ADA impact how our students learn and the shape their careers will take.

This essay explores how to teach the ADA's constitutionality without sidestepping how *Garrett* and *Lane* impact the lives of people with disabilities—including the people with disabilities in your classroom. The essay begins by describing how to lead a discussion about disability in classes in which *Garrett* and *Lane* are taught. Next, it

* Associate Professor and Director, Disability Law and Policy Program, Syracuse University College of Law..

1. Bd. of Trustees of Univ. of Alabama v. Garrett, 531 U.S. 356 (2001).

2. Tennessee v. Lane, 541 U.S. 509 (2004).

3. Ctrs. for Disease Control and Prevention, *Disability Impacts All of Us* (Oct. 28, 2022), https://www.cdc.gov/ncbddd/disabilityandhealth/infographic-disability-impacts-all.html (last visited Jan. 6, 2023).

reviews the ADA's history and purpose. It then describes the importance of *Garrett* and *Lane* to the development of abrogation doctrine and the everyday lives of people with disabilities, including disabled law students and lawyers. The essay is informed by my experience teaching Federal Courts and Constitutional Law, and my experience as a law student with disabilities.

Introducing Disability While Teaching the ADA

Though *Garrett* and *Lane* are cases that address Congress's ability to overcome Eleventh Amendment immunity, they are also cases that dictate which aspects of public life are accessible to people with disabilities. Class discussions of *Garrett* and *Lane* should confront rather than avoid disability.

Before my students jump into the law of *Garrett* and *Lane*, I offer some guiding principles and background information to shape our discussion. First, I explain that people with disabilities prefer to be called "disabled people" or "people with disabilities." "Differently-abled," "handicapped," and "special needs" are disfavored terms.[4] Similarly, George Lane is a "wheelchair user," not someone who is "wheelchair bound." Wheelchairs create mobility and access, not confinement.

I share information about reclaimed language, including the disabled community's use of the word "crip." I encourage students to explore #CriptheVote on Twitter and the stereotype-busting documentary *Crip Camp*.[5] I also explain that disability is underclaimed, and hardly ever faked.[6]

With respect to the ADA itself, I recount the incredible activism of people with disabilities that led to the ADA's passage.[7] I explain that the ADA's definition of disability is purposefully broad and protects individuals who are paraplegic wheelchair users like George Lane, as well as those with invisible disabilities like Lupus. I also introduce students to the ADA's reasonable accommodation principle, and the limits on a covered entity's obligation to provide accommodations. Since the beginning of the COVID-19 pandemic, I have used work-from-home accommodations for people who

---

4. The National Center on Disability and Journalism's Disability Language Style Guide is an excellent resource regarding language used to describe disability. *See* NAT'L CTR. ON DISABILITY & JOURNALISM, DISABILITY LANGUAGE STYLE GUIDE (rev. Aug. 2021), https://ncdj.org/style-guide/.

5. CRIP CAMP: A DISABILITY REVOLUTION (Netflix 2020).

6. Professor Doron Dorfman has described how American society suffers from a moral panic surrounding the faking of disability, "the fear of the disability con." This (unfounded) fear leads to "[t]he second-guessing of a person's disability and of that person's need for an accommodation," and forces disabled people to constantly prove that they are disabled. Doron Dorfman, *Fear of the Disability Con: Perceptions of Fraud and Special Rights Discourse*, 53 L. & SOC'Y REV. 1051 (2019). Your students may have had their disabilities questioned in connection with attempts to obtain accommodations.

7. Notable examples of disabled activism include the 1990 Capital Crawl, staged when the ADA's passage was in jeopardy, and the 504 Sit-in, held in 1977, which led to long-awaited regulations to ensure that the Rehabilitation Act of 1973 could be enforced.

are high-risk for serious death or illness from COVID-19 as a quintessential example of a reasonable accommodation.

Finally, I share how disability law arises in practice, and the importance of having people with disabilities represented in the practice of law. I tell my students that I am a person with disabilities who received accommodations in law school and in practice, and that accommodations ensure equality, not unfair advantages.[8]

The Americans with Disabilities Act

The ADA,[9] passed in 1990, was the culmination of decades of disability rights activism focused on employment, education, access to public and private buildings, and independent living.[10] The ADA follows the social model of disability, which treats disability as a social construct created by barriers that must be removed to provide people with disabilities full access to public life.

Though the ADA was not the first federal civil rights statute to offer legal protection to people with disabilities, it was necessary to fill gaps created by previous laws. For example, the 1968 Architectural Barriers Act required only new public buildings or buildings renovated with federal funds to be rendered accessible.[11] The Rehabilitation Act of 1973 prohibited disability discrimination, but only in programs or activities receiving federal funding.[12] An attempt to add disability discrimination to the conduct prohibited by the Civil Rights Act of 1964 failed.[13]

The ADA is radical, culture-shifting legislation, "necessary to end disabled Americans' second-class citizenship."[14] The ADA's key titles prohibit disability discrimination in employment (Title I), public services (Title II), and public accommodations (Title III). During hearings on the ADA, the Senate heard testimony about how disabled Americans were significantly poorer than other Americans.[15] Title I, which creates opportunities for gainful employment and financial independence, is key to ending disabled poverty.

---

8. *See, e.g.*, Katherine Macfarlane, *Testing Accommodations Are Not a Gift of Extra Time*, Ms. JD (Jan. 10, 2019), https://ms-jd.org/blog/article/testing-accommodationsare-not-a-gift-of-extra-time.

9. 42 U.S.C. §§ 12101–12213.

10. Kim E. Nielson, A Disability History of the United States 161–63 (2012).

11. *Id.* at 165.

12. 29 U.S.C. § 794(a).

13. Nielson, *supra* note 10, at 166.

14. Katherine A. Macfarlane, *Disability Without Documentation*, 90 Fordham L. Rev. 59, 64 (2021).

15. Michael Ashley Stein, *From Crippled to Disabled: The Legal Empowerment of Americans with Disabilities.*, 43 Emory L.J. 245, 248 (1994) (reviewing Joseph P. Shapiro, No Pity: People with Disabilities Forging A New Civil Rights Movement (1993)) (citing *Guaranteed Job Opportunity Act: Joint Hearing on S. 777 Before the Subcomm. on Employment and Productivity and the Subcomm. on the Handicapped of the Senate Comm. on Labor and Human Resources*, 100th Cong., 9 (1987), *noted in* S. Rep. No. 101-116 (1989) *and* H.R. Rep. No. 101-485 at 31 (1990)).

It took three years to negotiate the ADA's ultimate language,[16] and required concessions and compromise. For example, Title III's prohibition on discrimination in public accommodation reaches places that individuals visit to obtain basic essentials, but also covers those places people visit "to enhance the quality of their lives," like restaurants, hotels, and movie theaters. Therefore, Title III's reach is broad and has "an enormously important role in the integration of individuals with disabilities into society."[17] But in exchange, Title III remedies are limited to injunctive relief—a disabled person denied entry to a restaurant, for example, cannot sue for damages.

Teaching the ADA requires teaching both its promise and its unfulfilled potential. Even after the passage of the American with Disabilities Act Amendments Act (ADAAA) in 2008, which "was intended to reverse the effects of several Supreme Court decisions that limited the coverage of the ADA and to broaden the coverage of the ADA,"[18] the ADA is underenforced. Disabled people remain a disadvantaged group.

How the Outcomes in *Garrett* and *Lane* Impact People with Disabilities

Garrett and *Lane*, which address the constitutionality of Title I and Title II of the ADA, respectively, are part of a series of Supreme Court decisions limiting Congress's ability to pass civil rights legislation. Soon after its passage, the 1964 Civil Rights Act was challenged and then upheld as a valid exercise of Congress's Commerce Clause Power,[19] but by 2000, the Court held that Congress could not rely on the Commerce Clause to justify the Violence Against Women Act's civil rights remedy.[20] Just as it was limiting Congress's Commerce Clause power to pass civil rights legislation, the Court also restricted Congress's ability to pass legislation authorizing suits for damages against the states. In *Seminole Tribe v. Florida*, it held that Congress could not abrogate the states' Eleventh Amendment immunity by relying upon Article I powers.[21] Congress could, however, authorize suits against the states through Fourteenth Amendment legislation. But the Court curtailed Congress's Fourteenth Amendment power in *City of Boerne v. Flores*, holding that legislation passed pursuant to the Fourteenth

16. Chai R. Feldblum, *Medical Examinations and Inquiries Under the Americans with Disabilities Act: A View from the Inside*, 64 Temp. L. Rev. 521, 523–31 (1991).

17. Ruth Colker, *ADA Title III: A Fragile Compromise*, 21 Berkeley J. Emp. & Lab. L. 377, 377 (2000).

18. Stacy A. Hickox, *The Underwhelming Impact of the Americans with Disabilities Act Amendments Act*, 40 U. Balt. L. Rev. 419, 421 (2011).

19. *See, e.g.*, Heart of Atlanta Motel, Inc. v. United States, 379 U.S. 241 (1964) (holding that Title II of the 1964 Civil Rights Act, which prohibits discrimination on the basis of "race, color, religion, or national origin" in places of public accommodation, is constitutional).

20. United States v. Morrison, 529 U.S. 598 (2000). *Morrison* also held that the Fourteenth Amendment only authorizes legislation targeting state action, and would not save VAWA's civil remedy provision, which targeted private individuals.

21. Seminole Tribe of Fla. v. Fla., 517 U.S. 44 (1996).

Amendment must deter or remedy constitutional violations but cannot substantively change governing law.[22] Legislation is "substantive in operation" if it lacks a congruence and proportionality between "the injury to be prevented or remedied and the means adopted to that end."[23] Consequently, civil rights legislation like the ADA—which authorizes civil rights suits against the states—faces significant obstacles.

Title I of the ADA prohibits both private and state employers from discriminating on the basis of disability. The ADA also requires employers to make reasonable accommodations for its disabled employees unless the accommodations would create an undue burden. The failure to provide a reasonable accommodation is disability discrimination. Title I authorizes suits for damages against the states to remedy disability discrimination. In *Alabama v. Garrett*, the Court applied the congruence and proportionality test to hold that Title I's application to state employment was unconstitutional.[24]

In 1994, Patricia Garrett was diagnosed with breast cancer, and took leave from her work as Director of Nursing in the University of Alabama Birmingham Hospital's OB/Gyn/Neonatal Services to receive treatment. When she returned in 1995, she was demoted to a lower-paying position. Consider the impact of a salary cut to individuals recovering from serious health issues—they likely need every cent for medical expenses and a pay cut could jeopardize their financial security.

In applying *City of Boerne*, the *Garrett* Court first identified what kind of disability discrimination violates the Fourteenth Amendment—that is, "the scope of the constitutional right at issue." Under the Equal Protection Clause, disability discrimination is subject only to rational basis review. In other words, disability discrimination is unconstitutional only if it is irrational.

Next, the Court held that Congress had not identified a pattern and practice of irrational disability discrimination by the states, as its findings pertained mostly to private discrimination. The Court noted that Congress found that "some 43,000,000 Americans have one or more physical or mental disabilities," and that in 1990, "the States alone employed more than 4.5 million people."[25] According to the Court, it was noteworthy, "given these large numbers, [that] Congress assembled only such minimal evidence of unconstitutional state discrimination in employment against the disabled."[26]

The dissent described the record differently, noting that Congress identified "massive, society-wide discrimination."[27]

---

22. City of Boerne v. Flores, 521 U.S. 507 (1997).

23. *Id.* at 519–20.

24. Bd. of Trustees of Univ. of Alabama v. Garrett, 531 U.S. 356 (2001). Because employment is a "quintessentially economic activity that is almost certain, in the aggregate, to affect interstate commerce substantially," Title I's application to private employers is likely constitutional. Calvin Massey, *Two Zones of Prophylaxis: The Scope of the Fourteenth Amendment Enforcement Power*, 76 Geo. Wash. L. Rev. 1, 26–27 (2007).

25. Garrett, 531 U.S. at 370.

26. *Id.*

27. *Id.* at 377–78 (Breyer, J. dissenting).

> In addition to the information presented at 13 congressional hearings and its own prior experience gathered over 40 years during which it contemplated and enacted considerable similar legislation, Congress created a special task force to assess the need for comprehensive legislation.... [which] held hearings in every State, attended by more than 30,000 people, including thousands who had experienced discrimination firsthand.[28]

Congress, the dissent argued, found that "'[t]wo-thirds of all disabled Americans between the age of 16 and 64 [were] not working at all,' even though a large majority wanted to, and were able to, work productively."[29] Their unemployment "flowed in significant part from 'stereotypic assumptions' and 'purposeful unequal treatment.'"[30]

The *Garrett* majority held Congress to an impossible standard: identify disability discrimination in the very settings that have excluded disabled people.[31]

Justice Kennedy's concurrence also deserves attention. It acknowledged that disability prejudice "rises not from malice or animus alone," but also from "insensitivity" that causes individuals to "guard against people who appear to be different in some respects from ourselves."[32] Similarly, Justice Kennedy explained that it doesn't take historical documentation, but simply "knowledge of our own human instincts," to "teach[] that persons who find it difficult to perform routine functions by reason of some mental or physical impairment might at first seem unsettling to us."[33] In both passages, he distinguishes people with disabilities from "us." Invite your students to question distinctions that exclude people with disabilities from our understanding of who "we" are. Justice Kennedy's perspective also runs counter to the ADA's social model of disability, which does not require nondisabled people to reach enlightenment, but simply requires removal of unnecessary barriers—many of which are concrete as opposed to esoteric.

Garrett had a devastating impact. Without the threat of damages, state employers are less likely to refrain from disability discrimination. If there are no consequences for the failure to accommodate, employees who need accommodations may be fired or quit if they cannot work without accommodations. As you teach *Garrett*, students with disabilities may be realizing in real time that their employment options may be limited. If they choose to work for the state, they may face discrimination for which there is no recourse. *Garrett* weighs heavy on a disabled person's mind.

Just three years after *Garrett*, the constitutionality of Title II of the ADA was before the Court in *Tennessee v. Lane*. Title II provides that people with disabilities cannot

---

28. *Id.*

29. *Id.* at 378.

30. *Id.*

31. *Cf. id.* at 375–76 (Kennedy, J. concurring) (stating that "[i]f the States had been transgressing the Fourteenth Amendment by their mistreatment or lack of concern for those with impairments, one would have expected to find in decisions of the courts of the States and also the courts of the United States extensive litigation and discussion of the constitutional violations").

32. *Id.* at 374 (Kennedy, J. concurring).

33. *Id.* at 374–75.

"be excluded from participation in or be denied the benefits of the services, programs, or activities of a public entity, or be subjected to discrimination by any such entity."[34] "Public entities" for purposes of the ADA are state and local governments.[35]

Plaintiffs George Lane and Beverly Jones, "paraplegics who use[d] wheelchairs for mobility," were "denied access to, and the services of, the state court system by reason of their disabilities."[36] Lane was compelled to answer to criminal charges in a second-floor courtroom located inside a county courthouse without an elevator. For his first appearance, Lane crawled up two flights of stairs to reach the courtroom. For his second, he refused to crawl or be carried, and was arrested and jailed for failing to appear. Jones worked as a court reporter and could not access several county courthouses, losing "both work and an opportunity to participate in the judicial process."[37] Though unstated by the Court, Lane and Jones sued not for literal access, but for dignified access that would not require the assistance of others.

Lane, unlike *Garrett*, pauses to identify the conditions "central" to the ADA's passage, noting that:

> individuals with disabilities are a discrete and insular minority who have been faced with restrictions and limitations, subjected to a history of purposeful unequal treatment, and relegated to a position of political powerlessness in our society, based on characteristics that are beyond the control of such individuals and resulting from stereotypic assumptions not truly indicative of the individual ability of such individuals to participate in, and contribute to, society.[38]

The ADA was designed "to provide a clear and comprehensive national mandate for the elimination of discrimination against individuals with disabilities."[39]

The Court explained that like Title I, Title II sought to remedy Equal Protection Clause violations arising from the states' irrational treatment of people with disabilities. However, Title II went further, protecting against constitutional violations subject to stricter scrutiny, such as violations of the fundamental right to access the courts, protected by the Fourteenth Amendment's Due Process Clause. The *Lane* plaintiffs' inability to participate in the judicial process added due process considerations absent in *Garrett*. Practically, states will find it harder to identify a compelling government interest that justifies the denial of the fundamental right to access the courts than they will in identifying a rational basis for disability discrimination.

Lane, unlike *Garrett*, scours the legislative record, describing how, at the time of the ADA's passage, an astounding 76% of public services and programs were housed in inaccessible state buildings. Title II was enacted "against a backdrop of pervasive unequal

34. 42 U.S.C. § 12132.
35. 42 U.S.C. § 12131.
36. Tennessee v. Lane, 541 U.S. 509, 513 (2004).
37. *Id.* at 514.
38. *Id.* at 516 (quoting 42 U.S.C. § 12101(a)(7)).
39. *Id.* (quoting §§ 12101(b)(1), (b)(4)).

treatment in the administration of state services and programs, including systematic deprivations of fundamental rights."[40] Congress learned of "exclusion of persons with visual impairments and hearing impairments from jury service, failure of state and local governments to provide interpretive services for the hearing impaired, failure to permit the testimony of adults with developmental disabilities in abuse cases, and failure to make courtrooms accessible to witnesses with physical disabilities."[41] In *Lane*, the absence of people with disabilities from public spaces is obvious, and the record constitutionally sufficient.

Lane did not consider Title II's application in each state setting but focused on the more limited question of whether "Congress had the power under § 5 to enforce the constitutional right of access to the courts."[42] It held that the ADA's accommodation remedy was congruent and proportional to the evidence of constitutional violations. And the remedy was not limitless; for example, accommodations that would fundamentally alter the government service provided need not be made. Also, though buildings built or altered after 1992 "require compliance with specific architectural accessibility standards," in older facilities, "for which structural change is likely to be more difficult," a public entity may comply through "less costly measures, including relocating services to alternative, accessible sites and assigning aides to assist persons with disabilities in accessing services."[43] Title II as applied to *Lane*'s facts was constitutional.

When I read *Lane* in law school, it spoke to me, a person with mobility impairments who often needed an elevator. When I teach *Lane*, I celebrate its namesake. George Lane had so much to lose by asserting his civil rights in the context of a criminal prosecution.

Mobility impairments are the most common disability in the U.S. After covering *Lane*'s holding, ask your students about the impact *Lane* has on the practice of law. Because of *Lane*, state courthouses are more likely to be accessible to mobility-impaired jurors, parties, lawyers, courthouse staff, and judges.

Conclusion

When I teach *Garrett* and *Lane* as described herein, I receive a great deal of positive student feedback. Students come to my office hours and share that they are interested in disability law as a result of a family member's or friend's disability. Others disclose their invisible disabilities and share the discrimination they have experienced as students.

The disclosure of disability happens behind closed doors. No matter how pertinent their experience with disability may be to our class discussion, students do not disclose their disabilities in class. Law schools can be ableist spaces,[44] and a great deal of stigma

40. *Id.* at 524.

41. *Id.*

42. *Id.* at 530–31.

43. *Id.*

44. *See, e.g.*, Katie Rose Guest Pryal, Life of the Mind Interrupted: Essays on Mental Health and Disability in Higher Education (2017); Jay Timothy Dolmage, Academic

surrounds testing accommodations. Because professors with disabilities also fear stigma, they too may not publicly identify as disabled. As a result, students with disabilities often have no disabled role models or mentors. Each year, I counsel students with disabilities who have been told by their professors or law school administrators that as a result of their disabilities, they should not practice law. I find those conversations both heartbreaking and taxing as they make me wonder if my colleagues believe that I too do not belong.

As a professor who openly identifies as disabled, I am often the only person students with disabilities feel comfortable speaking to about their disabilities. Every year, I hear from students at my own institution as well as from students around the country. I am honored that they trust me. However, as powerful as my own disclosure may be, learning about disability from nondisabled law professors is just as meaningful. Adapting a lecture about *Garrett* and *Lane* to incorporate discussions about disability enriches the learning experience, but also signals to disabled students that they are seen.

Ableism (2017). I was diagnosed with Rheumatoid Arthritis and related eye disease at 13 months. In law school, my disabilities were invisible. I went to great lengths to ensure that my professors and potential employers would not discover that I was disabled because I feared that they would assume I was ill-suited to the practice of law. I received testing accommodations in the form of five-minute stretching breaks away from my computer. I kept my accommodations to myself, worried that my classmates would assume that my good grades were the result of my (paltry and likely counterproductive) accommodations.

Administrative Law Through a Social Justice Lens

*Natalie M. Chin**

Introduction

Administrative law is deemed the fourth branch of government, which is a new concept to many law students. Government agencies issue regulations that have the force of law in virtually all aspects of society. From issues of immigration,[1] abortion,[2] disability,[3]

* Associate Professor of Law and Co-Director, Disability and Aging Justice Clinic, City University of New York School of Law. Special thank you to Sarah Lamdan for her helpful feedback on this chapter and constant guidance, support, and positivity as a fellow administrative law colleague. Gratitude to my CUNY law students who never cease to impress me with their tenacity to think critically about the law.

1. *See, e.g.*, the Department of Homeland Security (DHS), an agency with a vast regulatory agenda over immigration policy. DHS's administrative powers are further carried out by U.S. Citizenship and Immigration Services, U.S. Customs and Border Protection, and the U.S. Immigration and Customs Enforcement through the issuance of regulations and the execution of other regulatory powers.

2. *See, e.g.*, *Protecting Access to Reproductive Healthcare Services*, Exec. Order No. 14,076, 87 Fed. Reg. 42,053 (July 8, 2022), *Securing Access to Reproductive and Other Healthcare Service,* Exec. Order No. 14,076, 87 Fed. Reg. 49505 (Aug. 3, 2022) (President Biden implemented two Executive Orders within weeks following the *Dobbs* decision, directing the Department of Health and Human Services to take measures protect access to reproductive rights and health care).

3. *See, e.g.*, Jasmine E. Harris, *Processing Disability*, 64 Am. U. L. Rev. 457 (2015) (discussing the outsized role of administrative adjudications in perpetuating stigma against people with disabilities in the areas of guardianship, special education, civil commitment, and Social Security).

and LGBTQ+ rights[4] to the food we eat[5] and internet speed and access,[6] virtually no part of U.S. society is unaffected by administrative regulations. Despite, or possibly because of, the power of the administrative state, scholars have long warned that there would be assaults on this fourth branch. These efforts, as most recently seen in *West Virginia v. EPA*,[7] aim to reduce the power and legitimacy of administrative agencies, referred to as "antiadministrativism" by Gillian Metzger.[8]

Despite its impact on social, racial, and economic justice, and the magnitude of the administrative state, administrative law is not considered a sexy class. The subject often elicits grunts and exasperation from many students who view the topic as dry and technical when compared against United States Supreme Court and other pivotal federal court rulings that can change the course of history, as we have most recently witnessed in *Dobbs v. Jackson Women's Health Organization*.[9] The consequences of *Dobbs*, the Supreme Court decision overturning *Roe v. Wade* and *Planned Parenthood v. Casey*, were immediately apparent, dramatically curtailing reproductive rights in an instant. Administrative law cases that tend to grapple with less politically visible issues such as statutory interpretation, separation of powers doctrine, and the procedural requirements of rulemaking and adjudication are less apparent in their impact.

This difference is noticeable when comparing the *Dobbs* decision to *West Virginia v. EPA*,[10] an administrative law case decided by the Supreme Court just six days after the high-profile abortion decision. The 6–3 opinion in *West Virginia* from the conservative majority garnered much less attention outside administrative scholar and pundit circles despite the potentially consequential impact of the decision on the ability of administrative agencies to effectively and aggressively address climate change. As one

---

4. *See, e.g.*, Advancing Equality for Lesbian, Gay, Bisexual, Transgender, Queer, and Intersex Individuals, Exec. Order No. 14,075, 87 Fed. Reg. 37189 (June 15, 2022); U.S. Dep't of Health and Human Services, Office for Civil Rights, HHS Notice and Guidance on Gender Affirming Care, Civil Rights, and Patient Privacy, Mar. 2, 2022, https://www.hhs.gov/sites/default/files/hhs-ocr-notice-and-guidance-gender-affirming-care.pdf; Margot Sanger-Katz & Noah Weiland, *Trump Administration Erases Transgender Civil Rights Protections in Health Care*, N.Y. Times (Sept. 28, 2021), https://www.nytimes.com/2020/06/12/us/politics/trump-transgender-rights.html.

5. *See, e.g.*, *Marketplace: The Uncertain Hour, Peanut Butter Grandma Goes to Washington*, https://www.marketplace.org/shows/the-uncertain-hour/s02-1-peanut-butter-grandma-goes-washington/ (Season 2, episode 1) (a three-part podcast series that details the years-long administrative process of the Food and Drug Administration to finalize rules that regulated the ingredients of peanut butter).

6. *See, e.g.*, Cong. Rsch. Serv., Net Neutrality Law: An Overview, R46973, May 27, 2002, https://crsreports.congress.gov/product/pdf/R/R46973 (providing an overview of Federal Communication Commission's actions in regulating broadband internet access service).

7. 142 S. Ct. 2587 (2022) (invoking the major questions doctrine to limit the Environmental Protection Agency's power to regulate carbon dioxide, a pollutant that hastens climate change).

8. Gillian E. Metzger, *1930s Redux: The Administrative State Under Siege*, 131 Harv. L. Rev. 1 (2017).

9. Dobbs v. Jackson Women's Health Org., 142 S. Ct. 2228 (2022).

10. West Virginia v. EPA, 142 S. Ct. 2587 (2022).

scholar noted, *West Virginia* is a blow to "democratic constitutionalism"—a decision that "str[ikes] at the heart of government agencies' ability to protect the public."[11]

West Virginia v. EPA directly hamstrings the power of administrative agencies to regulate greenhouse gas emission—a primary driver of climate change. By embracing a more robust application of the "major question" doctrine, which provides that "clear congressional authorization"[12] is required "to assign to an agency decisions of vast economic and political significance,"[13] the Supreme Court rejected the authority delegated to the Environmental Protection Agency (EPA) to adopt major regulatory policies to cap the carbon dioxide emissions of power plants.[14] The Court concluded that Congress did not grant EPA with an "unheralded power"[15] to "devise carbon emissions caps based on a generation shifting approach" (regulation that shifts electricity generation from carbon dioxide-heavy methods like burning coal to methods that produce less greenhouse gas). The Court further reasoned that decisions of such "magnitude and consequence" did not belong to administrative agencies, but to Congress.[16]

In a scathing dissent, Justice Kagan wrote:

> Today the Court strips the Environmental Protection Agency (EPA) of the power Congress gave it to respond to 'the most pressing environmental challenge of our time'.... The stakes here are high. Yet the Court today prevents congressionally authorized agency action to curb power plants' carbon dioxide emissions. The Court appoints itself—instead of Congress or the expert agency—the decision-maker on climate policy. I cannot think of many things more frightening.[17]

The immediate decision may not seem very impactful, focusing on regulatory acronyms and jargon like BSER (Best System of Emissions Reduction) and "generation shifting," but the ripple effects of *West Virginia* v. *EPA* are anticipated. In the long term, the *West Virginia* decision might put agencies' efforts to advance health and safety regulations that have a broad economic and political impact at risk. *West Virginia* encompasses "political and rhetorical attacks on the legitimacy of administrative agencies ... [and] growing constitutional skepticism among some jurists about the scope of agency authority."[18] Why is understanding the impact of attacks and the growing skepticism of agency authority important? And why should law students care? These challenges facing the administrative state are important (and students should care about them)

---

11. Blake Emerson, *The Real Target of the Supreme Court's EPA Decision*, Mother Jones (Jul. 1, 2022), https://www.motherjones.com/politics/2022/07/supreme-courts-epa-west-virginia-climate-ruling/.

12. *West Virginia*, 142 S. Ct. at 2614.

13. *Id.* at 2605 (internal quotation omitted).

14. *Id.* at 2595.

15. *Id.*

16. *Id.* at 2626.

17. *Id.* at 2626 (quoting Massachusetts v. EPA, 549 U.S. 497, 505 (2002) (internal citation omitted).

18. K. Sabeel Rahman, *Reconstructing the Administrative State in an Era of Economic and Democratic Crisis,* 131 Harv. L. Rev. 1671, 1672 (2018) (citing to Metzger, *supra* note 8, at 4)).

because, at their core, they are about who gets to make the detailed, specific decisions of government that impact our daily lives. Should courts or environmental experts decide how to fight climate change? Should choices about how to protect access to reproductive health care or gender affirming care[19] be made by politicians, courts, or by unelected civil servants working at the Department of Health and Human Services?

Administrative law provides a unique framework for students to examine and critique the weight of administrative power and the role of the judiciary, legislature, and the President of the United States as the head of the executive branch, on the most fundamental aspect of individual lives. This area of law also gives students another way to explore the breadth of agency power over marginalized populations who are often at the center of contentious issues bearing deep political and economic impact.

Students may explore many question that have no clear answer: should Congress be more exacting it its direction when delegating its powers to agencies, as expressed by Justice Roberts in *West Virginia v. EPA*? What are examples of administrative actions that may be viewed as having a deep political and economic impact? What populations are most at risk with Justice Roberts' new definition of the "major questions" doctrine, and why? Can we entrust agencies to evenhandedly carry out their delegated duties with less direction? What does history show us about the role of culture, society, and politics in administrative decision-making and agency outcomes? As I explain to my students, knowledge of black letter law is only part of legal learning. A knowledge of the history and sociopolitical climate to which the black letter law is rooted provides important analysis to grapple with these complex questions.

This chapter begins with a discussion of using history as a foundation to teach administrative law through a social justice framework. Through varied readings and class discussions, students are encouraged to examine and critique the role of the administrative state in upholding and perpetuating racial, economic, and other forms of identity-based subordination. The chapter then moves into an exploration of how to engage law students by making administrative law relatable. This section describes an exercise used in class that encourages students to think more deeply about the role of administrative law in the current sociopolitical climate. In conclusion, this chapter identifies cases that provide students with opportunities to apply a critical social justice lens to the doctrine.

---

19. U.S. Dept. of Health & Human Servs., *HHS Notice and Guidance on Gender Affirming Care, Civil Rights, and Patient Privacy*, https://www.hhs.gov/sites/default/files/hhs-ocr-notice-and-guidance-gender-affirming-care.pdf (Mar. 2, 2022).

Teaching Administrative Law Through a Social Justice Framework

In an effort to provide a social justice framework to my administrative law students that also grounds the doctrine, I start the semester with an examination of the white supremacist roots of administrative law and the mercurial nature of this fourth branch of government. We spend the first classes taking a short journey back in time to better understand the administrative state of today. When students think about administrative law, for example, the Administrative Procedure Act and *Chevron*[20] more immediately come to mind rather than issues of slavery, internment camps, medical racism, and the rights of Indigenous people.

My discussion of historical flashpoints in administrative law is informed by several readings. I start the semester by assigning students *The Racial Roots of the Federal Administrative State* and *An Ethic of Race for Public Administration.*[21] In the first piece, Professor Weinberg discusses the Fugitive Slave Act of 1850 and the Chinese Exclusion Act of 1882 as examples of how racism and xenophobia are the seeds from which the modern administrative state grew. I use Weinberg's piece as a jumping-off point to delve deeper into the Fugitive Slave Act and its relevance to the modern administrative state.

Congress authorized the appointment of "federal commissioners" to carry out police and adjudicatory powers under the Fugitive Slave Act.[22] This delegated congressional power included the right of the commissioners to seize, arrest, and imprison enslaved persons who fled captivity to seek freedom from their enslavers.[23] Commissioners were further authorized to adjudicate the "fugitive" status of the enslaved person, who were prohibited from submitting evidence or giving testimony at the hearing or trial.[24]

As one scholar wrote, "[t]he choice to delegate to federal commissioners created new opportunities to change the administrative process in favor of slave-holding interests," with Congress specifying in the Fugitive Slave Act that commissioners be given $10 to rule in favor of the enslaver and $5 if the ruling resulted in the enslaved person's freedom.[25] As Weinberg noted, the federal administration of the Fugitive Slave Act does not resemble the administrative state of today. Yet, learning about the administration of the Fugitive Slave Act and the Chinese Exclusion Act provides students with an early

---

20. Chevron v. Nat. Res. Def. Council, Inc., 467 U.S. 837 (1984).

21. Johnathan Weinberg, *The Racial Roots of the Federal Administrative State*, 45 ADMIN. & REGUL. L. NEWS 15 (Summer 2020); Jennifer Alexander & Camilla Stivers, *An Ethic of Race for Public Administration*, 32 ADMIN. THEORY & PRAXIS 578 (2010).

22. Scott J. Basinger, *Regulating Slavery: Deck-Stacking and Credible Commitment in the Fugitive Slave Act of 1850*, 19 J. LAW, ECON. & ORG., 307, 309 (2003).

23. The Fugitive Slave Act, ch. 50, 9 Stat. 462 (Sept. 18, 1850); *see also* Jonathan Weinberg, *The Racial Roots of the Federal Administrative State*, YALE J. REGUL. NOTICE & COMMENT (July 20, 2020), https://www.yalejreg.com/nc/the-racial-roots-of-the-federal-administrative-state-by-jonathan-weinberg/.

24. The Fugitive Slave Act, ch. 50, 9 Stat. 462 (Sept. 18, 1850).

25. Basinger, *supra* note 22, at 309.

lesson as to the reach of congressionally delegated power in subordinating individuals to uphold the existing power structure. These lessons are designed to serve as groundwork for class discussions as the semester moves forward.

In the early days of the semester, students also learn about the Freedman's Bureau, an agency established by Congress in 1865 "to assist in the political and social reconstruction of post-war Southern states and to help formerly enslaved people make the transition from slavery to freedom and citizenship."[26] Through a discussion of the Freedman's Bureau, students engage in a lesson in social justice versus presidential will versus congressional will. This examination provides students with an early example of the sometimes-competing interests between the President and Congress in effectuating or stifling social change through agency action.

When Congress passed the bill to create the Freedman's Bureau, for example, President Lincoln signed it into law. But just one month later, President Johnson, a staunch segregationist, became president following Lincoln's assassination. As a result, the success of the Freedman's Bureau waxed and waned, never reaching its intended potential. Johnson vetoed the reauthorization of the Freedman's Bureau with Congress overriding Johnson's veto. However, the Freedman's Bureau was severely underfunded and understaffed by Congress, and persons employed by the Bureau were threatened by the Ku Klux Klan and other white nationalists.

Dismantled after only seven years, the challenges and successes of the Freedman's Bureau are indicative of the violent politics and culture in mid-nineteenth century post-Civil War America. As one source indicated, the "politics of race and Reconstruction" ultimately undermined the Freedman's Bureau, with its dismantling in 1872 at the behest of white Southerners.[27] An examination of the Freedman's Bureau exposes students to the complex relationship between the executive and legislative branches of government. This lesson raises important questions of whether agencies are ever truly independent if Congress holds the purse strings and sociopolitical pressures can overwhelm the best of congressional and agency intentions.

The reading *An Ethic of Race for Public Administration* provides another critique of the administrative state as a system that upholds and perpetuates racial bias and subordination.[28] Two examples highlighted from this article are the Tuskegee experiment and Indian Land Trusts. In teaching about the government's role in the Tuskegee experiment, many students are unaware that the federal government, through the United States Public Health Service, a federal agency charged with advancing public health, carried out and sustained the Tuskegee experiment for 40 years, stopping only

26. *The Freedman Bureau's Records*, National Museum of African American History & Culture, https://nmaahc.si.edu/explore/initiatives/freedmens-bureau-records.

27. Freedman's Bureau, History.com (updated Oct. 3, 2018) https://www.history.com/topics/black-history/freedmens-bureau#section_4. *See also* Ira C. Colby, *The Freedmen's Bureau: From Social Welfare to Segregation* 46 Phylon 219, 229 (1985) (critiquing the Freedman's Bureau as a program that reinforced "segregation as the guiding force for black-white social relations.").

28. Alexander & Stivers, *supra* note 21.

after a whistleblower exposed the government's actions.[29] As a result of the agency's withholding of medical treatment, many men died from syphilis and their family and loved ones were impacted by infection.[30]

Through this reading, we also discuss Eloise Cobell, and the failure of the United States Department of the Interior to distribute trust funds to Indigenous persons for the money that resulted from resources accessed and sold from their leased land, which ended in a billion-dollar settlement by the federal government.[31] We also touch upon the Boldt decision and how state administrative agencies and local politics can stymie judicial outcomes.[32]

Examining the history of administrative law is aimed at providing students with the necessary insight to understand how the systemic structures of white supremacy continue to embed the administrative state, further reinforcing racism, ethnocentrism, heteropatriarchy, economic inequality, and ableism.[33] Further, a goal of starting the semester by incorporating history and narrative voices is to cultivate a space where students can feel safe to identify and explore issues of race, power, and privilege throughout the course.

---

29. *See* Jean Heller, *AP Exposes Tuskegee Experiment Syphilis Study: 50 Years Later*, AP (Jul. 25, 2022), https://apnews.com/article/tuskegee-study-ap-story-investigation-syphilis-53403657e77d76f52df6c2e2892788c9.

30. Tuskegee Univ., *About the USPHS Syphilis Study*, https://www.tuskegee.edu/about-us/centers-of-excellence/bioethics-center/about-the-usphs-syphilis-study (last visited Dec. 16, 2022).

31. *See* Julia Whitty, *Elouise Cobell's Bittersweet Victory*, MOTHER JONES (Dec. 9, 2009), https://www.motherjones.com/politics/2009/12/elouise-cobells-bittersweet-victory/.

32. *See* U.S. v. Washington (Boldt), 384 F. Supp. 312 (W.D. Wash. 1974), *aff'd sub nom.*, Washington v. Wash. State Commercial Passenger Fishing Vessel Ass'n., 443 U.S. 658 (1979). *See, e.g.*, Native Knowledge 360°, *Backlash to Boldt*, Smithsonian National Museum of the American Indian, https://americanindian.si.edu/nk360/pnw-fish-wars/backlash.

33. *See, e.g.*, Milicent Sasu, *HUD's "Mixed-Status" Rule Is the Latest Attack on the Immigrant Community*, THE TORCH—NAT'L IMMIGR. L. CENT. (July 8, 2019), https://www.nilc.org/2019/07/08/huds-mixed-status-rule-is-the-latest-attack-on-the-immigrant-community/; *The Trump Administration's Latest Attack on Transgender People Facing Homelessness*, CENT. AM. PROGRESS (Sept. 3, 2020), https://www.americanprogress.org/article/trump-administrations-latest-attack-transgender-people-facing-homelessness/; Hailey Fuchs, *Trump Attack on Diversity Training Has a Quick and Chilling Effect*, N.Y. TIMES (Oct. 13, 2020), https://www.nytimes.com/2020/10/13/us/politics/trump-diversity-training-race.html; David Weaver, *At Social Security, the deck is stacked against the disabled*, THE HILL (June 16, 2021), https://thehill.com/opinion/finance/558670-at-social-security-the-deck-is-stacked-against-the-disabled/.

Making Administrative Law Relatable to Law Students

In an effort to connect students to the real-life impact of administrative law, I incorporate current events that center administrative law. For one assignment, students examined Trump's midnight regulations[34] and the regulatory changes that Biden made after taking office as the President.[35] Students identified a rule/regulation that was delayed or overturned, or a rule that was passed during the Trump presidency that remained in effect. Students are asked to think through who was most impacted by this rule/regulation and what they thought about this rule/regulation being delayed/overturned/passed.

As students gain more knowledge about what agencies are and what they do, the discussion then leads students to think critically about how agencies relate to social justice work. They are asked to consider the following questions below and write a few paragraphs prior to class, which help frame the class discussion:

1. Can you envision a way that administrative agencies can exercise their duty to protect the public while also being purposeful in how their decisions and practices impact marginalized communities?
2. Can we look to these existing legal structures in administrative law to build social justice, or is administrative law a tool of oppression?[36]

I utilize Slack in class, where students post their thoughts on the assigned question. I then identify several student entries for classroom discussion. This exercise pushes students to think more deeply about the role of administrative law as a tool for social justice or as a system that perpetuates oppression. The discussion provides a space for students to express both perspectives. Through classroom exchanges, students further explore the reality of the administrative state as being complex by design, impacting society in both positive and detrimental ways.

---

34. The Leadership Conference on Civil and Human Rights, *Trump Administration Civil and Human Rights Rollbacks*, https://civilrights.org/trump-rollbacks/#2021.

35. Brookings Inst., *Tracking regulatory changes in the Biden era*, https://www.brookings.edu/interactives/tracking-regulatory-changes-in-the-biden-era/ (last visited Dec. 16, 2022).

36. This question was written by my wonderful colleague, Professor Sarah Lamdan.

Applying a Critical Social Justice Lens to Administrative Law Doctrine

As we move through the semester, students continue to engage the doctrine, revisiting the critiques explored during the first several classes. For example, in *Citizens to Preserve Overton Park v. Volpe*,[37] a case that focuses on the arbitrary and capricious standard, the Secretary of Transportation authorizes the expenditure of federal funds for the construction of a six-lane interstate highway through a public park in Memphis, Tennessee. Students are assigned a supplemental reading, *How Interstate Highways Gutted Communities and Reinforced Segregation*,[38] to balance the legal doctrine with its human impact on marginalized communities and how systemic racism can drive agency actions. I use cases like *Board of Regents State College v. Roth*[39] to teach about protected property and liberty interests under the due process standard, while also engaging students in the civil rights history of this case.

In *Roth*, students recognize, as expressed in Justice Douglas's dissent, that the university's decision should have qualified as a violation of the professor's First Amendment right.[40] This thought process, however, is not as evident without the reading of the *Roth* dissents and understanding the political context under which the case takes place. To supplement this case, and to encourage a deeper analysis of *Roth*, I assign a reading and play an audio recording of a Black student who was expelled from the university following the events that relate to Roth's teaching contract not being reinstated. This reading is called *Black Thursday*.[41]

Chocolate Manufacturers Ass'n of the United States v. Block,[42] a case about the logical outgrowth test, offers an enriching opportunity to engage the class in a robust dis-

---

37. 401 U.S. 402 (1971).

38. Farrell Evans, *How Interstate Highways Gutted Communities—and Reinforced Segregation America's interstate highway system cut through the heart of dozens of urban neighborhoods*, HISTORY.COM (Oct. 20, 2021), https://www.history.com/news/interstate-highway-system-infrastructure-construction-segregation.

39. 408 U.S. 564 (1972). In *Roth*, a state-run university professor, David Roth, claimed that university violated his due process and First Amendment rights after it did not renew his fixed one-year teaching contract. *Id.* Roth was rated by faculty as an "excellent teacher." *Id.* at 579. The university did not renew his teaching contract after he "publicly criticized the administration for suspending an entire group of 94 black students without determining individual guilt." *Id.* Roth also "criticized the university's regime as being authoritarian and autocratic [and] used his classroom to discuss what was being done about the black episode." *Id.*

40. The Supreme Court held that the state university did not violate the procedural due process rights of Roth because he did not have a liberty or property interest in his employment. *Id.* at 578. The Court further determined that "the interest in holding a teaching job at a state university" did not qualify as a free speech right. *Id.*

41. Stephen Kercher, BLACK THURSDAY, http://www.blackthursday.uwosh.edu/index.html (Univ. of Wisconsin-Oshkosh). According to this website, the content "draws substantially from Black Thursday Remembered, a multimedia, interactive exhibition which opened at UW Oshkosh on November 21, 2008."

42. Chocolate Mfrs. Ass'n v. Block, 755 F.2d 1098 (4th Cir. 1985).

cussion about the role of paternalism in rulemaking. While *Chocolate Manufacturers Ass'n of the United States* is about regulations concerning chocolate milk, it raises larger questions as to the extent of the government's reach in policing what the agency refers to as a "healthy and adequate diet"[43] for low-income and poor people who receive federal food subsidies.

In large doctrinal classes, there are challenges in engaging students in conversations around issues of race, power, and privilege. In administrative law, students may question why they are delving into history and learning about the Fugitive Slave Act and the Tuskegee experiment. Students may express nervousness as to how these materials will be tested and how they fit into the class doctrine. Though I may not successfully assuage these fears, I remind students that understanding the history of the law allows for a better understanding of our clients and the systems that successful advocacy may be up against. It also provides a necessary tool for better understanding the modern administrative state.

Students may ask, for example, what *Dobbs* has to do with administrative law? With the overturning of *Roe*, the Food and Drug Administration (FDA) is certain to play an outsized role in reducing barriers to reproductive health services and abortion medication. The swift issuance of Executive Orders by President Biden in an effort to buffer the immediate harm of *Dobbs* on reproductive rights and health care access is a real-time display of the role of the administrative state, its interplay between the judicial and executive branches of government, and how administrative processes can respond to a civil rights crisis.[44]

An understanding of history also allows for a deeper analysis of current political issues and how they may have roots in past administrative law decisions. As an example, the coronavirus pandemic resurfaced one reason why some in the Black community were reticent to accept the COVID vaccination as a safe government response to curb the virus's spread. The central role of government in the decades-long Tuskegee experiment—and the many other instances of government-sanctioned medical racism[45]—embedded a deep mistrust as to the motivation of the government in the implementation of vaccine efforts.[46]

As a final assignment, I ask students to select from a group of three topics provided in the assigned readings: "Disability Rights and the Administrative State, "COVID and the Administrative State," and "The Carceral State." Each topic includes readings that focus on current events as they intersect with an aspect of administrative law. Students are then required to post a comment in Slack as to how the knowledge they learned

43. *Id.* at 1103.

44. *See supra* note 2.

45. *See* Harriet A. Washington, Medical Apartheid: The Dark History of Medical Experimentation on Black Americans from Colonial Times to the Present (2006), for an in-depth examination on medical racism and the role of the federal government.

46. Debbie Elliott, *In Tuskegee, Painful History Shadows Efforts to Vaccinate African Americans*, NPR (Feb. 16, 2021), https://www.npr.org/2021/02/16/967011614/in-tuskegee-painful-history-shadows-efforts-to-vaccinate-african-americans.

throughout the semester impacted their perspective, understanding, or analysis of their chosen readings. This exercise provides students with the opportunity to reflect on how their newly acquired administrative law knowledge can provide an additional layer of critique when examining issues. It further highlights one of the course learning goals—for students to gain a greater understanding of the direct impact of the administrative state on social justice issues.

Conclusion

Layering the study of administrative law with history, engaging students to strengthen their relatability to this doctrine, and prompting students to critique the materials through a social justice lens elevates the study of this subject. As one former administrative law student commented in reflection of a past course:

> I have a better understanding of how our system of administrative law subordinates people based on their race and other classification [sic], [and] how elaborate the system is.... The origins of Administrative Law as a manifestation and concretization of discrimination and racism, though not un-expected [sic], was very eye-opening in just how precisely systemic racism is realized... it has been an education in the multiple layers that the American legal and social system is made up and function.[47]

Incorporating doctrine with teachings on race, class, and privilege draws out the sociopolitical complexity of the materials, giving students a richer learning experience.

47. Eric Page, City University of New York School of Law, student, spring 2022.

Dismantling Discriminatory Zoning: *City of Edmonds v. Oxford House, Inc.*—A Case Study on Defeating City-Imposed Family Composition Mandates

*D.O. Malagrinò**

In integrating issues of federal disability law and administrative law, *City of Edmonds v. Oxford House, Inc.*, 514 U.S. 725 (1995), has broad applicability. In *City of Edmonds*, a zoning code regulation defines "family" for a single-family zone in a manner that excludes a group home for adults recovering from alcoholism and drug addiction. We must never forget that the considerable number of lawsuits seeking to exclude group homes from single-family, residential-use districts attests to the level of fear and prejudice against others,[1] who may need congregant living—those recovering from sub-

---

* Associate Dean for Faculty Research & Development and Professor of Law, Charleston School of Law, Charleston, S.C., and co-author of the casebook LAND USE AND ZONING LAW: PLANNING FOR ACCESSIBLE COMMUNITIES (2d ed. 2022) (with Robin Paul Malloy), which comprehensively integrates issues of accessibility under the Americans with Disabilities Act (ADA) with land use and zoning laws, and systematically addresses the complexities of aging in place and of disability in the context of local land regulation. Thanks are due to Larry Cunningham, Nancy Zisk, Deborah Turkewitz, Zachary A. Porter, and Bates M. Holman for their contributions to this essay.

1. Oxford House-Evergreen v. City of Plainfield, 769 F. Supp. 1329, 1331 (D.N.J. 1991) ("There are few among us who do not have a friend or relative who has suffered the ravages of drugs or alcohol. They are persons who need our compassion and require our support.... [W]hat this matter truly needs is not judicial action, whether it be state or federal, but for the parties to search their consciences, recognize the needs and hopes of the plaintiffs and the concerns and fears of the neighbors, and arrive at an accommodation which serves and enriches all who are involved and affected by it.").

stance addiction,[2] HIV-positive persons,[3] and individuals with mental disabilities,[4] to name a few.[5] In an administrative law course, we learn about land use and zoning laws at about the halfway point, and this case provides a thorough introduction to the police power to regulate land use through lawful zoning and the federal protections against housing discrimination. *City of Edmonds* provides a good introduction to exclusionary zoning laws that try to define which living arrangements qualify as a "family" and to restrict occupancy to only those traditional family arrangements. Law students are sometimes surprised that legal phrases like "single-family" and "residential use" are words used to discriminate; but students also learn that those same phrases are legally ambiguous, and instead can be used as tools to fight those same discriminatory efforts. There is a strong public policy favoring small-group homes within the definition of the term "family," encouraging such group homes to be located in single-family residential areas, treating them as if they constituted traditional families, and opposing any barriers to these goals.[6]

In *City of Edmonds*, a housing policy limited the number of unrelated persons who can live together, which had the effect of excluding group homes from districts zoned for single-family, residential-use only. The Court makes a clear distinction between rules focused on the zoning nature of a neighborhood (single-family homes, for example) from rules that limit total occupancy for public health and safety reasons (addressing the challenges population density presents, for example). Teaching this case in an administrative law course introduces students to this distinction, reveals how

---

2. *E.g.*, Oxford House, Inc. v. Twp. of Cherry Hill, 799 F. Supp. 450, 454 (D.N.J. 1992).

3. Stewart B. McKinney Found., Inc. v. Town Plan & Zoning Comm'n of Town of Fairfield, 790 F. Supp. 1197, 1219 (D. Conn. 1992) ("[R]equiring the plaintiff to apply for a special exception [to operate a HIV group home in a one and two-family residential zone] has a discriminatory impact on HIV-infected persons because it holds the future tenants up to scrutiny in a way that seven unrelated non-HIV-infected persons would not be.").

4. *E.g.*, Macon Assn. for Retarded Citizens v. Macon-Bibb County Planning and Zoning Comm'n, 314 S.E.2d 218 (1984).

5. In *Doe v. Butler*, a group of battered women advanced the argument that a zoning ordinance limiting residency in transitional dwellings to six persons violated the familial-status provisions of the FHA by making the group home for battered women economically infeasible to operate. 892 F.2d 315 (3d Cir. 1989). The court stated, "We cannot discount the possibility that the six-person limit may in fact have a general dampening effect on the ability of women with children to take advantage of transitional dwellings." *Id.* at 324. The court remanded the case to decide this issue. 24 Am. Jur. Proof of Facts 3d 543 (originally published in 1994).

Indeed, many lawyers also suffer from addiction issues; so, from an instructional perspective *City of Edmonds* also provides a platform to discuss professional identity formation and the issue of ableism in the legal profession with your law students.

6. United States v. Scott, 788 F. Supp. 1555, 1561 (D. Kan. 1992) (citing H.R. Rep. No. 100-711, at 23–24 (1988), *as reprinted in* 1988 U.S.C.C.A.N. 2173, 2184, 2185). "As the House Report explains, the [Fair Housing] Act protects against efforts to 'restrict the ability of individuals with handicaps to live in communities.'" *See also* 42 U.S.C. § 3601; Hill v. Cmty. of Damien of Molokai, 1996-NMSC-008, ¶ 16, 121 N.M. 353, 360, 911 P.2d 861, 868; Support Ministries for Persons with AIDS, Inc. v. Vill. of Waterford, 808 F. Supp. 120, 129 (N.D.N.Y.1992).

seemingly neutral zoning laws are indeed discriminatory, and shows students the limits that federal laws, such as the Fair Housing Act,[7] impose on the local zoning power.

Oxford House, Inc.[8] ran a group home in Edmonds, Washington; the facility housed ten to twelve adults recovering from substance abuse addiction. Oxford House, Inc. was a nonprofit organization of more than three hundred private, self-run, single-sex group homes for individuals recovering from substance abuse addiction. The group homes were financially self-supporting, democratically governed, substance free, and immediately expelled any resident who violated its substance-free rules.[9] The home was in a typical single-family residential zone, where the only permitted primary use was as a single-family dwelling. The Edmonds Community Development Code (ECDC) defined a "family" as "an individual or two or more persons related by genetics, adoption or marriage, or a group of five or fewer persons who are not related by genetics, adoption, or marriage...."[10]

The City claimed that the group home violated local zoning regulations because it was in an area zoned for single-family dwellings. The provision governing areas zoned for single-family dwelling units defined "family" as "persons [without regard to number] related by genetics, adoption, or marriage, or a group of five or fewer [unrelated] persons."[11] The City asserted a violation of the zoning provision. The City issued criminal citations to the owner of the house and one resident because Oxford House violated the single-family zoning provision by housing more than five unrelated adults.[12] Oxford House challenged the City's actions, relying on the Fair Housing Act's (FHA) prohibition on discrimination because of disability.[13]

---

7. Texas Dep't of Hous. & Cmty. Affs. v. Inclusive Communities Project, Inc., 576 U.S. 519, 539 (2015). (stating that the Fair Housing Act prohibits exclusionary zoning laws that "unfairly ... exclude minorities from certain neighborhoods without any sufficient justification.").

8. Oxford House, Inc., is a nonprofit corporation "that serves as the umbrella organization of the worldwide network of more than 3,000 individual Oxford Houses" with the goal of facilitating supportive environments for recovering alcohol and drug addicts to "learn or relearn values and responsive behavior ... to assure comfortable sobriety—forever...." OXFORD HOUSE, INC. ANNUAL REPORT FY2021 (Jan. 30, 2021), https://www.oxfordhouse.org/doc/ar2021.pdf. Congressional support of the Oxford House model is reflected in the Federal Anti-Drug Abuse Act, which established state start-up loans for recovery group homes with at least six residents. Oxford House, *History and Accomplishments*, https://www.oxfordhouse.org/oxford_house_history.php. *See* 42 U.S.C. § 300x-25.

9. City of Edmonds v. Washington State Bldg. Code Council, 18 F.3d 802, 803 (9th Cir. 1994), *aff'd sub nom.* City of Edmonds v. Oxford House, Inc., 514 U.S. 725 (1995).

10. *City of Edmonds*, 18 F.3d at 803.

11. City of Edmonds v. Oxford House, Inc., 514 U.S. 725, 728, 115 S. Ct. 1776, 1778–79, 131 L. Ed. 2d 801 (1995); Edmonds Community Development Code (ECDC) § 21.30.010 (1991).

12. City of Edmonds v. Oxford House, Inc., 514 U.S. 725, 729, 115 S. Ct. 1776, 1779, 131 L. Ed. 2d 801 (1995).

13. "Disability" or "handicap," as is expressed in the FHA, covers persons recovering from substance abuse. 42 U.S.C.A. § 3602(h): "Handicap" ... does not include current, illegal use of or addiction to a controlled substance (as defined in section 802 of Title 21)." *Id.* Under Title 21 section 802, the term "addict" refers to "any individual who habitually uses any narcotic drug so as to endanger the public morals, health, safety, or welfare, or who is so far addicted to the use of narcotic drugs as to have lost the power of self-control with reference to his addiction." 21 U.S.C.A. § 802(1). "Persons

The FHA requires "reasonable accommodations" in rules and policies as necessary for disabled persons.[14] The City claimed that the ordinance at issue is exempt from the requirement for reasonable accommodation because the FHA expressly allows "any reasonable local, State, or Federal restrictions regarding the maximum number of occupants permitted to occupy a dwelling."[15] Oxford House replied that the City's zoning provisions are not exempt, and do not make the required reasonable accommodations.[16] The trial court held for the City,[17] the court of appeals reversed,[18] and the Supreme Court took this case[19] to determine whether the City's family-definition rule qualified for this exemption.

The FHA exempts from its requirements generally applicable occupancy limits, like those in the Uniform Housing Code, such as municipal codes or zoning rules that constitute reasonable restrictions on the maximum number of people permitted to occupy a dwelling.[20] The primary policy justification for residential occupancy standards is protecting public health and safety. Overcrowding creates significant problems, such as an inability for residents of a building to exit safely in an emergency, transmission of disease, and other psychological stress associated with living in higher density areas.

---

recovering from a drug or alcohol addiction are considered handicapped for the purposes of the FHA." Holy Ghost Revival Ministries v. City of Marysville, 98 F. Supp. 3d 1153, 1168–69 (W.D. Wash. 2015) (citing Pac. Shores Props., LLC v. City of Newport Beach, 730 F.3d 1142, 1156–57 (9th Cir. 2013)).

14. "It shall be unlawful ... [t]o discriminate in the sale or rental, or otherwise make unavailable or deny, a dwelling to any buyer or renter because of a handicap ... including a refusal to make reasonable accommodations in rules, policies, practices, or services, when such accommodations may be necessary to afford such person equal opportunity to use and enjoy a dwelling...." 42 U.S.C.A. § 3604. "Handicap means, with respect to a person— (1) a physical or mental impairment which substantially limits one or more of such person's major life activities, (2) a record of having such an impairment, or (3) being regarded as having such an impairment, but such term does not include current, illegal use of or addiction to a controlled substance (as defined in section 802 of Title 21)." *Id.* "An accommodation is reasonable when it imposes 'no fundamental alteration in the nature of a program' or 'undue financial and administrative burdens.' Forest City Residential Mgmt., Inc. *ex rel.* Plymouth Square Ltd. Dividend Hous. Ass'n v. Beasley, 71 F. Supp. 3d 715, 728 (E.D. Mich. 2014), *citing* Smith & Lee Assocs., Inc. v. City of Taylor, 102 F.3d 781, 795 (6th Cir.1996).

15. 42 U.S.C.A. § 3607(b)(1).

16. The City of Edmonds rejected Oxford House's request for a "reasonable accommodation" by allowing the group home to remain in the single-family dwelling and alternatively passed a zoning ordinance permitting the group home to use "multifamily and general commercials zones." City of Edmonds v. Oxford House, Inc., 514 U.S. 725, 729–30 (1995).

17. *City of Edmonds*, 514 U.S. at 730 (The "District Court held that ECDC § 21.30.010, defining 'family,' is exempt from the FHA under § 3607(b)(1) as a 'reasonable ... restrictio[n] regarding the maximum number of occupants permitted to occupy a dwelling.'").

18. *Id.* ("The United States Court of Appeals for the Ninth Circuit reversed; holding § 3607(b)(1)'s absolute exemption inapplicable, the Court of Appeals remanded the cases for further consideration of the claims asserted by Oxford House and the United States."). City of Edmonds v. Washington State Bldg. Code Council, 18 F.3d 802, 807 (9th Cir. 1994) ("Many factors must be weighed to determine whether reasonable accommodation under 42 U.S.C. § 3604(f)(3)(B) was achieved.").

19. *City of Edmonds*, 514 U.S. at 730–31.

20. 42 U.S.C.A. § 3607(b)(1) ("Nothing in this subchapter limits the applicability of any reasonable local, State, or Federal restrictions regarding the maximum number of occupants permitted to occupy a dwelling.").

Neighbors are generally concerned about "overcrowding" because of its expected spill-over effects: excessive noise, cramped parking, and traffic congestion. Cities also need to plan for the delivery of utilities and public benefits, like schools, parks, emergency resources, and infrastructure, among others.

The Court held that the City's family-definition rule did not qualify for this exemption. Rules that cap the total number of occupants per dwelling plainly fall within the FHA exemption, but rules designed to protect the family *character* of the neighborhoods do not.[21] The family-definition rules of the City were concerned with family living, not space per occupant; the former rules cannot simply become maximum occupancy restrictions by adding an occupancy cap to the regulation applicable only to unrelated residents. Justice Ginsburg stated in the majority opinion that, "it is curious reasoning indeed that converts a family values preserver into a maximum occupancy restriction once a town adds to a related persons restriction."[22] In other words, the City's argument was that all it had to do is add to the family composition description "and also five or fewer [unrelated] persons" to implicate the exemption. The Court was unconvinced. Hence, the regulation was not exempt from the FHA. As such, the Court remanded for the lower courts to determine, in light of the FHA's prohibition against discrimination based on disability and its requirement of reasonable accommodations, whether the City's single-family definition provided the required reasonable accommodation.

The impact of the decision in *City of Edmonds* was substantial. A state's police power includes the authority to lay out zones or districts wherein "only compatible uses are allowed[,] and incompatible uses are excluded."[23] These restrictions typically: (1) categorize uses and (2) zones in such a way as to designate districts as single-family residential, multiple-family residential, commercial, agricultural, or industrial. For example, reserving land for single-family residences preserves the character of neighborhoods, securing "zones where family values, youth values, and the blessings of quiet seclusion and clean air make the area a sanctuary for people"[24] free from conflicting uses. This case was an important victory for disabled persons because an unfavorable ruling would have allowed municipalities to exclude group living arrangements from

21. *City of Edmonds*, 514 U.S. at 734–35.

22. In footnote eleven of the majority opinion, Justice Ginsburg refers to the Thomas dissent (joined by Scalia and Kennedy), stating "This curious reasoning drives the dissent. If Edmonds allowed only related persons (whatever their number) to dwell in a house in a single-family zone, then the dissent, it appears, would agree that the § 3607(b)(1) exemption is unavailable. But so long as the City introduces a specific number—any number (two will do)—the City can insulate its single-family zone entirely from FHA coverage. The exception-takes-the-rule reading the dissent advances is hardly the 'generous construction' warranted for antidiscrimination prescriptions. *See* Trafficante v. Metropolitan Life Ins. Co., 409 U.S. 205, 212, 93 S. Ct. 364, 368, 34 L.Ed.2d 415 (1972)."

23. Daniel R. Mandelker, Land Use Law § 4.16, pp. 113–14 (3d ed. 1993).

24. *City of Edmonds*, 514 U.S. at 732–33 (quoting Vill. of Belle Terre v. Boraas, 416 U.S. 1, 9 (1974); *see* Moore v. East Cleveland, 431 U.S. 494, 521 (1977) (Burger, C.J., dissenting) (stating the purpose of East Cleveland's single-family zoning ordinance "is the traditional one of preserving certain areas as family residential communities.").

most residential neighborhoods.[25] Although the decision was significant, single-family zoning did not disappear; cities may still maintain single-family ordinances, but must just exhibit a willingness to be flexible and to provide reasonable accommodations where single-family zoning has a disproportionately negative effect on individuals covered by anti-discrimination laws.

Both the Fair Housing Amendments Act (FHAA)[26] and the Americans with Disabilities Act (ADA)[27] prohibit governmental entities from implementing or enforcing housing policies in a discriminatory manner against persons with disabilities. Under the FHAA, it is unlawful to discriminate, or otherwise make unavailable, in the sale or rental of a dwelling because of the disability of "a person residing in or intending to reside in that dwelling after it is sold, rented, or made available."[28] The House Report accompanying the 1998 Amendments to the FHA specifically states that the Act was intended "to prohibit the application of special requirements through land-use regulations, restrictive covenants, and conditional or special use permits that have the effect of limiting the ability of such individuals [disabled persons] to live in the residence of their choice in the community."[29]

Similarly, the ADA provides, "no qualified individual with a disability shall, by reason of such disability, be excluded from participation in or be denied the benefits of the services, programs, or activities of a public entity, or be subject to discrimination by such entity."[30] Both statutes require that "covered entities make reasonable accommodations ... to provide qualified individuals with an equal opportunity to receive benefits from or to participate in programs run by such entities."[31] And, because the statutes are similar, they should be interpreted together.[32]

In *City of Edmonds*, pursuant to the FHAA, Oxford House requested that the City provide a "reasonable accommodation" by permitting it to operate in the single-family zone. The City denied this request, but it did pass an ordinance allowing group homes in multifamily and general commercial zones. The City filed a declaratory judgment

---

25. Matthew J. Cholewa & Dwight H. Merriam, City of Edmonds v. Oxford House, Inc.: *A Victory for Group Homes for the Handicapped*, 5 J. Affordable Hous. & Cmty. Dev. L. 73, 73 (1995).

26. Discrimination under the FHAA includes a refusal to make "reasonable accommodation" for handicapped persons. The FHAA protections apply to city zoning codes. 42 U.S.C. § 3604.

27. Discrimination under the ADA prohibits discrimination "by any [public] entity" against "qualified individual disability, by reason of such disability." 42 U.S.C.A. § 12132. *See* United States v. City of Baltimore, 845 F. Supp. 2d 640, 647–48 (D. Md. 2012) ("Under the ADA and FHA, a public entity such as the City of Baltimore is prohibited from implementing a zoning scheme that treats disabled individuals differently than non-disabled individuals.").

28. 42 U.S.C. § 3604(f)(1).

29. H.R. Rep. No. 100-711, at 24 (1988) *as reprinted in* 1988 U.S.C.C.A.N. 2173, 2185; *see* City of Edmonds v. Oxford House, Inc., 514 U.S. 725, 729–30 (1995).

30. 42 U.S.C. § 12132.

31. Tsombanidis v. West Haven Fire Dept., 352 F.3d 565, 573 (2d Cir. 2003) (quoting Reg'l Econ. Cmty. Action Program, Inc. v. City of Middletown, 294 F.3d 35, 45 (2d Cir. 2002), cert. denied, 537 U.S. 813 (2002)).

32. *Id.*; *see* Adam v. Linn-Benton Hous. Auth., 147 F. Supp. 2d 1044, 1047–48 (D. Or. 2001).

action, seeking a ruling that the single-family zoning provision did not violate the FHAA. The United States filed an action claiming the City violated the FHAA by failing to make a reasonable accommodation for Oxford House. After consolidating the actions, the trial court ruled the zoning provision was exempt from the FHAA because it fit within the maximum-occupancy exemption.[33] Thus, no violation was found.

The Ninth Circuit rejected the City's argument that the provision is a restriction on the maximum number of occupants and accepted Edmonds' argument, holding the plain meaning of the exemption is only applicable to those limiting the number of all occupants, related or not.[34] On appeal, the outcome hinged on Congress' intent when drafting the FHAA. The City contended that its single-family provision was a "restriction regarding the maximum number of occupants." Oxford House argued the only restrictions exempted are those that limit the number of all occupants, whether related or not.[35] Finding the plain language of the statutory exception to be ambiguous, the Ninth Circuit examined the legislative history and concluded that Oxford House's argument was the correct one.

The Ninth Circuit held a single-family zoning ordinance limiting the number of unrelated persons who may live in a particular residence, with no similar restriction on related persons, did not fall within the maximum number of occupants permitted to occupy a dwelling exemption.[36] The Ninth Circuit rejected the Eleventh Circuit's holding in *Elliott v. City of Athens, GA*, 960 F.2d 975, 976 (11th Cir. 1992), where the Eleventh Circuit found similar facts to those in *City of Edmonds* to come within the exemption.[37]

On appeal to the Supreme Court, the majority did not address whether the plain meaning was ambiguous and, rather, just jumped into legislative history. Key to the Court's reasoning was the language of the House Committee report on the FHAA (the "House Report"):

> These provisions are not intended to limit the applicability of any reasonable local, State, or Federal restrictions on the maximum number of occupants permitted to occupy a dwelling unit. A number of jurisdictions limit the number of occupants per unit based on a minimum number of square feet in the unit or the sleeping areas of the unit. Reasonable limitations by gov-

33. *City of Edmonds*, 514 U.S. at 730.

34. City of Edmonds v. Washington State Bldg. Code Council, 18 F.3d 802, 804 (9th Cir. 1994). The Ninth Circuit stated "[w]e cannot discern from the plain language of the statute whether Congress intended to exempt Edmonds' zoning ordinance. Edmonds argues that its single-family use restriction is a 'restriction regarding the maximum number of occupants.' 42 U.S.C. § 3607(b)(1). Yet the zoning provision does not regulate the maximum number of related occupants. Oxford House argues that the statute exempts only those restrictions that limit the number of all occupants, whether related or not. Although both interpretations could be inferred, neither follows directly from the plain language."

35. City of Edmonds, 18 F.3d at 804.

36. *Id.* at 807.

37. "The single-family residential zoning provision at issue in *Elliott* defines 'family,' in relevant part, as '[o]ne (1) or more persons occupying a single dwelling unit, provided that unless all members are related by blood, marriage or adoption, no such family shall contain over four (4) persons.'" *City of Edmonds*, 514 U.S. at 731 n2 (citing Elliott v. City of Athens, Ga., 960 F.2d 975, 976 (11th Cir. 1992).

ernments would be allowed to continue, as long as they were applied to all occupants, and did not operate to discriminate on the basis of race, color, religion, sex, national origin, handicap, or familial status.[38]

In ruling that the FHAA's maximum-occupancy exemption did not apply to the Edmonds ordinance, the Court reasoned that the exemption applied only to occupancy restrictions of the kind typically found in housing codes. The single-family zoning ordinance in question was, instead, a *use* restriction because the restriction did not apply to all occupants. The ordinance placed no restriction on the maximum number of occupants related by genetics, adoption, or marriage. Viewed as a use restriction, the ordinance affected the level of occupancy, not based on density, but by the *relationship* of the occupants. Therefore, the zoning ordinance was not exempt from the reach of the FHAA.[39] The Court remanded "for further consideration of the claims asserted by Oxford House and the United States" as to whether passing the ordinance permitting the group home to operate in multifamily and general commercial zones sufficed as reasonable accommodation.[40]

When teaching *City of Edmonds*, I ask my students: what are the key takeaways from this case? And the responses I typically get focus on what this case does. First, the decision benefits disabled persons seeking to establish a group home in single-family zones they would otherwise be excluded from. Second, the Court's opinion and discussion of the FHAA's legislative intent signal a shift from a history of stereotyping disabled persons based on fear and ignorance.[41] Neighbors' unfounded fear of nontraditional families is what manifested into a concern over lower property values and the City's execution of discriminatory zoning provisions. And so, yes, *Edmonds* is important for two primary reasons: (1) it curbs discrimination and housing exclusion; and (2) it discourages strict application of pre-*Edmonds* ordinances that would disproportionately negatively impact a disabled person's rights under the FHAA.

And then I ask my students: but what did *Edmonds not* do? The Court did not provide a bright-line rule for what constitutes a reasonable accommodation. The question was not presented on appeal, thus leaving lower courts to decide what instances constitute a reasonable accommodation as a question of fact, which leaves open potential loopholes for cities to apply discriminatory zoning provisions and offer accommodations that fail to meet the needs of recovery group homes without violating the FHAA.[42]

---

38. *City of Edmonds*, 514 U.S. at 734 n.8.

39. *Id.* at 738.

40. "The parties have presented, and we have decided, only a threshold question: Edmonds' zoning code provision describing who may compose a "family" is not a maximum occupancy restriction exempt from the FHA under § 3607(b)(1). It remains for the lower courts to decide whether Edmonds' actions against Oxford House violate the FHA's prohibitions against discrimination set out in §§ 3604(f)(1)(A) and (f)(3)(B). For the reasons stated, the judgment of the United States Court of Appeals for the Ninth Circuit is Affirmed." *City of Edmonds*, 514 U.S. at 738.

41. Michelle R.K. Todus, City of Edmonds v. Oxford House, Inc.: *Opening Doors to Housing for Handicapped Persons*, 26 Golden Gate U.L. Rev. 737, 738 (1996).

42. Oxford Home requires homes to be located in single-family residential zones removed from "commercial zones, liquor stores, and illicit drug activity to minimize the likelihood of a relapse by a

Additionally, the Court did not provide guidance on how far its "narrow reading" of the reasonable maximum occupancy exemption reaches.[43] Was *Edmonds* just an isolated set of facts worthy of a narrow reading of the FHAA exemption? These questions went unanswered, so lower courts were left to decide which cases present instances where reasonable accommodation must be provided because it will not compromise the primary goal of the legitimate land use regulation; in addition, lower courts must decide which permits satisfy the requirement to provide reasonable accommodation.[44]

In administrative law, we are often blinded by statutory language, with its underlying social policy somewhat obscured. *City of Edmonds* provides one of many opportunities to use a case study effectively looking at administrative law through a diversity, equity, and inclusion lens. My experience is that students appreciate the in-class discussion going beyond statutory construction to explore social policy and the impact that these seemingly innocuous laws have on real people's lives.

---

resident." Brief of the United States in Opposition at 4, City of Edmonds v. Oxford House, Inc., 514 U.S. 725 (1995) (94-23), 1994 WL 16012017 at *4.

43. *City of Edmonds*, 514 U.S. at 731; Todus, *supra* note 41, at 739.

44. Lower courts must decide those "instance[s] in which an exception to 'a general statement of policy' is sensibly read 'narrowly in order to preserve the primary operation of the [policy].'" *City of Edmonds*, 514 U.S. at 731 (citing Comm'r v. Clark, 489 U.S. 726, 739, (1989)).

Section 2

Business, Commercial, and Labor

De-Neutralizing Business, or Teaching Business Organizations for Inclusive Engagement

*Lua Kamál Yuille**

Critical Encounter[1]

"In the beginning, there was business. And business was good!" Whether it is a flagship public university or a progressive social justice niche, the refrain spills—with almost alarmingly little hesitation or discomfort—from the halls of the business law classroom. Little do they know, I have led them into something of a trap. *What is business?* I asked, after giving the students five minutes to brainstorm all the ways they had encountered or been impacted by business that day. *Where is business?* comes next. "Everywhere." It is the only possible response after they have listed the myriad ways they have engaged with business since opening their eyes. *When is business?* "All the time."

Got it. Business is everything, everywhere, all the time? So, why, then, did you submit thirty, forty, one hundred—the result is essentially the same regardless of the number of students enrolled in the class—*pictures of middle-aged, white guys when I asked you to send me images showing what business looks like?*[2] And this is the moment when things

* Professor, Northeastern University School of Law and D'Amore-McKim School of Business. I developed the approaches described here as part of the inaugural Diversity Scholars Program in the University of Kansas Center for Teaching Excellence. The theoretical foundation of the work was articulated in generative dialogue with interdisciplinary PhD cohorts and faculty in curriculum and instruction at the University of Missouri-Kansas City. Specific activities benefit from, and are routinely revised through, pedagogical workshops with Ruhiyyih N. Yuille. FTJ. JGY.

1. What follows is an amalgamated and stylized account of my experience during a session I have delivered more than a dozen times at multiple schools, normally but not always during the first meeting of the introductory course on business entity law. This account is not intended to report or recollect the experiences of the students but my impressions as the instructor.

2. I do not assign any reading for this first class meeting. However, either at the outset of the session or the night before, I ask students to respond to the following prompt with a visual reply that

get ... awkward, as students recognize that this is not any old course in corporations (or business organizations, or business associations, or whatever the class is titled at the particular institution).

I let the students sit in their discomfort for a while. But I break the silence and ease the prickling and unjustified guilt with the disquieting knowledge that they are not wrong. And they are far from the only ones who "feel" this way.

Take *Forbes*, the highly influential American business magazine widely known for its lists and rankings of companies and people of interest to and influence in the business world. In 2019, the magazine released a list of "America's Most Innovative Leaders," which purported to identify (based on rigorous criteria) and profile the one hundred most creative and successful business minds.[3] Jeff Bezos and Elon Musk, unsurprisingly, tied for the number one spot. No women appeared on the list. Well, that is not exactly true. Buried down the list at number seventy-five, as an afterthought accompanied by a blank silhouette instead of the high-resolution power shots afforded to the men, was Barbara Rentler, the chief executive officer of Ross Stores Inc.

Despite the magazine's lengthy defense of the objectivity of its methodology,[4] the *Forbes* ranking is—I brook no dissent—tone-deaf, problematic, and embarrassing.[5] But it was not wrong. Relieved smiles mingle with furrowed brows. At this, I introduce students to *The Anatomy of an Entrepreneur*, a series of research reports of the findings of a Kauffman Foundation research study into the backgrounds of successful

---

they create themselves or source from any available media: *This is a visual association exercise. Think of business as a person. What does that person look like?* Regardless of the timing, most submissions represent middle-aged, white men. When the exercise is preassigned, I use the time students would have taken to complete the exercise in class to ask them to explain or justify their selection. Those explanations vary widely. However, I have noticed (informally) that students who select non-white male images tend to explain that choice with formative personal experiences or critical political beliefs.

3. Jeff Dyer et al., *America's Most Innovative Leaders*, FORBES (Sept. 3, 2019), https://www.forbes.com/lists/innovative-leaders/#3c07445e26aa.

4. Randall Lane, *Opportunity Missed: Reflecting on the Lack of Women on Our Most Innovative Leaders List*, FORBES (Sept. 8, 2019), https://www.forbes.com/sites/randalllane/2019/09/08/opportunity-missed-reflecting-on-the-lack-of-women-on-our-most-innovative-leaders-list/?sh=344e63ed1c6b.

5. Occasionally, students will ask about the creators of the *Forbes* list. If they do, I give them time and space to search Jeff Dyer, Nathan Furr, Michael Hendron, and Curtis Lefrandt. They glimpse their academic pedigree and scholarly reputation (three are business professors at BYU); they speculate on their racialized and gender identities. Quick-fingered students learn about the public religious identification of at least one member of the team. Then, we discuss whether, to what extent, how, and why these characteristics *could* impact their assessment of business innovation and our consumption of the list. Should we expect an all-male team to fairly evaluate the contributions of women in business? How do our own beliefs about the importance of representation make us more or less likely to "trust" their list? What if the team was more diverse? What if the team was comprised of professors from Harvard Business School or the Wharton School? These queries provide a nice opportunity to preview conversations about representation, inclusivity, and objectivity that will recur throughout the course. However, I only engage these matters at this juncture if it arises organically.

business founders.[6] The Kauffman reports provide empirical evidence for the truth my students have already unintentionally and, often, unwilling recognized: entrepreneurs are—overwhelmingly—middle-aged, middle-class, and male.[7]

Again, we sit with discomfort for a short while. This time I do not relieve it. I lean into it. *Why? Why is business so white and male?* Someone invariably seeks comfort in the myth of self-selection. Other students offer reasons that find support in the Kauffman data. Class. The American middle class, they suggest, is disproportionately white and male. Education. Higher education is disproportionately white and male.[8] A range of other possibilities are offered, but suggestions tend to externalize any lack of diversity in business to broader social problems. An air of satisfaction descends.

Then, we watch. Cell phone footage shows a University of California police officer taking money from the wallet of a distressed hot dog vendor over the audible protests of onlookers. The vendor protests in Spanish, as the officer proceeds to issue a citation without response. To the unhappy crowd, the officer announces, "This is law and order in action."[9] I do not traffic in racial trauma voyeurism, so I do not show any more footage. But I ask, pointedly, about Eric Garner. He was the Black entrepreneur New York police officers killed for selling untaxed, single cigarettes.[10] I ask about "CD man" Alton Sterling, the Black entrepreneur police killed in Baton Rouge, Louisiana, while operating his business out of his car.[11]

But! But! Most semesters a hand shoots up, as a student cannot resist breaking the silence: The police power allows the state to protect public health by regulating the sale of cigarettes. It's okay to monitor who is selling hot dogs to prevent food poisoning! It hurts artists to allow people to sell bootlegs! However, the intervention is framed, the point is the same: Healthy markets require some rules and, if people just followed the rules....

---

6. Vivek Wadhwa et al., The Anatomy of an Entrepreneur (2009), https://www.kauffman.org/entrepreneurship/reports/the-anatomy-of-an-entrepreneur/.

7. The Kaufmann reports I present to my students are, disappointingly but not surprisingly, silent as to key demographic information including race, ethnicity, sexual orientation, religion, immigration status. Therefore, I supplement what they discover in the Kauffman reports with data on those demographic matters from other sources.

8. Although we do not focus on this issue, when students offer this explanation, I inform them that race, gender, and class in higher education are more complicated than we have space to discuss. I offer resources so they can explore further on their own.

9. Gillian Edevane, *GoFundMe for Hot Dog Vendor Raises More Than $70K After Video of UC Berkeley Cops Seizing His Earnings Goes Viral*, NBC Bay Area (Sept. 11, 2017), https://www.nbcbayarea.com/news/local/gofundme-for-hot-dog-vendor-goes-viral-after-video-shows-ucpd-seizing-earnings/31610/.

10 Al Baker, J. David Goodman & Benjamin Mueller, *Beyond the Chokehold*, N.Y. Times, June 14, 2015, at A1, https://www.nytimes.com/2015/06/14/nyregion/eric-garner-police-chokehold-staten-island.html.

11. Roxane Gay, *Alton Sterling and When Black Lives Stop Mattering*, N.Y. Times (July 7, 2016), http://www.nytimes.com/2016/07/07/opinion/alton-sterling-and-when-black-lives-stop-mattering.html.

I am not sure why, but the reflexiveness with which each highly educated, critically capable, new community of learners seems to defend the prevailing order surprises me every time.[12] I do not *intend* for the class to be moved this way. Rather, I engage in generative problem posing. And semester after semester, here we are. Leaving me to pose the mic drop question to end our session: *But! But! You told me that business is everything, everywhere, all the time ... for everyone. After all, "in the beginning, there was business and business was good."*

Background

Business organizations is an introductory elective course in the laws governing the main forms of business entity. Such courses normally focus primarily or solely on the corporation. The areas of law, policy, and economics typically covered are thoroughly permeated by the myth of "neutrality": *Business, and therefore business law, is impartial with respect to race, gender, class, religion, sexual orientation, and the other political and social identity and categorizations that preoccupy other fields. Business entities exist to organize commercial activity in pursuit of profits, and business entity law provides background rules to facilitate those pursuits.* Race, gender, class, religion, sexual orientation, and the like are largely (or wholly) outside the business law interest or inquiry.

This myth of neutrality in business means students are generally not (or only tangentially) exposed to diverse perspectives on or critiques of business. Studies have proven that such lack of content diversity negatively impacts student engagement and achievement, especially for students from historically underrepresented and underserved groups.[13] After languishing by using the dominant paradigm, I radically redesigned my course into a site of critical, inclusive engagement that treats business entity law as a key element of the social order.

The series of exercises I facilitate during the first meeting of business organizations does a lot of work. It provides an experiential introduction to my dialogue-based, constructivist teaching philosophy and pedagogy. Those first exercises also preview the content of the course. They demonstrate to students that they already know a lot about business and the dominant goals and culture of business, while letting students know that they will be asked to consider the perspectives, needs, and values of people,

---

12. I do not suggest that these defenses represent the personal views of most students. Each semester, I poll students anonymously as to their position on the role of business in society. Even though academic and practical experience with business tends to be evenly distributed, only a relatively small fraction of any class reports any strong or particular affinity for business.

13. *See, e.g.*, Geneva Gay, Culturally Responsive Teaching: Theory, Research, and Practice (3d ed., 2018); Gloria Ladson-Billings, *Culturally Relevant Pedagogy 2.0: aka the Remix*, 84 Harv. Educ. Rev. 74 (2014); María del Carmen Salazar, Amanda Stone Norton & Franklin A. Tuitt, *Weaving Promising Practices for Inclusive Excellence into the Higher Education Classroom*, 28 To Improve the Academy 208 (2010); Regan A.R. Gurung, *Got Culture? Incorporating Culture into the Curriculum*, *in* Getting Culture: Incorporating Diversity across the Curriculum 11–22 (Regan A.R. Gurung & Loreto R. Prieto, eds., 2009).

communities, and interests that are often treated as outside of or subsidiary to the core concerns of business. Finally, by upending student expectations about the format and content of a typical law course (especially one focused on the law of corporations), the exercises destabilize the intangible and entrenched hierarchies that exist among students, helping lay the foundation for a course in which any student may feel empowered to make critical interventions.

Course Design Goals

I use the three interrelated aspects of the course—pedagogy, content, and climate—to which I expose students during the first class meeting as a guide for holistically integrating diversity, equity, and inclusion with the statutory, doctrinal, theoretical, and practical capabilities demanded of every competent business lawyer.

To motivate my course planning, I have articulated the following goals:

- **Pedagogy**—*incorporate high-impact practices and dialogue-based learning strategies to promote engagement and achievement.*
- **Content**—*expose students to diverse perspectives and voices in business law, so they can identify whose interests and which ideologies the law serves, critique the outcomes associated with those commitments, and utilize the law as a tool across the stakeholder spectrum.*
- **Climate**—*implement practices to systematically foster inclusivity among the community of learners by including diversity issues in core learning outcomes and engaging students in interdependent collaborative learning.*

Implementation is not a fixed or completed process; it is iterative and dependent on the needs and interests of each new community of learners.

I open the second class meeting with a basic recapitulation: *So far, you've told me that business is a major influence on every aspect of the social world; we've confronted (or been confronted with) the powerful belief that the influence of business is largely positive; and we've seen that, despite apparent openness, business might not be as universal and inclusive as people would like to believe. What's the law got to do with any of this? And where should we go from here?* Notwithstanding the eerie predictability of that first meeting, I have yet to accurately anticipate what the community of learners will present to me on day two. Instead, I organize the students into reasonably diverse,[14] stable learning teams. Throughout the semester, these "firms" complete structured small group learning activities that require members to rely on each other and engage in dialogue to

14. I actively avoid isolating students who self-identify as belonging to any identity group that is salient to the community of learners. In my experience, this choice tends to mean at least one small group will appear to be all male, all straight, or all white. Although I exercise discretion, I tend to identify salient identity groups using a demographic and experience survey distributed after the first class meeting. That survey asks, among other questions, students to provide demographic information they would like taken into account in creating groups.

apply course content studied outside of class in increasingly sophisticated, real-world contexts.[15] The first task firms complete is brainstorming what things they believe they should and what things they want to know about the law of business entities.[16]

The inquiries and interests identified by the students reflect their personal and professional experiences and aspirations. And I integrate the students' questions into a suite of content modules that ensure students will be introduced to and develop facility with the foundational concepts of business entity law. Learning developed in each content module is wrapped by a "critical encounter" presenting alternative approaches, critiques, or issues of diversity and inclusion for general discussion and practical deployment based on topics identified by the firms.

Learning Experiences

I use the guiding principles and goals I articulated, the core standards of business entity law I identify, and the students' interests to create real, practical exercises and learning experiences. In developing new experiences responsive to the demands of the community of learners, I have amassed several DEI-inflected experiences or prompts for nearly every major topic in business entity law.

Most of these experiences are presented in the day-to-day learning activities completed by firms. However, at the conclusion of each content module, I also provide students with more profound opportunities to grapple with and problem solve the matters of greatest concern to them. The following lesson and activity plans outline two particularly successful examples of learning activities regularly presented in my course.

Breast Milk for Sale

Objective. This high-impact writing activity challenges students to implement advisory skills, while exploring the exclusionary and limited nature of business law.

Theory/Doctrine. Sole proprietorship; Agency liability

Materials. Video summaries (e.g., news reports) that demonstrate the risks associated with entering into accessible (though unauthorized) sole proprietorship businesses. E.g., Beto Juarez (unlicensed hot dog vendor at the University of California,

---

15. I organize content delivery and learning activities using the principles of Team-Based Learning, which is itself a strategy for meeting my pedagogical and climate goals. TEAM-BASED LEARNING: A TRANSFORMATIVE USE OF SMALL GROUPS IN COLLEGE TEACHING (Larry K. Michaelsen et al. eds., 2004).

16. This exercise is an adaptation to content-specific demands of Paulo Friere's concept of "problem posing." In a problem posing learning model, students are presented with (or themselves present) large social realities that are relevant or interesting to their communities, and then collaborate with each other and the teacher to gain the knowledge and skills they need to reflect upon, act on, and respond to those realities. PAULO FREIRE, PEDAGOGY OF THE OPPRESSED (4th ed. 2018).

Berkeley), Eric Garner (selling loose cigarettes in New York), Alton Sterling (selling CDs in Louisiana).

Procedure. Students are presented with a contextualizing introduction (either as a lecture or in writing) that references the materials they viewed or explored demonstrating the differential experiences of entrepreneurship. Then they are asked to advise a client who is entering into an unauthorized business. At the conclusion of their advisory activity, students write a reflection on the experience.

> *Introduction*
>
> Is business law serving values accessible or targeted to everyone, or just a select few (whomever they may be)? After elaborating the idea that business law serves an underlying capitalist ideal in which business is good and more business—in the form of entrepreneurship—is better, you considered counter examples that strain that conclusion: Beto Juarez (Berkley's hot dog vendor), Eric Garner (selling loose cigarettes), Alton Sterling (selling CDs).
>
> Each man was ostensibly engaged in exactly the kind of market-disrupting entrepreneurship that business law, generally, and the low-entry-cost sole proprietorship, specifically, is supposed to support. Nonetheless, the consequences of their entrepreneurship were bankruptcy and death. Juxtapose those experiences with the experience of Uber or Lyft, which have been framed as market disruptors engaged in dubiously lawful enterprises. What does that say or mean about business law? How do we provide advice that is attuned to these realities? This assignment (on which you are expected to spend no more than 30 minutes) requires you to draw on both the practical knowledge and skills you have developed and the critical lessons you have explored to provide sound professional advice.
>
> *Key Information*
>
> Jessica Alban pumps breast milk two to three times a day. Unlike many nursing mothers who store the output from such intensive pumping sessions for when they are unavailable to nurse their children, Jessica stores her expressed milk in a deep freezer. Jessica stores her own milk with milk she has obtained from various paid and unpaid donors. The unpaid donors have been promised that, when the business becomes profitable, Jessica will hire them full time as employees. Jessica is preparing to launch Latte Mamas, an online business selling the milk for $6 an ounce. In addition to pure milk, Latte Mamas will also sell breast milk products including "pearls" for jewelry, cheese, butter, and ice cream. Jessica has invested almost her entire savings in the commercial deep freezers she obtained to start her business. She has funds left to set up her website, but not much else. Federal law does not regulate the commercial exchange of breast milk, but where Jessica lives it is unlawful to sell "bodily fluids." Whether breast milk is a bodily fluid has not been determined in the courts of that jurisdiction.

Tasks

1. Advise Jessica with respect to her proposed business plan. Should she move forward? May she? What risks does she face, if any? Note: Depending on the size of the class, students are expected to either produce a video recording of their advice or participate in a live client simulation.
2. In writing, explain how you balanced properly advising Jessica of the legal considerations associated with her breast milk business plan with the reality of informing her that she risks criminal and civil liability for her business. Specifically describe at least one aspect of your advice that:
   a. accounted for the implications of their advice on Jessica's life and business prospects, and
   b. showed respect for Jessica's situation and choices.

   Include a description of whether you found the task difficult and explain how your advice might look different if you were advising the entrepreneurs starting another business of unclear legality at the time of their founding, such as Uber or Airbnb.

Students will return to Jessica Alban's business throughout the course, advising her (and the business) as it grows. The following activity presents the next major engagement students will have with the client.

The Corporation and Diversity

Objective. This practical skills activity gives students the opportunity to complete the relatively straightforward task of incorporating a business. Students connect the statutory requirements to the administrative forms. Students also explore the legality and practicality of including limitations on the business in the constitutive documents of the company. In feedback, students are introduced to diversity statutes, which have been implemented in non-U.S. jurisdictions.

Theory/Doctrine. Incorporation; corporate purpose; ultra vires doctrine.

Materials. Delaware form articles of incorporation.

Procedure. Students are presented with a contextualizing introduction (either as a simulation from the client or in writing). Then, they must prepare the required documents for the client. The activity concludes with in-class discussion. Occasionally students will present their decisions to the client in a simulated client meeting.

Key Information

After considering your advice, Jessica Albans, has decided that she would like to proceed building Latte Mamas. She has enlisted Maria Santos, a woman with Hyper Lactation Syndrome, as co-venturer. Maria had several conditions pursuant to which she agreed to invest the funds necessary for the business to get off the ground:

1. The sole purpose of the corporation must be selling breast milk and breast milk-based products.
2. The company must give away a quarter ounce of breast milk for every ounce sold.
3. The company must be incorporated in Delaware.
4. The board of directors must always include at least one currently lactating mother and at least one non-lactating woman.

Jessica and Maria agreed that the corporate headquarters would be at Jessica's home:

1624 Foothill Blvd.

Monrovia, California 91016

Tasks

1. Prepare the necessary documents to incorporate Latte Mamas in Delaware. You should feel free to use the template provided by the State of Delaware, but it must be modified to fit the needs of Latte Mamas and annotated to: (a) explain its main provisions to Jessica and Maria and (b) indicate the statutory reference, where appropriate, for the language.
2. Draft a brief email cover letter to Jessica and Maria that explains anything you have not included in the formation documents, why they were omitted, and how you plan to address those issues.

For the purposes of this assignment:

- Assume that your choice accepts appointment as registered agent.
- Do not form as a C Corporation, S Corporation, Close Corporation, or Benefit Corporation.
- Assume that no license is needed to operate Latte Mamas and that selling of breast milk or breast milk products is not definitely prohibited under Delaware law.
- Assume that Latte Mamas complies with any Food & Drug Administration regulations.
- Do *not* use the State of Delaware's One Stop Business Registration and Licensing System

KKKorporation

Objective. This "critical encounter" wraps the module on forming a corporation. Students explore the authority of states to limit incorporation, reflecting on key questions: Who can start a corporation? Why? Does it matter?

Theory/Doctrine. Corporate formation; state and federal law on free expression, discrimination, etc.

Materials. Profiles of business-oriented or -focused hate groups. These are easily obtained via the Southern Poverty Law Center (SPLC). Note: For everyone's safety, students are encouraged to use only the material maintained by the SPLC.

Charles C. Alexander, *Kleagles and Cash: The Ku Klux Klan as a Business Organization, 1915–1930*, 39 The Business History Review 348 (1965).

Procedure. Students are presented with a contextualizing introduction posing questions about the business of hate. Contemporary examples are presented. Each firm is assigned a business-oriented or -focused hate group; ideally each group operates in a different jurisdiction.

Tasks

1. Practical Exercise
    - You work for the Secretary of State (or the appropriate authority in the jurisdiction you have been assigned). Find a way to reject the incorporation filing of the organization you have been assigned. You may rely on state or federal law.
    - Prepare a brief presentation, describing the organization and the basis for rejecting its incorporation, providing the relevant statutory reference and explanation, if any.
    - Optional extension activity: Either in firms or as a class, discuss the strength and validity of proposals to reject incorporation.
2. Reflection (after the practical exercise)
    - Read the Alexander article cited above.
    - React freely to the characterization of the KKKorporation (i.e., the KKK or any other hate group as a business entity). What is the role/responsibility of the state to support or oppose these entities through law?

Mirrors, Windows, and Sliding Glass Doors

As Saru Matambanadzo astutely observed,[17] the slow revolution that Christopher Columbus Langdell brought to American legal education with the Socratic-style case method coincided with the ascendance of the corporate capitalism that Adolf A. Berle and Gardiner Means would describe in their seminal work *The Modern Corporation and Private Property*.[18] This confluence of events shapes the contemporary business law classroom.

Langdell was determined to treat law as a scientific endeavor, operating on a small number of core theories and principles that—once mastered—could be applied "with constant facility and certainty to the ever-tangled skein of human affairs."[19] While the human *affairs* may have been complex, the law was nothing more than a system of rational, neutral ordering mechanisms. The scientification of law, reflected in Langdellian pedagogy, coincided with a similar process in economics led by the rationalization of Alfred Marshall and the mathematicalization of William Stanley Jevons, Léon Walras, and Irving Fisher.[20]

Meanwhile, capital rapidly became heavily concentrated in a small number of extraordinarily powerful corporations, transforming corporate and business law and policy from "a torpid backwater of law, mostly a matter of municipalities, charities, and churches"[21] into key drivers of sociopolitical-economic relations. The oligarchy of colossal corporations was run by a new managerial class, who were being trained in rapidly proliferating collegiate schools of business. And the Langdellian sensibility (including the adaptation of the case method as a primary pedagogical strategy[22]) became the dominant philosophy.

In the intervening century, the wisdom of the scientification of the sites for the systematic reflection on law, economics, and business has frequently been called into question. Race, gender, and class disparities in increasingly diverse communities of learners have been attributed to pedagogical commitments instead of meritocratic factors. Rational, neutral laws, economic policies, and business strategies have been

---

17. Saru Matambanadzo, *Fumbling Toward a Critical Legal Pedagogy and Practice*, 4 POL'Y FUTURES IN EDUC. 90 (2006).

18. ADOLF A. BERLE & GARDINER MEANS, THE MODERN CORPORATION AND PRIVATE PROPERTY (1932). Although it was published amidst the Great Depression, this work is a product of a cycle of corporate evolution Berle and Means observed from the late nineteenth century until the stock market crash of 1929.

19. CHRISTOPHER COLUMBUS LANGDELL, A SELECTION OF CASES ON THE LAW OF CONTRACTS vi (1871).

20. *See, e.g.*, Margaret Schabas, *Alfred Marshall, W. Stanley Jevons, and the Mathematization of Economics*, 80 ISIS 60 (1989).

21. Lawrence M. Friedman, *The Law of Corporations*, *in* A HISTORY OF AMERICAN LAW (4th ed., 2019).

22. Bruce A. Kimball, *The Proliferation of Case Method Teaching in American Law Schools: Mr. Langdell's Emblematic 'Abomination,' 1890–1915*, 46 HIST. OF EDUC. Q. 192, 193 (2006).

shown to produce, reproduce, and reify class, race, and gender stratification. And yet it is the settlements of that era (questionable, incomplete, or obsolete as they may be) that undergird the teaching of corporate, business, and economic law today.

Grounded in the liberatory pedagogical theories and practices of Paulo Friere, bell hooks, Michael Apple, Gloria Ladson-Billings, Henry Giroux, Antonia Darder, Ira Shor, Joe Kincheloe, Peter McClaren, Donald Macedo, Geneva Gay, and the like, my Business Organizations class follows a radically different path. I recognize and am responsive to the core set of skills and knowledge students who have studied business organizations are expected have. But I focus on facilitating opportunities for students to engage in authentic dialogue. This allows them to incorporate their own identities and lived experiences (and the lived experiences of the wide range of people and communities shaped and impacted by the law) into each learning encounter.

Because of these practices, my students report feeling valued and validated as legal thinkers. They describe seeing themselves—their communities and their interests—as relevant, active subjects of business law. And, perhaps most important, they are able to develop skills-grounded responses to routine, practical, and existential corporate problems both within and beyond the confines of existing legal settlements.

In 1990, Rudine Sims Bishop published an essay about the importance of diversity, equity, and inclusion in literature:

> Books are sometimes windows, offering views of worlds that may be real or imagined, familiar or strange. These windows are also sliding glass doors, and readers have only to walk through in imagination to become part of whatever world has been created or recreated by the author. When lighting conditions are just right, however, a window can also be a mirror. Literature transforms human experience and reflects it back to us, and in that reflection we can see our own lives and experiences as part of the larger human experience.[23]

When literature is a window, readers see people, experiences, or worlds removed from their own. The value of windows is in how they can challenge thinking and offer unique perspectives. It is vital, however, to experience literature as a mirror; people need to see something of themselves—physical, cultural, or emotional—reflected back. When books never serve as mirrors, Bishop recognized, readers "learn a powerful lesson about how they are devalued in society."[24] Sliding glass doors invite readers to enter and engage. When literature is a sliding glass door, readers can change, and they can make change. Bishop's lesson holds for the law. And through the critical, dialogic strategies I employ, my students experience Business Associations as mirrors, windows, and sliding glass doors.

---

23. Rudine Sims Bishop, *Mirrors, Windows, and Sliding Glass Doors*, 6 Perspectives ix (1990).
24. *Id.* at ix.

Business Law and Racism

*Robert R. Statchen**

Professor, we are processing this material in real-time. I really haven't covered this before.

Introduction

My goal in developing a Business Law and Racism course has been to create a learning environment that facilitates critical, informed, and brave[1] discussions on how domestic business laws, since the colonial period through modern times, have furthered white supremacist economic policies, societal outcomes, and institutional structures in the United States. In the first iteration during the pandemic, I taught it as a condensed online summer course with 16 students. After the first few classes, the discussions were not flowing as I had hoped. I privately asked a student why she was not participating in the seminar discussions as much as I would have hoped, and her response is quoted above. She went on to say that she had not previously been exposed to most of the historical and substantive legal material we were covering and therefore she was often reacting to the material in real-time and finding it difficult to immediately express her

* Clinical Professor of Law, Western New England College School of Law. J.D. Chicago-Kent College of Law, LL.M. in Taxation Boston University, M.B.A. University of Connecticut, B.A. Clark University.

1. Brian Arao & Kristi Clemens, *From Safe Spaces to Brave Spaces—A New Way to Frame Dialogue Around Diversity and Social Justice, in* The Art of Effective Facilitation: Reflections from Social Justice Educators 135–150 (Lisa M. Landreman, ed., 2013); Laura P. Graham, *"Safe Spaces" and "Brave Spaces": The Case for Creating Law School Classrooms that Are Both*, 76 U. Miami Law Rev. 84, 90–91 (2021); *see also* Micky ScottBey Jones, *Invitation to Brave Space*, HelpingOut (2017), https://helpingout.net/2018/12/02/invitation-to-brave-space-poem-by-micky-scottbey-jones / [https://perma.cc/NYW9-AK9N]. These concepts are now evolving to also highlight the importance of humility and creating humble spaces. Stuart Chinn, *Free Speech Controversies and Consequences on Campus*, 54 Tulsa L. Rev. 225, 230 (2019) (referencing Justice Holmes's dissent in *Abrams v. United States* stating that the heart of free speech "is a reminder for all to maintain some degree of humility in their beliefs," and citing Keith E. Whittington, Speak Freely: Why Universities Must Defend Free Speech 44–46 (2018)).

thoughts. Upon further reflection, she shared that it was the first time in her academic journey that she distributed class readings to friends and family.

It is self-evident that the course content is important.[2] Business lawyers, as counselors and advisors to business owners and leaders, must be able to advise their clients on the intersection of business law and racism.[3] Incorporating race in transactional law courses has received increased attention over the past few decades.[4] A recent statement by 271 law professors across the United States reflects this intersection:

> We are law professors, and many of us write and teach about business law.
>
> We think race and racism are important to the study of business law, just as they are important to the study of any area of law. From slavery and redlining to lack of opportunity in the workplace and limited access to capital, race and racism have always been part of business and business law.
>
> To our colleagues and our students: we welcome the opportunity to engage in these discussions and commit to thinking hard about how to incorporate them into our research and our teaching.[5]

This essay first discusses the process of adopting a critical pedagogy and thereafter assembling appropriate curricular material. Finally, it will provide some of my reflections and student feedback.

---

2. Effective February 2022, subsection (c) was added to the Standard 303 of the ABA Standards and Rules of Procedure for Approval of Law Schools. AM. BAR ASS'N, STANDARDS AND RULES OF PROCEDURE FOR APPROVAL OF LAW SCHOOLS 2022–2023. This section reads "A law school shall provide education to law students on bias, cross-cultural competency and racism: (1) at the start of the program on legal education and (2) at least once again before graduation."

3. Alina S. Ball, *Disruptive Pedagogy: Incorporating Critical Theory in Business Law Clinics*, 22 CLINICAL L. REV. 1, 31 (2015) ("For business law students, exposure to critical legal theory helps them to better understand the inner working of legal systems, their client's broader community, and better anticipate clients' needs.") (citations omitted).

4. *See, e.g.*, Veryl Victoria Miles, *Raising Issues of Property, Wealth and Inequality in the Law School: Contracts & Commercial Law School Courses*, 34 IND. L. REV. 1365 (2001); Cheryl L. Wade, *Attempting to Discuss Race in Business and Corporate Law Courses and Seminars*, 77 ST. JOHNS L. REV. 901 (2003). There is also an organic compilation of Race and Business Law resources being maintained by Professor Jessica M. Erickson at the University of Richmond School of Law, available at https://perma.cc/K8SP-XTSW.

5. Benjamin P. Edwards, *Business Law Profs' Statement on Race/Racism in Business Law*, BUSINESS LAW PROF BLOG (Aug. 29, 2020), https://lawprofessors.typepad.com/business_law/2020/08/business-law-profs-statement-on-raceracism-in-business-law.html# [https://perma.cc/8Y6E-2BVL].

Adopting a Critical and Antiracist Pedagogy

In directing a community economic development/small business legal clinic in a relatively small city for 17 years, I have worked with hundreds of minority-owned businesses run by highly motivated and talented entrepreneurs.[6] And yet these businesses often fail to thrive.[7] My decision to develop a course on Business Law and Racism stemmed from the desire to further explore this reality. My decision was also informed by the recent works of professors, attorneys, and journalists exploring more generally the intersection of race and law.[8] Combining my practical experiences with the concepts presented in these works, the course is an effort to move past the paradigm of racism presented as a tangential aspect of a business law course to instead being centered in all discussions.[9]

My hope is that students will increase their knowledge of substantive principles of business law and, concurrently, understand how business law continues to reinforce structural racism. For example, what better way to learn the responsibilities, duties, and power of corporate boards than to study who has been excluded from such positions, how such exclusion occurred, and evaluate current efforts to address this institutionalized marginalization?[10] Students can learn the concept of corporate personhood while examining the argument that such a construct can be a strong rationale for reparations.[11] One can study intellectual property[12] and the importance of creativity

---

6. See client testimonials at https://www1.wne.edu/law/centers/small-business-legal-clinic.cfm [https://perma.cc/FB3L-PAAS].

7. Dymond Green, *Why Black-owned businesses are struggling to stay afloat*, CNBC, (Feb. 3, 2021, 6:26 PM), https://www.cnbc.com/2021/02/03/black-owned-businesses-are-struggling-to-stay-afloat.html ("There are 30.2 million small businesses in the U.S. But only a fraction of them survive. Twenty percent of small businesses fail by the first year, 30% by the second, 50% by the fifth and, by the 10th year, a staggering 70% of businesses have shut off their lights. For minorities, the numbers can be even more daunting. Eight out of 10 Black-owned businesses fail within the first 18 months.").

8. *See e.g.*, MICHELLE ALEXANDER, THE NEW JIM CROW (2010); TA-NEHISI COATES, BETWEEN THE WORLD AND ME (2015); EDDIE S. GLAUDE JR., DEMOCRACY IN BLACK—HOW RACE STILL ENSLAVES THE AMERICAN SOUL (2016); IBRAM X. KENDI, STAMPED FROM THE BEGINNING—THE DEFINITIVE HISTORY OF RACIST IDEAS IN AMERICA (2016); IBRAM X. KENDI, HOW TO BE AN ANTIRACIST (2019); BRYAN STEVENSON, JUST MERCY—THE STORY OF JUSTICE AND REDEMPTION (2015).

9. Wade, *supra* note 4, at 905 ("This tendency in law school to discuss race only in specified courses trivializes the experiences of students of color and the importance of race in American society. Ignoring race in core courses squanders precious opportunities for students who do not take "race courses" to learn to speak intelligently about the important and difficult issues of race and racism.").

10. *See, e.g.*, Cheryl L. Wade, *Corporate Compliance that Advances Racial Diversity and Justice and Why Business Deregulation Does Not Matter*, 49 LOY. U. CHI. L.J. 611, 621 (2018) (explaining how the SEC Board Diversity Rules and Dodd-Frank's Section 342 provide two vivid examples of the inadequacy of the discourse on race and gender inequities in the business setting).

11. Susan S. Kuo & Benjamin Means, *A Corporate Law Rationale for Reparations*, 62 B.C. L. REV. 799 (2021).

12. Anjali Vats & Deidre A. Keller, *Critical Race IP*, 36 CARDOZO ARTS & ENT. L.J. 735, 740 (2018) ("Critical Race IP, as we define it, refers to the interdisciplinary movement of scholars connected by

and invention for copyright and patent ownership by learning about the exploitation of artists[13] and inventors of color.[14] Dissecting unconscionable real estate, installment, service, and commodity contract provisions that have created and continue to perpetuate economic inequality—while being enforced by the courts—will both expand the student's social consciousness and prepare them for the upcoming bar exam.[15]

Additionally, by linking the study of racism and antiracism countermeasures with business law, it is possible a wider range of students will engage with this material. The course could be valuable to the aspiring civil rights attorneys seeking to implement community-based legal projects or engage in impact litigation.[16] It should also be attractive to future corporate, real estate, tax or employment lawyers for social and moral reasons,[17] as well as to help their future clients succeed financially.[18] Unfortunately, both types of students may not previously have seen the relevance of these issues to their chosen course of legal study and professional aspirations.[19]

My first reservation about this course is that it attempts to cover too much material and therefore could be prone to superficiality. The curriculum seemed to break the "less is more" commandment. However, I reason that absent this effort, the alternative is students, and especially those interested in transactional and business law, will leave

---

their focus on the racial and colonial non-neutrality of the laws of copyright, patent, trademark, right of publicity, trade secret, and unfair competition using principles informed by CRT.").

13. K.J. Greene, *Intellectual Property at the Intersection of Race and Gender: Lady Sings the Blues*, 16 Am. U. J. Gender Soc. Pol'y & L. 365, 369 (2008) ("While individual black artists without question have benefited from the IP system, the economic effects of IP deprivation on the black community have been devasting.... It is only in recent years that scholarship exploring IP has examined it in the context of social and historical inequality.").

14. Kara W. Swanson, *Race and Selective Legal Memory: Reflections on Invention of a Slave*, 120 Colum. L. Rev. 1077 (analyzing the 1858 U.S. Attorney General opinion regarding inventions by slaves).

15. Deborah Zalesne, *Racial Inequality in Contracting: Teaching Race as a Core Value*, 3 Colum. J. Race & L. 23, 30 (2013) ("These various contracting scenarios raise complex and nuanced issues surrounding the issue of whether contract law has helped to perpetuate racial discrimination and the disempowerment of racial minorities or to minimize it.").

16. Wade, *supra* note 4, at 911 ("Feminists, environmentalists, and civil and human rights activists can find fulfillment in the study of corporate law.")

17. Lisa M. Fairfax, *Board Diversity Revisited: New Rationale, Same Old Story*, 89 N.C. L. Rev. 855, 859 (2011) (arguing that failure to increase board diversity can be in part attributed to overemphasis on business rationale for diversity and underemphasis on the important role that social and moral justifications must play in such efforts). *See also* Jamillah Bowman Williams, *Breaking Down Bias: Legal Mandates vs. Corporate Interests*, 92 Wash. L. Rev. 1473, 1483–1484 (2017) ("[M]oral underpinnings of civil rights law were downplayed and organizations began rationalizing integration efforts by emphasizing business-related benefits of racial inclusion, such as 'efficiency,' 'productivity,' 'innovation,' 'client service,' 'competitive advantage,' and 'increased profits.'").

18. Quinn Curtis et al., *Do ESG Mutual Funds Delivery on their Promises?* 120 Mich. L. Rev. 393, 440 ("[I]nvestors in ESG [Environmental, Social, and Corporate Governance focused] funds do not give up returns—either raw or risk adjusted. If anything, investors in these funds might do a bit better, on average, than investors in non-ESG funds.").

19. Ball, *supra* note 3 at 29 ("Future corporate lawyers are among the least likely to be exposed to critical theory during their law school careers because business law courses rarely utilize critical legal theory in their curriculum.").

law school with little to no exposure to these crucial intersections.[20] Further, as an upper-level course, students will be bringing some degree of substantive knowledge to the classroom so discussions can hopefully begin at an elevated level. And arguably, all of law school should simply be a preliminary starting point for further self-directed intellectual inquiry. Perhaps spending a two-hour class to discuss racism in the health care[21] or insurance[22] industries is woefully inadequate, but there will be students who take that knowledge and move on to the significant body of work that further addresses these issues.

My second reservation, which I continue to closely assess, is that business law professors such as myself do not have an appropriate background in critical race theory, Black history, ethnic studies, or business history to present the material and facilitate the discussions appropriately or properly. My entrance into the legal academy came through the clinical world after more than 10 years in both government and private practice, neither with a civil rights focus. As a white, male, heterosexual, cisgendered, abled, well-resourced, 50-something, military veteran, clinical professor, when I undertook to teach a law school podium class on Business Law and Racism, I knew I had a tremendous amount to learn both substantively and pedagogically.[23] In my assessment, I also considered that professors specializing in race and the law may not have extensive familiarity with corporate, real estate, intellectual property, and tax issues. I concluded the significant impact of racism on these transactional areas of law mandates an effort to bridge these substantive areas carefully and respectfully for our students.[24] The next section presents the imperfect first effort I made, with great trepidation, to assemble course materials to help my students, and myself, better understand these monumental issues.

---

20. *Id.*

21. Dorothy A. Roberts, Killing the Black Body: Race, Reproduction, and the Meaning of Liberty (1998); Vernellia R. Randall, *Slavery, Segregation and Racism: Trusting the Health Care System Ain't Always Easy! An African American Perspective on Bioethics*, 15 St. Louis U. Pub. L. Rev. 191 (1996).

22. Daniel Schwarcz, *Toward a Civil Rights Approach to Insurance Anti-Discrimination*, 69 DePaul L. Rev. 657 (2020).

23. *See, e.g.*, Matthew R. Kay, Not Light, But Fire—How to Lead Meaningful Race Conversations in the Classroom (2018).

24. I also presented my course proposal to several colleagues of color. The responses were positive, appreciating the effort, but also emphatically caveating that I better do it very well.

Developing a Curriculum

There are several excellent casebooks,[25] teaching aids,[26] and online materials[27] addressing race and the law. However, I did not find a casebook or curriculum specifically addressing the intersection of race and business law.[28] Fortunately, there are renowned legal scholars producing excellent, substantive work in this area.[29]

For example, there is significant work analyzing failed efforts at regulatory reform in banking and "Black Capitalism" resulting in the Black-white wealth gap barely changing from the end of the Civil War to the current day.[30] Furthermore, in the aftermath of George Floyd's murder in 2020, several law schools have held conferences attempting to address these specific issues relating to business law and racism.[31]

---

25. *See, e.g.*, Ralph Richard Banks et al., Racial Justice and Law: Cases and Materials (2016); Derrick Bell, Race, Racism, and American Law (6th ed. 2008) (The first edition of this book was published in 1973. Professor Bell passed away on October 5, 2011 at the age of 80.); Dorothy A. Brown, Critical Race Theory: Cases, Materials and Problems (3d ed. 2014); Juan Perea et al., Race and Races: Cases and Resources for a Diverse America (3d ed. 2015); Francisco Valdez et al., Critical Justice—Systemic Advocacy in Law and Society (2021); Richard Delgado et al., Latinos and the Law—Cases and Materials (2d ed. 2021); Robert T. Anderson et al., American Indian Law—Cases and Commentary (4th ed. 2020).

26. Gloria J. Browne-Marshall, Race, Law, and American Society (2d ed. 2013); Rachel F. Moran & Devon W. Carbado, Race Law Stories (2008); Kimberly O'Leary & Mable Martin-Scott, Multicultural Lawyering (2021).

27. *Law Deans Antiracist Clearinghouse Project*, The Ass'n of Am. L. Schs., https://www.aals.org/antiracist-clearinghouse/ (last visited Jan. 4, 2023); *Teach-in For Racial Justice*, Univ. Cin. Coll. L., https://law.uc.edu/racial-justice-teach-in.html (last visited Jan. 4, 2023); *Embedded Racism in the Law Panel Discussion*, Vermont Law Schl., https://www.youtube.com/playlist?list=PLRG0KiYx1Tp_KC--QQ7g8K-LORgoiHhrj (last visited Jan. 4, 2023); Law for Black Lives, http://www.law4blacklives.org (last visited Jan. 4, 2023); Race, Racism & The Law, https://racism.org/ (operating since 1995) (last visited Jan. 4, 2023).

28. The closest I have found is the following, which is an excellent casebook, but it is no longer in publication. Emma Coleman Jordan & Angela P. Harris, Economic Justice—Race, Gender, Identity and Economics—Cases and Materials (2d ed. 2010). Additionally, and even more focused, there is an excellent book addressing the intersection of race and tax policy. Anthony C. Infanti & Bridget J. Crawford, Critical Tax Theory—An Introduction (2009). I am beginning the process of developing a casebook (and possible business undergraduate and MBA textbook) for this material and welcome the input of potential collaborators, authors, and editors. I am also happy to share my current syllabus and materials, subject to an agreement to provide critical feedback in return. Please contact me at rstatchen@law.wne.edu.

29. See *supra* text accompanying notes 10–22.

30. Mehrsa Baradaran, The Color of Money—Black Banks and the Racial Wealth Gap 9 (2017); Jannis Sarra & Cheryl L. Wade, Predatory Lending and the Destruction of the African-American Dream (2020).

31. Iowa College of Law, *Examining Institutional Structures: Race, Business & the Law*, YouTube (Seven-part series from Sept. 10, 2020 to Dec. 3, 2020), https://www.youtube.com/channel/UC_CyJeRrkAts0y0Zl15qzmQ/videos; Univ. of Chicago School of Law & Univ. of Virginia School of Law, *Insights on Teaching Race in Business Law*, YouTube (Feb. 5, 2021), https://www.youtube.com/watch?v=quboSkqrYVU; Univ. of Chicago & Univ. of Virginia, *A Workshop on Race and the Law of Business and Finance*, YouTube (Feb. 19, 2021), https://www.youtube.com/watch?v=jVEOY5GSD_w; Stanford Law School, Columbia Law School & University of Pennsylvania Carey Law School, *Conference on Racial Equity in Corporate Governance* (three-part series on October 29, 2020, Nov. 16,

Notably, other social sciences appear to have a longer history and focus in this area of legal analysis. For example, in 2014, historian Edward E. Baptist examined decades of economic public policy and the laws that supported the expansion of slavery in the nineteenth century.[32] Economics Professor Jenny B. Wahl studied the nearly 11,000 pre-Civil War appellate cases involving commercial disputes over slaves, connecting those cases to modern Uniform Commercial Code provisions and positing that the southern courts thereby helped minimize the costs of trading in slaves.[33] Historian Bonnie Martin analyzed 8,840 mortgages recorded in the eighteenth and nineteenth centuries explaining how Southerners used human collateral to raise large amounts of cash and credit.[34] Journalist Douglas A. Blackmon, in his Pulitzer Prize-winning work, described the legal structures that facilitated post-Civil War exploitative sharecropping, convict leasing, and peonage.[35] Sociologist Richard Rothstein's seminal work methodically presents how federal, state, and local governments intentionally created and enforced neighborhood segregation through zoning, tax, real estate, landlord-tenant, and mortgage lending laws at the turn of the twentieth century.[36] Economists Brendan O'Flaherty and Gavin Wright have both explored the impact of 1960s civil rights legislation on business development for people of color.[37] Importantly, many of the ideas presented in all these relatively modern works are often reflections of economic justice analysis and concepts dating back 50 to 150 years in the works of Frederick Douglass,[38]

2020 and January 14, 2021), https://web.cvent.com/event/72292c44-a0cd-4f8c-981a-cb76564f4513/websitePage:70e9122c-4a39-495d-ad8b-17bfdd05b0f8 (last visited Jan. 4, 2023).

32. Edward E. Baptist, The Half Has Never Been Told—Slavery and the Making of American Capitalism (2014).

33. Jenny B. Wahl, *The Jurisprudence of American Slave Sales*, 56 J. Econ. Hist. 143 (1996).

34. Bonnie Martin, *Slavery's Invisible Engine: Mortgaging Human Property*, 76 J. Southern Hist. 818 (2010).

35. Douglas A. Blackmon, Slavery by Another Name—The Re-enslavement of Black Americans from the Civil War to World War II (2008).

36. Richard Rothstein, The Color of Law—A Forgotten History of How Our Government Segregated America (2017).

37. Brendan O'Flaherty, The Economics of Race in the United States 132 (2015); Gavin Wright, *The Regional Impact of the Civil Rights Act of 1964*, 95 B.U. L. Rev. 759 (2015).

38. Baradaran, *supra* note 30, at 23 (quoting Frederick Douglas: the "mission of the Freedmen's Bank [of which he was appointed President in March 1874] is to show our people the road to a share of the wealth and well-being of the world.").

Booker T. Washington,[39] W.E.B. Dubois,[40] Marcus Garvey,[41] Langston Hughes,[42] James Baldwin,[43] Dr. Martin Luther King Jr.,[44] Malcom X,[45] and the still-relevant 1968 Kerner Commission Report.[46]

One may argue, in response to the assertion that the legal academy has not addressed this area as fully as the social sciences, that the important work produced by these scholars and experts is properly developed in their respective fields of history, economics, sociology, and the like. However, when I read their works, I am struck by their significant and continual reliance on legal analysis of statutes, cases, and regula-

---

39. BLACK-BELT DIAMONDS—GEMS FROM THE SPEECHES, ADDRESSES AND TALKS TO STUDENTS OF BOOKER T. WASHINGTON 60–61 (Victoria Earle Matthews ed., 1898) ("The first year our people received their freedom they had nothing on which to live while they grew their crops. Funds for the first crops were supplied by the storekeeper or by former masters. A debt was created, and to secure this indebtedness a lien was given on the cotton crops. In this way there was started in the South the mortgage or crop-lien system,—a system that has proved a curse to the black and to the white man ever since it was instituted.").

40. W.E.B. DU BOIS, THE SOULS OF BLACK FOLK (1903), *reprinted in* THREE AFRICAN-AMERICAN CLASSICS 237 (Dover 2007) ("The Negro farmer started behind,—started in debt. This was not his choosing.... Once in debt, it is no easy matter for a whole race to emerge.").

41. Justin Hansford, *Jailing a Rainbow: The Marcus Garvey Case*, 1 GEO. J.L. & MOD. CRITICAL RACE PERSP. 325, 336 (2009), *citing* TONY MARTIN, RACE FIRST: THE IDEOLOGICAL AND ORGANIZATIONAL STRUGGLES OF MARCUS GARVEY AND THE UNIVERSAL NEGRO IMPROVEMENT ASSOCIATION 3–25 (1976) ("... Garvey created the Negro Factories Corporation in 1919 using slogans such as 'Race First' and 'Africa for the Africans, at home and abroad.' The Negro Factories Corporation later gave birth to a plethora of small businesses, including 'Universal Laundries, a Universal Millinery Store, Universal Restaurants, Universal Grocery Stores, as well as a hotel, tailoring establishment, doll factor and printing press.'").

42. LANGSTON HUGHES, THE COLLECTED POEMS OF LANGSTON HUGHES 172 (1995) (containing his short but impactful 1933 poem *Black Workers*: "The bees work. Their work is taken from them. We are like the bees—but it won't last Forever.").

43. Craig Werner, *The Economic Evolution of James Baldwin*, 23 COLL. LANGUAGE ASS'N J. 12, 15 (1979) ("Even in the early stage, he [Baldwin] recognizes several crucial economic issues which he emphasizes in his later work. He sees a complex apparatus working for the economic exploitation of the ghetto through high rents, low quality, and general lack of safeguards against abuse. 'The Harlem Ghetto' (1948) and 'Fifth Avenue Uptown' (1960) extensively catalog the economic injustices which have a debilitating effect on the life of the individual ghetto resident.")

44. Dr. Martin Luther King, Jr., *Beyond Vietnam—A Time to Break Silence*, Address at New York City's Riverside Church (Apr. 4, 1967), https://www.americanrhetoric.com/speeches/mlkatimetobreaksilence.htm ("When machines and computers, profit motives and property rights are considered more important than people, the giant triplet of racism, materialism, and militarism are incapable of being conquered.")

45. Malcom X, *Speech at Ford Auditorium* (Feb. 13, 1965), https://www.blackpast.org/african-american-history/speeches-african-american-history/1965-malcolm-x-speech-ford-auditorium/ [https://perma.cc/3UKQ-G2NF] ("In Harlem, for instance, all of the stores are owned by white people, all of the buildings are owned by white people. Black people are just there, paying rent, buying the groceries. But they don't own the stores, clothing stores, food stores, any kind of stores; don't even own the homes that they live in.").

46. *See* Symposium, *The Urban Crisis: The Kerner Commission Report Revisited* 71 N.C. L. REV. 1283 (1993); U.S. DEP'T OF HOUSING & URBAN DEVELOPMENT, REPORT OF THE NAT'L ADVISORY COMM'N ON CIVIL DISORDERS (1968), https://www.hud.gov/sites/dfiles/FHEO/documents/kerner_commission_full_report.pdf [https://perma.cc/HL3K-XP5G].

tions. If the law is such a foundational aspect of their work, it begs the question of why legal scholarship and pedagogy have not been even more focused on the intersection of race and business law. A retort to this question would properly reference the numerous legal resources cited in this essay and possibly the legal journals specifically addressing race and economics.[47] So perhaps the question is better framed as why the legal academy has been unable to bring this available, relevant, and compelling research into the law school classroom in a manner accessible for future transactional attorneys. While course development and textbook writing is generally considered secondary or even tertiary scholarship, I would argue that providing this crucial information in a coherent manner to students focused on transactional law deserves significantly more attention. My effort is not bringing any new scholarly theories to the intersection of business law and racism, but instead attempting to collate this material for law students and possibly, in the future, make it easier for other business law professors to integrate these materials into their teaching.

One of the largest inhibitors to bringing race discussions into any classroom is the lack of a common frame of reference among the students. Therefore, the first third of the course attempts to provide students with such a framework. In a perfect world, this common frame of reference would be developed as part of a law school's orientation, coordinated institutional coverage in the first-year curriculum, or as a stand-alone course. There are efforts being made in this area.[48]

As such, the first class in this course[49] examines data on economic racial inequities that continue to exist within the U.S. economy and how critical race theory and antiracism strategies provide paradigms for analyzing these inequities. The next three classes look at the development of systemic racism leading up to the 1960s civil rights era. We review statutes and cases from colonial Virginia, slavery jurisprudence in commercial transactions, and post-Civil War/Reconstruction segregation-based economic polices facilitated by convict leasing, peonage, involuntary servitude, sharecropping agreements, and redlining. We also review the financial exploitation of indigenous populations, overt white supremacist laws and policies impacting Asian-American owned businesses beginning in the mid-nineteenth century, and exploitative labor-based immigration policies impacting people from Mexico, the Caribbean, and

---

47. *See, e.g.*, Hastings Race and Poverty Law Journal, University of Maryland law Journal of Race, Religion, Gender and Class, and Widener Journal of Law, Economics and Race.

48. *See From Words to Action: Dickinson Law Course Examines Roots of Systemic Racism*, PENN STATE NEWS (Apr. 13, 2021), https://news.psu.edu/story/654548/2021/04/13/academics/words-action-dickinson-law-course-examines-roots-systemic-racism (describing a new required class for 1Ls called "Race and the Equal Protection of the Laws"); Edward Fitzpatrick, *Course about race and law to be mandatory at Roger Williams University School of Law*, BOSTON GLOBE (June 28, 2021), https://www.bostonglobe.com/2021/06/28/metro/course-about-race-law-be-mandatory-roger-williams-university-school-law/ [https://perma.cc/JA64-WZZK]; Kari Njiiri, *Western New England to Require Students Take Anti-Racism Course*, NEW ENGLAND PUB. MEDIA (May 24, 2001), https://www.nepm.org/regional-news/2021-05-24/western-new-england-law-to-require-students-take-anti-racism-course [https://perma.cc/26SH-K377).

49. In the first iteration, each class was a two-hour period.

South America. We then look at federal civil rights laws of the 1960s (e.g., Civil Rights Act, Immigration Act, Fair Housing Act) and specifically, the successful and unsuccessful aspects of those attempts regarding economic development.

The next third of the course looks at how racism impacts traditional business and transactional legal subjects (e.g., corporate, tax, intellectual property, contracts). This section also assesses issues related to wealth and income inequality as they impact access to capital to finance business creation and growth. Specifically, we look at housing as a tool for intergenerational wealth, banking, venture capital, and bankruptcy and we review attempts at solutions, including controversial efforts at "Black Capitalism" beginning in the early 1970s.[50]

The final third of the course assesses contemporary racism in specific industries (e.g., insurance, technology, agriculture, service, and healthcare). Within this final section, we are not able to cover all industries. However, after analyzing certain industries from this perspective, students will have developed the framework to self-study areas of interest that we were not able to cover. Further, this additional material creates flexibility for offering the course as a two- or three-credit course.

The primary deliverable for the students is a 20- to 30-page paper related to our course material. I give the students the option of writing the paper in the form of a scholarly article or in the form of an internal memo addressed to a senior partner or corporate general counsel. I meet individually with each student once to discuss and formulate their topic and a second time to review their first draft. I also ask each student to give a five- to seven-minute presentation on their topic. After the fourth week of classes, each class begins with two student presentations. In practice, these presentations facilitated some of the best discussions of the course.[51] Topics chosen included:

- How the Minority Business Resiliency Act fails to address minorities' struggle with access to capital
- Race and Retail: Shoplifter Profiling and Consumer Racism (examining civil rights cases brought alleging discriminatory impact of "shopping while Black")
- Tax Increment Financing and Corporate Development in Detroit: Little Caesars Arena and Negative Impact on the City
- The Merchant Marine Act of 1920: A Shipping Regulation Strangling Puerto Rico's Economy
- Whether Asian American labor organizations can have a productive relationship with national organized labor
- Can Public Act No. 21-35 (An Act Equalizing Comprehensive Access to Mental, Behavioral, and Physical Health in Response to the Pandemic) further advance health equity in Connecticut?

---

50. Baradaran, *supra* note 30, at 164–214 (Chapter 6: The Decoy of Black Capitalism).

51. Special appreciation to Professor Bill Chin at Lewis & Clark Law School for sharing his Race and the Law course syllabus with me, which provided this successful paper review and class presentation structure.

- The disparate impact credit scores have on African Americans and minorities when determining insurance eligibility and analysis of two federal cases assessing such impact
- An analysis of racial health inequity through the lens of Medicare and Medicaid
- Assessing Federal Trade Commission guidance for use of artificial intelligence and the impact of biased algorithms
- Analysis of pending litigation alleging state and federal funding disparities between Historically Black Colleges and Universities and primarily white institutions in Maryland

The assignment was meant to provide the students the opportunity to research and discuss legal issues related to the course which they found personally engaging. Ultimately, I think it accomplished its objectives. As one student said, this was the type of paper they came to law school to write.

Reflections and Student Feedback

There was a range of responses on the class evaluations from the initial delivery of this course. I also received feedback during the course. For example, after one class, two students complained to the Associate Dean for Academic Affairs when I read aloud the name of an 1862 California statute that contained a racial slur.[52] When their concerns were brought up in class, I attempted to discuss the historical nature of language and its importance in understanding the context within which institutional structures were forming and operating. Subsequently, two other students reached out to me outside of class to say they understood what I was trying to accomplish in the class and hoped we could focus more on the facts and history and law and less on "politically correct language." One student specifically advised me to not let other students "take me down a rabbit hole." I think these are all the important and necessary conversations that a class of this nature will inspire.[53]

Regarding the written evaluations, the responses reflected that a majority of the students generally enjoyed the course and understood it was in the development stage. As always, the more interesting aspect was the narrative portions of the evaluations. Specific comments regarding the weakest point of the course include:

- Broader class participation would have been beneficial—professor often had to carry the discussion due to apparent apprehension by students.

---

52. Lin Sing v. Washburn, 20 Cal. 534, 564 (1862) (striking down the Act of April 26, 1862, titled "an act to protect free white labor against competition with Chinese *coolie* labor and discourage the immigration of the Chinese into the State of California"). Offending language at issue is emphasized.

53. I do not intend to make this mistake again and will be more sensitive to this issue in the future. *See* Anthony C. Thompson, *Stepping Up to the Challenge of Leadership on Race*, 48 Hofstra L. Rev. 735, 754–756 ("Racist conduct by law professors and microaggressions inside and outside the classroom have far-reaching impacts. These comments transform learning environments into uncomfortable and unsafe spaces.").

- In the course description people need to understand that difficult history, language and issues will be discussed. I found it very difficult to navigate the class given all the "drama" that was generated from other students. You have to understand the past to understand the present and make an impact on the future.
- The history and overall antiracist approach would benefit from a guest lecturer or co-instructor (an idea I shared directly and I know there was not an opportunity to do that this time around). This would support a deeper engagement with the history and set the tone for how to engage with difficult, upsetting material. Once the material got into business law specifically, the course flowed much better.
- I enjoyed this class and would definitely recommend it. That said, this was challenging subject matter. At some times, I found the class discussion uncomfortable because I wasn't sure that all the students were trusting the direction the professor was trying to take the discussion (e.g., the focus on the overt racist language in the Asian American cases transitioning to less obvious racism but still disparate impact in later cases—this dialogue for this class in particular became a little distracting). I thought the disclosures in the syllabus were helpful but still felt a "gap" in the room. Maybe holding a class like this in person would have helped to bridge that. I know I approached the discussions assuming positive intent but not sure everyone reached that point.
- This course should have been co-taught. The business law piece should be taught by a business law professor and the antiracism piece should be taught by a civil rights professor. The co-teaching would provide an opportunity for the antiracism information to be taught respectfully and appropriately with accurate historical information as opposed to twisted information picked out with regard to the business law aspects. The course needs to have clear direction that is conveyed to students in preparation for class. This course needs to be discussion based as antiracism is largely opinion based as cultural changes occur.
- The execution of the course was disappointing, to put it mildly. Clearly the professor needs to evolve more in his understanding of antiracism and how to apply different intellectual frameworks to an area of practice he knows well. This was truly such a letdown.

Student comments regarding strong points include:

- We were all learning together. I think it made a big difference and the professor acknowledged when he did not know something. I appreciate the candor and detailed discussion.
- The strongest point about this class was that it provided in-depth history as a preface to current worldwide issues and dilemmas. The instructor was knowledgeable and encouraged meaningful discussion but often that discussion was thwarted due to the difficulties presented by one or two of the students.

- The material in the second part of the class was valuable. The research the students are conducting is important and valuable.
- The selected readings/videos were thoughtful and provided a helpful backdrop for the discussions.
- The course topic is extremely important and had all the potential to redirect legal understandings of business law. I appreciated being able to choose a topic that interested me for the final paper as I am genuinely excited about the research and I am looking forward to writing this paper.
- Interesting concepts. I liked the variety of resources and have incorporated some of them into my routine beyond the course.

I recognize I still have much more to learn on facilitating these discussions and continue to seek out resources and support from colleagues. After reviewing these evaluations with my dean, she encouraged me to continue developing the course, and it will be offered again. I continue to believe that the intersection of business law and racism is an important area to focus upon and hope others will find new and innovative ways to bring this discussion into the law school classroom and business law curriculum.

Doctrine and Diversity in the Labor Law Syllabus and Classroom

Kerri Lynn Stone[*]

Introduction

Labor law, as I teach it, is a survey course that can cover a variety of topics, law, and legal bodies, including the National Labor Relations Act (NLRA),[1] the National Labor Relations Board (NLRB), the union election process, and more. At its core, this course is about the enabling and regulation of workers banding together to join their voices in order to work to improve the terms, privileges, and conditions of their workplace and to leverage their strength as a group to negotiate effectively with management. The integration of diversity and doctrine is thus a natural instinct in a course like this that focuses as much as it does on justice.

Opportunities to do this exist in many places, but one key place is in the discussion of racial and other protected class discrimination by unions. Traditionally, unions are the entities that protect workers from exploitation, abuse, and discrimination. However, when the culture or priorities of a union are antithetical to the provision of this protection, the role and function of the union are compromised. Moreover, in the midst of union campaigns and elections, malicious people may seek to prevail by inflaming already-existing prejudices, and the law must act to regulate this exploitation. After all, union campaign elections are supposed to be overseen with the goal of creating "laboratory conditions," such that nothing thwarts or obstructs voters' free exercise of will and choice.[2] With an eye toward history, context, and current events, many principles bearing upon diversity and doctrine are naturally, easily, and beneficially integrated into this class.

* Professor of Law, Florida International University College of Law.

1. National Labor Relations Act, 29 U.S.C. § 152 (2012).
2. *See, e.g.*, NLRB v. River City Elevator Co., 289 F.3d 1029, 1031 (7th Cir. 2002).

Section 7 of the NLRA

Specifically, unions' claims that they needed to de-prioritize discrimination claims of members so as to optimize benefits and efficacy can be examined through a critical lens. The impact of Section 7 of the NLRA's protection of employees' concerted activities on employers' ability to prohibit bullying and online bullying should also be examined with an eye toward diversity. As should the regulation of behavior during a union campaign or election that seeks to inflame and stoke bias in order to persuade a voter of something. Additionally, the influence of and role in social justice movements that unions play is important when discussing diversity.

A bit of background is useful here. Section 7 of the NLRA confers a right upon employees to, "... self-organization, to form, join, or assist labor organizations, to bargain collectively through representatives of their own choosing, and to engage in other concerted activities for the purpose of collective bargaining or other mutual aid or protection."[3] On the other hand, per Section 8(a)(1) of the NLRA, it is an unfair labor practice for an employer "to interfere with, restrain, or coerce employees in the exercise of the rights guaranteed in [the Act's] Section 7."[4] "For example, employers may not respond to a union organizing drive by threatening, interrogating, or spying on pro-union employees, or by promising benefits if they forget about the union."[5]

Much of a basic survey course in Labor Law explores the contours of the statutory law and case law that deal with the interplay between Section 7 rights and Section 8 unfair labor practices, as well as the spaces in which each exists. When I teach this course, I also usually reference the intersection of labor law with employment discrimination law—and the amenability to suit that unions have under Title VII of the Civil Rights Act of 1964, in particular.

Discrimination, Unions, and Labor Law

With respect to the latter, I usually reference a case that is more typically found in Employment Discrimination casebooks, *Goodman v. Lukens Steel Co.*[6] The Supreme Court delineated between the core substantive antidiscrimination provision and the anti-retaliation provision of Title VII. In the former, a substantially adverse action must be cabined within the workplace and concern itself with terms, conditions, or privileges of employment. In the latter, a "materially adverse action" is an adverse action that "well might have dissuaded a reasonable worker from making or supporting

3. 29 U.S.C. § 157.

4. 29 U.S.C. § 158(a)(1).

5. *Interfering with employee rights (Section 7 & 8(a)(1))*, NAT'L LAB. REL. BD. (last visited Feb. 9, 2023), https://www.nlrb.gov/about-nlrb/rights-we-protect/the-law/interfering-with-employee-rights-section-7-8a1#:~:text=Section%207%20of%20the%20National,of%20collective%20bargaining%20or%20other.

6. Goodman v. Lukens Steel Co., 482 U.S. 656 (1987).

a charge of discrimination."[7] Specifically, while the employer was alleged to have engaged in discrimination, the union was alleged to have engaged in discriminatory practices when it deprioritized and refused to advance challenges to Lukens's allegedly discriminatory discharges of probationary employees, or to assert incidences of alleged racial discrimination as grievances, and tolerated and tacitly encouraged alleged racial harassment.[8]

Significantly, the Supreme Court, with the understanding that "there was no suggestion below that the Unions held any racial animus against or denigrated [African Americans] generally," flatly rejected the union's argument that "these grievances could be resolved without making racial allegations and because the employer would 'get its back up' if racial bias was charged, thereby making it much more difficult to prevail" at the bargaining table.[9] The Court made it clear that the unions' failure to pursue the claims and grievances was not, as the dissent tried to frame it, a "racially neutral policy,"—a strategy that aimed to optimize results overall for union members[10] by, as the dissent said, "processing racial grievances on nonracial grounds—to obtain the swiftest and most complete relief possible for the claimant."[11] Rather, per the Court, the unions' choices constituted intentional racial discrimination that was violative of both Title VII and 1981 because a union may not lawfully "refuse to file any and all grievances presented by a black person on the ground that the employer looks with disfavor on and resents such grievances."[12]

In the past, covering this case had led to some really nuanced conversations about the role of unions and the obligations imposed upon them by the law. The idea that many individual voices, needs, and interests are represented by one body is an idea that needs to be understood at the outset of the class, and the idea that groups within groups might be sacrificed for the strategic reason of optimizing results for all is vividly illustrated in this case. Moreover, there is always a fear present that an organization engaged in such sacrificing will bend toward the arc of the majority's interests and identity. The fact that this is discriminatory and unlawful, however, is an important point to drive home. Where the goal is to protect individuals and prevent their rights from being trampled upon, the fact that more members of a minority group might benefit from a so-called strategic choice will not outweigh the violation of any individual's rights against racial or other discrimination prohibited by Title VII. This sets the tone for the class. Students benefit tremendously from thinking through and discussing the diversity of interests and identities contained within a bargaining unit, as well as the importance of the nondiscrimination mandates to which unions are held.

---

7. *Id.* at 658–59.

8. *See id.* at 669.

9. *See id.* at 668.

10. The dissent noted that the evidence adduced suggested that "the percentage of grievances filed on behalf of black employees was proportional to the number of blacks in the work force," and that "black members had a slightly higher rate of success in arbitration than white members." *See id.* at 682.

11. *Id.* at 685.

12. *See id.* at 669.

Antidiscrimination Principles and the NLRA

Students similarly benefit from considering the role of antidiscrimination principles in the proper interpretation of the NLRA. There is significant caselaw that deals with Sections 7 and 8, the cornerstone upon which the survey course rests, and with the NLRA's treatment of the inflammation of racial and other biases and the interplay of its regulation with the freedoms that the NLRA affords employers and employees, respectively.

The Supreme Court has said that Section 7 allows employees to "use intemperate, abusive, or insulting language without fear of restraint or penalty if [they] believe[d] such rhetoric to be an effective means to make [their] point."[13] This can naturally come into tension with the goals and underpinnings of antidiscrimination law, like Title VII. Indeed, not only have employers felt torn between the two statutes when it came to what to permit in the workplace before clamping down on speech,[14] but they have sometimes even been (successfully) accused of violating the NLRA when all they had done was promulgate anti-bullying policies meant to increase civility and reduce offensive, hurtful speech in the workplace.[15]

It is important to note the unique and disproportionate impact that workplace bullying has on protected classes like women and other minority groups in the workplace, and the way in which the NLRA had historically thwarted certain employers' attempts to create policies that stem it. Specifically, although status-neutral bullying is wholly lawful, scholars and others have posited that it may be uniquely targeted at and absorbed by members of certain protected classes, including women, in a way that disproportionately harms them.[16] Some employers, though not required to, voluntarily undertake to promulgate and implement anti-bullying policies, so as to enhance goodwill, morale, and reputational benefits.[17] However, such policies may create tension with the dictates of the NLRA, to the extent that the Board finds, as it has in the past, that the policies may shut down what Section 7 terms "other concerted activities for the purpose of collective bargaining or other mutual aid or protection."

---

13. *See* Old Dominion Branch No. 496 v. Austin, 418 U.S. 264, 283 (1974).

14. *See* Chai R. Feldblum & Victoria A. Lipnic, *Select Task Force on the Study of Harassment in the Workplace*, U.S. Equal Employment Opportunity Comm'n (June 2016) (discussing workplace civility training, which can raise issues under the NLRA), https://www.eeoc.gov/select-task-force-study-harassment-workplace#_ftnref220.; Ryan H. Vann & Melissa A. Logan, *The Tension Between the NLRA, the EEOC and Other Federal and State Employment Laws: The Management Perspective*, 33 ABA J. Lab. Emp. Law 291, 295 (2018).

15. *See generally* Kerri Lynn Stone, *Floor to Ceiling: How Setbacks and Challenges to the Anti-Bullying Movement Pose Challenges to Employers Who Wish to Ban Bullying*, 22 Temp. Pol. & Civ. Rts. L. Rev. 355 (2013).

16. *Id.* at 364.

17. *Id.* at 371.

In mid-2020, however, the NLRB flatly denied the idea that employers must always put up with abusive speech pursuant to their obligations under Section 7; it held that a burden-shifting test from 1980[18] is the appropriate framework for cases involving the question of whether an employer violated the NLRA when it disciplined an employee who engaged in abusive speech (including racially and sexually offensive speech) in the course of, ostensibly, exercising their Section 7 rights.[19] Under this test, first it must be shown that: (1) the employee who was disciplined engaged in protected activity under the NLRA; (2) the employer was aware of this activity; and (3) the protected activity was a motivating or substantial reason for the disciplinary action.[20] At that juncture, the burden will shift to the employer to prove that it would have taken the same adverse action regardless of the presence of the Section 7 activity.

Prior to 2020, the NLRB was poised to essentially presume in cases like this that employees' abusive behavior was protected, unless and until the employer could prove otherwise. The current status of the Board's position, however, is that protection has evaporated. The disciplined employee now shoulders the initial burden of making the three-part showing outlined above before any burden is placed on the employer. This is significant in a way that will likely impact class discussion on this turn in the trajectory of the law. As one legal blog has noted:

> The Board's decision to revive Wright Line could not be more timely, particularly in light of social justice movements such as the Black Lives Matter movement, the #MeToo movement, and other causes that have the potential to increase social discord and tension in the workplace. Under this renewed standard, employers will regain the liberty to discipline abusive employee conduct without suffering from the Board's prior presumption that an employee's abusive conduct was protected unless that protection was lost.[21]

Student discussions will likely revolve around the role and ability of an employer to create and maintain a workplace climate that is not inimical to diversity, inclusion, and equality, in light of its dual obligations under the NLRA and Title VII.[22] The new standard is certainly more hospitable to fostering greater workplace diversity, equity, and inclusion, but the Board has historically vacillated on legal approaches that it has taken, and it is important for students to flesh out this tension, especially at this moment in history. This country is in the midst of a series of reckonings and, as another legal blog

18. *See* Wright Line, 251 N.L.R.B. 1083, 1087 (1980).

19. *See* General Motors LLC, 369 N.L.R.B. No. 127 (2020).

20. *Id.*

21. W. Eric Baisden, Eric Flagg & Adam Primm, *NLRB Makes it Simpler to Discipline Profane or Abusive Employee Conduct*, JD SUPRA (July 24, 2020), https://www.jdsupra.com/legalnews/nlrb-makes-it-simpler-to-discipline-32331/.

22. In class, students have shared stories about many aspects of this ensuing tension. For example, several students have shared stories about online debates and disputes that are simultaneously alleged to be bullying toward a manager or supervisor and a legitimate exercise in collective action as the discussants air their grievances and attempt to improve the terms and conditions of their workplaces.

has noted, in the past, "The Board's catalogue of precedent protecting obscene, racist, or sexually harassing speech would make even the stoutest of heart uncomfortable."[23]

Indeed, the Board solicited opinions from amici on the question of precisely at what point racial, sexual, or otherwise profane language would no longer enjoy Section 7 protection, and the responses were classified by a legal blog as falling within three broad categories: "(1) th[ose] ... who believed that 'speech protected by Section 7 of the Act can be coarse "because of the passions such topics inflame and that it should not be censored or hindered"'; (2) the general counsel and others who proposed a per se approach that would eliminate protection for language based on race, sex, or other protected categories under Title VII; and (3) those ... who urged the Board to jettison 'setting-specific standards altogether and uphold employers' enforcement of facially neutral work rules prohibiting profane, racist, or sexist conduct unless the evidence shows that the employer used such conduct as a pretext to interfere with Section 7 activity.'"[24]

A useful article that could be brought into class discussions is an empirical piece from 2018 that sets out to answer the question of whether the NLRA sanctions racist employee speech, and finds that it often does after looking at cases in which campaign speech made in the course of union elections is challenged and in which racist speech is engaged in on picket lines.[25] A great discussion to engage students in after educating them about the study and its results is one about the author's proposal that the NLRB afford "less legal protection for racist speech by adopting Title VII's standard for hostile work environment."[26] To support this, the author asserts, among other things, that "NLRB speech doctrines have unwittingly opened the door to form whites-only labor unions," and observes that "No federal law—in this case, the NLRA—should offer a platform to re-segregate the American workplace."[27] A robust discussion about opinions on this proposal and its underpinnings would call upon students to use critical thinking skills.

The *Sewell* Doctrine

The above discussion is far from the only point in the labor law syllabus where issues of diversity, equality, and inclusion come into play. The Board's *Sewell* doctrine and the way in which it deals with alleged attempts to inflame racial prejudices in the course of union election campaigns is also a rich topic. The *Sewell* case, decided by the Board in 1962, is best described by Professor Marion Crain:

---

23. *See* Stephen E. Baumann II, James A. Paretti, Jr. & Michael J. Lotito, *A Return to Workplace Civility: The NLRB Adopts the* Wright Line *Burden-Shifting Approach to Section 7 Speech*, Littler Mendelson P.C. (July 22, 2020), https://www.littler.com/publication-press/publication/return-workplace-civility-nlrb-adopts-wright-line-burden-shifting.

24. *Id.*

25. *See* Michael H. LeRoy, *Slurred Speech: How the NLRB Tolerates Racism*, 8 Colum. J. Race & L. 209, 211–13 (2018).

26. *See id.* at 211–12.

27. *Id.* at 213.

> [T]he Georgia-based employer appealed to the racial privilege of its white workers in an effort to defeat the union organizing drive. The employer circulated pictures of a white woman dancing with an unidentified Black man and of a white man identified by an accompanying caption as the union president dancing with a Black woman. The pictures were accompanied by suggestions that the union would seek to racially integrate the workforce, an idea that many southern whites found alarming. As evidence of its assertions, the employer pointed to the fact that the union had donated funds to the NAACP and the Congress of Racial Equality, groups that advocated for integration. Finding that the employer's conduct constituted a 'deliberate, sustained appeal to racial prejudice ... which made impossible a reasoned choice of a bargaining representative,' the Board set aside the election....[28]

The Board proclaimed that it would not set aside an election result where "a party limits itself to truthfully setting forth another party's position on matters of racial interest and does not deliberately seek to overstress and exacerbate racial feelings by irrelevant and inflammatory appeals," and that the party deploying a racial communication will shoulder the burden of showing that the communication was "truthful and germane."[29] The discussion of this proclamation can easily lead to classroom debates as to its application in a number of scenarios. It behooves a professor to ensure that students, while remaining respectful to one another, probe and interrogate the meanings of words like "overstress," "exacerbate," "irrelevant," and "inflammatory." Professor Crain noted that the NLRB "seemed particularly disturbed by the implication of the employer-distributed photos and letters that 'unionism is a foreign, Communist concept with the end objective of racial intermarriage.'"[30]

As cases continued to be filed, and the Board wound up trying to delineate the contours between communications that were relevant and sincere, as opposed to those that were spurious and designed to inflame prejudices so as to manipulate others, the Board also found itself faced with cases in which the race-related statements alleged to merit the overturning of an election came from the union involved in a campaign, and not the employer.[31] According to Professor Crain, cases like this afforded the NLRB "an opportunity to draw a meaningful distinction between appeals that sought to divide employees (typically made by the employer) and appeals that sought to unite them (typically made by the union)," with unions arguing that their attempts to unite workers in racial terms could be handily distinguished from employers' (like that in *Sewell*) previous attempts to cast a vote to not unionize as a vote against the advancement of and equality for African Americans.[32]

---

28. Marion Crain, *Whitewashed Labor Law, Skinwalking Unions*, 23 Berkeley J. Emp. & Lab. L. 211, 231–42 (2002).

29. *Id.* at 233.

30. *Id.*

31. *Id.* at 234.

32. *Id.* at 234–36.

However, per Professor Crain, as these cases made it past the Board, federal courts were prone to finding it "irrelevant whether the appeal to racial passions was made by the employer with the goal of dividing the workforce, or by the union with the goal of enhancing solidarity."[33] Her article, cited above, contains examples of compelling cases that are useful for discussion in class. Students benefit from thinking critically about the origins, evolution, and trajectory of the *Sewell* doctrine. Criticisms of the doctrine may be entertained (e.g., is the doctrine so muddled and unfocused as to blunt elections without predictability and causing delay?), as may ways to strengthen it in terms of its underlying goals. It is worth analyzing Professor Crain's conclusion that the doctrine has, in actuality, "functioned most powerfully to undermine union election victories in racially segregated workplaces, which usually contain the most oppressed workers."[34]

It is also worth discussing federal courts' split on the issue of whether the doctrine applies when third parties seek to stoke racial and religious prejudices in the context of a representational election, and if so, how. A legal commentator whose analysis would be good to share with a class provides some historical context and a good lens through which to consider this question:

> [C]hanges in the tenor of U.S. race relations since 1962 diminish Sewell's utility in two ways and support cabining Sewell within its original confines—prohibiting primary-party inflammatory appeals to prejudice. First, racism in the workplace has become less explicit. Sewell excels only as a test for explicit racism because it seeks out overt "appeals or arguments which can have no purpose except to inflame the racial feelings of voters in the election." As overt racism diminishes, there is less need for a doctrine focused on overtly discriminatory speech, especially third-party racist speech. Second, because of persistent latent racism, there is a great need to openly discuss race and conduct that has adverse effects on systemically disadvantaged racial groups.... Race is frequently germane to union elections because race is everywhere....[35]

It is a laudable goal in the classroom to expose students to viewpoints and insights with which they may not agree, but with which they can use their critical thinking skills to inform their own opinions. The scope and continued viability of this doctrine will depend on how future legislators, judges, NLRB members, and others construe everything from the "laboratory conditions" deemed necessary to a fair representational election, to the menace of racial prejudice to the integrity of the process. Is open, unfettered discussion the key to combating discrimination? Or is increased regulation desirable to blunt the power of inflamed prejudice as a tool of manipulation? Having

---

33. *Id.* at 236–37.

34. *Id.* at 242.

35. Marc J. Shinn-Krantz, *Third-Party Inflammatory Appeals to Prejudice: Race, Religion, and Union Elections*, 31 ABA J. Lab. & Emp. L. 385, 389–408 (2016).

these discussions during a time when the power of abusive speech, especially in and around the workplace, has taken center stage is fruitful.

Modern Union's Role in the Context of Social Justice Movements

A final topic that may come up in class is the modern union's role in the context of social justice movements going on around it. With the Black Lives Matter and #MeToo movements gaining momentum in recent years, and with inflation at such high levels, unions are forging a resurgence even as they sometimes bind themselves to social justice movements. With big names like Starbucks and Amazon tied to the union resurgence, students want to forecast trends and get at the compelling social forces and messages that have influenced the dynamics behind it. According to an article on indianexpress.com, discussing the renewed interest in unionization after such a lengthy period of disinterest:

> Recent social movements may also have played a role. At Google, employees have complained in the last few years about the company's attitude towards addressing sexual harassment at the workplace in light of the #MeToo movement. This, among other disagreements with the company administration, added to growing frustrations. The firing of Dr Timnit Gebru, an African-American artificial intelligence researcher, allegedly for her criticism of Google's diversity policy, caused outrage from workers in the aftermath of the Black Lives Matter protests of 2020. In January 2021, the Alphabet Workers Union was formed.[36]

Indeed, students benefit from discussing the historical and social context from which the current trends regarding unionization derive. Social movements have been propulsive catalysts that have impelled people to want to unionize. As Alejandro Ortiz, a former NLRB attorney who now works for the American Civil Liberties Union, which he helped unionize, put it on a June 2022 CNN podcast:

> Forming a union is a vehicle for self-help. It's a way to build solidarity. It's a way to have a voice in your working conditions.... And the main reason in my experience that employers often resist their workforce unionizing is because it means ceding power to the workers. And generally speaking, when people or organizations are in positions of power, they don't want to give it up. But I see it as a vehicle for marginalized, vulnerable groups of workers, workers of color, in particular, low wage workers who are disproportionately workers of color, to band together to improve their working conditions.... [P]romoting laborers and promoting solidarity, especially among the most

36. Rishika Singh, *Explained: Apple, Amazon, Starbucks and the trend of workers forming unions in US*, INDIAN EXPRESS, (June 25, 2022), https://indianexpress.com/article/explained/explained-apple-amazon-starbucks-workers-union-us-7991065/.

> marginalized people in society, is a racial justice issue, given who composes the most marginalized people in society. If you can lift them up through a union, through solidarity, through a sense of common cause, then you are promoting racial justice. MLK, what was he doing the day before he was assassinated? He was in Memphis helping promote the cause of striking sanitation workers who were disproportionately black. He also recognized that promoting labor rights is promoting racial justice.[37]

In sum, labor law is a class whose materials naturally invite questions and comments from students about issues of diversity, workplace equality, and inclusion. The material is rife with various social movements that gave rise to the legislative scheme surrounding the NLRA as we know it today, and issues touching upon the treatment of minority groups are pervasive. Allowing students to explore these and the other issues discussed above enriches their understanding of the material and enables them to have memorable discussions about the policies, historical context, and tensions undergirding the birth and trajectory of labor law.

37. Diversifying Podcast, *Why Unions Are Making a Comeback*, CNN Audio (June 13, 2022), https://www.cnn.com/audio/podcasts/diversifying/episodes/6594e0f8-b839-4146-8a9f-aeb000e1188c.

Equity and Inclusion at the Intersection of Law, Money and Technology

Rohan Grey & Julia Ricciardi†*

Introduction

The way we talk about [money] in law school has been blocked in a way, because we're not really honest with each other about the fact that our money system is a legal choice.

—Robert Jackson, Jr., Former S.E.C. Commissioner[1]

[D]esigning money is shaping community; it can bring people together or set them at each other's throats.

—Christine Desan, Legal historian of money[2]

Issuing a currency is always a political act.

—Ndongo Samba Sylla, Development economist[3]

Monetary law is at once pervasive and obscure; everywhere and nowhere. It stretches from the loftiest peaks of constitutional and democratic theory[4] down to the daily

* Assistant Professor of Law, Willamette University College of Law. My deepest gratitude to my student, research assistant, and pedagogical collaborator, Julia Ricciardi, for agreeing to write this with me. All mistakes remain my own.

† J.D. Candidate ('24), Willamette University College of Law. Thank you to my greatest teachers, including Phoenix Johnson, Hon. Darleen Ortega, and my mom.

1. Robert Jackson, Jr., Panel Remarks at the Columbia Law School Symposium on "Taking Money for Granted: Pedagogical Issues in Law and Economics" (Oct. 8, 2013).

2. Christine Desan, *The Impact and Malleability of Money Design*, LPE Project (Mar. 25, 2019), https://lpeproject.org/blog/the-impact-and-malleability-of-money-design/#more-2165.

3. Ndongo Samba Sylla, *Moving Forward to African Monetary Integration*, 45 Africa Dev. 39, 39 (2020).

4. *See, e.g.*, Christine Desan, *Money as a Constitutional Medium*, LPE Project (May 14, 2019), https://lpeproject.org/blog/all-debts-public-and-private; Stefan Eich, The Currency of Politics (2022).

grind of the common law.[5] Yet until the global financial crisis, it did not feature prominently in the American law school curriculum outside of cursory treatment in a few niche, technical subjects like banking and payments.[6]

Since then, the rise (and falls) of cryptocurrencies and central bank digital currencies, as well as other geopolitical developments, including the COVID-19 pandemic and Russia-Ukraine war, have pushed questions of monetary technology and governance to the forefront of public consciousness and political debate.[7] Consequently, money has (re)emerged as a central focus across a range of legal fields, including administrative law, regulation, corporate law, payments law, privacy law, criminal law, international law, and legal history.[8] Today, practitioners from areas as diverse as intellectual property and family law are grappling with the brave new world of digital money, and what it means for their clients and careers.[9]

The remainder of this essay provides those new to the topic with an introduction to the law-money-technology nexus, its implications for equity and justice, and some preliminary suggestions for how to approach teaching about related issues in the law school classroom.

---

5. *See, e.g.*, KATHARINA PISTOR, THE CODE OF CAPITAL (2019); Lua Yuille & Rohan Grey, *Money & Property*, LPE PROJECT (May 16, 2019), https://lpeproject.org/blog/money-and-property; DAVID FOX, PROPERTY RIGHTS IN MONEY (2008).

6. This was partly due to the then-hegemonic dominance of the Chicago School of Law and Economics, which largely deferred to macroeconomists on monetary issues, and instead placed near-exclusive emphasis on the application of neoclassical microeconomic concepts to judicial reasoning. *See, e.g.*, Richard Posner, *How I Became a Keynesian*, THE NEW REPUBLIC (Sept. 22, 2009), https://newrepublic.com/article/69601/how-i-became-keynesian. *See also* Roy Kreitner, *The Legal History of Money*, 8 ANN. REV. L. SOC. SCI. 415 (2012) (discussing the dearth of legal historical scholarship on money).

7. *See, e.g.*, Alan Rappeport, *US escalates sanctions with a freeze on Russian central bank assets*, N.Y. TIMES (Feb. 28, 2022), https://www.nytimes.com/2022/02/28/us/politics/us-sanctions-russia-central-bank.html; Erin Griffith, *We're All Crypto People Now*, N.Y. TIMES (Apr. 25, 2021), https://www.nytimes.com/2021/04/25/technology/cryptocurrency-mainstream.html; Jeanna Smialek, *Still Getting Your Head Around Digital Currency? So Are Central Bankers*, N.Y. TIMES (Apr. 26, 2021), https://www.nytimes.com/2021/04/26/business/economy/fed-digital-currency.html; Matt Phillips, *How the Government Pulls Coronavirus Relief Money Out of Thin Air*, N.Y. TIMES (Apr. 15, 2020), https://www.nytimes.com/2020/04/15/business/coronavirus-stimulus-money.html.

8. *See, e.g.*, CRYPTOCURRENCIES IN PUBLIC AND PRIVATE LAW (David Fox & Sarah Green eds., 2019); YAIR LISTOKIN, LAW AND MACROECONOMICS: LEGAL REMEDIES TO RECESSIONS (2019); CAMILLE WALSH, RACIAL TAXATION: SCHOOLS, SEGREGATION, AND TAXPAYER CITIZENSHIP, 1869–1973 (2018); MEHRSA BARADARAN, THE COLOR OF MONEY: BLACK BANKS AND THE RACIAL WEALTH GAP (2017); MONEY IN THE WESTERN LEGAL TRADITION (David Fox & Wolfgang Ernst eds., 2016); PETER CONTI-BROWN, THE POWER AND INDEPENDENCE OF THE FEDERAL RESERVE (2016); CHRISTINE DESAN, MAKING MONEY: COIN, CURRENCY, AND THE COMING OF CAPITALISM (2014).

9. *See, e.g.*, Birgit Clark, *Blockchain and IP Law: A Match Made in Crypto Heaven?*, WIPO MAG. (Feb. 2018), https://www.wipo.int/wipo_magazine/en/2018/01/article_0005.html; Alexis Garcia Connors, *A Divorce Lawyer's Crash Course in Cryptocurrency*, LAW.COM (July 1, 2022), https://www.law.com/dailyreportonline/2022/07/01/a-divorce-lawyers-crash-course-in-cryptocurrency/?slreturn=20220926042411.

The Law-Money-Technology Nexus

Law schools increasingly now offer dedicated courses in the law of money or related topics like cryptocurrency.[10] Legal textbooks, including for foundational subjects such as contracts and property, are incorporating modules and cases relating to digital currency and fintech. At the same time, networks of critical legal scholars are developing new conceptual frameworks that emphasize the social non-neutrality of money, and the role of legal and technological systems in the creation and perpetuation of inequality and injustice.[11]

Despite these developments, the law of money remains under-taught and under-studied, and its broader sociopolitical implications poorly understood. In part, this is by design: imperial, exploitative, and technocratic monetary regimes function most effectively when kept invisible from and unquestioned by the masses.[12]

In part, this is also because it is difficult to define the boundaries of "monetary" law when almost every social problem has a monetary dimension that, if altered sufficiently, could radically transform if not eliminate the problem entirely. Is involuntary unemployment inevitable, or a contingent by-product of bad monetary system design? Is it more emancipatory to give people a guaranteed income, or direct access to public goods and services like housing, food, healthcare, and education?[13] Is there really such thing as a "free market" when the global economy is built upon monetary regimes governed by and for a small number of militarized, hegemonic nation-states? The answers to these questions differ depending on which macroeconomist you ask.[14]

---

10. *See, e.g.*, Geoffrey Miller, Max Raskin, & David Yermack, *Digital Currency, Blockchains, and the Future of the Financial Services Industry*, NYU Law/Stern School (Spring 2020), https://w4.stern.nyu.edu/finance/docs/pdfs/Outlines/2021-1/2101-gb3324-yermack.pdf; Christine Desan, *The Constitutional Law of Money*, Harvard Law School (Fall 2017), https://justmoney.org/wp-content/uploads/2019/07/ConMon-2017-syllabus.pdf; Angela Walch, *Cryptocurrencies, Blockchain Technologies & the Law*, St. Mary's University School of Law (Fall 2018), https://ledgerprof.files.wordpress.com/2018/11/blockchain-and-the-law-syllabus-website-version-fall-2018.pdf. *See also* Rohan Grey, *Law, Money, & Technology*, Willamette University College of Law (Fall 2021), https://willamette.edu/law/internal/students/osa/pdf/syllabi/21fa/law319-grey-lmt-syllabus-fall2021.pdf.

11. For example, ClassCrits, the Law & Political Economy (LPE) Network, the Association for the Promotion of Political Economy and Law (APPEAL), Just Money, the Journal of Law & Political Economy (JLPE), the Modern Money Network (MMN), and the Law & Macroeconomics Conference.

12. JAKOB FEINIG, MORAL ECONOMIES OF MONEY: POLITICS AND THE MONETARY CONSTITUTION OF SOCIETY (2022) (arguing that contemporary American history oscillates between periods of monetary politicization and monetary "silencing," where the public is broadly excluded from participation in political discussions about money and related economic issues by policymakers and elite stakeholders); *see also* Michael Dorf, *Money, Law, and Other Noble Lies*, VERDICT (Oct. 13, 2021), https://verdict.justia.com/2021/10/13/money-law-and-other-noble-lies (arguing that "[f]alse belief[s]" about money "may be necessary to ensure [its] continued use and thereby avert . . . catastrophe").

13. *See, e.g.*, Rohan Grey, *Equality, Not Equal Pay: Distributional Justice Beyond Money*, *in* DEBATING EQUAL PAY: ECONOMY, PRACTICABILITY, ETHICS 283 (Anders Örtenblad ed., 2021).

14. Mark Kelman, *Could Lawyers Stop Recessions? Speculations on Law and Macroeconomics*, 45 STAN. L. REV. 1215, 1217 (1993). *See also The Monetary Case for a Job Guarantee*, Money as a Democratic Medium—Conference at Harvard Law School (Jan. 10, 2019), https://www.youtube.com/watch?v=ijSUfh33yO8.

More practically, the law of money, particularly digital money, is a technically complex, constantly evolving field that draws on multiple doctrinal areas and extra-legal disciplinary competencies. In order to properly contextualize the leading fintech issues of the day, lawyers must be at least somewhat familiar with not only black letter law, but also balance sheets, economic theory, and payments system engineering. [15] This is a daunting challenge for busy professors and students alike.

Equity and Inclusion in an Inequitable and Exclusionary World

These pedagogical challenges are exacerbated by the fact that monetary regimes have actively oppressed, exploited, and excluded many communities throughout history and continue to do so. Monetary law thus implicates the intersection of multiple systems of power and privilege including race, gender, class, national origin, disability, and the like. [16]

When first introduced to this world—sometimes not until law school, but often in undergrad, or even high school—many students feel alienated or unwelcome, and struggle to relate the topics being discussed to their professional interests and lived experience. For many students, a common response is to remain quiet, disengage, or even leave the space entirely. Others attempt to participate fully, but quickly get discouraged or derailed by technical aspects of the subject matter that are not commonly taught, fear and impostor syndrome, a hostile or unsafe learning environment, and/or lack of trust or connection with their instructor and/or classmates. Without deliberate counteractive intervention, this typically results in the structural overrepresentation of white male students in money and fintech course enrollments, and the centering of white male voices and perspectives in money-related discussions when they arise in other classes. Over time, this dynamic further engrains the same social inequities and exclusionary professional cultures that produced it in the first place.

To disrupt this cycle, we must reckon with the injustices, biases, and staggering lack of racial, Indigenous, class, and gender diversity that define the key institutions and actors in the field. The cryptocurrency industry, for example, has extreme right-wing ideological roots, [17] and is saturated with scams perpetrated against vulnerable and

---

15. *See, e.g.*, James Grimmelmann, *All Smart Contracts Are Ambiguous*, 2 J. L. & Innov. 1 (2019).

16. *See, e.g.*, Pavlina Tcherneva, *Money, Power, and Monetary Regimes*, Levy Working Paper No. 861 (2016), https://www.levyinstitute.org/pubs/wp_861.pdf; Raúl Carrillo, *Challenging Monetary Sanctions in the Era of Racial Taxation*, 4 UCLA Crim. J. L. Rev. 143–155 (2019); Emma C. Jordan, *The Hidden Structures of Inequality: The Federal Reserve and a Cascade of Failures*, 2 U. Pa. J. L. & Pub. Affairs (2017); Fanny Pigeaud & Ndongo Samba Sylla, Africa's Last Colonial Currency: The CFA Franc Story (2021).

17. *See generally* David Golumbia, The Politics of Bitcoin: Software as Right-Wing Extremism (2016).

impoverished communities.[18] The traditional finance and technology sectors—Wall Street and Silicon Valley—are infamous for their racist, toxic masculine cultures and predatory consumer behavior. Central banks, especially the Federal Reserve, regularly impose devastating economic pain on communities of color and nations in the global south (allegedly) in service of domestic macroeconomic and financial stability goals.[19] The economics discipline is only beginning to take account of decades of unchecked sexual harassment by many of its leading figures.[20] Each of these communities, industries, institutions, and professions is, unsurprisingly, dominated at the top by wealthy, cishet, white men.

Teaching for Monetary Justice

For law professors aspiring to center equity and inclusion while teaching at the intersection of law, money, and technology,[21] the challenge is threefold.[22]

First, we must frame our inquiry around issues and themes that are engaging and approachable to students with historically marginalized identities. We must actively seek to understand where our students are coming from, validate any sense of exclusion or apprehension they may feel, and recognize that each student has a personal experience of money and monetary systems (likely influenced by their family, culture, class background, race, and other identities). As students learn about the law of money, they may grapple with their own experience of and/or trauma related to money. If we invite students to engage authentically, we must also engage authentically and demonstrate a willingness to reveal our own identities and limitations.[23]

Responsive professors will build on students' prior experience with and interest(s) in money and technology, while simultaneously recognizing that many have little or no formal training, and are relying on our judgment regarding what legal questions, issues, and concepts are important to learn. We must acknowledge and take meaningful

18. Emma Fletcher, *Reports show scammers cashing in on crypto craze*, FTC.GOV (June 3, 2022), https://www.ftc.gov/news-events/data-visualizations/data-spotlight/2022/06/reports-show-scammers-cashing-crypto-craze.

19. *See, e.g.*, Jeff Stein, *Poorer nations could suffer from U.S. efforts to slow inflation*, WASH. POST (July 25, 2022), https://www.washingtonpost.com/us-policy/2022/07/25/federal-reserve-interest-developing-markets; Tim Barker, *Other People's Blood*, 34 N+1 (Spring 2019), https://www.nplusonemag.com/issue-34/reviews/other-peoples-blood-2.

20. Ben Casselman, Jim Tankersley & Jeanna Smialek, *A Year After a #MeToo Reckoning, Economists Still Grapple With It*, N.Y. TIMES (Jan. 1, 2020), https://www.nytimes.com/2020/01/07/business/economy/economics-race-gender.html.

21. Either in a standalone course, or as a module in another course.

22. This section is primarily built around Rohan's experiences teaching such courses, with input from Julia based on her experiences in these and related classes, and as a former elementary school and youth-leadership educator, artist, and activist.

23. We find that inviting feedback from students and swiftly apologizing when we have caused harm or invalidated someone's lived experience goes a long way in building trust and creating stronger professor-student relationships.

steps to reduce the technical and cultural barriers many students face when learning about money and digital technology.[24] In our syllabi and classrooms, we must center voices and issues that reflect communities most frequently erased or sidelined, as well as clarify and break down technical jargon. Focusing on both the technical and socio-cultural aspects of intersections between money, law, and technology helps reveal the core tensions, values, and forces at play, as well as the monumental stakes.

This can be facilitated through integration of multimedia resources, news and current affairs stories, cultural and popular references, poetry, music, and humor.[25] Even simple curricular touches can go a long way, such as shareable outlines and glossaries, clear signposting, frequent revision, periodic low-stakes reflections, and thoughtful feedback from professor to student or among peers.

Second, we must balance providing a general, interdisciplinary framework from which to critically evaluate monetary and fintech-related problems, and covering doctrinal concepts and rules in keeping with broader learning requirements. To quote futurist Alvin Toffler, we've got to "think about the big things while [we're] doing the small things, so the small things go in the right direction."

Curricular decisions about what topics to focus on, and how much, are inherently value-laden, and provide students an early window into the priorities and commitments of the instructor. Given the many entry points into digital monetary issues across the law school curriculum, there is no one-size-fits-all approach. However, I (Rohan) typically try to cover the following themes across all of my classes:

- *Non-Neutrality of Money:* In contrast to the orthodox account of money commonly found in economics textbooks, which ahistorically asserts its "apolitical" origins in voluntary private exchange, I locate money's roots in public authority and imperial, colonial, and intra-community violence.[26] I emphasize

---

24. Arming students with the most robust technical understanding can help them resist the systemic oppression that can manifest as imposter syndrome and defend against future attempts at professional discrimination or marginalization.

25. Given that white, cishet men take up a lot of space in these fields, it is critical—although by no means easy—to actively seek out and to decolonize our curriculum by centering diverse and heterodox scholars, leaders, and sources, especially those whose historical influence and significance has been marginalized. Oftentimes such individuals have contributed monumentally to these fields, yet have been marginalized or erased from the canon. While there are too many to list here, the authors wish to extend a special acknowledgment to Fadhel Kaboub for his tireless efforts to orient the emerging 'Modern Monetary Theory' paradigm around issues of anti-colonialism and development in the Global South, and Nina Banks for her work to bring public attention to the life, ideas, and contributions of Sadie Alexander, the first African-American woman in the United States to obtain a doctorate in economics. Both have been inspirational to the authors' own educational journey and pedagogical development. *See, e.g.*, Scott Ferguson, Maxximilian Seijo & William Saas, *The New Postcolonial Economics With Fadhel Kaboub*, Money on the Left (July 7, 2018), https://mronline.org/2018/07/07/the-new-postcolonial-economics-with-fadhel-kaboub; Economic and Monetary Sovereignty in 21st Century Africa (Maha Ben Gadha et al. eds., 2021); Nina Banks, Democracy, Race, and Justice: The Speeches and Writings of Sadie T.M. Alexander (2021).

26. *See, e.g.*, Christine Desan, *Money as Legal Institution*, *in* Money in the Western Legal Tradition 18 (David Fox & Wolfgang Ernst eds., 2015); K-Sue Park, *Money, Mortgages, and the*

class interests and the bureaucratic desire to assert social control as key drivers in the development of new modes of monetary governance.[27] At the same time I suggest that, notwithstanding its long history of weaponization in the service of oppression, money is always and everywhere a small-c constitutional project, and a public good whose design and administration affects everyone, particularly those from diverse or marginalized backgrounds who are more likely to experience economic insecurity, discrimination, or poverty. The modern political and legal struggle over the "money power"—who gets to make money, for what purposes, in what amounts—is, in a very real sense the struggle for democracy itself.[28]

- *Non-Neutrality of Technology:* I encourage students to think about how they depend upon monetary technologies to facilitate social interaction; the various demographic, cultural, and aesthetic considerations that go into their daily use of money, and the extent to which changes in monetary technologies and habits affect their senses of personal identity and autonomy.[29] I walk them through major historical developments in monetary technology, from clay tokens and tablets through to double-entry accounting, paper money, the wire, cards, mobile money, the internet, and cryptography.[30] In doing so, I highlight the interconnection between monetary systems and information technology regimes, the inherently political and contested nature of technological change,[31] and the ways in which monetary technological innovation can function as a leading indicator of broader techno-social trends.[32] I also touch on the history of digital activism and internet freedom movements, primarily to identify points of intersection with monetary activism around issues of censorship, privacy, and civil liberties.[33]

Conquest of America, 41 L. & Soc. Inquiry 1006 (2016); Mathew Forstater, *Taxation and Primitive Accumulation: The Case of Colonial Africa*, *in* The Capitalist State and Its Economy: Democracy in Socialism: Research in Political Economy, Vol. 22, 51 (2005).

27. *See generally* David Graeber, Debt: The First 5000 Years (2011).

28. *See* Desan, *supra* note 2; Desan, *supra* note 4.

29. *See also* Viviana Zelizer, *The Social Meaning of Money: "Special Monies"*, 95 Am. J. Socio. 342 (1989).

30. For a relatively accessible and comprehensive, if somewhat qualitatively uneven historical overview, *see generally* William Goetzmann, Money Changes Everything: How Finance Made Civilization (2016).

31. *See, e.g.*, Mireille Hildebrandt, Smart Technologies and the End(s) of Law: Novel Entanglements of Law and Technology 175–85 (2015).

32. *See, e.g.*, Denise Schmandt-Besserat, *The Evolution of Writing*, *in* International Encyclopedia of Social and Behavioral Sciences (James Wright ed., 2014), https://sites.utexas.edu/dsb/files/2014/01/evolution_writing.pdf.

33. *E.g.*, Jay Stanley, *We Need Digital Cash That is Actually Like Cash*, ACLU (Mar. 28, 2022), https://www.aclu.org/news/privacy-technology/we-need-digital-cash-that-is-actually-like-cash; Tamara Nopper, *Alternative Data and the Future of Credit Scoring*, Data For Progress (Aug. 17, 2020), https://www.filesforprogress.org/pdfs/alternative-data-future-credit-scoring.pdf.

- *High Stakes of Monetary Struggle:* The modern "currency" wars are being waged across every level of society, from governments, banks, and technology platforms down to hackers, celebrities, and even a few twelve-year-olds.[34] Cryptocurrency advocates and central bankers alike foresee a future in which physical cash is obsolete, and every digital payment is subject to potential censorship by large, faceless actors.[35] Without sounding (too) alarmist, I try to impress on students the urgency of the present monetary moment and the extent to which decisions being made today will shape the future in profound ways.[36] I stress the potential for smart lawyers to both do good and do well, and highlight career pathways to monetary law beyond the corporate firm route, including regulatory enforcement, community development, and public policymaking.

For my standalone "Law, Money, Technology" seminar, I usually introduce students to leading digital money debates through analogical case studies that clarify the underlying political dynamics and practical implications for different stakeholders. For example:

- *Monetary Sovereignty:* contrasting the cryptocurrency vision of an "apolitical" and "stateless" monetary system with the experience of colonial American monies, the Constitution's drafters' debate over paper money, and the Supreme Court's decisions in the *Legal Tender* (Civil War) and *Gold Clause* (New Deal) Cases;[37]
- *Shadow Banking:* comparing current attempts to regulate stablecoins and other forms of "shadow money" with earlier debates over state-chartered bank notes, deposit insurance, and central banks as lenders-of-last-resort to financial markets;[38] and
- *The War on Cash:* comparing debates over the design and privacy features of central bank digital currencies with historical attempts by governments to monetarily surveil and censor political dissidents, marginalized populations,

---

34. *See, e.g.*, Dion Rabouin, *The U.S. Is Losing the Global Race to Decide the Future of Money—and It Could Doom the Almighty Dollar*, Time (Sept. 21, 2021), https://time.com/6099105/us-china-digital-currency-central-bank/.

35. *See, e.g.*, Malcolm Harris, *The War on Cash*, N.Y. Mag. (June 22, 2022), https://nymag.com/intelligencer/2022/06/the-war-on-cash.html. Legal Tender Cases, 79 U.S. (12 Wall.) 457 (1871); Norman v. Baltimore & Ohio R.R. Co., 294 U.S. 240 (1935), Nortz v. U.S., 294 U.S. 317 (1935), Perry v. U.S., 294 U.S. 330 (1935).

36. *See, e.g.*, Rohan Grey, *Digital*, *in* Tipping Points in International Law: Commitment and Critique 116–131 (John Haskell & John D'Aspremont eds., 2021).

37. *See, e.g.*, Sarah Jeong, *The Bitcoin Protocol as Law, and the Politics of a Stateless Currency*, SSRN (May 8, 2013), https://papers.ssrn.com/sol3/papers.cfm?abstract_id=2294124.

38. *See, e.g.*, Jeff Benson, *Crypto's New Villain: Meet the Legal Scholar Behind the STABLE Act*, Decrypt (Dec. 4, 2020), https://decrypt.co/50384/cryptos-new-villain-meet-the-legal-scholar-behind-the-stable-act. *See also* Morgan Ricks, The Money Problem: Rethinking Financial Regulation (2016).

and colonial subjects, as well as the extraction of monetizable data by fintech and platform companies.[39]

In each context, I emphasize the distributional and power dynamics at play, the importance of technological context, and the various ways political disputes are crystallized and shaped by legal forces.

Third, we must aim to not only promote equity and inclusion in the classroom, but also empower students to do so more broadly through their careers. Additionally, we must create opportunities for students to bring their existing expertise, interests, and lived experience to bear on the realms of monetary and technological law.

The most direct way to do so is to prepare students to enter and thrive in practice areas related or adjacent to digital monetary law. I support this by giving students broad leeway in designing their own research and/or practicum experiences. Additionally, I invite a range of speakers from related legal fields, including advocacy, public policy and regulation, and industry, to speak to the class about their professional experience, career trajectory, and outlook on the state of the field.[40] I also invite students to join a legal working group that I direct, which assists local activists seeking to establish a state public bank.[41]

For students who are less interested in monetary law-related practice, I typically focus on helping them build linguistic and technical fluency by introducing them to a variety of legal and technological concepts, as well as key actors in the monetary and fintech spaces. I also provide them with opportunities to cultivate informed opinions on current affairs and complex policy issues, resulting in their deepened understanding of our cultural and political landscape.

To that end, I avoid using a textbook, and instead curate reading packets comprised of news and web articles, selected constitutional, statutory, and common law texts, extracts from scholarly legal and social scientific literature, and technological case studies. This is also partly out of practical necessity—textbooks quickly become outdated

---

39. *See, e.g.*, *Digitizing the Dollar: Investigating the Technological Infrastructure, Privacy, and Financial Inclusion Implications of Central Bank Digital Currencies, Testimony before the U.S. House of Representatives Committee on Financial Services*, 117TH CONG. (June 15, 2021) (testimony of Rohan Grey), https://rohangrey.net/files/testimony-6-15-21-written.pdf.

40. For example, we have had representatives from the U.S. Treasury, the Oregon State Department of Financial Regulation, the Oregon State Bar Section on Securities Practice, a cryptocurrency firm, a nonprofit legal firm serving low-income individuals of color facing financial predation, a journalist covering issues of race and economic justice, and the co-organizer of a national network of legal scholars working in the law and political economy tradition. These speakers have discussed, among other issues, cryptocurrency, the disparate impact of predatory financial inclusion on communities of color, the class biases inherent in white-collar criminal law enforcement, public mythologies and social narratives about money, the interdependency of poverty, financial system architecture, and the hierarchy-reproducing and privilege-reinforcing aspects of the traditional commercial law and 1L curricula.

41. Thus far, students in the working group have prepared a black letter constitutional law memorandum, testified to the legislature, and worked with elected and community stakeholders on legislative drafting and political strategy.

in such a rapidly evolving field—as well as my interest in modeling what an authentic media diet of a legal professional in the space looks like.

In addition to written assignments and in-class discussion, I allow students to participate asynchronously via a class wiki and a chat platform.[42] I encourage them to reflect on how the class materials relate to their own lived experiences and passions, and to help educate and learn from each other. In doing so, I try to model best practices in virtual team-based collaboration, while providing a concrete example of how digital technology can be effectively designed to prioritize certain political commitments (i.e., transparency, autonomy, decentralization, data-protection, security) while remaining relatively user-friendly.

Finally, I encourage students to experiment with new digital platforms and practices, in order to gain greater control and understanding of the technologies that govern their lives, families, and communities.[43] In my seminar, for example, I teach students how to set up their own website, including purchasing a customized domain name, setting up a dedicated server, and following a series of command line instructions to install and configure the software.[44] My goal in doing so is to peel back the layers of digitally networked systems and highlight how operationally complex and interdependent even the most common software applications really are.

Conclusion

The space at the intersection of law, money, and technology is rapidly evolving. Staying up-to-date, while also deconstructing our own biases and being accountable for our privileges, involves constant reorientation of our learning process toward greater equity and inclusion. This involves, but is not limited to, devoting a greater share of our learning, professional time, and material resources to antiracist and diverse texts, initiatives, and communities, holding ourselves and our communities accountable, and embracing apology and meaningful repair as critical tools in the educator's toolkit. It also involves finding and engaging with professional and educational networks that are

---

42. Both platforms run on privacy-respecting, self-hosted, enterprise-grade free software, and can be adapted and scaled up to any future organizational or professional setting. *See* MediaWiki, https://www.mediawiki.org; Element, https://element.io.

43. Rule 1.1 of the ABA's Model Rules of Professional Conduct provides that: "A lawyer shall provide competent representation to a client. Competent representation requires the legal knowledge, skill, thoroughness and preparation reasonably necessary for the representation." In Section 8 of the accompanying commentary, the ABA states that "[t]o maintain the requisite knowledge and skill [for competent representation], a lawyer should keep abreast of changes in the law and its practice, *including the benefits and risks associated with relevant technology* . . ." (emphasis added).

44. *See, e.g.*, Lyn Muldrow, *How to Install WordPress with LEMP on Ubuntu 20.04*, DigitalOcean (Nov. 23, 2020), https://www.digitalocean.com/community/tutorials/how-to-install-wordpress-with-lemp-on-ubuntu-20-04.

not only interested in the same substantive issues, but also are committed to similar social values and transformative political goals.[45]

In the future, we hope that more law school educators teaching at the intersection of the law-money nexus will resemble the students coming into law school and, more broadly, the communities in which they are embedded. If we are living up to our best pedagogical aspirations, our classes will meet our most diverse and deserving students where they are, rather than expecting them to come to us. Justice demands no less.

45. For example, the professional networks listed in note 13 all have free resources available for other law professors looking for help to integrate these or similar topics into their syllabi, and can provide invaluable community-building and accountability opportunities.

Identifying Bias, Inequity, and Discrimination in Insurance Law (with Some Thoughts on Doing the Same in a Business Associations Course)

*Deborah L. Johnson**

Introduction

I am always amazed when I hear professors and lecturers who teach in the business and commercial law fields say they do not think issues of diversity, equity, inclusion, and belonging fit into their courses. On one hand, I kind of get it; the issues may not be as plainly evident as they are in courses such as constitutional law and criminal procedure, or even property. But on the other hand, perhaps because I am a former diversity, equity, and inclusion administrator, I am well aware it takes almost no thought to recognize that there are several issues related to bias and discrimination that can arise in any area of law, and particularly in business law courses where there are often issues of power, institutionalized bias, and discrimination. Insurance contracts are typically adhesion contracts (as are many commercial contracts) and the imbalance of power between insurers and policyholders is inherent in the contract relationship between the parties. Making determinations about what entity to create when discussing business organization formation provokes reflection upon who has access to and can afford the legal, tax, and other assistance needed to make an informed decision about which

* Visiting Assistant Professor of Law, North Carolina Central University School of Law. J.D., Northeastern University School of Law; B.A., University of Notre Dame. I thank the editors involved in this project for giving me the opportunity to share my teaching approach related to this critically important topic. I also thank the students who demand that their professors address these issues in the classroom and my past, current, and future students who engage with me on them inside and outside the classroom.

entity may be best for a particular business. Furthermore, we may also ask—who tends to be in control when it comes to business management and leadership? Who creates the law, sets the policy, and controls the operation of business entities? Who typically is involved in and benefits from the mergers and acquisitions of companies? These questions implicate power, access, and bias, and raise the potential for discrimination—all issues worthy of discussion in a business or commercial law class.

In this essay, I share some of my strategies for and experience with addressing issues of power, access, bias, and potential discrimination in my insurance law and business associations courses. I bring these issues that fall under the broad umbrella of "diversity, equity, inclusion, and belonging" into my courses because they are important and relevant, but also because my students expect me to do so.

Insurance Law

One of the first things to explore when considering how to incorporate issues of bias and discrimination into a business or commercial law course is the textbook you use. In an insurance law course, there are several topics that can address these issues. I have found the area of insurance regulation to be a particularly fitting one for addressing issues of power, access to insurance, and risk classifications. However, other areas of insurance law, including the law addressing health insurance, disability insurance, and property insurance, provide ample opportunity for discussion. Consequently, as I discuss in more detail below, I use *Insurance Law and Policy*[1] because I have found that the editors are thinking about and incorporate access and discrimination issues into the casebook's content, which, in turn, facilitates my ability to talk about them in class.

Insurance Regulation

One of the primary reasons I selected *Insurance Law and Policy* when I first started teaching insurance law many years ago is the fact that there is a significant chapter dedicated to insurance regulation.[2] In the current (fifth) edition, the authors made what I think was a wise decision to move the chapter from the end of the book (Chapter 6) to the middle (Chapter 3). This prioritization has ensured that I cover insurance regulation during the semester. As other insurance law professors would likely admit, insurance regulation is often not covered in an introductory insurance law class. I think that is a mistake for many reasons; chief among them is the fact that this topic provides an opportunity to incorporate issues of bias and discrimination into the curriculum and classroom teaching.

---

1. Tom Baker et al., Insurance Law and Policy (5th ed. 2021).

2. Another casebook I know to have a good section on insurance regulation is Christopher C. French, Insurance Law and Practice (2d ed. 2020). Kenneth Abrams and Daniel Schwarz, Insurance Law and Regulation (7th ed. 2020) is another one. There may be other casebooks, but I have not explored them.

Having now taught the course multiple times, and admitting that I have not always gotten to insurance regulation when it was on the syllabus at the end of the semester, I have started using this chapter to create a launching point for my students to think about issues of bias and discrimination in insurance law and in the insurance industry. Insurance regulation is an important (but often overlooked) aspect of insurance law, as within its domain is the issue of risk classification, i.e., the idea that different people can be treated differently based on predictions on how much of a risk they are to an insurer,[3] and the legal limitations that exist on making such classifications. Insurers regularly make predictions about whether a person is likely to make a claim (or claims) against their insurance policy, how frequently the individual will make claims, and what the size of those claims might be. While there is often a valid justification for making these distinctions (e.g., charging a smoker a higher premium for their health or life insurance policy than a nonsmoker, which, incidentally, leads to more men being charged higher premiums), such risk classifications can and often do lead to discrimination and disparate impact against groups of people based on characteristics such as race and gender, or on one's socioeconomic status. For example, insurers charge auto insurance premiums based on the ZIP Code where a vehicle is primarily garaged, which typically results in higher premiums for those living in lower-income neighborhoods. This, in turn, often means that concentrated groups of people of color are experiencing a disparate impact because they may be unable to afford their auto premiums. Thus, they are unable to own a car or legally drive the car they have. This has further-reaching implications, such as the need to use public transportation to get to work, school, and appointments in a direct and less burdensome way. While I do not take this conversation too deep due to time constraints, I find it is an effective way to get my students thinking. The fact that the law allows for this type of risk classification and inherent (not to mention intentional) discrimination is one I let them grapple with for a while.

To be a bit more concrete, here are some examples of how I introduce and facilitate these discussions. When we discuss the functions of insurance regulation, we look at, among other topics, licensing regulation, rate regulation, and regulation of access to and availability of insurance.[4] When we discuss the licensing function of insurance regulation, we learn that one of the functions of insurance regulation is to review the leadership and experience of insurance companies to ensure the companies will be run efficiently and remain solvent. I use this as an opportunity to talk about who is in leadership and management at these companies.[5] This can lead to a discussion around the

3. Baker, *supra* note 1, at 257.

4. *Id.* at 142–145.

5. *See* U.S. House Comm. on Fin. Svcs., Diversity and Inclusion: Holding America's Largest Insurance Companies Accountable (Sept. 16, 2022), https://democrats-financialservices.house.gov/uploadedfiles/d.i_insurance_report_092022.pdf.

fact that the industry (not surprisingly, at least to some) remains heavily male-dominated and, specifically, heavily white male-dominated.[6]

When discussing rate regulation, we talk about the role and responsibility of insurance commissioners or departments/divisions of insurance to monitor and prohibit "excessive" and "discriminatory" rates. Again, I use that as an opportunity to provoke discussion around what discriminatory rates might look like and who is discriminated against. This raises the risk classification issue. Insurers are within their rights to evaluate individuals' or entities' risk levels, and to make rate decisions based on those evaluations. As noted above, when determining auto insurance premiums, insurers look at (among other things) where the automobile is primarily garaged. They typically do this by looking at the ZIP Code of the policyholder's main residence. However, as I discuss with my students, this is fraught with several issues. While on one hand, it makes sense for an insurer to look at crime statistics in a particular area, using a ZIP Code can be problematic. If a ZIP Code covers a three-square-mile area and there is a significant rash of car thefts or break-ins, but only on a couple of streets within that ZIP Code or within a smaller area, there can be discrimination against policyholders who are within the ZIP Code but are not within the area that has suffered the car thefts and break-ins. We talk about how this often impacts lower-income communities, which are often communities of color. The impact is that policyholders or residents who live in economically depressed areas often find themselves being charged higher premiums simply by virtue of where they live. And, as noted above, even though they may live in a certain ZIP Code, crime statistics used to set the premium rates may not be truly relevant to where they specifically live.

Consequently, students start to see how seemingly neutral bases for risk classification, such as looking at a policy applicant's credit score, often have a negative, discriminatory impact on racial and ethnic minoritized groups. To support this conclusion, it is reported that many homeowners and auto insurance companies look at an individual's credit score to determine the premium amount to charge policyholders.[7] While this type of underwriting is not permitted in every state, in states where it is allowed it has been estimated that approximately 95% of auto insurers and 85% of homeowners insurers follow this practice.[8]

Additionally, when we talk about insurance regulation, we also talk about access to and the availability of insurance. State governments have a strong interest in making sure insurance companies remain solvent and that insurance products on the market

---

6. *See* Lindsey White, *How a Historically White Male Sector is Grappling with Diversity*, S&P Global Market Intelligence (Nov. 18, 2020), https://www.spglobal.com/marketintelligence/en/news-insights/latest-news-headlines/how-a-historically-white-male-sector-is-grappling-with-diversity-61356969; Sam Boyer, *It is All White Men Over 40: Lack of Diversity Among Insurance Execs*, Ins. Bus. Mag. (June 8, 2017), https://www.insurancebusinessmag.com/us/news/breaking-news/it-is-all-white-men-over-40-lack-of-diversity-among-insurance-execs-69849.aspx.

7. *See* French, *supra* note 2, at 815.

8. *Id.*

are fairly priced, transparent, and readily available by many competing and reliable companies.[9] Consequently, state regulators are tasked with ensuring that everyone who needs insurance has access to it—and at a fair and reasonable price. While this is the goal of insurance regulation, achieving the goal typically comes at significant cost to certain policyholders. While I do not introduce specific statistics, I engage my students in a conversation about who has access to insurance and at what cost. For example, although auto insurance or homeowner's insurance may be available, there are some policyholders to whom insurers have no interest in extending coverage. In other words, there are certain individuals that no insurance company will write a policy to insure—and this is permissible. States have residual market mechanisms to ensure that even the "uninsurable" can gain coverage, but that typically comes at significant expense to the individual: it means higher premiums and lower limits, which may, in reality, make it impossible for an individual to secure such insurance. Again, this allows for a classroom discussion around who is deemed "uninsurable" and why, and for students to think about how biases along economic, social, and racial lines show up in how rates are determined, how available insurance really is, and who has meaningful access to various types of insurance.

In a recent class, I drew from an excerpt from a 1960s article in which a well-respected insurance scholar wrote the following:

> The insurance regulator is conceived by far too many insurance executives, and too often **he** conceived **himself**, as part of the industry, existing to serve the industry. Indeed, I have heard life insurance **men** express the notion that it would be useful to have a national regulator to 'represent' the industry in the executive branch of the national government. Nothing unsavory was intended—whatever else one may say about *the insurance business, it is a business run by honorable men*. However, the notion that a regulator should "represent" the industry is a subtly corrupted point of view.[10]

I put this language on a PowerPoint slide, with the male pronouns and references to men highlighted. I gave my students a chance to read it and then said to them that, although it was written in 1969, these sentiments are still held today by many and the same words could very well have been written today (in the 2020s), given statistics around who works in the insurance industry. I then used the next few slides to offer some statistics about who makes up the insurance industry. We looked at the percentage of entry-level positions, namely underwriters, claims adjusters, and agents, that are held by women. A 2020 report indicated that, in the U.S., for the first two categories,

---

9. Nat'l Ass'n of Ins. Comm'rs, *Market Conduct Regulation*, https://content.naic.org/cipr-topics/market-conduct-regulation (last updated June 23, 2022). The focus is on state governments because insurance is overwhelmingly regulated at the state level due the McCarran-Ferguson Act. *See* 15 U.S.C. §§ 1011–1012.

10. Spencer Kimball, *The Case for State Regulation of Insurance*, in INSURANCE, GOVERNMENT, AND SOCIAL POLICY; STUDIES IN INSURANCE REGULATION, 411, 432 (Spencer L. Kimball & Herbert Denenberg eds., 1969) (emphasis added). This excerpt appears in the Baker casebook, *supra* note 1, at 165.

approximately 50% are women and, in the last category, i.e., claims handlers, an overwhelming 80%-plus are women.[11] However, another 2021 report demonstrated that the numbers sharply declined as you go up the management chain where, for example, only 21.3% of board chairs and 15.8% of CEOs in the health insurance industry are women.[12] I also included an excerpt from an interview with an insurance industry expert who talked about the current state of diversity in the insurance industry, focusing specifically on gender diversity and racial diversity.[13] My next slide then provided statistics around how many women and how many women of color held certain positions, followed by a comparison of women and men of color holding positions at various levels within the industry.[14]

I used this data to: (1) expose my students to these statistics, and (2) open a discussion as to what practical impact this has on insurance offerings. During that class, a few of my students talked about how the language that is used in insurance policies can be dictated or at least influenced by who sits in certain management positions. Others noted that how rates are determined can similarly be influenced by who works within a state division or department of insurance. While I chose to introduce these statistics and open this discussion in response to the excerpt included above, I think another likely place for such a discussion could be when there is a discussion around the functions of insurance regulation and how insurance companies are licensed, i.e., how regulators look at the management and experience of the company when determining which insurance companies can do business in the state. In other words, looking at who is in positions of power and authority in the insurance companies opens a discussion as to who is leading the companies (i.e., largely white men) and what impact that may have on how insurance companies operate and serve their various policyholders.

Lastly, with respect to insurance regulation, there is an opportunity to discuss the legal limitations on insurers' ability and right to classify risks. The Baker casebook does a nice job of addressing the legal limits (or lack thereof) that exist on insurance companies' risk classification practices. Over the span of approximately twelve pages, the editors address the extent to which federal law restricts insurers' discrimination among insureds based on risk characteristics such as race, gender, sexual orientation, and religion. In this section, the authors discuss the Fair Housing Act, Section 1981 of the Civil Rights Act of 1866, Title VII of the Civil Rights Act of 1964, and the Affordable Care Act, and highlight the fact that few states have laws expressly forbidding insurers

11. Peter Littlejohns, *Seven women at the top of their game in the global insurance industry*, NS Ins. (Mar. 7, 2020), https://www.nsinsurance.com/news/women-in-insurance/#; *see generally* Ins. Info. Inst., Facts + Statistics: Careers and employment, https://www.iii.org/fact-statistic/facts-statistics-careers-and-employment (last visited Jan. 20, 2023).

12. Bismarck C. Odei et al., *Representation of Women in the Leadership Structure of the US Health Care System*, JAMA Network Open (Nov. 29, 2021), doi.org/10.1001/jamanetworkopen.2021.36358.

13. *Diversity in Insurance and Beyond with Kweilin Ellingrud*, McKinsey & Co. (Mar. 8, 2022), https://www.mckinsey.com/industries/financial-services/our-insights/insurance/women-in-insurance-leading-voices-on-trends-affecting-insurers/diversity-in-insurance-and-beyond-with-kweilin-ellingrud.

14. *Id.*

in all lines of insurance from engaging in discrimination on the basis of race, religion, or national origin. This is another launching pad for discussion.

Health Insurance

Another place where it seems logical to bring up issues around bias and discrimination in insurance law is when we talk about health insurance. I usually have a guest speaker when we reach this topic, so I don't have any direct experience in addressing bias and discrimination with respect to this insurance type. However, the earlier example of charging smokers higher health and life insurance premiums, which leads to more men being charged higher premiums, is a good example to use. Another way I might introduce the topic would be to talk about the health disparities that exist along racial and socioeconomic lines and how that influences insurers' regulation of premium rates. Moreover, the impact of the Affordable Care Act (ACA) and individual mandates also invites discussion as to who the ACA benefits and harms.

Disability Insurance

Another area where we talk about bias and discrimination can come up in a discussion around disability insurance. Disability insurance is provided by a plan or policy that pays all or some portion of an individual's income when the individual is disabled from an illness or injury and cannot work.[15] The two main types of disability insurance are short-term disability (STD) and long-term disability (LTD).[16] STD and LTD are often offered by employers to certain employees depending on the employee's position and the employer's ability to offer it. For those who may be in management, white collar, or other professional career positions, having disability insurance is generally not an issue. Some self-employed individuals can also afford to purchase their own disability policies. But lower wage earners, many of whom are people of color or people whose first language is not English, are typically not afforded disability insurance. This is significant because, as noted above, disability insurance, by its nature, is intended to provide financial security in the event that an individual is injured and cannot work. If individuals do not have disability insurance offered by their employer and are unable to purchase disability insurance on their own, the financial and economic impact on their livelihood, and their ability to support themselves and care for their families may be significantly damaged. This inevitably has a harsher impact on those who most need the financial security.

---

15. Nat'l Cancer Inst. Dictionary of Cancer Terms, *Disability insurance*, https://www.cancer.gov/publications/dictionaries/cancer-terms/def/disability-insurance (last visited Jan. 20, 2023).

16. Ins. Info. Inst., What Are the Types of Disability Insurance? https://www.iii.org/article/what-are-types-disability-insurance (last visited Jan. 20, 2023).

Property Insurance

Another great opportunity to discuss issues around inequity and discrimination in insurance law arises in our discussions around property insurance, namely homeowner's insurance. Thought must be given to who homeowners are, who can afford to have homeowner's insurance, and how much coverage a homeowner can afford. This year I had the opportunity to address these issues in the context of current (2022) legislative proposals for changes to the National Flood Insurance Program. Experts have said that, "[r]eforming the National Flood Insurance Program to better serve marginalized communities and ensure long-term support for homeowners should be a top priority for lawmakers ahead of a coming deadline to reauthorize the program."[17] When teaching on the topic of property insurance, the Baker casebook reading includes a subsection on the risk of weather disasters and catastrophic property damage.[18] Most property insurance policies sold by private insurers contain flood exclusions, and what private flood insurance is available is prohibitively expensive for most homeowners.[19] Thus, most homeowners in high flood risk areas of the United States who purchase flood insurance (as it is typically required by most mortgage companies and banks for those in flood-prone areas) depend on and purchase national flood insurance from the federal government via the National Flood Insurance Program (NFIP).[20]

Although the NFIP was intended to make flood insurance more affordable for properties in flood risk zones (and it has for many), for some homeowners, especially those in lower-income neighborhoods, the insurance remains problematic. While some of the current NFIP reform proposal could be beneficial by expanding coverage and reducing the number of underinsured households through policy discounts and higher policy limits, lawmakers are also considering barring the NFIP from insuring new buildings in high-risk areas, and barring coverage altogether for some properties that flood repeatedly.[21] As experts have stated, the consequences of that approach could be harshest for the poorest Americans because discriminatory housing practices and historic disinvestment in low-income communities have put people of color, and Black people especially, in areas at risk of high flood damage.[22] Using this article ("NFIP Reforms Take on Urgency as Program Deadline Nears") or a similar supplemental reading can expose students to the challenges and problems with this insurance type and weave it into our discussion around weather disasters and property insurance.

---

17. Eli Flesch, *NFIP Reforms Take On Urgency as Program Deadline Nears*, Law360 (Sept. 12, 2022), https://www.law360.com/insurance-authority/property/articles/1502306/nfip-reforms-take-on-urgency-as-program-deadline-nears.

18. *See* BAKER, *supra* note 1, at 296–301.

19. *See id.* at 297.

20. *Id.*

21. *Id.*

22. *Id.*

Cases

Another way to introduce issues of bias and discrimination is via the cases we cover in class. Again, looking at the casebooks is key to seeing what cases may be useful to introducing diversity, equity, inclusion, and belonging issues. While I have not done a comprehensive survey of cases, there are several cases in the Baker casebook that have some discrimination component in them:

Transport Ins. Co. v. Lee Way Motor Freight, Inc., 487 F. Supp. 1325 (N.D. Tex. 1980)[23] (defendant was found to have engaged in a pattern and practice of race discrimination and ordered to pay over $1.8 million in damages. Insurance question centered around whether the defendant's liability resulted from a single occurrence, a separate occurrence at different locations, or a separate occurrence for each of the individuals discriminated against. The answer to the question would dictate the amount the insurer would have to pay—less for a single occurrence, more for separate occurrences). Note: In a recent semester, our classroom discussion of this case led my students to engage in a student-initiated debate over whether insurance policies should protect against racial discrimination.

Appalachian Ins. Co. v. Liberty Mut. Ins. Corp., 507 F. Supp. 59 (W.D. Pa. 1981), *aff'd* 676 F.2d 56 (3d Cir. 1982)[24] (gender discrimination; court found multiple acts of discrimination were one occurrence for deductible purposes).

Mead Reins. v. Granite State Ins. Co., 873 F.2d. 1185 (9th Cir. 1989)[25] (police brutality; court found multiple acts of police brutality were one occurrence for deductible purposes).

Telles v. Comm'r. of Ins., 574 N.E.2d 369 (Mass. 1991)[26] (addressing whether life insurance companies are prohibited from considering gender-based mortality differences in the underwriting process and concluding that they are prohibited from such risk classification).

Hartford Acc. & Indem. Co. v. Ins. Comm'r of Pa., 482 A.2d 542 (Pa. 1984)[27] (supreme court agreed that the insurer's gender-based automobile insurance rates were "unfairly discriminatory").

Insurance Servs. Office v. Comm'r of Ins., 381 So. 2d 515 (La. Ct. App. 1979)[28] (appellate court affirmed commissioner's use of age and gender discrimination because statistics showed higher rate of accidents in males and young people, noting that although the classifications were discriminatory, they were not "unfairly discriminatory").

---

23. *See id.* at 570–575.
24. *See id.* at 575.
25. *See id.*
26. *See id.* at 271–274.
27. *See id.* at 274 n. 1.
28. *See id.*

Beaty v. Truck Ins. Exch., 8 Cal. Rptr. 2d 593 (Ct. App. 1992)[29] (appellate court concluded that defendant's refusal to issue a policy to a same-sex couple was justifiable discrimination). The casebook discusses how the California legislature enacted a statute that superseded the court's decision.[30]

Los Angeles Dept. of Water & Power v. Manhart, 235 U.S. 703 (1978) and *Ariz. Governing Comm. v. Norris*, 463 U.S. 1073 (1983)[31] (cases dealing with gender discrimination; suggesting an employer violates Title VII of the Civil Rights Act of 1964 by providing an insurance benefit, such as life insurance, unless it provides identical benefits to both men and women and contributions into a benefit plan are the same for both sexes.

Business Organizations

Business organizations (a/k/a Business Associations (BA)) is another course in which issues of power dynamics, privilege, access, and inequity arise and should be discussed. Teaching BA involves addressing agency law, the different types of business entities, how ownership is structured, and what the controlling provisions are regarding the business's operation and potential dissolution. Choosing the right business entity allows an entrepreneur to reduce personal liability exposure, minimize taxes, and ensure that the business can be financed and run efficiently. When discussing the different forms of business organizations, it is also important to talk about societal and economic factors, including who has access to and can afford the legal and tax assistance needed to make an informed decision about which entity may be the best for a particular business and how best to draft or otherwise address the provisions that govern the business's operation. Incorporating some of the practical considerations and implications related to the different entity types such as how they impact individual liability, and what barriers exist to forming entities that offer greater liability protection, financing opportunities, and decision-making power to business owners can assist students in understanding the different structures.

Another aspect of business associations that is ripe for diversity discussions is the dissolution of businesses. Why a business dissolves or is restructured can be driven by societal factors, and this is where I have some experience discussing disparate impact in a BA course. The first time I taught business associations was in the summer of 2020, when we were seeing, among other things, the large number of businesses that were forced to close or were otherwise significantly and negatively impacted by COVID-19. The course was offered asynchronously and, as such, a significant component of it was our discussion forum. I challenged my students to think about which businesses and, more significantly, which business entity types, were most impacted by COVID-19 and

29. *See id.* at 275 n. 3.

30. *See id.* at 276.

31. These cases appear in the "Insurance Law and Practice" casebook. *See* French, *supra* note 2, at 813.

in what ways. Although I used discussion boards for these conversations, I think they could be thoughtfully incorporated into a live classroom discussion.

One of the questions I posed to students in the discussion forum was around the number and types of businesses that were closing during the beginning and the height of the pandemic. I asked them to think whether they were large corporations or small, family-owned businesses; were they law and accounting firms or were they restaurants and hair salons? And who owned these businesses? While all businesses and sectors were impacted in one way or another, was there or could there have been any evidence that the harsher impact was on smaller businesses and businesses in sectors that are traditionally owned or occupied by those from lower-income backgrounds or in neighborhoods serving lower-income individuals and families, those from different racial, ethnic, or national origin backgrounds, or those who were immigrants? Some other questions I posed:

- Is it possible that a business might have survived or been in a better financial position if it had formed as a different entity type?
- What factors or barriers might have existed that prevented individuals from organizing their business as a different entity type?
- Who bore what liabilities (third-party, tax, etc.) when the businesses suffered a downturn in operations and revenue? Imagine (or share, if you have evidence) what were the backgrounds of those individuals with greater or lesser liability? Imagine what their national origin, gender, racial, ethnic or religious background may have been. Their immigration status?

I did not always elaborate on the questions or press for answers. Given the circumstances of the course (asynchronous learning), I thought it was sufficient, at least at that stage, to plant the seed. That being said, as outlined above, I think there are a myriad of access and availability issues that can be explored in a BA course, and I look forward to doing so in the future.

Conclusion

Despite thoughts to the contrary, there are indeed many ways to bring issues of diversity, equity, inclusion, and belonging into the business and commercial law curriculum and classroom discussions. It is imperative that law professors adopt one or more of them. Law students not only expect their professors to do so, but are increasingly demanding it. An instructor who fails to explore issues that are obvious to students runs the very real and potentially damaging risk of appearing to be ignorant or indifferent to realities that impact their students and the students' communities. I have not identified every way that it can be done, and not all of the approaches I have addressed can be accomplished in every course or in every semester. Sometimes the way to address the issues is by assigning certain readings. Other times it is beneficial and important to have a meaningful discussion in class even if it provokes some apprehension. As noted above, often a good place to start this process is with the casebook you select, and I appreciate the sentiments of Professor Carliss Chatman who recently co-edited a new Business Organizations casebook.[32] In a 2022 social media post, Professor Chatman wrote the following:

> When Carla Reyes and I decided to write a Business Organizations casebook [ ], we weren't setting out to write a book on race and equality. We just wrote It [sic] the way we think BA should be taught—with consideration of all people, stories and problems that are relatable, excerpts from articles from people we respect and admire who don't get the attention they deserve, and not hiding the ball. I don't think business and business law are all that complicated. We just use jargon that intentionally excludes....[33]

I think this is a wise approach that, if followed, can contribute significantly to an instructor's strong and successful teaching and classroom discussions that include bias, inequality, and discrimination issues. Ignoring these issues—even when out of fear of saying the wrong thing or not knowing how to address an issue—is no longer a practical option. The key, I think, is to be thoughtful, well-informed, and intentional with one's approach, whatever that approach may be, for it is what most of today's law students want and expect.

---

32. Carliss Chatman & Carla Reyes, Business Organizations: An Experiential Approach (2022). I have not yet reviewed the casebook, but will be doing so as I prepare to teach Business Associations in the next academic year.

33. Carliss Chatman, Facebook (Mar. 23, 2022), https://www.facebook.com/carlissc.

Doctrine and Diversity in the Employment Law Syllabus and Classroom

*Kerri Lynn Stone**

Introduction

A survey class in employment law should equip the students that take it to think through, litigate, and guard against legal issues that arise in the regulation of the workplace. The law of the workplace is fascinating because it forces legislators, triers of fact, and triers of law to grapple with the nuances of life at the workplace: the human psyche, interpersonal exchanges, and the dynamics that exist between groups and individuals. Typically covering everything from workplace speech, to whistleblowers, to employees' privacy rights (physical and electronic), a solid survey course in this area will likely address the development and application of the law on several levels.

In the first place, the black letter law must be imparted; but that is only the beginning. Students should also leave the class with a nuanced grasp of the theory, policy goals, and tensions underlying relevant legislation and case law, as well as an informed understanding of how to advise clients and litigate issues in practice today. In the case of employment law, the law's frameworks and interpretations, far from calcified and static, are dynamic and volatile. Policy and theory are intimately interwoven with black letter law and analysis.

Unlike its sister survey class of employment discrimination, which I tell my students is essentially the "chapter that ate the course" (and thus became its own course in many schools, including my own), employment law covers a broad array of topics. Hence, students go way beyond thinking about the chapter that is employment discrimination, and the concept of regulating changing the terms, conditions, or privileges of an employee's job "because of" some protected status and must think as well about the

* Professor of Law, Florida International University College of Law.

sanctity of and right to well-being at work that derives from conferrals of various forms of freedom, privacy, and safety that should be afforded to all.

The notion of incorporating principles of diversity and inclusion may seem completely intuitive in employment discrimination—a class dedicated to the composition and protected class-based treatment of employees in the workplace. It is just as intuitive and natural, however, to incorporate insights, thoughts, and themes that touch upon diversity and inclusion in an employment law survey class—separate and apart from the chapter(s) that one includes in that survey on the topic of employment discrimination law.

An employment law class provides many opportunities to integrate doctrine and diversity. A theoretical overlay enables students to not only see how the law operates to regulate workplace issues like free speech, privacy, and safety, but it can point to inequalities in the law's application and structural societal inequalities that start certain protected classes off at a disadvantage before the law even comes into play. I have found that bringing current events into class and using them to formulate case studies in which established law applies to novel factual scenarios can stimulate thinking and discussion that sharpens critical analytical skills.

COVID, Women, and the Workplace

For example, the issue of the COVID pandemic and the multitude of problems that it presents to the contemporary workplace yields numerous case studies and applications. What are the privacy rights of an infected employee versus the interest of co-workers in knowing that they have been exposed? Can an employee who lives with family members who are in a high-risk category for transmission claim an ability to work from home during a pandemic when others are not allowed? How may an employer permissibly respond to tensions and debate in the workplace over things like vaccine efficacy and mask wearing? What does the employer's duty to provide a safe workplace look like during a pandemic? Factoring in the increased vulnerability and higher susceptibility of certain people due to their age, disability status, or race makes these analyses more complex when conducted with an eye toward diversity. The so-called COVID Care crisis, whereby women, who overwhelmingly and disproportionately shoulder the burden of childcare and other caretaking responsibilities in families and society while working through the pandemic, has led to a huge professional backslide for women as a group.[1] There is much to discuss in the way of cultural and protected class consciousness when such a pervasive challenge poses itself, and the case

---

1. *See* Richard Fry, *Some Gender Disparities Widened in the U.S. Workforce During the Pandemic*, Pew Research Center (Jan. 14, 2022), https://www.pewresearch.org/fact-tank/2022/01/14/some-gender-disparities-widened-in-the-u-s-workforce-during-the-pandemic/; Gemma Zamarro, *Gender Differences in the Economic and Social Impact of the COVID-19 Pandemic*, WIA Report (Nov. 12, 2022), https://www.wiareport.com/2020/07/gender-differences-in-the-economic-and-social-impact-of-the-covid-19-pandemic/.

studies and extrapolations and projections that it generates can and should be conducted with much thought given to the mindful integration of doctrine and diversity.[2]

Using Current Events to Spur Thought and Discussion

There are many other non-COVID-related issues and topics that would benefit from such thoughtful integration. For example, freedom of speech, expression, and association in the public and private workplace are staples in a traditional employment law survey course. But does the law evince any patterns in its application or enforcement depending upon who the speaker is? What about with respect to the content of the speech? Recently we have seen intense debate in this country, both inside and outside of the workplace, about issues that range from science (and pseudo-science) to racial injustice and reckoning. Additionally, the so-called "gig economy" and the employment trends that come with it invariably come up during a discussion of the distinction between an employee and an independent contractor and its significance. This discussion, however, benefits tremendously from a discussion of which groups participate or are forced to participate more in the gig economy, and which groups are more prone to suffer abuse, harassment or ostracization in work situations that do not come with the benefits and protections accorded "employees" by the law. This discussion is best had by allowing examples to come up organically, and it is often a good practice to follow up the spontaneous emergence of an issue by subsequently bringing relevant material to read to or summarize for students, should one not wish to add to students' reading mid-semester. The examples are endless, but the integration of doctrine and diversity enriches the course and better equips students to be thoughtful attorneys in contemporary society.

Below is just a sampling of some issues bearing on diversity and inclusion that have come up in the course of teaching an Employment Law survey class.

---

2. *See* Equal Employment Opportunity Commission, *The COVID-19 Pandemic and Caregiver Discrimination Under Federal Employment Discrimination Laws* (Mar. 14, 2022), https://www.eeoc.gov/laws/guidance/covid-19-pandemic-and-caregiver-discrimination-under-federal-employment; Daiquiri J. Steele, *Preserving Pandemic Protections*, 42 Berkeley J. Emp. & Lab. L. 321, 321 (2021); Leanne Fuith & Susan Trombley, *Covid-19 and the Caregiving Crisis: The Rights of Our Nation's Social Safety Net and A Doorway to Reform*, 11 U. Miami Race & Soc. Just. L. Rev. 159 (2021); Angela Coco, *The Impact of Covid-19 on the Older Workforce: Reforms to Ensure a Safer Future for Older Workers*, 18 NAELA J. 1 (2022).

The Law of Retaliation: Walking in the Plaintiff's Shoes and Context Is Key

While anti-retaliation law is a topic that is covered in a typical employment discrimination class, it is not uncommon for an employment law class to probe somewhat deeply into the subject, looking at the notion of statutes and common law that make it unlawful for an employer to exact an adverse employment action in response to an employee's having engaged in a protected activity. This is a natural juncture at which to inject some perspective into the conversation that might make students think through the realities of what goes on in the aftermath of an employee's attempting to vindicate their rights. Students can be reminded of several things that will, irrespective of which side of the aisle they will be on, confer and cultivate empathy and a sense of realism in them when it comes to thinking about and confronting legal issues that arise. Below are but a few examples of numerous junctures in the teaching of this topic where it feels natural to encourage students to consider, as courts have done, the identities and unique situations of the litigants in a way that integrates diversity into the doctrine.

Adverse Action: From Whose Perspective?

Students often benefit from being reminded that the litigants in the cases that they are reading are, in fact, actual people that they could know, and who reside in the real world. The notion that litigants' identities and circumstances could diverge from those of the triers of their cases in ways that could make their lived experiences relevant to the application of the law to them is one that is important to explore. For example, in the popular Supreme Court case *Burlington Northern v. White*, the Court addressed several legal questions that had been left unresolved in lower courts until that point.[3] Among them was the question of precisely how adverse, or bad, an alleged adverse action had to be in order to rise to the level at which it could support a cognizable retaliation claim.[4] Whereas the defendant employer had initially argued that the plaintiff's claim, having been suspended without pay, could not rise to the level of actionable retaliation because she was eventually reinstated with compensation to make up for the pay that she had not been given, the Court disagreed.[5]

The Supreme Court delineated between the core substantive antidiscrimination provision and the anti-retaliation provision of Title VII. In the former, a substantially adverse action must be cabined within the workplace and concern itself with terms, conditions, or privileges of employment. In the latter, a "materially adverse action" is an adverse action that "well might have dissuaded a reasonable worker from making or supporting a charge of discrimination."[6] With that standard in mind, the Court was

---

3. Burlington N. & Santa Fe Ry. v. White, 548 U.S. 53, 57 (2006).
4. *Id.*
5. *Id.* at 71–72.
6. *Id.* at 66–68.

able to reject the defendant employer's argument that "it defies reason to believe that Congress would have considered a rescinded investigatory suspension with full back pay" because it, as I encourage my students to do, looked beyond the monolithic, "no harm-no foul" narrative of a temporary situation that had been restored and made right, and looked to the underlying realities experienced by the plaintiff.[7]

The idea that one could be retaliatorily suspended and placed under investigation without pay and sustain no harm in the moment is premised on the assumption that the person in question enjoys privilege, security, and a well-founded confidence that justice will prevail that so many simply do not. Quoting the plaintiff's testimony that "That was the worst Christmas I had out of my life. No income, no money, and that made us all feel bad.... I got very depressed," the Court looked at the plaintiff through a lens that honored her situation as she experienced it in real-time, without the benefit of privilege or hindsight.[8] It concluded that:

> White and her family had to live for 37 days without income. They did not know during that time whether or when White could return to work. Many reasonable employees would find a month without a paycheck to be a serious hardship.[9]

It is this lens of empathy and respect for diversity of situation and identity that the Supreme Court employed, that ought to be understood and used by students when addressing employment law issues that require an individualized assessment of factors. Diversity and inclusion are not optional concepts in this type of analysis; they are part and parcel of what must be considered. It may be the case that one or more students will want to share a personal experience that resonates with the facts of a case or with a discussion of public policy. Ideally, these narratives will be shared in a way that clearly relates back to the material and drives the discussion. Also ideally, these narratives will be met with respect and appreciation and enrich the lesson. For example, a student who has been retaliated against by being socially ostracized at work may share that experience with the class and what it really felt like as a means of conveying to other students how something that may strike some courts as petty or workplace-adjacent is actually cruel, punitive, and a very effective means of deterring others from engaging in certain behavior.

Self-Help: When Is It Taken Too Far?

One of my favorite cases to teach in employment law is that of *Hochstadt v. Worcester Foundation.*[10] This case, decided by the First Circuit Court of Appeals in 1976, considered the outer parameters of the protection a plaintiff enjoys from retaliation after engaging in so-called "self-help," visibly opposing discriminatory practices prohibited

7. *Id.* at 71–72.
8. *Id.* at 72.
9. *Id.*
10. *See* Hochstadt v. Worcester Found. for Experimental Biology, 545 F.2d 222 (1st Cir. 1976).

by Title VII.[11] At what point does one lose protection because one's self-help and opposition has crossed over into behavior that may be termed sabotage or be considered otherwise intolerable by the defendant employer? I believe that this case interests my students so much because the plaintiff, Dr. Joy Hochstadt, emerges as more than the colorful, irascible, ultimately unforgivable character that the Court paints her to be, but as a victim of her time and circumstances by dint of her sex, even as the opinion emerges as a product of its time. As the class's discussion of this case evolves, students increasingly view the importance of this case's historical and social context.

In this case, the Court describes Dr. Hochstadt as a microbiologist whose biomedical research is "pioneering," but who only succeeds in procuring a job at the prestigious Worcester Foundation for Experimental Biology after she is recommended by her husband, who comes in at a significantly higher salary than she does.[12] The opinion fails, however, to delve into the significance or details of Dr. Hochstadt being, in 1971, one of relatively few women with her credentials, position, or the rare insight into her pay disparity (which she had only by dint of her marriage). In fact, it describes the salaries offered to her and her husband as "reflect[ing] the needs of the institution."[13]

The Court's recounting of Dr. Hochstadt's behavior as she uncovers and takes aim at sex-based disparities of every variety from compensation to access to representation, is nothing short of vivid. As the Court recounts, she "early began to interpose personal grievances and salary complaints, to discuss the inadequacy of the Foundation's affirmative action program, and to criticize the Foundation's administration.... "[14] Resultingly, this behavior "interfered with the meetings, disrupted the discussions, and eventually caused the discontinuation of the meetings."[15]

After filing formal charges against the Foundation and initiating a lawsuit against it, which was eventually settled, Dr. Hochstadt continued to engage in behavior like soliciting salary information from other employees and, as the Court put it, "circulat[ing] rumors that the Foundation would lose much of its federal funding because it was not complying with regulations concerning affirmative action programs."[16] The Court further recounts that she acted clandestinely to procure a "covert affirmative action survey" from an expert embedded at a seminar, who then publicized the shortfalls revealed by the survey to members of Congress; invited a reporter to examine confidential salary files for a series of articles; utilized Foundation resources for inappropriate personal use; and alienated and allegedly drove away research assistants, among other instances of conduct the Court termed evincing "extreme hostility."[17]

11. *Id.*
12. *Id.* at 227.
13. *Id.*
14. *Id.*
15. *Id.*
16. *Id.* at 228.
17. *Id.* at 228, 234.

This case provides an excellent opportunity to go beyond teaching the legal standard for when, as the court put it, a "plaintiff's overall conduct [i]s so generally inimical to her employer's interests, and so 'excessive', as to be beyond the protection of [the anti-retaliation provision of Title VII] even though her actions [a]re generally associated with her complaints of illegal employer conduct."[18] I believe that diversity of opinion is critical to a rigorous and robust law school class, especially in this area of law.

There is always a healthy range of opinion in my classes from year to year as to whether students agree with the Court's holding that despite the fact that Dr. Hochstadt may have been justified with respect to her initial complaint about pay discrimination, "and although her later complaint over her poor rating—whether or not justified—was one which she was entitled to make in an appropriate way," her behavior simply did not merit "insulat[ion] ... from adverse scrutiny insofar as it went beyond the pale of reasonable opposition activity."[19] Some students are quick to point to the Foundation's managerial prerogative to run its enterprise free from what could be perceived as downright sabotage, as well as to the erosion of everything from trust to interpersonal relations to internal harmony that they feel Dr. Hochstadt's behavior engendered. Still, others are quick to discuss the context in which this took place—one in which women were grossly underrepresented, not only at workplaces like the Foundation, but in the classrooms that conferred the credentials necessary to do the high-level STEM work that Dr. Hochstadt did, and one in which the discrimination when it came to things like the pay disparity of which she complained, were overt and undeniable.

Irrespective of how students feel about the holding, they continually raise certain points in the discussion. For one thing, many students point to how hard it is to effect change in a situation in which discrimination and underrepresentation are overt and rampant without engaging in behavior that takes them "past the pale," and beyond the purview of "protected activity." The fact of the matter is that many women employed in professional positions in which women were underrepresented in the 1960s and 1970s found themselves paid and generally valued less than their male counterparts were.[20] Still more were underemployed. Justice Ruth Bader Ginsburg graduated from Columbia Law School tied for first place in her class and was endorsed for a clerkship with Supreme Court Justice Felix Frankfurter by Harvard Law Professor Albert Sachs, to whom "Frankfurter responded that he wasn't ready to hire a woman and asked Sachs to recommend a man."[21] As a tribute to Justice Ginsburg on the ACLU's website recites,

> Ginsburg had worked for a top law firm in New York during the summer of her second year in law school. "I thought I had done a terrific job, and I expected them to offer me a job on graduation," she recalled. Despite her per-

---

18. *Id.* at 230.

19. *Id.*

20. *See* Sharon M. Oster, *Is There a Policy Problem?: The Gender Wage Gap*, 82 Geo L.J. 109, 109–11 (1993).

21. American Civil Liberties Union, Women's Rights Project, *Tribute: The Legacy of Ruth Bader Ginsburg and WRP Staff*, https://www.aclu.org/other/tribute-legacy-ruth-bader-ginsburg-and-wrp-staff (last visited Jan. 20, 2023).

> formance, there was no job offer. Nor was there an offer from any of the twelve firms with which she interviewed; only two gave her a follow-up interview.[22]

After eventually finding another clerkship, she "joined the faculty of Rutgers Law School in 1963, but her status as a woman still put her at a disadvantage," and once she found out that she was being paid less than her male counterparts at work, she joined other female professors at the university to mount an equal pay campaign.[23] It is not lost on students that a woman like Dr. Hochstadt, situated as she was, likely did not have a community of women with whom to launch such a civil rights campaign. Whether this does or does not impact their own determination as to whether Dr. Hochstadt went "too far," these are points that make the facts of the case come alive for students in its context and appreciate what went on.

Finally, even the opinion is somewhat of a relic—replete with phrases like "Congress ... did not mean to grant sanctuary ... to engage in political activity for women's liberation on company time. ..."[24] The facts contain reminders of the period in which this all took place, and when they are left wholly unremarked upon, it is clear that the opinion, too, is a product of its time. For example, the court recites, with no note of irony, the fact that Dr. Hochstadt only received her position after her husband, already employed by the Foundation, let it know "of the availability and interest of his wife. ..."[25] At this period in history, it was actually quite common for those few women who did enter and ascend the ranks of a professional organization like the Foundation, that had few women to begin with, to have done so with the aid of a male mentor, relative, or ally.[26]

Moreover, Dr. Hochstadt's proximity to her husband/colleague was the only means that she had to even discover the discriminatory pay disparity of which she complained. Whereas today, opacity when it comes to employers discouraging or forbidding the soliciting or disclosure of employees' salaries to one another is frowned upon by those who seek the ideal of equal pay for equal work,[27] and is unlawful in many places,[28] the Court treated Dr. Hochstadt's attempts to ascertain and document pay inequality as more or less unforgivable: "[P]laintiff sought to elicit salary information

22. *Id.*

23. *Id.*

24. *See* Hochstadt v. Worcester Found. for Experimental Biology, 545 F.2d 222, 230 (1st Cir. 1976).

25. *Id.* at 227.

26. Virginia G. Drachman, *Women Lawyers and the Quest for Professional Identity in Late Nineteenth-Century America*, 88 Mich. L. Rev. 2414, 2434 (1990); Kenneth W. Mack, *A Social History of Everyday Practice: Sadie T.M. Alexander and the Incorporation of Black Women into the American Legal Profession, 1925–1960*, 87 Cornell L. Rev. 1405, 1424 (2002).

27. *See* Orly Lobel, *Knowledge Pays: Reversing Information Flows and the Future of Pay Equity*, 120 Colum. L. Rev. 547, 588–89 (2020); Marianne DelPo Kulow, *Beyond the Paycheck Fairness Act: Mandatory Wage Disclosure Laws--A Necessary Tool for Closing the Residual Gender Wage Gap*, 50 Harv. J. on Legis. 385, 419–21 (2013); Susan R. Fiorentino & Sandra M. Tomkowicz, *Can Millennials Deliver on Equal Pay? Why the Time Is Finally Right for Pay Transparency*, 38 Hofstra Lab. & Emp. L.J. 253, 256 (2021); Ledbetter v. Goodyear Tire & Rubber Co., 550 U.S. 618, 645 (2007) (Ginsburg, J., dissenting).

28. *See, e.g.*, National Labor Relations Act of 1935, Pub. L. No. 74-198, 49 Stat. 449 (codified as amended at 29 U.S.C. §§ 151–169 (2018)); Mass. Gen. Laws Ann. ch. 149, § 105A(c) (West 2019); Cal.

from other scientists and personnel at the Foundation, and on several occasions this conduct interfered with ongoing research and upset the other scientists and research assistants who were approached."[29] It enriches the discussion to note this shift in not only thinking, but legislation, and it reframes the analysis and the perception of the narrative for students, irrespective of whether they believe that the line at issue was correctly drawn in this case.

Freedom of Speech in Public Employment and Antiracist Speech

A final area of the employment law survey course that naturally implicates issues of diversity and inclusion is that of free speech and public employment. In my class's casebook,[30] the first case on this topic is the seminal Supreme Court case of *Pickering v. Board of Education*, which contains an exposition of the principles that undergird much of the analysis that courts use when determining whether a public employee engaged in a (conscripted) First Amendment-protected right to speak or whether the employer at issue exercised its legitimate managerial prerogative to exact an adverse employment action in response to the speech.[31] This analysis provides that to be protected speech, speech must be made as a citizen addressing matters of public concern.[32]

The second case in the chapter is *Givhan v. Western Line Consolidated School District*, in which an English teacher was terminated after she had several private conversations with her school principal during which she raised complaints about "employment policies and practices at the school" that Givhan perceived as "racially discriminatory in purpose or effect."[33] The Supreme Court in this case held that the First Amendment's protection of government employees extended to the private discourse at issue, noting that nothing in the First Amendment or relevant caselaw "indicate[s] that this freedom is lost to the public employee who arranges to communicate privately with his employer rather than to spread his views before the public."[34] The Court subsequently clarified that racial discrimination—as opposed to a "personal" employment conflict—was "a matter inherently of public concern."[35]

Significantly, in the course of discussing this case, students habitually raise the fact that the speech, though spoken more "in" than "out" was likely viewed as having a great

---

Lab. Code § 1197.5(k)(1) (West 2019); Conn. Gen. Stat. § 1(b) (2018); N.H. Rev. Stat. Ann. § 275:41-b (2015).

29. *See Hochstadt*, 545 F.2d at 227–28.

30. Samuel Estreicher, Michael C. Harper, Elizabeth Tippett, Cases and Materials on Employment Law, The Field as Practiced (5th ed. 2016).

31. *See* Pickering v. Bd. of Educ., 391 U.S. 563 (1968).

32. *Id.* at 568.

33. *See* Givhan v. Western Line Consol. School Dist., 439 U.S. 410, 413 (1979).

34. *Id.* at 415–16.

35. Connick v. Myers, 461 U.S. 138, 148 n.8 (1983) (distinguishing *Givhan*, 439 U.S. at 415–16 (1979)).

impact on the employer's institutional efficacy because of the nature of the complaint and the way in which it was directed at the teacher's supervisor. This typically gives way to a rich discussion about what the Court's determination actually hinged upon. In this regard, I find it useful to direct my class to some key questions raised by a legal scholar in the wake of a 2006 Supreme Court decision that cemented a public employer's absolute right to take action against an employee whose offending speech was made in the course of discharging his employment duties:

> In *Givhan*, a teacher made critical comments to her principal regarding race relations in the school, and the Court reasoned that the forum where the expression occurs does not determine whether it is of public or personal interest.[36] The Court did note, however, that the balancing process may involve additional considerations when private speech is involved, such as an assessment of the time, place, and manner of the remarks, given the nature of the employer-employee relationship.[37] Although the *Ceballos* majority attempted to reconcile these two cases by emphasizing that Givhan's remarks were not made pursuant to her job responsibilities, the *Givhan* opinion did not mention that consideration should be given to whether the controversial comments pertained to the employee's official duties. Would the current Supreme Court find that issue significant if a *Givhan*-like case were heard today? Perhaps the Roberts Court would conclude that teachers have responsibilities to advance equity goals, and thus speech akin to Givhan's would be viewed as relating to job responsibilities and would not evoke any type of balancing of interests before sanctions could be imposed.[38]

Closing Thoughts

The curriculum of a survey course in employment law is full of topics and cases that provide springboards for students to thoughtfully address issues of diversity, equality, and inclusion that arise naturally in the theory and the practice of the law. Above is but a small sample of such opportunities. The most important factor a professor should provide is a classroom climate in which all students are comfortable discerning, raising, and pondering these issues, irrespective of how or whether they influence or alter that student's opinion on something like the outcome of a case or the desired trajectory of legal doctrine. While the substantive law of employment discrimination may be the "chapter that ate the course," a proper Employment Law class that touches on workplace law topics like free speech, self-help, or retaliation can be fertile ground for thought and discussion of these issues in other contexts as well.

36. *Givhan*, 439 U.S. 414.

37. *Id.* at 415 n.4.

38. Martha McCarthy, Garcetti v. Ceballos: *Another Hurdle for Public Employees*, 210 Ed. L. Rep. 867, 879 (2006).

Section 3

Remedies

Widening the Lens of Consciousness: Strategies to Broaden Students' Agency in Considering Remedies as a Vehicle for Systemic Change

*Patricia Winograd**

> *I am cognizant of the interrelatedness of all communities and states. I cannot sit idly by in Atlanta and not be concerned about what happens in Birmingham. Injustice anywhere is a threat to justice everywhere. We are caught in an inescapable network of mutuality, tied in a single garment of destiny. Whatever affects one directly affects all indirectly.*[1]

Introduction

I will never forget the first time I read an annotated version of *Walker v. City of Birmingham*,[2] the infamous Supreme Court case reinforcing the collateral bar rule. I immediately noticed that the case arose in Birmingham, Alabama. The case name put me on high alert: it evoked my childhood memories of the Christmases I spent visiting my grandmother as a young, Black—frightened—girl in Mobile. Then, I noticed the year: 1963, a critical point in the civil rights movement. I expected to feel triggered, though the words of the decision did not, at least initially, incite emotion. Nonchalant and casual, even perfunctory, the words of the opinion seemed intentionally to convey a "nothing to see here" tone. Justice Stewart, in fact, used passive voice to describe the

---

* Associate Dean for Equity & Inclusion and an Associate Clinical Professor of Law at LMU Loyola Law School. I wish to thank LMU Loyola Law School Interim Dean Brietta Clark, and Professor Gary Craig, without whose insight, conviction, and support I might never have joined the legal academy. I am also eternally grateful to my family (my husband and two children, Hailey and Patrick) and friends who have supported me throughout my never-ending journey to educate myself and others.

1. Martin Luther King, Jr., *Letter from Birmingham Jail* (Apr. 16, 1963), https://kinginstitute.stanford.edu/sites/mlk/files/letterfrombirmingham_wwcw_0.pdf.

2. Walker v. City of Birmingham, 388 U.S. 307 (1967).

events. "*Meetings … were held*." "A statement was distributed. . . ." "*Violence occurred*." There were no names used in the decision—save Respondents and Petitioners. No one to whom to assign blame appeared readily identifiable.

I was suspicious. And then came the decision's blow that aroused my cognitive dissonance:

> This case would arise in quite a different constitutional posture if the petitioners, before disobeying the injunction, had challenged it in the Alabama courts, and had been met with delay or frustration of their constitutional claims. . . . It cannot be presumed that the Alabama courts would have ignored the petitioners' constitutional claims.[3]

Really?

Yes, I agreed with the general imperative that those bound by court orders must follow them. But the high Court's stated presumption that all litigants—to wit, Black Civil Rights leaders—in an Alabama court would be heard? I needed to know more. I started doing research. It was only then that I realized the Petitioner here was none other than Dr. Martin Luther King, Jr.; his claim: that Alabama city officials had obtained, discriminatorily, an *ex parte* order preventing him from peacefully protesting in Birmingham. Having deliberately chosen to disregard the order, King and others were held in contempt—a punishment that would require King to serve a five-day jail sentence that ultimately led to King's authorship of "Letter from Birmingham Jail," quoted above and one of Dr. King's best-known writings.

How could I have missed that? I perused the notes before and after the case; nothing described the events leading up to the case or their aftermath.

I read the case, again, and again, and again.

By the time the class in which I was to discuss *Walker* started, I was irate. I prepared my notes and PowerPoint, featuring Dr. King's photograph prominently on the title slide. I began class: "This is not just any case," I said. "Is anyone aware of a reason I might say that?"

Silence ensued.

*****

It was in that moment that I set an intention to teach remedies in a manner that awakened student consciousness about justice *and* injustice.

*****

Remedies are, without question, one of the most consequential aspects of the law. If the purview of remedies is the existing legal framework used to address wrongs, then surely the study of remedies should serve as fertile ground for students to learn and ideate about solutions to society's most egregious wrongs—social injustices. Traditional presentations of remedies can easily ignore the ways in which remedies work *injustice* and can do *justice*. (I was guilty of such a presentation!) But, in this moment,

3. *Id.* at 317–19.

I decided that I could no longer turn a blind eye to the concepts of equity and justice that pervade the landscape of remedies.

Of course, creating a classroom environment that pays homage to justice—in particular, the brand of justice I subscribe to that seeks to expose inequities against othered and marginalized communities, is no easy task. Practical realities impede best intentions. Time is finite. Where bar preparation is the goal, there is scant time to adequately cover even the triad of remedies[4] most often encountered on bar exams. Beyond such pragmatic concerns, incorporating issues of justice in a manner that emphasizes difference and inequity in any law school class requires more than a set of occasional questions, an individual case, or even an isolated discussion. It begins with showing up in the legal classroom—authentic, empathic, and caring—and is carried forward by strategic decisions signaling to marginalized students that you "see" and value them.[5] Further, any deliberate attempt to honor diversity, equity, and inclusion in the legal classroom is multifaceted, multipronged, and should be omnipresent.[6]

Here, I seek to share some of the strategies I use to incorporate equity into my class. My pedagogical choices are fueled by my steadfast commitment to equity,[7] engaged,[8] and antiracist[9] pedagogy. First and foremost, I want my students to see themselves in, and feel connected to, my curriculum. Many of the cases in traditional case books will seem untethered to the experience of othered and marginalized students. I take care to introduce relevant cases and materials that matter and that raise issues familiar to a broad swath of students (even if such materials come from a source other than the casebook).[10] Additionally, I attempt to orient students to the manner in which our

---

4. I use the phrase "triad of remedies" to refer to: (1) damages; (2) equitable remedies; and (3) restitution, which straddles both legal and equitable frameworks. With exceptions, these three categories are typically described as comprising the fundamental categories of remedies.

5. See Nicole P. Dyszlewski, *Wisdom for Teachers on the Journey to Integrating Diversity in the Law Classroom, in* INTEGRATING DOCTRINE AND DIVERSITY: INCLUSION AND EQUITY IN THE LAW SCHOOL CLASSROOM 3 (Nicole P. Dyszlewski et al. eds., 2021).

6. All of these decisions must be preceded by reflection on the part of the professor. Without reflection regarding goals to be achieved in implementing such strategies, execution may fail, and worse, be perceived by students as inauthentic. See generally ETTA R. HOLLINS, CULTURE IN SCHOOL LEARNING: REVEALING THE DEEP MEANING (2d. ed. 2008).

7. "Equity pedagogy" is an approach to contextualizing instruction for a particular population by "employing instructional strategies that incorporate aspects of their cultural and experiential backgrounds." *Id.* at 89. The University of Michigan's Center for Research on Learning & Teaching offers multiple guides including equity-focused teaching practices and strategies designed to achieve equity in the classroom. *See, e.g.*, Equity-Focused Teaching, https://crlt.umich.edu/equity-focused-teaching/principles-strategies-resources (last visited Jan. 6, 2023).

8. "Engaged pedagogy," as used here, is a term coined by bell hooks. *See generally* BELL HOOKS, TEACHING TO TRANSGRESS: EDUCATION AS THE PRACTICE OF FREEDOM (1994).

9. I wholeheartedly adopt the meaning of the word "antiracist" as described by Ibram X. Kendi. *See, e.g.*, IBRAM X. KENDI, HOW TO BE AN ANTIRACIST 13 (2019) (defining antiracist as "one who is supporting an antiracist policy through their actions or expressing an antiracist idea.").

10. Just prior to completing this article, Professors Candace S. Kovacic-Fleischer and Paul T. Hayden released CONTEMPORARY REMEDIES AND RESTITUTION (2023), which offers students a survey of relevant, contemporary cases that capture the essence of incorporating equitable learning techniques in the legal classroom. Professors Douglas Laycock and Richard L. Hasen are authors of

system of remedies reinforces bias and racist structures. Beyond that, I aspire to employ instructive techniques that render students more conscientious about the broad landscape of remedies and students' agency in utilizing remedies to lift minoritized populations.

These techniques are designed to awaken in students a consciousness that enables and motivates them to look beyond the superficial to critically question the impact of remedial choices. Ultimately, I see the study of remedies as an ideal opportunity to ready upper-division students to serve as culturally competent advocates with a sharp attunement to ways they might think about remedies as advocates for good (or of change). I believe such an "others"-centric disposition can be fostered by a professor who intentionally seeks to lay the foundation to empower students. My goal is to render students ready to: (1) consider legal problems and remedies empathically, from another's perspective; (2) appreciate their own bias, privilege, and access; and (3) understand that their own culture, perspective, and background may not resemble that of the parties in the case, the lawyer who represented them, or the judge who decided the matter—and that these distinctions *matter.*[11]

---

another rich, comprehensive remedies casebook titled MODERN AMERICAN REMEDIES (5th ed. 2019) that I believe can be used to further these ends.

In the past, I have also used a variety of published and unpublished cases in myriad ways—necessarily keyed to the interests and backgrounds of the students I teach. Such examples include, for example, Attorneys General v. Trump, No. 4:20-cv-01563, (N.D. Cal. filed Mar. 2, 2020, *sub nom.* California et al. v. Biden) and California v. Trump, 2019 WL 2715421 (N.D. Cal. 2019), concerning declaratory and injunctive relief sought over the diversion of funds used by the Trump administration in connection with the border wall; Epic Games, Inc. v. Apple, Inc., 2021 WL 5205487 (N.D. Cal. 2021), involving a dispute between Apple and the distributer of the video game Fortnite over the propriety of Apple's exclusive in-app purchase system; Goldberg v. Pace University, 535 F. Supp. 3d 180 (S.D.N.Y. 2021) involving a dispute requesting among other things, restitution, following the school's transition to remote learning; Clifford v. Trump, No. 2:18-CV-02217 (C.D. Cal., filed Mar. 16, 2018), the declaratory relief action involving the viability and enforceability of a contract; Olsen v. Singer, No. 5:19-cv-01351 (N.D. Cal., Filed Mar. 13, 2019), involving a class action for damages by students of universities alleged to have been involved in the college admissions scandal of 2018–19; Parler LLC. v. Amazon Web Services, Inc., 514 F. Supp. 3d 1261 (W.D. Wash. 2021), concerning a request for a temporary restraining order against Amazon to stop it from removing its account following the Jan. 6 riots.

11. For more on cultural competency training, *see* Serena Patel, *Cultural Competency Training: Preparing Law Students for Practice in Our Multicultural World*, 62 UCLA L. REV. DISC. 140 (2014); L. Danielle Tully, *The Cultural (Re)Turn: The Case for Teaching Culturally Responsive Lawyering*, 16 STAN. J. CIV. RIGHTS & CIV. LIBERTIES 201 (2020); Susan Bryant, *Five Habits of Cross-Cultural Lawyering and More: Clinical Law Teaching Materials from Sue Bryant and Jean Koh Peters*, https://fivehabitsandmore.law.yale.edu/ (last visited Jan. 6, 2023).

Setting the Tone

The quickest way to establish consciousness about the far-reaching effects of remedies is to make clear to students, from the beginning, that remedies carry broader implications than what may be facially apparent from the triad of categories traditionally tested on the bar exam. Although the triadic paradigm is foundational to a basic understanding of remedies, the more one is wedded to topics germane to the bar examination, the greater the tendency to stick to this template. This paradigm, however, can be dangerously narrow. Adherence to this triadic relationship leaves students unaware of the most important ends to which remedies may be used. Students neither readily see the potential for remedies to impact legal questions of significance to marginalized identity groups, nor are they invited to recognize their agency in bringing about change in our legal system.

Even an introductory announcement changes the narrative. On the first day of class, I announce the multifaceted and consequential role of remedies in our nation's most serious legal issues. I call out *Bush v. Gore*,[12] *The Estate of Henrietta Lacks v. Thermo Fisher Scientific Inc.*,[13] and other cases in which a litigant's substantive rights are determined, in large part, by the framing of a remedy and other remedial choices.

Broad Curriculum Coverage

A related pedagogical decision concerns what to cover in a remedies curriculum. Again, traditional, circumscribed presentations of remedies, may unnecessarily lead to the exclusive coverage of private remedies. This lean focus causes students to home in on legal issues impacting those with the means to pursue litigation—another point worth explicitly stating. Moreover, as critical scholars would argue, it smacks of [l]egal individualism, which:

> underpins the architecture of the U.S. legal system both as process (personal cases only) and substance ("individual rights" only), thereby ... creat[ing] ... a mismatch between remedies (for individuals only) and problems (that are built around group identities).[14]

In other words, if they are overly focused on individual problems with individual remedies, students are never required to think beyond the individual to collective problems facing certain marginalized identity groups and their responsibility in remedying the effects of discrimination and other forms of oppression of othered populations. Students are, thus, not trained to be inclusive and all-encompassing in their thinking about solutions. That practitioners would enter the profession without a sound sense of the ways in which even the traditional framework of remedies may be used to further

---

12. 531 U.S. 98 (2000).

13. No. 1:21-CV-02524 (D. Md., filed Oct. 4, 2021)

14. Francisco Valdes, Steven W. Bender & Jennifer J. Hill, Critical Justice: Systemic Advocacy in Law and Society 764 (2021).

antiracist and equitable agendas bodes poorly for training lawyers with the ability, let alone the inkling, to make change. The use of remedies as a means of solving systemic inequalities is virtually hidden, left to the creativity and will of those who do certain public interest work. As Valdes et al. explain, "legal individualism hamstrings advocacy consciousness and choices."[15] Students are thus not forced to consider their own agency in using remedies as a means of challenging and changing systems.

I am mindful of the need to incorporate public remedies[16] and remedies that impact group, rather than individual, outcomes in my curriculum. Luckily, remedies scholars need not go out of their way to accomplish this. Injunctions provide a rich source of such material. Remedies casebooks expansively cover preventive injunctions, which focus narrowly on violations against individuals or individual entities. However, structural and nationwide injunctions are also featured in casebooks and have the natural appeal of exposing students to remedies that impact broad swaths of people. Given that structural injunctions seek to address social injustices to reform systems (i.e., a school, prison system, or mental institution), they are perfect fodder for exposing students to the manner in which modern forms of injunctive relief can operate to dismantle systems of oppression. *Brown v. Board of Education of Topeka*[17] is one of the seminal cases utilizing structural injunctions, but scores of subsequent cases also reveal novel ways of using the structural injunction to bring about institutional change.[18] Students should unequivocally be familiar with the reach and impact of structural injunctions.

Nationwide injunctions, though controversial, are similar in impact and also relate to matters—such as immigration, health, and public land regulation—that involve issues of great interest to marginalized students and those of other backgrounds. It is worth pausing to consider the merits of several cases in this realm, particularly given the important policy and other questions supporting both criticism and arguments in favor of such injunctions.

Still other aspects of the triadic paradigm, including damages and restitutionary concepts, can lay the groundwork for an understanding of remedies that directly dismantle racism. Reparations are one such example. Reparations touch upon just about every aspect of the remedial context, including not only considerations of injury, but also problems of valuation and an exploration of policy. The subject of reparations, thus, readily can be incorporated into the study of remedies as a way of solidifying an

---

15. *Id.* at 765.

16. Public law litigation, as described by Judge Abram Chayes, includes cases involving: school desegregation, employment discrimination, prisoners' or inmates' rights, securities fraud, union government governance, consumer fraud, housing discrimination, electoral reapportionment, and environmental management. *See, e.g.*, Abram Chayes, *The Role of the Judge in Public Law Litigation*, 89 HARV. L. REV. 1281, 1282–84 (1976). Tracy A. Thomas et al.'s remedies casebook seeks to include both private and public remedies. TRACY THOMAS ET AL., REMEDIES, PUBLIC AND PRIVATE (6th ed. 2017).

17. 347 U.S. 483 (1954).

18. Robert E. Easton, *The Dual Role of the Structural Injunction*, 99 YALE L. J. 1983 (1990). *See also* Dewey Roscoe Jones, *Federal Court Remedies: The Creative Use of Potential Remedies Can Produce Institutional Change*, 27 HOWARD L.J. 879 (1984); Russell L. Weaver, *The Rise and Decline of Structural Remedies*, 41 SAN DIEGO L. REV. 1617 (2004).

understanding of the distinction between compensatory damages—where interesting questions of computation involving the value of property and services taken from slaves—and unjust enrichment—where compelling questions abound concerning the need to disgorge slaveowners and others who obtained a benefit from the labor and services of others must be quantified. Like structural and nationwide injunctions, reparations have the obvious appeal not only of addressing issues directly relevant to diverse students but also of provoking students' deep thinking about how our remedial system can be used to address concerns of justice.[19] How better to center issues of racial inequality in remedies than through a deep dive into how remedies can play a part in rectifying the past injuries caused by America's greatest wrong.[20]

Uncovering What Lies Beneath the Surface: Asking the Normative Question and Establishing Context

Even when considering the more limited set of remedies, opportunities abound to consider questions of race, bias, diversity, and justice. Aside from issues of coverage, additional strategies must be utilized to generate student thought about issues of equity. I use several such strategies.

First, I invite students to *feel*, evoking their visceral responses to cases. I want students thinking about the human side of the law—and be moved to praxis! Therefore, at the same time I might elicit considerations about the "rightful position"[21] in a case, I similarly encourage students to think also about the "right" position in a case. A leading social justice advocate, William Quigley,[22] directs students desirous of advancing justice to critique the law by asking questions that help: discern who benefits from each law, and what their interests are; learn about the real history behind laws; and look at the unstated implications of race, class, and gender.[23] Among other questions, I askstudents: how does this make you? Did anything about the decision bother you? Who did the case hurt? Who did it help? Why? How should it be different?

---

19. Cardozo Law School has a wonderful teaching guide that frames thoughtful questions for discussion that could be brought into any remedies class. Cardozo Law Institute in Holocaust and Human Rights, Confronting Structural Violence: Law Teaching Guides, *U.S. Torts Law, Module 11*, https://go.yu.edu/hubfs/Module%2011%20-%20Reparations-1.pdf?hsCtaTracking=8ecf2dd2-e6bb-45ce-a82a-60a010814dc9%7Ce354bc09-390b-46d7-b46f-b798d8798972 (last visited Jan. 6, 2023).

20. *See* Eric J. Miller, *Republican, Rebellious Reparations*, 63 Howard L. Rev. 363 (2020); Roy L. Brooks, *Racial Reconciliation Through Black Reparations*, 63 Howard L. Rev. 349 (2020).

21. "Rightful position" is a term established by Douglas Laycock to refer to the position a litigant should be restored to in order to compensate him, her or them from a breach or tortious act.

22. William P. Quigley, *Letter to a Law Student Interested in Social Justice*, 1 DePaul J. for Soc. Just. 7 (2007).

23. I also recommend I. Bennett Capers, *Reading Back, Reading Black*, 35 Hofstra L. Rev. 8 (2007).

Second, I invite students to critically read cases, though I do not always explicitly describe it as such. I try to elicit students' thinking on what is not explicitly in the text—either because it is implicit or lacking altogether. For example, I challenge students to discern bias in case language. I engage in self-talk and think-alouds, revealing an attitude toward the case. I am known for reading excerpts from the text and, literally, "talking back"[24] to them (as if a petulant teenager speaking under her breath to her mother). Exposing myself in this authentic, almost irreverent way reminds students that they, too, should think about the case on a deeper level; I am even hoping to cause students to reflect not just on the case before them, but the larger issues presented.

Finally, I expose other, more transparent ways in which remedies involve bias and racism. Indeed, the field of remedies is necessarily concerned with questions of value. I caution students to be on guard for issues of inequity in seemingly straightforward mathematical calculations. In evaluating the fairness of recoveries that are said to be objective, for example, I help students understand that the law of damages determines the relative worth of individuals and their time differently.[25] Cases such as *Stauffer v. Stauffer*[26] or *Frankel v. United States,*[27] opinions authored in 1970s and arising in courts in Pennsylvania, lay bare the value-laden judgments made by the Court concerning the parties. The heteronormative, cisgender judgments uncovered when dissecting such cases can be the subject of a fruitful discussion. I never shy away from an emphasis on the importance of legal or historical context.[28] When discussing damages for personal injuries, I introduce actuarial tables that lay bare the discrepancy between life expectancy and work-life expectancies of diverse populations as compared to others. I also introduce students to current litigation challenging racist practices in damages calculations. The recent NFL concussion settlements where, according to lawyers for former Black players, "race-norming" was built into the settlements, offer a compelling example.

This "under-the-hood" training is the underpinning of an engaged, antiracist pedagogy that I believe is necessary to awaken in students a disposition to question the law more deeply in a manner that reveals injustice.

---

24. The phrase "Talking Back to Texts" was coined by Professors Elizabeth Fajans and Mary R. Falk. *See* Elizabeth Fajans & Mary R. Falk, *Against the Tyranny of Paraphrase: Talking Back to Texts*, 78 Cornell L. Rev. 163 (1993).

25. *See, e.g.*, Jennifer B. Wriggins, *Tort, Race, and the Value of Injury, 1900–1949*, 49 Howard L. Rev. 99 (2005).

26. 465 Pa. 558 (1976).

27. 321 F. Supp. 1331 (E.D. Pa. 1970).

28. Fajans & Falk, *supra* note 24, at 169.

Thinking Outside of the Box: Crafting Problems, Developing Solutions

Ultimately, the suggestions identified above provide a starting point for cultivating a consciousness about the ways in which remedies, or any discussion of them, instill bias, further prejudice, and solidify racist structures. At the end of the day, I seek to engender praxis, or action, that compels students to use remedies to actually dismantle and rectify harmful systems. Perhaps the best way to have students think about and craft solutions to problems that impact identity groups to which they belong is to let students do just that: invite students to offer their own remedial solutions on the basis of their lived experiences.

Two years ago, I had the privilege of creating a seminar[29] that offered students license to address problems and propose solutions to these problems on the basis of their own lived experiences.[30] In a process that I heavily scaffolded, students were asked to think about their own intersectional identities; identify and describe lived experiences in which the law played a part; explore a significant aspect of the law (i.e., housing, healthcare, education, employment, voting, crime) that has had a material impact on their lives; and suggest solutions for amplifying any positive, and rectifying any negative, impact the law has had on the student's own life. After significant reflection and dialogue, students created critical auto-ethnographies in which they discussed their remedial approaches to struggles impacting their identity groups.

Conclusion

Modern-day activists like Bryan Stevenson and others urge that as recipients of the benefits of justice, we must also be mindful of injustice.[31] For me, the subject of remedies is just the place to bring about consciousness relating to both justice and injustice.

---

29. The seminar, the first of its kind at LLS, was titled "Professional Identity, The Lawyer's Role In Eradicating Systemic Inequities."

30. The true test of pedagogy that engages othered, marginalized students is whether and to what extent it calls upon those students to create knowledge on the basis of their own experience. As Paulo Friere instructs in *Pedagogy of the Oppressed*:

> As ... [students] ... are increasingly posed with problems relating to themselves in the world and with the world, ... [they] ... feel increasingly challenged and obliged to respond to that challenge. Because they apprehend the challenge as interrelated to other problems within a total context, not as a theoretical question, the resulting comprehension tend to be increasingly critical and thus constantly less alienated. Their response to the challenge evokes new challenges followed by new understandings; and gradually the students come to regard themselves as committed.

Paulo Friere, Pedagogy of the Oppressed 81 (Bloomsbury 2000).

31. Bryan Stephenson, *We Need to Talk About an Injustice*, TED, https://www.youtube.com/watch?v=c2tOp7OxyQ8 (last visited Jan. 6, 2023).

Section 4

Criminal Procedure

Using Images and Videos in Criminal Procedure

*Tung Yin**

Introduction

The United States incarcerates more people per capita than any other nation in the world,[1] and a disproportionate number of those who are incarcerated are Black persons.[2] Those statistics focus on the output of the criminal justice system. What about the input? Consider that a study of 2018–19 traffic stops in Portland, Oregon, found that 11% of traffic stops of Black drivers resulted in a search, which was a rate more than double that expected "based on comparing similar drivers' characteristics, such as gender, age, reason for the stop, and time of day."[3] More searches likely result in more criminal evidence, meaning that Black drivers are more likely to be pulled into the criminal justice system at the front end. And when they do get pulled in, they are more likely to sit in jail for pretrial detention than white defendants.[4]

---

* Professor of Law, Lewis & Clark Law School. Thanks to Radhika Shah (L&C '23) for research assistance.

1. *See* RONALD ALLEN ET AL., COMPREHENSIVE CRIMINAL PROCEDURE 1463 (4th ed. 2014) (noting U.S. per capita incarceration rate as of 2013 of 698 per 100,000, compared to 450 for Russia, 165 for China, 212 for Mexico, 151 for Australia, 148 for the United Kingdom, and 106 for Canada, among other nations).

2. *See, e.g.*, Paul Butler, *One Hundred Years of Race and Crime*, 100 J. CRIM. L. & CRIMINOLOGY 1043, 1046 n.22 (2010) (noting that "one in forty-five blacks, and about one in three hundred and twenty whites" are incarcerated); *see also* MICHELLE ALEXANDER, THE NEW JIM CROW: MASS INCARCERATION IN THE AGE OF COLORBLINDNESS 11 (2010) (noting that one-third of young Black men are in prison or jail, or on probation or parole).

3. *See* Conrad Wilson, *Oregon Traffic Stop Data Shows Largest Disparity at Portland, Hillsboro Police*, OR. PUB. BROAD. (Dec. 1, 2019), https://www.opb.org/news/article/oregon-portland-traffic-stop-data-disparity-portland-hillsboro/.

4. *See* Conrad Wilson, *Report Finds Some Increasing Racial Disparities in Multnomah County's Justice System*, OR. PUB. BROAD. (Nov. 25, 2019), https://www.opb.org/news/article/multnomah-county-justice-system-racial-disparities-report/.

Given those facts, it seems impossible *not* to integrate discussions of race and diversity into a standard course on criminal procedure when such an obvious disparate impact exists for whom gets subjected to the clutches of the criminal justice system.[5] One of the reasons that I assign *Comprehensive Criminal Procedure* by Ronald Allen, Joseph Hoffman, Debra Livingston, Andrew Leipold, and Tracey Meares, is that it goes beyond the usual Supreme Court opinions to include references to law review articles, statistics, and commentary about race, gender, and class.[6]

As welcome as such supplemental material is, however, more can be done in the classroom to take advantage of audiovisual technology and the ready availability on the Internet of photographs and videos. Below I discuss five examples of videos or pictures that I share in my criminal procedure courses to call attention to the role that race plays, or should play, in understanding particular cases and doctrine.

Traffic Infractions

When I started teaching criminal procedure (search and seizure and interrogation law), I would begin the course by asking how many students had been pulled over for a traffic infraction. I, of course, would raise my hand as well. I figured this was a way of showing how criminal procedure was an area of law that would directly impact most of us in an annoying but relatively nonthreatening context.

But I came to see that this was true only from a position of privilege. As an Asian-American male, I am a person of color, but when it comes to interactions with the police, I'm not part of a vulnerable population. I'm not sure how my frequency of getting just a warning compares with other drivers, but I've never had occasion to think that I was pulled over because of my race; and I've *never* had an officer ask if it would be all right to search my car.

The challenge for those of us who do not suffer from being pulled over for *driving while Black* is that it's easy to understand at an intellectual level how wrong it is to profile someone racially, but it's very hard to internalize that feeling.

During the COVID-19 era, however, I went looking for ways to make hybrid classes more interesting, and I discovered a YouTube video of a highway stop taken from the deputy sheriff's dashcam. I now show the beginning of the video near the start of the first day of class. The video starts with the deputy's police vehicle racing down a highway, catching up to a U-Haul truck, and pulling the truck over. The deputy gets out and approaches the truck from the passenger side, and then walks around to the driver side.

---

5. *See* Cynthia Lee, *Race and the Criminal Law Curriculum, in* The Oxford Handbook of Race and Law in the United States (Devon Carbado et al. eds., 2022) ("Race, however, infuses so many aspects of the criminal justice system that to teach Criminal Law without any acknowledgment of race reinforces the fiction that criminal law is race-neutral and blind to racial difference . . .").

6. *See* Stephanos Bibas, *The Real-World Shift in Criminal Procedure*, 93 J. Crim. L. & Criminology 789, 793 (2002) (reviewing the first edition of the Allen and Hoffman casebook and noting its "sensitiv[ity] to real-world considerations, including the roles played by politics, race, drugs, and money.").

So far, this is standard fare, except the deputy has the driver step out. The driver is a young Black man (who, as it turns out, is a law student moving back home because of the COVID-19 lockdowns).[7] I then leave the video running but switch the screen back to my PowerPoint slides and turn to more of the class material.

About half an hour into the class session, I return to the highway stop video—in real time. I point out how much time has elapsed in our class, and we see that the highway stop is continuing. There is a glimpse of the drug-sniffing dog, and then the young Black man appears back on the screen. He is on the phone (with his father), and the deputy orders the driver to put the phone down, and then orders him to lean forward with his hands on the hood of the police car. The young Black man narrates everything to his father, and there is a hint of panic in his voice. The deputy then takes the Black man's left hand behind his back, and the young man starts crying out, "Daddy, he's arresting me!" He repeats that several times and then starts wailing, "There's nothing in there, I promise you, I didn't do anything!" The deputy puts the young man in the backseat of the police car. "Daddy, I don't wanna die!" The deputy responds (somewhat dismissively in my view), "You're not gonna die ..."

I should note that if a picture is worth a thousand words, then a video is worth a million. My description of the scene doesn't come close to conveying a sense of the visceral panic that the young Black man clearly felt at the time. This video is heartbreaking to watch.[8]

I then return to the video about an hour into the class session. Now the back of the truck is open and there are multiple deputies searching through the contents, which appear to be chairs and other furniture. (Apparently the drug-sniffing dog alerted to the possible presence of narcotics, so the police are looking for drugs.)

Finally, just before the end of the class session, I come back to the video one last time. At Lewis & Clark, our typical class sessions are 85 minutes long. The highway stop—in real time—has not ended! I actually skip forward to just under 115 minutes into the video, where there is a discussion between the deputy and the driver about their respective perceptions of the incident. In the end, the driver didn't get a ticket, only a warning. However, the stop lasted far longer than the class session, and the arrest sequence is downright harrowing to experience.

A few students have shared their reactions to this video with me. A couple stated in evaluations that they appreciated having the class begin this way, as doing so signaled that the course would be recognizing the role that race plays in the criminal justice system. Another student found the video disturbing enough that they doubted they could practice criminal law.

---

7. The law student, Marion Humphrey, Jr., has since filed a civil rights lawsuit over his detention.
8. It can be found here: tinyurl.com/yprzm3hu (beginning around the 29-minute mark).

Voluntariness

"Reasonableness" shows up frequently in Fourth Amendment doctrine, which is not surprising given that the text of the amendment references the right to be free from "unreasonable searches and seizures." In determining whether a person has been seized by law enforcement officers, federal courts ask whether "a reasonable person would feel free 'to disregard the police and go about his business,'" or, in a more confined setting such as a bus, "whether a reasonable person would feel free to decline the officers' requests or otherwise terminate the encounter."[9] Similarly, in determining whether a suspect is in custody for the purposes of a law enforcement officer's obligation to provide *Miranda* warnings, the Supreme Court has explained that "the only relevant inquiry is how a reasonable man in the suspect's position would have understood his situation."[10]

But how do we envision the "reasonable person"? Because we each have only our own lived experiences, it can be easier or harder for each of us to imagine how a reasonable person would act, depending on, among other factors, how closely we align to the predominant cultural norm being envisioned by the authors of the particular judicial opinions. In practice, of course, this means that there is a tendency for "reasonable person" to mean "reasonable cisgender heterosexual white male."[11]

One way I try to demonstrate how culturally dependent this concept of "reasonable person" can be is by showing a short video clip of an interrogation scene from a foreign crime drama. The specific goal is to present a common situation but with linguistic and cultural obstacles to full comprehension, and thus the fewer students who are likely to understand the foreign language, the better. I use "Age of Legends," which is a 2018 Chinese television crime drama,[12] and play a short scene in which the suspect is a woman being questioned about her alleged role in drug smuggling by two male police officers in an interrogation room. How does the woman reasonably understand her situation?

---

9. U.S. v. Drayton, 536 U.S. 194, 201–02 (2002) (quoting California v. Hodari D., 499 U.S. 621, 628 (1991); Florida v. Bostick, 501 U.S. 429, 434–36 (1991)).

10. Berkemer v. McCarty, 468 U.S. 420, 442 (1984).

11. *See, e.g.*, Robert S. Adler & Ellen R. Peirce, *The Legal, Ethical, and Social Implications of the "Reasonable Woman" Standard in Sexual Harassment Cases*, 61 Fordham L. Rev. 773 (1993) (discussing the Ninth Circuit's unusual use of "reasonable woman" in place of "reasonable person" in determining whether hostile work environment existed); Randall S. Susskind, *Race, Reasonable Articulation, and Seizure*, 31 Am. Crim. L. Rev. 327 (1994) (arguing that Fourth Amendment doctrine should take race into account in the "reasonable person" analysis); *see also* Sherrilyn A. Ifill, *Racial Diversity on the Bench: Beyond Role Models and Public Confidence*, 57 Wash. & Lee L. Rev. 405, 425–26 (2000) (discussing how perceptions of the criminal justice system differ between Blacks and whites, and how Black judges might bring different perspectives to the bench); *cf.* Susan F. Mandiberg, *Reasonable Officers vs. Reasonable Lay Persons in the Supreme Court's* Miranda *and Fourth Amendment Cases*, 14 Lewis & Clark L. Rev. 1481 (2010) (arguing that the Court's conception of the "reasonable lay person" is an idealized paragon devoid of any cultural or personal experiences, including those based on race).

12. *Age of Legends* (Dragon Television 2018); *see Age of Legends*, IMDB.com, https://www.imdb.com/title/tt8981944/.

If we try to answer this in the context of how the reasonable person would feel in that situation, we run into some problems. The entire conversation is in Mandarin with English subtitles. One has to hope that the translation is accurate—and sometimes they are not.[13] Even if the translation is accurate, it cannot convey inflection or nuances in the wording. Impeding the ability of a non-Mandarin speaker to capture the nuances of the conversation is that spoken Mandarin consists of four tones, which one must be trained to recognize;[14] thus, tone shifts in English that might signal sarcasm or levity may have entirely different purposes in Mandarin. Even getting past the language/translation issues, one is left wondering if there are different cultural norms in China regarding deference and submission to authority, and whether such norms impact the assessment of voluntariness. To be sure, there are some objective facts that a non-Mandarin speaking viewer can discern from the scene: the suspect is handcuffed to the chair, and she is outnumbered by the detectives. But overall, the interrogation scene seems alien to most students, and provides them with potential insight into how a typical American interrogation may seem to someone who is not versed in American culture—and whether the law inaccurately assesses any "voluntary" confession in such settings.

Race Impact

A picture is worth a thousand words. It can also bring cases to life: who is the defendant other than a name—often only a surname? When I introduce a new case for class discussion, I include a photograph of the defendant whenever possible, and in some instances, other people involved, such as Detective McFadden, who instigated the stop-and-frisk that was upheld in *Terry v. Ohio*.[15]

The very first photo I wanted to show my students was of a telephone booth that I saw in Anacortes Bay, Washington. I was so excited to be able to show my students what a phone booth looked like (in case many had never seen one) so that they could envision what Charles Katz stepped into, as a demonstrative aid concerning reasonable expectations of privacy.[16] Having committed to using PowerPoint to create a picture slide, I decided to go all in. The next picture I came up with was of boxing promoter Don King, who had a minor role in the facts of *Mapp v. Ohio*.[17] After that, I remembered that I had taken pictures of various controlled substances on display at the Vancouver Police Museum; for those who led relatively sheltered lives (as I did), it might

---

13. One example of a type of inaccuracy would be literal translation that fails to capture the actual meaning. In Chinese, *tā zǒule* (他走了) literally means "he left," but it also euphemistically means, "he passed away." The literal translation would be inaccurate if the actual meaning was the euphemistic one.

14. Confusingly, the words for buy (*mǎi*) and sell (*mài*) sound the same, differentiated only by tone.

15. 392 U.S. 1 (1968).

16. *See* Katz v. United States, 389 U.S. 347 (1967).

17. 367 U.S. 643 (1961).

be interesting to see what cocaine, heroin, and crystal meth actually look like, given how frequently they figured in the cases.

I wasn't able to find pictures for every defendant in the major cases covered in both criminal procedure courses, but here are the ones I did find: Ray Agard, Gail Atwater, James Batson, John Brady, Frank Costello, Willie Darden, Willie Gene Davis, Michael Elstad, Clarence Gideon, Booker Hudson, Curtis Kyles, Robert Lile, Dollree Mapp, Thomas Miller-El, Ernesto Miranda, Evangelisto Ramos, Anthony Salerno, Rudolph Santobello, Jeff Skilling, John Terry (and Richard Chilton and Carl Katz), Van Thompkins, Timothy Carpenter, and the "Scottsboro Boys." Of the 24 individuals listed, (not counting the Scottsboro Boys), 10 were white;[18] the rest were people of color, primarily Black. Apart from Batson and Miller-El (both of whose cases involved racially discriminatory jury selection), race was not raised as a legal issue in these cases, and the Supreme Court frequently does not identify the race of defendants. Yet, there is a cumulative impact from seeing how many of the major criminal procedure cases involve defendants who are people of color—it is a stark reminder of the disproportionate impact of the criminal justice system, especially on Black men.

One defendant is worth discussing in more detail: Willie Darden. The issue in *Darden v. Wainwright* was whether the prosecutor's inflammatory closing argument warranted reversal of the murder conviction. In addition to referring to Darden as "this animal," the prosecutor argued to the jury that Darden "shouldn't be out of his cell unless he has a leash on him and a prison guard at the other end of that leash."[19]

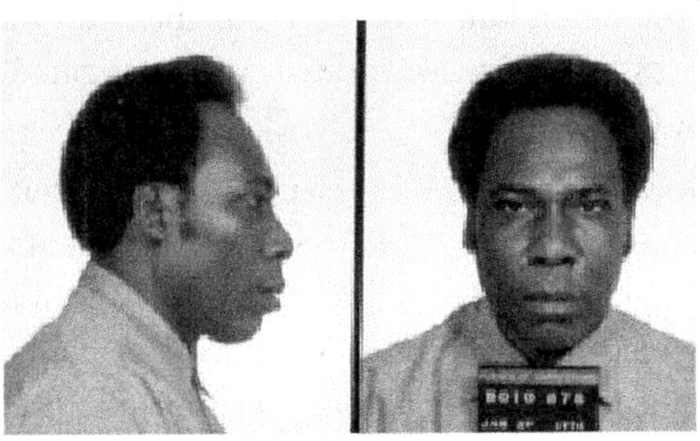

Willie Darden's race didn't figure into the analysis. In fact, the Court mentions race only once in the opinion, and it isn't even about Darden, but rather the description of the perpetrator: "On September 8, 1973, at about 5:30 p.m., a [B]lack adult male entered Carl's Furniture Store near Lakeland, Florida."[20] The reader must infer Darden's race from the fact of his arrest. It can be easy to miss that one almost throwaway description. The summary description of the case in the classic criminal procedure hornbook does not mention Darden's race.[21]

And yet, the true impact of the prosecutor's inflammatory argument cannot be appreciated without acknowledging that Darden was a Black man. An enduring racist

18. Atwater, Brady, Costello, Elstad, Gideon, Lile, Salerno, Santobello, Skilling, and Katz.
19. Darden v. Wainwright, 477 U.S. 168 (1986).
20. *Id.* at 171.
21. *See* Wayne R. LaFave et al., Criminal Procedure § 24.7 n. 18 (5th ed. 2009).

stereotype of Black persons (especially Black men) is that they are "apelike";[22] thus calling a Black man an "animal" is more likely to trigger such dehumanizing stereotypes than calling a white man an "animal." Similarly, the leash comment invited jurors to visualize Darden being forced to wear a leash—imagery that again is likely to have a different effect when applied to a Black man than to a white one considering the country's sordid history of slavery. For example, promotion for the acclaimed 1977 miniseries *Roots* used pictures of star LeVar Burton as slave Kunta Kinte shackled with an iron neck ring.[23]

Was the prosecutor seeking to dehumanize Willie Darden by evoking racial stereotypes and slave imagery? It's impossible to say from the Supreme Court's opinion. But that alone is an indictment of the Court's failure to acknowledge Darden's race and to explore the impact that his race may have had on the impact of the prosecutor's argument.

"High Crime" Neighborhoods and Race

Does running from the police provide reasonable suspicion to justify a *Terry* stop-and-frisk?[24] Not by itself, but according to the Supreme Court's decision in *Illinois v. Wardlow*, running from the police while in a "high crime" neighborhood can provide reasonable suspicion.[25]

After discussing the facts and reasoning of *Wardlow* with my class, I then turn to the implications of such a doctrine. I put up a slide with a scan of a Portland Police Bureau document titled "Monthly Neighborhood Offense Statistics." This is a map of Portland, with neighborhoods color-coded by crime rate, ranging from light gray for the lowest to dark blue for the highest. Parts of the city in the southeast, north, and just north of downtown are shaded darker; most of the west side of the city is light gray.

Next, I put up a slide titled "Neighborhood Coalitions," which is a map of Portland with pie charts superimposed on the various neighborhood coalitions in the city. The parts of the city that have the greatest racial diversity happen to be the southeast, north, northeast, and just north of downtown, while the west side has the least racial diversity.[26]

Of course, the correlation (as opposed to causation) between race and crime is linked by a third variable, which is income. Not surprisingly, a map of Portland color-coded by average family income shows that the parts of the city with the lowest average income are the southeast, north, and just north of downtown; and the west side has the highest average income.

---

22. *See, e.g.*, Phillip Atiba Goff et al., *Not Yet Human: Implicit Knowledge, Historic Dehumanization, and Contemporary Consequences*, 94 J. Personality & Soc. Psych. 292, 293 (2008).

23. *Roots* (ABC 1977).

24. *See* Terry v. Ohio, 392 U.S. 1 (1968).

25. *See* 528 U.S. 119 (2000).

26. Credit where credit is due: I was inspired to look into this approach by Professor Karrigan Börk (UC Davis law), who mentioned doing something similar with regard to environmental pollution and neighborhood diversity.

Whatever the causation and correlation, the juxtaposition of the crime rate and racial diversity maps shows how (at least in Portland) BIPOC communities bear the brunt of the "high crime neighborhood + running from the police = reasonable suspicion" holding.

Venue and Jury Selection

Finally, I use a short video produced by independent film maker Rob Bliss concerning his visit to Harrison, Arkansas, a town that he describes as "the most racist town in America." The video is a compilation of reactions he received from passing drivers as he stood on public streets while holding a "Black Lives Matter" sign. These include frequent spewing of the worst racial epithet to attempts to shame him for betraying Caucasians, and even more than one not-so-veiled threat of violence.[27]

A sampling of the comments that Bliss receives includes:

- "What about white lives? We matter, too. And you're a white man [racial epithet]!"
- "All lives matter, you racist mother******!"
- "Explain to me why a ****'s life matters"
- "No they don't!"
- "Get your ass out of town. That **** don't matter here"
- "Dude, you're white!"
- "I'd be ashamed to be a white boy carrying that stupid sign"
- "This is the biggest hoax there ever was. It's the next thing to ISIS"
- "**** black lives! And I have black friends"

Because of the vile language used throughout this video, I don't show it during class time. Instead, I offer it as a voluntary exercise through a link on my classroom learning management system (Moodle) with a trigger warning. For those students who choose to engage with the video, I provide a forum in which they can respond with their observations and comments. I pose questions about how a defense lawyer might use the video to seek a change of venue and how a prosecutor might respond.

Some students find the video quite shocking, while others comment that they grew up in similar environments and are therefore not at all surprised that there are towns where people feel comfortable openly expressing such racist or bigoted views.

---

27. *See* Rob Bliss, *Holding a Black Lives Matter Sign in America's Most Racist Town*, YouTube (Jul. 27, 2020), https://www.youtube.com/watch?v=ltmlvk9GAto.

Conclusion

The use of videos, pictures, and diagrams is literally a way to show rather than tell some of the ways in which race matters in criminal procedure, even if the doctrine does not discuss race explicitly. Showing, rather than telling, has another advantage—as an East Asian-American, I am a person of color, but I am not in one of the racial demographics that bears the brunt of disparate treatment. I have been subjected to traffic stops, but I have no reason to believe that any of those instances were because of my race; and I not only have never had my vehicle searched (by consent or otherwise), I also not received a citation during some stops. I can understand at an intellectual level the injustice of being stopped for "driving while Black," but the video of the highway stop of the young Black man is far more effective at conveying it than I could be.

At a time when my students have become more interested in—and have come to expect—discussions of race, gender, and the law, I feel fortunate to have been teaching criminal procedure. As with all subjects in law school, it is one in which we as teachers can do more to integrate diversity with doctrine, but it is also one in which there are so many avenues for doing so.

Conclusion

Section 5

Evidence

Teaching Antiracism in Evidence Law

*Jasmine B. Gonzales Rose**

Introduction

The foundational evidence law course provides abundant opportunities to teach antiracism. This essay shares reasons to teach antiracism in evidence law and a method for doing so. In my dozen years of teaching evidence law, I have found that incorporating antiracism engages students from diverse demographic and ideological backgrounds, trains students to think critically about the law, and encourages an equity mindset. When we fail to teach our students how evidence doctrine and practices replicate and perpetuate racism, we risk inadvertently teaching them that racism is unimportant and acceptable.

Reasons to Teach Antiracism in Evidence Law

The standard evidence law course provides abundant opportunities to explore race, racism, and antiracism while covering core topics like relevance, prejudice, character evidence, impeachment, and hearsay. Evidence law also presents an enriching opportunity for law students to think critically about the ways that *procedural* doctrine, policy, and practice can replicate and perpetuate racism—in addition to other forms of subordination—and ultimately affect substantive outcomes in cases.

Not only is such teaching productive and enriching, but it is also *vital* to examine race, racism, and antiracism in evidence law for at least five reasons. First, and centrally, racism is too often relied upon as a source of proof. In other words, people may rely on racist beliefs instead of facts to make determinations. Rather than focusing on

* Professor of Law, Boston University School of Law; Chair of Policy and founding faculty member, Boston University Center for Antiracist Research.

properly admitted evidence in a case, factfinders sometimes rely upon racially biased assumptions—often unconsciously—about who is worthy of belief and who is guilty/innocent or liable/not liable. Allowing racism, rather than truth, to determine facts calls into question the legitimacy of our legal system. While learning evidence law, students should consider how evidence law may incentivize or enable racist factfinding and begin to imagine fairer ways to ensure that cases are determined on the facts appropriately presented rather than racial bias.

Second, race and racism are sometimes employed as de facto evidence by counsel, and students should learn to identify and object to this practice. An example of this is the use of "racial character evidence." "'[R]acial character evidence' refers to the way a person's race is used as de facto proof of [their] character. More specifically, it describes how race—in tandem with racial stereotypes and biases—is relied upon or emphasized to establish the person's character propensity to be peaceful, violent, truthful, deceptive, or a variety of other traits."[1] There are different types of racial character evidence, such as "inherent reliance," "stereotype emphasis," and "opinion."[2] Prime examples of inherent reliance and opinion forms of racial character evidence were presented in *Peña-Rodriguez v. Colorado*,[3] where a juror stated that he thought the defendant was guilty because he was Mexican (inherent reliance) and that, in his experience as a law enforcement officer, Mexican men were violent toward females (opinion).[4] Stereotype emphasis as racial character evidence occurs where a prosecutor or defense counsel introduces evidence to enflame racial prejudice. For instance, introducing evidence of "urban" dress or rap music to surreptitiously suggest that a Black defendant or victim is the "type" of person of color that is dangerous, threatening, or criminally inclined.

Third, racial injustices take on evidentiary value. The archetype of this is impeachment by prior conviction.[5] Due to systemic racism—embodied by, for example, over-policing, racial profiling, unreasonable searches and arrests, plea inequities, sentencing disparities, and other injustices in the criminal "justice" system—people of color are more likely to have criminal convictions.[6] Many of these convictions are the manifestations or products of systemic racism in policing and prosecution. Federal Rule of Evidence 609 and its state equivalents allow witnesses' credibility for truthful-

1. Jasmine B. Gonzales Rose, *Racial Character Evidence in Police Killing Cases*, 2018 Wis. L. Rev. 369, 371 (2018) [hereinafter Gonzales Rose, *Racial Character Evidence*].

2. *Id.* at 401–16 (categorizing racial character evidence).

3. 580 U.S. 206 (2017).

4. *See id.* at 212–13; Gonzales Rose, *Racial Character Evidence*, *supra* note 1, at 392–94 (discussing racial character of evidence expressed in *Peña-Rodriguez*, 580 U.S. at 212–13).

5. *See* Jasmine B. Gonzales Rose, *Race, Evidence, and Epistemic Injustice*, *in* Philosophical Foundations of the Law of Evidence 381–84 (Christian Dahlman, Alex Stein & Giovanni Tuzet eds., 2022) [hereinafter Gonzales Rose, *Race, Evidence, and Epistemic Injustice*].

6. *See id.* at 382; Jasmine B. Gonzales Rose, *Toward a Critical Race Theory of Evidence*, 101 Minn. L. Rev. 2243, 2272 (2017) [hereinafter Gonzales Rose, *Toward a Critical Race Theory of Evidence*]; Montré D. Carodine, *"The Mis-Characterization of the Negro": A Race Critique of the Prior Conviction Impeachment Rule*, 84 Ind. L.J. 521, 535–36 (2009).

ness to be impeached with their former convictions in a variety of instances.[7] This can chill testimonial speech of people of color, especially for criminal defendants who have convictions and are afraid to be found guilty based upon their prior record rather than the facts of the present case.

Fourth, white experience is given preferential evidentiary treatment. Racialized reality evidence is "evidence of the lived experience of a person that is directly shaped by the racially stratified system in which [they] live[]. Racialized reality is how one experiences our nation's current racial caste system as a benefit or detriment."[8] An example of this is Black and Brown flight from police.[9] While the white racialized reality is that police officers enhance safety in a community, Black and Brown reality is that interactions with the police can be dangerous and even deadly and, thus, avoiding contact can be a rational safety strategy.[10] While the white racialized reality evidence that only the guilty would run may be argued with what I call "implicit judicial notice,"[11] the reality of avoiding racialized police violence requires formal evidence and can be challenging to prove. This is an example of how evidentiary burdens for white people and people of color are not equal.

Finally, evidence law has historically been overtly racist and because similar inequities persist today, these racialized dynamics warrant exploration. In the nineteenth and twentieth centuries, Black, Asian, Native American, and Latino people were not allowed to testify against whites or, in some instances, against anyone.[12] Under race-based witness competency rules, people of color were deemed to not be credible and capable witnesses and, thus, were hindered from protecting themselves against criminal and civil wrongs.[13] Today, people of color continue to experience more weighty evidentiary burdens than white people. We do our students a disservice when we teach evidence law in ways that makes it seem equally fair for all people. We should educate our students about racist evidence, both historically and presently.

Racist evidence includes: "(1) evidence that suggests one racial group is inferior to or superior to another racial group in any way, (2) products of structural racism, (3) racially disparate evidentiary burdens in proving one's racialized reality, and (4) the ways that racism distorts observation, perception and—accordingly—belief, which is then utilized as a basis of proof in legal proceedings."[14] As we teach our students

---

7. FED. R. EVID. 609; *see also, e.g.*, N.M. R. EVID. 11-609.

8. Gonzales Rose, *Toward a Critical Race Theory of Evidence*, *supra* note 6, at 2282.

9. *See id.* at 2269–72.

10. *Id.*; *see* Commonwealth v. Warren, 58 N.E.3d 333, 342 (Mass. 2016) (noting that for Black males, flight is not necessarily probative of guilt because their motivation to flee could be to avoid racial profiling).

11. Gonzales Rose, *Toward a Critical Race Theory of Evidence*, *supra* note 6, at 2285–86 ("The concept of '*implicit* judicial notice,' shows how evidence of white racialized reality is admitted into evidence without substantive proof.").

12. *See id.* at 2245–48 (discussing historical race-based witness competency rules).

13. *See id.*

14. Gonzales Rose, *Race, Evidence, and Epistemic Injustice*, *supra* note 5, at 380 (internal citations and quotations omitted).

evidence law, we must equip them with the skills necessary to recognize and consider ways to combat racist evidence. This will help our students become critical thinkers and more effective antiracist lawyers.

A Method to Teach Antiracism in Evidence Law

There are undoubtedly many ways to successfully teach antiracism in evidence law. Some instructors might want to incorporate a single reading,[15] while others may want to make antiracism a central theme of the course. Here, I will share a three-part approach that I have found effective over my dozen years of teaching evidence law. First, I incentivize students to explore potential disparities and reforms under evidence law. Second, I introduce critical race theory as a lens to reveal these disparities and inspire students to think expansively about possible advancements in the law. Third, I learn with the students as they prepare essays on critical evidence issues and possible reforms.

On the first day of classes, and in the syllabus, I assign students an essay. Some years I assign it as a required paper, other years as an extra credit assignment, and sometimes as part of the final exam that students can prepare in advance. Irrespective of the format of the assessment, the questions to answer are always: *(1) How might evidence law have a disparate impact or pose an injustice on (one or more) marginalized or subordinated population(s), and (2) How could evidence law be reformed to address this disparate impact or injustice?* Students are then motivated to explore examples throughout the course so they can prepare their paper or exam.

I do not require students address race or racism in their assessment. Many students choose to explore race and racism because of my emphasis on it in class and their own interests. I give examples of traditionally marginalized groups to include people of color, ethnic minorities, women, LGBTQ+ people, non-citizens, immigrants, people with limited English proficiency, people with disabilities, religious minorities, the people experiencing poverty, and people with unpopular political beliefs. Some politically conservative or right-leaning libertarian students seem to appreciate the option of exploring how people with unpopular political beliefs are impacted by evidence law. The freedom to think flexibly about groups encourages students to explore a variety of topics, including race.

---

15. For a concise and accessible introduction to how race and racism are improperly used as evidence, see Jasmine B. Gonzales Rose, *Race and Evidence*, *in* The Oxford Handbook of Race and Law in the United States (Devon Carbado, Emily Houh & Khiara M. Bridges eds., 2022), https://doi.org/10.1093/oxfordhb/9780190947385.013.14. *See also* Bennett Capers, *Evidence without Rules*, 94 Notre Dame L. Rev. 867 (2018) (noting how evidentiary rules result in unfair prejudice in courtroom that often go unseen and unchecked); Aníbal Rosario Lebrón, *A Wee Bit Racist: What Are the Rules of Evidence, Alex?*, 1 LSU L.J. Soc. Just. & Pol'y 7, 8–10 (2022) (addressing racial subordination embedded in evidentiary system using a CRT framework).

There are endless possibilities for paper topics; it is exciting to learn with and from the students. Some examples that I explore during the course are:

- *Impeachment (Rule 609*[16]*)*: The way that prior conviction impeachment is the product of racial disparities in the criminal justice system which results in diminished testimonial capacity and is reminiscent of historical race-based witness competency statutes.[17]
- *Hearsay (Rule 801(d)(2)(B)*[18]*)*: The way that the adoptive admissions by silence hearsay exemption might be influenced by "white normativity" and negatively affect ethnic and cultural minorities.[19]
- *Character Evidence (Rules 404*[20] *and 608*[21]*)*: The way that racial character evidence is utilized as de facto proof of negative character in violation of Rule 404(b)(2), or to bolster positive character in violation of Rule 608.[22]
- *Relevance and Unfair Prejudice (Rules 401,*[23] *402,*[24] *and 403*[25]*)*: The way that the flight doctrine can be critiqued as lacking probative value or being outweighed by unfair prejudice when the one fleeing is a person of color seeking to avoid

---

16. FED. R. EVID. 609.

17. Gonzales Rose, *Toward a Critical Race Theory of Evidence*, *supra* note 6, at 2272–73; Carodine, *supra* note 6, at 537–38 (critiquing prior conviction rule as racially disparate); *see also* Anna Roberts, *Conviction by Prior Impeachment*, 96 B.U. L. REV. 1977, 1977–78 (2016) (critiquing practice of impeachment through presenting prior convictions); Anna Roberts, *Reclaiming the Importance of the Defendant's Testimony: Prior Conviction Impeachment and the Fight Against Implicit Stereotyping*, 83 U. CHI. L. REV. 835, 835 (2016) (observing how, by testifying, defendant's race risks triggering stereotypes that threatens presumption of innocence); Anna Roberts, *Will the Most Controversial Rule of Evidence Be Reformed?*, THE APPEAL (Dec. 6, 2017), https://theappeal.org/will-the-most-controversial-rule-of-evidence-be-reformed-5930fd36df50/ [https://perma.cc/KT23-HWBM] (observing how Rule 609 impedes restorative justice efforts); Julia Simon-Kerr, *Credibility by Proxy*, 85 GEO. WASH. L. REV. 152, 158 (2017) (demonstrating how impeachment rules enforce status-based racially disparate view of truth).

18. FED. R. EVID. 801(d)(2)(B).

19. Maria L. Ontiveros, *Adoptive Admissions and the Meaning of Silence: Continuing the Inquiry into Evidence Law and Issues of Race, Class, Gender, and Ethnicity*, 28 SW. U. L. REV. 337, 345–50 (1999) (examining ways that adoptive admission rule fails to acknowledge how race, class, gender, and ethnicity affect silence in listeners' reactions to declarants' statement); Gonzales Rose, *Toward a Critical Race Theory of Evidence*, *supra* note 6, at 2253–54.

20. FED. R. EVID. 404.

21. FED. R. EVID. 608.

22. Gonzales Rose, *Racial Character Evidence*, *supra* note 1, at 434–35; Mikah K. Thompson, *Blackness as Character Evidence*, 20 MICH. J. RACE & L. 321 (2015); Montré D. Carodine, *Race Is Evidence: (Mis)Characterizing Blackness in the American Civil Rights Story*, *in* CIVIL RIGHTS IN AMERICAN LAW, HISTORY, AND POLITICS 64 (Austin Sarat ed., 2014); Chris Chambers Goodman, *The Color of Our Character: Confronting the Racial Character of Rule 404(b) Evidence*, 25 LAW & INEQ. 1 (2007).

23. FED. R. EVID. 401.

24. FED. R. EVID. 402.

25. FED. R. EVID. 403.

racialized police abuse.[26] Another example to explore these rules is the introduction of rap lyrics to indicate guilt.[27]

- *Juror No-Impeachment (Rule 606(b)*[28]*)*: The way that overt juror racial bias against the accused violates the Sixth Amendment pursuant to *Peña-Rodriguez* but leaves unanswered whether racial bias toward victims of police violence might be protected under the Fourteenth Amendment, or otherwise.[29]

Having provided examples and facilitated discussions about these topics in class, students can examine evidence doctrine and policy on their own using the tools of critical race theory (CRT). To prepare students for this analysis, I use the "Seven Ps of Critical Race Theory Inquiry," which are outlined in a ten-page excerpt of my article *Toward a Critical Race Theory of Evidence*.[30] The 7Ps are a summary of the foundational principles of CRT: inquiries into the power behind racialization and racism, the purpose of racism, the privilege of whiteness, the property of whiteness, the pervasiveness of racism, the permanence of racism, and the perspectives of people of color. The 7Ps of CRT inquiry present questions for students to ask in learning evidence (and other) law to reveal racial inequities.

1. *Power*: Is this evidence rule or doctrine being applied in ways that preserve existing racial power structures?[31]
2. *Purpose*: How is the purpose of racism (to confer privilege on the insider group) being satisfied here (in this evidentiary approach or decision)? Is there a disparate impact on people of color?[32]
3. *Privilege*: Who benefits here (from an evidentiary approach or decision)?[33]
4. *Property*: How do the legal entitlements of whiteness arise in the application of evidence law in this instance?[34]
5. *Pervasiveness*: If racism is ordinary, how might it be manifesting in this evidence rule, doctrine, or application?[35]
6. *Permanence*: If racism is permanent, how might it be manifesting in this evidence rule, doctrine, or application?[36]

---

26. Gonzales Rose, *Toward a Critical Race Theory of Evidence*, *supra* note 6, at 2269–72.

27. *See* Andrea Dennis, *Poetic (In)Justice? Rap Music Lyrics as Art, Life, and Criminal Evidence*, 31 Colum. J.L. & Arts 1, 24–27 (2007); Erik Nielsen & Andrea L. Dennis, Rap on Trial: Race, Lyrics, and Guilt in America 81–85 (2019).

28. Fed. R. Evid. 606(b).

29. Gonzales Rose, *Racial Character Evidence*, *supra* note 1, at 371.

30. Gonzales Rose, *Toward a Critical Race Theory of Evidence*, *supra* note 6, at 2248–58.

31. *Id.* at 2249–50.

32. *Id.* at 2250–51.

33. *Id.* at 2251–54.

34. *Id.* at 2254–55.

35. *Id.* at 2255–56.

36. *Id.* at 2256–57.

7. *Perspectives*: In the formation or application of an evidence rule or doctrine, are people of color being heard? Are people of color believed? Are people of color's sources of knowledge legitimized?[37]

An advantage of using the 7Ps of CRT framework is that it works for both those new and experienced in teaching antiracism. One need only provide the 7Ps of CRT framework[38] and some illustrations and leave it up to the students to make their own inquiries and find their own conclusions. While I focus on racism in the evidence law course because it is my area of expertise, I also raise issues of sexism, classism, heterosexism, ableism, antisemitism, religious intolerance, and other categories of structural bigotry[39] in the course because a commitment to antiracism is a commitment to ending subordination of all peoples in all their intersectional and multidimensional experiences. When students think about how evidence law has a disparate impact on traditionally marginalized populations, they will more rigorously interrogate the adequacy of rape shield laws, spousal testimonial privilege and how it tracks marriage equality, access to expert testimony, the ways religious affiliation strengthens or weakens credibility, and a plethora of other issues beyond racism. A focus on structural racism and other forms of structural bigotry prepares students to support diverse clients and recognize the challenges their clients face in and outside the courtroom. I find students are eager to examine evidence law structurally and share what they learn. In turn, I learn from and am inspired by my evidence law students each and every year.

---

37. *Id.* at 2258.

38. *Id.* at 2248–58.

39. Structural bigotry is "the promotion, creation, implementation, and perpetuation of laws, policies, practices, narratives, norms, and state and institutional actions that: (1) deny the value, dignity, liberties, and opportunities of people based on their perceived membership in a social or socially-constructed group or on a human characteristic that has historically been subjected to oppression and subordination; and (2) drive and are driven by expressions of animus, including shared symbolism and hateful vocabulary, verbal and physical assaults including hate crimes, and exclusion which serves to entrench power in privileged insiders." Paul Y. Watanabe & Sungkwan E.J. Jang, *Anti-Asian American Racism*, *in* MOVING TOWARD ANTIBIGOTRY 58 (Bos. Univ. Ctr. for Antiracist Rsch., 2022), https://www.bu.edu/antiracism-center/files/2022/06/Moving-Towards-Antibigotry.pdf.

Trial by Fire: Lessons Learned from Teaching Race and Evidence in a Hostile Environment

*Montré D. Carodine**

Introduction

This essay discusses strategies for teaching race as an intractable part of American law. I place a particular focus on lessons that I have learned teaching race and evidence in what I deem to be a hostile classroom environment. For me the hostile classroom environment is one in which the professor and certain students, typically members of outsider groups, are made to feel unwelcome and are regularly subjected to disrespect. In such environments, even when there are students present who are receptive or even eager to discuss race within the law, they can be effectively silenced by those who are aggressively antagonistic to such ideas and anyone who wishes to discuss them.

In this essay, I offer strategies for teaching in such classroom environments. The strategies that I offer can certainly be applied to any type of classroom environment, but they are especially useful in hostile ones. I first discuss some of my own difficult experiences teaching for the past fifteen years. I then discuss ways that I have learned to address race within a hostile classroom. I also discuss what I have found to be the most effective solution for thriving in law schools with environments that are hostile to outsider groups: the creation of safe and nurturing teaching environments, through specialized upper-level courses, that offer progressive students the opportunity to engage in critical explorations of the intersection of race and the law.

* Professor of Law, The University of Alabama School of Law.

Riptides: Fifteen Years at Alabama Law

I am a Black woman. I have been a professor of law at the University of Alabama School of Law for over fifteen years. While the experiences that I discuss in this section happened in a deep south law school, there are women of color all over the country who have had similar experiences.[1] Hostile classroom environments are not limited to Alabama and the south.

My time teaching law has confirmed for me that there is no area of U.S. law that has not been fundamentally shaped by race and racism. Teaching any area of the law without acknowledging, centering, and exploring the topic of race does a tremendous disservice to students and renders our overall teaching efforts deficient. Nevertheless, the challenge for me, particularly as a Black woman teaching at a flagship university in the deep south (Alabama, no less), is that there is a very real resistance to discussions of race among certain segments of our student population. Certain segments of the law school environment here, particularly the classroom setting for large enrollment courses, were hostile for people of color when I began teaching here. And they are hostile today. That said, there are also remarkably supportive and affirming segments of our law school community. And I would be remiss in not highlighting those. For they have truly helped to sustain me over the years.

While there have been a very small number of Black women who taught here before me, I am the first Black woman to reach Full Professor status (with tenure). It is not necessarily a designation that I am proud of (being the "first" that is), nor do I think that the University of Alabama should be proud of it. But it is my reality.

I did not set out to be a trailblazer. I merely wanted to teach law in a college town. As a small-town Louisiana native, I have always felt most at home in the south—the food, the weather, the culture (Black culture in particular). The conflict for me and so many Black people is that, despite our invaluable contributions to southern culture, and American culture generally, we have never been fully welcomed in privileged spaces in this country, especially in the south. And the University of Alabama, with its storied football team and pristine campus, replete with antebellum-style fraternity and sorority mansions (some of which employ Black maids and cooks), is about as privileged a space that you can imagine in the American South. It is unsurprising that a Black woman would not be fully welcomed to teach in this space. Sure, she might be tolerated for "diversity and inclusion" purposes, but not fully welcome. And yet, with much naivete and a youthful optimism, I began my journey here over fifteen years ago. This essay is about some of the lessons that I have learned—with the ups and downs, the defeats and the triumphs—over the last fifteen years.

---

1. *See* Presumed Incompetent II: Race, Class, Power, and Resistance of Women in Academia (Yolanda Flores Niemann, Gabriella Gutiérrez y Muhs & Carmen G. González eds., 2020).

My "bread and butter" class—a large fifty-plus student class—is evidence. I fell in love with evidence as a law student. As I learned the rules, I began to understand this area of the law as a strategy game (obviously with potentially serious consequences), requiring a mastery of the rules and the ability to stay several steps ahead of your opponent. I continually strive to understand evidence law on deeper level and to recognize how evidence fits within a broader framework for law and society. Evidence rules are a vital component to the justice system's infrastructure, but they are often overlooked as a vehicle for change. I have written several articles that grapple with the intersection of social justice, particularly as it relates to race.[2]

For several years, evidence at Alabama Law was taught as a required first-year class, which is a unique approach to the first-year curriculum. In the vast majority of law schools across the country, evidence is an upper-level course. Teaching evidence in the first year meant that students did not choose to take my class. It was clear to me that some students were angry from day one of my class because they did not "choose" my class (even though they chose Alabama's law school, and I am a member of the faculty who taught a first-year course). Indeed, when I taught evidence as a required first-year course here, I encountered strong resistance to my very existence as a Black woman teaching a complex class like evidence, which has traditionally been taught by white men. I represent the intersection of race and evidence each time I walk in the classroom. Indeed, no matter the subject that I am teaching, I have learned over the years that I literally embody race and the law. To be clear, I have taught some amazing students who truly appreciate the value that I bring to the classroom. On the other hand, I have had students—a minority, but a difficult minority—who have made their resentment of my existence quite clear.

Though the resentment is often clear from the first day of class, it is particularly stark when the course material becomes more challenging. I have had students openly challenge me, most often when they misread (or did not read) assigned material. They become angry when I am forced to point out their errors. Students who are resentful of Black women in authority are especially resentful when the clear gap between our knowledge and theirs is exposed. Of course, it is to be expected that there will be a gap in knowledge between professors and students. They presumably are in law school to narrow that gap. That is certainly my goal as a professor. But if a student cannot fathom a Black person, let alone a Black woman, simply knowing more than them in her area of expertise, it is nearly impossible to effectively teach them.

---

2. *See* Montré D. Carodine, *Race Is Evidence: (Mis)Characterizing Blackness in the American Civil Rights Story*, *in* Civil Rights in American Law, History, and Politics 64–102 (2014) (hereinafter *Race is Evidence*); Montré D. Carodine, *Contemporary Issues in Critical Race Theory: The Implications of Race as Evidence in Recent High-Profile Cases*, 75 U. Pitt. L. Rev. 679 (2014); Montré D. Carodine, *Keeping It Real: Reforming the "Untried Conviction" Impeachment Rule*, 69 Md L. Rev. 501 (2010); Montré D. Carodine, *«Street Cred,»* 46 U.C. Davis L. Rev. 1583 (2013); Montré D. Carodine, *"The Mis-Characterization of the Negro": A Race Critique of the Prior Conviction Impeachment Rule*, 84 Ind. L.J. 521 (2009).

If a student harbors biases against Black women in authority, it will also be nearly impossible to teach the reality of law as steeped in racial biases. For my general evidence class, *my very existence* is resistance to the idea that the law should be taught in a race-neutral manner. Moreover, many students are well aware of my work in the area of race and evidence. Students who are hostile to any discussion whatsoever of race are far more likely to come into the classroom setting already antagonistic and, with the preconception of any discussions in class as a part of some larger "agenda." On top of that, my mere mention of race has been enough to leave some students absolutely incensed and determined to undermine me at all costs. So given my very existence as a professor in the law classroom space, I am always teaching race and the law. As long as I am a professor in the deep south, or in any area of the country that has difficulty letting go of its white supremacist past, I cannot escape that reality. I have, instead, learned to embrace my reality and use it to deepen my understanding of the areas of the law that have always intrigued me.

Despite the disrespect, the bias, and the outright racism, I show up. I show up with a high level of enthusiasm and love for the subject matter I teach and a high level of preparation and dedication. I no doubt leave those students who seek to undermine my authority more challenged in their thinking as budding lawyers than when they first entered my class and wholly unsuccessful in their efforts to challenge my existence as a professor.

Rocking the Boat but *Not Really* Rocking the Boat

My philosophy is that to properly deal with the reality of race *in the* law, you either acknowledge that race is a central and fundamental aspect of American law, or you simply come up short. On the one hand, I would argue that my persistence in showing up in this way year after year and semester after semester, is more effective and meaningful in a hostile space like Alabama Law than futilely trying to engage on race issues with hostile students directly in a "general law" class like evidence. On the other hand, teaching evidence as a generally race-neutral topic with only occasional "footnote" or "note case" style acknowledgments of race issues feels deficient.

And to be clear, I believe that there are legitimate and justifiable reasons to avoid acknowledging the reality of race in the law. For faculty members of color, one of those legitimate and justifiable reasons is survival. I admit that my approach in my evidence course comes up short to my own ideal vision of dealing with the reality of race in the law. If, from my first day of law teaching at Alabama, I had taught evidence in a way that centers race, I doubt that I would still be on the faculty here or anywhere else for that matter given how difficult it is to find a lateral position when one has the "baggage" of a bad teaching experience at another institution.

In the aftermath of the brutal murder of George Floyd in 2020, the trend across the country was to grapple with a supposed "racial reckoning."[3] Many law schools facilitated discussions about how best to incorporate issues of race and racism in traditional law school classes. I have always been skeptical of attempts to incorporate race discussions in typical law school classes. How does one *incorporate* a topic that is so clearly already there, an issue that is so prominent, that dominates every aspect of life in this country?

At an institution like the University of Alabama, based on my own experiences, I predict that a faculty member who centers race in a "doctrinal" law school class, like evidence or civil procedure, will be met with extreme hostility. I have been subjected to hostility from students at the very mention of cases where race was a prominent issue. Many students just don't want to hear about race. Many come from backgrounds where they had the privilege of not having to think about race and doing so at this point for them is "uncomfortable." Students, particularly at a law school steeped in tradition like Alabama's and also highly ranked nationally, have a tremendous amount of power, and they have no problem wielding that power. Untenured faculty members, particularly women of color, at hostile institutions or even tenured faculty members who have not yet reached full professor status (or even those who simply want the raises that they deserve) should probably think twice before centering race in traditional law school courses.

Moreover, if students are hostile to the very idea of race as central issue in a case, it is difficult if not impossible to have a meaningful and productive dialogue, even if there are other students who are receptive to the idea. Hostile students can be very effective at silencing their classmates. That said, I have found ways to subtly address race in my evidence class in a way that does not result in an open revolt.

Casebook Selection

I use Professor George Fisher's evidence casebook, which has incorporated some cases that openly deal with race issues.[4] I must note here how crucial casebook selection is, particularly as it relates to opportunities to incorporate race in class discussions. The type of classroom environment is key. For hostile environments like the ones that I typically experience, a book like George Fisher's is an excellent choice. First, the book is an impeccable presentation of evidence law. It is challenging but also accessible. The vast majority of the cases in Professor Fisher's book are criminal cases. Despite that fact, most of the book's material does not overtly address race issues. But when Fisher does

---

3. *See* Alisa Chang, Rachel Martin & Eric Marrapodi, *Summer of Racial Reckoning: The Match Lit*, NPR (Aug. 16, 2020), https://www.npr.org/2020/08/16/902179773/summer-of-racial-reckoning-the-match-lit; Elliott C. McLaughlin, *How George Floyd's death ignited a racial reckoning that shows no signs of slowing down*, CNN (Aug. 9, 2020), https://www.cnn.com/2020/08/09/us/george-floyd-protests-different-why/index.html.

4. George Fisher, Evidence (3d ed. 2013).

address race, he typically does so in a detached and matter-of-fact manner, a manner that I mimic in class given the typical presence of hostile students.[5]

Fisher's *Evidence* begins with an exploration of the role of the jury in our judicial system. Each edition of his casebook begins with a discussion of the mistrust of jurors and hence our reliance on elaborate evidence rules to heavily scrutinize what evidence jurors are allowed to consider. The discussion centers on the case of *Tanner v. United States*, a case in which jurors convicted a defendant but later revealed that several of them (the jurors) had engaged in outrageous behavior, such as drinking and doing illegal drugs, during the trial and jury deliberations.[6] The Supreme Court in *Tanner* refused to compel the jurors to testify about their behavior during trial and jury deliberations, citing Federal Rule of Evidence 606(b).[7] The Court also found that the Sixth Amendment was not violated by the application of Rule 606(b) to the facts of the Tanner case because protections, such as the *voir dire* process for selecting jurors and the potential availability of non-juror testimony regarding juror misconduct, sufficed to satisfy the Sixth Amendment.

Recently, the Supreme Court decided, in the case of *Peña Rodriguez v. Colorado*, that the shielding, under Federal Rule of Evidence 606(b), of statements by jurors indicating their racial biases would violate the Sixth Amendment.[8] Fisher has recently added to his casebook a section discussing juror's racial bias, in light of the *Peña Rodriguez* decision.[9]

For professors teaching in a racially hostile classroom setting, the *Tanner/Peña Rodriguez* discussion, as presented in Fisher's casebook, is a great example of an effective way to introduce race issues (or more accurately, to acknowledge the presence of race issues) in evidence law. Importantly, *Peña Rodriguez* is a recent Supreme Court case in the evidence law. It makes perfect sense that it should be included in the casebook. Moreover, and perhaps most important, the decision to include the case was made by an apparently white male professor at one of the top institutions in the country. No one will seriously question Professor Fisher's credentials or judgment in the way that they would a woman of color. To be clear, I chose and continue to use Professor Fisher's book because it is an excellent book. But the reality is that many students are less hostile toward the inclusion of a case like *Peña Rodriguez* if the casebook is authored by a white male.

---

5. The newest edition of Fisher's casebook, which was published as I was finalizing this Essay, purports to address "student demand" for the inclusion of racial justice issues, according to the publisher. The newest edition is much like the previous editions but does now contain short excerpts of an article on the intersection of critical race theory and evidence. GEORGE FISHER, EVIDENCE (4th ed. 2022).

6. Tanner v. United States, 483 U.S. 107 (1987).

7. *Id.* at 115–116.

8. 580 U.S. 206 (2017).

9. FISHER, *supra* note 5.

When Race "Comes Up"

Now, I do not shy away from cases involving race, but I do not overtly and directly center race in the way that I would in a more progressive classroom setting. I have discussed cases involving race, focusing on the ostensibly "objective" evidentiary issues that they raise. Hostile students in those situations typically revert to a passive aggressive silence, often showing their anger through body language. They do not show the open hostility that they often reserve for other times (when discussing a "race-neutral" case about hearsay, for example), perhaps thinking that they might be viewed as "racist" if they openly show hostility during the discussion of a case involving race. However, supportive students have reported back to me that some of their classmates have expressed their anger in discussions outside the classroom at even the very mention in class of cases involving race and even though I had not overtly discussed race.

I should also say that in more recent years, likely due to shifts in the national discourse on race, there have been students in my classes who are more comfortable bringing up race and centering race issues in the discussions. I generally engage students' comments and questions, and those times are no exception. I engage those comments with the same level of enthusiasm and attention as I would with any others.

Using Film

Another subtle but highly effective way to acknowledge race in evidence is through film. As with casebooks, the film does the speaking and not necessarily the professor. And as with casebooks, film selection is key. I always show a full movie, *12 Angry Men*,[10] in my Evidence course. I show the original 1957 black-and-white version of the film. The movie centers on the jury deliberations in a murder trial where the evidence seems to point definitively to the defendant's guilt. One juror, played by Henry Fonda, is unconvinced of guilt and methodically challenges the prosecution's evidence. The film is set almost entirely in the jury deliberation room, though it feels as though the case is being tried by the jurors with Fonda's character acting as the lead defense attorney. Some of the jurors have clear racial bias against the defendant, though viewers are never told the defendant's race.

Over the years, I have timed the showing at different points in the semester, ranging from the very beginning of class to the end. The most effective time seems to be near or at the very end of the semester. At that point students have learned a lot of evidence law and are able to recognize important evidentiary issues. It is also an excellent way to help them review in preparation for the exam. And significantly, race is a central aspect of the movie, though the race of the defendant is ambiguous.

In my most recent evidence class, I had two students address the racial aspects of the film in response to my general call for reactions. In fact, the first student (a white woman) to offer a comment on the film immediately asked me whether I thought that

10. 12 ANGRY MEN (Orion-Nova Productions 1957).

the jury deliberations in the movie would have been handled differently had the jury not been a jury of "white men." Another student discussed the racialized way that the jury viewed the defendant. I readily engaged their comments on the issues. To be clear, there were far more "race-neutral" comments about the film, but I do not recall ever having any students so eagerly discuss the race issues in the film. I believe (hope) that we are starting to see a positive shift within our student body, where more students feel empowered to engage in critical discussions surrounding race.

Later in the semester for that same class, I showed a video clip of expert testimony from Derek Chauvin's state criminal trial for the murder of George Floyd. I wanted to show a video clip of expert testimony to demonstrate the practical application of the rules surrounding the admissibility of such testimony. I chose to show the expert testimony of Dr. Martin Tobin, a pulmonologist, because it perfectly exemplified the evidence rules' requirement that expert testimony be "helpful" to the jury in evaluating evidence and not merely tell jurors what conclusion to reach. During Dr. Tobin's testimony, the prosecution showed clips of the brutal murder of Mr. Floyd. Dr. Tobin methodically and objectively pointed out various details in the video to help the jury evaluate the reasonableness of Mr. Chauvin's use of force. One of the assigned cases in our casebook was a police use-of-force case, so my use of the expert testimony clip from the Chauvin trial helped to illuminate principles from our assigned reading.

I offered no commentary on the race issues in the Chauvin case—the race issues that had dominated our national discourse right after Mr. Floyd was murdered. I asked the students to offer their evaluation of the expert's testimony. I recall an uneasy tension in the classroom as I showed the video clip, and that tension lingered during the class discussion. Interestingly, a student whom I had not heard speak for the entire semester offered her comments, which were keenly on-point in describing what we had seen. Students like her feel empowered in these situations and know that I have their back in class. I believe that they feel empowered knowing that I will not shy away from engaging in tough discussions and that I will validate their decision to speak up because they have seen me do it before. Students know that I value a robust discussion generally. I give them no reason to think that any topic is off limits. I have learned that the best way to teach the intersection of race and evidence is in a class where each assignment, each class discussion, encourages students to share their ideas.

Creating an Island

For me, the most effective and rewarding way to teach the intersection of race and evidence, *race as evidence* as I often put it, is in an advanced evidence course. Several years ago, I decided that I had to get beyond merely existing and being controlled by students resentful of a Black woman in authority. I had to find my most authentic teaching self. Thus, several years ago, I created a course titled "Major Race Trials," which explores the intersection of evidence and race issues in some of the most significant cases in American history. In this advanced course, I generally attract students who acknowledge the centrality of race in the law and who want to explore law from that perspective, which is its truest and most accurate light. In my advanced evidence course, we study cases that have been transformative in American law, that have exposed the centrality of race in American law, or both.

Before studying the major cases for the course, I introduce students to critical race theory scholarship. We cover topics such as the social construction of race,[11] whiteness as property,[12] and Professor Derrick Bell's interest convergence theory.[13] We then look specifically at the rules of evidence and explore the concept of race as evidence. I assign my own piece on race as evidence,[14] which offers a race critique of the long-standing prior conviction impeachment rule and was one of the first articles to explore the intersection of race and evidence. I also assign Professor Jasmine Gonzales Rose's groundbreaking work, *Toward a Critical Race Theory of Evidence.*[15] Once the students have a solid foundation in critical race theory, particularly as it relates to evidence law, we then begin our journey of exploring major race trials in American history.

We study cases such as the *United States v. Amistad,*[16] *State of Missouri v. Celia, a Slave,*[17] *Korematsu v. United States,*[18] *People v. O.J. Simpson,*[19] *Florida v. Zimmerman,*[20] among many others. Our class materials are a compilation of various sources, including Annette Gordon-Reed's *Race on Trial,*[21] Professor Douglas O. Linder's Famous Trials website,[22] and multiple law review articles and news articles. As in my general evidence course, I rely on film, and I find that in my Major Race Trials class, film is particularly effective. I have used clips from the 1997 film *Amistad,*[23] a C-Span documentary on *Korematsu,*[24] and an ESPN documentary on the OJ Simpson case.[25] One of most impactful films that I have shown is *Unforgivable Blackness,*[26] which provides historical context for

11. Ian F. Haney Lopez, *The Social Construction of Race: Some Observations on Illusion, Fabrication, and Choice*, 29 HARV. C.R.-C.L. L. REV. 1 (1994).

12. Cheryl I. Harris, *Whiteness as Property*, 106 HARV. L. REV. 1709 (1993).

13. Derrick A. Bell, Jr., Brown v. Board of Education *and the Interest Convergence Dilemma*, 93 HARV. L. REV. 518 (1980).

14. *See* Carodine, *Race is Evidence*, *supra* note 1.

15. Jasmine B. Gonzales Rose, *Toward a Critical Race Theory of Evidence*, 176 MINN. L. REV. 2243 (2017).

16. United States v. Schooner Amistad, 40 U.S. 518 (1841).

17. Douglas O. Linder, *Celia, A Slave, Trial (1855): An Account*, FAMOUS TRIALS, https://famous-trials.com/celia/180-home.

18. 323 U.S. 214 (1944).

19. Douglas O. Linder, *O.J. Simpson Trial (1995)*, FAMOUS TRIALS, https://famous-trials.com/simpson.

20. Douglas O. Linder, *George Zimmerman ("Trayvon Martin") Trial (2013)*, FAMOUS TRIALS, https://famous-trials.com/zimmerman1.

21. ANNETTE GORDON-REED, RACE ON TRIAL: LAW AND JUSTICE IN AMERICAN HISTORY (2002).

22. FAMOUS TRIALS, https://famous-trials.com.

23. AMISTAD (Dreamworks Pictures 1997).

24. *Landmark Cases: Korematsu v. United States* (C-Span television broadcast Apr. 2, 2016).

25. OJ: MADE IN AMERICA (ESPN Films 2016).

26. *Unforgivable Blackness: The Rise and Fall of Jack Johnson* (PBS television broadcast Jan. 17, 2005).

the racist prosecution of the trailblazing Black heavyweight champion Jack Johnson.[27] Similarly impactful in my class was my showing of the PBS First Peoples series' episode on the Kennewick Man, which provides background and historical context for the near decade-long legal battle of a Native American tribe to secure the return of the ancient remains of one of their ancestors,[28] "the Ancient One."[29] The film typically sparks a discussion about the influence of race on the interpretation of scientific evidence and perhaps an even broader discussion about the ways that American law has been shaped by the sustained effort to protect and legitimize the atrocities committed against Native Americans throughout American history.

In addition to cases that have already been tried or resolved, I typically spend a significant amount of time discussing current events, as there are almost always race trials unfolding in the court of public opinion. Indeed, each day, I devote the first part of class to a discussion of current events. Invariably, my students realize that there is nothing new under the sun. Cases from over a hundred years ago that we have discussed are just as relevant today, as our country continues to grapple with difficult issues of race and its influence on the law.

I have found that courses such as Major Race Trials are the best way to study the intersection of race and evidence in depth. Indeed, my Major Race Trials class has been the most rewarding teaching experience of my career to date. The larger takeaway, however, is that in law schools like Alabama's, it is vitally important to create teaching spaces like the one that I created with Major Race Trials. Progressive students who want to engage in an intense semester-long dialogue about the impact of race on evidence law or any other area of the law deserve a nurturing classroom environment in which to do so.

Conclusion

While I would never have (consciously) chosen a teaching environment where students treat me with hostility, I have no doubt that the difficulties that I have faced in the classroom have led me down a path to understanding evidence law on a much deeper level than I would otherwise. I undoubtedly have a much deeper appreciation for not only how race intersects with evidence law but how it is embedded in the very fabric of evidence law. The antagonistic challenges by some students to my knowledge of evidence law have motivated me to learn evidence far better than I would have learned the subject had I been given the same presumption of competence that white male professors enjoy in the classroom. Moreover, the blatant disrespect by some students prompted me to create classes that have become safe and supportive learning spaces at

27. *See id.*

28. *First Peoples: Americas* (PBS television broadcast June 24, 2015).

29. Tasneem Raja, *A Long, Complicated Battle Over 9,000-Year-Old Bones Is Finally Over*, NPR—Code Switch (May 5, 2016), https://www.npr.org/sections/codeswitch/2016/05/05/476631934/a-long-complicated-battle-over-9-000-year-old-bones-is-finally-over.

our law school. And perhaps most importantly, my classroom experiences, as negative as they may have been at times, have given me great empathy for students who have been pushed to the margins of the law school community. My trial by fire has helped me to develop tools to show those students how to blaze their own trails in a profession that may not always welcome them with open arms.

Making Evidence Meaningful: Diversity and Realism in Action

Deborah Ahrens[*]

Introduction

I have a confession: I never wanted to teach evidence in the first place. While evidence rules have clear distributional consequences for litigants, and the rules often fail to achieve their promised aim of fairness, those points were not as obvious to me from the practice I was leaving as they are now to me as a professor. When I first started teaching evidence, it was what I referred to as my service course—a class I agreed, with some reluctance, to teach as part of my hiring package, but about which I felt a mixture of resignation and dread as the time approached. I had by that point been thinking and writing about inequality issues in substantive criminal law and criminal procedure, particularly in drug policy and policing,[1] and I had incorporated that scholarship and had tried to center inequality in those courses. At the time, I was not sure how to carry those themes into what I thought was a more neutral rules-based course. In the criminal courses I regularly teach, we may not always handle diversity issues as well as we ought, but it would be nearly impossible to avoid addressing them

* Vice Dean for Intellectual Life and Professor of Law, Seattle University School of Law. I would like to thank Grace Dublin for her research assistance on this piece and all of my evidence students for, as they have said, "trusting the process." I have built up a repertoire of scripts, exercises, and problems over the past fifteen years of teaching Evidence, and am willing to share any of them that readers may want. If any of the scripts or problems I describe here sound like they might be helpful to you as you organize your semester, I am happy to send them to you, for you to use, tweak, redraft entirely, or read as a jumping-off point for writing your own materials.

1. For some of my early work on these subjects, see Deborah Ahrens, *Drug Panics in the Twenty-First Century: Ecstasy, Prescription Drugs, and the Reframing of the War on Drugs*, 6 Alb. Gov't L. Rev. 397 (2013); Deborah Ahrens, *Schools, Cyberbullies, and the Surveillance State*, 49 Am. Crim. L Rev. 1669 (2012); Deborah Ahrens, *Methademic: Drug Panic in an Age of Ambivalence*, 37 Fla. St. U. L. Rev. 841 (2010).

at all.[2] In evidence, I have found, it takes a bit more conscious planning to ensure that students have ample opportunity to see and discuss the race, class, gender identity, religion, and other issues raised by the rules, yet opportunities abound. I have discovered that evidence provides opportunities for active learning that involve students in their coursework in ways that are different from traditional Socratic cold-calling. These learning opportunities are accessible, appealing, and inviting to many students, particularly students who may otherwise be uncomfortable in a law school classroom. I came to the evidence classroom because I was dragged there—not unlike my students, who are often enrolled solely because the course is required—but, now, it is one of my favorite courses to teach.

Opportunities to Incorporate Diversity into the Evidence Curriculum

On the first day of evidence class, I tell students the true story of my summer as a licensed legal intern.[3] I was staffed to my first trial with an accomplished and (remarkably) undefeated public defender who was my model for how to practice law successfully. She was chatting with the prosecutor prior to the start of our trial. I was anxious about the hearsay objection I knew I needed to make during trial, which I had been practicing making in my head for hours. As I fretted, I was startled to hear the attorneys agree on a proposition: trials would be better without rules of evidence.

After some brief framing about how the rules work, I open class discussion to see whether students agree or disagree with that statement, and one of the major points of contention regards the distributional effects of the rules. Can you as a party leverage the rules to your advantage if you are able to afford more skilled and experienced counsel than your opponent? Do some of the rules make assumptions about how "good" witnesses testify that are founded more in assumption and folklore than reality? Do parties face unfair limits on how they can tell their stories? Students quickly see that evidence rules may help prevent fact-finders from acting based on prejudice or stereotype by sifting out some evidence they consider to be unfair, but that, on the other hand, the rules of evidence reward well-resourced parties who can afford capable counsel, and can reinforce stereotypes about what makes for a credible witness. We carry these themes through the semester, reflecting on the distributional effects of the evidence rules, and the extent to which the rules often reflect very recent policy choices. In particular, evidence gives us a chance to think about how the rules are designed to shape how juries receive and sift information, and whether the rules do so in ways that disfavor already-disfavored groups.

---

2. For a discussion of how I incorporate these ideas in the Criminal Law classroom, see Deborah Ahrens, *Centering Race and Diversity in the Criminal Law Classroom*, *in* Nicole Dyszlewski et al. eds., Integrating Doctrine and Diversity: Inclusion and Equity in the Law School Classroom 169–178 (2021).

3. *See* N.H. Sup. Ct. R. 36 ("Appearances in Court by Eligible Law Students and Graduates").

Rules of Evidence and the Role of the Jury

The *Peña-Rodriguez v. Colorado*[4] case permits students to reflect on jury selection, how juries receive evidence, and what, exactly, transpires in the black box of jury room deliberation. In *Peña-Rodriguez,* two jurors approached the defendant's attorney after rendering a verdict and reported that a third juror had made several racist remarks about men of Mexican descent and undocumented immigrants.[5] This case permits us to have a number of excellent class discussions. How racist must statements be before they may be usable to impeach a jury verdict? Are there other protected categories, such as gender and religion, that *Peña-Rodriguez* should extend to in order to impeach jury verdicts, or is the unique history of race in American criminal justice (as recognized in cases like *Buck v. Davis*[6]) a reason to limit the case to that category? Can jury instructions or *voir dire* questions ameliorate these harms? How does the racial composition of the jury affect the likelihood of such behavior? The holding of the case—that, while FRE 606(b) generally renders jurors incompetent to impeach a verdict, that rule violates the Sixth Amendment right to an impartial juror where the statements are racist[7]—is itself one that leads to robust discussion about the extent to which the rules of evidence should consider categories like race, gender, and immigration status. It also offers an opportunity to consider the role of the jury more broadly and to reflect on how the rules of evidence shape what it sees.

Witness Testimony, Cultural Bias, and Impeachment

Evidence rules and the Sixth Amendment confrontation clause[8] place great faith in the ability of jurors to evaluate witness credibility by viewing testimony live. Certainly, being able to ask questions of a witness to expose issues is part of that process, but the preference for in-person testimony also reflects that evidence rules reflect the presumption that jurors will be able to determine if witnesses are telling the truth and remember events accurately. A confident demeanor might suggest a witness who is forthright and correct; tentative speech and a failure to make eye contact might suggest evasion and indecision.

Are those assumptions empirically founded? Or are we making assumptions about how truthful, accurate witnesses behave? What kinds of people, from what kinds of backgrounds, feel comfortable and confident in a courtroom, and what kinds of people

---

4. Peña-Rodriguez v. Colorado, 580 U.S. 206 (2017).

5. *Id.* at 861–862.

6. 580 U.S. 100 (2017).

7. *Peña-Rodriguez,* 580 U.S. at 225.

8. The Sixth Amendment's Confrontation Clause provides, in pertinent part, that, "[i]n all criminal prosecutions, the accused shall enjoy the right ... to be confronted with the witnesses against him." U.S. Const. amend. VI.

feel ill at ease? Do jurors pick up on things like dress and hairstyle and use those in evaluating witness credibility?[9] And, as usual, does the composition of the jury matter when jurors are evaluating witness credibility—if your communication patterns are common in your community, and your community is dominant on the jury, perhaps it is more likely that you will be believed.

The use of criminal convictions via FRE 609[10] in order to impeach witnesses provides an unfortunately excellent vehicle for discussing the role of race in law. Students at most law schools have taken criminal law and/or criminal procedure by the time they reach evidence; they usually are aware of the extent to which Black and Latine[11] Americans are more likely to be convicted of crimes and often have explored the persistent structural issues that create such inequality. Now, they learn, among the many things a criminal conviction signifies is that you are a less credible witness—that crimes of dishonesty must be admitted for impeachment purposes, and that felony offenses in general may be used to cast doubt on the willingness of a witness to testify truthfully.[12] That use, as they learn, has been heavily critiqued,[13] partly based on the disconnect between most criminal activity and dishonesty, but also because of the racial inequality in conviction rates that renders many witnesses less credible, including people attempting to tell their own stories in their own cases.

All Hail the Podcast, a Redux[14]

Finally, students appreciate the opportunity to explore evidence concepts through outside media and podcasts, and some excellent podcasts have given us episodes centering on evidence issues and diversity. In the fall of 2021, as the Elizabeth Holmes trial unfolded, we followed *The Dropout*.[15] In so doing, we explored a number of evidence issues, including character evidence, admissions, and FRE 403,[16] but also thought about some of the gendered issues, including commentary on her deepened voice, her relationship with Sunny Balwani and allegations of abuse, and the ways in which women

9. My public defense office, like many offices, had a large walk-in closet brimming with suits, dresses, and other outfits that our clients and witnesses could borrow for court; we often discuss, in class, the reason why a lawyer would need to maintain such a collection.

10. *See* Fed. R. Evid. 609 (laying out rules for "Impeachment by Evidence of a Criminal Conviction").

11. Throughout this essay, I use "Latine" as a gender inclusive term meant to encompass Latino and Latina Americans, as well as Americans of Latin American descent who embrace a non-binary or gender fluid identity.

12. *See* Fed. R. Evid. 609.

13. *See, e.g.*, Anna Roberts, *Impeachment by Unreliable Conviction*, 55 B.C. L. Rev. 563 (2014).

14. In an earlier book chapter, I discussed how I use podcasts in my first-year Criminal Law course. *See* Ahrens, *supra* note 2.

15. Rebecca Jarvis, *The Dropout* (2019–2022), https://cms.megaphone.fm/channel/ESP5480008395?selected=ESP2462762431.

16. Fed. R. Evid. 403 (discussing rules for "Excluding Relevant Evidence for Prejudice, Confusion, Waste of Time, or Other Reasons").

are constructed in court. That semester, we also followed *Suspect*,[17] a podcast about a Black man tried twice (and ultimately acquitted) for a murder in suburban Seattle. *Suspect* features one episode that focuses on DNA evidence specifically,[18] addressing both how experts evaluate DNA and the potential issues with their analysis. While we cover that issue in my class through cases as well, the podcast makes a complicated subject accessible for students in a context that allows them to consider what the analysis means for the DNA evidence in an interesting case. The podcast also has an excellent episode interviewing jurors from the trial and exploring how they discussed and viewed the evidence in the case, which students find eye-opening, and which raises the question of how much our evidence rules really control how jurors deliberate, what they consider to be important, and whether they follow instructions.[19] The second season of *In the Dark*,[20] which follows the Curtis Flowers case before the Supreme Court reversed his conviction,[21] also has several episodes with useful material for evidence class. The podcast explores the reason the Supreme Court ultimately reversed: the all-white composition of most of the six Flowers juries, and the racist pattern the prosecutor used to strike Black potential jurors.[22] The episodes related to these issues are an excellent companion piece for discussing *Peña-Rodriguez*.[23] Another episode addresses the confessions Flowers supposedly made to another man while incarcerated,[24] permitting us to talk about the admissions doctrine as well as impeachment (the witness had several convictions and was alleged to have been paid for testimony). As my students come to realize, the rules about admissions are about adversarial fairness and have little—if anything—to do with the reliability of the statements or even whether they were made in the first place. Still another episode deals with the case's questionable testimony from ballistics experts, a wonderful jumping-off point for our conversations about the possibilities and pitfalls of expert testimony.[25]

17. Matthew Shaer et al., *Suspect* (2021), https://wondery.com/shows/suspect/.

18. Matthew Shaer et al., *Suspect, The Break* (Sept, 21, 2021), https://wondery.com/shows/suspect/ (Season 1, episode 5).

19. Matthew Shaer et al., *Suspect, The Benefit of the Doubt* (Oct. 5, 2021), https://wondery.com/shows/suspect/ (Season 1, episode 7).

20. Madeleine Baran, *In the Dark: Season 2* (2018), https://features.apmreports.org/in-the-dark/season-two/ (last visited Dec. 16, 2022).

21. Flowers v. Mississippi, 588 U.S. (2019).

22. *See id.* at 2246.

23. *See* Peña-Rodriguez v. Colorado, 580 U.S. 206 (2017) (discussed in text accompanying note 2).

24. Madeleine Baran, *In the Dark: Season 2, The Gun* (May 8, 2018), https://features.apmreports.org/in-the-dark/season-two/ (Season 2, episode 3).

25. Madeleine Baran, *In the Dark: Season 2, The Confessions* (May 15, 2018), https://features.apmreports.org/in-the-dark/season-two/ (Season 2, episode 4).

Active Learning in the Evidence Classroom

Students find evidence terrifying. They come into the course aware that it is bar-tested; they are appropriately suspicious that a rules-based course might require some correct answers, rather than a fallback to "it depends"; and they often have been told by other students and practicing lawyers that the class will be hard. As a professor at a school that requires evidence for upper-division students, I have also found that many students are taking the class at sufferance; they have lost the shine of their 1L year or have become disconnected from or disaffected by their prior law school experience. Law schools have become more aware of these effects, particularly for students who are first-generation, Black, Latine, or otherwise have not historically seen themselves represented in the law. Many such students are still trying to find a place during their second and third years (a reason why, after years of thinking the professional thing would be to keep my biography out of the classroom, I began letting students know from the beginning that I am a first-generation college student). One of my primary goals in teaching an upper-level, bar-tested, required class has been to make my classroom into an inclusive, active space for students, which has been a challenge in a course where I usually have 80–90 students enrolled. In the remainder of this article I share some of the ideas that I believe have been successful in creating a course that works for our diverse student body.

A Taste of Practice Through a Series of Scripts

I learned evidence largely by practicing law, an experience that is not uncommon for those of us who transitioned from law school to an active trial practice. I found this theme of learning by doing to be particularly true for evidence, which required me not just to know the law, but how to apply it on my feet in a courtroom. The problem, as I discovered once in practice, was not just that I did not know when to stand or how to phrase my arguments—it was that the entirely case-based way in which I had learned evidence had left me with a less firm understanding of the substantive law as well. As I developed my evidence course, I knew I needed to find ways to give students a picture of how evidence works in practice; some ability to perform objections and argumentation as they might in court; and some teaching and evaluation that might be different from what they experienced in their first year.

I may have known I needed to do something different, but I found "doing something different" to be a logistical challenge. In a large lecture class, it is difficult to provide students with extensive skills training—I am thankful that clinics and advocacy courses offer deep support for students as they master courtroom work. What I have found helpful has been to create a progression of scripted class exercises for students to act out, add on to, and eventually culminate in student-made scripts. To encourage students to get comfortable in class, and to ease them into participation, I have set a number of courtroom scripts in the same fictionalized universe (the primary one for my course is set at the Soap 'n Suds, the bar/laundromat venue from one of my real-life cases), and we follow the case as it unfolds during the semester. At the beginning, the exercises are entirely scripted—I will call on a few students to come down to the well of the classroom and serve as a witness and an examining attorney, seating the witness at a table at the front; they will read the lines from the script, and afterward I will call on students to reflect on and respond to what they have seen. It has been a great way to get students used to speaking in class in a zero-stakes way; as I tell them, they are using my words, so if there is a problem, that problem is entirely with me. As the semester progresses, the scripts become more interactive, requiring the students to object to testimony, to make arguments, and to support and counter objections. I am always clear with students that I will never evaluate them on how well they perform trial skills (I tell them stories about my own initial awkward efforts); we treat the classroom as a lab where we allow experimentation, and where we are all included in the experiment.

About three-quarters of the way through the semester, I give the students a problem to help them process their understanding of impeachment; the problem contains facts that can support every possible mode of impeachment, and I ask them to draft a cross-examination that they think would appropriately impeach the witness given the rules that we have learned. I solicit a half-dozen volunteers prior to the class session to perform sections of their scripts with me, playing their impeachable witness in front of the class (enticing them with a promise of being off-call for the remainder of the semester, in full disclosure); I then call on other students after each section to get feedback (always positive and supportive) about what they have seen and to offer how it differs from what they have written in their own scripts. This impeachment exercise—which takes about two hours—is always a highlight of the semester, and, as a bonus, students appear to positively delight in the opportunity to make me squirm as a witness (I permit students to create physical evidence, demonstrative aides, and even to get classmates to serve as other witnesses within the confines of the fact pattern that I give them). I have found, over the years, that the set of students who leap at the chance to try their hands at cross-examination is rarely the set of students who are happy to be cold-called to discuss the holding of a case. While, in an 80-student evidence class, it is not possible to offer everyone extensive training and opportunity in trial practice, I have found that this progression of active-learning scripts culminating in a student-driven exercise have helped a greater number of people feel more at home in the classroom and have permitted students who might not feel as comfortable offering traditional case analysis to have ways to engage productively and helpfully in class.

Approaching Challenging Conversations

I think it is important to cover FRE 412–15[26] in class, both substantively and historically. Covering these rules, however, means that students are going to be reading about rape and then engaging in very difficult class discussions, which may affect students who are female or LGBTQ+ differently than straight cis male students. I have developed a problem that gives them a written fact pattern followed by a series of questions that required them to figure out whether the evidence would be admissible with and without the FRE 412–15 set of rules; I give them the problem to read before class, and, when we get to class, let them break themselves into groups of three or four students to discuss the problems one by one. After they have each discussion—and the discussions are always loud and thoughtful—I ask the groups to have someone report back to the class on the kinds of things they discussed in the group. I have found this to be helpful in several ways. First, students are able to process what can be distressing details and arguments in a smaller configuration of people. Second, the students choose those people, and are able to select classmates they trust for having the initial conversation. Finally, by being able to report to the class with "my group talked about these different arguments," students find it easier to discuss a variety of arguments, including those that are uncomfortable or challenging, when they are able to provide some formal distance between themselves and the arguments.

Coming Full Circle

By the end of my course, the vast majority of students have not just read and debated the Rules of Evidence, but have utilized, strategized about, and genuinely experienced those Rules. While every student is different, the majority of them seem to come out of the class with the attitude that (contrary to my first mentor) having rules of evidence beats the alternative but that the particular substance of the rules really matter and that our current rules need to be modified in myriad ways to reflect our emerging knowledge about their distributional consequences.

---

26. *See generally* FED. R. EVID. 412–415 (laying out special relevance rules for sex offense cases).

Creating a Space of Possibility in the Evidence Law Classroom

*Pavel Wonsowicz**

The Federal Rules of Evidence ("FRE") determine the fair and efficient administration of proceedings by providing a framework for ascertaining the truth and securing a just result. As such, they determine which facts will be considered to decide guilt or innocence in federal criminal cases as well as determining liability in federal civil actions. Significantly, the FRE carry the imprimatur of the entire United States government—the Supreme Court drafted these rules, Congress debated and revised them, and the President signed them into law.

So how should a law school class explore the idea that the FRE may disproportionately give an evidentiary advantage or disadvantage to a certain group? This piece will look at this problem, figure out a lens by which to view it in the evidence classroom, and then give an example of how that lens can be put into practice.

The Problem

Legal critical reasoning depends on inferences. For the FRE, "common sense psychology" guides many of those inferences by asking what a reasonable person would do in similar circumstances.[1] Yet "common sense psychology" can often incorporate majoritarian norms that may ignore practical realities based on race, ethnicity, gender, sexuality, and/or socioeconomic class. A host of these majoritarian preferences arguably exist in the FRE, and they create diversity fault lines that need to be explored in the evidence classroom.

One common example is the use of evidence of flight from the police as evidence of consciousness of guilt. The logic of introducing flight evidence is as old as the Bible:

---

* Lecturer in Law and Director of the Academic Support Program, UCLA School of Law.

1. Jasmine B. Gonzales Rose, *Toward a Critical Race Theory of Evidence*, 101 Minn. L. Rev. 2243, 2253 (2017). *See also* Todd A. Berger, *Politics, Psychology, and the Law: Why Modern Psychology Dictates an Overhaul of Federal Rule of Evidence 609*, 13 U. Pa. J.L. Soc. Change 203, 207–14 (2010) (exploring how psychological tenets do not support the rationales behind FRE 609).

"The wicked flee when no one pursues, but the righteous are as bold as a lion."[2] Put differently, only the guilty would flee the police, and therefore a defendant's flight is relevant under FRE 401 as to the defendant's consciousness of guilt. But can the motivations of one who flees be so easily distilled? When one factors in racial profiling in police stops, over-policing in minority neighborhoods, the war on drugs, conscious or unconscious prosecutorial bias, racially disproportionate sentencing, and mass incarceration, perhaps the motivations of one who flees has next to nothing to do with their consciousness of guilt.[3] Thus, encapsulating the majoritarian norms of what an innocent person would do into evidence law may lead to an inequitable result—evidence with no probative value toward guilt is admitted to prove guilt.

A similar argument can be made with silence as an admission under the hearsay exemption FRE 801(d)(2)(B). A form of adoptive admissions, silence can implicitly be an admission (and therefore exempted from the hearsay rule) if the party: (i) heard and understood the statement, (ii) circumstances called for a reply, (iii) the party had an opportunity to deny, and (iv) the party remained silent or made an evasive or equivocal reply. The second element is usually the contested one, as it essentially asks, "When would a reasonable person renounce a statement?" As one court put it, "It does seem, when we consider the condemnation and abhorrence with which the commission of such an atrocious crime is received by mankind, that an innocent man would resent such an accusation ... with all the power of his nature."[4] Yet what happens when the party has multiple motives for her silence, such as a mistrust of the police or a belief that the declarant would not take a denial seriously due to a conscious or unconscious bias? Again, are majoritarian norms encapsulated into evidence law leading to an inequitable result?

Yet another example stems from impeachment of a witness by a prior criminal conviction under FRE 609. The rationale behind this rule centers on the inference that if a witness cannot obey the law, that witness cannot be trusted to follow the rules in court to tell the truth. Accordingly, this rule relies on the criminal justice system for identifying credibility.[5] But, as noted earlier, if inequities exist in our criminal justice system, then that systemic racism silences the narratives of minorities who fear testifying due to the potential misuse of a prior conviction. Although the jury will be instructed to use a prior conviction to only weigh credibility, a significant risk exists that the jury will use the evidence for an improper propensity purpose (e.g., "If she committed a crime before, she is the type of person who commits crimes, and therefore must have committed the crime for which she is on trial").

---

2. *Proverbs* 28:1 (New International Version).

3. Gonzales Rose, *supra* note 1, at 2272.

4. State v. Mortensen, 73 P. 562, 567–568 (Utah 1903).

5. Montré D. Carodine, *"The Mis-Characterization of the Negro": A Race Critique of the Prior Conviction Impeachment Rule,* 84 Ind. L.J. 521, 560–66 (2009).

The Supreme Court struggled with the interaction of the FRE and racial discrimination in *Peña-Rodriguez v. Colorado.*[6] In *Peña-Rodriguez*, the Court grappled with the limits of FRE 606(b), which, subject to some exceptions, prevents juror testimony during an inquiry into the validity of a verdict or indictment. Miguel Angel Peña-Rodriguez was found guilty of sexually assaulting two teenaged sisters and, following the discharge of the jury, two jurors informed defense counsel that a fellow juror had expressed anti-Hispanic bias toward petitioner and petitioner's alibi witness. Should the Court follow the prohibition against juror testimony in the FRE or should it craft an exception for racial bias? A divided Court chose to carve an exception to the prohibition on juror testimony, finding that racial bias was "a familiar and recurring evil that, if unaddressed, would risk systemic injury to the administration of justice."[7]

A common link among these examples is the role played by FRE 403. FRE 403 adopts a balancing test that makes evidence inadmissible when its unfair prejudice substantially outweighs its probative value. Typically, emotionalism and misuse of the evidence by the finder of fact are the major unfair prejudices for which the rule is concerned. With this balancing comes an extremely broad amount of discretion for the trial judge that is reversed only for an abuse of that discretion. Thus, the concerns with FRE 403 as a safety net are evident: if probative value is evaluated through a common psychology incorporating majoritarian norms, then the minority experience is not given sufficient weight; if unfair prejudice does not account for the risk of misuse of evidence due to conscious or unconscious prejudice, then the evidence is not fairly weighed. Students of evidence law are often mystified as to why FRE 403 is not a better arbiter of unfair prejudice. It is from this sense of confusion that we as professors can build a powerful dialogue.

The Lens

For me, the classroom has always felt like a radical space of possibility.[8] In the best classes, anything felt possible, and no question seemed unanswerable—we grappled with ideas, rethought our assumptions, and examined our mental models of reality. It was not the professor's class or the students' class, but *our* class. Not surprisingly, my best moments as a teacher always come when the focus is on learner empowerment rather than knowledge transmission.[9] After all, we want our students to move to the higher order thinking that is critical to effective advocacy, such as evaluating and synthesizing. A class spent just learning the elements of a rule, rather than exploring the

---

6. 580 U.S. 206 (2017).

7. *Id.* at 868.

8. I first encountered the terminology "radical space of possibility" in the works of bell hooks. *See* BELL HOOKS, TEACHING TO TRANSGRESS: EDUCATION AS THE PRACTICE OF FREEDOM 12 (1994).

9. For a deeper exploration of my teaching philosophies, *see* Pavel Wonsowicz, *To Show Virtue Her Own Feature*, 59 UCLA L. REV. DISCOURSE 162 (2012).

grayness of those elements and how to best use facts and policy to maneuver in that gray space, feels like a lost opportunity to move a learner from novice to expert.

Accordingly, class should open up a student's toolbox and incorporate more skill development than just unfolding a case through the case method. Layering in creativity, practical judgment, factfinding, persuasively advocating, speaking, listening, strategic planning, the ability to see the world from the eyes of others, integrity, self-evaluation, passion, and engagement into a course's learning outcomes opens the door to the skills lawyers use every day.[10] One way to do this is to create a natural, critical learning environment. A natural environment would encompass authentic, real-world tasks, like arguing motions. A critical learning environment would not only examine the law, its application, and its synthesis, but also try to provoke an imagination that leads to possibilities and solutions while keeping in mind the practical realities of the people in the courtroom.[11]

Put another way, learning outcomes need to focus on reasoning more than memorizing. The content is not the end—it is the means to advance the learning outcomes. Content should be used to teach how to learn. When our students become practitioners, they will be spending their time comparing, applying, evaluating, analyzing, and synthesizing. Creating a classroom environment that hones those skills will lead our students to creative and successful advocacy.

There are many different classroom techniques we can use to put these ideas into practice. I typically rely on a form of the Socratic method to accomplish these outcomes.[12] Learners learn best when they answer their own questions and receive feedback on their efforts. In this way, knowledge is constructed, not received. With the Socratic method, I can give students a good problem, guide them through it, focus on higher-order thinking (such as evaluating and synthesizing), and allow the students to come up with the next question on their own. As explored in the next section, with Socratic dialogue on a challenging problem, discussions can turn from what the law is to why it is that way and how we can influence it. As a group, we can explore the material, handle it, relate it to our own life experiences, and feel challenged by it.

I also try to adopt approaches that reach different learning styles.[13] Learners have different strengths and weaknesses in obtaining information, and we do not want them

---

10. The skills mentioned are part of a list crafted in MARJORIE MAGUIRE SHULTZ & SHELDON ZEDECK, FINAL REPORT—IDENTIFICATION, DEVELOPMENT, AND VALIDATION OF PREDICTORS FOR SUCCESSFUL LAWYERING 15–16 (2009), http://papers.ssrn.com/sol3/papers.cfm?abstract_id=1353554. In their work, Shultz and Zedeck interviewed hundreds of lawyers in order to identify "effectiveness factors" that related to competent lawyering.

11. *See generally* KEN BAIN, WHAT THE BEST COLLEGE PROFESSORS DO 99–109 (2004) (exploring how posing questions and guiding students to understand the significance of the questions can lead to higher-order intellectual activity rather than merely having students listen and remember).

12. I place students into three-person law firms and randomly call on the law firms. While on call, each person in the law firm will engage in the Socratic dialogue.

13. *See generally* Robin Boyle & Rita Dunn, *Teaching Law Students Through Individual Learning Styles*, 62 ALB. L. REV. 213 (1998) (discussing how a learner may struggle under one particular teaching methodology and be more successful under an alternative methodology).

to rely exclusively on a method that is not a strength. While the Socratic dialogue may work well for auditory learners, learners who are more visual, kinesthetic (e.g., those who learn best by doing), or read-write (e.g., those who learn best by reading and writing) should have an opportunity to use those strengths. Therefore, incorporating video clips, conducting a cross-examination, and/or synthesizing a complex rule through a brainstorming exercise will allow the material to reach students through their strengths. In this way, one can keep circling back to their learning objectives in different ways so that students can try it on their own, develop questions, receive feedback, and try it again. In so doing, they move from novice to expert.

An evidence class is tailor-made for many of these techniques. Short, discrete problems can be created for rules that possess a limited scope. Students can be assigned roles for these problems (i.e., the proponent or opponent of the evidence) and argue them in class, thereby creating a more active learning environment. Countless video clips of trials and movies can be shown to amplify the gray areas of some of the rules. The rules themselves can be broken down to their component parts and then a grouping of rules can be synthesized through a brainstorming exercise. Indeed, when I was writing my casebook,[14] I decided early on to write one that could assist my teaching. Problems are prioritized over cases. I obtained the rights to a documentary, *The Staircase*, so that clips from that documentary could provide a continuous thread throughout the book.[15] I also created a short film, *The Trial*, which consists of numerous direct and cross-examinations that pause after each objection to allow the viewer to articulate the objection and the proponent's response.

But how can we incorporate this lens to bring diversity, equity, and inclusion issues in the evidence law classroom? What strategies can foster this radical space of possibility?

The View

Based on the numerous diversity fault lines in the FRE and the desire to create an inclusive classroom, I typically choose to take a deep dive into these issues early in the semester. I introduce these concerns in my opening discussion of FRE 403, which is something of a Pandora's box for resolving questions of racism, homophobia, or other biases. Note that this deep dive is not meant as a substitute for later discussion of diversity issues in the course; rather, it provides a scaffold to revisit these issues throughout the semester, even in a slightly less intensive manner.

I center this deep dive around *State v. Peterson*, which is the subject of *The Staircase*.[16] In *Peterson*, defendant Michael Peterson's wife, Kathleen, is found dead at the bottom of a staircase in their Durham, North Carolina, home. Michael is accused of beating Kathleen to death, but he claims that she accidentally fell down the staircase. The case

14. Pavel Wonsowicz, Evidence: A Context and Practice Casebook (3d ed. 2022).

15. The Staircase (Maha Productions 2003) (Jean-Xavier de Lestrade, director).

16. 634 S.E.2d 594 (N.C. App. 2006), *aff'd* 652 S.E.2d 216 (N.C. 2007).

possesses a remarkable number of twists and turns, leading to fascinating evidentiary issues and a riveting documentary.

The FRE 403 issue upon which I focus deals with Michael Peterson's bisexuality. More specifically, when the police searched the Peterson home, they found male pornography and emails from Michael in which he sought a liaison with a sex worker named "Brad."[17] The prosecution sought to enter this evidence under a number of theories, including that this evidence provided a motive for the killing and that it rebutted the defense attorney's opening that Michael and Kathleen possessed an "idyllic" marriage. The defense filed a motion to exclude it, arguing that the evidence was not relevant and unduly prejudicial, but the motion was denied by the trial court.

I want the students to see this issue through the eyes of an *advocate*—how does one articulate the unfair prejudice here and how does one voice the probative value? What is the precise inference that the prosecution is trying to make? Is there a risk that homophobia will enter the jury's reasoning? How does the defense explain the likelihood of that inference? Is admitting the evidence a subtle nod to the idea that someone seeking a same-sex liaison with a sex worker has a motive to kill his or her spouse? Would the same inference hold true if it were a heterosexual liaison with a sex worker? In other words, I want them to navigate the gray area by articulating what arguments work within the context of the FRE, so that we can then examine the appropriateness of the inherent norms of the FRE.

To begin, we explore the facts by reading the prosecution's brief. By relying on the prosecution's words, we can get a firmer sense of their implicit inferences through the facts they choose to emphasize. For example, the prosecution went into a great deal of detail regarding the type of pornography found and the type of sex sought (i.e., anal sex), which are facts that seem at the very periphery of a motive argument (after all, the motive exists from a desire to have an affair, not a desire to have a certain type of sex). We then explore how the defense could craft their version of the facts. What would they emphasize and de-emphasize? What would they concede relating to the potential probative value of the evidence?

We next read the appellate opinion that affirmed the trial court's admissibility decision. That opinion was strangely silent on the probative value of the evidence to prove motive, probably because there was no indication that Kathleen knew of the solicitation of Brad and, even if she did, that she would care enough that it would provide the defendant a motive to kill her (although Michael did not testify at trial, in an interview in the documentary he strongly implied that Kathleen knew of his bisexuality and was not troubled by his same-sex liaisons). Instead, the court focused on how "evidence of defendant's attempts to have sexual relations with a male escort and interest in homosexual pornography" contradicted defense counsel's portrayal of an "idyllic" marriage in his opening statement.[18] The court remained silent in its inferences but reaffirmed

17. Michael and Brad set up a time and place to meet, but Brad did not show up.

18. 634 S.E.2d. at 613.

that such decisions rest in the sound discretion of the trial court and no abuse of that discretion occurred here. The court even cited another North Carolina case from 1965 that referred to making homosexual advances as "abnormal propensities."[19]

The decision gives the class even more to unpack: How can a 2006 court reach the default position that homosexuality is an "abnormal propensity"? How does an advocate reframe that in the context of unfair prejudice under FRE 403? Would possession of opposite-sex pornography provide an equal motive to kill one's spouse or is there something unique to same-sex pornography that provides a motive? Will a jury instruction to use the evidence only for the purpose to rebut an idyllic marriage work or might the jury rely on a forbidden inference, such as homophobia? Is the deference afforded a trial judge in these and other determinations too strong?

As one can imagine, the undercurrent of the norms within the FRE and the deference afforded a judge to rely on her personal experiences in evaluating evidence takes up a great deal of the conversation in class. *The Staircase* gives an opportunity to make these abstract concerns more concrete. I show four different clips from the documentary in class. The first[20] shows defense counsel brainstorming for their motion argument. It is a remarkably candid clip that demonstrates how lawyers spend much of their time—spit-balling ideas, thinking about their inferences, and prioritizing their arguments. They openly worry about the potential for homophobia on the jury and explore how strong an inference exists between possession of same-sex pornography and a motive for the defendant to kill his wife.[21] The students end up seeing many of the concerns that they voiced in discussing the appellate opinion voiced by defense counsel. As a class, we list some of the arguments the attorneys should make at the motion hearing.

We then view the motion hearing[22] to see if our predictions were correct. How successful were our attempts to navigate this gray area? What we see is that defense counsel were absolutely explicit about their concerns—at one point defense counsel notes the unfair prejudice "if even one juror [thinks], 'Oh my God, this guy's gay!'" The prosecutor was much coyer, at one point analogizing defendant's motive to kill his wife to that of the plot line of a soap opera where such motives are routinely found. Once the trial judge rules the evidence admissible, we explore how we did in our prediction of what arguments were made and their efficacy.

But there is more to advocacy than motion work—there is also the art form of trial advocacy. We next view the direct and cross-examination of Brad[23] in order to see how

19. *Id.* at 614 (citing State v. Rinaldi, 372 S.E.2d 523, 527 (1965)).

20. The Staircase, *supra* note 15, episode 6, 7:47–9:21.

21. A moment that tends to get the students laughing is when one of the attorneys finds it shocking that a spouse seeking out a sex worker is probative to the strength of the marital relationship. After the laughter subsides, we often explore the idea that Michael and Kathleen may have had a sexually open relationship, in which case the evidence would indeed have little probative value.

22. The Staircase, *supra* note 15, episode 6, 9:21–12:16.

23. *Id.* at episode 6, 12:16–17:25.

the admitted evidence is actually presented. We know what inferences are permissible for the evidence, but will the prosecution be constrained by them? In perhaps the most powerful moment of Brad's direct examination, the prosecutor explicitly asks what "type of sex" they intended to engage in when they met. After some uncomfortable moments from Brad, he responds, "Anal sex." The camera flashes to defense counsel, who is actively scanning the jury to gauge their reaction. Defense counsel chooses not to object.

The moment sparks a sense of outrage in some of my students. How is the sexual act remotely relevant toward the limited inference that seeking sex outside a marriage shows a less-than-idyllic marriage? Is this not pandering to the potential homophobia of the jury?[24] Why did defense counsel not immediately object? Our exploration of these and other questions allows the students to understand that the presentation of evidence can lead to multiple inferences, like trains running on parallel tracks. Some of these tracks lead to the allowable destination (a less-than-idyllic marriage), and others do not (homophobia).

To further bring this point home, we watch the prosecutor's closing[25] where she discusses the defendant's relationship with Brad. We now move from the presentation of fact to arguments about those facts. The prosecutor's theme is "common sense." She asks if it "makes common sense" to the jury that Kathleen knew that Michael was bisexual and that she would go off to work each day[26] knowing that her husband was seeking to have anal sex with men. She describes the same-sex pictures as "filth" and "hardcore porn" and again asks whether it "makes common sense" to the jury that Kathleen would know that the defendant possessed these items. The inference is not hard to discern: these are deviant behaviors that, if discovered by Kathleen, would have led to defendant's motive to kill her. Arguably, the train is running full steam down the impermissible track.[27]

Exploring the entirety of what my students call "the Brad problem" takes one 75-minute class. In that span, we enhance skill development by thinking about how to frame facts for the judge, applying facts to gray terms like "unfair prejudice," exploring how to present facts to the jury, and analyzing how to make inferences on those facts to the fact finder that (hopefully) follow the evidentiary hypothesis that led to the evidence's admissibility.

---

24. A level of discomfort regarding the topic of bisexuality was present throughout the trial. For example, on cross-examination, Brad testified that one of his former clients was a judge. The presiding judge interjected, "Not this judge," leading to laughter in the courtroom.

25. THE STAIRCASE, *supra* note 15, episode 8, 16:21–17:57.

26. The prosecution repeatedly emphasized at trial that Kathleen was a highly paid executive while Michael was a novelist with limited income. This again raises the issue of the train running down parallel tracks: motive (Kathleen had a lucrative life insurance policy) versus gender and socioeconomic status (Michael was a husband who depended on his wife for support).

27. The prosecutor does end her closing by focusing on the permissible inference: Michael's actions are "not the way soulmates conduct themselves."

But we also do more. We explore how majoritarian norms may not capture the practical realities of sexuality and thereby allow a judge to impart too much probative value or too little unfair prejudice to evidence. We give a voice to a sense of outrage when evidence is taken down an impermissible track that leads to its misuse. We build a scaffold to encounter these issues in a productive way when they intersect later in the course with race, ethnicity, gender, sexuality, and/or socioeconomic status. We learn how to be empathetic in our advocacy by examining the impact of marginalization in the rules that govern the admissibility of evidence. We strive for solutions. In short, we create a radical space of possibility.

Evidentiary Support

*Malikah Hall Retteen**

Introduction

Federal and state evidence rules govern what can be admitted and considered proof in a legal proceeding. Unfortunately, bias and discrimination arise even though the rules are supposed to prevent such issues.

The following resources provide teaching support in the form of source material that discusses medical and scientific issues within evidence law, suggests changes to federal and state rules of evidence, and suggests strategies for integrating issues of diversity, equity, and inclusion into the evidence classroom. This bibliography intends to be as inclusive as possible in the selection of materials. As such, the resources included here address issues of racism, ageism, sexual orientation bias, gender bias, cultural difference bias, mental disabilities and competencies, and citizenship status bias—all within the field of evidence law.

Articles

Anna Roberts, *Reclaiming the Importance of the Defendant's Testimony: Prior Conviction Impeachment and the Fight Against Implicit Stereotyping*, 83 University of Chicago Law Review 835 (2016).

> This work discusses the racial stereotypes that "threaten the presumption of innocence" during legal proceedings (835). Roberts explains that "unconscious associations" are invoked when the defendants are Black, including

* Malikah Hall Retteen is an Associate Law Library Professor at CUNY School of Law. She is a legal research professional, an author, a blogger, and an educator. She is the Founding Editor and Early Contributor for www.wocandlib.org. You can read more about her here at www.malikahhall.com. I would like to thank the editors and writers of this book for continuing the conversation started in volume I. I would also like to thank my husband, my dog Bubba, and my cat Bella for being my writing partners. They didn't write anything, but they did remind me to take writing breaks when I needed them.

the belief that Black defendants "use violence, weaponry, hostility, and aggression, are immoral, and [are] criminally guilty" (838). Rule 609 (governing impeachment by prior conviction) is problematic in that Black defendants usually choose not to testify for fear that evidence of prior convictions can be used to impeach their testimony. This, coupled with the previously mentioned unconscious association that Black defendants with previous convictions are violent and criminally guilty, can lead to unjust outcomes in legal proceedings. Roberts suggests ways for defense attorneys to combat bias, including "reclaiming the importance of a defendant's testimony by explaining how stereotypes threaten the presumption of innocence" (880), providing "individuating testimony that highlights the life experience of the defendant to show the defendant's human side" (882), and other changes to Rule 609 to eliminate bias and lead to more equitable outcomes.

Bennett Capers, *Evidence Without Rules*, 94 Notre Dame Law Review 867 (2018).

This article discusses how the rules of evidence were designed to be "all-seeing, all-encompassing gatekeepers, checking all of the information juries may hear and see for relevance and trustworthiness" (872). However, Professor Capers posits that the rules are "selectively blind, with consequences that flow from this blindness" (873). In particular, he looks at evidence of style of dress of sexual assault victims, the demeanor of the defendant, witnesses, and attorneys, and the presence of family members during a trial, and race. To combat these issues, the author suggests "changes to pattern jury instructions that state that jurors are not allowed to consider unseen evidence at all" and provides a suggested instruction for others to follow (898).

Chris Goodman, *The Color of Our Character: Confronting the Racial Character of Rule 404(b) Evidence*, 25 Law & Inequality (2017).

In this article, Professor Goodman discusses how the character-based evidence rules are not living up to what they were designed to prevent (i.e., the use of irrelevant and racially biased evidence in criminal trials), and how unjust Rule 404(b) (permission of bad character evidence of other crimes, wrongdoings, or acts) has become, allowing inaccurate racial generalizations and stereotypes to be admitted.

The paper is divided into four parts, with a conclusion that aids the reader in taking advantage of the many ways in which the rules can be unfair, providing sample draft jury instructions. In Part I, Goodman posits how Rule 404(b) can be used to unfairly characterize witnesses. For example, a white housewife in the middle of a divorce who is accused of welfare fraud may be perceived differently than a Black single mother with multiple children from multiple fathers. Part II discusses methods for having jurors confront their own racial stereotypes and prejudices to produce less biased decision making. Several examples challenge the use of prior arrest evidence in drug cases involving Black and Latino defendants.

Part III discusses racial references in the rules of evidence, specifically how the balancing test in rule 403 is insufficient to address racial character references. The author provides another method of avoiding character evidence from being admitted: the defense can decline to offer good character evidence and/or submit evidence that undermines the legitimacy of the racial stereotypes and generalizations. Part IV provides potential solutions including creating a new Racial Reference Exclusion rule and banning the use of Rule 404(b), creating rules that exclude the chance of evidence of prior bad acts that are based on racial stereotypes, expanding the admission of good character evidence, and creating new jury instructions to directly address the issue of racial character evidence.

Demetria D. Frank, *The Proof is in the Prejudice: Implicit Racial Bias, Uncharged Act Evidence & the Colorblind Courtroom*, 32 Harvard Journal on Racial & Ethnic Justice 1 (2016).

Although the rules of evidence are supposed to be colorblind, Professor Frank illustrates how this is far from the truth. Specifically, this article looks at bias suffered by Black defendants under Rule 404(b) because of what the author calls "the over admission" of evidence or prior uncharged criminal acts (9). Frank suggests an amendment to Rule 404(b) to restrict the admittance of such evidence when the likely effect of admission is based on implicit bias.

Denis Magyar, *The Use of Neuroscientific Discoveries in Criminal and Civil Evidence Law*, 11 Medicine, Law & Society 121 (2018), https://doi.org/10.18690/mls.11.2.121-136.2018.

Professor Magyar believes that neuroscientific discoveries (such as the study of brain activity, mental health, mental capacity, etc.) can lead to more objectivity in both criminal and civil evidence law. The paper discusses the history and development of neurolaw (where neuroscientific discoveries intertwine with legal problems) with a focus on how issues of mental disorders and mental competence can lead to not guilty verdicts. The author calls for the creation of more interdisciplinary courses in the fields of neurolaw in order for both law and medicine to gain knowledge and understanding of the other.

The author looks at how applying neuroimaging methods can help a medical expert determine the mental capacity of an accused child of a certain age and brain development. Another example of how neurolaw can help mitigate punishment due to substantially diminished mental competence includes how MRI and PET[1] evidence caused the defendant to lose control.

1. *See* Stanford Medicine, *PET/MRI Scan*, https://stanfordhealthcare.org/medical-tests/p/pet-mri-scan.html (last visited Jan. 27, 2023).

Gabriel J. Chin, *A Chinaman's Chance in Court: Asian Pacific Americans and Racial Rules of Evidence*, 3 UC Irvine Law Review 965 (2013).

In this article, Professor Chin documents historical racist, xenophobic, and discriminatory laws facing Asian people in the United States from 1854 to 1954. The title is a reference to *Chin Kock Quon v. Proctor*,[2] where the court granted a writ of habeas corpus because an apparent U.S. citizen was excluded without good reason by overzealous administrators: "When Federal officers mete out such treatment to a man previously established to be an American citizen, we can well understand the bitter irony of the current phrase 'A Chinaman's chance'" (965 n.1). The paper is divided into two sections, one section addressing the unfair treatment of Asians in immigration and other cases and a second section addressing legal presumptions about the citizenship of Asians.

Section one begins with a discussion of *People v. Hall*,[3] a California Supreme Court case that held Chinese immigrants were:

> a race of people whom nature has marked as inferior, and who are incapable of progress or intellectual development beyond a certain point, as their history has shown; differing in language, opinions, color, and physical conformation; between whom and ourselves nature has placed an impassable difference, is now presented, and for them is claimed, not only the right to swear away the life of a citizen, but the further privilege of participating with us in administering the affairs of our Government.[4]

Another example is the passing of the 1892 Geary Act,[5] which amended the 1882 Chinese Exclusion Act[6] to require Chinese laborers lawfully present in the U.S. to obtain and carry a residence card. Those found without their residence card faced a year of hard labor and possible deportation if the Chinese person could not present a credible white witness to establish residency.[7]

The article then segues into the topic of Anti-Asian land law including the case of *Morrison v. California*,[8] in which the Supreme Court unanimously held that the law could presume persons of Asian racial ancestry found in the United States were aliens and placed the burden on Asians to prove otherwise. The court held that "if the admixture of oriental blood might be too

2. 92 F.2d 326 (9th Cir. 1937).
3. 4 Cal. 399 (1854).
4. *Id.* at 405.
5. Ch. 60, 27 Stat. 25 (May 5, 1892).
6. Ch. 126, 22 Stat. 58 (May 6, 1882).
7. In *Fong Yue Ting v. United States*, 149 U.S. 698 (1893), the Supreme Court held that the Voting Rights Act of 1870 that prohibited racial discrimination against witnesses did not apply to Fong Yue Ting as "Congress was within its authority in not allowing a fact to be provided solely on the testimony of aliens in a like situation or of the same race. *Id.* at 730. The Chinese Exclusion Act and subsequent amendments were repealed in 1943. Magnuson Act, ch. 344, 57 Stat. 600 (1943).
8. 291 U.S. 82 (1934).

slight for a defendant's race to be apparent, then the person may be mostly white, or in fact, entirely white and charged in error."[9] Whiteness and white adjacency was the rule of the day. The author ends by explaining that although progress has been made and a lot of these laws have been overturned or repealed, there are cultural and societal effects that are still felt today.

Gillian Chadwick, *Reorienting the Rules of Evidence*, 39 CARDOZO LAW REVIEW 2115 (2018).

The article discusses sexual orientation bias faced by LBGBTQ+ defendants based on coded language, innuendo, stereotypes, and prejudice. This includes the erroneous and discriminatory conflation of sexual orientation as evidence of guilt in sexual assault cases involving LGBTQ+ defendants as well as the improper admission and overreliance upon evidence of a defendant's sexual orientation in sexual assault cases. The author calls for the proper application of the rules of evidence, particularly relevance and character evidence rules (Rules 401, 403, 404, 413, 414, and 415) to lead to fairer outcomes. The paper also provides helpful definitions regarding rape etiology (rape as a hate crime, date or companion rape, etc.), gay panic defenses, and sexual orientation, among others.

The paper looks extensively at two cases, *J.O. v. O.E.*[10] and *State v. Ford.*[11] In *State v. Ford*, the defendant in a sexual assault case was forced to reveal that he was bisexual. In response, the prosecution stated that the defendant "admitted he is bisexual and that is exactly what he is charged with doing."[12] The defendant was charged with sexual assault, not being bisexual. Being attracted to the male victim is not the same as sexually assaulting them. In *J.O. v. O.E.*, a man sought a protection order from his roommate, who the man had accused of repeated sexual assault. The defendant simply testified that he was not gay. The judge stated that if the accused was not gay, he would not have approached his accuser for sex.

The author ends by calling for judges to properly weigh the probative value evidence of a defendant's sexual orientation, not just sexual assault cases, but in the court system as a whole. This will lead to fairer outcomes that can overcome the biases faced by LGBTQ+ defendants.

Helene Love, *Aging Witnesses: Exploring Difference, Inspiring Change*, 19 INTERNATIONAL JOURNAL OF EVIDENCE & PROOF 210 (2015), https://doi.org/10.1177/13657127 15591462.19.

This article looks at the physical and mental changes (to vision, hearing, and the brain itself) that occur as we age, and how these health challenges can

9. *Id.* at 95–96.
10. 100 A.3d 478 (2014).
11. 926 P.2d 245 (1996).
12. *Id.* at 248.

affect the treatment of evidence presented by older witnesses in legal proceedings. The author documents a laboratory study of persons older than sixty and younger adult participants who watched a staged crime and were asked to recall what they witnessed. Participants over sixty had issues remembering the details of the crime and provided less accurate answers. Older witnesses were also susceptible to suggestibility based on leading questions.

Love closes by providing several strategies and techniques for improving the reliability of evidence given by older witnesses in legal proceedings. These include conducting the witness interview as close to the event as possible or in the morning when the cognitive level of older witnesses is higher, conducting simultaneous and sequential lineups, and seeking legal accommodations for older witnesses.

Hugh Mundy & L. Alexandra McDonald, *Why Would You Say That? Addressing Systemic Injustice in the Evidentiary Standard for Opposing Party Statements*, 53 UIC John Marshall Law Review 773 (2021).

The article begins with a discussion of the false confessions given in the Central Park Five case.[13] The subsequent exoneration of all defendants in that case and the production of the films *The Central Park Five*[14] and *When They See Us*[15] have brought new interest and outrage to the case and the subject of false confessions, wrongful convictions, coercive statements and tactics, police abuse of power, and racial discrimination.

The article then segues into a discussion about how Rule 801, the rule that governs the admissibility of statements by defendants, has and will continue to lead to wrongful convictions for people of color. The authors explain that arrest and conviction rates of Black and Hispanic men of color were higher as compared to white men where Rule 801 was used. Rule 801 also applies when introducing statements in an immigration removal case. (In 2018, it was used in 43% of immigration removal proceedings in the United States.)

The authors end by suggesting an amendment to Rule 801 that would require a guarantee of trustworthiness in order to combat inequalities. A guarantee of trustworthiness would require the government to prove by a preponderance of evidence prior to trial that a statement is reliable to scrutinize interrogation tactics that lead to false confessions and wrongful convictions.

Jasmine B. Gonzales Rose, *Toward a Critical Race Theory of Evidence*, 101 Minnesota Law Review 2243 (2017).

"This article challenges [the] assumption that everyone has an equal voice in the courtroom irrespective of race and reveals how evidence law and practice

---

13. *See The Central Park Five*, History.com, https://www.history.com/topics/1980s/central-park-five (last visited Jan. 27, 2023).

14. The Central Park Five (PBS 2012).

15. When They See Us (Netflix 2019).

disadvantages people of color" (2243). Professor Gonzales Rose suggests applying critical race theory to the law of evidence, something few scholars have attempted to do. The article is divided into three sections: (1) Race and Racism in the Law of Evidence; (2) Critical Race and Analysis of Evidence Law; and (3) Critical Race Reconstruction of Evidence Law. Each section explains how evidence law has adversely affected people of color and provides practical advice for implementing change in the classroom and in the courtroom. Topics of discussion include analysis of stand-your-ground defenses, racial profiling by the police, and how police violence that results in the death of the accused is disproportionately higher for Black and Latino victims, and the reasoning for flight from the police by Black and Latino persons.

Kathryne M. Young, *Outing* Batson*: How the Case of Gay Jurors Reveals the Shortcomings of Modern Voir Dire*, 48 WILLAMETTE LAW REVIEW 243 (2011).

Professor Young takes readers through a "thought experiment" that *Batson v. Kentucky*[16] should apply to jurors who are members of the LGBTQ+ community. *Batson* held it unconstitutional to strike a juror based on membership in a protected class. Sexual orientation was not at the time a protected class category. The author believes juries are less diverse because some jurors will not participate in the jury process if they fear being outed (forced to reveal their sexual orientation) and are forced to cover (mask one's sexual orientation). She suggests changes to peremptory challenges, including limiting the number of peremptory challenges to "give for-cause challenges more teeth" (268) and requiring an explanation for every peremptory strike in order to create more diversity within juries.

Michelle Fine, *Troubling Calls For Evidence: A Critical Race, Class and Gender Analysis of Whose Evidence Counts*, 22 FEMINISM & PSYCHOLOGY 3 (2012).

The article discusses what evidence and whose evidence counts when addressing issues of criminality, domestic violence, sexual assault, and when seeking orders of protection. Professor Fine uses a few examples to demonstrate how "[poor] women, women of color, marginalized women who 'fail' to fulfill mounting piles of responsibilities are being disciplined and punished publicly, in courts and in the media" (7).

To "reclaim evidence" (13), she suggests the fields of psychology, higher education, and women's rights advocates work in solidarity: to create studies that tell these real stories; ensure the persons involved in future studies are representative of different backgrounds, cultures, and experiences; and better document issues of social injustice to improve the systems frequently used by the marginalized.

Mikah Thompson, *Blackness as Character Evidence*, 20 MICHIGAN JOURNAL OF RACE AND LAW 321 (2015).

16. 476 U.S. 79 (1986).

This article provides an analysis of Federal Rule 404, particularly how the exception to the prohibition against the use of propensity evidence has led to implicit and jury bias based on what Professor Thompson calls "stereotypical Blackness," (322) or bias based on what are considered stereotypical Black characteristics (e.g. unintelligent, inarticulate).

She then provides an example of stereotypical Blackness bias by looking at the testimony of Rachel Jeantel during the trial of George Zimmerman for the death of Trayvon Martin. She discusses the vitriol Jeantel received on social media following her testimony and an interview that Juror B-37 gave that showed stereotypical Blackness bias.

She concludes with suggestions for reducing the stereotypical Blackness bias including allowing for rebuttal evidence and being more selective during the jury selection process.

Tarika Daftary-Kapur, Maureen O'Connor & Mindy Mechanic, *Gender-Intrusive Questioning: A Survey of Expert Witnesses*, 32 Behavioral Sciences & the Law 180 (2014), doi.org/10.1002/bsl.2114.32.

This paper presents the results of a study of male and female psychologist expert witnesses and the perceived bias based female experts face "that might diminish the credibility of the expert and subsequently the proffered testimony, thus undermining the legal system as an effective fact-finder by leading to decision-making based on extra-legal factors" (181). The discussion begins with a history of the role of expert witnesses before transitioning into a discussion of the study.

The results showed that male expert witnesses are treated as more credible than female expert witnesses. The study also found that although male experts were asked more frequently about their financial status, female expert witnesses face more intrusive questions. This occurred more frequently when the cases centered around gender issues. Female experts are asked more gender-intrusive questions when opposing counsel is male.

The authors conclude by calling for the legal community to take steps to eliminate gender bias and gender-intrusive bias in legal proceedings.

Ted Sampsell-Jones, *Implicit Stereotyping as Unfair Prejudice in Evidence Law*, 83 University of Chicago Law Review Online 174 (2017).

This article is written as a critical response to Anna Roberts' *Reclaiming the Importance of the Defendant's Testimony: Prior Conviction Impeachment and the Fight against Implicit Stereotyping.*[17] That work discussed making changes to Rule 609 of the Federal Rules of Evidence to eliminate bias and lead to a more equitable application of the rules. This article discusses how Rules 609,

---

17. Anna Roberts, *Reclaiming the Importance of the Defendant's Testimony: Prior Conviction Impeachment and the Fight against Implicit Stereotyping*, 83 U. Chi. L. Rev. 835 (2016) (discussed *supra* at {x-ref}).

403, and 409 are intertwined, and potential change to Rule 609 alone can lead to more inequity and implicit bias.

Roberts argued that bias should be considered as part of the fourth factor of the "Luck-Gordon Test."[18] Professor Sampsell-Jones writes that an additional factor should be created instead to exclude racial and implicit bias based on Rule 609. The author also suggests a change to the rule that admits all defendant's prior convictions, regardless of whether they testify, and a complete repeal of rule 404.

Terrence W. McCarthy, *The Racial Bias Exception to the General Rule That Precludes Jurors from Offering Testimony to Impeach Their Own Verdict*, 42 AMERICAN JOURNAL OF TRIAL ADVOCACY 1 (2018).

In this article, the author discusses Rule 606(b) and how, in *Peña-Rodriguez v. Colorado*,[19] a Hispanic male defendant was convicted of child sex crimes. The defense filed a motion for a new trial that included affidavits from two jurors accusing another juror of making biased statements about Mexican men ("I think he did it because he's Mexican," and "Mexican men take whatever they want").[20] The motion was denied and the ruling was affirmed on appeal. The Supreme Court reversed the decision and added an exception to the rule, holding:

> [W]here a juror makes a clear statement that indicates he or she relied on racial stereotypes or animus to convict a criminal defendant, the Sixth Amendment requires that the no-impeachment rule give way in order to permit the trial court to consider the evidence of the juror's statement and any resulting denial of the jury trial guarantee.[21]

The court also explained that offhand comments about racial bias or hostility will not offset the no-impeachment standard of 606(b). The comment must be overtly racist in nature as to raise doubt about the fairness of the jury vote *and* this racial animus must be a significant factor in the juror's vote.[22] This exception is subject to the Supremacy Clause as it relates to State rules of evidence. The language of the exception limits the holding to racial bias.

---

18. *See* Luck v. United States, 348 F.2d 763, 769 (D.C. Cir 1965) (proposing a multi-factor balancing test); Gordon v. United States, 383 F.2d 936, 939–40 (D.C. Cir 1967) (reiterating aspects of the *Luck* decision and proposing additional factors).

19. 580 U.S. 206 (2017).

20. *Id.* at 213.

21. *Id.* at 225.

22. *Id.*

The author then discusses the leading cases that have interpreted the Peña-Rodriguez exception, including *United States v. Robinson*[23] and *Richardson v. Kornegay*.[24]

Books and Book Chapters

CHRISTIAN DAHLMAN, ALEX STEIN & GIOVANNI TUZET, PHILOSOPHICAL FOUNDATIONS OF EVIDENCE LAW (2021).

Written by leading scholars on philosophy and the law, this text discusses and debates the rules of evidence. Part VII, Biases and Epistemic Injustice, includes several relevant chapters.

Chapter 23, *Evidence Law and Empirical Psychology*, by Professor Justin Sevier, reviews major contributions psychologists have made to areas of evidence law and offers for future contributions toward sound evidential policy (350). Chapter 24, *Relevance through a Feminist Lens*, written by Professor Julia Simon-Kerr, discusses feminist theory as it related what and whose evidence is considered relevant. She illustrates how the credibility of women in U.S. law could be impeached based on their perceived chastity. "This form of impeachment happened not just when women were bearing witness to their sexual assaults, but also when they testified as witnesses in actions involving title to land, assault, arson, or wrongful death" (373). Thus "[a women's] failure to maintain a chaste reputation meant that they were not worthy of being believed" (376). Unfortunately, the belief systems of society can dictate what evidence is relevant and whose evidence is to be believed can lead to different outcomes in the legal system. To illustrate this, she compares the two trials of Bill Cosby.[25]

---

23. 872 F.3d 760 (6th Cir. 2017) (holding racial comments made about Black jurors being reluctant to convict because they "owed something" to their Black brothers did not offset the no-impeachment standard as the comments were not directed at the defendant).

24. No. 5:16-HC-2115, 2017 WL 1133289 (E.D.N.C. Mar. 24, 2017) (In this case, a Black juror stated other jurors felt the Black juror would vote to acquit because the defendant was Black. This also did not offset the no-impeachment rule.).

25. The author points out that the two trials happened just one year apart and were argued in front of the same judge. In the first trial, potential testimony evidence of past accusers was excluded from the trial. The defense argued that the women were gold diggers who "have been willing to offer their bodies on the casting couch." (376) The second trial came at the time of the "#MeToo social media movement had brought attention and credence to accounts of powerful men using their position to coerce or force sex on women or sometimes on men—the casting couch was starting to look ... like a hunting ground." (*Id.*) In the second trial, the witnesses were allowed to testify, the prosecution argued that the "other accusers should be admitted not as proof of modus operandi, but on a doctrine of chances theory that says it is unlikely there would be so many false complaints alleging very similar conduct against an innocent actor." This time, the past accusers who were excluded during the first trial were allowed to testify during the second trial and Cosby was convicted. That conviction has since been overturned. *See Why Bill Cosby's conviction was overturned*, PBS NEWSHOUR (June 30, 2021), https://www.pbs.org/newshour/arts/why-bill-cosbys-conviction-was-overturned.

In Chapter 25, *Race, Evidence, and Epistemic Injustice*, Professor Jasmine B. Gonzales Rose argues that the use of "racist evidence in legal proceedings in the U.S. results in pervasive, but often overlooked, racialized epistemic injustice" (380). Examples of racist evidence include: the impeachment of witnesses by prior convictions (a review of Rule 609 and its state equivalents and the heightened risk faced by Black and brown defendants); cross-racial identification of suspects (where the eyewitness is white and the suspect is a person of color); determining whether a victim was threatening such that deadly police force was warranted (examines if the use of deadly force by the police was warranted); and flight from law enforcement (discusses the history of Black and brown people's fear of law enforcement and legal proceedings).

Gonzales Rose defines two types of epistemic injustice—*testimonial injustice* and *hermeneutical injustice*. Testimonial injustice occurs when prejudice causes a hearer to give a deflated level of credibility to a witness based on race, a previous conviction, or flight from the police. Hermeneutical injustice occurs when someone has a significant area of their social experience obscured—as when courts fail to recognize the historical reason why Black and brown people run from the police.

Finally, Chapter 26, *De-Biasing Legal Factfinders* by Professor Frank Zenker, describes types of human biases and the de-biasing measures to address the negative effects of cognitive biases (involves some broad erroneous form of reasoning) and social biases based on stereotypes. De-biasing addresses a bias's negative effects to improve the legal process.[26] This chapter also includes helpful charts and descriptions of the different types of biases. The author ends by calling for more research in this area as current research is scarce and unclear.

LAW AND THE VISIBLE (Austin Sarat, Lawrence Douglas & Martha Merrill Umphrey eds., 2021).

This work consists of individual essays that discuss the responsibility (or lack thereof) of those who record violence, including recording police officers beating a person, livestreaming a murder in progress, documenting the rape of an unconscious person, red-light cameras, eyewitness videos, and using doorbell-recorded video as evidence. These essays are especially poignant as they come in the aftermath of the George Floyd, Philando Castille, and Ahmaud Arbery trials and the protests and discussions about the use of video surveillance as evidence that arose from these cases. As the editors point out, although videos of police beatings and shootings should provide a concrete

26. Five conditions are presupposed to change a person's reasoning process, including: (1) awareness of bias; (2) motivation to correct its effects; (3) awareness of the bias's direction and magnitude; (4) ability to apply an appropriate de-biasing technique, and (5) successful debiasing. *See* T.D. Wilson & N. Brekke, *Mental Contamination and Mental Correction: Unwanted Influences on Judgments and Evaluations*, 116 PSYCH. BULL. 117 (1994).

verdict of guilt in the eyes of the public who are consuming the images, that trial verdict (if there is one) may be not guilty for other mitigating reasons.

The essays discuss the value of videos as evidence, the potential complicity of those who record sexual assault, the use of bodycam video in the death of Michael Brown, the historical public consumption of images depicting Black suffering and murder (lynching postcards and the slave market) and the images' effect on how Black people are seen in our society, and the right to anonymity and privacy for the persons recording the videos to protect the right to protest.

Michael J. Saks & Barbara A. Spellman, The Psychological Foundations of Evidence Law (2016).

This book focuses on how psychological beliefs have informed the development and application of the rules of evidence. The rules determine what questions lawyers may ask, what evidence is admitted in a legal proceeding, who can provide expert testimony, and require witnesses to swear an oath. The beliefs of the judge can affect what evidence is heard by the jury. If the judge, expert witness, factfinder, or jury member holds biased or racist beliefs about the defendant, this can affect the fairness of the legal proceeding. The authors also discuss current psychological research aimed at accomplishing evidence law's goal of facilitating fairness.

Helpful definitions include the psychological process of *metacognition* (trying to conceive of what others (jurors) are thinking and feeling and how the others will respond to evidence presented to them) and *mental contamination* (which occurs when the jury is asked to disregard evidence that should not be considered when the evidence may be relevant to the matter at trial). The authors suggest judges instruct the jury at the time of deliberation that the evidence must not be considered when reaching a verdict.

Other chapters discuss: hearsay exceptions, in particular Rule 803 and the hearsay exception of excited utterance; character evidence under Rule 404 and how research has found that jurors tend to ignore a judge's instructions if the accused has been accused of or committed a previous crime; the use of scientific evidence; and how cognitive psychology might help make data more available by presenting scientific evidence in a way the human mind is capable of processing.

Teaching Evidence Law: Contemporary Trends and Innovations (Yvonne Daly, Jeremy Gans & P.J. Schwikkard eds., 2020).

Part of the Routledge series on legal pedagogy, this comparative law text is edited by evidence scholars from common law countries. The work includes new teaching tools and innovative strategies for engaging students in undergraduate programs, evidence-law-based workshops and training sessions, pre-law programs, and the law school classroom.

In Part I, *New Tools*, Chapter 3 discusses how Australian teacher Jeremy Gans used the American trial of Michael Peterson[27] in an evidence class, believing there is pedagogical value in telling complex stories and outlining the costs and benefits of studying evidence law through true crime. Gans chose this complex case because it covers issues including the use of expert witness testimony, marital infidelity evidence, bisexuality, and murder.[28] He received positive feedback from the participants in his 10-week program and recommended evidence professors incorporate this particular true crime case into their classrooms.

Part II, *New Audiences*, includes the chapter *Bridging the Law and Forensic Science Divide*, in which authors Carole McCartney and John Cassella argue that criminal lawyers and forensic scientists should learn to communicate better and that each field should establish a basic understanding of each other's functions in the criminal justice system. The authors discuss the finding of the U.S. National Research Council Report,[29] which called for law schools to offer courses in forensic science disciplines and develop joint degree programs to help establish better connections.

The authors discuss how different common law jurisdictions are attempting to integrate forensic science into legal education with varying degrees of success. For example, The Osgoode Hall Law School of York Criminal Law Clinic has students visit a live autopsy and spend time in forensic laboratories. They have used open-source materials to create an elective called Forensic Process and the Law. The materials included 1,000 staged images, evidence schedules, witness and police statements, and documents from a criminal case. They conclude by encouraging legal and forensic scholars to "[amend their curriculum] to equip our students with the tools to become the best forensic scholars and the best legal professionals" (120).

Part III, *New Fields*, includes Chapter 12, *Introducing Science and Technology Studies into the Expert Evidence Course.* Author David S. Caudill agrees with the earlier point that interdisciplinary science classes should be included in legal education to "break down the persistent barriers to communication between lawyers and scientists" (149). Here, Caudill discusses his experience integrating Science and Technology Studies (STS) in the U.S. and Australia evidence expert courses. The piece starts with a discussion of *Daubert v. Merrell Dow Pharmaceuticals* and the four-factor test,[30] and the

27. *See State v. Peterson (2006)*, FINDLAW, https://caselaw.findlaw.com/nc-court-of-appeals/1435797.html.

28. There is also a six-part documentary about the case. THE STAIRCASE (Maha Productions 2003) (Jean-Xavier de Lestrade, director).

29. NATIONAL RESEARCH COUNCIL, STRENGTHENING FORENSIC SCIENCE IN THE UNITED STATES: A PATH FORWARD (2009), https://www.crimrxiv.com/pub/z6cvxsr8.

30. 509 U.S. 579 (1993).

skepticism of forensic evidence and forensic expertise due to misapplication of forensic science.[31]

The book ends with a description of author-taught evidence courses that address expert scientific witness testimony and the different types of witness expertise, interactional expertise, or contributory expertise.

Jasmine B. Gonzales Rose, *Race and Evidence*, *in* The Oxford Handbook of Race and Law in the United States (Devon Carbado, Emily Houh & Khiara M. Bridges eds., 2022).

This chapter illuminates how attorneys perpetuate racism and racial stereotypes as "racial character evidence" and how the lived experiences of white people are given "preferential admissibility treatment" (1). Examples of racial character evidence includes the type of music a person listens to (rap, hip-hop), how the person was dressed (hoodie or baggy jeans), and if the accused has prior convictions or arrests. This racial character evidence often goes unchecked. To illustrate this, Gonzales Rose presents hypothetical involving a Black man being shot by a white police officer, an awful situation that has played itself out on our television screens far too often to count. She also reviews the cases involving Michael Brown, Tamir Rice, and Trayvon Martin, all unarmed Black teens who were killed by either white officers or a white Hispanic person.

Montré D. Carodine, *Race Is Evidence: (Mis)Characterizing Blackness in the American Civil Rights Story*, *in* Civil Rights in American Law, History, and Politics 64–103 (2014).

While civil rights have changed significantly over the past century, Professor Carodine presents a counter-narrative to the idea that the changes in civil rights have resulted in actual progress for people of color. This is part of the author's "larger agenda to make the case that race itself is suspected, pursued, arrested, convicted and even exonerated in our judicial system" (67). Important legal precedents, including *Gentry v. McMinnis*[32] (which held that Blackness is prima facie evidence of the person being a slave) and *Hudgins v. Wright*[33] (making the presumption that a Black person is a slave and must prove their right to freedom), and the Trayvon Martin trials are reviewed. She defines and discusses in depth the terms "black tax" (that Black people have to work, study, and must pay just by virtue of being Black) and "white credit" (white people are provided with undeserved and unearned benefits because they are white). She also includes a commentary on this chapter that reviews the article in the context of racial bias in the foster care system.

---

31. *See Overturning Wrongful Convictions Involving Misapplied Forensics,* The Innocence Project, https://innocenceproject.org/causes/misapplication-forensic-science/ (last visited Jan. 27, 2023).

32. 33 Ky. (3 Dana) 382 (1835).

33. 11 Va. (Hen. & M.) 134 (1806).

Websites

Guerrilla Guides to Law Teaching, *No. 5: Evidence* (Sept. 5, 2018), https://guerrillaguides.wordpress.com/2017/09/05/no-5-evidence/

Law professors from across the country created the *Guerilla Guides to Law Teaching*, led by four principles: building solidarities, advancing resistance, broadening and deepening discourse, and pursuing radical interventions. The evidence guide seeks "to enrich our study of these rules by introducing diverse voices that illustrate their impact, and visions that illuminate alternative approaches." The guide includes 21 possible approaches to teaching evidence law under several umbrella topics, including having students assume different perspectives or roles, questioning the reliability of forensic evidence, or examining the role of disparate access to legal resources between communities.[34]

Videos

Lindsay Malloy, *Why teens confess to crimes they didn't commit*, TED (2018), https://www.ted.com/talks/lindsay_malloy_why_teens_confess_to_crimes_they_didn_t_commit.

The speaker is a forensic development psychologist whose work centers on how children function in a legal system made for adults. The talk begins with the names of seven teenagers who served more than 80 years for murders they falsely confessed to committing. The speaker then shows a video of Brandon Dassey's confession. Dassey, an intellectually disabled 16-year-old, was later featured in the docuseries *Making a Murderer*.[35]

---

34. The full list of topics includes: unsettling inevitability or teaching that a rule does not lead to inevitable outcomes by showing jurisdictions that take different approaches to rules of evidence; problematizing credibility by discussing the racialized history of credibility; highlighting the pervasive influence of unequal resources by discussing access to legal resources in underserved communities; diversifying rules and voices by asking students to think critically by assuming different perspectives and roles or by discussing the silencing of underrepresented witnesses and defendants; exploring the influence of bias by evaluating the rules to look for potential biases and asking for student thoughts on the effects of racial biases during jury deliberations; critiquing traditional notions of truth-seeking by interrogating Rule 102, questioning forensic evidence for reliability, and questioning flight from police by Black and Brown defendants as evidence of guilt; and problematizing gender roles by discussing rape shield laws and addressing issues of campus assault.

35. Making a Murderer (Netflix 2015). Dassey was subject to a four-hour interrogation. Several times during the interrogation, police officers used minimization tactics with hints of leniency, including telling Dassey that "his mom said he would be honest—we already know you did it—so be honest" and "I'm your friend and I want to help you." Police officers can lie, threaten, pressure, and intimidate witnesses, even intellectually disabled defendants. Dassey eventually confessed to murder and sexual assault. There was no physical evidence, only the confession. Dassey was sentenced to life in prison. He appealed the conviction. State v. Dassey, 2013 Wis. App. 30, 346 Wis. 2d 278, 827 N.W.2d 928 (2013). He served 10 years before the conviction was overturned. Dassey v. Dittmann, 877 F.3d 297 (7th Cir. 2017).

Despite viewer outrage at Dassey's treatment, the speaker says she has seen much worse treatment of children and developmentally disabled suspects who falsely confess to murder, rape, and other serious crimes. The speaker states that 25% of DNA exonerations involve false confessions. As 97% of legal cases are resolved by pleas, this 25% may be the tip of the troublesome iceberg. Only 7% of incarcerated teens had a parent, child advocate, or attorney present during an interrogation. Ninety percent of U.S. juveniles waive their *Miranda* rights, and no law requires a parent to be present during an interrogation. Additionally, hundreds of scientific studies have shown that children do not think or behave like adults. Children's brains are different anatomically in the prefrontal cortex. All of this can negatively affect how children react in an interrogation, oftentimes leading to false confessions.

To demonstrate how easily children can falsely confess to something they did not do, researchers at Florida International University conducted a study. The researchers obtained ethical clearance and parental permission for the minors involved in the study. The study involved academic dishonesty by cheating. Fifty-nine percent of the students confessed to cheating, even though they had not, and only 3% asked to talk to a parent that was in the next room.

The speaker calls for more parents, lawyers, and child advocates in the room during an interrogation. Moreover, police officers should be subject to specialized training when dealing with children and the intellectually disabled. These suspects should also receive specialized treatment based on their status.

Jasmine Gonzales Rose, *Objection! How Evidence Law Perpetuates Racism in the Courtroom* (2017), Univ. of Pittsburgh School of Law—Center on Race and Social Problems Speaker Series (2017), https://pitt.hosted.panopto.com/Panopto/Pages/Viewer.aspx?id=fe7017c7-ccab-4e78-bb2c-c20e5be9f8af.

This video addresses racism in the courtroom and the racialized reality of why Black, Latino, and Native American people flee from police. Professor Gonzales Rose points out that Blacks are subject to force 3.6 times more often than whites and are 2.5 times more likely to be shot by the police. Native Americans are most likely to be shot and killed by police. Courts have recognized that flight is related to the desire to avoid racial profiling rather than the desire to hide criminal behavior.[36] On the other hand, white people are less likely to be subject to force and usually trust the police. There are more white officers than officers of color, leading to cross-racial eyewitness identification testimony against defendants of color.

False cross-racial eyewitness identifications based on bias, racism, and racial stereotypes are difficult to overcome.[37] Racial profiling is difficult to prove, as

36. *See* Commonwealth v. Warren, 58 N.E.3d. 333, 342 (Mass. 2016).

37. *Eyewitness Identification Reform*, The Innocence Project, https://innocenceproject.org/eyewitness-identification-reform/ (last visited Jan. 27, 2023).

statistics show that whiteness is seen as the norm and that white witnesses are seen as more trustworthy. Additionally, the cost of expert witnesses can be cost-prohibitive for the poor and defendants of color. To illustrate these issues, Gonzales Rose looks at the case *State v. Cotton*[38] through the memoir *Picking Cotton.*[39] In this case, Jennifer Thompson, a white rape victim, gave eyewitness testimony that helped convict Ronald Cotton, a Black man. The conviction was overturned after DNA evidence that showed another person had committed the crime. It took more than a decade to do so.[40] The book's website includes links to free downloads of documents from the original case file, which may be used as teaching materials.[41] Professor Gonzales Rose suggests changes to Rule 403, recognizes racialized realities, racism, and bias (individualized, systemic, unconscious, and conscious).

Ronald Wright, Public Records and Racial Disparities in Jury Selection—Ronald Wright, University of Pittsburgh School of Law—Center on Race and Social Problems Speaker Series (2019), https://pitt.hosted.panopto.com/Panopto/Pages/Viewer.aspx?id=5bb427f3-1054-47fe-a2c9-aa070103d201.

This video lecture addresses racial disparities in the jury selection process. Dean Wright discusses his five-year study to look for racial disparities in who serves on juries and who removes potential black jurors during the *voir dire* process. Despite *Batson v. Kentucky*[42] prohibiting exclusion from jury service based on race and gender, the speaker demonstrates a pattern of peremptory challenges that show jurors are being eliminated based on race. Dean Wright surveyed county courthouses in North Carolina to obtain juror data. His team gathered data on over 1,300 felony trials and over 290,000 prospective jurors. The study found that Black jurors were twice as likely to be removed from jurors than white jurors. Moreover, Black male jurors are excluded more frequently than Black female jurors.

Dean Wright provides a few solutions that can counteract issues of jurors being removed based on race, including limiting or eliminating peremptory challenges, or supercharging the rule of *Batson* to give judges more leverage when determining if the jurors are being removed based on their race.

Scott Fraser, *Why eyewitnesses get it wrong*, TED (2012) https://www.ted.com/talks/scott_fraser_why_eyewitnesses_get_it_wrong

Scientific evidence and studies in human memory and lawyers from the Innocence Project have used expert witnesses and the study of forensics to free

38. 394 S.E.2d 456 (N.C. 1990).

39. Jennifer Thompson-Cannino, Ronald Cotton & Erin Torneo, Picking Cotton: Our Memoir of Injustice and Redemption (2010).

40. *See Ronald Cotton Celebrates 24th Exoneration Anniversary*, The Innocence Project, https://innocenceproject.org/cases/ronald-cotton/ (last visited Jan. 27, 2023).

41. Picking Cotton—Explore the Case File, https://www.pickingcottonbook.com/case-file.

42. 476 U.S. 79 (1986).

dozens of wrongfully convicted defendants. Fraser, a forensic neurophysiologist and scientific expert, has worked extensively in the field of witness memory. He also uses tools like lunar data, special cameras, and high-speed film to recreate crime scenes.

Fraser stressed that memories are reconstructed, and therefore volatile and fallible. His talk centers around the case of Francisco Carillo. Carillo was convicted of a drive-by shooting murder and sentenced to life in prison due to the false eyewitness testimony of the victim's son and his friends. Carillo had been added to the photo lineup by police who had previously mistaken Carillo as a shooter in another incident. No gun was ever found, and no vehicle was ever identified.

The Innocence Project took on the case after Carillo had served over a decade in prison,[43] and brought in Fraser as the expert witness. Fraser was able to show that it was impossible to have made an eyewitness identification because it was too dark. Carillo's conviction was overturned, finally freeing him after 20 years.

Podcasts

Excited Utterance, https://excitedutterance.com.

Excited Utterance is an evidence law podcast from Vanderbilt Law School that began in 2016. The podcast is updated weekly throughout the academic year. Each episode lasts approximately a half-hour—each on a different topic or issue affecting evidence law. The podcast also presents periodic virtual workshops.

On-topic episodes include: episode #112: Itiel Dror discusses cognitive bias in forensic pathology decisions; episode #94: Jeffrey Belin highlights his work about how evidence Rule 609 leads to the conviction of innocent defendants;[44] episode #72: Morgan Birck discusses problems with juror bias in viewing body-camera evidence; and episode #43: Christine Ruva speaks about her work on bias and pretrial publicity.[45]

---

43. *See California Exoneree Featured in Netflix Series "The Innocence Files,"* The Innocence Project (Apr. 1, 2020), https://innocenceproject.org/california-exoneree-franky-carrillo-netflix-series-the-innocence-files/.

44. *See* Jeffrey Bellin, *The Evidence Rules that Convict the Innocent*, 106 Cornell L. Rev. 305 (2021).

45. *See, e.g.*, Christine Ruva, *From the Headlines to the Jury Room: An Examination of the Impact of Pretrial Publicity on Jurors and Juries*, *in* Advances in Psychology and Law 1–39 (M. Miller & B. Bornstein, eds., 2018).

Section 6

Family Law

Teaching Family Law Through the Lens of Minoritized Identities

*Jeffrey A. Dodge**

Introduction

Family law is a regularly tested subject on bar exams around the country. The field is also one of the most heavily practiced areas, especially outside large law firms and big cities. In fact, the reality is that nearly every law student has a point of reference from their own lives that connects to family law.

There is a fair bit of irony that, as a gay man, I now teach family law, an area of law that through my formative years excluded me from accessing the rights to marry and parent. This essay will start with my reflections on that perspective and how it influences my course design and delivery. While family law courses naturally lend themselves to important conversations around sex and gender, this essay will explore the importance of also incorporating present and past inequalities based on race, sexual orientation, disability, and more. The essay will share some of the inclusive teaching and learning practices employed in my classroom to create a supportive environment for difficult conversations. These efforts allow us to harness my experience and those of students from marginalized identities into meaningful, inclusive learning opportunities. The essay will then outline ways to design a course's reading assignments, teaching delivery, and assessments to integrate doctrine and diversity. Examples include the use of technology to start challenging conversations, using experiential assessments to bring current legal issues involving inequalities in family law to the classroom, and prioritizing historical and sociological contexts in the readings.

---

* Associate Dean for Academic Affairs, Assistant Professor of Law, and Joseph H. Goldstein Faculty Scholar, Penn State Dickinson Law. Special thanks to Coryn Hubbert, Taylor Mosley, Aria Plants, and Lucille Sherman, my research assistants from Penn State Dickinson Law, for their assistance with this essay and many other projects. Their thorough and expeditious support made this project possible. Thanks also to Suzanne Harrington-Steppen for her patience and support in the writing and editing process. I'm grateful to be included in this book.

Personal Perspective with Family Law

The rallying cry "the personal is political"[1] resonates with me deeply as it is part of my call to teach, research, and serve as a law professor. As a white cisgender man, I have many privileges in our society that enhance my social, legal, and political existence. My upbringing also included religious teachings and cultural practices from the Church of Jesus Christ of Latter-day Saints (popularly referred to as Mormonism[2]). That faith both insulated me from the diversity of the world around me and reinforced white savior[3] ideas that only through the spread of the teachings of Christ could "others" find salvation. I grew up unaware of the vast levels of privilege I carried in my life and, in many ways, perpetuated them in my youth. It wasn't until my own realization that I was gay that I began to understand the racist, patriarchal, and homophobic societal infrastructures that surrounded me.

Through my journey of self-discovery, I began to feel "othered" for the first time. The experience of coming out and having loved ones mourn my perceived lost potential strengthened how I see myself, the LBGTQIA+ community, family and friends, and others with minoritized identities. Concurrently with my personal exploration in college, I started the mind-shattering study of white privilege, fragility, and superiority, societal gender roles in family constructs, the destructive spread of Christianity, the shameful U.S. response to the AIDS crisis, and more.[4] Reasoning with our nation's difficult history was further influenced by my own activism in contemporary issues like affirmative action, bilingual education, marriage equality, and "Don't Ask, Don't Tell."

---

1. Popularized in the 1960s and 1970s, this phrase historically represented a challenge to the nuclear family, gender roles within the family, and family values more broadly. Carol Hanisch's essay by the same name is credited with popularizing the phrase although she actively refutes the assertion that she created it. *See* Carol Hanisch, *The Personal Is Political: The Women's Liberation Movement classic with a new explanatory introduction* (Jan. 2006), https://www.carolhanisch.org/CHwritings/PIP.html.

2. Elizabeth Dias, *"Mormon" No More: Faithful Reflect on Church's Move to Scrap a Moniker*, N.Y. Times (Jan. 20, 2023), https://www.nytimes.com/2019/06/29/us/mormon-church-name-change.html.

3. Rudyard Kipling's poem *The White Man's Burden* is one of the most recognized articulations of the white savior complex. In it, Kipling essentially characterizes the people of the Philippines as needing colonial control by the United States. The poem characterizes white people as having the burden of lifting up and supporting non-white people, thus a white savior. White savior complexes can be seen throughout world history from periods of colonialism to religious missionary work. It is worth noting that critics of our child welfare system rightly point out that the laws and processes are essentially acting as an institutional white savior given the disproportionate number of families of color under investigation.

4. I attended the University of California at San Diego's Thurgood Marshall College. A core general education requirement remains the three-quarter Dimensions of Culture course. The first quarter is focused on issues of Diversity, the second Justice, and the third Imagination and Action. The course reflects a commitment to social justice while enhancing critical thinking, reading, and writing skills. This course changed my perspective on the world around me in ways that inform my scholarship, teaching, and service today. Dimensions of Culture Program, https://marshall.ucsd.edu/doc/index.html (last visited Mar. 22, 2023).

Living through periods where my very own marriage and parenting fundamental rights have been unavailable or in question offers me a unique perspective on the subject of family law. In class, I share how I did not grow up thinking marriage or even a loving relationship would be something available to me. In fact, when I shared that I was gay there were some who worried I would meet the same untimely end as loved ones coming of age in the AIDS epidemic. The idea of having kids was even further from the realm of possibility. The trauma endured when seeing the Church I most closely associated with fund state and national efforts to prevent the expansion of those rights made the "culture war" around my existence feel lost before it began. It is only through my own journey of self-acceptance, societal defiance, and finding love that I came to the ability to engage in teaching and research matters of family law. It is the freedom to marry my husband and adopt two beautiful children that defined my motivation to center my family law course on the experiences of minoritized identities. Leading the course through this lens is all that makes sense to me.

Inclusive Teaching and Learning Practices

Inclusive teaching and learning practices are the subject of countless panels, speakers, and research nowadays. Weekly faculty in law schools are presented with opportunities to develop strategies that enhance the classroom experience for all. While many other practices exist, the one thing I have learned from nearly ten years of teaching is that faculty should lead classrooms with practices that challenge them to grow while being authentic to their voice.

In a family law course, it is especially important for the delivery of the material to invite students from all backgrounds and identities. Getting students engaged in the course as more than just bar exam testable material requires intentionality, though. The practices outlined below are the foundation of my approach.

Language

A cornerstone of creating an inclusive teaching and learning environment is the recognition that language matters. Word choices can have consequential impacts when navigating difficult conversations. They can reflect unintended meanings, implicit bias, and a closed mind without ever articulating those effects. Similarly, word choices can have the effect of welcoming engagement, making space for all views, and creating safety in our conversations. Introducing the importance of language is covered on my syllabus, on the first day of the class, and when approaching difficult topics and cases. My syllabus says the following:

> In any environment in which people gather to learn, it is essential that all members feel as free and safe as possible in their participation. To this end, it is expected that everyone in this course will be treated with mutual respect and civility, with an understanding that all of us (students, faculty, guests,

> and teaching assistants) will be respectful and civil to one another in language, in discussion, in action, in teaching, and in learning. There is an important line between challenging an idea and challenging the person who expresses that idea. Conflicting views will create dynamic discussions and help each of us refine our thinking. However, personal attacks whether express or subtle will stifle communication. Let us work together to think and speak critically of ideas and not of each other and be intentional about our language choices.

In addition to the above statement that I reinforce throughout the semester, I also draw on the culture of our institution to support inclusive learning. For the last few years I have led an inclusive classroom and difficult conversation workshop for new students. Over the course of an hour, I introduce our new colleagues to the exciting but challenging learning ahead of them. The workshop explores the need for more diversity in the legal profession, the importance of a class culture that supports everyone's academic progress, and some of the unique challenges identified for minoritized populations in law school. Along the way, the students interactively participate in the workshop by sharing some of themselves with their new classmates for the first time. The concluding activity asks the new class of students to identify values of inclusion that they can commit to while in law school. The values are then disseminated regularly for students, staff, and faculty to draw on in our teaching and learning practices. Recalling these values allows me to bring students' own commitments into the classroom in a way that replaces the "from the podium" feeling.

Finally, language choices are most effective when modeled for students. In my family law course, I seek to use words that reflect the inclusive culture, but also take moments to acknowledge failures. Based on the religious trauma I've experienced in the past, I have a difficult time validating elements of faith in cases. When I began teaching, I used callous word choices that invalidated the important role religion plays in some families. The language reflected my own experiences and thoughts, but did not invite inclusive conversations on the topic. A student anonymously pointed this out in a course evaluation and upon reflection I was more mindful moving forward. I share this experience with students to model that no one is perfect in this space and that what is important is how we grow moving forward.

Lived Experiences

Embedded in everyone's life experience is one or more touch points to topics in family law. Increasingly, more people grew up with family or friends who divorced or were the subject of child custody and support disputes. Many of my students themselves were directly impacted by family creation and dissolution circumstances. The study of family law is uniquely enhanced by creating an environment where these lived experiences provide illustration for the reading topics or help humanize an experience in a case. Drawing upon the lived experiences in the classroom harnesses the diversity of the class as a valuable resource in our learning.

To most effectively access the lived experiences of the class, I start each course unit by asking students to reflect on and share answers to big questions: What does it mean to be a family? What does marriage mean to them? What does divorce represent to them? What makes someone a parent? I let discussions around these topics really challenge the class to think legally, socially, culturally, religiously, and more about the answers. Inevitably, students share some of their lived experiences in their answers. Often students are surprised by the responses of their peers as they can directly contradict their own responses.

As examples, in fall 2022, I asked the class about marriage and an international student from Pakistan engaged in a fascinating comparative conversation with a Pakistani-American student from New York City. Their discussion was illustrative that even with the same ethnic origin, where they grew up made a huge difference in how cultural and religious beliefs entered their lives. In a conversation about parentage, a group of Black students shared experiences where relatives beyond their biological or legal parents held parenting roles in their lives. They bravely showed the class how culture influences a definition of a parent, and I was able to use that discussion as a way to show disconnects between law and policy. Lastly, discussions around what it means to be a family regularly involve members of the LGBTQIA+ community in the class sharing that family in the culturally and legally traditional sense may have less value to them. Their lived experiences may not evoke the same loving feelings toward biological and legal families, instead favoring self-selected family constructs. This conversation always brings different context to our statutory interpretation work on laws that define family.

Finally, welcoming students to share their lived experiences acknowledges an expertise they bring to our family law class and grows their confidence to engage with content where they do not have a personal point of reference. In my experience, students who feel valued in the classroom are more likely to volunteer to brief a case, share in the future, and remember the content they contributed to in class. Anecdotally, my shift from mostly lecture teaching to more of a hybrid discussion and lecture style has improved performances on assessments and resulted in more interest in family law as a practice area. I tell the students such to motivate their engagement and create comfort in our learning space.

Acknowledgements of Trauma

An important final point on creating an inclusive classroom is the acknowledgement of actual and potential trauma. As faculty and students bravely engage in teaching and learning with one another, it is important to remember that past trauma can cause harm when discussing related topics. For some of the same reasons where lived experiences are valuable in a family law course, they also need to be handled with care by a professor. When students open up to the class, we want that to be a valuable learning opportunity that doesn't trigger or retraumatize a student. Additionally, the family law course also includes topics that when discussed and assessed can touch on past trauma.

A first step in managing trauma is to acknowledge that we all carry some with us when entering the classroom. Saying that out loud begins making students feel seen in the class. I then invite students to leave the classroom, be silent in discussions, or engage in coping strategies when we touch on topics that may be difficult for them. This invitation is heard as welcome and acceptable and not something negative. Intentionally acknowledging trauma gives students the space to protect themselves without fear of faculty consequences.

As I turned to the divorce unit in a recent semester, a student visited with me after class to privately share that he was nervous about our equitable distribution and spousal support discussions. He shared that a close family member had just separated from their spouse and as that person's confidant he was enraged at the potential misjustice of the unfaithful spouse receiving property and funds. With tears in his eyes, he was clearly affected personally by the laws as applicable to his family member. This person's vicarious trauma felt understandable, and I invited him to leave the room if needed or watch the class recording on his own. I also made myself available to meet separately on the material. We left that conversation with the plan that he would listen for the next couple of classes instead of participating. Interestingly, the next two classes were his most active of the semester and he didn't say a word of context about his family member when doing so.

While there are inspiring times when acknowledging trauma allows someone to engage in unexpected ways, there are more instances where students need the comfort of the classroom culture just to exist.

Intentional Course Design

My family law course is intentionally designed to meet the following four learning objectives:

1. By the end of this course students should have a working understanding of the major themes and areas in family law, including a strong foundational knowledge for the bar exam.
2. Family law is different from many other areas of law and can often be seen as a "rules free zone" of the law. This is not to mean that there are no rules in family law. Rather there are rules that establish the context and shape the nature of the policies and controversies. Different from many other areas of law, the complexity of the human dynamics involved in many family law cases often means that the "rules" do not neatly resolve the issues. Students will develop a keen understanding of how the facts of the cases, family law policies, and cultural context interplay to resolve family law issues in a diverse society.
3. The practice of family law requires lawyers to interact with experts from other disciplines, in particular mediators, counselors, social workers, and

psychologists. Students will leave the class with a basic understanding of the interdisciplinary nature of family law practice and appreciate the value of others' expertise.

4. Lastly, the class is designed to encourage students to develop a variety of communication skills around family law topics. Assessments are intentionally multimodal ways for students to meet the learning objectives of the class. The Ripped from the Headlines presentation[5] will enhance students' oral communication skills. The memorandum, mid-term, experiential learning project, and final exam will enhance students' written communication skills through the knowledgeable analysis of family law itself as well as through legal research. To emulate the real-life demands of clients, all of these assessments require students to engage with difficult facts, diverse populations, and contemporary issues in family law.

To meet these objectives, the course draws upon a unique teaching pedagogy, curated reading assignments, and specially selected assessments to shape the learning experience. The section to follow will expound on the course design elements that guide students in meeting the learning objectives of the course.

Pedagogical Approach

The teaching pedagogy for family law is almost as important as the content of the course. The method of instruction intentionally relies on and builds space for student engagement in ways more like a seminar course. As unrelated to the teaching of law as it may sound, each class begins with music related to the topic of the day. Students report that they enjoy the diversity of music shared in the ten minutes leading up to class beginning. The music is also intentional as it gives the class some cultural context for reference later and allows for a wide breadth of music. The music also reflects the perspectives and lived experiences of the diverse artists featured. As an example, on the day we cover the fault-based divorce system I often play Outkast's "Ms. Jackson," Tammy Wynette's "D-I-V-O-R-C-E," and Dolly Parton's "Jolene." Less obviously connected to music, on the day we start our review of child support I play Brandy's "Baby Mama," The Temptations' "Papa Was a Rolling Stone," and Everclear's "Father of Mine." After teaching family law for so many years, I now have a catalog of songs to select from for nearly every topic. The hope is that students hear themselves in the selections and that it offers a window into the lived experience of others.

I use the songs of the day as a reference point to transition into our material. Each class begins with an interactive activity on Nearpod[6] that requires every student to

5. *See infra* Part III, Assessments.

6. Nearpod is a classroom learning tool that allows instructors to create interactive classes through games and activities. Students can log into Nearpod through phones, tablets, and laptops to participate in my question of the day. The system also doubles as my attendance tool as a report is generated indicating who participated that day. *See* NEARPOD.COM (last visited Feb. 6, 2023).

answer a question, share a thought, or reflect on a discussion prompt. Nearpod allows for a variety of ways for us to engage with one another, including collaboration boards, matching pair games, polls, and competition games driven by multiple-choice responses. I have three substantive purposes at play for these activities: to refresh our understanding of previously covered material, to help us frame new material for the day, and to check in or receive feedback on how the class is going. After students respond, I review the results and often ask students to share why they put what they did. In addition to having pedagogical value, the Nearpod activity also serves as my way to take attendance. Participation in these activities at the start of each class is required to count a student present.

After my class start-up rituals, we begin the content of the day. I intentionally teach family law in a hybrid lecture and seminar style. Meaning that while the content I share through lectures and PowerPoint slides is important, equally so is student engagement and sharing. I invite students to bring things they know from their own lives or popular culture to discussions so we can contextualize family law as people perceive it in society. I also often break the class into small group discussions, especially on topics and cases with greater sensitivity, and let them learn from each other more directly. Sometimes I will even prepare hypotheticals as ways to practice understanding and skills. These hypotheticals challenge students to think more deeply about the inequitable impact of family law on diverse families and unique circumstances. These group activities then result in a coming back together as a whole class for additional sharing and reflection.

A student from my fall 2022 class recently shared that they were clerking for a local judge who primarily dealt with family law matters. She thought that the material for the class was retained because, in her opinion, my teaching approach made the content memorable and relatable. Intertwining doctrine and diversity in how the class is presented is at the cornerstone of my pedagogical approach and, as anecdotally evidenced here, makes it more accessible in a practice environment too.

Reading Assignments

My family law course's reading assignments are intentionally selected to reflect testable material on the bar exam, the legal arch of family formation and dissolution, and a range of related topics with implications for diverse and minoritized populations. The course begins with marriage, navigates to divorce, spends time on parenting, child support and custody, and spousal support, and ends with family contracts and jurisdiction. After syllabus review, the course begins our semester-long work by discussing what it means to be married. The responses usually begin by citing the assigned reading materials, but ultimately drift deeper into a discussion about the cultural, religious, and political relationship the class has with the act of marriage. The question provides a referential point of understanding that the class harkens back to throughout the semester. Connected discussions are also had around divorce and parenting, each similarly defined by participants' background, identity, and values. These framing conversations then naturally guide discussion when looking at the *Loving*[7] and *Obergefell*[8] cases on marriage, *Roe*[9] and *Dobbs*[10] on reproductive choice, *Palmore*[11] on race and child custody, and *Brackeen*[12] on adoption and the Indian Child Welfare Act.[13] Reading assignments on difficult topics that intersect with minoritized identities both challenge the class to think critically about the legal issues in question as well as contemplate their own role as attorneys working with a diverse future client base.

Prior to fall 2022, the course did very little to directly address questions of reproductive choice as previously settled by *Roe v. Wade*. In a post-*Dobbs* era, the class would feel incomplete without a discussion of the material alongside topics like unwed fathers and the establishment of functional families. *Roe* and *Dobbs* are not just important cases for our study of family law but have broader implications for people capable of giving birth. The actual opinions and what they tell us about reproductive choice rights are critical to parse out. I start the conversation by pointing out that many of the assumptions in family law are predicated on a parent choosing to give birth and care for a child's needs. Post-*Dobbs* we see the potential for a rise in the involuntary nature of parenthood in our country, especially for people already experiencing the negative effects of health inequity. Additionally, the readings lend themselves to deeper conversations about reproductive justice, the presence of male identifying transgender identities capable of giving birth, and more. While this section of the class may be sensitive to navigate for some, it is important to engage in the varied dimensions of diversity it presents. The topic also gives me, as a cisgender male, the opportunity to reflect on the importance of allyship and advocacy for the rights of others as well a space to acknowledge my own societal privilege.

Assessments

Assessments for the family law course are intentionally constructed to give students multimodal opportunities to demonstrate knowledge and skills. More specifically, assessments ensure that varied types of learners have ways to not just read and write about the law, but also hear and speak about it. Keeping in mind that family law is currently a tested subject on the bar exam, the midterm and final exam seek to assess students' knowledge and skills in more traditional approaches. The midterm involves a detailed hypothetical modeled after the essay format used on the Multistate Essay Exam (MEE). Grading and feedback are focused both on the substance of the responses, but also on the writing structure used to communicate. Believing strongly that mid-semester assessments should not preordain final grades, students are told that

7. Loving v. Virginia, 388 U.S. 1 (1967).
8. Obergefell v. Hodges, 576 U.S. 644 (2015).
9. Roe v. Wade, 410 U.S. 113 (1973).
10. Dobbs v. Jackson Women's Health Org., 597 U.S. ___, 142 S. Ct. 2228 (2022).
11. Palmore v. Sidoti, 466 U.S. 429 (1984).
12. Brackeen et al. v. Haaland et al., 994 F.3d 249 (5th Cir. 2021).
13. Indian Child Welfare Act of 1978, 25 U.S.C. § 1902–1963.

improvement in both knowledge and skills on the final exam will be considered in grading. This motivates students of varied midterm performance levels to seek specific feedback to improve as they are motivated by the potential of a reward to do better. The three hypothetical final exam questions, similarly modeled after MEE questions, allow students to practice again with demonstrating knowledge in a way the bar examiners will require of them in the future.

In addition to the midterm and final exam, students are asked to do two other assessments. The Ripped from the Headlines Project requires students to collaborate in a group of three to four on both a presentation and an eight-page memorandum. The goal of the assignment is to have self-selected groups look more closely at headline-making family law issues around the country and world. Student groups must identify a current family law matter making headlines, research further into the legal aspects in controversy, and provide thoughtful analysis to the class via an eight-to-ten-minute presentation. Aligned with Penn State Dickinson Law's antiracism commitments,[14] students are further instructed to select family law matters that involve diverse or minoritized populations and issues. Presentations are scheduled at the start of the second class meeting each week. After the presentation, the students in the class ask questions and provide feedback to the presenters. This gives the class an opportunity to engage further with the topic as well as help the group think more deeply about the topic. The memorandum is then due early in the week after the presentation. In it, students must demonstrate their understanding of the legal issues, display sufficient legal research to support their analysis, and employ legal citation formatting (Bluebook). The Ripped from the Headlines Project has been well received by students as it gives them agency to explore contemporary topics of interest. It also challenges students to think critically about law and policy in the context of impacting diverse and minoritized populations. By letting the students select their own topic, they are more interested in the matters they are exploring, well researched about the discriminatory effects, and prepared to engage their colleagues in a brief discussion around what might otherwise be seen as a sensitive or difficult issue. This weekly peer modeling provides the instructor room to expound on issues not in the casebook without perceptions of an agenda. It also can lead to deeper conversations about material assigned in the class.

In addition to the Ripped from the Headlines Project, students are also asked to complete an experiential learning activity focused on the development of a settlement agreement. Students are randomly assigned a partner to represent the interests of a client in a hypothetical case file. Students negotiate in pairs with another duo of students in the class to prepare a settlement agreement that reflects the varied parties' interests. The experiential learning project is conducted in the last month of class and, as a result, has the added benefit of preparing the students for the final exam. The case file covers a broad range of considerations in divorce, like child custody, spousal support, child support, and equitable distribution. The potential for bias is also contemplated when

---

14. *Antiracism Development Institute*, PENN STATE DICKINSON LAW (Jan. 19, 2023), https://dickinsonlaw.psu.edu/antiracist-development-institute.

designing the hypothetical by intentionally selecting names, pronouns, and facts that challenge attorneys to think beyond majority identities. Students are instructed first to contemplate the interests of their clients with their co-counsel before turning to the negotiation of the settlement agreement. By requiring students to work with colleagues, the activity is designed to normalize and professionalize discussions around the potential for bias against their client as part of their assessment of the interests. Students are recognized for considering both the facts that are useful and harmful to these interests as well as for offering legal strategies in their negotiations to mitigate them.

Conclusion

It is difficult to fully assess whether the class as designed is resonating with students, but some anecdotal evidence indicates success. The course's enrollment is always one of the highest in the second- and third-year curriculum. It has reached enrollment capacities and maintained a waitlist. Most importantly to me, the students enrolled in the course reflect the gender, racial, and sexual orientation diversity of the student body. Word of mouth among students is rumored to be strong for the course both as a measure of preparation for the bar exam and for the approachable course design. Over 90% of enrolled students complete the course evaluations each semester and the results are almost unanimously positive. Constructive student feedback is incorporated into the course design for future semesters and students are informed that the feedback on their evaluations has an impact. Student interest in family law has grown and the law school adopted a certificate program to meet student demand. Interest in related curricular offerings like our clinics and seminars also grew as have co- and extracurricular opportunities through CASA,[15] the Pennsylvania Bar Association, and more. I point to all of this simply to acknowledge that something in the class is resonating and we're seeing it materialize in a number of ways.

15. CASA stands for Court Appointed Special Advocates. Volunteers who serve in CASA roles are appointed by judges to advocate for the best interest of children in the legal system due to alleged abuse or neglect at home. This is a national program run through regional nonprofit organizations.

Teaching Reproductive Justice Lawyering in Family Law: Moving Toward a Race-Conscious Curriculum

*Brittany L. Raposa**

Introduction

We are currently in a period where family planning and reproductive rights are under attack in the United States, both at the federal and state levels. The United States Supreme Court invalidated nearly 50 years of abortion and bodily autonomy precedent when it overturned *Roe v. Wade* and *Planned Parenthood v. Casey* in *Dobbs v. Jackson Women's Health Organization.*[1] Even prior to this decision, when reproductive rights were facing immense challenges in 2019, fewer than one-third of law schools offered classes on the topics of reproductive health and law.[2] Unfortunately, most law schools do not include reproductive rights and/or justice and intersectional discussions as part of their curriculum.[3] However, law schools must prepare their students to engage in reproductive justice advocacy. The upper-level family law course is a tremendous avenue to teach reproductive rights, justice, and reproductive justice lawyering into the law school curriculum.

Reproductive justice centers on the notion that all people should be able to make decisions about their families.[4] The reproductive justice framework has its origins in communities that have experienced intersecting layers of oppression and is grounded

---

* Adjunct Professor, Roger Williams University School of Law.

1. Dobbs v. Jackson Women's Health Org., 142 S. Ct. 2228 (2022).

2. Nina Henry, *Law schools are failing to prepare the next generation of leaders in reproductive rights and justice*, The Lily (Jan. 24, 2022), https://www.thelily.com/law-schools-are-failing-to-prepare-the-next-generation-of-leaders-in-reproductive-rights-and-justice/.

3. *Id.*

4. Loretta J. Ross & Rickie Solinger, Reproductive Justice: An Introduction 9 (2017).

in the idea of changing structural power inequities to achieve social justice.[5] Lawyering for reproductive justice is critical, especially now with state and national restrictions on access to abortion and contraception.[6] In family law—the body of law centered on governing the family—it is imperative that lawyers listen to and support reproductive justice activism, especially for women of color, the LGBTQ+ community, and low-income individuals.

While this essay does not cover every area of family law where reproductive justice may be taught—as it may be taught in many areas—it focuses on the areas that are prominent and good starting points. In addition, it is also important to note that this essay only incorporates the concept of reproductive justice as it relates to race. However, reproductive justice is a framework that is also utilized for low-income individuals, individuals in the LGBTQ+ community, and individuals from other oppressed groups.[7] First, this essay will describe the reproductive justice framework and will discuss the concept of reproductive justice lawyering. It will suggest ways professors may incorporate teaching this concept in their family law courses. Next, this essay will provide key sections of family law in which professors can incorporate teaching the law from a reproductive justice framework, which further teaches students how to engage in reproductive justice lawyering. Each section includes a series of sample discussion questions to use when integrating reproductive justice into family law courses.

What Is Reproductive Justice Lawyering?

The reproductive justice framework specifically asks whether the outcomes are tied to "the inequality of opportunities that we have to control our reproductive destiny."[8] The reproductive justice movement, founded by women of color, merges reproductive health and rights and social justice to achieve reproductive justice.[9] It has three main principles: (1) the right not to have a child; (2) the right to have a child; and (3) the right to parent children in safe and healthy communities.[10] In addition, "reproductive justice demands sexual autonomy and gender freedom for every human being."[11] Reproductive justice asserts the claim that "all fertile persons and persons who reproduce and become parents require a safe and signified context for these most fundamental

---

5. *Id.*

6. *See* Laura Deal, Cong. Rsch. Serv., LSB10779, State Laws Restricting or Prohibiting Abortion, Congressional Research Service (2022), crsreports.congress.gov/product/pdf/LSB/LSB10779.

7. In my family law course, we discuss how these other communities are impacted and look at their experiences from a reproductive justice lens. For purposes of this essay, however, I will only focus on incorporating race in key areas within the family law curriculum.

8. *Id.*

9. Ross & Solinger, *supra* note 4, at 68–69.

10. Loretta Ross, *Understanding Reproductive Justice: Transforming the Pro-Choice Movement*, Sister Song (May 2013), https://d3n8a8pro7vhmx.cloudfront.net/rrfp/pages/33/attachments/original/1456425809/Understanding_RJ_Sistersong.pdf?1456425809.

11. *Id.*

human experiences."[12] As a result, the family law class does not simply focus just on whether someone has a reproductive right. Instead, we are incorporating issues such as access to healthcare, housing and education, health of communities, the environment, and more. We are looking at the cases we read and are not only asking what the court's ruling was, but we are also looking at the conditions of the parties in their communities and asking whether the outcome was a product of inequality.

First, it's important that students learn the difference between reproductive rights and reproductive justice. Reproductive rights are based on the idea that everyone should have the right to make decisions about their reproduction freely, without interference from other individuals or government. Traditionally in the United States, the reproductive rights movement has focused on the right to access contraception and abortion.[13] This movement was largely led by white women, and isolated the issues of contraception and abortion from other imperative social justice issues that impact communities of color: economic justice, environmental justice, disability rights, discrimination based on race and sexual orientation, and other similar concerns.[14] Instead of looking at whether an individual has a right to make a decision, the reproductive justice framework focuses on reproductive oppression—"the control and exploitation of women, girls and individuals through our bodies, sexuality, labor and reproduction."[15]

Reproductive justice lawyering takes *intersectionality* into account—recognizing that women and families of color have been harmed by activism that fails to recognize interacting identities. In reproductive health advocacy throughout United States history, the impact of issues on women of color have been overshadowed because arguments were designed for white women and failed to account for the access needs of others.[16] Therefore, reproductive justice lawyering commits to advocating for improved policies and laws in such a way that centers the experience of individuals of color, low-income individuals, and for all individuals regardless of sexual orientation. Essentially, lawyers must uplift and support the voices of those who are from oppressed communities. This gives the family law class a framework with which to look at law throughout the course of the semester:

1. Which structural and systemic issues need to be addressed in order to support reproductive rights?
2. How do race, sexual orientation, class, and other axes of difference impact reproductive health and family decisions and outcomes?

---

12. *Id.*

13. Gemma Donofrio, *Exploring the Role of Lawyers in the Reproductive Justice Movement*, 42 N.Y.U. Rev. L. & Soc. Change 221, 228 (2018).

14. Ross, *supra* note 10.

15. *Id.*

16. Kimberlé Crenshaw, *Mapping the Margins: Intersectionality, Identity Politics, and Violence Against Women of Color*, 43 Stan L. Rev. 1241, 1253–58 (1991).

3. How have power relations within family law related to the historical oppression contributed to the systematic devaluation and regulation of oppressed communities' role in the notion of family?

How does this framework relate to family law? Family law involves the legal regulation of the family and its members, and these members include husband, wife, parent, and child, and even significant others whose relationships push family law beyond its traditional notion of what it means to be a family. Reproductive justice, which is the decision to have a child, to not have a child, and to raise our children safely, directly relates to family decision-making and nearly all aspects of family law. A fundamental area we look at in family law is how the law allocates responsibility for decision making about private family matters. History, systematic inequality, and oppression have influenced family laws and have certainly influenced the outcome of family law cases. Further, race, class, gender, sexual orientation, and other categories have challenged conceptions of the family and parenthood. Reproductive justice is therefore a core family law issue.

In this vein, we spend our first class discussing the role of a family law attorney, as well as the perspectives upon which we are going to look at family law throughout the semester—through the reproductive justice framework above. Beginning the class this way has another tremendous benefit, outside of pedagogy, because it sets the tone for the class: it lets students know we are going to be discussing issues of inequality, race, and social justice throughout our course. I explicitly tell the students we are going to not only be learning the law, but also how the law is applied and how it incorporates inequality, race, and social justice.

Throughout the rest of this essay, I will provide three examples within the family law curriculum where this framework can be used effectively. Within each area, I will also provide sample discussion questions I have used in my course to engage students and bring discussions of reproductive justice into the classroom, moving toward a race-conscious curriculum.[17]

17. I provide the students with discussion questions before class. I do this so students can think about these issues while they are completing the reading and can come prepared for class discussion of what may be difficult topics.

Incorporating Reproductive Justice Lawyering into Family Law to Integrate Issues of Race into the Curriculum

The Enslaved Body: Historical Roots of Family Law

After our first class discussing the role of the family law attorney and reproductive justice lawyering, the next class week is titled "The Historical Roots of Family Law." Specifically, we discuss the terms "family" and "mother" and how these terms have been construed in our nation's history dating back to slavery. To look at this, we read an excerpt from Rickie Solinger's book, *Pregnancy and Power*.[18] I use a portion of the book to teach about the treatment of female slaves and slaveholders' breeding schemes, the taking of Native American children from their families in the nineteenth century, and the sterilization of poor and Latina women in the 1970s.[19] Overall, I teach the concept that race and class have been at the center of the effort to control sex, pregnancy, and the notion of family in America over time.

Students must understand the oppressive systems in which women of color were placed in order to understand how current family laws and court decisions are biased against them due to systemic inequalities. In summary, the Black female body was seen as property to a slaveholder, and any children of the Black female became a profit. Therefore, Black women did not have control over their bodies, their families, or their reproductive choices. In addition, Native American women were considered unfit mothers and many lost their children to boarding schools. Further, Black, Native American, and Latina women were forced to undergo involuntary sterilization, completely losing their ability to create a family and make any reproductive choice. Family laws were created and evolved when these practices were in place, and this reading and lesson allows students to see how individuals within these marginalized groups are oppressed under current family laws and practices. As a result, I teach how the meanings of "mother" and "family" vary across national, racial, cultural, gendered, religious, and political boundaries.

Ultimately, beginning the course with this lesson will allow students to see how the foundation of many areas of family law are rooted in the effort to control sex, pregnancy, and family for individuals of color. Beginning with this history sets the foundation for the course—how those in our history who were vulnerable without institutionalized power continue to be in the probate and family court system.[20]

18. RICKIE SOLINGER, PREGNANCY AND POWER (2007).

19. This book discusses many historical timelines, and a faculty member can choose which portions of history they would like to focus on for their course.

20. There are many examples where we see those who are vulnerable without institutionalized power continue to be oppressed by certain family laws. For example, when teaching child custody, the

Discussion Questions:

1. In what ways do you think slavery, genocide, and eugenics may influence current family law policies and rulings?
2. What does "motherhood" mean? What is society's definition of "parent"?
3. What is your definition of family? What do you think the government's definition of family is?

Privacy Rights and Family Law's Future: Teaching *Dobbs v. Jackson Women's Health Organization*

Teaching *Dobbs v. Jackson Women's Health Organization*,[21] the new decision overturning *Roe v. Wade*, is critical to a family law course. Not only is teaching the decision important, but teaching and discussing the disproportionate impact this decision will have on communities of color, low-income communities, and the LGBTQ+ community is also essential to their understanding of family law and policies. This lesson, titled "Privacy Rights and Family Privacy," should be taught in the beginning of the semester, as the *Dobbs* decision has a potential impact on family law topics likely covered throughout the semester, including interracial marriage, same-sex marriage, and the right to parent.

Traditionally, the decisions of the family were viewed as private, and the Supreme Court expanded the notion of privacy when it made abortion a private choice in *Roe v. Wade*.[22] The Court in *Roe* held that the substantive due process right to privacy encompasses a woman's right to choose to terminate her pregnancy.[23] Despite establishing abortion as a fundamental right, I focus on the fact that the Court interpreted the Constitution as not requiring the government to establish women's positive rights to reproductive health care. Instead, it established a negative right, holding that a woman's right to choose had to be left alone by the government. The decision balanced the new abortion right against the government's interest in fetal life and the physician's authority over women's pregnancies, leaving deep holes in the capacity of many women to make their own decisions.[24] After *Roe*, reproductive rights remained conditional, dependent upon a woman's access to money and other resources.

The students should see how *Roe v. Wade* not only had its limitations in relation to certain populations of individuals, but also how it was always in jeopardy because the cases that came after it worked to slowly erode the "fundamental right" to an abortion and reproductive choice. Therefore, these cases should be taught from this erosion

---

course can discuss how men and women of color are imprisoned at a highly disproportionate rate, and this directly impacts their right to parent and reproduce.

21. 142 S. Ct. 2228 (2022).
22. Roe v. Wade, 410 U.S. 113 (1973).
23. *Id.* at 154.
24. *Id.*

perspective.[25] In *Planned Parenthood v. Casey*, the Court overturned *Roe's* central holding, where the Court was mistaken in *Roe* when it classified a woman's decision to terminate her pregnancy as a 'fundamental right.'"[26] *Casey* worked to weaken reproductive choice by implementing the "undue burden" standard where states' regulations regarding abortion are constitutional so long as they do not place an undue burden on a woman seeking the procedure.[27]

In *Dobbs*, despite Justice Alito's assurance that "[n]othing in this opinion should be understood to cast doubt on precedents that do not concern abortion,"[28] the Court's decision in *Dobbs* implicates other fundamental rights, including rights to contraception, interracial and same-sex marriage, sexual intimacy, and parental rights. It's important to explain to the students that, according to Justice Alito, there is no constitutional protection for abortion rights because the right to an abortion is not explicitly enumerated in the Constitution and is not "deeply rooted" in the history and traditions of the United States.[29] However, the same could be said for contraception, interracial and same-sex marriage, sexual intimacy, and parental rights. In his concurrence, Justice Thomas acknowledges the implications of other fundamental rights and calls upon the Court to reconsider and "correct the error" of its substantive due process precedents.[30]

The important part of the *Dobbs* discussion in the family law classroom is also the disproportionate impact it will have on certain communities, and I provide students with a reading, "What Are the Implications of the Overturning of *Roe v. Wade* for Racial Disparities?"[31] With this reading, we can see how *Dobbs* may impact individuals and communities of color with devastating consequences. As we have not yet seen all the implications and impact of *Dobbs*, this area of law remains unsettled. This allows students to analyze how this decision may impact certain areas of family law.

Discussion Questions:

1. What does *Dobbs* say about valuing the decision to parent? What values does the case uphold, and how do these values conflict with the decision to parent?
2. How will *Dobbs* have a disproportionate impact on certain communities? Which communities can you identify and what impact can you foresee?

---

25. *See* Timeline of Important Reproductive Freedom Cases Decided by the Supreme Court, ACLU, https://www.aclu.org/timeline-important-reproductive-freedom-cases-decided-supreme-court [https://perma.cc/32P2-5LKJ] (last visited Feb. 8, 2023).

26. Planned Parenthood of Se. Pa. v. Casey, 505 U.S. 833, 944, 953 (1992) (Rehnquist, J., concurring in judgment in part and dissenting in part).

27. *Id.* at 922.

28. Dobbs v. Jackson Women's Health Organization, 142 S. Ct. 2228, 2277–78 (2022).

29. *Id.* at 2242.

30. *Id.* at 2301. This includes Griswold v. Connecticut, 381 U.S. 479 (1965) (right to contraception), Lawrence v. Texas, 539 U.S. 558 (2003) (sexual intimacy), and Obergefell v. Hodges, 576 U.S. 644 (2015) (same-sex marriage).

31. Samantha Artiga et al., *What Are the Implications of the Overturning of* Roe v. Wade *for Racial Disparities?* KAISER FAMILY FOUNDATION, https://www.kff.org/racial-equity-and-health-policy/issue-brief/what-are-the-implications-of-the-overturning-of-roe-v-wade-for-racial-disparities/.

3. Which aspects of family law can this decision impact outside of the choice to reproduce?
4. Does anyone have reproductive freedom in the United States? If so, who?

Child Custody and Termination of Parental Rights

Reproductive justice is premised on two central ideas: first, that access to comprehensive healthcare, including reproductive health care, is a human right, and second, that neither this nor any other human right can achieve the status of a right if it does not apply to all people equally. In my first child custody class, I assign a chapter from Loretta Ross and Rickie Solinger's book called *The Right to Parent.*[32] This reading describes how certain parents, particularly parents of color and parents from a low socioeconomic status, are quick to be labeled unfit, losing custody of their children and rights to their children at higher rates than their middle- to upper-class white counterparts.[33]

At the center of every child custody dispute is the "best interests of the child" standard, which is quite subjective. When discussing the best interests of the child standard, it's important to incorporate the discussion of race and the role it plays in judicial decision-making. To do this, my lesson leads with the case of *Palmore v. Sidoti.*[34] This case deals with taking custody from a mother because of her remarriage to a person of a different race, and whether a child's welfare is jeopardized when a parent is in a relationship with an individual of a different race. The Supreme Court explicitly stated that the issue is "whether the reality of private biases and the possible injury they might inflict are permissible considerations for removal of an infant child from the custody of [a parent]."[35] The Court ultimately held that the effects of racial prejudice cannot justify a racial classification removing an infant child from the custody of their natural parent who would otherwise be fit to have custody despite their relationship with someone of a different race.[36]

This case then leads to a good discussion of how the family court system has treated parents of color and how bias may exist for parents of color when making custody or parental rights determinations. Prior to this decision, courts could have considered race as one single factor in determining a child's best interests. Students are typically surprised by this, and it evolves into a discussion about how race and bias still may play a factor in a court's decision, even though it is not a factor that is to be considered. We then discuss how reproductive justice lawyering—bringing race to the court's attention in the family court—can be one way to combat these biases and bring issues into the court system.

---

32. Ross & Solinger, *supra* note 4, at 168–188.
33. *Id.*
34. 466 U.S. 429 (1984).
35. Palmore v. Sidoti, 466 U.S. 429 (1984).
36. *Id.* at 434.

How parents lose custody, via terminating parental rights, is also a tremendous reproductive justice issue. The family law semester typically ends with the discussion of termination of parental rights. Bringing the class back to the discussion of privacy, I remind them that in the *Dobbs* decision, Justice Alito presented parental relinquishment as an alternative to abortion access. However, the conditions that lead to the relinquishment of children are shaped by the inequitable hierarchies and oppressive systems that we discuss throughout the semester. I provide the students with an interesting reading that looks at child relinquishment and the foster care system through a reproductive justice lens.[37] As we see in other areas discussed in this essay, throughout the family law course reproductive control and violence commonly intersect the lives of Black women, who are disproportionately in the prison system and in the family policing system.

Discussion Questions:

1. How does the best interests of the child standard in custody determinations allow for biases about race?
2. How much should a court weigh the factor of promoting a child's cultural and racial heritage?
3. What are some examples of where a judge may be biased regarding race in a family law case, and how can reproductive justice lawyering work to combat this bias?

Final Considerations

While teaching family law in this way is a step in the right direction for the law school curriculum, its implementation does not go without difficulties. First, I have experienced other faculty feedback with regard to this curricular approach, worrying that it is taking away from teaching students what they need to know for the bar exam. Specifically, faculty have expressed that I would not be able to cover all of the topics tested in family law on the bar exam, since it is incorporated into the essay portion of the exam. However, incorporating issues of race and social justice does not have to come at the expense of teaching the material tested on the bar exam. In fact, incorporating the laws the students are responsible for knowing on the bar exam is an important component of the course for me. The scope of the doctrinal law I teach in the course covers the entire scope of what is tested on the bar exam. Further, I provide students with writing assessments throughout the semester to test their understanding of the law, and I use prior bar exam essays released by the National Conference of Bar Examiners to do so. Both goals of teaching reproductive justice and bar readiness can be accomplished in this course.

---

37. Caitlin Becker et al., *Healthy Mothers, Healthy Babies: A Reproductive Justice Response to the "Womb-to-Foster-Care" Pipeline*, 20 CUNY L. Rev. 77 (2016).

Because we do discuss a lot of these social justice issues throughout the semester, a question I receive from students is whether they will have to analyze problems from a reproductive justice lens on their final exam. My final exam consists of two types of exam questions: (1) bar exam-style questions and (2) practical questions. Students analyze problems through a reproductive justice lens on my exam in a practical question, where I give them a fact pattern consisting of a real-life client who has come to them for assistance with a family law matter. The call of the question in that fact pattern typically reads, "How would you advise your client on all of their issues, approaching their case from a reproductive justice lens?" Students are then able to apply what we learned all semester to a hypothetical client problem.

Finally, I have not received much student push-back in the way I teach family law. In fact, most students appreciate looking at family law issues through this social justice lens. In student evaluations, they have used words like "practical," "real," and "important" to describe the incorporation of the reproductive approach. Some students have commented that it's "too much" talk of societal issues rather than law, and I continue to structure the course in a way where there is a balance. While reproductive justice issues can arguably be taught in every area of family law covered in the course, I incorporate it where the issues are the most prominent.[38]

Incorporating the concepts of reproductive justice and reproductive justice lawyering may be challenging at first, mainly because these issues are sensitive and can be difficult to discuss. However, as we move forward in this country in light of current attacks on family planning and reproductive freedom, we must train our students to be conscious of reproductive justice principles when practicing law. Incorporating these conversations in family law, for example, may allow a student to see how it relates to other areas of law throughout their courses in law school. Many issues relate to our ability to parent safely—housing conditions, food security, employment discrimination, criminal law, and incarceration, and so on. Having one course that at least incorporates reproductive justice truly helps students once they become attorneys.

---

38. I frequently incorporate reproductive justice in the following topics in my class (not including the topics discussed in this Essay): intimate partner violence, marriage, child support, the foster care system, and adoption.

Family Law Bibliography

Margaret (Meg) Butler[*]

Introduction

At the intersection of public and private, family law presents innumerable opportunities to consider issues of diversity, equity, and inclusion in the context of specific legal issues. Legal scholars and others have questioned some family law practices, such as the historic practice of a wife's prior interest in personal or real property merging with that of the husband on marriage, much longer than more recently raised issues such as the rights of disputing divorced parents to make medical determinations regarding puberty blockers and related hormone treatment for their transgender minor children.

Although family law is frequently imagined as the law regarding marriage, divorce, and the custody of any children of the marriage, the bounds extend further.[1] Exploration of diversity, equity, and inclusion in family law necessarily takes a broader view. One topic from this perspective would be described as the making of families, which includes pre-and post-marital contracts, parenting agreements among single people, ownership, custody, or adoption of embryos, surrogacy, posthumous conception, disabled peoples' rights to access birth control or marry, a woman's rights during pregnancy, etc. Children's rights issues may be considered family law matters, perhaps because the rights of children and their parents' rights may blur and overlap or become more distinct and independent as children age. This bibliography does not extend to include criminal law matters involving children as perpetrators or victims, though it does extend to consideration of the rights to create families including children.

Society may have a duty to protect children, the elderly, or others who cannot protect themselves. However, because members of each of those classes (children, elderly, others) typically have family members who may also wish to offer protection, these

---

* Associate Director for Public Services, Georgia State University College of Law Library.

1. Family law casebooks have changed their coverage from the 1960s to the 2010s to expand beyond the basic issues of marriage, divorce, alimony, and child custody and support, though bar exams focus on those core topics. *See* Laura T. Kessler, *Family Law by the Numbers: The Story That Casebooks Tell*, 62 ARIZ. L. REV. 903, 949 (2020).

issues sometimes are considered by the same sources as family law matters. For example, conservatorship, guardianship, and estate planning matters often implicate family relationships. The issues of family abuse, whether domestic violence (a broad topic), child abuse and protection, and elder abuse affect all types of people and families. Legal scholars critically analyze whether the legal systems' protections are fair, just, equitable, effective, and moral and offer suggestions ranging from minor tweaks to entirely new legislative schemes. This bibliography primarily addresses pedagogical and related concerns about the ways the law is used to protect minors.

With the recognition of marriage equality by the United States Supreme Court's decision in *Obergefell v. Hodges*,[2] family law underwent significant changes—lesbians and gay men could marry their partners, divorce their partners, be recognized as parents of the children of their partnerships, and more. This bibliography includes some resources that do not reflect that change, such as the Legal Guide for Military Families, because the resources contain additional useful unique information. Additionally, state legislatures and Congress are considering other legislation that may affect marriage equality or other family law precepts.

The annotations included in this chapter reflect a very broad view of family law. As such, items included in the bibliography may be used a couple of ways. The items listed represent a small taste of many of the areas described broadly as "family law" and various pieces may be used to supplement classroom readings or assignments. Instructors could consider providing students with additional contextual information for some pieces, such as Professor Clarke's piece "They, Them, and Theirs" about non-binary gender bias. Other pieces, such as the Community Legal Services of Philadelphia podcast critiquing the child welfare system, may not require significant recontextualization but may broaden the scope of student understanding. Consistent with the broad view, some annotations also address teaching students about trauma-informed lawyering.

Another approach to the annotations would be to use them as starting points for additional or further research. The law review articles contain extensive footnotes that may be consulted to identify additional related materials, and the citators in Lexis and Westlaw will facilitate a researcher identifying subsequent scholarship citing to an annotated entry. When teaching, it may be possible to present students with the analysis of a family law issue through a particular lens, e.g., race, sexuality, ability, gender identity, age, ability, and ask students to explore the same issue through other lenses. In that type of activity, it is critical to consider intersectionality and its effects in relation to the issue.

Family law is sometimes described as a low-status practice area,[3] perhaps because it is an area of law that is unremittingly common—it has touched the lives of every

---

2. 576 U.S. 644 (2015).

3. *See* Lucille A. Jewel, *Bordieu and American Legal Education: How Law Schools Reproduce Social Stratification and Class Hierarchy*, 56 Buff. L. Rev. 1155, 1185 (2008).

student in the classroom in some way or another. When teaching from a perspective valuing diversity and inclusion, students will evaluate how legal systems in family law both punish and protect clients at the intersection of the public and the private.

Articles

Susan Ayres, *Inside the Master's Gates: Resources and Tools to Dismantle Racism and Sexism in Higher Education*, 21 JOURNAL OF LAW & SOCIETY 20 (2021).

> Professor Ayres' article focuses on the storytelling aspects of critical legal studies, in the context of the 2020 protests for racial justice arising following the deaths of Breonna Taylor and George Floyd. Professor Ayres considers "Substance of Fire: Gender and Race in the College Classroom" by Claire Millikin, using it to unmask racism and sexism in legal education. Family law professors may consider the resources cited and suggested and extrapolate from the examples included to identify strategies to incorporate in their own classrooms.

Anna Burke, Zachary Hughbanks, Therese Kilbane Myers, Caroline Neville & Harry Samuels, *Child Custody, Visitation & Termination of Parental Rights*, 21 GEORGETOWN JOURNAL OF GENDER AND THE LAW 201 (2020).

> This annual review article lays out an overview of the law regarding child custody, visitation, and termination of parental rights, taking into consideration the experiences of some marginalized groups under the law. For example, marriage rights for LGBTQ couples are addressed, and the authors note as well that the implications of marriage equality on child custody and visitation has not been clearly applied in families with transgender parent(s). The authors briefly address the experiences of asylum-seekers who were separated from their accompanying children.

Jessica A. Clarke, *They, Them, and Theirs*, 132 HARVARD LAW REVIEW 894 (2019).

> Raising the profile of nonbinary gender identities, Professor Clarke provides an introduction to those who are not familiar with the historical existence and variety of nonbinary gender identities and follows that with an explanation of the ways in which legal responses to those identities would adjust if American law gave full and fair consideration of nonbinary gender. Clarke suggests ways in which nonbinary gender rights could be treated under the law (such as by sex neutrality) and concludes that the law "does not require a universal definition of sex or gender that limits the options to two" (904). Family law issues are addressed most closely in the discussion of the sex or gender neutrality approach.

Claire P. Donohue, *The Unexamined Life: A Framework to Address Judicial Bias in Custody Determinations and Beyond*, 21 GEORGETOWN JOURNAL OF GENDER AND THE LAW 557 (2020).

The specter of judicial bias in the determination of legally significant facts weighs heavily in family law litigation, where judges make normative determinations based on and consequentially affecting the daily lives of litigants. Professor Donohue describes ways in which mothers have been viewed and treated under the law, including the assumption that women should be mothers (rather than attorneys as Ms. Myra Bradwell) and further that they should be "good mothers," including notions of chastity, whiteness, and more. She notes that the best interests of the child standard creates room for judges' observations and values to underlie decisions. Noting that bias comes into play even inadvertently, Professor Donohue calls for family court judges to receive bias training and conduct self-identity work, as well as for the court to slow down judicial processes, such as by taking all matters under advisement, using judicial bias inventories in decision making, and peer review or consultation sessions with judicial colleagues.

Kris Franklin, *Method Lawyering: Immersion Teaching Illustrated*, 69 JOURNAL OF LEGAL EDUCATION 334 (2020).

This article focuses primarily on pedagogy, particularly the immersive approach that integrates doctrinal, practical, and values training and also uses case method, simulation, and clinical strategies. The framework that Professor Franklin and others are using to teach students includes a scenario in which a lesbian couple wants to marry and is considering having children. Professor Franklin demonstrates the ease with which critical legal analysis can be implemented in the family law classroom, through thoughtful planning and use of client simulation scenarios such as the question of how parental relationships are created and modified.

Gabriella Garbero, *Rights Not Fundamental: Disability and the Right to Marry*, 14 ST. LOUIS UNIVERSITY JOURNAL OF HEALTH LAW & POLICY 587 (2021).

The "disability marriage penalty" refers to the fact that Social Security and Medicaid beneficiaries must include spousal income and assets when calculating eligibility form benefits, often eliminating the option of legal marriage for those who depend on benefits for their health care and related services. The author reviews the legal history of marriage equality movements, the disability rights movement, and past and present reforms to address the penalty.

Marie-Amélie George, *Queering Reproductive Justice*, 54 UNIVERSITY OF RICHMOND LAW REVIEW 671 (2020).

Professor George uses a queer lens when approaching reproductive justice, broadening the 'reproductive rights' conversation from abortion access to include the "diverse set of issues and rights that fall within the scope of reproductive decision-making" (671). Although Professor George does not address pedagogy directly in this article, she addresses family formation, sex education, and medical decision making. The examples and considerations raised by Professor George may be used in the classroom to raise the question of whether or how queer rights advocacy may serve goals of the reproductive justice movement.

Paula Gerber & Claerwen O'Hara, *Teaching Law Students about Sexual Orientation, Gender Identity and Intersex Status within Human Rights Law: Seven Principles for Curriculum Design and Pedagogy*, 68 Journal of Legal Education 416 (2019).

The seven principles the authors rely upon to guide the design and implementation of curriculum that considers sexual orientation, gender identity, and intersex status are largely applicable to the development of curriculum for and the pedagogy of a family law course. The principles, particularly the principle of critical analysis, include discussion of family law issues such as marriage and the promotion of "heterosexuality as 'normal'" (453). Among the references in this article are treaties, advisory decisions of international courts, and law review articles describing the implementation of critical pedagogy.

Sonia M. Gipson Rankin, *Creating Lightbulb Moments: Developing Higher-Order Thinking in Family Law Classrooms Through Court Observations*, 51 Journal of Law & Education 13 (2022).

Heeding the call for students to engage deeply with subject matter and be more practice-ready upon graduation, Professor Gipson Rankin identified and analyzed an experiential learning assignment in her family law class. The article describes the pedagogical theory, including Bloom's Taxonomy for developing higher-order thinking, underlying the assignment in which she has students observe and reflect on their experiences in a family law courtroom. This may be particularly helpful to those who would like to improve their skills in developing interactive, experiential assignments. The student observations provide opportunities to develop critical legal thinking skills.

Sonia M. Gipson Rankin, *Would You Make It to the Future? Teaching Race in an Assisted Reproductive Technologies and the Law Classroom*, 56 Family Law Quarterly 1, 7 (2022).

Professor Gipson Rankin provides provocative and inspiring suggestions for those who teach family law, focusing particularly on assisted reproductive technologies (ART). Noting dangers of unstructured discussion (frustration, hindering belonging) and offering detailed contextual and statistical information, Gipson Rankin advocates for the use of cognitive dissonance as an ART teaching tool. She provides an in-class activity that "brings the racialized ideologies into sharper view" (15). Masterfully, Gipson Rankin discusses grading and outcomes, helping readers comply with the American Bar Association (ABA) Learning Outcomes requirements in legal education as well as useful texts, ideas for interdisciplinary connections, and assessment tools, including a rubric.

Julia Hernandez, *Lawyering Close to Home*, 27 Clinical Law Review 131 (2020).

Professor Hernandez focuses on narrative, which she notes has a central place in critical race theory and also acts in opposition to epistemic injustice that arises when the law seeks to answer questions of power and justice without considering the social and lived experiences of those at the margins. After shining a light on the lack of diversity within the legal profession, Hernandez observes that law students who are motivated to do social justice lawyering or are members of marginalized groups may be overlooked by law schools' enthusiasm for professional identity formation which may perpetuate marginalization through its description of "cross-cultural lawyering." Hernandez explores the challenges of representing clients as a family law defense attorney and offers suggestions for the law school curriculum. These include viewing law school curriculum with an anti-disciplinarity lens, facilitating law student understanding of communities that centers race-class marginalized communities rather than centers current educational models, and evaluating the ways in which law schools "level" student aspirations so that marginalized students' aspirations are limited.

Laila L. Hlass & Lindsay M. Harris, *Critical Interviewing*, 2021 Utah Law Review 683 (2021).

Professors Hlass and Harris promote the use of critical interviewing in the classroom, "using an intersectional lens to collaborate with clients, communities, interviewing partners, and interpreters, with an eye toward interrogating privilege differentials in these relationships and accounting for existing historical and structural biases" (684, citations omitted). They present guidance for critical interviewing in the context of the clinical pedagogical model based on planning, performance, and reflection. The authors introduce the Legal Interviewing and Language Access film Project (LILA), a video project including two videos specifically addressing family law issues that may be used when teaching critical interviewing skills. This article and related video content may be of particular interest to those who want to give their students exposure to issues of gender, race, power, and privilege that may arise in interviewing family law clients.

Clare Huntington & Elizabeth S. Scott, *Conceptualizing Legal Childhood in the Twenty-First Century*, 118 Michigan Law Review 1371 (2020).

Keeping in mind the historical development of the law governing children, from the Progressive Era's approach of parental primacy to the more recent trend of children gaining adult rights and privilege, Professors Huntington and Scott suggest a Child Wellbeing conceptual framework for the laws regulating children. The authors consider a variety of laws regarding children, including juvenile justice, parent rights regarding punishment, medical care, and homeschooling, and children's rights, including some consideration of racial equality.

Negar Katirai, *Retraumatized in Court*, 62 Arizona Law Review 81 (2020).

Professor Katirai describes domestic violence (DV) or intimate partner violence (IPV) and the ways in which attorneys can improve the experiences of their clients who seek legal help. Suggested options include cross-cultural communication techniques (explaining that court is a difficult experience and often traumatizing itself) and expanding the scope of services offered to include case management and counseling.

Sarah Katz & Deeya Haldar, *The Pedagogy of Trauma-Informed Lawyering*, 22 Clinical Law Review 359 (2016).

With their clients, clinical professors and student attorneys often face traumatic experiences, including domestic violence, and the professors and student attorneys experience vicarious trauma. Teaching law students to act as trauma-informed lawyers encourages students to deliver legal services more effectively, maintain a social justice focus (a common goal of clinical legal work), practice client-centered lawyering, and improve student advocacy skills. Professors Katz and Haldar describe how to integrate trauma-informed lawyering in a family law clinic.

Lundy Langston, *Political and Social Construction of Families Through Pedagogy in Family Law Classrooms*, 73 Denver University Law Review 179 (1995).

Recognizing the variety of family structures, Professor Langston suggests that the family law class center family, not marriage. She notes that focusing students on the question of what constitutes a family would foster discussion that would include consideration the breadth of backgrounds, experiences, and cultural norms that exist in society and the classroom. With a pluralistic approach, Professor Lundy offers several possible course outlines that professors may find helpful in centering their courses on relationships.

Laura Nixon, *The Right to (Trans) Parent: A Reproductive Justice Approach to Reproductive Rights, Fertility, and Family-Building Issues Facing Transgender People*, 20 William & Mary Journal of Women and the Law 73 (2013).

Recognizing the fact that social context informs reproductive decisions, Laura Nixon explores the ways in which a reproductive justice, rather than an abortion-centric framework, is more inclusive and responsive, "a natural home for advocacy on some issues at the intersection of reproduction and gender identity" (79). Nixon uses the reproductive justice lens to critique issues particularly affecting transgender people, including requirements for changing gender designation and preservation of fertility. Nixon observes historic disparate impacts of fertility technology, raising questions of intra-movement priorities.

Bernard P. Perlmutter, *George's Story: Voice and Transformation Through the Teaching and Practice of Therapeutic Jurisprudence in a Law School Child Advocacy Clinic*, 17 St. Thomas Law Review 561 (2005).

Therapeutic jurisprudence considers the mental well-being and function of clients and others who are affected by the legal system, with the goal of improving client psychological well-being. Through the three-year case study of George, a 15-year-old under the custody of Florida's Department of Children and Families as he approached the age of majority, the author illustrates how to use therapeutic jurisprudence in clinical client representation and also shares benefits of the model.

Robyn M. Powell, *Disability Reproductive Justice*, 170 University of Pennsylvania Law Review 1851 (2022).

Starting from the prevalence of reproductive oppression and the well-known example of Britney Spears, Professor Powell calls for reproductive justice, rather than reproductive freedom, particularly focusing on the oppression that is experienced by people with disabilities. In addition to providing a eugenics-focused origin story and contemporary contexts of reproductive oppression, Powell offers "a way forward" (1887). She calls for: (1) disrupting intersectional oppressions through policy implementation; (2) centering marginalized people, including disabled people, as leaders; (3) protecting the autonomy and self-determination for people with disabilities; (4) ensuring information and access for people with disabilities to sexual and reproductive health services; and (5) assuring that disabled people are guaranteed rights, justice, and wellness. As a family law professor, Powell provides significant context that may be leveraged to inform class discussion on a variety of reproductive justice contexts.

Antoinette Sedillo López, *Making and Breaking Habits: Teaching (and Learning) Cultural Context, Self-Awareness, and Intercultural Communication Through Case Supervision in a Client-Service Legal Clinic*, 28 Washington University Journal of Law and Policy 37 (2008).

Starting with Sue Bryant's "'habits' to enhance cultural competence," Professor Sedillo Lopez guides the reader through teaching objectives used to address these habits with students. Following that discussion, Professor Sedillo Lopez shares several vignettes that demonstrate cultural issues that may arise in the representation of clients in family law contexts including an adoption of a baby under the Indian Child Welfare Act (ICWA), a family abuse situation in which a student must reconcile the client goal of stopping violence and preserving the family with the typical advice of restraining order and separation, and a grandfather seeking to adopt his grandchildren following their removal from his daughter's custody.

Chantal Thomas, *Reloading the Canon: Thoughts on Critical Legal Pedagogy*, 92 University of Colorado Law Review 955 (2021).

Professor Thomas does not directly describe the specific subjects that should be included in a family law canon, as that was done by Professor Jill Elaine

Hasday in her 2004 article "The Canon of Family Law."[4] Instead, Professor Thomas suggests that the canon of legal education should be reloaded with consideration of law and social context. She notes other scholars who have addressed these questions, including Duncan Kennedy, Pierre Schlag, Kimberlé Crenshaw, and Charles Mills. Ultimately, she describes methods and calls for critical legal pedagogy to make the classroom a place of empowerment and also to reload the canon, noting that the choices of what to include in the canon reflect the learning goal(s) for the discipline.

Mary Pat Treuthart, *A Perspective on Teaching and Learning Family Law*, 75 UMKC Law Review 1047 (2007).

The assessment of classroom teaching and student learning underlies Professor Treuhart's description of her family law teaching. She includes experiential opportunities, simulations, and other small group work. The difficulties of teaching assessment are highlighted, as well as professionalism demands for professors including the "good practices" formulated by the American Association of Law Schools (1055). Students, in their evaluative responses for Professor Treuhart's family law course, addressed emotion. Emotion is a necessary consideration in teaching family law, she concludes, and she offers suggestions for professional conversation about the interrelationship between law and emotion. Although this essay does not directly discuss critical legal pedagogy, the discussion of the role of emotion in the classroom may be of interest to those who are considering adding or increasing their courses' focus on family law issues of justice highlighted by critical legal pedagogy.

Shanta Trivedi, *The Harm of Child Removal*, 43 N.Y.U. Review of Law & Social Change 523 (2019).

In addition to detailed description of the various types of harm that occur to children due to their removal from their parents, Professor Trivedi lays bare the systemic inequities and bias involved in child welfare decisions. She further describes the state's responsibility to assure that children are protected and the ways in which the child removal process fails to consider the harm experienced by the child as a factor in making a removal or reunification decision. Her statutory analysis and recommendations may provide useful jumping-off points for classroom discussion or assignments.

Lois A. Weithorn, *A Constitutional Jurisprudence of Children's Vulnerability*, 69 Hastings Law Journal 179 (2017).

Under the law children are treated differently from adults, and Professor Weithorn provides scholarly analysis of the ways in which the U.S. Supreme Court has characterized children's vulnerability, noting that the vulnerability identified by the Court is often used to substantiate the Court's determinations regarding the treatment and rights of children. In addition to noting

4. *See* 57 Stan. L. Rev. 825 (2004).

the potentially generative feature of vulnerability, Professor Weithorn contextualizes the societal concern for children's vulnerability and provides interdisciplinary information about child development. Ultimately, Professor Weithorn raises the question of the Court's evaluation of constitutional questions using the lens of children's vulnerability is based on the best available evidence. The taxonomy of children's vulnerability may present an interesting lesson to students.

Lynda Wray Black, *The Birth of a Parent: Defining Parentage for Lenders of Genetic Material*, 92 NEBRASKA LAW REVIEW 799 (2014).

Recognition of parentage, according to Professor Wray Black, has historic origins in the biologic connection between the child and parent. Writing prior to recognition of marriage equality, the article advocates full parental rights and obligations for parents regardless of gender, describes major parentage cases, and identifies statutory conditions that lead to inequality and foster conflicts between genetic and gestational mothers. Lenders of genetic material are defined as those who expect to get something in return for their loan of genetic material, while true donors have no expectation of any parental responsibilities arising from their donation. Wray Black's suggested parentage decision tree, with its basis in genetics, is positioned as consistent with existing doctrines recognizing family relationships such as psychological parenting.

Books/Book Chapters

AMERICAN BAR ASSOCIATION, LEGAL GUIDE FOR MILITARY FAMILIES: EVERYTHING YOU NEED TO KNOW ABOUT FAMILY LAW, ESTATE PLANNING, AND THE SERVICEMEMBERS CIVIL RELIEF ACT (2013).

Targeted at the individual rather than the attorney, the Standing Committee on Continuing Education of the ABA provides a plain-language review of the ways in which being a service member affects rights, and family law matters are about one-third of the book. Although the book was written prior to the *Obergefell v. Hodges* opinion and thus does not reflect federal recognition of same-sex marriages, there are few sources that specifically consider the issues experienced by service members and their families. Written with a lay audience in mind and including hypotheticals, charts, and examples, this may be an especially useful way to supplement classroom teaching about issues such as pension division. The tips for readers are tips that attorneys may also want to pass along to their clients.

FEMINIST JUDGMENTS: FAMILY LAW OPINIONS REWRITTEN (Rachel Rebouché ed., 2020).

Part of the Feminist Judgments series, this collection of essays and rewritten judicial opinions ostensibly reflects the canon of family law. The feminist judgments may be of interest for professors who wish to show their students that alternate perspectives may exist for these canon cases. Variation in terms of approach exists, as the authors were not required to espouse one particular feminist approach, and also the cases selected appear to reflect that variety. Of particular interest may be Professor Jessica Dixon Weaver's opinion that the State of Wisconsin violated Joshua DeShaney's Fourteenth Amendment right to liberty in its "deliberate indifference" to the abuse he suffered, Professor Seema Mohapatra's opinion recognizing gestational surrogacy under New Jersey law, and Professor Nancy Polikoff's decision maintaining a transgender father's parental rights.

Courtney G. Joslin, Shannon P. Minter & Catherine Sakumura, Lesbian, Gay, Bisexual and Transgender Family Law (2021–2022).

Although LGBT people face family law situations that may be similar to those faced by heterosexuals, representing LGBTQ people in those family law situations may present additional challenges. This book is meant to help practitioners rise to those challenges while also providing background information. Traditional family law topics such as adoption, marriage, custody and visitation, and dissolution are covered, as well as alternative reproduction. Issues of marriage and custody for transgender people have their own dedicated chapter. This resource would be helpful in guiding students in a project in which they had to represent LGBTQ clients in particular scenarios. Also, the chapter providing a history of marriage equality may be useful to those seeking to ground themselves in a history of marriage equality that the authors begin in 1971 and carries through "to the present" (8:2).

Kimberly E. O'Leary & Mable Martin-Scott, Family Law in Multicultural Lawyering: Navigating the Culture of the Law, the Lawyer, and the Client (2021).

The brief consideration of family law, set among case studies of cultural legal issues from a variety of legal practice areas, may be a helpful reading to share with students. Juxtaposing the notion of private family relationships with state regulation, the authors describe ways in which cultural practices may or may not be recognized and honored in family law litigation contexts. Students may be asked to interrogate the text's description of the functions of family law as normative statements: Family law may purport to be factors-based and normatively lean toward equity and balance, but how does it treat people who come to family court and are—in some way—outside the norm?

Dorothy Roberts, Torn Apart: How the Child Welfare System Destroys Black Families—and How Abolition Can Build a Safer World (2022).

Professor Roberts advocates for abolition of the child welfare system, which she characterizes as a family-policing system. Identifying the racial injustice reflected in the extant system and failed reform efforts, Roberts walks readers through the racist terrors of the existing child welfare system, the ways in which the system is designed to perpetuate "unjust political structure in the name of saving children" (28), and the mutually reinforcing relationship of family policing and criminal law enforcement. Roberts concludes by highlighting abolitionism in the context of child welfare, calling for the freeing of "family caregivers from state supervision and children from foster care (30)."

Loretta Ross & Rickie Solinger, Reproductive Justice: An Introduction (2017).

This joint project of a scholar and an activist serves as a primer to reproductive justice, offering three principles defining reproductive justice work and a human rights analysis. Although published prior to the *Dobbs v. Jackson Women's Health Organization*[5] decision, Ross and Solinger include significant legal analysis and may be helpful for those seeking to fully understand the ways in which contemporary reproductive justice centers storytelling and "pursues fresh critical thinking regarding power and powerlessness" (72). Fertility management, including eugenics, the War on Drugs, the use of politics to make health policy, and the right to parent, which captures the "deeply politicized" nature of motherhood (168), are addressed. Though lacking particular pedagogical suggestions, this provides excellent background and additional information that may be useful to anyone interested in this area.

Websites, Blogs, Podcasts

Margaret Ryznar, *New Book from the Gottmans*, Law Professor Blogs Network: Family Law Prof Blog (Oct. 12, 2022), https://lawprofessors.typepad.com/family_law/.

Issues related to diversity, equity, and inclusion are at the core of family law, and this blog consistently includes posts that may be of interest to those teaching in family law. The blog aggregates news stories and other web content that may be useful in highlighting or adding perspective to the classroom, such as the posts "Marriage Equality for Disabled People," "24 States Support ICWA [Indian Child Welfare Act]," and "Domestic Violence Has Many Types." The blog also reflects family law in international contexts.

Community Legal Services of Philadelphia, *Four Generations In, How Is That Legal?: Breaking Down Systemic Racism One Law at a Time*, Buzzsprout (June 29, 2022), https://howisthatlegal.buzzsprout.com/2003652/10831629-four-generations-in.

5. 142 S. Ct. 2228 (2022)

This podcast episode, produced by the Community Legal Services of Philadelphia, is one of many that provide a client-focused perspective and question underlying systemic issues, including racism, equity, and social justice. This particular episode relays the experience of a CLSP employee who in the past had her children removed from their home by the child welfare system and her advocacy to support parents individually and to challenge child welfare systems. Other episodes in this podcast series may also be of interest.

Kiilu Davis Discusses Racism and Discrimination in Family Law, FAMILY LAWYER MAGAZINE, https://familylawyermagazine.com/articles/racism-discrimination-family-law-kiilu-davis/ (Aug. 12, 2022).

In this episode, Editorial Director Diana Shepherd interviewed Kiilu Davis, the former Chair of the American Academy of Matrimonial Lawyers' Diversity Committee. The transcript is included. Interview topics range from discrimination within the profession, critical race theory (CRT), discrimination by the bench, and ways to open minds.

Pennsylvania Bar Association Family Law Section, *A Contested Adoption: The Pennsylvania Supreme Court Reverses a Parental Termination, Law in the Family*, LAW IN THE FAMILY (Sept. 22, 2022), https://podcasts.apple.com/us/podcast/episode-18-a-contested-adoption-the/id1588267654?i=1000580311995.

Attorney Chelsey Christiansen described the facts of a case in which she was court appointed to represent a father on appeal following the termination of his parental rights, where the mother had relinquished her rights and the child's maternal grandparents had sought to adopt the child. In the interview, Christiansen relays the basic facts surrounding the petition to terminate a father's parental rights and Christiansen's successful efforts to maintain the father's rights. Issues raised during the interview include statutory interpretation, sufficiency of evidence, legal strategy, and client representation in an appellate context.

Videos

LOVING (Focus Features 2016) (directed by Jeff Nichols and starring Joel Edgerton and Ruth Negga).

THE LOVING STORY (HBO 2011) (directed by Nancy Buirski).

These films share the real experience of Richard Loving and his wife Mildred Jeter Loving, who married each other in defiance of Virginia's anti-miscegenation law, were arrested and sentenced for the violation, and ultimately challenged the convictions at the United States Supreme Court. Nancy Buirski's *The Loving Story*, an award-winning documentary that inspired the feature film *Loving*, includes archival footage of the couple and others involved in their story.

FOSTER BOY (Gravitas Ventures 2019).

Based on true stories and written by an attorney, this fictionalized account of events arising when a for-profit foster care agency puts a minor who was a known sex offender into a foster home with other children, where the minor then abused other children in foster home and the for-profit agency allowed the abuse to continue although the children sought help. Though described by some as uneven, the acting is compelling and provides context for common family law considerations such as the role of the state in assuring the best interests of a child are met and a platform for discussion of the disproportionality in the child welfare system.

HOME TRUTH (Women Make Movies 2017).

A sometimes difficult to watch documentary, *Home Truth* reflects the experience of Jessica Gonzales following the parental kidnapping of her daughters in violation of a restraining order and the subsequent murders of the children. Gonzales's litigation and advocacy to strengthen rights for domestic violence victims features heavily, including her unsuccessful case before the United States Supreme Court, followed by the Inter-American Commission on Human Rights decision that the United States was responsible for human rights violations due to its law and policy regarding domestic violence. The movie is available through Kanopy.

THE MOST DANGEROUS YEAR (Collective Eye Films 2018).

In Washington State in 2016, six so-called "bathroom bills" were considered by the state legislature. This documentary reflects the perspectives of a group of parents who worked to protect their transgender children. Because the director is a member of the parent group and advocates on behalf of her own child, the reflection of the children, their families, and the goal of protecting transgender childrens' rights are both intimate and urgent. The documentary received multiple awards and is available through Kanopy.

NO MÁS BEBÉS (PBS 2015).

This documentary reflects the experience of Mexican-American immigrant mothers who were sterilized at Los Angeles County General Hospital. Although the plaintiffs did not prevail on their class action claim of forced infertility, the action was noteworthy for alleging a right to parenthood and, following the litigation, a number of positive changes affirming women's autonomy and bodily integrity were made in California.

Section 7

Indigenous and International Law

Decolonizing the Legal Academy (Is the Future)

*Nazune Menka**

Introduction

Why should the legal academy begin to understand, implement, and collectively seek to decolonize the law? Most directly because the legal academy in the United States teaches from a baseline constitutional doctrine that claims the country is founded on principles of democracy and equity when the truth is that *what is now known as* (*w.i.n.k.a.*)[1] the United States is a settler colonial nation-state whose canons of law rest on foundations of imperialism, racism, and xenophobia. More fully, the foundations of a settler colonial nation-state can only truly be understood by naming it so and analyzing it as such. To ignore this truth in any law course is a disservice to our students, to our collective collegiality, and to the legal academy.

We posit that justice is achievable under the law, but the law is imported from an imperialist regime of settler colonialism. If we do not confront these foundations of the law and frame it in the reality that the United States is an ongoing settler colonial project, justice remains elusive. In every classroom, and at every law school, we are standing on the ancestral homelands of Indigenous Peoples who have existed since "time immemorial" and whose Indigenous knowledges, languages, ways of knowing, cultural and governance institutions are inextricably linked to these lands.[2] The United States destructively dispossesses Indigenous Peoples and Native Nations from these

* Nazune Menka, J.D., M.S. (*Denaakk'e & Lumbee*), UC Berkeley School of Law, Environmental Law Clinic Supervising Attorney.

1. A liberatory acronym the author uses to mean "What Is Now Known As," intended to call the reader to consider what Indigenous Peoples have called places and spaces since time immemorial.

2. Cherokee Nation v. Georgia, 30 U.S. 1, 3 (1831) (providing that from "time immemorial the Cherokee nation have composed a sovereign and independent state, and in this character have been repeatedly recognized, and still stand recognized by the United States, in the various treaties subsisting between their nation and the United States.").

lands, and settler colonialism continues to support the erasure of vitally important and critical understandings of the lands upon which we now collectively reside.

To ignore settler colonialism is to ignore Native Nations as the first sovereigns in *w.i.n.k.a.* the United States. To ignore settler colonialism when teaching in the legal academy, we begin a student's legal education with lies. How righteous can the sense of justice we teach and seek truly be if we are ignoring the colonial elephant in the room? How can the legal academy adequately teach about systems of justice and the rule of law without acknowledging the United States' settler colonial foundations and its relationships with and treatment of Native Nations?

Settler colonialism analyzes the intersections of structural racism, law, and colonization. It illuminates how the United States engaged in strategies of elimination, displacement, containment, and the conceptual disappearance of Indigenous and non-Indigenous racialized or othered communities in the name of colonization.[3] As a theory it posits that if racialized power and privilege in the United States are rooted in the historic and ongoing colonization of Native North America, then we must begin to address and seek redress for the colonial structures, institutions, and relationships that still serve as its foundation. As such, our legal structures and systems are embedded in this colonial framework, which serve to reinforce historical and contemporary strategies to occupy the land, extract and appropriate its resources, and exercise the settler sovereign prerogative, which reinforces and legitimates the existence of the settler nation state's structures, institutions, and relationships—and delegitimates all others.[4]

This delegitimating disappears a plethora of worldviews, cultures, and ways of knowing, most radically those of the Indigenous Peoples and Native Nations, who have existed here since time immemorial, to perpetuate a Western hegemonic existence. By introducing our students (and our colleagues) to the difficult truths of settler colonialism, we can engage in a praxis of decolonization that reframes, (re)writes, or (re) rights the narrative of the origin story of the United States and empowers disappeared worldviews, cultures, and ways of knowing.[5]

The legal academy, and Western systems of knowledge more generally, have begun to understand how a diversity of cultural worldviews can bring about dynamic problem solving and solutions in ways that a myopic, hegemonic society cannot. And in the aftermath of the murder of George Floyd in May 2020 and the subsequent racial reckoning, we have begun to seek more formalized and institutionalized ways to increase cultural competency, reduce bias, and encourage antiracist training in law schools.

---

3. Natsu Taylor Saito, Settler Colonialism, Race, and the Law: Why Structural Racism Persists (2020).

4. *Id.; see* Maryam Kanna, *Furthering Decolonization: Judicial Review of Colonial Criminal Laws*, 70 Duke L.J. 411, 416 (2020) (defining colonialism as an effort of settlers to "transplant their own laws into their colonial possessions in an effort to control the native population and maximize the colonial power's ability to exploit and profit from native resources.").

5. *See* Cutcha Risling Baldy, We Are Dancing for You: Native Feminisms and the Revitalization of Women's Coming-of-Age-Ceremony (2018); Eve Tuck & K. Wayne Yang, *Decolonization is not a metaphor*, 1 Decolonization: Indigeneity, Educ. & Soc'y 1 (2012).

For example, over 150 law school deans sent a letter to the American Bar Association's Section of Legal Education and Admissions to the Bar requesting every law school require such training and education in April 2020.[6] Decolonization can and should be a part of this work. Reframing the foundational legal tenets of American law to include the three sovereigns, Native Nations, the United States, and the several states, not only combats erasure and reduces the impact of this ongoing harm, it allows for the legal academy to begin to seek solutions to governance from ways of knowing that predate *w.i.n.k.a.* the United States and that originate with Native Nations.

Native Nations and Federal "Indian" Law

Much of the work has already been done for us. There is an entire doctrine of law that does not ignore these facts but analyzes them and seeks to understand what justice might be if the federal government were engaged in actual government-to-government with Native Nations as Tribal sovereignty and the current era of Tribal self-determination call for. This doctrine of law, somewhat erroneously called "federal Indian law," should be one of the required courses for law students. Furthermore, as the recommendations in this chapter provide, bringing case law from federal Indian law into other law courses provides our students an opportunity to learn how vast and varied this field of law is—while also reducing the erasure of Native Nations and Tribal sovereignty from our field more generally. For many years, Indian law attorney Felix Cohen's metaphor of Native Nations as the canary in the coal mine has been cited as an apt illustration of how elusive justice has been in the United States. "Like the miner's canary, the Indian marks the shifts from fresh air to poison gas in our political atmosphere; and our treatment of Indians, even more than our treatment of other minorities, reflects the rise and fall in our democratic faith."[7] This metaphor, however, ignores the colonial elephant in the room and negates the lived experience and resiliency of Native Nations.

More recently, Professor Matthew Fletcher[8] dubbed Cohen's metaphor inaccurate as it analogizes Native Nations to a passive entity, preferring to analogize Native Nations to the scrappy, ingenious, and proactive muskrat who saves all of creation in Anishinaabe cultures.[9] These two metaphors also originate within two distinct policy eras of federal Indian law—the termination era and the current era of Tribal self-determination.[10] These metaphors illuminate very different perspectives. What was prescient

6. Alicia Ouellette et al., Letter to the Members of the American Bar Association, Section of Legal Education and Admissions to the Bar (Aug. 20, 2020) (on file with author).

7. Felix S. Cohen, *The Erosion of Indian Rights, 1950–53: A Case Study in Bureaucracy*, 62 YALE L.J. 348, 390 (1953).

8. *See also* Matthew L.M. Fletcher, *Teaching Indian Law in the 21st Century*, this volume.

9. Matthew L. M. Fletcher, *Muskrat Textualism*, 116 NW. U. L. REV. 963 (2022).

10. Charles F. Wilkinson & Eric R. Biggs, *The Evolution of the Termination Policy*, 5 AM. INDIAN L. REV. 1, 140 (1977) (discussing the federal government's attempt to terminate the federal-tribal relationship, eliminate reservations, and turn Indian affairs over to the states).

about Cohen's canary metaphor is that the failures of our democracy are indeed illuminated by the settler colonial nation-states' treatment of Native Nations, but it fails to address settler colonialism on its face. Consider instead Professor Fletcher's metaphor that rightfully acknowledges the resiliency of Native Nations who, having navigated and survived centuries of settler colonialism, including eras of genocide, forced removal, and forced assimilation, are emerging as "leaders in good governance."[11] Fletcher's metaphor recognizes Native Nations as engaged and proactive leaders of governance institutions. Despite the ongoing settler colonialist machinations of disappearance, assimilation, and dispossession, Native Nations continue to develop robust, innovative, and culturally responsive governance institutions. As Native Nations rebuild and move toward actualized measures of self-determination through assertions of Tribal sovereignty, the legal academy has—but for rare instances where Indigenous law centers, certifications, programs, and clinics have been established—lagged in educating our law students on Native Nations.

Settler Colonialism and Decoloniality

When I teach "federal Indian law" I weave themes of settler colonialism and decolonization into the doctrine on Native Nation rebuilding. First, the words we use matter and despite the course (and text) being called "federal Indian law" I renamed the course "Indigenous Peoples, Law, and the United States" (IPLUS) to reflect more accurately Alaska Native, Kanaka Maoli, and other Indigenous Peoples and institutions we discuss in the course. The term Indigenous Peoples is an international human rights term that is more inclusive and acknowledges the context of colonialism. In introducing the course, I discuss with students the differences between and the historical and contemporary use of the terms American Indian, Native American, Indigenous Peoples, and First Nations while also noting the importance of using the specific name a Tribe calls itself whenever possible. Second, the feedback I've received from IPLUS students and students from my undergraduate course, "Decolonizing UC Berkeley," reflect their desire for understanding how both settler colonialism and decolonization operate under the law. For example, students often share that these classes provide both the critical lens and optimism for the future that they hope to experience in a university setting but had not, up until taking these courses, yet encountered. While both courses cover a substantial amount of material on topics that can be both intellectually and emotionally difficult, the students respond with an eagerness to understand how they might create a more equitable and just future.

By centering a foundational understanding of settler colonialism, the students are encouraged to critically examine how the law has historically oppressed, marginalized, and dismantled Native Nations. Similarly, by centering decolonization, students are

11. Fletcher, *supra* note 9, at 968–68.

encouraged to reconsider how re-Indigenization of legal institutions occurs and how decoloniality might operate to achieve justice. To learn this area of law—its vast and varied past and potential liberatory future—is to fully understand the legal institutions of the three sovereigns. Decolonization addresses these issues, and more, and should be a part of the legal academy's liberatory future.

There are many ways we think of decolonization in academia, most of which center around the foundational theories of settler colonialism and the social sciences.[12] Tuck and Yang's article is a cornerstone article on what decolonization is and isn't.[13] As their article posits, decolonization is not a metaphor. It requires the return of Indigenous land and lifeways. It is also to be led, shaped, and understood as Indigenous Peoples and Native Nations want it to be led and understood. Tuck and Yang posit that decolonization is about Indigenous sovereignty and futurism, but there is not one predetermined result. The journey toward decolonization is as determinative of the destination as anything. Natsu Taylor Saito's "Settler Colonialism, Race, and the Law" describes the core tenets of settler colonialism and encourages the non-Indigenous reader to contemplate not the faux choice of whether to "stay or leave" the United States, but whether to choose to function as a colonizer or to consciously pursue decolonization.[14] She defines decolonization as "a relinquishment of the settlers' self-assigned entitlement to encompass everything and everyone" towards a liberatory future where we all have the right to be self-determining.[15] Decolonization is thus centered on true self-determination, and therefore must stem from, and be determined by, the people themselves. It cannot trickle down from a hierarchical institutional entity or structure. Both decolonization and self-determination are processes to be defined by the people. Legal scholars Carpenter and Wald have provided that decolonization of the law is a process of internal legal reform that revitalizes Native Nation communities by identifying core Tribal competencies and Tribal values and transmuting them into Tribal law.[16] In more recent scholarship, Carpenter and Riley provide that decoloniality requires that we acknowledge and respect Indigenous worldviews, cosmologies, and values. Such acknowledgements support Indigenous Peoples who are working to shape human rights, advance collective rights to self-determination, restore their cultures, and regain access to their traditional homelands.

Lastly, in the academy the call to decolonization often centers on the re-Indigenization of institutions, land, thought, ways of knowing, and relationships.[17] Re-indige-

---

12. Steven Mintz, *Decolonizing the Academy: Who's afraid to decolonize higher education?* Inside Higher Ed (June 22, 2021), https://www.insidehighered.com/blogs/higher-ed-gamma/decolonizing-academy.

13. *See* Tuck & Yang, *supra* note 5.

14. Saito, *supra* note 3, at 56.

15. *Id.* at 256.

16. Kristen Carpenter & Eli Wald, *Lawyering for Groups: The Case of American Indian Tribal Attorneys*, 81 Fordham L. Rev. 3085, 3108–09 (2013).

17. *See* Linda Tuhiwai Smith, Decolonizing Methodologies (2d ed. 2012); Theresa Stewart-Ambo, *The Future Is in the Past: How Land-Grab Universities Can Shape the Future of Higher Education*, 8 Native Am. & Indigenous Stud. 1, 162–168 (2021).

nization acknowledges Tribal legal institutions as the vast and varied rules of law, and culturally informed worldviews, that they are comprised of. Indeed, as Native Nations continue to rebuild from the attempted dismantling by the settler colonial state, the most effective tool to combat settler colonialism in the classroom is to reduce the erasure of Native Nations by cementing them in their rightful place in the legal academy as resilient social, cultural, and legal institutions. As Professor Maggie Blackhawk illuminates, Native Nations have successfully advocated for their inherent sovereignty, power, and self-determination under a colonialist regime with various amounts of success but with a fierce civil advocacy that all citizens could learn from.[18]

Bringing Decolonization (Re-Indigenization and Self Determination) into the Academy and Upper-Level Law Courses

What knowledge and reframing of perspective might occur if we attempted to eschew colonial erasure and lean into learning a new, more liberatory, language of the law that seeks a relationship of reciprocity instead of power over people and ownership over property? What can we learn from Native Nations' and Indigenous Peoples' leadership? What might we learn if we were to begin using and understanding the Indigenous place names for these landscapes, asking for Indigenous partnership in decision making via a diplomatic engagement structure? By bringing the first sovereign into our doctrinal courses in meaningful ways we are preparing ourselves, the legal academy, and our soon-to-be practicing attorneys for the future.

Goal: Beyond Land Acknowledgements: *Place-Based Recognition of Indigenous Peoples, Institutions, Languages, and Cultures*

Objectives

What we can do in the classroom is important. I outline a few examples of how I am attempting to engage a decolonial framework in my classrooms: by reducing the erasure of Native Nations by introducing Tribal law and Tribal sovereignty, and choosing my use of words and theories in the classroom with honesty, respect, and intentionality. One other small but meaningful action is to open your courses each semester with the land acknowledgment and to include it in your syllabus. Many universities have instituted land acknowledgements, but these must be created in partnership with the appropriate Native Nations. If your university doesn't have an official land acknowledgment, I recommend visiting Native Land Digital for resources such as the

18. Maggie Blackhawk, *Federal Indian Law as Paradigm Within Public Law*, 132 HARV. L. REV. 1787, 1875 (2019).

2019 Teacher's Guide on acknowledgments and their map resources. However, land acknowledgments are simply performative words unless they are coupled with substantive actions engaging these same Native Nations in institutional to government relationships. While such relationship building might occur on a case-by-case basis, say for example in the work I do in the Environmental Law Clinic at UC Berkeley with California Native Nations, it is of the utmost importance that these relational endeavors occur by and between university leadership and Native Nation leadership.

Beyond land acknowledgments, especially for those universities established as land grant institutions, a university should be honoring Native Nations by engaging in reciprocal relationships and supporting Indigenous students with tuition waivers like several universities have begun to do. University leadership, including law school deans, should work to develop, fund, and continually engage in institutional to government relationships with Native Nations, especially those whose lands they occupy.

For example, UC Berkeley School of Law recently announced that it will cover professional degree supplemental tuition for students that qualify for the new University of California policy covering tuition for California residents that are members of federally recognized Tribes. Land grant institutions occupy and benefit from unceded (i.e., stolen) Indigenous lands and beginning to acknowledge this with substantive actions such as covering tuition for Indigenous students is part of how the relationship with Native Nations can be rebuilt.

In an excellent example of this work, the University of Arizona has recently opened a microcampus "to serve the Pascua Yaqui Tribe [which] represents a significant milestone in our ongoing commitment to Native American communities—especially those whose traditional homelands include Southern Arizona." Universities that center Indigenous programs and certificates increase not only the number of Indigenous students they serve, but also support and serve local and national Indigenous communities through the offering of Tribal and Indigenous law clinics and centers.

Finally, one last but important action university leadership should focus on when engaging with relationship building with Native Nations is to rematriate information extracted from Indigenous communities. Universities are repositories to an egregious amount of Indigenous cultural knowledge, data, languages, Ancestors, and more. I teach about this in my decolonization undergraduate course and encourage my students to engage in research projects that liberate the stories about this history and to center voices that have historically been silenced or intentionally forgotten. Creating courses that center these historically silenced voices and communities and allowing students to research and share their projects is in its own way a form of liberation. I recommend Linda Tuhiwai Smith's *Decolonizing Methodologies: Research and Indigenous Peoples* for anyone interested in learning more about this type of education. What is most impactful, however, is liberating Indigenous data and knowledge housed within the university directly back to the appropriate Native Nations or other impacted communities whose data and knowledge has been withheld.

Goal: Re-Indigenizing the Legal Academy *by Introducing the First Sovereign into the Law Classroom*

Objectives

For professors seeking to understand and introduce the concepts of decolonization, re-Indigenization, Tribal sovereignty, and self-determination in the classroom, I've compiled a short, introductory list of resources for use in numerous different courses.

Tribal Law

Including Tribal governments in discussions of state and federal governments reduces the erasure settler colonialism relies upon to uphold the settler state. Teaching Tribal Law as its own course centers and re-Indigenizes the legal academy. While many of the resources shared here contain valuable information about Tribal laws, the primer on the matter is Professor Matthew Fletcher's text *American Indian Tribal Law.*[19]

Statutory Interpretation

While there are many sources to learn about the Indian Canons of Construction, this short primer, *The Indian Treaty Canon and* McGirt v. Oklahoma*: Righting the Ship*, written by Judge Lauren King, should be required reading for all legal professionals.[20]

Indigenous Worldviews, Religious Freedom, Oral Traditions, and Ways of Knowing

International Human Rights Law & The United Nations Declaration on the Rights of Indigenous Peoples (UNDRIP)[21] has been utilized by Native Nations to increase Tribal sovereignty (and was created by their advocacy efforts) in what Professors Carpenter and Riley call a "jurisgenerative moment" in human rights.[22] The Declaration is a direct response to the global imperialistic endeavors by both settler colonial and colonizing extractive nations that disenfranchised and dispossessed Indigenous Peoples of their land and ways of life. UNDRIP was officially endorsed in 2007 with four settler colonial nation-states abstaining from that endorsement: the United States, Canada, Australia, and New Zealand/Aotearoa. These nations eventually supported UNDRIP but did not ratify it, rendering it unenforceable in courts. Despite this limitation the Declaration continues to be a widely utilized tool and benchmark for gauging when Indigenous

---

19. Matthew L.M. Fletcher, American Indian Tribal Law (2d ed. 2020).

20. Lauren King, *The Indian Treaty Canon and* McGirt v. Oklahoma*: Righting the Ship*, 56 Tulsa L. Rev. 401 (2021).

21. United Nations Declaration on the Rights of Indigenous Peoples, G.A. Res. 61/295, ¶ 12, U.N. Doc. A/RES/61/295 (Sept. 13, 2007).

22. Kristen A. Carpenter & Angela R. Riley, *Indigenous Peoples and the Jurisgenerative Moment in Human Rights*, 102 Calif. L. Rev. 173 (2014).

Peoples' rights are being violated and is being increasingly utilized by Tribal advocates in state and federal court systems and legislatures.

Illustrative of the comprehensive nature of Native Nation advocacy and worldviews that make the separation of the concepts of religious freedom, sacred sites, environmental law, and international human rights difficult is a Resolution by Yurok Tribal Council in 2019 establishing the rights of the Klamath River. The Resolution reinforces the Yurok cultural worldview by citing the Yurok Constitution, the strong Yurok relationship with "We-roy" (the Klamath river), and the Yurok's inherent sovereign rights buttressed by UNDRIP Article 29. Article 29 provides that "Indigenous peoples have the right to the conservation and protection of the environment and the productive capacity of their lands or territories and resources." Similarly illustrative of this point, Professor Angela Riley's work to illuminate Tribal laws protecting Indigenous cultural property identifies such laws as "uniquely situated to capture and reflect Indigenous cultures and lifeways" while also promoting Tribal sovereignty and Tribal self-determination.[23] Her work identifies that Indigenous Peoples' cultural property concerns are unique and cover "tangible and intangible aspects of culture" that "are not strictly siloed as they might be in Western law" because "[l]and religion, creation, design—... are all connected as an interrelated whole for Indigenous Peoples."[24] A practical resource outlining the rights and important aspects of implementation, both of which are contained in the Declaration, along with examples of Native Nation advocacy, was developed jointly by UCLA Law, the University of Colorado Law, and Native American Rights Fund.[25]

Environmental and Natural Resource Law/ Religious Freedom and Sacred Sites

As discussed above, Indigenous worldviews are not siloed as they are in Western law but are rather interrelated and interconnected, especially when advocating in the areas of cultural and environmental protection, religion, and sacred sites. In *Lyng v. N.W. Indian Cemetery Protective Ass'n,* Native Nations advocated for the protection of sacred "High Country" from logging development by the U.S. Forest Service.[26] The Supreme Court held that despite the entire area being "significant as an integral and indispensable part of Indian religious conceptualization and practice" and that any logging road "would cause serious and irreparable damage to the sacred areas which are

23. Angela Riley, *The Ascension of Indigenous Cultural Property Law*, 121 Mich. L. Rev. 75 (2022).

24. *Id.* at 86–87.

25. UCLA Law, the University of Colorado Law, & Native American Rights Fund, Project to Implement the United Nations Declaration on the Rights of Indigenous Peoples: Tribal Implementation Toolkit (2021), https://un-declaration.narf.org/wp-content/uploads/Tribal-Implementation-Toolkit-Digital-Edition.pdf (outlining the rights and important aspects of implementation, both of which are contained in the Declaration along with examples of Native Nation advocacy).

26. Lyng v. N.W. Indian Cemetery Protective Ass'n, 485 U.S. 439, 440 (1988) (holding that the Government's right to the use of its own lands need not and should not discourage it from accommodating religious practices like those engaged in by the Indian respondents, but there is no enforceable right available to the Tribes).

an integral and necessary part of the belief systems and lifeway of Northwest California Indian peoples," that "[w]hatever rights the Indians may have to the use of the area, however, those rights do not divest the Government of its right to use what is, after all, its land."[27] In response to this ruling, the now Chief Judge of the Yurok Tribe, Abby Abinanti, wrote a letter to Justice O'Connor sharing her cultural, legal, and historical perspectives on the *Lyng* case.[28] Her letter, published in UCLA's Indigenous Peoples' Culture and Resistance Journal, is an excellent primer on the cultural dissonance between Indigenous worldviews and environmental and religious protection in Western law, as well as the history of federal "Indian" law.

Speaking to the Indigenous worldviews and western legal paradigms of environmental protection and natural resource laws, even the nomenclature can be problematic. For example, calling land, water, and wildlife "natural resources" conveys that they are property subject to the Western human endeavor of exploitation in pursuit of productivity, which is antithetical to many Indigenous worldviews. Land, animals, and plants providing physical sustenance are treated with reciprocity and equity by the people. Under this paradigm people are encouraged to engage as stewards on behalf of these life-sustaining but vocally silent allies as was illustrated by the Yurok Resolution. This is becoming more recognized internationally under the law as "Rights of Nature," where land and waterways are given personhood and institutions, or organizations, are named as stewards who serve in the best interests of the recognized entity. A comprehensive database of such laws enacted by countries and Native Nations is available at The Center for Environmental Rights website.[29]

Legitimating Oral Traditions as Valid and Legible Evidence

Indigenous cultural and legal history is largely based on oral traditions. The legitimacy of such traditions continues to face challenges in U.S. federal courts. Consider bringing this to any class by comparing the legitimacy of oral history testimony between *Delgamuukw v. British Columbia*[30] and the federal court's determinations in *Bonnichsen v. United States*[31] of the statutory requirements of the Native American Graves Protection and Repatriation Act. The *Delgamuukw* Court held that Indigenous knowledge in the form of oral history traditions carried the weight of law while the *Bonnichsen* court held Indigenous knowledge in the form of oral history was not "ade-

27. *Id.* at 453.

28. Abby Abinanti, *A Letter to Justice O'Connor*, 1 Indigenous Peoples' J. L. Culture & Resistance 1 (2004).

29. The Center for Environmental Rights, *Rights of Nature Law Library*, https://www.centerforenvironmentalrights.org/rights-of-nature-law-library (last visited Jan. 16, 2023).

30. Delgamuukw v. British Columbia, 3 S.C.R. 1010 (1997).

31. Bonnichsen v. United States, 217 F. Supp. 2d 1116, 1152–55 (D. Or. 2002), *aff'd*, 367 F.3d 864, 882 (9th Cir. 2004) (holding that oral traditional Tribal knowledge was not "adequate to show the required significant relationship of the Kennewick Man's remains to the Tribal Claimants" within the meaning of the Native American Graves Protection and Repatriation Act).

quate to show the required significant relationship" of Ancestral remains ripped from Tribal claimants' ancestral territories.

Business Law, Tribal Sovereign Immunity, and Divestment

There are few areas of law where business law, advocacy, and social justice meet. However, as Native Nations continue to rebuild institutions, community, and economies after centuries of destruction, tribally owned businesses have been the funding mechanism supporting the rebuilding. Tribally owned businesses are imbued with a tribe's sovereign immunity and thus must consent to suit or waive immunity to be brought to federal or state court. Chapter 4 on Tribal Economic Development in the AMERICAN LAW INSTITUTE, RESTATEMENT ON THE LAW OF AMERICAN INDIANS (2021) provides a plethora of cases and examples of Native Nation law and advocacy and will likely become one of the most widely used tools for advocates in any area of "Indian" law but especially for the succinct outline of how Tribally owned businesses might retain their Tribal Sovereign immunity in the courts.

Treaties (and Federal Statutes) as the Supreme Law of the Land

While the United States Congress formally ended treatymaking in 1871, treaties still serve as the supreme law of the land and Native Nations with unabrogated treaties engage in various advocacy strategies to enforce and preserve treaty-based rights. The government-to-government relationship that serves as the foundation of treatymaking is truly unique and remarkable. Similarly remarkable, albeit more nefarious, is the judicial divestiture of inherent Tribal sovereignty the courts often engage in when interpreting such treaties and treaty-based rights. The following cases provide a contemporary glimpse at this area of law and the various places the academy might bring lessons of Tribal sovereignty and treaty advocacy into the classroom.

Criminal Jurisdiction

McGirt v. Oklahoma, 140 S. Ct. 2452 (2020) (citing treaties as the supreme law of the land and reestablishing the clear rule test to disestablish a reservation for the purposes of upholding federal criminal jurisdiction for certain enumerated crimes in Indian Country as established under the Major Crimes Act).

Oklahoma v. Castro-Huerta, 142 S. Ct. 2486 (2022) (holding, under 1882 case precedent, that the federal and state governments have concurrent jurisdiction to prosecute crimes committed by non-Indians against Indians in Indian Country despite treaty language to the contrary).

State Taxation

Washington State Dept. of Licensing v. Cougar Den, Inc., 139 S. Ct. 1000, 1004 (2019) (holding that a business established on the reservation, owned by a Tribal member, and serving the Tribe was preempted from state taxation as provided for in the treaty).

Hunting and Fishing Rights

Herrera v. Wyoming, 139 S. Ct. 1686 (2019) (holding that Wyoming's admission to the Union did not abrogate the Crow Tribe of Indians' right to hunt under the treaty).

Administrative Law & Movement Lawyering

Standing Rock Sioux Tribe v. U.S. Army Corps of Engineers, 985 F.3d 1032 (D.C. Cir. 2021), *reh'g en banc denied*, Nos. 20-5197 & 20-5201, 2021 BL 152245 (D.C. Cir. Apr. 23, 2021), *cert. denied*, No. 21-560, 2022 BL 57673 (U.S. Feb. 22, 2022) (This case arose out of the NODAPL movement at Standing Rock in 2016 that saw Indigenous Peoples from around the world join forces to protect the Standing Rock Sioux Tribe's treaty rights to water. In an administrative law victory, a district court held the easement issued by the U.S. Army Corps of Engineers was deficient under the National Environmental Protection Act and required an environmental impact statement be completed).

Conclusion

Decolonizing the legal academy is the future of our field. It is about recognizing the first sovereigns of *w.i.n.k.a.* the United States, and recognizing their history, resilience, and innovations in good governance. It is also about providing our students what they are requesting: an education that centers truth, reciprocity, and promise for the future while simultaneously acknowledging our settler colonial past and present. People invariably ask me if decolonizing a university, or the law, is possible given the systemic and institutional nature of settler colonialism. I have many thoughts about such a question, but if decolonization is determined by the people engaging in decolonial actions then I am, at least, doing my part.

Native American and Indigenous Law: A Selected, Annotated Bibliography of Sources for Promoting and Maintaining Native American Law as Part of the Core Curriculum in Law School

*Rebecca Chapman**

Introduction

As a law school subject, Native American law is often treated as an elective course with less value to the overall student legal education than other subjects considered part of the core curriculum.[1] In truth, Native American law and legal issues intersect across core subjects like constitutional law, property law, civil procedure, criminal procedure, administrative law, business law, and others. Moreover, federally recognized tribal nations reside and operate within approximately 37 of the 50 States of our Union.[2] Whether a student dreams of representing tribes in Indian Country, representing state or federal government agencies, or representing business clients in private practice, they are likely to encounter Native American law issues as part of that practice. It

---

* Rebecca Chapman is the Outreach Liaison Librarian for the Indigenous Studies Department of the College of Arts and Sciences and the Outreach Liaison Librarian for the Undergraduate Law Program at the University at Buffalo School of Law. She wishes to thank Charles B. Sears Law Library Director Elizabeth Adelman, Assistant Law Librarian Joe Gerken, and Assistant Law Librarian Theodora Belniak for their support with this endeavor. Finally, she wishes to thank her husband, Marc Chapman, and her daughter, Sofia Chapman, for every moment of support and care.

1. Core curriculum in this context is meant to encompass basic coursework from the first year of law school through the third and final year.

2. National Congress of American Indians, *Native People and Tribal Governments Today*, Tribal Nations and the United States: An Introduction, 10–11 (2020).

is critical that students receive the necessary training to identify and navigate issues within Native American law. Despite this need, many law professors feel some degree of anxiety at teaching Native American law or incorporating Native American legal issues into the core curriculum for students.

To ease that anxiety, this selected and annotated bibliography presents several resources that can provide law professors with foundational materials for a Native American law course or incorporating Native American Law issues into another subject area. It should be noted that these materials only serve as a starting point to design the course or provide topical areas of discussion. These materials provide a basic framework for educators seeking to illuminate the issues and prepare students to tackle challenges they will find in practice.

Articles

Raymond Cross, *The Fate of Native American Diversity in America's Law Schools*, 27 Journal of Civil Rights and Economic Development 47 (2013).

Cross contends that law schools across the country are lagging in social justice initiatives and outreach or service to minority communities. The solution to this dilemma lies within Indian law as part of the curriculum. Cross notes that the federal Indian law policies made their way into the University of New Mexico Law School in 1967. That school began an intensive Indian Law training court—the Pre-Law Summer Institute (PLSI). Today, the program still develops young tribal members seeking to practice in Indian law. While many schools offer a course or two in their course guides, few maintain an active and consistent curriculum with faculty, staff, and programing to support native students and anyone else interested in Indian law and the issues. Moreover, Cross argues that the PLSI structure and model, one that promotes community building and empowerment at its core, is a desirable and necessary tool of modern legal education. Community-focused lawyers, understanding the needs of a special community and able to collaborate on a granular level, are needed across the United States. Cross insists that more schools should establish a program like PLSI and dedicate themselves to providing Indian law training as part of the core curriculum. Taking these steps would enable more law schools to foster social justice, create long-lasting partnerships with tribal communities, and create more skills-based learning for students.

Angelique Townsend Eaglewoman, Sheri Fremont, Gloria Valencia-Weber & Joseph Williams, *Recognizing the Importance of Indian Law on State Bar Examinations*, The Federal Lawyer, April 2013, at 30–34, 45.

In their work, Eaglewoman writes that, "Indian law is an umbrella term that includes both Tribal and Federal Indian law." (31) She notes that because of constant friction between claims of jurisdiction, Indian law requires a special competency among practitioners. (31) To aid that competency, Eaglewoman insists that federal Indian law needs to be treated as a core subject in law school curriculum, and it needs to be on the bar exam.

Placing Indian law on the bar and making it part of the core requirements in law school will promote a better understanding from law enforcement and legal practitioners working with them. Knowledge of overlapping or conflicting jurisdictions is vital to law enforcement, and the lack of knowledge in this area is inexcusable.

Indian law also contains several subject-specific areas where federal law preempts state law. This is vital information to those practicing in Indian country, or on behalf of local, state, or federal government agencies.

Cynthia Ford, *Integrating Indian Law into a Traditional Civil Procedure Course*, 46 Syracuse Law Review 1243 (1996).

Ford's article suggests that law schools must move beyond offering Indian law as an elective course and work to incorporate it throughout the core curriculum. (1243–1244) She recommends using Indian law examples and hypotheticals in a host of subjects. Ford even offers a teaching packet available upon request to engage professors, and thus students, in intellectual curiosity on the subject. Competing jurisdictional questions between tribes, states, and the federal government make this area of law a rich training ground for students of civil procedure. Learning when and how a case can transfer to tribal court, or how courts honor the decisions of other jurisdictions, is vital to any law students or civil practicing attorney. (1247) As such, Ford notes that hypothetical and case examples from Indian law can become part of a civil procedure curriculum with minimal changes to any syllabus. Indian law impacts non-Indians acting within tribal borders or "engaging in transactions" with a tribe or tribal members subject to a specific tribal or federal statute. (1247–1249) This means that Indian law can affect almost anyone at any time given the right set of circumstances.

As of 1996, only 23.8% of law schools accredited in the United States offer at least one Indian law course. (1253) Of that 23.8%, it is not clear how many of these electives are offered regularly and continuously. It is just as likely that the course remains unoffered and unused.

James M. Grijalva, *The Pedagogy of American Indian Law: Article: Compared When? Teaching Indian Law in the Standard Curriculum*, 82 North Dakota Law Review 697 (2006).

Grijalva, a former Indian law practitioner, makes a strong case for Indian law as part of a regular and continuous standard curriculum for law school. "My representation of Tribal governments on a host of environmental and natural resources issues implicated contracts, property, torts, corporate law, bankruptcy, state and federal constitutional law, and taxation as well as civil procedure and professional responsibility." (698) As a professor, Grijalva incorporated tribal law and Indian law examples in his "other" courses such as environmental law and administrative law. He noted that based on simple geography, and the location of Tribes throughout the United States, students would likely encounter Indian law issues even if they had not chosen to practice Indian law. Grijalva argues that adding Indian law as part of the core curriculum, and adding case examples to other courses, adds integrity to the overall legal education. Law schools should address a historical deficiency on general student education surrounding tribes and tribal issues. (699) Moreover, he notes that Indian law issues can promote law students' critical thinking across various legal subjects and promote higher legal analysis. (700) Additionally, Grijalva argues that Indian law courses can promote higher matriculation rates for Native American law students. (703–704) Yet his most compelling statements come when he insists on preparing students to practice in a diverse world. In short, Grijalva insists that without Indian law, law students are not fully prepared to practice "in a multicultural world." (704)

Aliza G. Organick, *Tribal Law and Best Practices in Legal Education: Creating a New Path for the Study of Tribal Law*, 19 Kansas Journal of Law and Public Policy 63 (Fall 2009).

Organick writes about her experiences with creating a tribal court practice clinic in law school and the insights she gained into the process. She noted that practice training and skills instruction around Indian law issues is vital to student learning and to the "indigenous legal framework" that exists "in tribal court structures." (64) She also notes that students need to understand the importance of culture in the practice of Indian law and how culture is infused into every component of Indian law construction and interpretation.

In addressing the students' knowledge gap, Organick admits that she "greatly underestimated the amount of time" needed to explain "basic Federal Indian law and tribal court structure to students." (64) It became clear to her that federal Indian law as a course must be required and taught consistently every year to enable a clinic course to operate efficiently. Giving adequate attention to Indian law as a course, and to Indian law examples across the curriculum, provides students a necessary cultural context for the law of every jurisdiction in their geographic area. (65) Organick asserts that students are not adequately prepared to practice without that cultural context—regardless of whether they choose to practice Indian law or select another area of practice. (66–67)

Organick observes that Indian law and tribal law are sporadically taught, lacking consistent support and development as compared to the "mainstream curriculum." (68–69) To address the issue, she insists that faculty start integrating Indian law examples into business law, administrative law, civil procedure, and legal writing courses. (72)

Paul Spruhan, *Indian Law on State Bar Exams in the Age of the Uniform Bar Examination*, THE FEDERAL LAWYER, March 2015, at 14–15, 23.

Spruhan notes that a push to include Indian law on the bar exam gained momentum around 2002, only to have it fade by 2013. He cites fervor over uniformity on the bar exam as one source for the fading support and growing marginalization of Indian law as a school subject and exam topic. (14) Specifically, Spruhan observes that the adoption of the UBE, or uniform bar examination, by the National Conference of Bar Examiners impacted how Indian law has been supported. (14) The growing marginalization appears at odds with the fact that adopting the UBE does not preclude the use of additional topics for the exam.

Spruhan looks at South Dakota as an example of a state that requires Indian law as an essay topic on its bar exam for every test. Spruhan notes that students taking the exam in South Dakota learn basic Indian law as part of their coursework prior to the examination. (15)

For places without Indian law on the bar exam, Spruhan suggests that some level of Indian law coursework is still needed for practitioners. Independent coursework would test areas of knowledge that a bar exam cannot. (15)

Rennard Strickland & Gloria Valencia-Weber, *Observations on the Evolution of Indian Law in the Law Schools*, 26 NEW MEXICO LAW REVIEW 153 (1996).

"If you look at Indian law and the teaching of Indian law in the history of legal education, you will find a void." (153) Strickland notes that "much of what has happened in Indian law and legal education is the result of strong support from Deans." (157) Indian law first became a focus of property law courses at the University of Tulsa, Oklahoma. (158) Constitutional law came next and described the government-to-government relationship between the Tribes and the federal government. The legal services movement of the 1960s enabled Indian law to flourish in separate clinical programs and skill-based training. (158)

Valencia-Weber takes over to explain Strickland's history lesson and why it is needed.

> Law schools must affirmatively act to (1) teach Indian law … (2) educate American Indians in law … and (3) change their curriculum and environment to incorporate … the viewpoints of Indigenous peoples which can enhance the law of the United States. (160)

The support for Indian law as a core piece of the legal education model must be continuous and unwavering. Indian law precedes the creation of the United States, and as such, it should be a core component of our legal education. Without it, our jurisprudential picture is incomplete. (161) It is also important to "decolonize" Indian law and teach from a tribal, cultural perspective to promote understanding and support for the principles of sovereignty. As of this 1996 article, only about 17 law schools offered more than one Indian law course regularly and continuously. (165) Funding, support, and continuous coursework must increase. (166)

Gloria Valencia-Weber & Sherri Nicole Thomas, *The Pedagogy of American Indian Law: Article: When the State Bar Exam Embraces Indian Law: Teaching Experiences and Observations*, 82 North Dakota Law Review 741 (2006).

In this article, Valencia-Weber recounts the creation of the Pre-Law Summer Institute at the University of New Mexico. PLSI focuses on "preparing entering students for law school, developing tribal governmental institutions, and strengthening the various relationships of tribal governments with federal, state, local and other governments." (744) Valencia-Weber expresses some dismay, however, at the lack of funding for these programs. Beyond funding, one concern is that the PLSI program remains an outlier in the field, and not enough schools appear ready and willing to create their own programs. In 2006, Valencia-Weber noted only about 64 of about 200 law schools offer Indian law coursework. Additionally, she observes that some courses are legal history taught sporadically by adjunct or visiting faculty and not considered part of the main curriculum. (745)

In contrast, Valencia-Weber uses University of New Mexico as an example of commitment and support. This University requires more than one Indian law course for special certification of students and over nine elective courses beyond clinics to support student specialization in the subject area. (746–747) Further, she notes that the University "mainstreams" Indian law into basic courses like Torts and Contracts to provide students general exposure to the subject area.

Valencia-Weber observes that practicing attorneys, not identifying as Indian law practitioners, are encountering Indian law issues with increasing frequency. These practitioners need help and often more Indian law education. It is an ethical issue of competency as well as a public interest issue. (750) A full and complete commitment to the subject of Indian law by law schools and state bar examiners is needed to promote "respect for the Tribes and members whose lives are most affected by this unique body of law." (775)

Books

Reading American Indian Law: Foundational Principles (Grant Christensen & Melissa L. Tatum eds., 2020).

This work is a collection of scholarly essays identifying tribal sovereignty and Indian law issues. In Bethany Berger's chapter on racism and sovereignty, she indicates that much of the United States Supreme Court's selective memory on sovereignty is rooted in an effort to treat tribes and tribal members as a racial group instead of a political classification. (72) The attempt to do so is a thinly veiled attempt to diminish or remove the inherent sovereignty of Tribes and Tribal members.

The rest of the book continues to press the narrative of reading Indian law from a native perspective with Native scholars' voices. The Honorable Robert Yazzie of the Navajo Nation Supreme Court discusses the concept of common law—the law developed by judges in court decisions outside of statutory or civil law. (121–139) He notes that the tribal court common law decisions—using traditions and customs of the tribal community—will often contrast, or even conflict, with the better-known common law standards of state courts or Anglo-American courts. (121) This contrast and conflict can cause heartburn and confusion for the uninitiated. To resolve that discomfort, some practitioners prefer to ignore, minimize, or insult tribal courts in a way that attempts to diminish their impact and authority.

Sarah Krakoff tackles this issue in her chapter on the Supreme Court and its lack of understanding of Indian law. (188–210) Krakoff notes that diminishing sovereignty or declaring it nonexistent would be akin to termination of Native peoples' separate status and rights. (189) She insists that tribes and advocates must create a robust explanation of sovereignty, how tribal governments exercise it, and why they do so. This approach would educate others and better protect tribal sovereignty. Kevin Washburn's chapter notes that this area of law suffers from a lack of tribal representation and cultural traditions related to justice. (357–380)

National Council of Juvenile and Family Court Judges, Indian Child Welfare Act Judicial Benchbook (2017).

This book is free and downloadable at https://www.ncjfcj.org/wp-content/uploads/2018/09/NCJFCJ_ICWA_Judicial_Benchbook_Final_Web.pdf. Written primarily for judges and practitioners, the easy-to-use handbook walks the reader through the basic steps of ICWA, how to define standards under the Act, and how to understand the process in ICWA according to each type of adjudication governed by ICWA.

Stephen L. Pevar, The Rights of Indian Tribes (4th ed. 2012).

The most recent edition of Pevar's work starts with an overview of federal Indian policy from the settlement at Jamestown, Virginia, in 1607 through the 2000s. It moves on to describe the federal trust responsibility and treaties. Pevar details the duties of a trustee, what that duty requires of federal officials, what standard to apply in a trust responsibility case, and when or how a trust responsibility is triggered in an event. (30–34) Pevar goes to great lengths to discuss the legal remedies available to a tribe asserting that the federal government broke its trust responsibility in a given case. (36–40) When discussing treaties, he notes the mechanics of signing a treaty, what the treaty legally addresses, how they are interpreted, and what happens when someone claims that a treaty was violated. (45–53) Pevar later moves onto self-governance and what role a state can play when a tribe exists in its space. Pevar notes the conflict between the federal plenary power and tribal sovereignty. He insists that sovereignty for tribal nations—predating the federal government—cannot be diminished or released by the federal government's plenary power. It cannot remove what it could not grant or bestow. (82–83)

When tackling state government's response to tribal nations, Pevar states that: "Ever since the United States was founded, state governments have attempted (1) to compel Indians to obey state law, (2) to erode Tribal law, and (3) to extend their authority within Indian reservations." (109)

Pevar discusses jurisdictional issues in the context of specific areas of Indian law. He looks at the right of taxation and what entities can exercise the sovereign power of taxation. (165–183) He discusses water rights under the *Winters* Doctrine and how that impacts tribal nations depending on their region of the United States. (205–209) Pevar then details how and when a tribe can regulate water and water use in a manner that does not conflict with the Clean Water Act and federal legislative power. (215–219). He addresses Indian law legislation in specific examples over the remaining chapters.

In this same work, he also addresses the Indian Child Welfare Act (ICWA), from its inception and the supporting reasoning to supporting its requirements in court. (291–306). Pevar explains in detail why ICWA became necessary, and he lays out the basic requirements and criteria within the statute. He goes on to explain which children qualify under the statute, and what state courts can and cannot do when a child custody proceeding falls under ICWA. (291–298). He discusses what "active efforts" requires under the statute and how placement works under the law. (297–301). All of this information, Pevar notes, is needed to ethically manage an ICWA case and any of its tangential issues. Finally, Pevar explains how tribes become involved in ICWA cases, the rights of the noncustodial parent, and what happens in an ICWA case when Public Law 280 also impacts the proceedings. (301–304). For many practitioners in Public Law 280 states, this interplay between the statutes is a necessary area to learn.

Robert Odawi Porter, Sovereignty, Colonialism, and the Indigenous Nations: A Reader (2005).

Sovereignty can take many forms and meanings. Porter attempts to capture a fraction of those forms and meanings by presenting statements from leaders and scholars on the subject. Billy Evans Horse—Leader of the Kiowa Nation of Oklahoma—was quoted as saying, "our inherent sovereignty is not defined by the United States government or the State of Oklahoma." (33) This is an unalienable right amongst tribal nations and exists without the approval or grant from any outside actor or government.

The work continues with discussions on how outside actors and governments have attempted to distinguish or erase that sovereignty. But it is not within their power to bestow sovereignty, diminish sovereignty, or take it away.

Porter expands on the discussion of sovereignty by featuring preeminent scholars' works in Indian law and American Indian Studies.

In his section, Vine Deloria Jr. remarks that judges often struggle with fully grasping and applying tribal sovereignty. (52–53) The confusion comes in part from an outsider's focus on finding the source of sovereignty and not simply acknowledging the exercise of it as being proof of its existence. (53) Sovereignty, as exercised by tribal people, needs a "continued, cultural integrity" for it to flourish. (54) "Cultural integrity involves a commitment to a central ... purpose that motivates a group of people, enables them to form ... social institutions, and provides for them a clear identity." (54) Under this framework, Porter notes that tribal sovereignty depends on these elements:

> (i) the degree to which Indians believe in the right to define their own future, (ii) the degree to which Indians have the ability to carry out those beliefs, (iii) the degree to which tribal sovereigns' acts are recognized both within the Tribe and by the outside world. (55)

In the next seven chapters, he establishes that threats to tribal sovereignty come from greed, fear, animosity, paternalism, assimilation, self-destructive tendencies, and other related threats to equality. Porter's solution to these ailments is to redefine, reframe, and redevelop the subjects within Indian law and tribal governance with a focus on a uniquely Tribal and Indigenous perspective. It means ensuring that Indian law, and all its facets, contain an Indigenous perspective, an Indigenous reasoning, and an Indigenous construction and design. That is how sovereignty is strengthened and enhanced.

Websites and Online Resources

Difficult Dialogues National Resource Center, *Beyond Land Acknowledgements* (2022), https://www.youtube.com/watch?v=GzVTXF_3WDI (also available at https://www.difficultdialogues.org/webinars).

> This webinar provides an overview of decolonization practices, focusing on Indigenous voices and perspectives, and providing real examples of creating acknowledgements and working in collaboration with Indigenous communities. This same area also contains additional links to land acknowledgement examples from the University of Pennsylvania.

Every Learner, Everywhere, *An Introduction to Indigenous Land Acknowledgements for College and University Leaders* (2021), https://www.everylearnereverywhere.org/blog/an-introduction-to-indigenous-land-acknowledgements-for-college-and-university-leaders/.

This site provides a downloadable toolkit and interactive maps for locating tribal communities and referencing correct site locations. It provides links to Native Land Digital as a tool for interactive exploration. Moreover, the site references the Land-Grab Universities as a historical starting point for the purpose and use of land acknowledgements. The report on Land-Grab Universities is linked from this page to one at High Country News, and it explains the Morrill Act of 1862 and how universities under that Act benefited from the active seizure of Indigenous lands.

Julia Giffin, *The obstacles of being a Native law student and how attorneys can help*, ABA Student Lawyer (Nov. 9, 2021), https://abaforlawstudents.com/2021/11/09/the-obstacles-of-being-a-native-law-student-and-how-attorneys-can-help/.

Giffin writes about the National Native Law Student Association's (NNALSA) efforts to increase diversity and inclusive support in law schools through the use of standards featured in a petition to promote a "Native friendly" environment. She remarks generally that students need to see Native representation throughout the schools and more financial support that promotes Native success. In the petition, NNALSA asked for more support for diversity initiatives and for Indian law to be a consistent part of the law school curriculum. NNALSA insists that the related coursework should be taught consistently by Native full-time faculty. Indian law should be incorporated into the rest of the curriculum as a way to teach all law students about three systems of government: federal, state, and tribal. Erasure of these tribal systems fails to adequately train attorneys to practice across the country whenever they encounter a case containing any element of tribal or Indian law. Law school must actively promote and create a space that sees, acknowledges, and welcomes tribal community members. Failing to teach about tribal law, tribal governments, and Indigenous perspectives on law fails to create that space. Showing active efforts in this area requires financial support as well as participatory support in creating and promoting access to Indian law or tribal law employment.

Gabriel Kuris, *What Native American Law Applicants Should Know*, U.S. News (Mar. 8, 2021), https://www.usnews.com/education/blogs/law-admissions-lowdown/articles/what-native-american-and-indigenous-law-applicants-should-know.

Kuris notes five things for Native American applicants to consider:

- Reaching out can be beneficial.
- Resources are available to Native American applicants.
- Native American affiliation encompasses more than Tribal enrollment.
- There are more Native American law students than official statistics show.
- Advocating for Native American communities can take many forms.

Networking in the small and close-knit community of Indian law can have practical benefits to students seeking to become practitioners. Data collected on the student body of a school often obscures a Native applicant's identity in a manner that makes the overall student body numbers appear smaller. Kuris advocates for applicants speaking up and speaking out to achieve more effective results toward community building and networking. He notes that these efforts enrich the school environment for all involved.

"I Am a Native Law Student": Diverse Perspectives Panel on the Native Law School Experience," Association of American Law Schools (Aug. 3, 2021), https://www.aals.org/sections/list/indian-nations-and-indigenous-peoples/I-am-a-native-law-student-diverse-perspectives-panel-on-the-native-law-school-experience/.

A webinar following statements from Native law students from around the country. The webinar digs into Native students' reasons for attending law school, selecting their programs, what's been missing, and what they'd like to see in the future. Straight from the student body, this webinar discusses what needs to change in law school and how to support Native students and a Native curriculum.

Decolonizing Education—Teacher Resources, Facebook (last updated Sept. 27, 2022), https://www.facebook.com/pages/category/Tutor-Teacher/Decolonizing-Education-Teacher-Resources-261007904594610/.

This Facebook page provides links and resources for teachers looking to make active efforts towards decolonizing their curriculum and instruction.

Native Governance Center, *A Guide to Indigenous Land Acknowledgement*, (Oct. 22, 2019), https://nativegov.org/news/a-guide-to-indigenous-land-acknowledgment/.

This site is an online guide with links to additional resources crafted and driven by tribal communities to incorporate Indigenous perspective into any statement. The guide provides general steps to begin the process of crafting a specific and personal statement that honors the Indigenous communities of the area. It explains how to express the statement in respectful terms that enable collaboration and continued conversation. It also includes a self-assessment tool to incorporate into the beginning process of researching Indigenous communities and exercises of sovereignty. The self-assessment and the guide are online and free to download for anyone wanting to begin the process.

Trent University, *How to Do a Land Acknowledgement* (May 3, 2021), https://www.trentu.ca/teaching/how-do-land-acknowledgment.

For institutions beginning this journey, Trent's page explains what a land acknowledgement is meant to be at its core and why we engage in the practice of it. The site explains how to engage in the practice of presenting your land acknowledgement in a way that is impactful, meaningful, and not merely performative. It also provides three general steps that a researcher must embrace to create a statement that is personal, specific, and ultimately the beginning of celebration and collaboration with tribal communities of the area.

U.S. Department of Arts and Culture, *Honor Native Land: A Guide and Call to Acknowledgement* (Aug. 29, 2022), https://usdac.us/nativeland/.

This site contains a free, downloadable guide to crafting a land acknowledgement statement. It also explains why these statements combat the "Discovery Doctrine" and reawaken an understanding in the larger community about colonization and the role of academic institutions in continuing along the same path. Moreover, it reminds scholars and advocates that the statement is meant to be the start of further action and not a performative gesture that ends a larger conversation. The guide explains the general research process and links to start that process.

Engaging with Equity in International Law—Personal Reflections

*J. Nilmini Silva-Send**

Each era interprets history according to its own concerns.[1]

Introduction

Equity has become an overarching concern of our times, as is the changing climate.[2] Both are interconnected, and both are simultaneously global and local in scale. Many classes are offered at universities—in law schools, in the sciences, in economics, and in social sciences about the complex law, economics, and science of climate change; all of these classes use the United Nations Framework Convention on Climate Change (UNFCCC)[3] as their basis. The UNFCCC and its latest iteration, the Paris Agreement,[4] explicitly and implicitly recognize equity issues.[5] Nations that have least contributed to the climate change problem expect to pay the highest price in terms of the ability to

---

* Dr. J. Nilmini Silva-Send, Associate Director, Energy Policy Initiatives Center, University of San Diego School of Law.

1. Antony Anghie, *Asia in the History and Theory of International Law*, THE OXFORD HANDBOOK OF INTERNATIONAL LAW IN ASIA AND THE PACIFIC 68 (Simon Chesterman et al. eds., 2019).

2. This is not to say that aspects of equity have not been part of scholarly writings in the past, but today's concerns, I find, are more holistic, overarching, and global than in the past.

3. United Nations Framework Convention on Climate Change, May 9, 1992, 31 I.L.M. 849 [hereinafter UNFCCC], https://unfccc.int/files/essential_background/background_publications_htmlpdf/application/pdf/conveng.pdf

4. Framework Convention on Climate Change, Adoption of the Paris Agreement, Dec. 12, 2015, U.N. Doc. FCCC/CP/2015/L.9/Rev.1, https://unfccc.int/resource/docs/2015/cop21/eng/l09r01.pdf.

5. *Id.* at n. 3. There are at least five mentions of equity, for example:

- From the Preamble: "... principle of equity and common but differentiated responsibilities and respective capabilities, in the light of different national circumstances ..."; "Emphasizing the intrinsic relationship that climate change actions, responses and impacts have with equitable access to sustainable development...."; "Taking into account the imperatives of a just transition of the workforce and the creation of decent work ..."

become wealthy using the fossil-fuel pathway previously taken by the United States and European countries and their ability to deal with climate change impacts.[6] At both the local and global levels, attempts to right past wrongs are seen as needed to deal with mitigation of greenhouse gases[7] and to adapt to the consequences of climate change.[8]

In teaching about international law, and to strive for an ever-more-equitable world, we need a shared understanding of the basis of international relations among countries. I would argue that public international law should be a *foundational* law class, more than just an elective, *necessary* to comprehend today's international relations. The historical evolution of international law is instructive in its demonstration of equity among nations. Understanding, while not condoning, inequity in international law has provided my students and I with lessons for any scale of society. I propose that we use history as the starting point for ways to redirect thinking about equity across countries and communities, increase the sensitivity of all peoples to the impacts of inequity, and reduce the fear that may prevent us from dealing with it for future generations.

I will not attempt to define equity, or inequity, other than to say that it is not the same as equality but comprises a *feeling* of injustice, of unfairness, and therefore can be recognized without a definition. However, it must be recognized that there are what I may call inherent inequities, based on mere geographical size or location of a nation, its population size, its level of maturity. In this essay, I am concerned with human-caused historical inequities rather than inherent inequities. In the following sections, I draw on my experience teaching international law, international energy investment law, law of the sea, a simulation of an international negotiation, and an experiential cross-border pollution class, respectively, to demonstrate historical inequities. In so doing, I must provide some history in a nutshell. By basing each topic on its history, we can propose better ways to incorporate equity into future teaching. As a co-benefit, history

---

- From Article 2: "This Agreement will be implemented to reflect equity and the principle of common but differentiated responsibilities . . ."

Other aspects of equity are referenced indirectly, such as in the Preamble, ". . . noting the importance for some of the concept of 'climate justice,' when taking action to address climate change," and "Taking into account the imperatives of a just transition of the workforce and the creation of decent work. . . ."

6. The impacts of climate change affect some countries and communities more than others. Sea level rise, for example, affects islands and low-lying coastal communities, increasing heat affects the older populations disproportionately to others.

7. In 1997, Brazil proposed that mitigation requirements be proportional to each country's historical responsibility for warming. See Proposed Elements of a Protocol to the United Nations Framework Convention on Climate Change, Presented by Brazil in Response to the Berlin Mandate (submitted May 28, 1997), https://unfccc.int/resource/docs/1997/agbm/03b.pdf.

8. In several U.S. states, equity has become a component of major climate change legislation. Starting with A.B. 32 (2006) (codified as amended at Cal. Health & Safety Code § 38500 *et seq.*), the Global Warming Solutions Act, California committed to cutting greenhouse gases and "to the extent feasible, direct public and private investment toward the most disadvantaged communities in California." A most recent example is the prohibition of new oil and gas wells within 3,200 feet of day care facilities, homes, schools, and hospitals, a goal of environmental justice activists for nearly a decade due to the disparate impacts in low-income communities of color. S.B. 1137, 2021–2022 Reg. Sess. (Cal. 2022), codified at Cal. Pub. Res. Code § 3280 *et seq.*

can be used to partly address a significant problem among upper-level students who come to me: their lack, but sore need, for a much greater depth and breadth of both general knowledge and current affairs to deal with equity in their daily lives.

Exposing Inequity in International Law

I am certainly not alone in noticing that the international law texts of the last decades[9] all start around the mid-1600s with a reference to the Peace of Westphalia,[10] and to Dutch jurist Grotius as the "father of modern international law" with his works on war and peace, prizes of war, freedom to trade, and freedom of the seas.[11] The Peace of Westphalia certainly brought an end to the hegemony of the European-based papal empire. However, I believe that more significant than this treaty is the reference to an incident in the Eastern oceans where a commercial vessel of the Dutch East India Company (VOC) seized a Portuguese commercial vessel carrying prized goods from the East for trade and sale in Portugal. This incident was the impetus for the most far-reaching chapters of Grotius's writings on the right to trade and the freedom of the seas.[12] Most international law textbooks do not delve into the reasons Grotius wrote: it was to justify this seizure by its ship's captain, a cousin of Grotius. Grotius defended the seizure on the basis of principles of self-defense, and self-preservation, including that ownership of goods could be attained through labor and industry, and also through fighting evil (the Portuguese being considered evil by the Dutch).[13]

9. MALCOLM N. SHAW, INTERNATIONAL LAW (7th ed. 2014); LORI F. DAMROSCH & SEAN D. MURPHY, INTERNATIONAL LAW (6th ed., 2014) IAN BROWNLIE, PRINCIPLES OF PUBLIC INTERNATIONAL LAW (8th ed. 2012); INTERNATIONAL LAW (Malcolm Evans ed., 4th ed. 2014); ANTONIO CASSESE, INTERNATIONAL LAW (2d ed. 2004).

10. The Peace of Westphalia was a 1648 treaty signed to end the massive religious wars and battles between European powers and the Holy Roman Empire based on the consent of all the "states" present. Some authors support the view that the Peace of Westphalia "... still remains the model for international politics around the world and the concept of state sovereignty, solidified by the peace ..." and "... is still the basis for modem international treaties and conventions." Steven Patton, *The Peace of Westphalia and it Affects* [sic] *on International Relations, Diplomacy and Foreign Policy*, THE HISTORIES, Fall 2010, at 91, https://digitalcommons.lasalle.edu/the_histories/vol10/iss1/5.

11. HUGO GROTIUS, DE JURE BELLI AC PACIS [The Laws of War and Peace] (Richard Tuck ed., 2005) (originally published 1625) consists of three books. The prizes of war are discussed in HUGO GROTIUS, COMMENTARY ON THE LAW OF PRIZE AND BOOTY [De Jure Praedae Commentarius] (Martine Julia van Ittersum, ed., 2006). The freedom to trade and freedom of the seas are discussed in GROTIUS, FREEDOM OF THE SEAS [Mare Liberum] (David Armitage ed., Richard Hakluyt trans., 2004) (originally published 1609).

12. *See* GROTIUS, FREEDOM OF THE SEAS, *supra* note 11. The freedom of the seas was not new in Asian oceans and existed long before Grotius. However, Grotius reacted to the attempts by Portugal and Spain, including through Papal decrees, to monopolize the oceans to their trade advantage at the time.

13. *See id.* at xvii, n.9. *De jure belli ac pacis*, Book II, provides justifications for a just war.

In addition, Grotius defended the principle of the freedom of the seas and the freedom to trade against the claimed exclusive ownership of the seas and trade by Portugal and Spain.[14] While Grotius's systematic and impressive defense of the specific incident does draw on older historical writings such as Roman law and Aristotle, and acknowledges that islands such as "... Java, Tabrobana and the greatest part of the Moluccas ... have, and always had, their kings, their commonwealth, their laws and liberties,"[15] today's international law textbooks pay scant reference to even the existence of non-European laws.

At the present time, a textbook is not a piece of scholarly writing and research in defense of a particular incident and need not draw on classical or other rules of international conduct. However, pointing to or asking some of the same questions Grotius asked can be used within today's international law teaching. Thus, questioned Grotius, "How can it be said by any means that the Portugals have found out India which was so famous many ages since, even from the time of Horace?"[16] And what laws did the "Persians and Arabians," referred to by Grotius as the "borderers," have?[17] How did the Portuguese, the Spanish, the Dutch, and the British evolve from being mere traders welcomed along faraway coasts, to occupiers and invaders? Certainly there was no prevention by the Indians, the Chinese, the Persians, and Arabs to deter Europeans from sailing the seas. But European powers were at war with each other, fighting for economic growth, domination, and expansion through trade in spices, textiles, porcelain, precious stones, minerals, and other goods across the East, Africa, and South America. European battles were fought on the basis of what would today be considered illegal treaties and declarations, including Papal declarations on ownership of the oceans, in order to regulate and block other European powers in the East, in Africa, and in South America. These aspects are not mentioned in today's international law textbooks.

I believe that international law texts *can and should* integrate historical context to a much greater degree than they do, and must not ignore the contribution of philosophies, laws, and customs older-and-other than those from the start of European colonization in the 1600s. Alexandrowicz[18] provides an early post-colonial critique of Western international law, followed more recently by Koskenniemi,[19] Anghie,[20] Neff,[21] and Bederman.[22] Each assesses aspects of international law such as treaty making, rules of warfare, and diplomacy that include the influences of laws from the Near East, ancient

---

14. *See id.* at xviii, n. 10
15. *Id.* at 13.
16. *Id.* at 14.
17. *Id.*
18. Charles Henry Alexandrowicz, An Introduction to the History of the Law of Nations in the East Indies (1967).
19. Martti Koskenniemi, The Gentle Civiliser of Nations: the Rise and Fall of International Law, 1870–1960 (2000).
20 Antony Anghie, Imperialism, Sovereignty, and the Making of International Law (2004).
21. Stephen C. Neff, Justice among Nations (2014).
22. David J. Bederman, International Law in Antiquity (2001).

Rome, and Greece. However, nuggets of "equity" from these writings have still not become part of the typical textbooks. And while we wait for such changes,[23] a teacher of international law has a duty to include as much history as possible in the curriculum to help expose current equity issues in international law. Below, I provide some specific examples from my course teachings.

Seeing International Law Textbooks through an Equity Lens

The traditional international law class curriculum, based on any current international law textbook,[24] starts with the *sources* of international law, then the *subjects* of international law, the *relationship* between international and domestic law, the *recognition* of states, *jurisdiction* and *immunities* of states, and finally *responsibility* of states.[25] These topics are followed by chapters on more specific international law, such as environmental law, law of the sea, and human rights.

Starting with the first topic on *sources* of international law, there is always reference to the Statute of the International Court of Justice (ICJ) where Art 38 1(c) states that "... the general principles of law recognized by civilized nations...." are one of the sources of international law to be applied to the resolution of disputes submitted to the Court. The use of the term "civilized" nations by the original, predominantly Christian negotiators of the 1948 statute begs the question of what is meant by "civilized."[26] In teaching about Art 38 1(c), I have found it sufficient to simply bring up this question and ask students to find out what is considered "civilized" in Buddhist, Hindu, or Islamic teachings.

Having thus opened an equity aspect to the sources of international law, I run into the next equity issue with the concept of a *state* as a *subject* of international law. By this point, I have dutifully explained to students that public international law regulates relations between states, and together we look for characteristics that must be present before an entity can be recognized as a state, such as an effective government, a population, and territory. As I teach, I struggle with the word *state*: should we rather call it nation-state, country, or nation? What are the differences? I look into what social sciences tell us about states, and read that nation-states can be those built on ethnicity,

23. Shaw's *International Law* textbook has changed significantly since its first edition in 1977. The latest edition includes a 36-page chapter on historical context. *See* Malcolm N. Shaw, International Law (9th ed. 2021). Evans' edited book on international law includes chapters by the writers who have examined historical aspects before the start of European colonization efforts and its influences on international law. *See supra* note 9.

24. *See supra* note 9.

25. Consult the table of contents in any of the titles *supra* note 9.

26. See Anghie, *supra* note 1, at 80. As per Anghie's exploration of what it takes to become civilized, he quotes a Japanese general after Japan's military victory over Russia in the Battle of Tsushima Strait, 1905: "Once we defeat you in war, we become civilized."

or those built on a willingness to live together.[27] It appears to me that the social sciences are written mainly by Western writers, and that both concepts are European subjective constructs that have been taken into international law, perhaps without regard for what other civilizations considered "nations," if they did at all. For example, I have read anecdotally that Native Americans did not have a concept of property ownership,[28] and that land, like air and water, could not be owned so that it would have been nearly impossible for Native Americans to imagine a state as defined today. It is easy to find examples of similar problems related to statehood—a glance at a map of the continent of Africa and the symmetry of its nations suggests a certain artificiality. As author Martin Meredith has described, almost all African countries are artificial states constructed by European governments during the Scramble for Africa at the end of the nineteenth century. In all, some 10,000 African polities were amalgamated into 40 European colonies and protectorates...."[29] Although European powers aggressively broke up Africa into relatively artificial nations without the consent of the people, the requirements to be recognized as a state by the European Union (EU) today include requirements such as "respect for the inviolability of all frontiers which can only be changed by peaceful means and by common agreement.... The Community and its member states will not recognize entities which are the result of aggression.[30]

Under these criteria, most African nations and the United States would not be recognized as states by the EU and its member states. What type of equity considerations are we faced with in this example?

Related to the concept of a state as an entity based on nationality, I speak to students about Anghie's explanation of nationality as a prerequisite for post-colonial "states," that:

> ... nationalism in these new states created an immediate problem by seeming to demand a singularity that did not exist. Whereas in earlier times different ethnicities and cultures had interacted with and accommodated each other

---

27. Any definition by the social sciences, such as in the *Encyclopedia Britannica*, provides these explanations but also demonstrates the exclusive dominance of European thinkers on the subject. *See, e.g.*, *Dmitry Mikhaylovich, Prince Golitsyn*, BRITANNICA.COM, https://www.britannica.com/biography/Dmitry-Mikhaylovich-Knyaz-Golitsyn.

28. *See, e.g.*, National Museum of the American Indian, *The Different Views of Land*, NATIVE KNOWLEDGE 360°, https://americanindian.si.edu/nk360/manhattan/different-views-land/different-views-land.cshtml#:~:text=Native%20Americans%2C%20did%20not%20appreciate,rights%20to%20use%20the%20lands.

29. Martin Meredith, author of the "The Fate of Africa," Live Q&A with Martin Meredith, WASHINGTONPOST.COM (Jan. 20, 2006), https://perma.cc/K8RS-AM5C.

30. The conditions for acceptance as a state to the European Union are provided in the European Community's Declaration on the "Guidelines on the Recognition of New States in Eastern Europe and in the Soviet Union," and consist of *respect for the provisions of the Charter of the United Nations ... especially with regard to the rule of law, democracy and human rights, guarantees for the rights of ethnic and national groups and minorities ... acceptance of all relevant commitments with regard to disarmament and nuclear non-proliferation as well as to security and regional stability, commitment to settle by agreement, including where appropriate by recourse to arbitration, all questions concerning State succession and regional disputes,* "and that the Community and its Member States will not recognize entities which are the result of aggression." *See* U.N. Doc. S/23293 (Dec. 16, 1991).

> in various ways, the edict of the nation-state created a massive insecurity amongst both majority and minority communities in ethnically divided states. It is notable that many Asian countries, shortly after achieving independence, passed nationality laws that left minorities stateless or disadvantaged. The tragic plight of the Rohingya is one product of this phenomenon. The spectre of secession and security have continued to haunt many Asian states. Sri Lanka's particularly bloody war against Tamil separatists, with its ongoing and unresolved issues of accountability and reconciliation, is emblematic in this regard. At the very heart of such conflicts is the meaning of the 'nation-state'.[31]

I have found many other ways to teach about equity in international law. One can use a group of treaties by subject matter, such as petroleum extraction treaties, or maritime delimitation treaties, or consider the history of a single comprehensive treaty regime, such as the climate change regime. One can use practicum courses on a single issue, such as cross-border pollution, and one can examine fairness in outcomes of litigation. The following sections briefly describe how each topic I teach is well-suited to learning about equity.

Petroleum Extraction Treaties and International Energy Law

European expansion in the 1600s created zones of different European legal systems throughout the world and coincided with discoveries and inventions related to oil. Even though oil had been known in the ancient world of Mesopotamia and Greece, and in the late 1800s in Eastern Europe,[32] its commercial and competitive exploitation did not begin until the late 1800s by inventions in America.[33] By the mid-1800s, the British East India Company, formed for trade in South Asia, had set up posts in the Persian Gulf, eventually gaining control of large parts of these geographies.[34] As the technology for oil extraction and its uses became better known, oil was discovered in large quantities around the world. In the mid-1800s, the Nobel brothers of Sweden expanded the Baku oil boom with their technology to transport the oil in oil tankers.[35] This led the way to shipping out the oil discovered in Iran and Iraq, and setting up Anglo-Persian, now British Petroleum (BP).[36] Similarly, the Dutch East India Company had founded settlements, later colonies, in Indonesian islands such as Sumatra and Java, where oil discoveries were also made, leading to the establishment of oil compa-

31. Anghie, *supra* note 1, at 88.
32. Daniel Yergin, The Prize: The Epic Quest for Oil, Money & Power 23 (1990).
33. *Id.* at 15–55.
34. David Veevers, The Origins of the British Empire in Asia, 1600–1750 1–23 (2020).
35. *Id.* at 59, n. 29.
36. *See id.* at 211–269.

nies such as Shell.[37] The history of oil and gas has been well documented by Yergin[38] and forms an integral part of my class on international energy law.

Petroleum extraction and production agreements provide an excellent source to ponder procedural and participatory equity over time. One of the initial petroleum extraction agreements was made with the Shah of Persia alone, at a time when the significance of petroleum was little appreciated by the Persians themselves. The 1901 D'Arcy agreement[39] was a concession agreement by the state of Persia with a private person, Mr. D'Arcy, and preceded similar concession agreements with private companies. Most of these early petroleum concessions gave exclusive rights for exploration, extraction and sale, to huge geographical regions, such as the whole area of Iran, for long periods of time, like 60 years, and for minimal royalties. Under the D'Arcy Concession, the royalty to Iran was less than the taxes of the profits by the British government.[40] Similar concessions were in use in colonies of various European powers.[41] Could there be negotiating equity in drawing up treaties when the knowledge and capacity of the colonial populations were so different compared with those of the powerful colonizers?

As the awareness of the terms and impacts of the early concession agreements increased, nascent nation-states began to flex their muscles and themselves to use the concept of nationality to nationalize oil companies[42] in acts that could be considered acts of desperation under historically unequal treaties, and to renegotiate for improved terms.[43] The European governments, however, considered such nationalizations illegal, demanding return of the property or compensation. Principles of international law were developed to justify the European position,[44] and when renegotiations took place, the principle of immediate and adequate compensation for expropriation evolved painfully toward recognition of a right to expropriate (investments)[45] for the public interest.

---

37. *See id.* at 57, 63–77, 117–128.

38. *See* Yergin, *supra* note 32.

39. Agreement of 28th May, 1901 (the D'Arcy Concession), https://perma.cc/P33N-JTTR.

40. Yergin, *supra* note 32, chapter 14.

41. Cătălin Gabriel Stănescu, Eduardo G. Pereira & Aaron Koenck, *Petroleum Concessions, Licenses and Leases: "Same-Same but Different"?* 8 LSU J. Energy L. & Resources 100 (2020).

42. *See, e.g.*, Yergin, *supra* note 32, at 508.

43. *Id.* at 101, n.40.

44. The search for stability for investors globally is the underlying reason for the development of international law principles such as most favored nation, national treatment, fair and equitable principle, or due process, where these principles are used to justify the investor action in investor-state disputes. In energy investment cases, these principles have traditionally arisen in state expropriation. Historically, investors have been European states looking for markets globally and needing such stability.

45. The application of the principle of "prompt, adequate and effective" compensation for government takings of foreign property in a foreign state was used to defend many companies since the 1930s; its importance has decreased now. For example, in *Banco National de Cuba v. Sabbatino*, the United States reduced the import quota for Cuban sugar, upon which Cuba nationalized certain US companies in Cuba. 376 U.S. 398 (1964). In a database of energy investment arbitration matters I have kept over the years, I have not found a single instance of justification of the state action against the investor using of the same principles, even if a state has had success in a few cases against an investor for other reasons.

Determination of the contours of these principles spawned a huge area of international arbitration, at first mostly in secret, where energy contracts between companies and governments were made subject to superior investment treaties between their governments,[46] which protected companies backed by their governments. The international energy arbitrations of the last few decades have seen unprecedented compensation awards against developing, ex-colony, resource-rich countries, a compensation so large that several countries have denounced these treaties.[47]

In energy resource extraction treaties, therefore, students can research equity in multiple ways: the negotiation process for these treaties, resistance to the treaties in practice, the renegotiation options, and outcomes of international arbitration litigation.

Law of the Sea—Maritime Entitlements

The Law of the Seas Convention (UNCLOS, 1982) was hailed as the first modern treaty, bringing nearly all nations together to agree on principles of maritime delimitation and entitlements.[48] While UNCLOS saw a more equitable negotiating process and outcomes than in the past, areas of contention, including those based on equity remain. It is useful to review law of the sea cases[49] through the lens of history. For example, in January 2013, the Philippines instituted arbitral proceedings against the People's Republic of China under Annex VII to the United Nations Convention on the Law of the Sea (The Republic of Philippines v. The People's Republic of China).[50] The arbitration concerned the role of historic rights and the sources of maritime entitlements in the South China Sea, the status of certain maritime features in the South China Sea, and the lawfulness of certain actions by China in the South China Sea that the Philippines alleged to be in violation of the Convention. China adopted a position of nonacceptance and nonparticipation in the proceedings, but in accordance with international law, the arbitration could nonetheless continue, and the South China Sea Arbitration resulted in all counts decided against China. However, as Anghie suggests, should the South China Seas issues be resolved on the basis of current international law, with a 12 nautical mile territorial sea, with freedom of any type of navigation by any nation

---

46. In the eighteenth and nineteenth centuries, European powers typically protected their overseas companies with weapons and armies.

47. United Nations Conference on Trade & Development, IIA Issues Note: Denunciation of the ICSID Convention and BIT, https://investmentpolicy.unctad.org/publications/40/iia-issues-note-denunciation-of-the-icsid-convention-and-bits.

48. James K. Sebenius, Negotiating the Law of the Sea (1984).

49. Int'l Tribunal for the Law of the Sea, List of Cases, https://www.itlos.org/en/main/cases/list-of-cases/ (last visited Oct. 10, 2022). Some law of the sea cases have arisen at the International Court of Justice; for example, its Advisory Opinion on Legal Consequences of the Separation of the Chagos Archipelago from Mauritius in 1965, which deals specifically about consequences of colonization and decolonization. Int'l Court of Justice, Legal Consequences of the Separation of the Chagos Archipelago from Mauritius in 1965 (Feb. 25, 2019), https://www.icj-cij.org/en/case/169.

50. The South China Sea Arbitration (The Republic of Philippines v. The People's Republic of China), 2013–19 (Perm. Ct. Arb. 2016), https://pca-cpa.org/en/cases/7/.

and classified as an international waterway?[51] Or should it be decided on the basis of much older regional customary law and cultural attributes, which were never included in the development of the arbitration?[52] Using a recent most weighty and impactful (in theory) decision or opinion is another excellent source for the study of equity in international relations.

Using a Single Treaty to Expose Inequities Holistically—International Climate Change Law

International climate change is a global phenomenon that affects all people and has brought nearly all countries together to develop an international treaty. It is recognized in the UNFCCC regime that the developed countries, which are the same European colonizing powers and their progeny—the United States, Canada, most Latin American countries, and Oceania—have profited from their past colonial exploits through massive exploitation of fossil fuels and accumulation of greenhouses gases (GHGs) far in excess of what the earth can quickly absorb. This historical inequity affects developing countries that may be unable to enjoy the consumption of goods and economic expansion seen as the basis for the highest standard of living today. Should those most responsible for the GHGs that are already in the atmosphere be held accountable for the changing climate? When China overtook the United States as producing the most GHGs per year in 2018, it was headline news, even if this absolute amount translated to a per capita value of less than half of the United States.'[53] The treaty could be studied only on the basis equity of its provisions on mitigation and adaptation, asking: How does the UNFCCC regime (including the Paris Agreement) address equity in theory and in practice?

51. Anghie, supra, Note 1, 88–89

52. Hans Dieter-Evers, *Understanding the South China Sea: An Explorative Cultural Analysis*, 10 Int'l J. Asia Pacific Stud. 77 (2014), https://www.zef.de/fileadmin/user_upload/hdevers_download_Evers2014-SouthChinaSea-IJAPS.pdf.

53. In 2018, the U.S. per capita CO2 emissions were 15.2 metric tons while China's was 7.2 metric tons. *Compare* The World Bank, CO_2 emissions (metric tons per capita)—United States https://data.worldbank.org/indicator/EN.ATM.CO2E.PC?locations=US, *with* The World Bank, CO_2 emissions (metric tons per capita)—China, https://data.worldbank.org/indicator/EN.ATM.CO2E.PC?locations=CN.

Using an Experiential Course: Cross-Border Marine Pollution—USA-Mexico

My initial goal for this experiential course was to investigate whether there is a legal basis under UNCLOS or other treaty, or under customary international law, for a potential claim by the United States against Mexico for marine pollution originating from northern Baja California to California waters and beaches. While the facts of the pollution incidents are clear, and a case could be made against Mexico on the basis of international law, a myriad of other factors related to equity arose in this class based on the need for peaceful settlement of disputes at this large binational border.[54] Students learn that marine pollution is caused by a swelling population on the Mexican side, with wastewater infrastructure in Mexico that is insufficient and cannot keep up, as well as increasing industrial wastes. Why is there a swelling population? Why is there a large industrial sector along the border? We find that industrial wastes come from a large increase in the number of factories producing goods for export especially to the United States—a result of the NAFTA treaty, where Mexico, United States, and Canada agreed to free trade so that goods that could be produced cheaper in Mexico could be, and the United States could expand their goods and services into the other two countries.[55] As a result, not only have industrial goods produced at the border created jobs and more movement between the countries, with ensuing cross-border pollution through air and water, but also Mexican agricultural goods started to be produced more for export, with increased water use, land clearing, and pesticide use. Similarly, U.S. mass-produced goods, such as grain for livestock and snack foods, and mining equipment, were exported to Mexico.[56] Overall the impact of economic liberalization appears to have created new inequities related to destruction of the environment. Why did Mexico negotiate and accept provisions of NAFTA without adequate protections for itself? Who negotiated for Mexico? Who was behind the negotiations for the Unit-

54. The population of San Diego County in 2020 was over 3 million. *See* U.S. Census, QuickFacts, San Diego County, California, https://www.census.gov/quickfacts/fact/table/sandiegocountycalifornia/PST045221. The population of Tijuana, Mexico, was almost 2 million. *See* Data México, Tijuana, https://datamexico.org/en/profile/geo/tijuana.

55. The Maquila program has a history before the North American Free Trade Agreement (NAFTA) and was set up to combat labor shortages in the United States following World War II, later followed by unemployment in Mexico leading Mexico to open its economy to foreign investment. Under each phase, incentives were given to attract foreign businesses to the Mexican border region. Whether NAFTA caused accelerated growth of maquiladoras or was just a formalization of the existing situation is not clear. *See* William C. Gruben, *Did NAFTA Really Cause Mexico's High Maquiladora Growth?* Center for Latin American Economics Working Paper (2001), https://www.dallasfed.org/~/media/documents/research/papers/2001/wp0106.pdf. Many writers have argued that NAFTA has had negative environmental impacts along the border even if attribution is complex. *See* Fiona Gladstone et al., *NAFTA and Environment after 25 Years: A Retrospective Analysis of the US-Mexico Border*, 119 Env't Sci. & Pol'y 18–22 (2021).

56. Congressional Research Service, U.S.-Mexico Trade Relations, IF11175 (Updated Sept. 29, 2022), https://sgp.fas.org/crs/row/IF11175.pdf.

ed States? Should there be a duty of care by developed countries toward developing countries for the environment? Should the United States, with its knowledge, experience, and capacity to better deal with environmental impacts, educate Mexico before and during treaty negotiations? What is the role of civil society and nongovernmental organizations in exposing inequities on both sides of the border? This experiential class provided students with an excellent understanding of current inequities based on a historical understanding of the treaties, discussions with agencies involved in implementation of the treaties, interviewing, and researching the role of civil society on both sides of the border as well as keeping up with regular news items on the issue.[57]

Simulations of Negotiations

Finally, I find that a simulation of international negotiations is particularly beneficial to exposing issues of equity when students take on the role of representative and negotiator for a particular country or group of countries. Over several years, we were fortunate that negotiations for the development of an international treaty on the conservation and sustainable use of marine biological diversity of areas beyond national jurisdiction were occurring during the duration of the course.[58] Students were required to get to know their select country or group of countries and were given a series of questions to think about as they approached the negotiation (Table 1).

I did not set up the questions to particularly expose equity issues; however, with hindsight, equity in all aspects was a very important factor in the negotiation. Small island representatives found they had to partner with a large state to negotiate common provisions; large countries had financial and legal resources that small and poorer countries lacked. Unlike in the real negotiation, the student representatives came to the table with a common legal expertise. However, differences in the depth and breadth of each student's knowledge and research also contributed to inequitable outcomes where those who had done their research were well able to easily outshine those who had not. Even accounting for such differences, an interesting and significant outcome was that students were unable to come to consensus on even a single provision that needed

57. Countless reports of spills have been reported by NGOs and local newspapers over the years. For example, Surfrider Foundation frequently reports on sewage spills at the border (https://www.surfrider.org/). *See also, e.g.*, Joshua Emerson Smith, *Tijuana sewage spill shutter Imperial Beach and Coronado shorelines, yet again*, San Diego Union Trib. (August 4, 2022), https://www.sandiegouniontribune.com/news/environment/story/2022-08-04/tijuana-sewage-border; The California Water Board Sewage Pollution within the Tijuana River Watershed, https://www.waterboards.ca.gov/sandiego/water_issues/programs/tijuana_river_valley_strategy/sewage_issue.html (reporting on spills).

58. The fifth and most recent Intergovernmental Conference on an international legally binding instrument under the United Nations Convention of the Law of the Sea on the conservation and sustainable use of marine biological diversity of areas beyond national jurisdiction took place August 15–26, 2022. The first session was in September 2018, the second session was in March-April 2019, the third session in August 2019, and the fourth session in March 2022. *See* United Nations, Intergovernmental Conference on Marine Biodiversity of Areas Beyond National Jurisdiction, https://www.un.org/bbnj/.

Table 1. Factors to consider when you represent your nation-state as a high official, with powers to negotiate the High Seas treaty

• Why are you in these negotiations?
• Have you been instructed by your government on what your position should be?
• Are you representing one country or a group of countries with the same objectives?
• Are you a coastal state, a flag state, a port state, a small island state, a maritime power with a large navy, ships, and global commerce? Can you defend yourself from external threats?
• What is the history of your state with the seas?
• What is your level of development using both GDP and the Human Development Index (HDI)?
• Do you depend on submarine cables that bring internet access/communications?
• Do oil and gas pipelines that cross the high seas come to or go through your country?
• Are you a state with a large fishing fleet that fishes in the high seas?
• Are you representing a state that depends on fisheries in the high seas?
What do you want your state/society to be like in the next 20–30 years?

negotiation, *largely based on issues of equity.* A second outcome was that being *open, collaborative, facing historical wrongs, acknowledging historical wrongs, being transparent* about the country's needs and sharing knowledge might lead to more successful longer-term results than withholding information for self-advantage. Finally, if I were to set up the simulation on the basis of equity itself, a whole semester of class time may not be enough.

Conclusions—Learning from Teaching

Reflecting on my teaching, I offer a few observations of how we might strengthen the equity components in law school classes, even without defining what equity is. Equity may be based on the complex history of relations between nations and communities, but another realization is that this process does not seem to stop, and new inequities may be established in the present, which affect future generations. Therefore, heightened sensitivity to issues of equity can be integrated into every class on international law through a few actions by teachers:

- The *history of international law* must be an essential component of every university international law topic
- *General knowledge about current affairs* is imperative and can be placed into a historical context.

- Using *role-playing for simulations of treaty negotiations* directed through a series of history and general knowledge questions, can provide an excellent understanding of the challenges to deal with existing inequities.
- *Experiential classes* that require *interaction with civil society* exposes students to a variety of opinions and feelings, and may lead to alternative and more equitable solutions to a particular cross-border problem.

I firmly believe that because equity among nations and communities is an overarching concern of our times, *acknowledging and exposing historical inequities in the teaching of international law* can go a long way in the improvement of international relations and negotiations of treaties today and in the future.

Section 8

Writing, Research, and Simulations

Reconstructing Advanced Legal Research

*Kristin C. McCarthy**

> *Legal education should be liberating, and legal research classrooms and law libraries can be sites of liberation. They can be places where students discover the potential to oversee their own development, both professional and personal. They can be places where students see the possibilities in their world and envision themselves as agents of social change.*[1]

Identifying Bias Is Essential to the Research Endeavor

The ability to do legal research is a skill that is fundamental to the practice of law.[2] Competency in research is more than knowing which button to push or link to follow within a database to generate facially relevant results. It requires being able to evaluate both the results and the process of searching. If an attorney does not know the limitations (including biases) of a source or tool, they have no ability or incentive to investigate elsewhere or expand their research beyond initial results. Awareness of bias in results is a necessary part of the critical thinking that underlies skilled research. The American Association of Law Libraries' Principles and Standards for Legal Research Competency encapsulates this in Principle III: A Successful Legal Researcher Critically Evaluates Information.[3] Principle III(A)(1)(f) specifically notes that an informa-

---

* Director of the Law Library and Assistant Professor of Law, New England Law | Boston.

1. Yasmin Sokkar Harker, *Invisible Hands and the Triple (Quadruple?) Helix Dilemma: Helping Students Free Their Minds*, 101 B.U. L. Rev. Online 17 (2021), https://www.bu.edu/bulawreview/files/2021/04/SOKKAR-HARKER.pdf.

2. Am. Bar Ass'n Sec. of Legal Educ. & Admissions to the Bar, Legal Education and Professional Development—An Educational Continuum 135, 163 (1992) (also known as the MacCrate Report) (noting that "[i]t can hardly be doubted that the ability to do legal research is one of the skills that any competent legal practitioner must possess.").

3. Am. Ass'n of Law Libraries, Principles and Standards for Legal Research Competency, July 11, 2013 (rev. Apr. 2020), https://www.aallnet.org/wp-content/uploads/2020/04/AALL2020-

tion-literate legal professional should be able to consistently apply criteria to evaluating reliability of information considering, among other factors, bias. Thus, discussions of potential bias are a necessary component of any comprehensive research curriculum. In my recently taught Advanced Legal Research course, issues of potential bias against marginalized groups in the research process were discussed from day one.

Fellow legal research instructors and scholars have enumerated the benefits of integrating discussions of potential bias in search methods and results in legal research programs.[4] Students can benefit by developing "... a critical consciousness about legal information. They can question and critique the social, economic, and political forces that shape legal information. They can see past claims of neutrality and objectivity and understand legal information as a social construct...."[5] Understanding the limitations of search tools as products of human thinking is not a new concept. Human thinking, though sometimes striving for objectivity, has bias. Professor Susan Nevelow Mart challenges the supposed objectivity of research tools and processes when she refers to their structures as "human artifacts."[6] As human artifacts, searches and search tools reflect the society from which they originate. "Critical commentators assert that the legal research and analysis regime is not normatively neutral but instead insidiously reflects and indeed perpetuates hegemonic societal interests along lines of class, race, gender, LGBTQ+ status, Indigenous status...."[7]

As an upper-level course, Advanced Legal Research (ALR) is ideal forum for discussions of bias in search tools and results. First-year legal research is devoted to introducing students to the tools for competent legal research, vastly unfamiliar content for most students since legal research differs significantly from most undergraduate research. The first volume of *Integrating Doctrine and Diversity*[8] includes several excellent chapters on first-year introductory legal research focused on choosing research problems that give students the opportunity to think about legal issues from a variety of cultural perspectives and analyze problems in terms of how bias can affect margin-

---

PrinciplesStandardsLegalResearchCompetencyFull.pdf. Another competency listed is possession of "... a basic understanding of the means by which online search platforms process queries and generate results, including the potential of algorithmic bias associated with machine learning." *Id.*

4. *See, e.g.*, Yasmin Sokkar Harker, *Legal Information for Social Justice: The New ACRL Framework and Critical Information Literacy*, 2 Legal Info. Rev. 19, 41–53 (2016–2017); Latia Ward, *A Librarian's Experience Teaching Critical Information Literacy*, 41 Legal Reference Servs. Q. 52 (2022); Annalee Hickman, *How to Teach Algorithms to Legal Research Students*, 28 Persps. 73 (2020); Paul D. Callister, *Law, Artificial Intelligence, and Natural Language Processing: A Funny Thing Happened on the Way to My Search Results*, 112 L. Libr. J. 161, 204–05 (2020).

5. Harker, *supra* note 1, at 17.

6. Susan Nevelow Mart, *The Algorithm as Human Artifact: Implications for Legal [Re]Search*, 109 L. Libr. J. 387 (2017).

7. Nicolas F. Stump, *"Non-Reformist Reforms" in Radical Social Change: A Critical Legal Research Exploration*, 101 B.U. L. Rev. Online 6, 8 (2021), https://www.bu.edu/bulawreview/2021/04/06/non-reformist-reforms-in-radical-social-change-a-critical-legal-research-exploration/.

8. Integrating Doctrine and Diversity: Inclusion and Equity in the Law School Classroom (Nicole P. Dyszlewski, Raquel J. Gabriel, Suzanne Harrington-Steppen, Anna Russell & Genevieve B. Tung eds., 2021) [hereinafter Integrating Doctrine and Diversity].

alized groups.[9] However, ALR, offered in the second or third year of law school, offers additional and significantly different opportunities for discussing issues of equity and inclusion in research. Drawing on Bloom's Taxonomy,[10] first-year legal research focuses on critical but basic skills, such as remembering, understanding, and applying fundamental research concepts; whereas in ALR, students can move beyond these basic skills to evaluating research strategies and tools and understanding not only their strengths, but also their shortcomings. Students learn through Socratic research[11] to critically question research processes and corresponding results and reformulate searches using different methods where useful to improve results. Thoughtful iterative searching is an essential skill for any competent researcher. As my colleagues often say, "one search is not research."[12]

Research Tools Structure Legal Realities for Systematic Searching

> [L]egal resources can reinforce and reify dominant ideologies, can narrow perspectives, and can make contingent results seem inevitable.... Key numbers, indexes, annotations, footnotes, and cross-references set the limits of inquiry; they "narrow the window," so to speak.[13]

The best legal research tools aggregate relevant resources for researchers, but they can also narrow the scope of inquiry and create insular sets of data. Professors Richard Delgado and Jean Stefancic first noted how traditional research can narrow the scope of research inquiries and elevate results over others in their groundbreaking 1989 *Stanford Law Review* article, "Why Do We Tell the Same Stories?: Law Reform, Critical Librarianship, and the Triple Helix Dilemma," comparing the replication of results in

---

9. *See* Shamika Dalton, *Teaching Cultural Competency through Legal Research Instruction, in* INTEGRATING DOCTRINE AND DIVERSITY, *supra* note 8, at 279, 280. *See also* Raquel Gabriel, *Integrating Diversity into Legal Research: Building on Essential Skills for Law Students, in* INTEGRATING DOCTRINE AND DIVERSITY, *supra* note 8, at 267; Alyson Drake & Brie Sherwin, *Service-Learning in the First Year Legal Research and Writing Classroom, in* INTEGRATING DOCTRINE AND DIVERSITY, *supra* note 8, at 287.

10. *See generally* TAXONOMY OF EDUCATIONAL OBJECTIVES HANDBOOK I: COGNITIVE DOMAIN (Benjamin S. Bloom ed., 1956). While Bloom's Taxonomy is a useful model for discussing depth of learning, the author of this article does not believe the model should be understood as a linear progression.

11. *See infra* notes 55–59 and accompanying text.

12. I am not sure of the origins of this formulation of the iterative search process, but Mary Whisner, Librarian Emeritus at Marion Gould Law Library, mentions that one of her vendor representatives used to say this in training sessions. Mary Whisner, *Harvesting Relevant Cases on Lexis and Westlaw: Comparing Results*, 20 PERSPS. 31 (2011).

13. Steven M. Barkan, *Deconstructing Legal Research: A Law Librarian's Commentary on Critical Legal Studies*, 79 L. LIBR. J. 617, 632 (1987).

legal research to the replication of identical strands of DNA producing exact copies of the original double helix.[14]

Homogeneity of results occurs because one of the foundations of the legal research process is the "one good authority" method. Legal research professors encourage students to begin research from "one good authority," starting with a single case or statute, and using the sophisticated tools available on legal search engines such as Westlaw or Lexis to find additional relevant authority. Two broad categories of research tools used with "one good authority" are indexes, sometimes referred to as classification systems (e.g., Topics and Key Numbers) and citators (e.g., Shepard's). Subject searching through indexes and citation searching, using citators, are powerful methods of retrieving additional legal authorities.

Teaching the benefits of indexing is an opportunity to examine how indexes can be at the same time useful and confining. Indexes structure legal reality for systematic searching, and they can map the scope of inquiry. Professor Robert Berring describes the structure built by indexes as creating the "world of thinkable thoughts."[15] However, the world of thinkable thoughts as framed by the index, while possibly larger than that of a newly minted attorney, is not as large as world of legal inquiry itself.[16] The scope of inquiry is limited by the indexing choices made by legal vendors both currently and historically.

The West Digest System, the epitome of legal subject searching, was designed to categorize all of legal thought, and by virtue of its own success now often defines the parameters of legal inquiry. In the 1890s, John B. West developed the eponymic West Digest System, an indexing system arranging and categorizing all published United States cases into an "alphabetical arrangement of subjects" called Topics and Key Numbers.[17] This organization was revolutionary to legal research. In the first-year curriculum, the Digest System is introduced, but in Advanced Legal Research (ALR), students have opportunities to use it to its fullest advantage through complex, multifaceted problems. Indexes such as the Digest System are powerful tools that are often overlooked by novice researchers accustomed to Google searching. Other vendors such as LexisNexis have developed similar indexing systems to allow users to find cases

---

14. Richard Delgado & Jean Stefancic, *Why Do We Tell the Same Stories?: Law Reform, Critical Librarianship, and the Triple Helix Dilemma*, 42 Stan. L. Rev. 207, 217 (1989).

15. Robert C. Berring, *Legal Research and the World of Thinkable Thoughts*, 2 J. App. Prac. & Process 305 (2000).

16. *See* Richard Delgado & Jean Stefancic, *Why Do We Ask the Same Questions? The Triple Helix Dilemma Revisited*, 99 L. Libr. J. 307, 308–09 (2007) ("Existing indexing systems thus function like eyeglasses that we have worn for a long time. They enable us to see better but conceal the possibility that we might be able to see even better with a different pair. Yet, even when we discover that better pair, it too begins to set limits on what we can see. We move from one set of limitations to another slightly less confining one in an unending process that seems inherent in our condition.").

17. Susan Nevelow Mart, *Teaching the Benefits and Limits of Human Classification and Machine Algorithms: Theory and Practice*, *in* The Boulder Statements on Legal Research Education: The Intersection of Legal and Practical Skills 153, 157–58 (Susan Nevelow Mart ed., 2014).

and secondary sources using topics.[18] Indexing is not merely a research tool, but an organization of legal inquiry and thought and the implications of its structure resonate throughout legal education and practice:

> [T]he entire West digest system was the product of the end of the nineteenth century.... The system also dovetailed neatly with the model of legal education that Dean Langdell had installed at Harvard Law School in the 1870s. The major divisions of the digest system's topics mirror the first-year courses at Harvard, indeed the first-year curriculum at most law schools today. Thus, the stamp of the nineteenth century was indelibly placed on American law.[19]

An example of how indexes can limit is demonstrated by Professor Justin Simard in his *Stanford Law Review* article, *Citing Slavery.*[20] The 1863 Florida case *Smith v. Hines*[21] has to do with a widow complaining that the administrator of a will was defrauding her. LexisNexis has subject headings that index this case into subject areas such as "Family Law," "Estate, Gift & Trust Law," "Marital Property," and "Contracts Law." Westlaw's Topics and Key Numbers index under "Fraud" and "Marital Distribution." These subject headings narrow the case to formalistic legal categories severed from the context in which the case arose. The case was brought over enslaved persons.[22]

In addition, indexing involves choices about terminology and categories that can reflect biases. As has been written in numerous places, Topics and Key Numbers mirror the society they emerge from and change at a glacial pace. For example, until the 1980s workers' compensation cases were assigned the topic "master and servant."[23] Even as of this writing, while the Library of Congress has removed the term "illegal aliens" from its subject headings in favor of "non-citizens,"[24] Digest Topic 24 remains "Aliens, Immigration, and Citizenship" and many underlying Key Numbers use this terminology as well.[25] Despite cases involving discrimination because of gender identity, the

---

18. *See* Susan Nevelow Mart, *The Case for Curation: The Relevance of Digest and Citator Results in Westlaw and Lexis*, 32 Legal Reference Servs. Q. 13, 18 (2013). This article has a helpful guide to the vocabulary of indexing on Westlaw and Lexis.

19. Robert C. Berring, *Collapse of the Structure of the Legal Research Universe: The Imperative of Digital Information*, 69 Wash. L. Rev. 9, 22 (1994) (internal citations omitted).

20. Justin Simard, *Citing Slavery*, 72 Stan. L. Rev. 79, 95–96 (2020). "[C]iting slavery creates both legal and dignitary harms. These harms are hidden by a judicial approach that does not see "slave case" as a relevant category of analysis." *Id.* at 107.

21. Smith v. Hines, 10 Fla. 258 (1863) (enslaved persons at issue).

22. Simard, *supra* note 20, at 96.

23. *See* Delgado & Stefancic, *supra* note 14, at 215–16. *See also* Note, *Protecting Employees at Will against Wrongful Discharge: The Public Policy Exception*, 96 Harv. L. Rev. 1931, 1941 n. 76 (1983) (discussing research of wrongful discharge cases under the public policy exception to at-will employment as being researched using the West Topic, Master and Servant).

24. Press Release, Am. Libr. Ass'n, ALA Welcomes Removal of Offensive 'Illegal aliens' Subject Headings (Nov. 12, 2021), https://www.ala.org/news/member-news/2021/11/ala-welcomes-removal-offensive-illegal-aliens-subject-headings.

25. The Immigration and Nationality Act (INA) § 101(a)(3), 8 U.S.C. § 1101(a)(3) (2018) defines the term "alien" to mean "any person not a citizen or national of the United States." However, a recent executive order from the DOJ directs staff to use noncitizen as language that is consistent "with our

Digest System has no relevant Key Number but classifies cases under "Discrimination by reason of sexual orientation or identity."[26] Some categories do not exist, making it difficult to find cases beyond the indexing. One example often cited in the literature is intersectionality. While researchers can locate cases involving discrimination based on one characteristic (e.g., race), indexing, such as the Digest system, does not account for discrimination based on multiple characteristics (e.g., race and gender). While changes to indexing have been made over time, they are infrequent. Both the structure and the inertia in part reflect the priorities and biases of a larger society.[27] New theories and areas of study are subsumed in archaic structures and legal thought replicates itself, to quote Professors Delgado and Stefancic "like molecular biology's double helix."[28]

The second method of using "one good authority," citation analysis, also has a homogeneity that works against diversity. In a circular manner, works cite to reasoning and scholarship that reflect similarity of background and ideas.[29] One has only to look at a recent citation analysis of "most cited" law review authors to note how few women are ranked highly.[30] Is it because women have not contributed to legal scholarship as robustly? Or are women's contributions less likely to be published in flagship law re-

---

character as a Nation of opportunity and of welcome." Director of the Executive Office of Immigration Review (EOIR) Jean King, *Policy Memo to clarify the agency's use of terminology regarding noncitizens* (July 26, 2021), https://www.justice.gov/eoir/book/file/1403401/ (noting that some Supreme Court cases are also changing using the term "noncitizen" in place of "alien"). *See, e.g.,* United States v. Palomar-Santiago, 141 S. Ct. 1615, 1619 (2021); Barton v. Barr, 140 S. Ct. 1442, 1446 n. 2 (2020) ("This opinion uses the term 'noncitizen' as equivalent to the statutory term 'alien.'").

26. According to Wikipedia, sexual identity is "... how one thinks of oneself in terms of to whom one is romantically and/or sexually attracted." *Definition: Sexual Identity*, WIKIPEDIA (Dec. 2, 2022), https://en.wikipedia.org/wiki/Sexual_identity. The Wikipedia entry is prefaced by the following wording and hyperlinks to other topics: "Not to be confused with sexual orientation or gender identity."

27. While this article has mentioned some larger legal research vendors, other indexing systems have similar issues, *e.g.*, Library of Congress classifications. *See generally* Amanda Ros, *The Bias Hiding in Your Library*, THE CONVERSATION (Mar. 20, 2019, 6:33 AM), https://theconversation.com/the-bias-hiding-in-your-library-111951.

28. Delgado & Stefancic, *supra* note 14, at 217.

29. *See, e.g.*, Stephen J. Choi & G. Mitu Gulati, *Bias in Judicial Citations: A Window Into the Behavior of Judges?*, 37 J. LEGAL STUD. 87 (2008).

30. Fred R. Shapiro, *The Most-Cited Legal Scholars Revisited*, 88 U. CHI. L. REV. 1595, 1609 (2021). Professor Shapiro's study found that of the fifty most-cited legal scholars of all time only two are women, Professors Catharine MacKinnon and Deborah Rhode. He attributed the low number of women scholars on that list "to the historical scarcity of women in legal academia and the legal profession, prejudice against those women who did participate in law, and sociological factors such as the greater demands on women to juggle work and family obligations." *Id.* Professor Shapiro found some improvement in the list of younger cited scholars, where six of the top twenty were women. *Id.* Notably, Professor Orly Lobel, one of the most cited younger scholars, takes issue with the framing of the data as being a solely historical problem, stating that prejudice as mentioned in the article "... is misleadingly phrased as in the past. And there is much to say about the vicious cycles in the advancement of women's careers, especially in places like academia.... The thing about inequity is that it isn't caused by one thing." Orly Lobel, *On Citations & Gender*, PRAWFSBLAWG (Nov. 10, 2021, 12:42 AM), https://prawfsblawg.blogs.com/prawfsblawg/2021/11/on-citations-gender.html.

views?[31] Or does citation analysis (as useful as it is) reflect certain values as to what is relevant and worthy of citation? Although less studied than gender, there is evidence that citation counts are impacted by both race and socioeconomic status.[32] The result is homogeneity over diversity, and intransigence over creativity.

Citation, as a tool, can be even more pernicious where the citations are to cases whose core premises and values are inimical to human and civil rights. For instance, cases involving enslaved persons "... are still commonly cited in the twenty-first century."[33] The *Citing Slavery Project*[34] is a database of cases citing to cases involving enslaved peoples. Slavery cases are still cited without acknowledgement of their undermined legal authority. An example given in Professor Simard's law review article on the topic is how a 1994 Supreme Court of Mississippi case cites an 1860 slave case for the proposition that a contract to devise property in a will is valid.[35] The contract in the 1860 case for the inheritance of enslaved persons is used in 1994 to explain what a "valid contract" is.[36] Professor Simard points out how courts "... cite cases about the forcible transport of enslaved people for routine choice-of-law rules. They rely on cases about the sale of the enslaved to explain the requirements of deeds. They cite cases in which enslaved people served as collateral in debts to illustrate how property may be permissibly seized."[37]

---

31. Shontee M. Pant, *Calculating the Gender Gap in Legal Scholarship: An Empirical Study*, 65 St. Louis U. L.J. 199, 211 (2020) (finding that, over a five-year period, flagship law reviews were over twice as likely to publish a male author as a female author).

32. Lawprofblawg & Darren Bush, *Law Reviews, Citation Counts, and Twitter (Oh My!): Behind the Curtains of the Law Professor's Search for Meaning*, 50 Loy. U. Chi. L.J. 327, 342–45 (2018). *See also* Richard Delgado, *The Imperial Scholar: Reflections on a Review of Civil Rights Literature*, 132 U. Pa. L. Rev. 561 (1984).

33. Simard, *supra* note 20, at 81.

34. Citing Slavery Project, http://www.citingslavery.org/ (last visited Nov. 15, 2022).

35. Simard, *supra* note 20, at 82.

36. *Id.* Professor Simard proposes the following corrective: "When led to slave cases through research or citation, judges should reconsider their validity in light of contemporary constitutional and legal principles. Where courts determine that a slave case's holding remains persuasive, they should acknowledge and explain the case's slave context and explicitly justify their reliance on case law that has been abrogated by the Thirteenth Amendment." *Id.* at 84.

37. *Id.* at 106.

AI—A New Frontier or the Same Terrain Remapped?

An alternative to subject and citation searching is "natural language searching," enhanced through artificial intelligence (AI). Both Westlaw and Lexis, as well as relatively newer legal research engines such as Casetext's CARA, advertise their search engines as being powered by AI.[38] Is AI a panacea to the shortcomings of the legal search methods outlined above in that it relies on objective, mechanical processes, thereby disentangling the researcher from the ridged hierarchies of the past? AI's contribution to legal research cannot be understated; in many ways, it is groundbreaking.[39] Researchers, including the author, who can remember earlier iterations of legal search engines, realize that there has been exponential growth in the sophistication of these search engines that has been transformative in legal research. Nevertheless, impressive is not synonymous with infallible or unassailable.

For legal researchers there are many unknowns in terms of algorithmic searching. Legal database providers are protective of their algorithms as trade secrets,[40] making it difficult to ascertain their shortcomings and strengths except through trial and error, and AI, as the term is commonly used relative to search engines, can have a variety of meanings depending on context.[41] Although we do not know the exact algorithms used by legal search engines, what we do know about *any* AI is this—AI is not devoid of human influence, existing in a purely objective analytical realm, and can be influenced by both programming bias and data bias.[42] As with other AI development, "legal research AI" is built on algorithms designed by human beings and the data sets (cases, statutes, law review articles, etc.) are products of human intelligence. Aspects of legal research

---

38. *See* Thomson Reuters, *Westlaw—Plans and Pricing*, https://legal.thomsonreuters.com/en/westlaw/plans-and-pricing (last visited Apr. 14, 2022) (describing Westlaw Edge as "[t]he most used and advanced research tool powered by cutting-edge AI technology."). *See also* LexisNexis, *The Power of Artificial Intelligence in Legal Research*, LEGAL INSIGHTS, (Oct. 9, 2020) https://www.lexisnexis.com/community/insights/legal/b/thought-leadership/posts/the-power-of-artificial-intelligence-in-legal-research ("Both Lexis and Lexis+ demonstrate that artificial intelligence-powered legal research is a game-changer for lawyers and their firms, helping them find relevant information faster, more efficiently and cost-effectively."); Casetext, *Have CARA A.I. find you the most on-point authorities*, https://casetext.com/cara-ai/ (last visited July 9, 2022).

39. *See* Melissa E. Love Koenig & Colleen Mandell, *A New Metaphor: How Artificial Intelligence Links Legal Reasoning and Mathematical Thinking*, 105 MARQ. L. REV. 559 (2022). ("Artificial intelligence's (AI's) impact on the legal community expands exponentially each year. As AI advances, lawyers have more powerful tools to enhance their ability to research and analyze the law, as well as to draft contracts and other legal documents.").

40. Susan Nevelow Mart, *Results May Vary*, A.B.A. J., Mar. 2018, at 48, 52. ("For the most part these algorithms are black boxes—you can see the input and the output. What happens in the middle is unknown, and users have no idea how their results are generated.").

41. Naveen Joshi, *7 Types of Artificial Intelligence*, FORBES (June 19, 2019) https://www.forbes.com/sites/cognitiveworld/2019/06/19/7-types-of-artificial-intelligence/. In this schema, the AI of legal research systems would be "limited memory" AI.

42. *See* Ronald Yu & Gabriele Spina Alì, *What's Inside the Black Box? AI Challenges for Lawyers and Researchers*, 19 LEGAL INFO. MGMT. 2, 3–4 (2019).

AI that work against objectivity are: (1) algorithms built on preexisting data structures (some of which were discussed in the previous section); (2) algorithms that incorporate customer usage patterns; and (3) algorithms that encode bias either intrinsically or through training on data sets reflecting bias.[43]

AI is built on the preexisting legal information structures discussed in the previous section. For instance, Westlaw's AI is not divorced from its traditional research systems but predicated on them. In a press release announcing Westlaw Edge, Vice President of Research & Development and head of Thomson Reuter's Center for Artificial Intelligence and Cognitive Computing said, "By tuning our AI to the West Key Number System, citation networks and other attorney-authored content, our legal and technology experts have created something that no other legal research provider relying on AI and raw data alone could ever make...."[44]

The second potential source of bias is the incorporation of customer usage patterns into legal search algorithms, sometimes referred to as crowdsourcing.[45] While it is impossible to know exactly how customer usage patterns factored into particular research algorithms because vendors are protective of this information, it is not a secret that usage patterns are used by legal research search engines in relevance ranking of results.[46] Fastcase, a legal search engine, for example, uses among other factors "... the aggregate history of more than 100 million searches on the system."[47] How users of a research system interact with that system thereby affects the results obtained by other users

---

43. *See* Harker, *supra* note 1, at 18–20. *See also* Hickman, *supra* note 4, at 75 ("At one point, we knew that Westlaw had the following factors that affected its algorithms: West key number system, statutory indexes, KeyCite, secondary sources, and document usage patterns. And that Lexis had these factors: phrase recognition, case names and citations, concentration of terms, coverage of terms, prominence, recentness, document segment the search term appears in, and number of hits within document.").

44. Jeff McCoy, *Thomson Reuters Unveils New Legal Research Platform with Advanced AI: Westlaw Edge*, Thomson Reuters | Legal Current (July 12, 2018), https://www.legalcurrent.com/thomson-reuters-unveils-new-legal-research-platform-with-advanced-ai-westlaw-edge/.

45. A 2010 commentary discusses Westlaw crowdsourcing through usage patterns in this way: "[It] takes actions like 'print', 'save', 'folder', and 'view' that a searcher performs and logs that information for future reference. If another researcher runs a similar search later, the actions from the previous users is taken into account and the results are influenced by those previous user actions to potentially rank items higher or lower in the results list. The thoughts behind leveraging previous user actions against search results is that the 'crowd' will tend to identify and use the same documents when searching specific legal issues." Greg Lambert, *WestlawNext—A Study in Applying Knowledge Management & Crowdsourcing*, 3 Geeks and a Law Blog (Jan. 28, 2010), https://www.geeklawblog.com/2010/01/westlawnext-study-in-applying-knowledge.html.

46. *See* Susan Nevelow Mart, Joe Breda, Ed Walters, Tito Sierra & Dr. Khalid Al-Kofahi, *Inside the Black Box of Search Algorithms*, AALL Spectrum, Nov.–Dec. 2019, at 10, 11. *See also* Callister, *supra* note 4, at 187 n. 102 (Professor Callister speculates that the reason rerunning searches in legal search engines at later dates leads to different results may be that "systems are reacting to training in the form of aggregating user responses" and surmises that "[p]robably all of the services take advantage of aggregated user history.").

47. Nevelow Mart et al., *supra* note 46, at 13.

of the system.[48] Incorporating usage patterns into AI has flaws when the users of the search engine have a training that intentionally guides them to certain aspects of cases, statutes, and analysis. If bias exists in larger society against marginalized groups, that bias can also influence the choices that attorneys, law students, and researchers make in deciding what is most relevant. These choices could also be affected by economics: access to online research databases means paying a premium for expensive research products. Law firms with more resources who represent clients with more resources will have an outsized influence on search results as the data obtained from their search habits drives the results of the algorithm.

Finally, algorithms themselves are human creations and even machine learning algorithms are programmed by human beings and interact with data created by human beings. As noted by Professor Nevelow Mart, "every algorithm has a point of view."[49] That point of view can mirror the inequities and prejudices in our world.[50] AI is not infallible, and its perspective is only as broad as its programming.[51]

---

48. *See* Thomson Reuters, *A legacy of customer-inspired innovation*, INSIGHTS (Aug. 15, 2022), https://legal.thomsonreuters.com/en/insights/articles/westlaw-edge-standard-for-legal-research. ("We look at overall usage patterns—which are anonymized, encrypted, and secure, from the thousands of research sessions conducted by legal professionals every day and use those patterns to improve our search algorithms . . .").

49. Susan Nevelow Mart, *Every Algorithm Has a POV*, AALL SPECTRUM, Sept.–Oct. 2017, at 40.

50. *See* Sigal Samuel, *This AI makes you look like a masterpiece—while teaching you about its own bias*, Vox (July 25, 2019), https://www.vox.com/future-perfect/2019/7/25/20708589/ai-portraits-art-bias-classical-painting. "Amazon abandoned a recruiting algorithm after it was shown to favor men's résumés over women's. Researchers concluded an algorithm used in courtroom sentencing was more lenient to white people than to black people. A study found that mortgage algorithms discriminate against Latino and African American borrowers. Transgender Uber drivers had their accounts suspended because the company's facial recognition system is bad at identifying the faces of people who are transitioning." *Id.*

51. Take, for instance, a Westlaw natural language search in Ohio cases (both federal and state) for LGBT discrimination. This search results in twenty-one cases, of which four are relevant, two peripherally relevant, and fifteen not relevant. The first case retrieved in a relevancy-ranked search is *Riddick v. S&P Data Ohio, LLC*, No. 1:20-CV-1000, 2021 WL 7286744 (N.D. Ohio Dec. 22, 2021), a currently unreported federal district court case involving alleged "straight discrimination." The third case in the results, an unpublished Sixth Circuit case, holds that the rights of protestors, who were protesting a gay pride parade, were violated when they were required to move their protest to a public sidewalk. McGlone v. Metro. Gov't of Nashville, 749 F. App'x 402 (6th Cir. 2018). The fourth case, again unpublished, *Winkelmann v. Big Lots Stores, Inc.*, No. 1:08-CV-00419, 2009 WL 3788673 (S.D. Ohio Nov. 10, 2009) is irrelevant, dealing solely with age discrimination (Westlaw search conducted July 10, 2022, 12:57 PM). Similar results were obtained using "LGBTQ discrimination" as a natural language search (only four cases were relevant to LGBTQ discrimination) (Westlaw search conducted Nov. 27, 2022, 3:43 PM). One of the relevant cases was *Byers v. Ohio Dep't of Rehab. & Corr.*, No. 1:19-CV-661, 2019 WL 4267344 (S.D. Ohio Sept. 10, 2019) brought by a prisoner subject to discrimination on the basis of sexual orientation. The complaint was dismissed with the court stating: "A prison official's use of racial slurs and other insults, although unprofessional and reprehensible, does not rise to the level of constitutional magnitude and is insufficient to support a constitutional claim for relief." *Id.* at *2. On the other hand, the Boolean search, *adv: lgbtq! or gay or lesbian or homo-sexual or bi-sexual or trans-gender or trans-man or trans-woman or non-binary or queer /s discrimin!* retrieves 160 cases. Of the first twenty-one results, seventeen were relevant to LGBTQ discrimination in some way, one was peripherally relevant, and two were not relevant (Westlaw search 7/10/2022, 3:17 PM). My conclusion

Advanced Research Training, Offered in ALR, Provides an Ideal Forum for Discussions of Bias

Without more advanced research training, legal researchers often erroneously expect that powerful search engines will produce indisputably accurate and relevant results with little thought to the human aspects of the research process or the human origins of the tools they use. Use of prominent legal search engines confers a perception of validity in results. Professor Paul Callister maintains that in the twenty-first century search engines bestow a "cognitive authority" on results comparable to the perception of authority bestowed in prior times through other mechanisms.[52] He analogizes the authority conferred by search engines to historical indicia of legal authenticity and reliability such as the Mesopotamian clay wrappers or seals around legal texts and the elaborate systems of citation found in the Bluebook and ALWD.[53] He notes that "natural language processing may become society's new mediating scribe of the law—[ostensibly] able to understand relationships of legal texts invisible to human intelligence without its aid. Such a technology would quite naturally be endowed with cognitive authority by the legal community."[54]

ALR offers students the chance to challenge the cognitive authority of computerized research processes and their results by teaching new search techniques and analytical skills. First-year legal research is devoted to introducing students to the tools for competent legal research, a learning curve since legal research differs from undergraduate research; in ALR, students can move beyond learning about the tools of research to examining them. In first-year legal research, students acquire a foundational skill set. In ALR, students have an opportunity to build on these fundamentals. With ALR, an educational window opens to examine more deeply the structures scaffolding these skills, structures that can mirror our society itself, supporting the privilege of a few over the rights and needs of many, structures imbued with the biases ingrained in our society. So, what is the method for promoting this deeper examination in the law school research classroom? Recognizing the necessity of instruction on bias, research professors may still struggle with how to implement this discussion within the ALR classroom. One method is through posing questions to generate critical thinking about these issues, Socratic research.

---

is that LGBTQ as a concept is not currently recognized in Westlaw's natural language searching in a meaningful way (copy of searches on file with the author).

52. Callister, *supra* note 4.

53. *Id.* at 166.

54. *Id.*

Teaching the Questions: Socratic Research

The oft-maligned Socratic method,[55] the hoary standard of the doctrinal classroom, seems far removed from skills-based and experiential classes such as ALR. While use of the Socratic method in its traditional form can further disenfranchise students from historically marginalized groups in legal education,[56] the method does not have to assume a traditional form. The questions can center on how marginalization impedes reliable research, and the answers can be both personal and creative. Internalizing and utilizing the Socratic method of asking probing questions, of analyzing weaknesses and inconsistencies in methodology and outcomes, to arrive at stronger search results, is the core of outstanding research. Examples of such questions in the literature are offered by Professor Harker, including: "*Who created the West Topic and Key Number system? What kind of society did they live in? Who was excluded from the process of creating the original taxonomy? How do these categories reflect societal values?... What happens to points of law that do not fit into the taxonomy?*"[57] Through Socratic questioning, legal research becomes what it should be: a fundamentally iterative process involving analysis of results and reformulating of searches based on preliminary results, not mere knowledge of resources and information structure.

Effective solutions begin with questioning the status quo. The questions initiate the process of working toward solutions. Where can the questions be found? The literature is out there. Professors Delgado and Stefancic have done interesting work in this area both in the past[58] and more recently.[59] The footnotes to this article offer many articles that can be rich sources of discussion and insight. This literature can be mined and incorporated into ALR syllabi.

---

55. *See, e.g.*, Jeffrey D. Jackson, *Socrates and Langdell in Legal Writing: Is the Socratic Method a Proper Tool for Legal Writing Courses?*, 43 Cal. W. L. Rev. 267, 283 (2007) (stating that "[p]erhaps more than any other teaching technique, the Socratic method has drawn a host of criticism on a variety of fronts.") On the other hand, Professor Jackson acknowledges the Socratic method as a useful tool in legal writing courses to promote active learning, cognitive development, and encouragement of discourse. *Id.* at 307.

56. *See generally* Jenny Morgan, *The Socratic Method: Silencing Cooperation*, 1 Legal Educ. Rev. 151 (1989).

57. Harker, *supra* note 1, at 23–24 (emphasis added).

58. Delgado & Stefancic, *supra* note 14.

59. Delgado & Stefancic, *supra* note 16.

Effective Research Acknowledges and Addresses Search Bias

Where are solutions to be found? How do researchers get beyond the limitations of the systems that frame our legal knowledge? An answer to embedded bias requires starting with an understanding of both the strengths and the limitations of research tools. Armed with this understanding, students can develop ways to compensate for the weaknesses of these tools.

Some of the answers may be:

- Adopting a holistic approach to legal research, i.e., looking beyond a single document or research method, as well as analyzing results and rebuilding searches. This is an essential aspect of being a good researcher and must be stressed in ALR. Sometimes this is termed *redundant* or *iterative searching.*[60]
- Using Boolean searching as a supplement to other forms of searching. Boolean operators allow researchers control of their search terms and the relationships of these terms to one another, and ultimately control of search output, particularly when the student suspects the search algorithm is giving biased results.[61] ALR is an ideal forum to hone Boolean search skills.
- Using innovative empirical research as a model.[62] Empirical research starts from a question and builds the answers through deeper analysis of source documents.

---

60. *See* Susan Nevelow Mart, *Understanding the Human Element in Search Algorithms and Discovering How It Affects Search Results*, 33 Pol'y, Pols., & Int'l Rels. Newsl., Spring 2018, at 14, 18, https://scholar.law.colorado.edu/faculty-articles/978/ ("Redundancy in searching is necessary to ensure you are getting a good set of relevant results."). *See also* Hickman, *supra* note 4, at 74 ("To be thorough while researching, law students should run searches in multiple legal research databases when they have the opportunity to do so. Further, they should not necessarily give deference to the top ten search results presented in a particular legal research database, nor to the order in which the results are listed as relevant.").

61. *See, e.g.*, Nicholas F. Stump, *Following New Lights: Critical Legal Research Strategies as a Spark for Law Reform in Appalachia*, 23 Am. U. J. Gender Soc. Pol'y & L. 573, 640 (2014) ("[T]he critical researcher should consciously and continuously negotiate with online search systems; in exerting agency over retrieved results, as possible, through such means as targeted Boolean searching . . ."). A good example of the strength of Boolean searching at New England Law | Boston can be found in the work of the Judicial Language Project (JLP). For JLP, members of the Women's Law Caucus monitor cases related to sexual violence for language that stereotypes, demeans, or otherwise inappropriately characterizes the victims of the violence. These cases can be difficult to find using traditional search methods because the structures are not supportive of this type of research but are discoverable more readily using Boolean search techniques.

62. Unlike traditional scholarship, which analyzes doctrine, empirical research starts with the hypothesis and tests the results. Professor Tracey George differentiates empirical research in other disciplines from traditional legal scholarship stating that: "Non-law academic research in the physical and social sciences focused on formulating hypotheses and testing them against relevant data collected through observation and experiment. Most academic law writings, by contrast, concentrated on legal issues and evaluated them in the same way as judges writing opinions." Tracey E. George, *An Empirical Study of Empirical Legal Scholarship: The Top Law Schools*, 81 Ind. L.J. 141, 144 (2006).

- Advocating for diverse voices and diversity in recruitment for programmers of search engines.[63] This is the development of what is termed "human-centered AI," defined as the "practice of seeking input from people of different backgrounds, experiences, and lifestyles when designing AI systems."[64]
- More broadly and beyond the course—championing algorithmic transparency and accountability.[65]
- As a corollary to algorithmic transparency, advocating for dynamic and intentional approaches to legal indexing.[66]
- Addressing bias with search engine vendors. Researchers no longer need to see themselves as complaisant consumers of research. They can make their voices heard. Larger search engines such as Google have streamlined mechanisms for user input: when given search predictions, researchers are also given the option of reporting predictions as inappropriate, notifying the company that their search algorithms need reconsideration. Similar concerns can be raised with any information vendor.

---

63. *See* SAFIYA UMOJA NOBLE, ALGORITHMS OF OPPRESSION: HOW SEARCH ENGINES REINFORCE RACISM 65–66, 69 (2018). *See also* Mark Muro, Alan Berube & Jacob Whiton, *Black and Hispanic Underrepresentation in Tech: It's Time to Change the Equation*, BROOKINGS (Mar. 28, 2018), https://www.brookings.edu/research/black-and-hispanic-underrepresentation-in-tech-its-time-to-change-the-equation/ ("While tech companies across the nation have over and over said they must do better, Blacks and Hispanics still remain underrepresented in tech jobs by nearly 50 percent.").

64. Sara Brown, *Machine Learning, Explained,* MIT SLOAN SCH. OF MGMT. (Apr. 21, 2021), https://mitsloan.mit.edu/ideas-made-to-matter/machine-learning-explained.

65. *See* U.S. Pub. Policy Council, Ass'n for Computing Mach., STATEMENT ON ALGORITHMIC TRANSPARENCY AND ACCOUNTABILITY, (Jan. 12, 2017) https://www.acm.org/binaries/content/assets/public-policy/2017_usacm_statement_algorithms.pdf. *See also* Algorithmic Justice and Online Platform Transparency Act, S. 1896, 117th Cong. (2021) (proposed by Senator Markey and designed to prohibit discriminatory use of personal information and to require transparency in the use of algorithmic processes and content moderation); Nevelow Mart, *supra* note 6, at 395 ("Algorithmic accountability' is the term for disclosing prioritization, classification, association, and filtering. What we need is a frank discussion with database providers about what it means to search in their databases.").

66. While dialogue with vendors was not a part of my ALR course, students have been at times grassroots organizers of changes in indexing terminology. In 2014, a group of undocumented Dartmouth students petitioned the Library of Congress to change the term "illegal aliens." In 2021, the Library of Congress changed their subject headings to "noncitizens" and "unauthorized immigration." *See* Tina Gross, *Search Terms up for Debate: The Politics and Purpose of Library Subject Headings*, PERSPS. ON HISTORY (Feb. 15, 2022), https://www.historians.org/research-and-publications/perspectives-on-history/march-2022/search-terms-up-for-debate-the-politics-and-purpose-of-library-subject-headings.

Socratic Research Empowers, Restoring Agency to Searching

The law, like the world itself, is not stagnant,[67] and researchers must be equally dynamic. They need to think creatively about legal issues in the context of a wider world, "reinventing, modifying, flipping, and radically transforming legal doctrines and theories imaginatively. . . ."[68] In other words, "[a] computer is good at showing you what is. It cannot show you what might be. Believing so is an abdication of one's responsibility as a lawyer and an agent for change."[69] Questions about processes and tools challenge students to deeper analysis, and ALR can be the catalyst of positive social change.

Having the competency to understand and manipulate the tools is empowering. Students need no longer be passive recipients of algorithmically produced knowledge. They can reclaim agency in their searches. In the end, this is a deconstruction of legal research, but more importantly, a reconstruction, one that acknowledges the prevalence of bias and the historically unfair structures supporting knowledge thereby seeking a firmer foundation in a methodology that supplements and corrects the traditional one.[70]

---

67. This is particularly true in a common law system such as the United States, where numerous cases are initiated, argued, and decided daily.

68. Delgado & Stefancic, *supra* note 16, at 328.

69. *Id.*

70. *See* Nicholas Mignanelli, *The Case for a Social Justice Research Course?*, RIPS LAW LIBRARIAN BLOG (Aug. 31, 2020), https://ripslawlibrarian.wordpress.com/2020/08/31/the-case-for-a-social-justice-research-course/ ("Having deconstructed the legal research process, we move on to a reconstruction by reading and discussing Nicholas F. Stump's articles proposing that attorneys supplement the traditional legal research process by internalizing critical insights . . .").

The Unstandardized Client: Collaborating with an Actor on Lessons About Diversity, Equity, and Inclusion

*Carol M. Suzuki**

Introduction

In this chapter, I share my experience teaching with an actor who participated in simulated client interviews to promote law student understanding of diversity, equity, and inclusion issues. Among my curricular responsibilities at the University of New Mexico School of Law (UNM) is teaching in our mandatory clinical law program. The clinic serves clients from low-income communities in this state that is rich in racial, ethnic, and cultural diversity.[1] Working with students and clients of many backgrounds, I routinely include discussions of diversity, equity, and inclusion in my courses.[2] I incorporate elements of clinical pedagogy when I teach courses outside of the clinic.

I developed Legal Issues for the Elderly, a non-clinic legal drafting course, giving consideration to experiential methods of learning, as I believe students are better able to meet the learning objectives of a drafting course when they draft documents that incorporate a client's goals and values gathered from a simulated client interview with a professional actor portraying the client. The experiential dimension requires students

* Keleher & McLeod Professor of Law, University of New Mexico School of Law. J.D., Columbia Law School. The author would like to thank Sheldon Blackhorse, Dr. Aroop Mangalik, Professor Susan Erickson, Professor April Land, and the students who engaged so thoughtfully in this learning opportunity.

1. *See QuickFacts New Mexico*, U.S. Census Bureau, https://www.census.gov/quickfacts/NM (last visited Jan. 9, 2023).

2. The American Bar Association revised its curricular standards in February 2022 to require "education to law students on bias, cross-cultural competency, and racism...." *See* Am. Bar Ass'n, ABA Standards and Rules of Procedure for Approval of Law Schools 2022–2023, Standard 303(c) (2022) (hereinafter ABA Standards). Standard 303 in this revised form did not exist when I taught Legal Issues for the Elderly, but the methods set forth in this chapter support the goals of the revised standard.

to understand the relevant law in order to engage in fact gathering, and the experiential learning process resulted in thoughtful documents that reflected care in drafting and an appreciation for the objectives of the course. Although adding an experiential component to this class does not satisfy the ABA experiential learning requirement,[3] I find that incorporating experiential methods earlier in the law school experience helps students to prepare for success in the law school's mandatory clinical law program and as lawyers.

In clinic, client interviews and post-interview discussions are vital to helping students learn how to provide client-centered advocacy and culturally competent representation. Students can better understand and focus on client goals when they appreciate how race, socioeconomic status, gender, sexual identity, disability, and other attributes of a person can affect the legal process and a legal matter.[4] Discussion of the relevance of race and culture to legal matters enriches the learning experience and helps students learn how their own backgrounds and experiences shape their learning and perspectives on the law.

I was honored to teach this drafting course with a medical doctor, Aroop Mangalik, and a Native American actor, Sheldon Blackhorse.[5] Involving an actor to bring the client to life allowed me to incorporate discussion of how race and culture inform beliefs surrounding substantive issues in elder law. Working with Dr. Mangalik, a retired oncologist and emeritus professor from the University of New Mexico Health Sciences Center and Medical School, enhanced student learning of the effects of aging and illness on clients' lives and their legal services needs. Our collaborative course was an opportunity to teach students about the diversity of culture in our New Mexico communities, the need to diversify the legal bar to serve the state, and the inequities that communities of color face in accessing legal services.

In this chapter, I will set forth how we developed the course; discuss the benefits of teaching the class with an actor; raise the controversy of involving an actor who may not possess particular cultural characteristics; and suggest ways to replicate this teaching methodology.

---

3. *See id.* Standard 303(a)(3).

4. *See* Susan Bryant, *The Five Habits: Building Cross-Cultural Competence in Lawyers*, 8 Clinical L. Rev. 33 (2001).

5. Dr. Mangalik and I use formal titles when we teach. Sheldon preferred to be referred to by his first name.

Description of the Course

Legal Issues for the Elderly is an upper-level law school course that satisfies the law school's writing requirement that students engage in "a substantial written product or series of products which are collectively substantial"[6] and involve research. I developed the course to expose students to documents an elder law lawyer may typically draft beyond a last will and testament, and as a means for teaching document content, layout, and grammar. I intended for students to progress in their writing abilities, substantive law understanding, and legal analysis performance as they learned the law and drafted documents through a series of fact patterns using an actor to portray the client. I also wanted students to learn how to identify and respectfully approach issues of diversity, equity, and inclusion they will encounter as lawyers, and to practice basic client interviewing skills.

In selecting the types of documents students would draft, I considered foundational laws and documents in the area of elder law.[7] I required students to write an interview memo for each client, using a consistent format throughout the semester. I observed that the students improved in their memo drafting over time. These memos also revealed the progression of student learning on issues of diversity, equity, and inclusion. They showed the students' increased awareness of how these issues affect legal matters and the students' increased ability to question their clients about these issues respectfully in order to provide culturally competent services.

I engaged Sheldon Blackhorse, a local Native American actor who is Diné,[8] to be interviewed by the students as a potential client regarding various substantive areas of elder law. Sheldon has professional acting experience, starting as a child actor in New Mexico commercials supporting Indian tribes. He told me that he enjoys acting, and he participated in this classroom venture in order to hone his craft. Taking acting courses at Central New Mexico Community College, participating in CNM's theater program, and acting in student films all help Sheldon to develop as an actor.[9]

Once we were introduced and agreed to collaborate on this class with Dr. Mangalik, we developed a process to meet and prepare for each of the five classes in which Sheldon participated. I met with Sheldon to discuss the law and he began to develop the scenario and his character. Taking into consideration Sheldon's input, I created a basic fact pattern for his role. I sent that collaboratively created material to Sheldon in advance along with the relevant law for him to review as context. The students researched the substantive law prior to our discussion in class the week before each interview.

6. *See* Univ. of N.M. School of Law, Bulletin and Handbook of Policies: Juris Doctor Program 2022–2023, at 8 (rev. Aug. 5, 2022).

7. I chose advance directives, Emergency Medical Treatment & Labor Act (EMTALA), aid in dying, anatomical gifts, kinship guardianship, and adult guardianship.

8. Navajo for "the People."

9. *See* Classless Chaps, *Idle Hands: Hello*, YouTube (Dec. 13, 2020), https://www.youtube.com/watch?v=2nB3jAMMgzc (monologue).

Also the week prior to each interview, Sheldon, Dr. Mangalik, and I met to discuss the scenario and add details, and we finalized some themes that we wanted Sheldon to consider in his role. For example, when Sheldon portrayed a potential client with questions about aid in dying,[10] Dr. Mangalik provided the illness, symptoms, and prognosis so that Sheldon, in character, would be able to discuss in a factually correct manner the medical concerns that led him to seek legal representation.[11] Sheldon's acting skills enabled him to use the facts to give a credible portrayal of a client dying of an incurable illness within six months, a requirement of most if not all states that allow aid in dying.[12]

The course was a weekly three-hour class in a fifteen-week semester. For the five classes in which Sheldon participated, the class began with a one-hour interview. The students had predetermined the format, which was for each student to take turns asking a few questions. We then had a short break after which we discussed the interview and the assignment. This post-interview debriefing provided an opportunity for me to clarify the law and facts and for us to discuss the social and cultural issues that surfaced when Sheldon was interviewed. For example, the Diné traditional concept of hózhó (ho-jzoh) combines "the concepts of beauty, blessedness, goodness, order, harmony, and everything that is positive or ideal."[13] Discussion of end-of-life issues such as advance directives is viewed as negative and violative of hózhó.[14] A lawyer sometimes assists a client to process conflicts between legal goals and cultural beliefs.

For each class, Sheldon and I agreed that he would have broad authority to develop his character. I advised Sheldon that he had freedom to try out different facets of a character, as long as he conveyed information to the students so that they gained the facts necessary for their assignments and learned and practiced some interviewing skills. Sheldon portrayed a different character for each interview. For each client, he created a six-month backstory[15] and a biography of the character that provided context surrounding the character and the impetus for the legal goal.[16]

Sheldon brought to his characters knowledge of problems that affect the Diné community, including the effects of poverty on struggling families, limited access to legal services in rural areas, and challenges in outreach to people living on the Navajo Nation or Pueblo lands. For example, service of process on a resident who lives on Pueblo

10. Aid in dying laws allow a competent individual living with a terminal illness to request a prescription for a lethal medication.

11. Dr. Mangalik was a plaintiff in New Mexico's aid in dying litigation due to his work with terminally ill patients. *See* Morris, Mangalik & Riggs v. Brandenburg, 2016-NMSC-027, 376 P.3d 836 (N.M. 2016).

12. Aid in dying was contested in New Mexico, *id.*, and enacted into law in 2021. *See* N.M. Stat. Ann. §§ 24-7C-1 to 24-7C-8 (2021) (Elizabeth Whitefield End-of-Life Options Act).

13. Joseph A. Carrese & Lorna A. Rhodes, *Western Bioethics on the Navajo Reservation: Benefit or Harm?*, 274 J. Am. Med. Ass'n 826, 828–29 (1995).

14. *See id.* at 829.

15. Discussion with Sheldon Blackhorse, in Albuquerque, N.M. (Mar. 27, 2017); *see* Constantin Stanislavski, Building a Character 7 (Elizabeth Reynolds Hapgood trans., 1989).

16. *See* Larry Moss, The Intent to Live 136–40 (2005) (*Back Story* and *Biography: Believing in Your Character's Life*).

land may pose challenges, as there might not be a physical address that the United States Postal Service would recognize.[17] Or if an elderly person were in medical distress, an emergency medical vehicle might have a difficult time finding a residence due to the lack of an address.

Sheldon also raised cultural considerations that affected choices in the various substantive legal areas covered in the course. His portrayals surfaced the complexities of how race and inequity affect an individual's ability to access legal services and strategies to resolve a substantive legal matter. For the students, Sheldon's role provided facts that served as bases for discussions of how race and culture affected legal issues, including beliefs about dying, opting for aid in dying, and choosing to donate one's organs.

Through the pre-interview reading and preparation, client interviews, and post-interview debriefings, students gained an understanding of the goals of writing, became more engaged writers, exercised legal interviewing and oral communication skills, and showed an appreciation of issues of diversity, equity, inclusion, and professional identity.

Other Benefits of Involving an External Actor

Sheldon is a versatile actor who was able to portray a number of characters for this course. Being Diné, he brought aspects of his Indigenous background and experiences to his roles. Sheldon's portrayal during the interview, and his participation in post-interview discussions, allowed the students to ask questions about Sheldon's intent in including certain facts into the pattern that raised issues of culture and equity, and for Sheldon to share and teach about his Diné community.

I am grateful for Sheldon's participation in the course and was pleased with his performance and work throughout the semester. I was fortunate that Sheldon graciously volunteered to participate in order to hone his craft. Sheldon was keen to portray a client who faces a complicated or challenging legal issue, or is confronting death. Going to "painful places" is part of the craft and the work of an actor,[18] and Sheldon rose to the occasion. One student remarked about Sheldon in an end-of-semester teaching evaluation, "He approached each role in a way that was believable and made the experience seem real. I appreciate having the ability to work with and interview him." Sheldon created a reality for each character whom he portrayed.

Working with Sheldon was a benefit to the students and to me on various levels. Because Sheldon shared information about his Diné culture, the students learned about

17. *See, e.g.*, Matt Vasilogambros, *For Some Native Americans, No Home Address Might Mean No Voting*, Pew Charitable Trusts (Oct. 4, 2019), https://www.pewtrusts.org/en/research-and-analysis/blogs/stateline/2019/10/04/for-some-native-americans-no-home-address-might-mean-no-voting ("Turn off U.S. Highway 191 between mile markers 1 and 2. It's a blue house with a tan roof.").

18. *See* Moss, *supra* note 16, at 59–60. "Of course you should be upset. Of course you should weep.... Acting represents all that human beings experience...." *Id.* at 60.

a significant population in the Southwest. Furthermore, involving an actor helped the students to better learn laws that are germane in an elder law practice. The students appreciated that they needed to understand the law in order to gather relevant information during the client interview. One student remarked in the teaching evaluation, "It is important to understand the issues before speaking to a client." Another wrote that working with Sheldon "made me make sure to prepare fully for each interview."

Sheldon's character portrayal in various hypothetical situations also gave the students an introduction into client interviewing and counseling with regard to issues of diversity, equity, and inclusion affecting communities that make up the population of the state. The exercises helped the students to learn how to ask challenging questions without risks inherent in a situation with a real client where trust may need to be developed over time for a client to divulge uncomfortable facts. A student wrote in the teaching evaluation, "I thought having Sheldon participate in this course was a great way to get comfortable with client interviewing. He did an awesome job in the different roles." The simulated client interviews fostered student confidence in their abilities to transfer their understanding of the law into questions they needed to ask a client in order to gather information.

The Dilemma of the Roles an Actor Can Inhabit

Sheldon brought to his portrayals his background and lived experiences as a Diné person, which enriched the class discussions about diversity, equity, and inclusion. In including an Indigenous actor in the course, I am cognizant of evolving discourse in the performing arts regarding whether an actor must share particular attributes with the portrayed character. Although a great actor might be able to inhabit any role, the dilemma is whether an actor should portray a person with specific characteristics, such as in the aspects of race, gender, gender identity, or disability that the actor does not possess, to the exclusion of other actors who are not afforded the opportunity to participate.

Some portrayals in history are now generally considered to be racist. The use of blackface in minstrel shows starting in the 1830s[19] led to white actors portraying characters of other races in the entertainment industry. White actor Mickey Rooney portrayed Japanese neighbor I.Y. Yunioshi in Blake Edwards's 1961 film adaptation[20] of Truman Capote's novella *Breakfast at Tiffany's*.[21] Tilda Swinton[22] and Scarlett Johans-

---

19. Stephen Foster, *Blackface Minstrelsy*, PBS American Experience, https://www.pbs.org/wgbh/americanexperience/features/foster-blackface-minstrelsy/ (last visited Jan. 9, 2023).

20. Breakfast at Tiffany's (Paramount Pictures 1961); *see Asian Activists Say "Breakfast at Tiffany's" Is a Racist Film*, The Mercury News, https://www.mercurynews.com/2008/08/22/asian-activists-say-breakfast-at-tiffanys-is-a-racist-film/ (Aug. 22, 2008, 2:42 AM).

21. Truman Capote, Breakfast at Tiffany's (1958).

22. *See* Doctor Strange (Marvel Studios 2016); Cole Delbyck, *Tilda Swinton Releases Email Exchange with Margaret Cho About Whitewashing in "Doctor Strange,"* Huffpost (Dec. 17, 2016),

son[23] were both accused of "whitewashing" their roles by portraying characters in their respective films who are Asian in the source material. The entertainment industry, with a history of exclusion and inequity, has evolved to questioning not only hiring practices that surface issues of racism and cultural appropriation, but of ableism and gender identity. Singer and producer Sia was criticized for hiring a neurotypical actor to portray a girl with autism in the movie *Music.*[24] Actor Eddie Redmayne now regrets portraying a transgender individual in the film *The Danish Girl.*[25] Whether a part can only be played by an actor whose authentic life embodies the characteristics of that role is a concern that deserves continuing scrutiny.

I raise this issue and acknowledge the choices I made in working with Sheldon. When he talked about issues Native Americans faced, it was from his life or his knowledge of Native American culture. I would not have conceived of asking someone who was not an Indigenous person to portray one for my class. However, the client roles required Sheldon to portray an elderly person, which he is not. Sheldon portrayed characters who were older than his authentic self. I informed Sheldon that he could portray a woman or any other character he wanted to inhabit, as he was volunteering his talent in order to work on his craft. Faculty interested in collaborating with an actor may want to consider whether the evolving casting choice discourse in the entertainment business matters in the law school setting.

Clinical law faculty often look to medical school training methods for insight, as that field is in many ways further advanced in clinical methodology. Medical educators have studied role casting in training simulations. Medical schools may use standardized patients in their educational programs, actors or actual patients who portray patients who present with predetermined physical or mental health symptoms, in order to train students in a consistent manner.[26] A medical student might interview a standardized patient portraying a patient with a disability to teach the student how to communicate with patients with disabilities and about the Americans with Disabilities Act.[27] Medical school programs that involve real patients with disabilities note that they experience challenges of time and resources expended to plan, recruit, and teach with

---

https://www.huffpost.com/entry/tilda-swinton-releases-unedited-email-exchange-with-margaret-cho-about-whitewashing-in-doctor-strange_n_58555bdae4b08debb7897962.

23. *See* Ghost in the Shell (Paramount Pictures 2017); Summer Noblé, *Why Scarlett Johansson Starring in "Ghost In The Shell" Is So Problematic,* Huffpost (Dec. 6, 2017), https://www.huffpost.com/entry/why-scarlett-johansson-st_b_6466498.

24. Music (Vertical Entertainment 2021); *see* Samuel Spencer, *"Music": The Backlash Against Sia's Autism Movie Explained,* Newsweek (Feb. 15, 2021), https://www.newsweek.com/music-sia-movie-autism-controversy-maddie-ziegler-1569289.

25. The Danish Girl (Focus Features 2015); *see* Toyin Owoseje, *Eddie Redmayne Says Playing a Trans Character in "The Danish Girl" Was a Mistake,* CNN (Nov. 22, 2021, 10:51 AM ET), https://www.cnn.com/2021/11/22/entertainment/eddie-redmayne-trans-mistake-intl-scli-gbr/index.html.

26. *See* Linda M. Long-Bellil et al., *Teaching Medical Students About Disability: The Use of Standardized Patients,* 86 Acad. Med. 1163, 1163 (2011); Lawrence M. Grosberg, *Medical Education Again Provides a Model for Law Schools: The Standardized Patient Becomes the Standardized Client,* 51 J. Legal Educ. 212, 212 (2001).

27. *See* Long-Bellil, *supra* note 26, at 1163, 1167.

patients with disabilities who portray standardized patients in contrast to non-disabled standardized patients.[28]

I am not sure whether I am overthinking this aspect of involving an actor in a law school course.[29] By working with an Indigenous actor, I avoided some cultural challenges regarding the question of whether a person portraying a role must share, experience, or possess the diversity, inequity, or exclusion characteristics that are the intended discussion points. I was able to involve an actor who embodies diversity, inequity, and exclusion. An instructor should consider the relevance of this evolving matter if collaborating with actors, as a matter of respect and consistent with the antiracist goals we are trying to achieve.

Practical Considerations for Replication

Law is a profession where many will earn their living by talking about and on behalf of their clients. Role-play is a common teaching method in clinical law programs to prepare for client interviewing and counseling. When students engage in client interviewing, they learn how to respectfully ask intensely personal questions of their clients in order to represent them competently. They also gain judgment regarding what to reveal to their clients about themselves. The law school experience often teaches students to be reticent in sharing their backgrounds and what they find challenging about law school, for fear they will be judged negatively. Among my students and myself, our collective experiences bring diversity of background, including race, culture, gender, gender identity, sexual orientation, age, ability, and socioeconomic status.

As a clinical teacher, I might play the role of a client, a judge, or an opposing counsel. For the drafting course, I could have performed the part of the client in the interviews. However, involving Sheldon in the class provided some perspective and allowed students the opportunity to determine what they wanted to share about themselves with a stranger in a controlled setting while still participating in the discussion. By not playing the client, I was able to focus on taking notes for formative assessment of and feedback to students in a consistent manner.[30]

In some courses, students portray clients in simulation exercises, bringing to their portrayals their own or imagined backgrounds and experiences. However, in this drafting course I was hesitant to have students feel they must share their experiences regarding diversity, equity, and inclusion. Also, students would not have experienced the depth and consistency of learning in the course had they portrayed various clients instead of having an external actor participate. Involving Sheldon as an external par-

---

28. *See id.* at 1168–69.

29. Role-play occurs often in law school. For example, when students are enrolled in a trial practice course, they recruit their friends to play the parts of parties, witnesses, and jurors.

30. *See* ABA Standards, *supra* note 2, Standard 314.

ticipant allowed me to be directive with him regarding his role, such as when I passed him notes in class to ensure coverage of particular facts for pedagogical reasons. The exercises helped the students learn how to ask challenging questions without risks inherent in a situation with a real client. They instilled within students confidence in their abilities to transfer their understanding of the law into coherent and relevant questions for the character Sheldon was portraying.

I researched hiring a theater department student, paying the student through the University's work-study program or my available professional development funding, or arranging for independent study credit to act in a law school class. I also looked into the possibility of paying an actor not affiliated with UNM. That option was procedurally prohibitive due to the university's process to pay a non-UNM student or contract employee/independent contractor. Despite my challenges with funding and course credit for a non-law student, I suggest looking into funding possibilities, as volunteers may be hard to locate. If I were to teach a course again involving a simulated client, I would research available funding and non-monetary benefits to an actor. Providing funding would support a move toward actual equity to support a student or actor.

Fortunately, my clinical law colleague, Professor April Land, knows faculty in the Central New Mexico Community College Theater Department, also in Albuquerque. I reached out to Professor Susan Erickson, who communicated with a few acting students she thought would be good actors and responsible collaborators. She recommended Sheldon Blackhorse, sharing, "He is able to play a wide age and character range. He's a great guy."[31] Also, Sheldon is a professional math tutor at CNM, so he appreciates a teacher's focus on learning outcomes.

In order to find an actor external to a law school, I would suggest looking to the theater department if there is one affiliated with the law school. If there is none, I would suggest looking into identifying actors through a local college or community theater. Even if one person were not able to commit to an entire semester, perhaps a few actors would be willing to participate once or twice during a semester.

In their teaching evaluations, students expressed their appreciation for the combined efforts of Sheldon Blackhorse, Aroop Mangalik, and myself to incorporate diversity, equity, and inclusion pedagogy into the elder law drafting course. One student commented about Sheldon, "He was realistic—coming in as someone with no legal training—made me sensitive to avoiding 'legalese' and being culturally sensitive." Other student comments regarding Sheldon's participation in the course included, "It helped give perspective about how difficult these issues can be to talk about," and "Helped me to understand the human and emotional aspect that gets overlooked in other courses." This elder law drafting course, taught through a collaboration among an actor, a medical doctor, and a law school clinician, provided law students with an experience rich in discussion of diversity, equity, and inclusion that will resonate in their practice of law in the Southwest.

31. Email from Susan Erickson (Aug. 15, 2016) (on file with author).

Incorporating Federal Indian and Tribal Law into Litigation-Drafting Curricula

Gail Stephenson & Michael D.O. Rusco†*

Introduction

Incorporating federal Indian[1] and tribal law[2] (Indian law) into a litigation-drafting course is a great way to increase diversity, promote inclusion, and further social justice coverage in law school curricula. Diversity, inclusion, and social justice issues permeate Indian law. This piece will provide guidance on incorporating Indian law by describing the typical litigation-drafting course, explain why Indian law is a good choice for a course hypothetical, propose methods to develop an Indian law problem, and recommend ways to teach Indian law research and Indian law itself.

* Director of Legal Analysis & Writing and the Louisiana Outside Counsel A.A. Lenoir Endowed Professor, Southern University Law Center.

† Associate Professor, Southern University Law Center; Senior Fellow, SULC Native American Law & Policy Institute; Former Senior Tribal Counsel, Ho-Chunk Nation Department of Justice; 2010 William H. Hastie Fellow and 1995–98 LEO Fellow, University of Wisconsin Law School; Cherokee Nation citizen.

1. This article will use the terms "Indian" and "American Indian" to refer to the indigenous peoples of the contiguous forty-eight states. *See* Michael Yellow Bird, *What We Want to Be Called: Indigenous Peoples' Perspectives on Racial and Ethnic Identity Labels*, 23 AM. INDIAN Q. 1, 1 (1999).

2. "Federal Indian law" is the body of federal constitutional provisions, treaties, statutes, regulations, governmental agreements, and court decisions that define the relationship between the federal government, the state governments, and the 574 federally recognized tribes in the United States. "Tribal law" is the body of tribal constitutional provisions, statutes, regulations, agreements, and court decisions made by the tribe to govern any person or entity within its territory and its internal affairs.

The Typical Litigation-Drafting Class

Litigation-drafting courses (LDCs) teach students about the basic litigation process and how to draft documents used in litigation. Such courses are distinct from civil procedure and trial skills courses. LDCs introduce students to the litigation process from an experiential perspective, as opposed to the abstract or conceptual perspective presented in civil procedure courses. LDCs focus on advanced writing skills and differ from trial skills courses that focus on the oral presentation of evidence and argument before judges and juries.

LDCs are typically structured around a substantial and detailed hypothetical. Students follow the development of the hypothetical case from client intake through trial, and sometimes through appeal. Typical assignments include drafting initial client correspondence, a complaint, a summons, an answer, a dispositive motion, proposed court orders, affidavits, a judgment, and an appellate brief. Courses may also include drafting discovery requests and handling discovery disputes.

LDCs have several teaching goals beyond introducing students to the basics of drafting litigation documents. These additional goals include further development of the skills introduced in the first year, including research, rhetoric, and persuasion. The courses also introduce students to basic trial strategy and ethical considerations found in litigation.

Reasons to Use Indian Law in Litigation-Drafting Classes

Indian law is a good choice for an LDC hypothetical for two reasons. First, use of Indian law promotes diversity, inclusion, and social justice in law school curricula. Second, Indian law is well suited to working on the skills that advanced legal writing courses are designed to develop.

A. Promoting Diversity, Inclusion, and Social Justice

Using an Indian law problem promotes diversity and inclusion because few students at mainstream law schools will have any substantial experience with or understanding of tribal people, their governments, or their laws. Just 0.8%[3] of the U.S. population are

3. There are 2.56 million tribal citizens of 574 federally recognized tribes as of January 2020. Indian Health Servs., https://www.ihs.gov/newsroom/factsheets/ihsprofile/ (last visited Dec. 8, 2022). The U.S. population as of January 2020 was 330.22 million. U.S. Census Bureau, *Census Bureau Projects U.S. and World Populations on New Year's Day* (Dec. 30, 2019), https://www.census.gov/newsroom/press-releases/2019/new-years-2020.html.

citizens of tribal governments, and only 2.9%[4] of the U.S. population self-identifies as having Indian ancestry. Litigation-drafting students using an Indian law hypothetical delve deeply into the culture and people behind the issues presented, allowing a greater opportunity for understanding and empathy.

Using an Indian law hypothetical confronts non-tribal students with difficult social-justice issues. Tribes and their citizens are among the most marginalized and dispossessed groups in American society. Tribal populations have been more than decimated, in a literal sense. Estimates of the native population of North America prior to 1492 vary widely; most agree at least 50 million lived here, and some estimates exceed 110 million.[5] Today there are approximately 3.7 million people who exclusively identify as American Indian or Alaska Native.[6]

Tribes are also among the most dispossessed people in the world, having gone from controlling all 1.9 billion acres of the continental United States, to governing just 138 million acres of land in 1865, to holding just 48 million acres in 1934.[7] Moreover, tribes were promised freedom from non-tribal authority—federal or state—in both in the federal Constitution and myriad treaties, and those promises have been broken far more than kept. The continued existence and relevance of tribal people and their governments is a testament to their resilience and ongoing fight for social justice in the face of prolonged, active efforts to destroy them.

Studying Indian law also shows students how law can be weaponized against vulnerable groups to a genocidal degree. Indian law is rife with examples of courts sidestepping universally accepted, intuitively fair solutions to basic sovereignty issues in order to reach results in line with federal policy positions hostile to tribal people. The difference in outcomes between Indian cases and non-Indian cases about equivalent issues raises useful questions. If the only valid government is one to which people consent, is it fair to subject tribal people to state law if they do not consent to state government? Is it fair to prohibit a tribe from prosecuting non-Indians who commit crimes on reservations?[8] These questions provide students an opportunity to see what "law" looks like when it struggles to reach specific results.

Incorporating federal Indian and tribal law into law school curricula directly benefits tribal students, who get a chance to enjoy the status of "insiders" rather than being

---

4. U.S. Census Bureau, *Percentage of Population and Percent Change by Race: 2010 and 2020*, www2.census.gov/programs-surveys/decennial/2020/data/redistricting-supplementary-tables/redistricting-supplementary-table-02.pdf.

5. The Native Population of the Americas in 1492, 1–4 (William M. Denevan ed., 2d rev. ed. 1992).

6. U.S. Census Bureau, *Population by Race: 2010 and 2020*, https://www2.census.gov/programs-surveys/decennial/2020/data/redistricting-supplementary-tables/redistricting-supplementary-table-01.pdf.

7. Matthew L.M. Fletcher, *Sawnawgezewog: "The Indian Problem" and the Lost Art of Survival*, 28 Am. Indian L. Rev. 35, 105 n.29 (2004).

8. The Supreme Court held that tribal courts cannot try or punish non-Indians in *Oliphant v. Suquamish Indian Tribe*, 435 U.S. 191, 122–23 (1978).

"routinely relegat[ed] ... to the role of perpetual 'outsider.'"[9] Students engage with materials more when they feel connected to those materials. Better engagement translates into better performance.

The converse is also true. Students disengage from materials they feel disconnected from. Similar dynamics apply at the institutional level, i.e., students learn more from institutions when they feel the institution values them.[10] Indeed, a course or law school that fails to incorporate issues like race as a factor in the development and enforcement of law will likely lose credibility with minority students.

B. Developing Advanced Writing Skills

Another reason Indian law is a good choice for an LDC hypothetical is because it is well suited for working on skills taught in advanced legal writing. It teaches upper-level students how to handle problems in areas of law that are new to them. Using simple problems in familiar subjects helps beginning students grasp fundamental skills; this approach acknowledges that students are beginners. But the practice of law often presents lawyers with questions about areas of law with which they are entirely unfamiliar. Consequently, law students benefit from having to develop expert knowledge in new areas of law. Few students will have any experience with Indian law.

Indian law also pushes students to grapple with fine legal distinctions and make those distinctions persuasively. For instance, Indian law requires students to distinguish "civil" rights from "sovereign" rights. A common misconception is that Indian law is a type of civil-rights law. It is not. It is a species of the law of sovereignty, connected to both the Law of Nations and concepts of federalism. Some students have difficulty making this distinction. The case law makes clear that federal authority over Indian affairs and tribal authority over tribal territory is political in nature, not racial.[11] In other words, while tribal peoples are distinct racially, federal Indian law and tribal law are concerned only with tribes' existence as separate sovereign governments and the government-to-government relationship between tribes and the federal government.[12]

Another advantage of using Indian law in an LDC hypothetical is that it presents students with complex and imperfect areas of law highly influenced by policy considerations and history. Complex issues lead students to develop critical thinking skills.[13]

---

9. Charles R. Calleros, *In the Spirit of Regina Austin's Contextual Analysis: Exploring Racial Context in Legal Method, Writing Assignments and Scholarship*, 34 J. Marshall L. Rev. 281, 292 (2000).

10. Gail S. Stephenson & Linda C. Fowler, *Keeping It Real: Developing a Personally and Culturally Relevant Legal Writing Curriculum*, 10 J. Gender, Race & Just. 67, 74–76 (2006).

11. Michigan v. Bay Mills Indian Cmty., 572 U.S. 782, 788 (2014); Santa Clara Pueblo v. Martinez, 436 U.S. 49, 56 (1978); Cherokee Nation v. Hitchcock, 187 U.S. 294 (1902); Cherokee Nation v. Georgia, 30 U.S. 1, 55–57 (1831).

12. 25 U.S.C. § 3601(1) provides: "The Congress finds and declares that ... there is a government-to-government relationship between the United States and each Indian tribe."

13. Professor Charles Calleros notes that students "tend to care deeply about the issues and can challenge each other to analyze the issues from different perspectives." Calleros, *supra* note 9, at 291.

While beginning students need fairly straightforward problems as an introduction to legal concepts and skills, students also need to be presented with situations with the legal complexity they will encounter in practice. Along the same line, Indian law provides numerous opportunities to teach students that even Supreme Court decisions can be wrong. Students can be shown how to identify, analyze, deconstruct, and attack poorly reasoned, adverse binding precedent.[14]

Indian law problems help students better understand federalism issues.[15] Students often assume how federalism works based on their understanding of the federal-state relationship prior to law school. These assumptions are usually well-seated in their worldview and, sadly, oversimplified for purposes of legal analysis. Indian law disrupts these assumptions by introducing tribes as an additional source of sovereignty that must be accounted for in federalism's geographic and qualitative distribution of authority. A hypo based on Indian law offers the opportunity to discuss social inequality and injustice while presenting students with issues of first impression in the context of a three-way power split between states, tribes, and the federal government.

Lastly, practicing lawyers encounter Indian law issues today more than ever and, as a result, need exposure to the topic.[16] The benefit to students from states with large tribal populations or reservations is obvious, but even students from other states benefit because the Indian population is so widespread.[17] Tribal economic and political influence is at an all-time high.[18] More businesses recognize the advantages of investing within tribal territories and see tribes as valuable partners. At the same time, more tribes are reaching beyond their borders for economic opportunities.

---

14. *Nevada v. Hicks*, 533 U.S. 353, 361–62 (2001), and *Federal Power Commission v. Tuscarora Indian Nation*, 362 U.S. 99, 116–17 (1960), are prime examples. *See* Michael D. Oeser, *Tribal Citizen Participation in State and National Politics: Welcome Wagon or Trojan Horse?*, 36 WM. MITCHELL L. REV. 793, 805–06 n.50 (2010).

15. *See* Frank Pommersheim, *"Our Federalism" in the Context of Federal Courts and Tribal Courts: An Open Letter to the Federal Courts' Teaching and Scholarly Community*, 71 U. COLO. L. REV. 123, 124, 129 (2000); Carol Tebben, *An American Trifederalism Based upon the Constitutional Status of Tribal Nations*, 5 U. PA. J. CONST. L. 318, 318–21 (2003); Jen Reidel, *Teaching Civic Ideals Using Primary Sources: Cherokee Removal and Federalism*, LIB. OF CONG. (Oct. 22, 2019), https://blogs.loc.gov/teachers/2019/10/teaching-civic-ideals-using-primary-sources-cherokee-removal-and-federalism/.

16. *See* Stephenson & Fowler, *supra* note 10, at 78–79.

17. The U.S. government recognizes 345 tribes spread over 35 of the 48 contiguous states, in addition to 229 tribes in Alaska. NAT'L CONF. OF AM. INDIANS, *Tribal Nations & the United States: An Introduction*, https://ncai.org/about-tribes (last visited Dec. 8, 2022). However, half of the total U.S. Indians and Native Alaskans live away from their tribal lands. U.S. DEP'T OF INTERIOR, INDIAN AFFAIRS, *Must All American Indians and Alaska Natives Live on Reservations?*, https://www.bia.gov/faqs/must-all-american-indians-and-alaska-natives-live-reservations. (last visited Dec. 8, 2022).

18. *See* Oeser, *supra* note 14, at 808–12; David Wilkins, *An Inquiry into Indigenous Political Participation: Implications for Tribal Sovereignty*, 9 KAN. J.L. & PUB. POL'Y 732, 732–33 (2000) (discussing the use of Indian gaming finances to make significant funding contributions to American political campaigns).

Finding a Topic and Creating Materials

Finding a Topic

Developing an Indian law hypothetical for an LDC starts with finding a topic, which is not substantially different from finding a topic for a hypothetical in any other area of law. However, not everyone is familiar with sources that address Indian issues.

Several media outlets and blogs focus on tribal issues, such as Indian Country Today,[19] Indianz.com,[20] American Indian Quarterly,[21] Native Studies Review,[22] Wicazo Sa Review,[23] and Turtle Talk.[24] Many journals either specifically focus on Indian law or are recognized for Indian law content. These include American Indian Law Review,[25] American Indian Law Journal,[26] Tribal Law Journal,[27] North Dakota Law Review,[28] Tulsa Law Review,[29] and Arizona State University Law Journal.[30] The appellate dockets of federal and state jurisdictions with large tribal populations—such as Arizona, California, New Mexico, North Dakota, Oklahoma, South Dakota, and Wisconsin—can provide useful ideas as well. Many organizations support tribal issues, and many publish regular newsletters and make their policy positions public. These include the National Congress of American Indians, the Native American Rights Fund, the American Indian Movement, the Conference of Western Attorneys General,[31] and 7Gen Leaders.[32]

---

19. Indian Country Today, https://indiancountrytoday.com/ (last visited Dec. 8, 2022).

20. Indianz.com, https://www.indianz.com (last visited Dec. 8, 2022).

21. American Indian Quarterly, Univ. of Nebraska Press, https://nebraskapressjournals.unl.edu/search-results/?collection=american-indian-quarterly&collectionTitle=American+Indian+Quarterly (last visited Dec. 8, 2022).

22. Native Studies Review, Univ. of Saskatchewan, https://publications.usask.ca/nativestudiesreview/ (last visited Dec. 8, 2022).

23. Wicazo Sa Review, Univ. of New Mexico, https://nas.unm.edu/wicazo-sa-review.html (last visited Dec. 8, 2022).

24. Turtle Talk, https://turtletalk.blog/ (last visited Dec. 8, 2022).

25. American Indian Law Review, Univ. of Oklahoma, https://www.law.ou.edu/faculty-and-scholarship/journals/american-indian-law-review (last visited Dec. 8, 2022).

26. American Indian Law Journal, Seattle Univ., https://law.seattleu.edu/academics/lawyering-skills-training/writing-research/student-run-academic-publications/american-indian-law-journal/ (last visited Dec. 8, 2022).

27. Tribal Law Journal, Univ. of New Mexico, https://lawschool.unm.edu/tlj/index.html (last visited Dec. 8, 2022).

28. North Dakota Law Review, https://law.und.edu/law-review/ (last visited Dec. 8, 2022).

29. Tulsa Law Review, https://digitalcommons.law.utulsa.edu/tlr/?_ga=2.188513384.1998377546.1668646341-354211644.1668646341 (last visited Dec. 8, 2022).

30. Arizona State Law Journal, https://arizonastatelawjournal.org/ (last visited Dec. 8, 2022).

31. Including the Conference of Western Attorneys General on this list might seem odd because it has historically opposed tribal interests. Nonetheless, the group's policy positions can provide ideas for Indian law hypotheticals.

32. A more comprehensive list can be found at National Congress of American Indians, *Tribal Organizations*, https://www.ncai.org/tribal-directory/tribal-organizations (last visited Dec. 8, 2022).

Creating Course Materials

The next task is creating materials. Developing an Indian law hypothetical for an LDC is not substantially different from developing a problem based on any other area of law. However, Indian law hypos need to include certain facts and present a few unique complications. Indian law issues almost always include the following facts:

- Ancestry and tribal citizenship, if any, of the people in the problem;
- Whether the events in the problem occur on reservation land, or in Indian country;[33]
- Ownership of the land where the events in the hypo occur;
- The demographics of the area with regard to race, land ownership, and governmental authority, particularly within relevant reservation borders;
- The language of relevant treaty and statutory provisions;
- The history of Indian and non-Indian relations in the geographic area of the problem.[34]
- Cultural information relevant to the issue under consideration, particularly information that reveals tribal beliefs or practices that reflect relevant tribal values.[35]

Professors choosing to use an Indian law hypothetical need to be aware of unique complications related to certain topics. For example, Congress delegated the federal government's power to exercise partial civil and criminal jurisdiction over Indian country to six states in 1953 in an act commonly known as Public Law 280 or PL-280.[36] Since its passage, criminal jurisdiction has been expanded to include additional states.[37]

---

33. "Indian country" is a slightly broader term than "reservation land." "Indian country" includes reservation land, but also includes all "dependent Indian communities" and all Indian allotments still held in trust by the United States, whether located inside or outside a reservation. 18 U.S.C. § 1151.

34. The rules of treaty interpretation include a canon that treaties must be interpreted as the Indians understood them at the time. Washington v. Washington State Commercial Passenger Fishing Vessel Ass'n, 443 U.S. 658, 675–76 (1979); Minnesota v. Mille Lacs Band of Chippewa Indians, 526 U.S. 172, 206–07 (1999). The difference in practices before and after contact with non-Indians can be probative.

35. Custom, tradition, and common practice have always informed the interpretation of law, largely because they were the original sources of law. George Rutherglen, *Custom and Usage as Action Under Color of State Law: An Essay on the Forgotten Terms of Section 1983*, 89 Va. L. Rev. 925, 930–32 (2003). This is true for both native and non-native nations.

36. The states are Alaska, California, Minnesota, Nebraska, Oregon, and Wisconsin. 18 U.S.C. 1862(a) (2022). Pub. L. No. 83-280 (Aug. 15, 1953) (codified as 18 U.S.C. § 1162, 28 U.S.C. § 1360, and 25 U.S.C. § 1321–26); *see* Vanessa J. Jiménez & Soo C. Song, *Concurrent Tribal and State Jurisdiction Under Public Law*, 47 Am. U. L. Rev. 1627, 1632–33 (1998); M. Brent Leonhard, *Criminal Jurisdiction in Indian Country*, 69 DOJ J. Fed. L. & Prac. 45 (2021). A few specific reservations within the mandatory states were exempted from the law.

37. Florida, Idaho, Washington, and two Montana reservations were added later. M. Brent Leonhard, *Returning Washington P.L. 280 Jurisdiction to Its Original Consent-Based Grounds*, 47 Gonz. L. Rev. 663, 694 (2011).

Furthermore, the law related to tribes in Alaska, California, and Hawaii differs significantly from the law related to tribes in other states.

Avoid negative stereotypes. We all have blind spots when it comes to cultural issues. Avoiding missteps becomes harder where tribes are involved because of the number of culturally distinct tribes. Tribes can be broadly categorized (e.g., woodland/coastal/plains, patrilineal/matrilineal, Algonquin/Five Civilized), but individual tribes often have strongly held, substantially different practices and values. If the hypothetical involves real tribes or tribal lands, seek out that tribe's government and people familiar with that tribe. If the hypothetical uses a fictional tribe, run things by several people familiar with Indian culture and communities beforehand,[38] even if you already have some familiarity.

Indian Law Research

The variety of primary sources that come into play in Indian law makes Indian law an excellent subject for teaching research. Every primary source of law is on the table. Starting with secondary sources and asking for assistance from library staff become even more important when dealing with Indian law. Most students have little familiarity with it. Encourage them to start with treatises instead of diving directly into the plethora of cases and law review articles available online. Grounding students in fundamentals via a reputable secondary source will help them parse what is at times a confusing subject.

The most specific and well-known secondary source is Cohen's *Handbook of Federal Indian Law.*[39] The American Law Institute published the first *Restatement of Indian Law* in 2022. The American Civil Liberties Union publishes a treatise, as well—*The Rights of Indians and Tribes. The American Indian Law Deskbook*, published by the Conference of Western Attorneys General, is a good source for opposing arguments.

Tribal history, traditions, and practices come into play regularly in Indian law cases. Conventional research methods are sufficient, but advise students to focus their research on the particular tribe at issue. Sites like HeinOnline and JSTOR can be particularly helpful when looking for information related to specific tribes. Firsthand, historical accounts of early contact with particular tribes also exist in many cases.[40]

---

38. We suggest reaching out to law professors at schools with Indian Law programs, particularly programs in an area of the country with tribes similar to your fictional tribe.

39. Many scholars and tribal advocates eschew the 1958 and 1982 editions. They consider these editions biased against tribes. Joseph R. Membrino, *A Brief History of Indian Trust Administration Reform: Will the Past Be Prologue?*, 50 Tulsa L. Rev. 227, 234 (2014); Native Village of Venetie I.R.A. Council v. Alaska, 687 F. Supp. 1380, 1390 n.2 (D. Alaska 1988).

40. For collections of historical sources see *Research Guide: Native American Resources in Haverford College Special Collections (HC)*, TriCollege Librs., https://guides.tricolib.brynmawr.edu/c.php?g=285374&p=1900836 (last visited Dec. 8, 2022); Erik Ponder, *Native American Studies Research Guide*, Mich. State Univ. Libr., https://libguides.lib.msu.edu/c.php?g=95603&p=624342#:~:text=Firsthand%20accounts%20reveal%20how%20Indians,while%20living%20in%20a%20society (last visited Dec. 8, 2022).

These accounts are useful sources for establishing the traditions and practices of the tribe involved.

Teaching Indian Law

Teaching Indian law as part of an LDC is much the same as teaching any other area of law for the course. Begin with a good history of the various federal policy Indian periods. Cohen's *Handbook* has a good one, as do most Indian law casebooks.[41] Then move to foundational rules in good secondary sources. The ALI Restatement[42] is a good source, as is Cohen's *Handbook*. From there, suggest that students locate and study one or two law review articles, preferably from reputable journals with well-known authors.

Conclusion

Indian law has much to offer as a topic when it comes to LDCs and promoting diversity, inclusion, and social justice. From the LDC perspective, it offers intermediate to advanced material for students to work on. From the diversity and inclusion perspective, it offers an opportunity to expose students to cultures they may never learn anywhere else and challenges them to see those cultures as worthy of legal respect.

---

41. *See, e.g.*, FELIX S. COHEN, HANDBOOK OF FEDERAL INDIAN LAW ch. 1 (2012); *see also* WILLIAM C. CANBY, JR., AMERICAN INDIAN LAW 10–32 (3d ed. 1998); ROBERT N. CLINTON, NELL JESSOP NEWTON & MONROE E. PRICE, AMERICAN INDIAN LAW 137–65 (3d ed. 1991); DAVID H. GETCHES, CHARLES F. WILKINSON & ROBERT A. WILLIAMS, FEDERAL INDIAN LAW chs. 2, 3 & 4 (4th ed. 1998).

42. RESTATEMENT OF THE LAW OF AMERICAN INDIANS (Am. Law Inst. 2022).

Grappling with DEI Issues Through an Environmental Negotiation Case Study

*Robin L. Juni**

This article will describe a teaching module that grapples with diversity, equity, and inclusion (DEI) issues in the context of an environmental negotiation case study, seeking to provide guidance useful to professors in both doctrinal and skills courses. The teaching tools offered could readily be adapted to case studies other than the hazardous waste permitting scenario described here, and could be applied in an environmental law or administrative law course, as well as in a negotiation or other skills course.

This teaching module is structured in four parts: first, assigning advance readings and handouts; second, utilizing case studies that require students to engage with DEI issues as they negotiate; third, conducting a facilitated review of the process in which students have engaged, including discussion of how the DEI issues were managed; and fourth, requiring completion of a written journal from each student that follows up the oral discussion and further mandates integration of relevant concepts from the assigned readings.

* Associate Professor, Fundamentals of Lawyering Program, the George Washington University Law School.

Setting the Stage

Providing relevant background to prime students for appreciation and discussion of DEI issues is crucial.[1] That background consists of both practical issues to be negotiated and the theoretical issues that may come into play when issues of culture and identity come to the fore.[2]

A useful scenario—providing rich detail yet a sufficiently straightforward dispute for students to manage in three hours of class time (spread over one or two class periods) and six to eight hours of outside preparation time—involves the proposed siting of a hazardous waste incinerator in a small town in Texas, close to the Mexican border.[3] A summary of the issues follows:

> Up in Smoke, Inc. (UIS) is a multi-state waste management company specializing in the treatment and disposal of hazardous waste. UIS has conducted pilot testing of a new incinerator facility that it wishes to locate in LeHaze, Texas, a community located near the border with Mexico. Economic pressures have generally garnered support for the new facility from the Mayor and City Council in LeHaze.
>
> UIS has filed its "Part A" and "Part B" applications for a hazardous waste incinerator under the Resource Conversation and Recovery Act (RCRA). The permits were approved by the U.S. Environmental Protection Agency (EPA), subject to a final showing of full compliance based on the results of a test burn.[4]
>
> The test burn using the new incineration technology was scheduled to occur three months ago. One week prior to that date, the national environmental group GreenAction sued UIS to stop the test burn, primarily on the basis of an affidavit and testimony from a former UIS engineer, who stated that UIS knew the new technology could not meet EPA standards and that emissions would endanger plant workers and nearby residents.

---

1. *See* Bonny L. Tavares, *Integrating Diversity through Design of Legal Writing Assignments*, in INTEGRATING DOCTRINE AND DIVERSITY: INCLUSION AND EQUITY IN THE LAW SCHOOL CLASSROOM 225 (Nicole P. Dyszlewski, Raquel J. Gabriel, Suzanne Harrington-Steppen, Anna Russell & Genevieve B Tung eds., 2021) ("Designing [course] assignments with diverse characters broadens students' perspectives about their potential place in the profession, and helps them to prepare for a diverse client base and increasingly global legal marketplace.").

2. Relevant materials that could be assigned to students in whole or in part include: CULTURE & NEGOTIATION (Guy Oliver Faure & Jeffrey Z. Rubin eds., 1993); Daniel L. Shapiro, *Identity Is More Than Meets the "I": The Power of Identity in Shaping Negotiation Behavior*, 87 MARQ. L. REV. 809 (2004); and Leo F. Smyth, *Intractable Conflicts and the Role of Identity*, 10 NEGOT. J. 311 (1994). Many negotiation textbooks excerpt these and similar books and articles in a chapter on intercultural issues in negotiation.

3. The author holds the copyright to this negotiation exercise.

4. In the context of this exercise, the state of Texas has chosen to defer to EPA's analysis of the hazardous waste incineration permit, so the state environmental agency is not a participant in the negotiation.

> At the court hearing on GreenAction's request for a preliminary injunction, UIS produced company scientists who refuted the former employee's testimony, stating instead that the technology had been successful in the pilot stage, that there was no reason to believe the incinerator would not meet emissions limitations, and that there were no indications that any person's health would be endangered. EPA technical experts were cautiously supportive of UIS's technical arguments, while reserving the right to come to a different conclusion after the test burn. After that hearing, the judge refused to issue an injunction to stop the test burn.
>
> The test burn thus went forward one month ago. Unfortunately for UIS, the measurement data from that first test burn, which was made public by the regulators, was inconclusive (it did not show either safety or harm). GreenAction immediately issued press releases arguing that the data thus supported warnings that the incinerator was a threat to the community because it was not shown to comply with the emissions standards established in EPA's regulations. UIS then proposed, and EPA reluctantly agreed to, a second test burn.
>
> However, using the first test burn data, GreenAction again went to court to stop the second test burn. The court this time issued a Temporary Restraining Order (TRO) prohibiting further burning, based on the inconclusive data from the first test burn. The parties agreed to schedule a hearing 10 days later (as required) on whether the court should allow the TRO to expire or issue a permanent injunction. A local citizens' group from LeHaze, "People Upset From Filth" (PUFF), has at this point intervened in this suit as a plaintiff with GreenAction.
>
> The President of UIS has proposed that stakeholders sit down in person to discuss the situation and has offered to voluntarily commit to a two-week extension of the TRO and to continue similar two-week extensions, or otherwise delay the second test burn, for up to 90 days, so long as UIS believes the parties are negotiating in good faith. The parties will meet in LeHaze.

In addition to the background information summarized above, students are each provided with a one-page role assignment for the negotiation, providing information on the interests and positions of their individual clients: City of LeHaze, PUFF, GreenAction, UIS President, UIS Board Chair, UIS Outside Counsel, UIS In-House Counsel, and EPA Counsel.

More broadly, to encourage students to reflect thoughtfully on the facts presented, it is useful to assign readings that will help students to contextualize the environmental justice issues,[5] using both current and historical materials. For example, President Joe

---

5. EPA defines "Environmental Justice" as "the fair treatment and meaningful involvement of all people regardless of race, color, national origin, or income with respect to the development, implementation and enforcement of environmental laws, regulations and policies." U.S. ENVIRONMENTAL PROTECTION AGENCY, *Learn About Environmental Justice*, https://www.epa.gov/environmentaljustice/learn-about-environmental-justice. *See also* Robert D. Bullard & Beverly Wright, *Disastrous Response*

Biden signed two executive orders articulating the Administration's commitment to environmental justice during his first week in office,[6] building on a discussion that has been ongoing for decades.[7] Moreover, if desired in an environmental law or hazardous waste course, much more detail could be provided about RCRA permitting steps, the typical content of a RCRA permit, and opportunities for public participation that are part of the RCRA permitting process outside litigation.[8] Finally, in the context of both negotiation and environmental negotiation courses as deployed by the author, students have read and discussed materials from a standard negotiation textbook,[9] and have already completed eight or nine negotiation exercises during the semester before engaging in the incinerator siting negotiation exercise discussed in this article.

Engaging the Issues

Having provided sufficient grist for discussion in the incinerator siting negotiation exercise, students are placed into groups and instructed to begin the exercise with all parties at the table at a specific time and to end approximately 1.5 hours later. After the initial meeting with all parties, students can meet privately, in a caucus, with any other parties. The professor typically moves among these large and small group meetings without interceding, in order to observe the various processes as they unfold.

---

to Natural and Man-Made Disasters: An Environmental Justice Analysis Twenty-Five Years after Warren County, 26 UCLA J. ENV'T L. & POL'Y 217, 224 (tracing the generally accepted beginnings of the environmental justice movement to 1982 protests in Warren County, North Carolina, regarding siting of a hazardous waste landfill in a community "exhibit[ing] the 'quadruple whammy'—in that it is mostly black, poor, rural, and politically powerless").

6. *See* Exec. Order No. 13,990, 86 Fed. Reg. 7037, 7037 (Jan. 20, 2021); Exec. Order No. 14,008, 86 Fed. Reg. 7619, 7629 (Jan. 27, 2021); Press Release, Biden-Harris Administration Outlines Historic Progress on Environmental Justice in Report Submitted to Congress (May 23, 2022), https://www.whitehouse.gov/ceq/news-updates/2022/05/23/biden-harris-administration-outlines-historic-progress-on-environmental-justice-in-report-submitted-to-congress-2/.

7. *See* Deborah Behles, From *Dirty to Green: Increasing Energy Efficiency and Renewable Energy in Environmental Justice Communities*, 58 VILL. L. REV. 25, 25 (2013) (describing historic environmental justice efforts and defining "environmental justice communities" as "[p]oor communities of color that are . . . vulnerable and disproportionately impacted by pollution"); Chad Small, *5 Places with the Most Alarming Instances of Environmental Racism in America*, BLAVITY (Sept. 4, 2019, 7:35 PM), https://blavity.com/blavity-original/5-places-with-the-most-alarming-instances-of-environmental-racism-in-america.

8. *See* U.S. ENVIRONMENTAL PROTECTION AGENCY, *Resources on Public Participation in the Hazardous Waste Permitting and Corrective Action Processes*, https://www.epa.gov/hwpermitting/resources-public-participation-hazardous-waste-permitting-and-corrective-action (Feb. 6, 2022): "[P]ublic interaction occurs during pre-application meetings, public comment and response periods, and public hearings. RCRA includes specific provisions to involve the public in all stages of the hazardous waste treatment, storage and disposal facility ("TSDF") permitting process: prior to the initial permit application; after draft permit issuance; and during permit modifications, permit renewals, post-closure permits, and trial burns."

9. CARRIE J. MENKEL-MEADOW, ANDREA KUPFER SCHNEIDER & LELA PORTER LOVE, NEGOTIATION: PROCESS FOR PROBLEM-SOLVING (3d ed. 2021).

Within this framework, students can seek to build coalitions among the disparate parties and must at the same time grapple with their own values and feelings about the process. For example, students who are representing EPA or PUFF often try to build coalitions by serving as a "partisan mediator" in the process, both to maximize the potential for settlement and to enhance their own negotiation power.[10] This strategy can pay off, particularly for a party like PUFF; research suggests that in the environmental justice context, better organized communities can fight information asymmetry to prevent harmful siting decisions.[11]

Students often recognize during this negotiation exercise that establishing litigation-oriented "sides" to the dispute, rather than remaining flexible and engaged with all parties, can lead to group polarization that undercuts the likelihood of reaching a deal.[12] However, while recognizing the benefit of an engagement strategy, some students may nonetheless feel as though taking that course of action means they are selling out their community or the broader environmental movement by letting go of their role as a litigation advocate and engaging in a negotiation at all.[13]

Strategies employed by one or more of their colleagues that seek to sabotage the negotiation process, such as strategic misrepresentation by a participant—here, the UIS Board Chair—who is at the table but secretly would prefer the negotiation to fail,[14] challenge students to reach a negotiated result that is better for their client than a litigation outcome.[15]

---

10. *See* I. William Zartman & Saadia Touval, *International Mediation and Power Politics*, 41 J. Soc. Issues 27, 36 (1985) ("Often a mediator motivated by its own concern for position in the area seeks to use its intervention to maintain close ties with one side, while at the same time improving ties with the other.").

11. *See* Christopher Timmins & Ashley Vissing, *Environmental Justice and Coasian Bargaining: The Role of Race and Income in Lease Negotiations for Shale Gas* 40–41 (Nat'l Bureau of Econ. Rsch., Working Paper No. 29487 (2021)), https://www.nber.org/system/files/working_papers/w29487/w29487.pdf

12. Cass R. Sunstein, *Deliberative Trouble? Why Groups Go to Extremes*, 110 Yale L.J. 71, 105–06 (2000) ("It is important to ensure social spaces for deliberation by like-minded persons, but it is equally important to ensure that members of the relevant groups are not isolated from conversation with people having quite different views.").

13. *See* Carolyn Brommer, George Buckingham & Steven Loeffler, *Cooperative Bargaining Styles at FMCS: A Movement Toward Choices*, 2 Pepp. Disp. Resol. L.J. 465, 484 (describing labor negotiators' need to "report to their constituents that they are not 'selling out' by engaging in [a mediated bargaining process], rather, they are engaging in a certain quantity of collaborative problem solving, and if they are not successful, they will naturally transition to traditional bargaining").

14. *See* Leigh Thompson, The Mind and Heart of the Negotiator 223–32 (5th ed. 2012) (discussing challenges of multiparty negotiation processes and explaining that engaging participants at an emotional level may discourage divisive behavior).

15. The well-known concept of Best Alternative to a Negotiated Agreement ("BATNA") requires a negotiator to evaluate whether the deal being offered is better than the alternative available outside the negotiation, and—if the alternative is indeed better—to walk away. *See* James K. Sebenius, *BATNAs in Negotiation: Common Errors and Three Kinds of "No,"* 33 Negotiation J. 89 (2017).

Consistent with research on group polarization,[16] students completing this exercise often report that the most significant progress is made when parties caucus with those outside their natural coalitions; for example, GreenAction and the City of LeHaze, who initially seem diametrically opposed to each other, sometimes ally together with PUFF to stay the litigation in a way that will allow a second test burn, conditioned on a substantial commitment from UIS to a community medical monitoring program, an outcome that would not be able to be ordered by the Court. And the UIS President can readily be persuaded to adopt a medical monitoring plan, even if it will be expensive, because success of the incinerator project in LeHaze will provide a basis for further expansion of the new incinerator technology on a nationwide basis.

In contrast, students who allow the UIS Board Chair and GreenAction—the two most anti-settlement parties—to control the negotiation often do not reach agreement. Students are frustrated with that result,[17] but that outcome provides an equal number of opportunities for learning.

Having the Hard Conversation

Immediately after the negotiation, all students convene in the classroom to debrief the exercise, usually over the course of 45 minutes to an hour. With a total course enrollment of 20–30 students, there are typically 8–10 students in each negotiation room, so two or three contrasting processes—and additional caucuses within each negotiation—to debrief. While sometimes challenging to provide sufficient discussion time to engage these myriad viewpoints, it is pedagogically useful to have multiple different processes to review, so that different approaches can be examined and discussed.[18]

Coupled with the journals discussed in the next section, the classroom debrief is the key learning vehicle for the exercise, and thus puts the onus squarely on the professor to lead a fulsome conversation, in which students can explore why either they them-

---

16. Sunstein, *supra* note 12, at 106 ("[C]onversation [between members of initially opposed groups] promote[s] the interests of those inside and outside the relevant enclaves, by subjecting group members to competing positions, by allowing them to exchange views with others and to see things from their point of view, and by ensuring that the wider society does not marginalize, and thus insulate itself from, views that may turn out to be right or at least informative.").

17. Desire to settle is often driven by a perception of "sunk costs," due to the effort already expended on the process, but that perception is a fallacy. MAX H. BAZERMAN & MARGARET A. NEALE, NEGOTIATING RATIONALLY 9 (1992) ("[S]unk costs ... *cannot* be recovered and should not be considered when selecting future courses of action.") (emphasis in original).

18. *See* Bonny L. Tavares, *Changing the Construct: Promoting Cross-Cultural Conversations in the Law School Classroom*, 67 J. LEGAL EDUC. 211, 214 (2017) (explaining that explicit discussion of DEI issues, such as environmental justice, "increase[s] engagement in the law school classroom and [helps] the law come alive for students"); Nellie Munin & Yael Efron, *Role-Playing Brings Theory to Life in a Multicultural Learning Environment*, 66 J. LEGAL EDUC. 309, 330 (2017) (observing that negotiation role-plays "exposed participants to an intercultural arena, sharpening their cultural sensitivity and developing their cultural literacy. This experience might have also raised their awareness to the great impact that cultural differences may have in negotiations.").

selves or other participants reacted as they did, and how a similar situation might be managed the same or differently in the future. For example, a student may believe that they were acting as a partisan mediator, "encouraging dialogue and mutual consideration, asking open-ended questions, using reflective listening, trying to be relatively open-minded (and even neutral), identifying underlying interests, [and] using those interests to develop mutually beneficial solutions,"[19] but another student simply did not hear or appreciate that effort, perhaps because of some implicit bias.[20] A discussion of why that dynamic occurred is useful to all, even if just two students are the focus of the conversation.

The author has had success in these conversations by asking each student to put one "worked well" and/or "do differently" point on the board, and then going around the room to talk about each point; alternatively, individual discussions that the professor viewed while circulating among the groups can be used to illustrate a desired point. Similarly, the professor can start with one party for each of the processes in the classroom—the UIS President, for example—and ask each of the two or three students playing that role (in different processes) to explain the strategy they had decided upon in approaching the negotiation, and whether or not it worked.

Reflecting on the Process

Finally, particularly because not all students have the opportunity—either because they are less extroverted than their colleagues or because review is by necessity conducted in a limited time—to fully engage in the oral classroom discussion, requiring a written journal from each student can be a useful pedagogical tool.[21] Specific guidance can be provided to encourage each student to engage in thoughtful reflection; for example, the author's syllabus provides, in part:

---

19. Nancy A. Welsh, *Introduction to Symposium on "ADR's Place in Navigating a Polarized Era,"* 35 Ohio St. J. Disp. Resol. 581, 584 (2020).

20. Alexandra Dickinson, *3 Strategies to Change Implicit Biases in a Negotiation*, Forbes (Aug. 17, 2017), https://www.forbes.com/sites/alexandradickinson/2017/08/17/3-strategies-to-change-implicit-biases-in-a-negotiation/#470565692038. *See also* Tavares, *supra* note 1, at 225 ("[C]lassroom discussions about equity viewed through the lens of [the course] assignment[ ] will allow students to practice cross-cultural conversations in a professional setting and give them opportunities to participate in educating each other about diversity and inclusion.").

21. Reflection through both the oral discussion in class and the written journal can directly contribute to development of professional identity in law students. *See* Neil W. Hamilton, Verna E. Monson & Jerome M. Organ, *Empirical Evidence That Legal Education Can Foster Student Professionalism/Professional Formation to Become an Effective Lawyer*, 10 U. St. Thomas L.J. 11, 18 (2012) (discussing development of professional formation through "reflection on a professional's responsibilities to the person served and others, encouragement of the habit of actively seeking feedback, dialogue with others on the tough calls, and reflection and consideration of each student's developmental stage"); Eduardo R.C. Capulong, Andrew King-Ries & Monte Mills, *Starting at the Start: Integrating Race and Reflection for an Antiracist Approach to Professional Identity Development in the First Year Curriculum*, in Integrating Doctrine and Diversity: Inclusion and Equity in the Law School Classroom 28 (Nicole P. Dyszlewski, Raquel J. Gabriel, Suzanne Harrington-Steppen, Anna Russell

> This class will focus on practical analysis of negotiation issues and strategies that arise in the exercises we conduct in class, with integration and discussion of concepts from the readings as appropriate (e.g., by citation to page number and/or author). To that end, a key work product will be two negotiation journals incorporating such analysis. Your journals should address:
>
> - What negotiation skills come most naturally to you?
> - What negotiation skills do you find most challenging?
> - What did you (or someone else) do in a role-play or exercise that worked well? How will you seek to replicate that experience in the future?
> - What did you (or someone else) do in a role-play or exercise that did not work well? How will you avoid that outcome in the future?
> - What skills or concepts covered in the course do you think will be most useful to you as a legal practitioner, and why?
>
> Thoughtful reflection on your experiences in a way that evinces preparation and engagement with the readings is important. Journals are confidential.
>
> ———
>
> Confidentiality is crucial to the success of this course, both so that others in the class feel comfortable "trying on" strategies that they might not normally pursue, and so that those who take the class in the future get the same benefit from the exercises as you.

As set forth in the syllabus, requiring engagement with the readings and articulating confidentiality to the students are both key elements to foster learning. The former seeks to ensure that students thoughtfully reflect on their reactions, especially emotional reactions, so that they will be better positioned to represent clients when similar situations arise, while the latter allows students greater freedom to engage in various negotiation behaviors and to discuss them in the journal. Students sometimes choose to approach the professor to talk about their reactions and feelings, and that, too, is fine.[22]

& Genevieve B Tung eds., 2021) (pointing out that "[l]egal skills courses—such as lawyering and legal writing—are especially primed for an exploration of professional identity. Because they are experiential, these courses already incorporate reflective practice and often professional ethics—and therefore professional values and identity.").

22. *See* Nicola A. Boothe-Perry, *The "New Normal" for Educating Lawyers*, 31 BYU J. Pub. L. 53, 55 (2016) ("[I]t is critical that law professors remain aware of the roles they serve to students as mentor, inspiration, and counselor, to name a few.").

Conclusion

This article has sought to provide an example of a negotiation exercise involving environmental justice issues and concrete tools for professors seeking to employ such an exercise. These tools could further be applied to address other sorts of DEI issues in a variety of course settings.

Index

1st amendment, 166, 189, 273
4th amendment, 292
14th amendment, 4, 111, 174–177, 306, 391

Abortion, 33, 181, 182, 190, 371–373, 376, 377, 379, 384
Abrogation doctrine, 172
Academic Support, 54, 329
Addiction, 151, 155, 160, 193, 195
Administrative law, 169, 181, 182, 184, 185, 187–191, 193, 194, 201, 242, 408, 409, 412, 473
Administrative State, 182–188, 190, 191
Advocacy, 27, 29, 30, 73, 141, 157, 190, 222, 249, 281, 282, 326, 331, 332, 335, 337, 347, 367, 371, 373, 385, 387, 393, 394, 402, 404, 405, 407, 454
AIDS, 55, 56, 63, 194, 222, 340, 360, 361
Alternative dispute resolution, 74, 479
American Association of Law Libraries, 445, 446
American Bar Association, 31, 32, 37, 38, 69, 75, 95, 102, 122, 126, 129, 136–138, 142, 143, 146, 152, 155, 162, 164, 218, 234, 238, 250, 385, 390, 418, 453, 454, 460
American Bar Association Model Rules of Professional Conduct, 32, 136, 138, 144, 167
American Bar Association Standards and Rules of Procedure for Approval of Law Schools, 102, 122, 142, 143, 218, 453, 460
American Civil Liberties Union, 117, 247, 271, 377
Americans with Disabilities Act, 19, 152, 171–178, 193, 198
Antiracism, 68, 93, 96, 220, 225, 228, 299, 301, 304, 307, 368
Artificial intelligence, 443–446, 450
Asian-Americans, 342
Asynchronous teaching, 133, 263

Bar admission, 154, 155, 161
Bar exam, 142, 154, 155, 157, 164
Bias, 63, 68, 86, 125, 166, 167, 341, 347, 361, 479
Black Americans, 116, 190, 223
Black Lives Matter movement, 3, 84, 235, 239, 296
Bloom's Taxonomy, 53, 385, 439
Bodily autonomy, 3, 4, 13, 371, 394
Business organizations, 5, 17–19, 34, 41, 44, 89, 146, 147, 181–184, 186, 187, 189, 190, 205, 206, 208–211, 215, 216, 217–222, 225, 228, 229, 253, 254, 262–264, 277, 280–282, 368, 394, 402, 407, 409, 412, 441, 449, 451, 474–476

Capitalism, 113, 114, 141, 215, 222, 223, 226, 242
Carceral state, 190
Case law, 44, 234, 273, 351
Character and fitness, 154, 155, 157, 164
Chinese Exclusion Act of 1882, 185
Civil Rights Act of 1866, 258
Civil Rights Act of 1964, 173, 223, 232, 258, 262
Civil rights movement, 111, 116, 173, 277
Civil war, 88, 91, 222, 223, 248
Client-centered lawyering, 28, 33, 387
Cognitive bias, 165, 356
Colorblindness, 45, 289
Constitutional Law, 6, 14, 17, 50, 62, 64, 65, 90, 91, 99, 116, 171, 172, 243, 249, 253, 409, 411, 413

Copyright, 219, 220, 474
Course design, 45, 79, 84, 209, 359, 364, 365, 369, 410
COVID-19, 134, 135, 171, 190, 242, 266
Criminal law, 5, 23, 24, 50, 64–66, 99, 159, 242, 249, 253, 290, 291, 321, 322, 324, 351, 380, 381, 392
Criminal procedure, 253, 287, 289, 290, 294, 297, 321, 324, 409
Critical Legal Theory, 5, 218, 220
Critical pedagogy, 110–112, 116, 215, 218, 385, 388, 389
Critical race theory, 5, 67, 84, 99, 106, 116, 163, 221, 222, 225, 302–306, 311, 314, 317, 329, 344, 345, 386, 393
Cryptocurrency, 242–244, 248
Cultural humility, 28, 73, 74
Custody, 23, 292, 362, 366–368, 375, 378, 379, 381, 383, 388, 391, 416

Decolonization, 398–404, 408, 417, 429
Democracy, 20, 88, 111, 113, 117, 119, 219, 246, 247, 397, 400, 426
Diné, 455–458
Disability law, 171, 173, 178, 193
Disparate impact, 226–228, 249, 255, 262, 290, 304, 306, 307
Divorce, 151, 242, 340, 363–366, 368, 381, 382
Due process, 3, 23, 177, 189, 376, 377, 428

Empathy, 37, 38, 42, 45, 50, 73, 74, 76–79, 121, 268, 269, 319, 465
Employment law, 8, 232, 265–269, 273, 274, 418
Entrepreneurship, 207, 211
Environmental Protection Agency, 182–184, 474–477
Equal Employment Opportunity Commission, 147, 234, 267
Ethics, 17, 134, 138, 139, 141, 143, 154, 157, 158, 162, 163, 166, 167, 243, 479
European Union, 426

Federal Reserve, 242, 244, 245
Federal Rules of Evidence, 305, 323, 324, 328, 329–331, 333–335, 340, 341, 344, 346, 347, 349, 350, 355, 356
Federal trade commission, 245
Feminist Judgements Project, 5, 14
Feminist legal theory, 5

Free expression, 214
Freedman's Bureau, 186
Freire, Paulo, 111, 210
Fugitive Slave Act of 1850, 185

Gender, 4, 6, 9, 28, 29, 31–34, 45, 48, 51, 52, 57, 60–63, 65, 66, 68, 70, 98, 118, 135–137, 145, 147, 152, 154, 159, 166, 182, 184, 206–208, 215, 216, 219, 220, 222, 225, 244, 255, 258, 261–263, 266, 271, 272, 283, 289, 290, 297, 305, 322–324, 329, 336, 337, 339, 345, 346, 353, 355, 359, 360, 369, 372, 374, 382, 383, 385–387, 390, 438, 441–443, 449, 454, 458–460, 466
Gig economy, 267
Grotius, 423, 424

Harris, Angela, 66, 121, 222
Health law, 5, 37, 45, 89, 164, 254, 371, 384
Homophobia, 4, 5, 123, 333–336
hooks, bell, 216, 279, 331

Immigration, 5, 77, 89, 181, 207, 225–227, 263, 282, 323, 342, 344, 441, 450
Imperialism, 397, 424
Implicit bias, 63, 68, 86, 125, 166, 167, 341, 347, 361, 479
Indian, 137, 146, 303, 318, 354, 375, 400, 403, 405, 406, 409, 410, 412, 418, 454, 455, 459, 463, 468, 470
Indian law, 17–20, 222, 399, 400, 402, 404, 406, 407, 410–419, 463–471
Indigenous Peoples, 6, 7, 397, 398, 400–406, 408, 413, 463
Inequality, 8, 10, 60, 84, 85, 89, 92, 95, 101, 109–111, 114, 117, 118, 139, 167, 187, 218, 220, 226, 243, 244, 264, 272, 283, 321, 324, 340, 372–374, 390, 467
Innocence Project, 352, 354–356
Insurance, 21, 221, 226, 227, 248, 253–262, 336
Intellectual Property, 37, 45, 219–221, 226, 242
Intimate Partner Violence, 345, 382, 387, 392, 394

Juries, 294, 296, 323, 346, 355

Labor law, 231, 232, 236, 237, 240
Labor organizations, 90, 231–233, 236–240, 271, 282, 408, 409, 426, 432, 470

Law firm, 27, 34, 123, 124, 141, 144–149, 209, 210, 214, 248, 249, 263, 271, 272, 326, 332, 359, 444, 446
Leadership, 28, 146, 148, 188, 227, 254, 255, 258, 402, 403
Legal writing, 3, 5, 8, 9, 11, 12, 14, 19, 27, 29, 30, 34, 37–39, 41, 43, 44, 54, 62, 63, 69, 78, 79, 88, 90–92, 139, 157, 210–212, 225, 226, 229, 247, 321, 333, 339, 359, 360, 367, 379, 390, 412, 424, 435, 439, 441, 448, 449, 455, 457, 463, 464, 466, 474, 479
LGBTQIA, 32, 38, 43, 71, 146, 163, 166, 167, 181, 182, 304, 328, 343, 345, 372, 376, 383, 391, 438, 446
Litigation, 19, 25, 39, 123, 126, 144, 147, 171, 176, 220, 227, 281, 282, 284, 384, 391, 394, 427, 429, 456, 464, 476–478

Marriage Equality, 307, 360, 382–384, 390–392
Medicaid, 227, 384
Medicare, 227
Mental health, 52, 100, 135, 151, 152, 155, 156, 158, 215, 410
Misogyny, 4–6, 123
Model Code of Judicial Conduct, 31
Monetary law, 241, 243, 244, 248, 249
Movie, 114, 296, 315–318, 333, 356, 386, 393, 458, 459
Multi-State Professional Responsibility Exam, 133, 134, 139, 142, 153, 158, 160

NAFTA, 431
Negotiation, 28, 73, 76, 369, 422, 429, 432, 433, 473–481
New Deal, 114, 248

Open educational resources, 69, 70, 135, 139

Pass-fail grading, 97, 98, 100
Patent, 37, 45, 219–221, 226, 242
Pedagogy, 41, 45, 47, 60, 86, 87, 97, 110–112, 116, 128, 159, 164, 208–210, 215, 218, 219, 225, 279, 284, 285, 350, 365, 374, 384, 385, 387–389, 411, 414, 453, 461
Podcast, 103, 136, 158, 182, 239, 240, 324, 325, 356, 382, 393
Police, 3, 24, 92, 114, 185, 194, 197, 207, 261, 289–293, 295, 296, 302, 303, 305, 306, 316, 329, 330, 334, 344, 345, 349, 351–354, 356
Poverty, 5, 77, 99, 111, 124, 173, 247, 304, 456
Prejudice, 4, 25, 176, 193, 237, 238, 285, 301, 302, 304, 305, 322, 324, 331, 334–337, 341, 343, 346, 349, 378, 442
Privacy, 117, 182, 184, 242, 247–249, 265, 266, 293, 350, 376, 379
Pro bono, 141, 144, 145, 147, 148
Problem Based Learning, 37–39, 43–45
Professional identity, 28, 81, 89, 95, 96, 98, 99, 101, 102, 104, 105, 134, 142, 143, 149, 151–153, 158, 161, 164, 165, 167, 194, 272, 285, 386, 457, 479
Pronouns, 28–34, 63, 257, 369
Property law, 6, 8, 220, 221, 223
Public policy, 11–14, 22, 24, 25, 194, 223, 249, 269, 412, 441, 468

Queer legal theory, 5

Race, 4–6, 8–10, 21, 45, 48, 49, 51, 57, 60–63, 66–68, 70, 78, 81, 83–93, 96–99, 101, 106, 109, 110, 112–119, 121, 126, 136, 145, 147, 152, 154, 159, 160, 162, 163, 165, 166, 174, 185–187, 190, 191, 200, 207, 208, 215, 216, 218–227, 236, 238, 244–246, 248, 249, 255, 258, 259, 261, 264, 266, 267, 274, 283, 284, 289–295, 297, 301–306, 309–318, 322–324, 329, 330, 337, 340, 342–345, 349, 352, 354, 355, 359, 367, 372–375, 378, 379, 382, 383, 385, 386, 393, 398, 401, 438, 442, 443, 454, 457, 458, 460, 465, 466, 469, 475, 477, 479
Racism, 84, 87–90, 92, 187, 305
Religion, 60, 136, 147, 152, 174, 200, 207, 208, 225, 238, 258, 259, 322, 323, 362, 405
Remedies, 37, 45, 174, 242, 275, 277–285, 415
Reparations, 89, 219, 282, 283
Reproductive Justice, 5, 367, 371–375, 378–380, 384, 385, 387, 388, 392
Retaliation, 232, 268, 271
Roman law, 113, 424

Search and seizure, 290
Securities, 6, 249, 282
Sex, 28, 61, 182, 385
Sioux, 17, 21, 408
Social justice, 3–6, 43, 59, 71, 78, 79, 84, 95, 111, 134–136, 139, 152, 163, 164, 167, 181, 184–186, 188, 189, 191, 205, 217, 232, 235, 239, 283, 311, 360, 372–374, 379, 380, 386, 387, 393, 407, 410, 438, 451, 463–465, 471

Social media, 30, 31, 114, 172, 264, 419, 443
Social work, 75–78, 188
Socratic method, 50, 159, 332, 333
STEM (Science, Technology, Engineering, Mathematics), 76, 234, 271, 401
Stereotype, 47–49, 51–53, 56, 57, 159, 294, 295, 302, 322
Storytelling, 14, 44, 45, 77, 78, 121, 122, 162, 164, 383, 392
Syllabus, 59, 243, 246, 251, 448

Taxation, 14
Teaching assistants, 102
Technology, 162, 226, 241–243, 245–248, 250, 290, 351, 359, 387, 427, 444, 445, 447, 474, 475, 478
Textbook, 14, 19, 60, 63, 64, 66, 86, 135, 136, 139, 193, 222, 254, 257, 258, 260–264, 273, 279, 282, 290, 313, 314, 316, 333, 368
Torts, 5, 40, 64–66, 103, 105, 283, 411, 414
Trauma, 41, 44, 207, 245, 361–364, 387
Tribal sovereignty, 399, 400, 402, 404, 405, 407, 414–417, 467
Trusts and estates, 5, 6, 50, 186, 457

Uniform Commercial Code, 39, 223
United Nations, 399, 404, 405, 421, 422, 426, 429, 432, 467
United States Supreme Court, 3, 14, 15, 18, 23, 88, 182, 371, 382, 393, 394, 414

Voting rights, 3, 116, 342

Xenophobia, 185, 397

Zoning, 193–200, 223